Blackwell Handbook of Language Development

Blackwell Handbooks of Developmental Psychology

This outstanding series of handbooks provides a cutting-edge overview of classic research, current research and future trends in developmental psychology.

- Each handbook draws together 25–30 newly commissioned chapters to provide a comprehensive overview of a sub-discipline of developmental psychology.
- The international team of contributors to each handbook has been specially chosen for its expertise and knowledge of each field.
- Each handbook is introduced and contextualized by leading figures in the field, lending coherence and authority to each volume.

The *Blackwell Handbooks of Developmental Psychology* will provide an invaluable overview for advanced students of developmental psychology and for researchers as an authoritative definition of their chosen field.

Published

Blackwell Handbook of Infant Development
Edited by Gavin Bremner and Alan Fogel

Blackwell Handbook of Childhood Social Development
Edited by Peter K. Smith and Craig H. Hart

Blackwell Handbook of Childhood Cognitive Development
Edited by Usha Goswami

Blackwell Handbook of Adolescence
Edited by Gerald R. Adams and Michael D. Berzonsky

The Science of Reading: A Handbook
Edited by Margaret J. Snowling and Charles Hulme

Blackwell Handbook of Early Childhood Development
Edited by Kathleen McCartney and Deborah A. Phillips

Blackwell Handbook of Language Development
Edited by Erika Hoff and Marilyn Shatz

Blackwell Handbook of Language Development

Edited by

Erika Hoff and Marilyn Shatz

Blackwell
Publishing

© 2007 by Blackwell Publishing Ltd

BLACKWELL PUBLISHING
350 Main Street, Malden, MA 02148-5020, USA
9600 Garsington Road, Oxford OX4 2DQ, UK
550 Swanston Street, Carlton, Victoria 3053, Australia

The right of Erika Hoff and Marilyn Shatz to be identified as the Authors of the Editorial Material in this Work has been asserted in accordance with the UK Copyright, Designs, and Patents Act 1988.

First published 2007 by Blackwell Publishing Ltd

1   2007

Library of Congress Cataloging-in-Publication Data

Blackwell handbook of language development/edited by Erika Hoff and Marilyn Shatz.
   p. cm.   (Blackwell handbooks of developmental psychology)
Includes bibliographical references and index.
ISBN-13: 978-1-4051-3253-4 (hardcover : alk. paper)
ISBN-10: 1-4051-3253-1 (hardcover : alk. paper)   1. Language acquisition.   I. Hoff, Erika, 1951–   II. Shatz, Marilyn.
P118.B583 2007
401′.93—dc22

                                2006028202

A catalogue record for this title is available from the British Library.

Set in 10.5 on 12.5 pt Adobe Garamond
by SNP Best-set Typesetter Ltd, Hong Kong
Printed and bound in Singapore
by Markono Print Media Pte Ltd

The publisher's policy is to use permanent paper from mills that operate a sustainable forestry policy, and which has been manufactured from pulp processed using acid-free and elementary chlorine-free practices. Furthermore, the publisher ensures that the text paper and cover board used have met acceptable environmental accreditation standards.

For further information on
Blackwell Publishing, visit our website:
www.blackwellpublishing.com

Contents

Contributors

Mikko Aro is a researcher at the Niilo Mäki Institute, Jyväskylä, Finland.

Dare Baldwin is Professor of Psychology at the University of Oregon, Eugene, Oregon, USA.

Ruth A. Berman is Professor Emeritus in the Department of Linguistics at Tel Aviv University, Tel Aviv, Israel.

Gil Diesendruck is Senior Lecturer of Psychology and Member of the Gonda Brain Research Center at Bar-Ilan University, Ramat-Gan, Israel.

Jane Erskine is a researcher at the Niilo Mäki Institute, Jyväskylä, Finland.

Julia L. Evans is Associate Professor at the School of Speech, Language, and Hearing Sciences at San Diego State University, San Diego, California, USA.

Karen Garrido-Nag is a doctoral candidate at The Graduate School and University Center, City University of New York, New York, USA.

Virginia C. Mueller Gathercole is Professor of Psychology at the University of Wales, Bangor, Wales.

Fred Genesee is Professor of Psychology at McGill University, Montreal, Canada.

LouAnn Gerken is Professor of Psychology and Linguistics and Director of the Cognitive Science Program at the University of Arizona, Tucson, Arizona, USA.

Susan A. Graham is Associate Professor of Psychology at the University of Calgary, Calgary, Canada.

Helen Goodluck is Anniversary Chair of Linguistics at the University of York, York, UK.

Erika Hoff is Professor of Psychology at Florida Atlantic University, Davie, Florida, USA.

Linda Jarmulowicz is Assistant Professor of Audiology and Speech-Language Pathology at the University of Memphis, Memphis, Tennessee, USA.

Heikki Lyytinen is Professor of Developmental Neuropsychology at the University of Jyväskylä, Jyväskylä, Finland.

Jeffrey Lidz is Associate Professor of Linguistics at the University of Maryland, College Park, Maryland, USA.

Karen Mattock is a postdoctoral fellow in the McGill Centre for Language, Mind and Brain, Montreal, Canada.

Meredith Meyer is a doctoral student in Psychology at the University of Oregon, Eugene, Oregon, USA.

Letitia R. Naigles is Professor of Psychology at the University of Connecticut, Storrs, Connecticut, USA.

Elena Nicoladis is Assistant Professor of Psychology at the University of Alberta, Edmonton, Alberta, Canada.

D. Kimbrough Oller is Professor and Plough Chair of Excellence in Audiology and Speech-Language Pathology at the University of Memphis, Memphis, Tennessee, USA.

Johanne Paradis is Associate Professor of Linguistics at the University of Alberta, Edmonton, Alberta, Canada.

Linda Polka is Associate Professor of Communication Sciences and Disorders at McGill University, Montreal, Canada.

Diane Poulin-Dubois is Professor of Psychology at Concordia University, Montreal, Canada.

Mabel L. Rice is Fred and Virginia Merrill Distinguished Professor of Advanced Studies at the University of Kansas, Lawrence, Kansas, USA.

Ulla Richardson is a researcher at the University of Jyväskylä, Jyväskylä, Finland.

Susan Rvachew is Assistant Professor of Communication Sciences and Disorders at McGill University, Montreal, Canada.

Jenny R. Saffran is Professor of Psychology at the University of Wisconsin – Madison, Madison, Wisconsin, USA.

Valerie L. Shafer is Associate Professor of Speech and Hearing Science at The Graduate School and University Center, City University of New York, New York, USA.

Marilyn Shatz is Professor of Psychology and Linguistics at the University of Michigan, Ann Arbor, Michigan, USA.

Michael Siegal is Marie Curie Chair in Psychology at the University of Trieste, Trieste, Italy, and Professor of Psychology at the University of Sheffield, Sheffield, UK.

Anna Vogel Sosa is a doctoral student in Speech and Hearing Sciences at the University of Washington, Seattle, Washington, USA.

Carol Stoel-Gammon is Professor of Speech and Hearing Sciences at the University of Washington, Seattle, Washington, USA.

Luca Surian is Associate Professor of Psychology at the University of Trieste, Trieste, Italy.

Lauren D. Swensen is a doctoral student in Psychology at the University of Connecticut, Storrs, Connecticut, USA.

Helen Tager-Flusberg is Professor of Anatomy and Neurobiology and Pediatrics at Boston University School of Medicine and Professor of Psychology at Boston University, Boston, Massachusetts, USA.

Erik D. Thiessen is Assistant Professor of Psychology at Carnegie Mellon University, Pittsburgh, Pennsylvania, USA.

Preface

As they watch their children begin to acquire and use language, that benchmark of human behavior, parents voice both delight and wonder. Researchers, too, have expressed wonder at the children's accomplishments, and although the scientific study of language acquisition is relatively recent as topics of academic investigation go, they have made it a lively one, marked by often heated debate. Between us, we have observed nine children and grandchildren learning to talk, and we have gained much insight from them. Also, taken together, our work over three decades tallies up to more than 50 years of scientific research. We have witnessed many developments since one of us, as an assistant professor, advised the other, her first PhD student at the University of Michigan. We worked together then, investigating questions of the role of input. Now, more than 25 years later, we have collaborated again to assess changes in the field and to gather chapters into a Handbook for present-day students that conveys the current state of the science in the context of the field's history.

From the start, we envisioned a volume organized around periods of development instead of the more conventional organization around the different aspects of language. We aimed with such an organization to emphasize how the field has been changing from one that focused primarily on the logical problem of language acquisition to one that addresses not only this issue but more directly considers the development of language in actual children by examining both their ability to learn any language and also their accomplishments in learning one or more particular ones over time. An introductory chapter setting recent work broadly in its historical context, evaluating the state of the science, and raising questions for future research helps to keep the organization true to our original aim. It and the chapters that follow offer a contemporary account of the field.

Our primary thanks go to our authors, who heeded our requests for state of the art chapters that set topics in historical context, critically summarized the current state of research, and offered suggestions for the future. They graciously dealt with our prodding over deadlines, as well as our advice on revisions. We met several times over the course of several years to work on the Handbook, sometimes at conferences we both conveniently attended, and twice in Florida, where Brett Laursen generously offered us a place to work face-to-face, a happy change from the endless e-mailings. Funds from the Consortium for Language, Society, and Thought at the University of Michigan facilitated face-to-face meetings.

Erika's thanks go also to Sarah Bird, who as acquisitions editor for Blackwell first suggested undertaking this Handbook, and to Brett Laursen, who shared the benefit of his greater experience in the role of editor of a collected volume. Marilyn's thanks go also to her many classes of students in her graduate language development classes at the University of Michigan, especially the students in the 2005 class, none of whom were specialists in language development, but who nevertheless brought deep interest and fresh perspectives to the topic. Her colleagues at Michigan, especially Sam Epstein, Rick Lewis, and Twila Tardif, as well as visitors to the university, particularly Lila Gleitman, Elena Nicoladis, John Trueswell, and Charles Yang, deserve thanks too for informative seminars and stimulating conversations.

Finally, we would both like to express our appreciation to Sarah Bird for her advice and encouragement during the early stages of the project and to others at Blackwell Publishing who helped in the making of this book: Andrew McAleer, Elizabeth-Ann Johnston, Jenny Phillips, and Simon Eckley. Special thanks are due to Melanie Weiss, of Florida Atlantic University, who ably and cheerfully provided secretarial assistance to the project.

Erika Hoff
Marilyn Shatz

1

On the Development of the Field of Language Development

Marilyn Shatz

"Plus ça change, plus c'est la même chose."

A conversation between a 2-year-old boy and his grandmother (1991):
  GM: (*reading*) There were many, many buildings in the city.
  C: Many, many builds.

A conversation between a 3¹/₂-year-old girl and her grandmother (2006):
  GM: They're building a house.
  C: No, not "*building*." Say "*making*."

Speculation about how children come to know a language antedates by centuries the systematic investigation of the topic; only in the last century did the methodical study of language development explode. In roughly 100 years (dating the field's origins from the diaries of the Sterns, 1907) there have been a myriad of studies on children's language development and many consequent changes in both method and theory. Within this relatively short history, the field has reflected the changing "hot" intellectual trends of the times. Thus, the first half of the twentieth century saw descriptive, normative work like McCarthy's (1930), whereas much work in the latter half of the twentieth century, influenced by theoretical work in linguistics, attempted to prove or disprove claims about predispositions specific to language (see Pinker, 1994). Now, in the early twenty-first century, much research in language development is concerned with brain development and computational skills, cross-linguistic and cultural comparisons, and bilingualism and education. This Handbook strives to capture the state of the art by bringing together chapters written by a generation of researchers who mainly address current concerns.

However, a reading of the chapters in this Handbook reveals that questions of predispositional specificity, though changed, are still with us. The first arguments for language-specific predispositions made an obviously false but simplifying assumption that language acquisition was instantaneous (see Chomsky, 1975). Instead, more recent work makes development an important factor in the language acquisition story, thereby requiring renewed evaluation of the roles played in an ongoing acquisition process by the child's physiological, cognitive, and social status, as well as caregiver input. There is, then, increased appreciation for how multiple interacting factors may contribute to language acquisition and how weightings among them may change with development.

Moreover, it is clear that the predisposition issue can be divided into a question about what the predispositions are and a question about whether any of these are necessarily specific to the task of acquiring language. In this volume, there are chapters reporting findings sometimes relevant to one question and sometimes both. With regard to language-specific constraints, for example, Diesendruck, in his chapter, asks whether mechanisms that limit possible word meanings are specific to that domain or are more general, and Lidz, in his chapter, asks whether children's early syntactic knowledge supports evidence of early abstract grammatical representations. Whereas the evidence argues against domain-specific predispositions for word learning, it is premature to decide the case for syntactic competence (see the section *Do we still need domain-specific constraints?* for more discussion). Despite the changes the field has undergone in recent years, the continuing concern about the nature of the child's abilities is an apt instance of the idea that the more there is change, the more there is constancy.

There is other evidence of constancy in the face of change. Four decades ago, systematic research on language development was almost exclusively focused on how young children acquire English as their native language. More recently, research has expanded to include work on older children and has produced findings on how linguistic knowledge develops with experiences such as learning a second language and learning to write, and how earlier developments in oral language are related to the later acquisition of reading (see chapters by Oller & Jarmulowicz and by Paradis on second-language learning, by Berman on later language use, and by Lyytinen, Erskine, Aro, & Richardson, on learning to read). Researchers have also asked whether and how the course of acquisition changes as a function of cultural differences or differences in language types (see, e.g., Slobin, 1985, 1992, 1997). Work in this vein revealed some interesting facts about early language development. For example, child-directed language is not necessary to acquisition (e.g., Ochs & Schieffelin, 1984), and children are sensitive very early on to language-particular features, even those encoding such basic notions as space, time, and manner (e.g., Bowerman, 1996; Bowerman & Choi, 2001). Children acquire a language under many different conditions of exposure; yet regardless of those conditions, they seem to make ordered decisions about the particular language to which they are exposed (Baker, 2005).

Moreover, children learning the same language in different times and under different conditions also exhibit similar concerns during development. The quotes above, from two children who were learning English in different decades and rearing conditions, reveal that both children by age 3 were troubled by the potential ambiguity in grammatical class of the word *building*, although they apparently had previously analyzed the word in different ways. One seemed concerned that the morphological ending *-ing* be non-ambiguous in indexing verbs, whereas the other seemed to have coded the word as a noun, regardless of ending, and refused to accept a usage that would result in an ambiguity of grammatical class. Such anecdotes suggest that, at least by age 3, young children do not mindlessly accept the language they hear, but they think about it somewhat abstractly and creatively.

Thus, while the field has expanded to address a broader range of topics concerning language development and use, it is important to note that the central phenomenon needing explanation has not much changed – children acquire a great deal of the language of their community in a comparatively short time without much direct tuition and with remarkable commonality in the concerns they have. Both the similarities and differences in their patterns of development require explanation.

Also, it is common, though not often recognized by scientific researchers, that current states of knowledge rest on the contributions and efforts of prior generations. In the abstract, science proceeds via the falsification of theories; but in practice, wholesale changes or substitutions of alternative world views are rare. Instead, increasingly sophisticated empirical investigations provide the engine for theoretical change. While debates within a field are often portrayed as dichotomous – with positions declared to be either formalist or functionalist, black or white, right or wrong, proven or disproven – the reality is often not so discontinuous, and progress in a field typically comes via rapprochement, as both earlier questions and earlier answers are modified to accommodate more recent findings. As much as language development research has progressed in recent years, the footprints of its past are still visible.

In this chapter, I elaborate on these observations by addressing some themes of language development research, taking note of some of the precursors to the more recent work, and suggesting promising research topics for the future.

The Enduring Question about Language Development

Every human language is a complex system. Each includes regular ways of combining a limited set of signs or sounds to create an unlimited set of meanings. Any relatively normal child born into a relatively normal language-using community will, even without formal education, develop the ability to use that community's language. How this feat is accomplished so readily has been and still is the central question of the field of language development.

The legacy of theories of syntactic formalism

Are areas of language autonomous?   The work of two language theorists greatly affected the organization of twentieth-century research in the field of language development. First, the philosopher and semiotician Charles Peirce described four distinct components of language: phonology, semantics, syntax, and pragmatics. Second, linguists, most notably Chomsky, reified these distinctions by offering compelling theories, particularly of syntax, that assumed for analytic purposes the autonomy of separate parts. Scholarly work and curricula in linguistics departments came to be organized around the distinctions, and even handbooks and textbooks of language development (e.g., Fletcher & MacWhinney, 1995; Hoff, 2005) commonly organized the field around them.

Peirce's distinctions help even today in understanding the complex phenomena of language and its acquisition. After all, children learn the signs or sounds of a language, they learn words and word meanings, they learn how to combine words into meaningful and acceptable sentences, and they learn how to interpret such sentences in a variety of circumstances. A reasonable, scientifically sound, first approach was to analyze all these accomplishments separately and to see how far one could go with the simplifying assumption of autonomy of components. The autonomy approach fueled a lively community of researchers in syntactic theory, and its application to the field of language acquisition did have some success, perhaps most clearly with regard to the knowledge gained about the capacities of infants to analyze the sound patterns of their language (see Polka, Rvachew, & Mattock, this volume).

Yet, the autonomy assumption was made for analytic purposes; it is an empirical question whether children necessarily abide by it when developing language. Increasingly, researchers propose interactive theories, where one kind of linguistic knowledge can influence, or is even crucial to, the development of another (see, e.g., Gleitman, Cassidy, Nappa, Papafragou, & Trueswell, 2005). In addition, formal linguists are increasingly recognizing that the ways in which the components interface, and even interact, are crucially important to analytic characterizations of adult language (e.g., Chomsky, 1995).

To capture this trend, as well as to emphasize the factor of development in the acquisition of language, we chose to organize the sections of this volume according to an age continuum rather than by components of language. Although the chapters within each Part by and large still reflect the fact that researchers focus more on a specific component of linguistic knowledge than on interactions among components, the growing tendency to account for the phenomena of one with explanations partly dependent upon another is nevertheless well represented. Currently, the topic of word learning is the best example of an area in the acquisition field where researchers propose that knowledge of one language component helps to account for development in another. So, in this volume, a chapter by Naigles and Swensen, one by Stoel-Gammon and Sosa, and one by Diesendruck argue for syntactic, phonological, and pragmatic knowledge, respectively, as factors aiding word learning.

The idea of interaction across components of language has found more advocates in recent years, and so has the idea of interaction among areas of development. Currently, infants' social abilities play a large role in some language development theorists' thinking (e.g., Baldwin & Meyer, this volume), and the question of the separateness of language and cognition is receiving renewed interest (see Saffran & Thiessen, this volume). There are several ways to achieve more interaction among areas of development. Basing language acquisition on cognitive or social knowledge (e.g., Tomasello, 1992) is one way, but that has been argued to be troubled (see Poulin-Dubois & Graham, this volume; Shatz, 1992). Another way is to integrate language intimately into the very fabric of a system of development and thereby provide a more unified account of how the child moves toward adulthood (Shatz, 1994, in press). While the question of how children acquire the complex system of language is still central, an increasingly common goal among researchers in the field of language development is to take more account of other areas of development; theoretical accounts of acquisition that recognize neither a broader picture of language development nor the child's ability to operate across areas are waning in influence.

The poverty of the stimulus.   Another argument about acquisition that was generated by the dominance of work in syntactic theory was the one from the poverty of the stimulus (see Chomsky, 1980). The claim here was that infants and children do not hear language which sufficiently or directly reveals to them the underlying and abstract grammatical structure governing all and only the grammatical sentences of a particular language. Without such information, children cannot converge on the correct structure of the language they do hear. The idea that language acquisition was constrained by innate universal grammatical principles guiding their acquisition filled this input gap.

Early controversy over the poverty of the stimulus argument concerned whether the environment or the child provided the engine of development (see Shatz, 1987, for early arguments in favor of the child). Decades of research on the language spoken to the child, beginning in the 1970s, attempted to find evidence against the poverty of the stimulus argument, first by showing that child-directed speech was largely grammatical, and then by proposing that it was richer in structure than earlier envisioned (see Baldwin & Meyer; Gathercole & Hoff; Gerken, this volume, for more history on this topic).

Recently, the arguments against the poverty of the stimulus claim have been changing in an important way. Input theorists no longer argue simply for a much richer overt input to a relatively passive child. Rather, the argument now is that the child has general capacities for extracting over time from a range of input sentences a deeper set of relations than are revealed superficially in the input (see, e.g., Elman, 2003). Thus, that the child provides the impetus for acquisition is more readily accepted, but the characterization of the child is also changing, from a child endowed simply with an abstract blueprint for grammar to one with a broader complement of sensitivities and capacities applicable to the language development task.

Nonetheless, the critical issue remains how to characterize the capacities the child needs to traverse the developmental landscape efficiently (see Baker, 2005). Whatever those capacities, the linguistic environment will have to be sufficient in both variety and quantity to offer the child so equipped what it is she needs to abstract her particular language's structure; and there are consequences for the rate and quality of development if it is not (see Hoff, 1999, 2006). Still controversial are questions of whether any of the capacities are domain-specific and which are innate or emergent during development. On the one hand, some researchers have provided evidence that children have general abilities for extracting information from input (see Gerken; Saffran & Thiessen, this volume). On the other hand, some researchers offer particular acquisition phenomena as evidence of the continuing need for language-specific constraints (see Lidz, this volume). At least as yet, there are no explicit general accounts of these (see also Lidz & Gleitman, 2004), although there are those who believe that such general capacities ultimately will account for all of language development (e.g., MacWhinney, 2004; Tomasello, 2003; but see Hoff, 2004; Legate & Yang, 2002).

No negative evidence.   Related to the poverty of the stimulus argument is the no-negative-evidence-in-input argument. If, when children make mistakes of grammar as they acquire language, they neither get corrected nor pay much attention to corrections, how do they recover from their mistakes? One early proposed solution to the no-negative-evidence problem was the subset principle: Children are constrained to consider first only those grammars that generate a subset of grammatical sentences so that upon hearing in input the positive evidence of the broader set of sentences, they can adjust their grammars (Berwick, 1986). Alternatively, a generation of researchers sought to find evidence against the whole idea of the no-negative-evidence problem by showing that children had at least probabilistic information from parental responses as to the grammaticality of their utterances, but such efforts proved to be inadequate (see Marcus, 1993). In this volume, Goodluck does not eliminate the no-negative-evidence problem. Instead, she tries to avoid Berwick's otherwise unmotivated subset principle by arguing for the possibility that the processing system responsible for comprehending and producing language itself provides a developmental constraint on the workings of the linguistic system. Namely, limited processing ability constrains access to universal grammar, and this accounts for errors and omissions under a variety of circumstances. As is made clear in the next section, how processing constraints are construed can have deep implications for a basic tenet of formalist theory.

Competence and performance.   Obviously, scientific study requires that the phenomena under investigation be identified. Chomsky identified his topic of linguistic interest not as human language use, but as the knowledge of grammar adults possess; and the evidence of the nature of that knowledge was to be found not in utterances but in judgments of grammaticality. In consequence, what is known became divorced from what is said, and errors of speech were argued to be subject to chance factors – vagaries of the moment that might afflict any speaker at any time, and of no relevance to questions of linguistic competence or knowledge. With regard to language development, the issue of how to assess competence and not just performance was a particularly knotty one, since no matter how clever the experimenters, they still were left with only overt behaviors by which to assess underlying knowledge. With very young children, there are no opportunities to obtain judgments of grammaticality. Unsurprisingly, then, the latter half of the twentieth century saw many controversies about what constituted evidence for or against linguistic competence and what could be discounted as reflecting "only" performance variables.

Recent work in psycholinguistics has sought to bridge the gap between competence and performance. If, for example, a language processor is constrained by limitations of human working memory, that processor itself may have an impact on the very nature of syntactic structure (see Lewis & Vasishth, 2005). Such a processor apparently differs from Goodluck's proposal because it influences the very nature of language structure itself and not just access to it. Its effects, then, would be constant, not developmental. Possibly there are several sorts of processing constraints, some accounting for structural characteristics and others for how children at different levels of development handle various kinds of task demands (see Werker & Curtin, 2005, for an example of the latter). In any case, what seemed like a clear formalist distinction between competence and performance has become blurred. Indeed, doing away altogether with the distinction is the radical solution proposed by dynamic systems theorists (who do away with the standard notion of representation as well). By integrating knowledge and performance in favor of real-time processing, Evans argues in this volume that language is "performance in context."

There is still the question, however, of just what is meant by "processing." Is there a domain-specific processor that affects the very structure of language? Is there as well a more general processor with additional limitations that also affects processing of linguistic as well as non-linguistic information? Are there unique limitations on processing due to immaturity? What is the relation between processing and representation? The increased interest in "processing" – and the attendant demise of the competence–performance distinction – is indicative of the promise of processing arguments, although such arguments are in need of more empirical support and more theoretical clarification.

What constrains the acquisition of language?

In 1965, Chomsky proposed a language acquisition device (largely for syntax) that was endowed with a universal grammar such that it received specific-language input which was underdetermined with regard to that language's underlying structure but nonetheless could instantly output any and only grammatical sentences of that language. The universal grammar itself consisted of both constraints on allowable human languages – what they could not be – and specifications of what they could consist of, thereby limiting the allowable conclusions the device could draw from the input received about the nature of the particular language to be learned.

We knew in 1965 that the device had to be flexible enough to acquire any human language. As a result of subsequent research on the acquisition of sign languages, we now know that the device is not limited even to one modality (e.g., Petitto & Marentette, 1991); and as a result of research on bilingual development, we know that it is not limited to acquiring one language at a time (Genesee & Nicoladis, this volume). Also, by applying new genetic and neurobiological techniques to the study of language development, we have discovered that various atypical outcomes can arise from genetically based, neurodevelopmental disorders (Rice; Shafer & Garrido-Nag; Tager-Flusberg, this volume).

We have also seen that the question of what constrains the acquisition of language receives a much broader answer today. Not only do researchers in language development generally accept a broader scope to the field, but they also accept the fact that language acquisition is not instantaneous but is subject to development, with the weightings of various influential factors changing as the child's knowledge states change. Interactions among components of language knowledge, as well as among different areas of development – in particular the physiological, social, and cognitive spheres – are increasingly recognized as relevant to the complex process of language acquisition. Currently, the "language acquisition device" can be described as a probabilistic thinker, capable of making inductive inferences across utterances over time based on a broad array of cues changing with development.

In the next section, I consider some of the trends in past research that foreshadowed the current, more comprehensive, view of the language learner, and I ask whether the current view suffices to do without the idea of domain-specific abilities.

The Nature of the Child Developing Language

The active, social child

The field of language development can thank Jean Piaget for the notion of a child actively navigating a course of development. Beyond that important but general view, however, Piaget's characterization of a child progressing through stages of cognitive development governed by dialectical mechanisms of assimilation and accommodation offered little help in explaining the phenomena of language development. Indeed, attempts to find cases in which language milestones could be based directly on cognitive developments bore relatively little fruit (see Poulin-Dubois & Graham, this volume, for discussion). Bruner's attempts to base language development on the child's active social interactions similarly met with failure (see Baldwin & Meyer, this volume, for a review). It is not because language development is autonomous that such attempts failed. Rather, it is because they did not recognize how integrated these areas of development are for the child; the divisions of social, cognitive, and language development are divisions of the researcher, not of the child. The task of a developing child is to become an active, knowledgeable participant of a language community. To do so, she uses whatever pre-dispositions and knowledge she has to increase her understanding even as she engages in it. It is in this sense that she bootstraps her way to adult competence as an active, social child (Shatz, 1987, 1994).

Two decades ago, I summarized the evidence available then for active child language learners who "use what they have to learn more" (p. 1), and I proposed a set of capacities a normal language learner would use to control the process of acquiring a native language (Shatz, 1987). The capacity to elicit speech in referentially transparent situations through gesture and eye gaze, and eventually, simple utterances, was an ability that I suggested served the function of eliciting data potentially rich, not only in syntactic information, but also in pragmatic and semantic information ("elicitation operations"). Second, I suggested that the capacity to store strings in units large enough for off-line comparison and analysis was necessary ("entry operations"). Finally, I proposed a set of "expansion operations" that provided the child the opportunity to explore and analyze what she knew of language – its structure and use – through language play, practice, and organization, thereby to generalize and self-repair.

Much of what appears in this volume is not only compatible with these proposals, but supports, elaborates, and clarifies them. New findings on children's statistical learning abilities (Saffran & Thiessen, this volume) and sensitivity to form (Gerken, this volume) give added specification and substance to the ideas of entry and expansion operations. Evidence for pragmatic and syntactic bootstrapping (see Diesendruck; Naigles & Swensen, this volume) is consonant with the claim that children use what they know to learn more, and so is evidence that children, by virtue of their immaturity, inexperience, or incomplete knowledge, sometimes make inaccurate syntactic self-repairs (Shatz & Ebeling, 1991) or inappropriate pragmatic inferences (Siegal & Surian, this volume). Research on language disorders also supports and expands on my argument that different disorders result from the disruption of different kinds of operations the child can carry out (see Rice; Tager-Flusberg, this volume). An active child, then, is one who brings a variety of capacities to the complex task of language acquisition, and based on whatever her capacities and knowledge at the time, she makes inferences about her linguistic situation at that moment.

What role remains for the environment? In a comprehensive review of the influences of variable social environments on language development, Hoff (2006) provides considerable evidence for the myriad social factors that affect development, from the amount of time children spend in conversation to the contexts in which they hear talk. Hoff proposes that, regardless of differences in such social circumstances, all environments supportive of language must provide two things: opportunities for communicative interaction and an analyzable language model. However, as Hoff notes, no matter how rich an environment is in such opportunities, it cannot by itself be effective as a support for language development if the child does not take advantage of them.

To optimize their learning opportunities, then, children have to be social beings, interested and able to engage in communicative interactions involving language, very possibly using the proposed elicitation operations to maintain and enhance the learning environment, as well as having the skills to analyze the language model it offers. How much opportunity they have to exercise their skills, and how well their language model matches their abilities for analysis will have an effect on the rate and course of their particular language development.

None of this seems especially arguable. Infants typically engage with their interlocutors early and often; infants and toddlers who don't do so have problems with language development, sometimes very severe ones (see Baldwin & Meyer; Tager-Flusberg, this volume). Yet, even some children who don't engage normally can acquire a fair amount of language, including a vocabulary of reasonable size (Diesendruck, this volume). How sociable does a child have to be to acquire any language at all?

If indeed children use what they know to learn more, one possibility is that children who are less sociable substitute other skills when learning language. For example, when learning new words, children with autism may make few inferences (or none at all) about the speaker intentions that apparently inform typically developing children about word meaning; rather, they may focus more on associations or distributional cues. This view fits well with the argument that there are multiple clues to the nature of language. Individual differences in quality and rate of acquisition would depend, then, not only on differences in social environments but also on which clues children with varying skills could use in varying environments to access them. Social–linguistic environments need to provide multiple cues a child can use to discover how to act and interact both linguistically and non-linguistically in her community. But the developing child actively and selectively attends to the cues as she grows in both brain (Shafer & Garrido-Nag, this volume) and mind (Poulin-Dubois & Graham, this volume).

Do we still need domain-specific constraints?

Conversations as information conduits.   Infants have a preference for speech sounds over non-speech sounds. This attentional bias toward language suggests that the human child may be prepared to engage with conspecifics via language, the benchmark behavior of humans. Such a bias may be the initial entrée into developing one's own language competence. Also, it may facilitate a very early infant behavior – engaging in reciprocal interactions involving vocalizations, which is typically rewarding for both caregiver and infant. Such "proto-conversations" become increasingly sophisticated, and conversations are major sources of information for the developing child (see Shatz, in press; Siegal & Surian, this volume). There are many ways young children can learn – by observing others, or by trial and error, for example. But no ways other than conversation provide information via indirect experience, or what Harris (2002) has called "testimony." Moreover, the richness and variety of information that can be conveyed in relatively short time is unmatched by other means. In short, engaging in conversations via language is a powerful tool for learning and not just learning language.

So far, the picture we have of the optimally successful language learner is one of an active, social child equipped with early attention to language, possessing probabilistic inferencing skills, and engaged in frequent communicative interactions rich with linguistic information. Can a child so equipped traverse the linguistic landscape efficiently enough to learn the substance of any of thousands of human languages by school age?

Language typologies as a constraint on the learning task.   Whether the learning problem, especially with regard to the acquisition of syntax, can be settled solely by recourse to the kind of child described above is far from clear (see Baldwin & Meyer, this volume, for more discussion). Chomsky's early insights led him to argue for an innate universal grammar based on abstract principles underlying all human languages. A later proposal clarified how both the commonalities and the differences among languages could be accommodated in such a system: All human language can be described in terms of a small number of dimensions or parameters having a limited number of settings, with each setting potentially accounting for apparently disparate superficial characteristics. Any specific language, then, can be described by its particular combination of set values; and the vast numbers of languages result from the various possible combinations of settings on those parameters (see Chomsky, 1981). According to this view, the learning task is more manageable because, rather than considering a virtually unlimited number of hypotheses, a child equipped with knowledge of that small number of parameters would have only to determine which of the possible parametric values pertain to the particular language to be learned. Despite the elegance of this approach, attempts to apply it directly to account for the data of language acquisition have been controversial at best (see Goodluck, this volume, for more on parameters and their application to the problem of language acquisition).

Baker (2001, 2005) has offered a version of parameter setting that seems more compatible both with recent findings on universals of grammar and, at least on the surface, with the picture of the child as a probabilistic thinker who learns language over time, keeping track of correlational properties and making inferences from them. Rather than couching parameters in terms of formal universal principles, Baker bases them on generalizations from implicational universals. These are descriptive statements about language commonalities and differences with respect to the ways linguistic properties correlate with one another, and they are stated in terms of probabilities; for example, 70% of languages do one thing and not another. He notes that some parameters can have a greater impact on a particular language's form than others, and he orders the parameters hierarchically according to their ability to affect one another; parameters higher in the hierarchy than others have at least one setting which eliminates the need to consider other parameters at all.

If children first set the parameters higher in the ordering, they would not, depending on the language they were learning, necessarily need to consider lower-ordered ones at all, thereby narrowing still further the learning task. If the language to be learned did require further parameter setting, the errors children made would be consonant with not yet having considered parameters lower in the hierarchy. Baker's ideal learner is one who, in developing a grammar, observes the ordering. Baker provides some preliminary evidence from children's errors at early stages of grammatical development showing that they do appear to observe that ordering.

Baker explicitly leaves open the question of whether the particular learning mechanisms needed to account for what he proposes are domain-general or domain-specific. In either case, the particular-language input, or what Baker refers to as the "primary linguistic data" (p. 119, footnote 9), must contain the information the child needs so as to learn according to the ordering. This requires, then, a symbiosis between the input and the child's learning abilities. Recent work on sensitivity to the frequency of linguistic information and its consistency in the input suggests that frequency and consistency monitoring are within the ken of young children (see Gathercole & Hoff, this volume). If different types of information in the input vary enough on these dimensions, the input may "order" appropriately the apparent parametric decisions children seem to make. The reported ordering evidence may be explainable, then, as a consequence of a child, sensitive to the frequency and consistency with which the input displays particular phenomena, repeatedly operating over such input and inferring structural relationships in a manner consistent with the hierarchy. This sort of explanation helps to dispense with any need for prior knowledge of the parametric hierarchy.

However, before one can conclude that domain-specific knowledge is not required, one must ask what the entities themselves are that are being monitored for frequency and consistency. Are they abstract linguistic concepts, and if so, how can the abstractness be accounted for? Implicational universals are typically written in terms of abstract grammatical entities like *verb* and *direct object*, and even the most general description of them, as in Baker's parameters, utilizes some linguistic abstractions like *word* or *phrase*. Baker's solution does not seem neutral with regard to the source or kind of representational abilities needed to deal with the abstractions. Baker suggests that children have "an innate phrase building mechanism, which stands ready to group whatever words the child happens to learn into useful larger phrases" (Baker, 2005, p. 104). So, his proposal relating typological data and acquisition relies on an innate structure-building device handling abstract linguistic representations. In this regard, it seems little different from and hardly more plausible than earlier claims for innate, language-specific abilities.

Despite the issue of their implausibility, is it nonetheless necessary to grant innate domain-specific capacities to the learner? A "yes" answer may be premature. Saffran and Thiessen (this volume) make several important arguments relevant to the question. First, they note that questions of innateness and domain-specificity are orthogonal issues: Logically, either kind of abilities, general or specific, can be innate or emergent. Second, they offer evidence that "domain-general learning abilities" should not be construed as completely unconstrained; rather, they are limited by specifically human perceptual and cognitive constraints, and those constrained abilities can shape a specific domain like language to include just those properties (such as phrase-based structures) needed to mesh with the learning capacities. When coupled with the notion of development in which such abilities operate repeatedly over inputs themselves previously modified by virtue of cycles of increasingly sophisticated organizations, this proposal suggests a powerful mechanism, able to account for the emergence in the learner's competence of linguistic notions like "verb" or "phrase" (see Saffran & Thiessen, this volume). The symbiotic relationship between language typology and acquisition may thereby be preserved without the need to stipulate innate, domain-specific abilities to account for domain-specific representations.

However, at this point in the course of research into language development, the questions of whether and how a resolution to the domain-specificity debate will bring us closer to a true understanding of language development remain unanswered. Because the constraints on human domain-general abilities are not fully understood, it is as yet unclear how substantive are the differences between the domain-general view and the domain-specific view. The commonalities among languages attest to the existence of constraints somewhere, but whether to situate them in language because of the nature of the learner or in the learner because of the nature of language may turn out simply to be a question of perspective, reminiscent of the controversy between proponents of Chomskyan and Gibsonian theories about whether constraints on our view of the world are situated in our minds or in the world. The unhappy possibility here is that this question is merely a metaphysical one, not amenable to serious empirical inquiry capable of resolving the issue. The hope that it is not rests on the expectation that further empirical investigations into constraints on domain-general abilities will reveal that their differences from a domain-specific view are not merely superficial. If the differences are substantive, then how the views weigh in on two scientific criteria should help to decide in favor of one or the other: namely, whether one view accounts for more phenomena than the other, and whether the explanatory constructs offered by one rather than the other are more compatible with constructs at other levels of explanation. The goal of domain-general theorists seems to be to win the day on both those counts.

Tasks for Future Research

Many of the authors of chapters in this volume note gaps in our current understanding of language development and make specific suggestions for future research. Here I note several general concerns that have emerged in this review.

Above all, we need an explanatory theory of language development in which language acquisition neither stands alone nor is said simply to result from other kinds of development or knowledge – cognitive or social. If we take seriously the claim of interactions among areas of development, then language knowledge cannot simply emerge out of, say, social development, although various aspects of social understanding, of intention and mind, can come into play to expand language knowledge. We need to expand our understanding of how various areas of development interact mutually to sustain development, and we need as well to continue to address how areas within language knowledge impact development of one another. Only then can we expect to have a truly comprehensive, explanatory theory of language development.

Another obvious goal for the future is a more complete understanding of human information processing abilities. We need to know how these human abilities differ from those of other creatures, what unique characteristics ours may have, whether and how they change with development, and how human processing characteristics may influence the very nature of human languages.

We also need to know more about the genetic basis of human abilities. Surely, increasing knowledge about how genes work will help us to discover more about the genetic bases of language, but already our growing understanding of human genetics suggests that the idea of a single "language gene" is a journalistic fantasy. Genes multi-determine behavior, including language behavior, and deficits in single genes typically have multiple consequences, some on the linguistic system, some not. Increasingly, efforts to dissociate language from cognition seem as infelicitous as earlier efforts to correlate language milestones with Piagetian cognitive developmental ones.

Our knowledge of the development of the human brain is itself in an infant stage. We need to know more about the developing human brain, and to have more evidence on the limits brain immaturity imposes on the functional ability to extract information from the environment. We also need to know whether, when, and how different aspects of the environment, such as the availability of more than one input language, have an impact on the developing brain.

As we become more knowledgeable in these areas, we will gain even more understanding than we now have about how the predispositions that human infants bring to the task of developing language interface with their language communities to produce mature language knowledge. Recognizing their intimate relationship, we nowadays pay little attention to the nature–nurture dichotomy that for so long characterized debates in the field of language acquisition. In the future, we may very well discard the domain-general versus domain-specific dichotomy, as we learn more about how human information processing capacities are innately constrained and how they in turn constrain the structure of language. We may even decide that the best characterization of the course of language development is that there is no single course, but instead multiple paths through varying epigenetic landscapes determined by a particularly endowed child acquiring a specific language in a specific cultural context. Still, what constrains the number and kinds of those paths will be the limited ways a genetic program interacting with an "expected" environment in order to build a functional human adult can be modified by accidents of nature or nurture.

The chapters in this book represent the state of the art early in the second century of systematic work on the question of how language is acquired by human infants. They summarize the history of the field and its progress to date. To their credit, regardless of their theoretical bents, the authors have by and large eschewed an antagonistic tone in favor of presenting and interpreting data reasonably even-handedly, recognizing gaps, and noting continuing challenges. Such open-minded candor itself presages well for a field with very old questions and still-developing answers.

Note

I owe much to Sam Epstein and Richard Lewis for a provocative seminar on competence and performance at the University of Michigan in fall, 2004, and to the authors with whom I discussed revisions to their chapters. I also thank Erika Hoff and Richard Feingold for comments on earlier versions of this chapter. Of course, remaining errors and interpretations are mine.

References

Baker, M. (2001). *The atoms of language.* New York: Basic Books.

Baker, M. (2005). Mapping the terrain of language learning. *Language Learning and Development, 1*, 93–129.

Berwick, R. (1986). *The acquisition of syntactic knowledge.* Cambridge, MA: MIT Press.

Bowerman, M. (1996). Learning how to structure space for language: A crosslinguistic perspective. In P. Bloom & M. A. Peterson (Eds.), *Language and space: Language, speech, and communication* (pp. 385–436). Cambridge, MA: MIT Press.

Bowerman, M., & Choi, S. (2001). Shaping meaning for language: Universal and language specific in the acquisition of spatial semantic categories. In M. Bowerman & S. Levinson (Eds.), *Language acquisition and conceptual development* (pp. 475–511). Cambridge: Cambridge University Press.

Chomsky, N. (1965). *Aspects of the theory of syntax.* Cambridge, MA: MIT Press.

Chomsky, N. (1975). *Reflections on language.* New York: Pantheon Books.

Chomsky, N. (1980). *Rules and representations.* London: Basil Blackwell.

Chomsky, N. (1981). *Lectures on government and binding.* Dordrecht, The Netherlands: Foris.

Chomsky, N. (1995). *The minimalist program.* Cambridge, MA: MIT Press.

Elman, J. (2003). Generalizations from sparse input. In *Proceedings of the 38th Annual Meeting of the Chicago Linguistic Society.* Chicago: University of Chicago Press.

Fletcher, P., & MacWhinney, B. (1995). *Handbook of language acquisition.* London: Blackwell.

Gleitman, L. R., Cassidy, K., Nappa, R., Papafragou, A., & Trueswell, J. C. (2005). Hard words. *Language Learning and Development, 1*, 23–64.

Harris, P. (2002). What do children learn from testimony? In P. Carruthers, S. Stich, & M. Siegal (Eds.), *The cognitive basis of science* (pp. 316–334). Cambridge: Cambridge University Press.

Hoff, E. (1999). Formalism or functionalism? Evidence from the study of language development. In M. Darnell, E. Moravscik, M. Noonan, F. Newmeyer, & K. Wheatlery (Eds.), *Functionalism and formalism in linguistics* (pp. 317–340). Amsterdam: John Benjamins.

Hoff, E. (2004). Progress, but not a full solution to the logical problem of language acquisition. *Journal of Child Language, 31*, 923–926.

Hoff, E. (2005). *Language development*. Belmont, CA: Thomson Wadsworth.

Hoff, E. (2006). How social contexts support and shape language development. *Developmental Review, 26*, 55–88.

Legate, J. A., & Yang, C. D. (2002). Empirical reassessment of stimulus poverty arguments. *The Linguistic Review, 19*, 151–162.

Lewis, R., & Vasishth, S. (2005). An activation-based model of sentence processing as skilled memory retrieval. *Cognitive Science, 29*, 375–419.

Lidz, J., & Gleitman, L. R. (2004). Yes, we still need a universal grammar. *Cognition, 94*, 85–93.

MacWhinney, B. (2004). A multiple process solution to the logical problem of language acquisition. *Journal of Child Language, 31*, 883–914.

Marcus, G. F. (1993). Negative evidence in language acquisition. *Cognition, 46*, 53–85.

McCarthy, D. (1930). *The language development of the preschool child*. Institute of Child Welfare Monograph (Serial No. 4). Minneapolis, MN: University of Minnesota Press.

Ochs, E., & Schieffelin, B. B. (1984). Language acquisition and socialization: Three developmental stories and their implications. In R. A. Shweder & R. A. LeVine (Eds.), *Culture theory: Essays on mind, self, and emotion* (pp. 276–320). New York: Cambridge University Press.

Petitto, L. A., & Marentette, P. F. (1991). Babbling in the manual mode: Evidence for the ontogeny of language. *Science, 251*, 1493–1496.

Pinker, S. (1994). *The language instinct: How the mind creates language*. New York: Morrow.

Shatz, M. (1987). Bootstrapping operations in child language. In K. E. Nelson & A. van Kleeck (Eds.), *Children's language: Vol. 6* (pp. 1–22). Hillsdale, NJ: Erlbaum.

Shatz, M. (1992). A forward or backward step in the search for an adequate theory of language acquisition? *Social Development, 1*, 151–154.

Shatz, M. (1994). *A toddler's life*. New York: Oxford University Press.

Shatz, M. (in press). Revisiting *A Toddler's Life* for *The Toddler Years*: Conversational participation as a tool for learning across knowledge domains. In A. Brownell & C. B. Kopp (Eds.), *Transitions in early socioemotional development: The toddler years*. New York: Guilford.

Shatz, M., & Ebeling, K. (1991). Patterns of language learning related behaviours: Evidence for self-help in acquiring language. *Journal of Child Language, 18*, 295–314.

Slobin, D. (1985). *The crosslinguistic study of language acquisition: Vols. 1 and 2*. Hillsdale, NJ: Erlbaum.

Slobin, D. (1992). *The crosslinguistic study of language acquisition: Vol. 3*. Hillsdale, NJ: Erlbaum.

Slobin, D. (1997). *The crosslinguistic study of language acquisition: Vols. 4 and 5*. Hillsdale, NJ: Erlbaum.

Tomasello, M. (1992). The social bases of language acquisition. *Social Development, 1*, 67–87.

Tomasello, M. (2003). *Constructing a language*. Cambridge, MA: Harvard University Press.

Werker, J., & Curtin, S. (2005). A developmental framework of infant speech processing. *Language Learning and Development, 1*, 197–234.

PART I

Basic Foundations and Theoretical Approaches to Language Development

Introduction

How does the child achieve language? In this Part, five chapters describe five different, though not mutually exclusive, approaches to answering this question. Shafer and Garrido-Nag tackle the question at the physiological level. They begin with a primer on the neurodevelopmental processes that underlie language development, and they review evidence of both similarities and differences between children and adults in how the brain is organized for language functions. They describe the developmental changes that occur in the relation of function to underlying structure as sometimes resulting from changes in the type of processing the child engages in and sometimes resulting from the maturation of the structures themselves. They suggest neural underpinnings for critical-period phenomena and disorders of language development, and they describe a course of development in which input shapes a genetically based initial structure.

Goodluck answers the question of how children achieve language with the generative grammar position that children have innate knowledge of Universal Grammar (UG). She then reviews the problem with this position, namely, that it must be reconciled with the fact that children make errors. She proposes an account of the child language learner as having full access to UG but also as having processing limitations which account for the child's failures to realize UG in actual comprehension and production of sentences.

Saffran and Thiessen review the evidence for the position that children achieve language by applying general learning procedures to the speech they hear. Although the processes they describe are not language specific, applying to both speech and nonspeech stimuli and used by both humans and nonlinguistic species, there are language-specific aspects to the application of these procedures. For example, infants selectively attend to speech with the result that domain-general learning processes are particularly brought to bear on language stimuli in infancy, and domain-general processes make use of language-specific knowledge throughout the course of development in guiding the analyses of input that yield further linguistic knowledge.

Baldwin and Meyer argue that children's social nature is an important part of the explanation of children's linguistic accomplishments. They bring clarity to this position by making distinctions among three kinds of social factors relevant to language acquisition: the social input children receive, children's own social responsiveness, and children's social understandings. They review evidence that usable language input is social (it must come from a person, not a screen), that children's attentiveness to input is socially based, and that children's social understandings provide crucial support to the task of mapping sound to meaning. They present both the view and the controversies associated with the view that language is social and achieved through social means in each aspect: phonology, the lexicon, and syntax.

Gathercole and Hoff argue that the way children achieve language is, to a significant degree, by inducing structure from their analysis of input. They review evidence from analyses of the input available to the child, from computer simulations of acquisition, and from studies of the relation between variation in children's input and children's grammatical development. They also conclude, however, that internal constraints must operate in the course of language development because input affects only the pace of development, not the sequence in which the structures of language are acquired.

Evans brings the theoretical framework of dynamic systems theory to bear on the question of how children achieve language. In doing so, she reformulates the question, asking how the self-organizing processes that are intrinsic to the child, in combination with the child's past input, current state, and extrinsic dynamics of the immediate context, result in the emergence of language. In this view, language emerges in the child both ontogenetically and at the moment of speech as a result of similar dynamic processes. The distinction between competence and performance and the distinction between acquiring language and using language are discarded.

In addition to presenting an array of current theoretical approaches to the field, the chapters in this Part illustrate the wide variety of methodologies that current research employs. The methods include the physiological technique of evoked potential recording (Shafer & Garrido-Nag), many different laboratory-based experimental techniques used with infants and children (Gathercole & Hoff; Goodluck; Saffran & Thiessen), computer simulations of language acquisition, and naturalistic, observational approaches (Gathercole & Hoff; Evans). The chapters in this Part also illustrate the broad range of phenomena that characterize the field's current definition of the accomplishment that needs to be explained. Some chapters focus on the acquisition of syntax (Goodluck; Gathercole & Hoff); others address phonological, lexical, and pragmatic development as well (Baldwin & Meyer; Evans; Saffran & Thiessen). Most focus on competence, but of necessity use performance as an indicator of competence. Evans argues that the distinction is false. Together, the chapters in this Part on foundations and theoretical approaches provide a survey of how researchers in the field of language development currently frame the questions they ask and pursue answers to those questions.

2

The Neurodevelopmental Bases of Language

Valerie L. Shafer and Karen Garrido-Nag

Imagine someone claiming to know how a car works on the basis of knowing how to drive, but having no notion of the internal mechanisms that make it work! If the car breaks down, external signs (e.g., engine light, steam escaping from under the hood) are of little use in determining the cause, particularly for someone with no understanding of the internal mechanisms. It would also be virtually impossible to build a similar or identical system for powering a car on the basis of observing another car's external performance because there are many different solutions that can lead to the same performance. Our understanding of language processing and language development when based entirely on behavior is limited in a similar manner. Knowledge of the neurobiology (i.e., internal mechanisms) is critical for arriving at a real understanding of language processing and language development.

The goal of this chapter is to illustrate how neurobiological evidence can help address three questions regarding language development. One issue concerns how biological and environmental factors interact during development to lead to the neurobiological specialization for language found in the mature system. For example, why are certain language functions lateralized to the left and others to the right hemisphere? Direct observation of the brain mechanisms supporting linguistic processes and how they develop will help address this question.

A second question is which processes contributing to language are limited by sensitive or critical periods? Evidence from behavioral data suggests that there are sensitive periods for both first- and second-language learning. However, the complex nature of language processing makes it difficult to isolate the specific causes of these limitations. Identifying which brain structures/functions correspond to different language functions and which of them have sensitive or critical periods for learning is necessary to answer this question.

Answers to both these questions are necessary to help further understand a third question: What are the biological and environmental causes of developmental language disorders and delays? Current understanding of these disorders is primarily in terms of descriptions of impaired behaviors. Since a number of different causes could lead to the same observed impairment, this level of knowledge is inadequate. Knowledge of the underlying causes in terms of brain function should lead to earlier and more accurate identification of a disorder and improved strategies for remediation. Returning to the car analogy, it is easy to see that a mechanic will have greater success in repairing a car that has overheated if the underlying cause is known. For example, a hole in the radiator versus a broken fan can lead to the same breakdown, but each requires a different repair.

The first section of this chapter provides a neurobiological model of the adult language system. This model includes a description of structures involved in language processing and their corresponding functions as revealed by neurobiological studies. This section also provides definitions of basic principles of neuroscience that are necessary for understanding brain function and for interpreting neurophysiological data, and a description of the event-related potentials (ERPs) method, which is most frequently used in neurodevelopmental studies.

The final sections focus on the three questions posed above. Our knowledge of neurodevelopment of language is rather limited at this time because, until recently, research in this area has been sparse; even so, there is sufficient information to demonstrate how these data can aid in addressing the questions of interest.

Neurobiology of the Adult System

Until recently, knowledge of neurobiology of language was gained from observing breakdown in function due to brain damage. This method of study led to the view that major functions of language were primarily localized to the left hemisphere, and that two large brain regions, Broca's area (roughly left inferior frontal cortex) and Wernicke's area (roughly left posterior superior temporal cortex), were responsible for most language functions. Damage to Broca's area led to deficits in production, such as articulation, sequencing of speech sounds, and sentence production, whereas damage to Wernicke's area resulted in deficits of speech perception, and word and sentence comprehension. These observations led to the claim that Broca's area was responsible for executing language and Wernicke's area for speech perception and language comprehension, despite some inconsistent evidence. For example, some Broca's aphasics also showed deficits of comprehending certain syntactic structures (e.g., passives).

Recent advances in neurobiological methods have dramatically increased our knowledge of brain structure–language function relationships in the mature adult system, and it has become clear that the broad two-system view is inaccurate. Functional brain imaging data from non-clinical populations indicate that the language system consists of many interconnected small modules, each with a specialized task contributing to language function (see Bookheimer, 2002). To understand language function in terms of the brain, the location and function of each of these supporting modules must be identified, as well as the connectivity between modules. These relationships will be briefly reviewed below, following a discussion of basic principles of neuroscience that are necessary to understand how the brain works.

Principles of neuroscience

This section describes brain function in terms of neural–electrical circuits and how these circuits are used to store information and are modified in learning. This explanation of brain function will focus on the electrical function of neural circuits because information storage is in terms of firing of neurons, and much of our knowledge of neurodevelopment comes from examining electrical potential at the scalp using ERPs.

The basis for storing and communicating information in the brain is via electro-chemical signals passed between neurons (cell bodies) via a long process called an axon. A chemical message (neurotransmitter) is released at a terminal (synapse) at the end of an axon and received on another neuron, often at a dendrite (extension of the neuron). This chemical message leads to changes in the electrical potential of the receiving neuron. Sufficient change in potential (typically from receiving chemical messages from multiple synapses) can lead to either excitation (and firing) or inhibition (which will make firing more difficult). A neural circuit consists of axonal connections between thousands of neurons. Within a circuit, neurons fire in synchrony to particular stimulus characteristics (e.g., frequency) or processing demands (e.g., discriminating two stimuli). Different neural circuits can be linked together to accomplish more complex process-ing tasks.

Language, like other functions, requires that information be learned and stored in memory. The manner in which this learning occurs is often called Hebbian learning. Neurons become part of a neural circuit in two ways: First, there is some pre-wiring of circuits that is determined biologically, typically found at lower levels of the nervous system. Second, circuits are created by strengthening or weakening the synaptic connec-tions between neurons in the presence or absence of correlated firing patterns. Even in the case of pre-wired circuits, stimulation is often needed to maintain the circuit, and further tuning of the circuit can occur based on input (see Hebb, 1949; Pulvermüller, 1996; Vaughan & Kurtzberg, 1992).

Memory for an association is the result of these synaptic modifications. Learning and memory are intrinsic properties of the same neural networks, rather than being functions of distinct brain structures. In other words, brain structures activated in learning a spe-cific stimulus or task are also activated in memory for the stimulus or task. Humans and other higher animals have evolved sophisticated systems to support learning and memory of both linguistic and non-linguistic information. These include medial temporal lobe structures (limbic structure and hippocampus) involved in declarative/explicit memory and basal ganglia/cerebellar structures involved in procedural/implicit memory (Squire & Kandel, 1999).

In summary, memory for information is seen as synchronous electrical activity across neurons in a neural circuit responding to some stimulus attribute or task. Learning is the result of modification (strengthening or weakening) of synaptic connections across neurons, leading to the creation of new neural circuits, or to the linking of a number of circuits into higher-order circuits. The brain structures involved in learning information are the same as those involved in memory for the information.

Neuroanatomical and neurophysiological evidence

Identifying the brain location and function of specialized modules that contribute to different behavioral functions can be achieved by examining the connectivity within and across neural circuits in the brain (structure) and by examining their activation patterns (function). This section describes how structural and functional evidence are used to identify specialized modules in the brain.

Structural evidence.   Structural evidence for specialized modules is seen as distinctive patterns of connectivity and cell types (i.e., cytoarchitectonics) and has been used to define Brodmann's Areas (e.g., primary auditory cortex is BA 41). The organization of neocortex into four to six layers of neurons, each reflecting a different type of connectivity, has facilitated identification of these distinctive patterns. Primary sensory regions (e.g., visual, auditory) have a thick layer of neurons that receives information from the peripheral senses (Layer IV), whereas primary motor regions have a thick layer of neurons that sends information to the motor system (Layer V). By contrast, association regions have a thick layer of neurons that sends and receives information to and from other cortical areas (Layers II and III). Layer I (closest to the scalp) consists primarily of dendrites of neurons in deeper layers and axons synapsing on these dendrites, or passing through this layer (but with some other target), and Layer VI contains a heterogeneous mixture of neuron cell bodies and dendrites from cell bodies in Layers II and IV. The neurons in these different layers also differ (e.g., pyramidal neurons are efferent projection neurons and are larger and more abundant in Layer V than in Layers II and III) (Kandel, Schwartz, & Jessell, 2000; Kolb & Whishaw, 1996).

In summary, these structural studies have identified brain regions (specifically, Brodmann's Areas) that are likely to carry out different functions. However, the pattern of connectivity into and out of these areas can only be used to make limited guesses about function. Real-time functional measures are necessary to identify the precise function of brain regions, as will be illustrated in the next section.

Functional evidence.   Imaging methods, such as functional magnetic resonance imaging (fMRI) and positron emission tomography (PET), provide fairly precise information on which brain areas are activated in a language-processing task, but not when they are activated. These methods indirectly index activation of neural circuits by measuring blood flow to discrete brain regions (Bookheimer, 2002). Both PET and fMRI have been extremely useful for identifying brain regions activated in adult language processing. However, neither method tolerates movement from participants, and PET is invasive; both factors limit their use with non-clinical child populations.

The optimal method for studying typical neurodevelopment in infants and young children is electrophysiology. In addition to its excellent temporal resolution, it is relatively tolerant of movement (unlike magnetoencephalography, MEG), and unthreatening to a parent or child. The development of multichannel systems for recording the electroencephalogram (EEG) has improved the spatial resolution of this method, although it remains poorer than fMRI, PET, and MEG. This section provides a brief description of the most commonly used electrophysiological method, event-related potentials (ERPs).

Electrophysiology takes advantage of the phenomenon that firing of neurons leads to changes in the electrical potential (post-synaptic excitatory and inhibitory potentials) of the extracellular solution. These changes propagate to the surface of the scalp where they can be amplified and measured using a voltage meter. Adjacent neurons in neural circuits in many regions of the neocortex are arranged in parallel, so that the axons of the neurons are aligned all on one end, and the inputs into dendrites on the other end. This arrangement leads to the circuit behaving like a dipole (positive at one end, negative at the other) when neurons in a neural circuit fire in synchrony. Thus, on one end (e.g., positive end), ions of the opposite polarity will be attracted, and this perturbation will propagate to the scalp, while on the other end the opposite phenomenon will be observed. These tiny fluctuations from a set of circuits participating in one process (e.g., speech discrimination) are too small to resolve in the unprocessed EEG, because it is the summation of activity from firing of many brain circuits.

A number of signal-processing methods have been developed to isolate the electrical patterns related to a single event of interest. The most commonly used is that of averaging portions of the EEG time-locked to an event which has been repeated, with the goal of decreasing the contribution from processes that are not time-locked. Specifically, the activity from events that are not time-locked is sometimes positive, and sometimes negative, and will sum to zero as more trials are added. Time-locked events that are consistently of the same polarity and latency are maintained with averaging. For example, in infants and children a positive polarity at fronto-central sites is found around 100 ms (P1 or P100) following the onset of an auditory event. This method is called averaged ERPs. Figure 2.1 illustrates the instrumentation, unprocessed EEG, and an averaged ERP to a vowel sound at multiple sites (fronto-central in gray and posterior-inferior in black) that show opposite polarity for the child P100. This pattern of polarity (positive on top of the head and negative at the back and below the ears) is consistent with a neural source in auditory cortex.[1]

Event-related potentials are useful for examining learning and memory because they can provide information that participants can discriminate particular stimuli, with or without attention. They also have the power to reveal the sequence of processes leading up to a behavioral response. Figure 2.2 shows auditory and language-dependent ERP components to consonant–vowel–consonant (CVC) words in a match-to-sample phonological task. Participants were asked to decide whether the second word of a pair was the same or different from the first word in the pair (e.g., cheese vs. cheev). The sequence of early occurring peaks, N1 and P2 in adults, are evoked by the physical properties of the stimulus and are called obligatory components. Components which are modulated by task or context and occur at later latencies are called cognitive or endogenous components. For example, the N400 component amplitude is modulated by a phonological decision. Each component has a distinctive topography. For example, as shown in the right-hand graph of Figure 2.2, the endogenous phonological N400 is largest at lateral

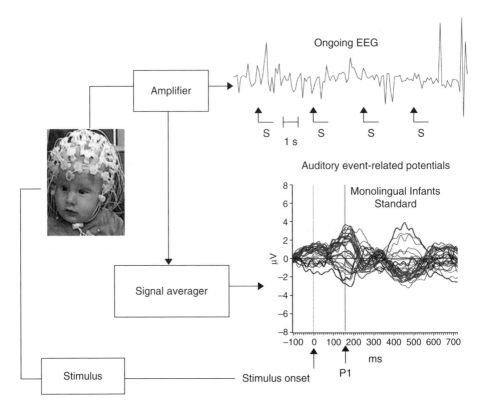

Figure 2.1   Instrumentation and signal processing for recording ERP data. Brain activity is recorded through electrodes (top left) and amplified, and the precise time of stimulus events is recorded with the digitized EEG (top right). Multiple events are averaged so that the ERP emerges from the background noise (bottom right). Components indexing time-locked brain activity are seen as the time-points of greatest divergence (i.e., standard deviation) in amplitude across the sites, as seen at P1 in this graph plotting multiple sites.

posterior sites (P7 and P8) and the N1 obligatory component is largest at superior frontal sites (FC1 and FC2).

Possible neural sources of ERPs can be inferred from the scalp topography because of their dipolar nature. Electrodes placed on the scalp at opposite poles of the dipole will record opposite potentials. Source localization with ERPs is imprecise, but can be informed by knowledge of neuroanatomy and information from other imaging methods with better spatial resolution (e.g., fMRI), and from clinical and animal research. Despite the limitations in source localization, different distributions of activity across the scalp to two events, such as that seen in Figure 2.2, can be used to make inferences that different sources are activated in processing these events.

In summary, the optimal method for studying neurodevelopment of language is event-related potentials because they have excellent temporal resolution and are suitable for use with children. The latency and topography of ERP components can be used to make

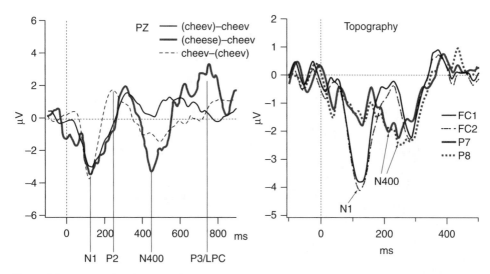

Figure 2.2   Event-related potential components to CVC words in a match-to-sample task. The left-hand graph shows the obligatory N1 and P2 components and the cognitive components N400 and P3/LPC. The thick and thin black lines show ERPs recorded to the second word in a pair and the dotted line to the first word in a pair. The right-hand graph shows subtraction of the ERP to the second word in a different pair from that of the second word in a same pair and illustrates differences in topography for N1 and N400 (adapted from Shafer, Schwartz, & Kessler, 2003). PZ, superior posterior midline site.

inferences about the sequence of processes and cortical sources supporting language functions.

Brain indices of language processing in adults

One goal of this chapter is to explain how neurodevelopment leads to the organization and function of language observed in the adult brain. This section provides a description of this endpoint of development, and is organized in terms of imaging and ERP studies indexing (1) phonetic/phonological processing related specifically to speech perception, (2) morphosyntactic processing, focusing on anterior cortex involvement, and (3) semantic/discourse processing, focusing on comprehension. Figure 2.3 displays brain regions typically activated in imaging studies.

Phonetic/phonological processing.   Imaging investigations of speech perception have identified a number of brain structure–function relationships related to speech perception (see Bookheimer, 2002; Scott & Wise, 2004). These include primary auditory cortex (BA 41) and secondary auditory cortex (BA 42). Different portions of these regions are activated in different types of processing. Activation in the bilateral superior temporal gyrus (STG) is seen to pre-lexical processing of phonetic features. The left posterior

(a)

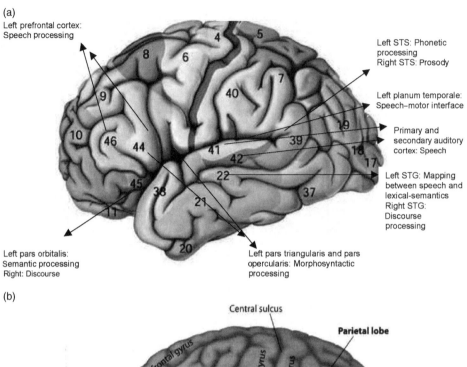

Left prefrontal cortex:
Speech processing

Left STS: Phonetic
processing
Right STS: Prosody

Left planum temporale:
Speech–motor interface

Primary and
secondary auditory
cortex: Speech

Left STG: Mapping
between speech and
lexical-semantics
Right STG:
Discourse
processing

Left pars orbitalis:
Semantic processing
Right: Discourse

Left pars triangularis and pars
opercularis: Morphosyntactic
processing

(b)

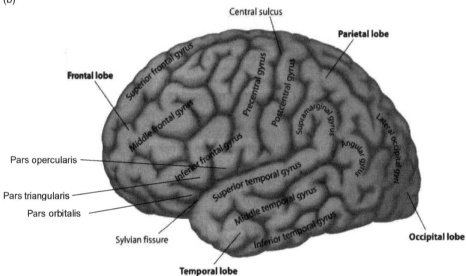

Figure 2.3   Brain structure–language function relationships. (a) Brain regions typically activated during (1) phonetic/phonological processing related specifically to speech perception, (2) morphosyntactic processing, and (3) semantic/discourse processing. (b) The premotor cortex (BA 6), pars opercularis, pars orbitalis, and pars triangularis (BA 44/45).

superior temporal sulcus (STS) shows particular sensitivity to phonetic features and the right STG to melodic variation of speech. Mapping of speech onto lexical-semantic representations activates the left anterior portion of the STS (BA 22). The planum temporale (PT), which is in posterior superior temporal cortex, appears to serve as a motor/sensory interface for any acoustic stimulus. A few studies also suggest that left prefrontal cortex (BA 44/6) is activated in processing rapid transitions, such as those found in consonant–vowel syllables, and in accessing, sequencing, and monitoring phonemes. This latter function may be better characterized as working or phonological memory.

Event-related potential evidence of activation of posterior cortex in phonetic/phonological processing comes largely from studies designed to elicit the ERP discriminative response, mismatch negativity (MMN). The MMN is seen as a negative shift between 100 and 300 ms at fronto-central scalp sites following the onset of a stimulus (called the deviant) that is delivered among a series of repetitions of a more frequent sound (called the standard), and can be elicited without attention.

Mismatch negativity reflects the phonological status of a pair of sounds in a listener's language (e.g., Näätänen et al., 1997; Winkler et al., 1999). Specifically, MMN is earlier and/or larger to a pair of contrasts for speakers who have had experience with the sounds as phonemically contrastive. This difference in experience is typically observed over left hemisphere sites (e.g., Näätänen, 2001; Shafer, Schwartz, & Kurtzberg, 2004). Dipole modeling suggests that neural circuits in superior temporal cortex are a major contributor to MMN.

In summary, the mature neurobiological system activated in phonological processing includes posterior brain regions (BA 41, 42, 22) for speech perception, and PT for interfacing with the motor system. These regions display somewhat different functions for left versus right hemisphere cortex. Activation of anterior regions in speech perception is probably related to phonological memory for sequential information. The ERP component MMN indicates that language-specific phonological categories affect processing at a pre-attentive level within 250 ms of a syllable onset. The MMN is not the only ERP component sensitive to phonological variables, but tasks designed to elicit other components, such as the phonological N400 (see Figure 2.2), have not been widely used in investigations of young children.

Morphosyntactic processing.   Neurobiological studies indicate that anterior brain regions play a critical role in morphosyntactic processing. Some researchers suggest that this anterior activation reflects structure-building processes, whereas others suggest that it reflects integrating syntax and semantics (see Bookheimer, 2002).

Imaging studies show that processing of morphosyntactic information includes regions in left prefrontal cortex, as shown in Figure 2.3. The premotor cortex (BA 6), pars opercularis, and putamen (basal ganglia structure) are activated in learning and recognizing simple grammars with phonological encoding, and pars opercularis and triangularis (BA 44/45) are activated in recognizing higher-level grammatical patterns. In posterior cortical regions, the anterior portion of the left superior temporal gyrus is also activated in processing morphosyntactic information (Friederici, 2004; Friederici, Ruschemeyer, Hahne, & Fiebach, 2003).

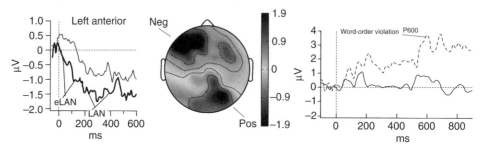

Figure 2.4 The left-hand graph displays ERPs at a left anterior site to a grammatical (thin line) compared with an ungrammatical sentence (*The zebra that the hippo kissed <u>the camel</u> on the nose] ran far away," thick line). The topographical display (center) shows the negative (neg) and positive (pos) distribution of the LAN (interpolated from all sites at 400 ms; adapted from Hestvik, Maxfield, Schwartz, & Shafer, in press). The right-hand graph shows the P600 to a word-order violation (adapted from Kessler, Martaharjono, & Shafer, 2004).

Event-related potential indices of morphosyntactic processing also suggest a major role for anterior cortex. An early left anterior negativity (eLAN) occurring 100 to 300 ms following a violation is believed to index early stages of phrase-structure building, and a later left anterior negativity (LAN) reflects violations of morphosyntactic processes, such as use of gender information. A late positive component (P600), which can co-occur with eLAN or LAN, is found to violations of syntax and less preferred morphosyntactic structures and indexes integration of syntactic and semantic information (Friederici, 2002). Figure 2.4 displays the eLAN, LAN, and P600 to morphosyntactic violations. Studies comparing function words and content words have also shown a larger early left anterior negativity to function words than to content words (Neville, Mills, & Lawson, 1992; Pulvermüller, 1996).

By contrast, sustained anterior positivities (SAPs) are seen to function words at the onset of sentences in discourse, and continue as long as the words in the utterances are meaningful, as shown in Figure 2.5 (Shafer, Kessler, Morr, Schwartz, & Kurtzberg, 2005). Shafer and colleagues (2005) suggested that the left SAP reflects automatic building of grammatical structure and the right reflects building discourse structure because only the right drops out when attention is directed away from the auditory story to the story-line of a silent movie.

The anterior scalp locations of eLAN, LAN, and SAP are consistent with sources in inferior frontal cortex or in the anterior portion of superior temporal cortex. Anterior cortex and basal ganglia structures (involved in implicit learning of patterns) appear to play a role in the generation of P600 since damage to left inferior frontal regions (Broca's aphasia) but not to left temporo-parietal regions leads to reduced and delayed P600 (Friederici, Kotz, Werheid, Hein, & von Cramon, 2003; Wassenaar & Hagoort, 2005) and damage to basal ganglia structures reduces or abolishes the P600, but not eLAN and LAN components (Friederici, Kotz, et al., 2003).

In summary, both imaging and neurophysiological studies indicate that left anterior regions, including Broca's area and basal ganglia subcortical structures, are highly activated in early and late aspects of morphosyntactic processing.

Semantic/discourse processing.   Research from clinical studies led to the view that posterior brain regions, particularly Wernicke's area, are the major contributors to semantic and discourse processing. Recent studies of non-clinical adults, however, have shown that anterior as well as posterior regions carry out important semantic and discourse functions. This section describes the principal regions and timing of activation of these regions in semantic/discourse processing.

Imaging studies have revealed that widespread anterior and posterior regions are activated in semantic processing, and that this activation is systematic and predictable in terms of semantic and sensorimotor properties (Bookheimer, 2002). For example, imageable words (lexemes), such as animals and concrete concepts, activate visual cortex (occipital lobe) and association cortex involved in object identification (e.g., inferior temporal gyrus), whereas graspable lexemes also activate anterior motor and premotor cortex (e.g., BA 6) associated with reaching and grasping. The pars orbitalis of the left inferior frontal gyrus is also activated in processing semantic relationships and/or retrieving semantic information. As mentioned above, the left superior temporal sulcus (posterior cortex) is activated in mapping between speech and lexical-semantic representations.

Right cortical regions, typically homologous to the left language regions, are activated in pragmatic/discourse and prosodic functions. These functions include interpreting metaphors and morals, creating coherence, topic maintenance, and using prosody to interpret emotion. For example, right regions, including BA 44/45, dorsolateral prefrontal cortex (BA 46), superior temporal cortex (BA 22), and angular gyrus (BA 39) are highly activated in topic maintenance (Caplan & Dapretto, 2001). Bookheimer (2002) suggested that the right hemisphere activation reflects integration of information over time, whereas left activation during language comprehension indexes interpreting the meaning of individual units.

Event-related potential studies of semantic/discourse processing typically show the effects of semantic processing beginning around 200 ms following a word form. The most commonly examined index of semantic processing is the N400, which peaks between 200 and 500 ms following the word of interest (e.g., Kutas & Hillyard, 1980). The increased N400 to unprimed compared with primed words in priming studies is probably due to activation of phonological and semantic neighbors in the process of lexical access (e.g., Praamstra, Meyer, & Levelt, 1994; Shafer et al., 2003, see Figure 2.2). In sentence-processing studies, the N400 negativity additionally reflects integration of a word into sentence context. Several studies have observed differences in N400 topography to semantic categories (e.g., motor vs. imageable) consistent with fMRI findings (Pulvermüller, 1996).

Dipole analysis of the N400 identifies sources in left prefrontal cortex, beginning around 250 ms after word onset, followed by activation of sources in left and right lateral prefrontal cortex and right inferior temporal cortex from 350 to 450 ms (Frishkoff, Tucker, Davey, & Scherg, 2004). The activation of frontal sources was sustained (250 to 800 ms), similar to the SAP seen by Shafer and colleagues (2005, Figure 2.5). These data support the view that the left frontal region is involved in executive control over semantic processing and the right over discourse processing.

In summary, multiple cortical regions are activated in semantic and discourse processing. The pars orbitalis portion of the inferior frontal gyrus probably functions in

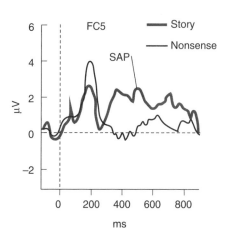
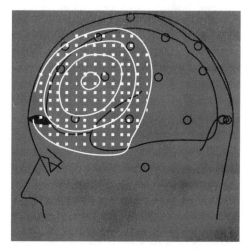

Figure 2.5   The graph shows the sustained anterior positivity (SAP) of the ERP to "the" followed by story context (e.g., "the curious little kitten, etc.") compared with that of "the" followed by nonsense (e.g., "the gikopo, etc."). The head image shows the anterior topography of this positivity (peak at the center of concentric circles; adapted from Shafer, Kessler, et al., 2005).

executive control, and activation is sustained throughout processing. Activation of other regions reflects retrieval of the semantic properties of a word. Right hemisphere activation is specifically involved in pragmatic/discourse aspects of processing.

General Principles of Developmental Neuroscience

Several important principles of neurodevelopment are described in this section, before we examine neurodevelopment of language. These principles lead to predictions about the timecourse of development of different types of information processing and are necessary to help interpret neurodevelopmental ERP data.

The timing of development of different brain regions typically proceeds from lower to higher levels. This timecourse of maturation places limitations on when functions can emerge, and later emergence is expected for higher-level functions. Specifically, neurons and axon projections mature earlier in peripheral systems (e.g., brainstem) compared with central systems (e.g., neocortex); within neocortex, primary motor and sensory regions mature earlier than secondary regions, which in turn mature earlier than association regions (e.g., Kolb & Whishaw, 1996). This progression of development has been determined largely through examining synaptogenesis, myelination, and neuron death.

Synaptogenesis is creation of synaptic sites on which axons can connect. Subcortical and primary cortical areas are relatively mature in newborns and reach a peak in synaptogenesis by 3 months of age. Association cortex, such as prefrontal regions, does not reach peak synaptogenesis until around 3 years of age. These peaks are followed by loss of synaptic sites and loss of neurons related to absent or weak connections (e.g., Huttenlocher & Dabholkar, 1997).

Myelination is the creation of a myelin sheath on axons, which leads to faster transmission of signals. Primary regions complete myelination quite early, beginning before birth, followed by secondary auditory cortex, and lastly by association cortex. Some regions do not complete myelination until well past puberty (Vaughan & Kurtzberg, 1992).

Brain regions can function before reaching peaks in synaptogenesis and before myelination is complete. However, a peak in number of synapses suggests that the brain region is ripe for learning, since many sites for axonal connections are available. Completion of myelination within a neural circuit indicates that rapid processing can take place. Infants and children typically show later latencies than adults for a number of ERP components, in part reflecting incomplete myelinations (e.g., N1: Ponton, Eggermont, Kwong, & Don, 2000; MMN: Shafer, Morr, Kreuzer, & Kurtzberg, 2000; N400: Coch, Maron, Wolf, & Holcomb, 2002; Friedrich & Friederici, 2004; eLAN, LAN: Hahne, Eckstein, & Friederici, 2004). They also show larger-amplitude ERP components, probably reflecting a greater abundance of neurons and synapses, less specificity in firing, and poorer insulation of the axons by myelin. Finally, some adult ERP components may be absent or attenuated in children's responses and others enlarged, particularly to stimuli presented at fast rates. For example, the early obligatory component P1, generated in Layer I cortex, dominates children's ERPs, whereas N1, generated in Layers II and III, is absent at fast rates (compare Figures 2.1 and 2.2). This pattern is related to early maturation of Layer I compared with Layers II and III (Ponton et al., 2000).

These maturational changes in brain neurobiology will affect processing of speech and language stimuli. One challenge in developmental neurobiology is to tease apart which changes are due to general maturation and which are related to learning a specific language; in other words, what aspects of development are related to environmental input versus genetic instruction. Higher levels of processing are increasingly dependent on input (Greenough, Black, & Wallace, 1987; Knudsen, 2004). For example, in some neural circuits, a certain type of information is expected (experience-expectant) and necessary to maintain the circuit and "tune" it. Other circuits (experience-dependent), generally in association cortex, need input, but do not require a certain type of information. There are also lower-level brain regions that are hard-wired to process a certain type of information (e.g., hard-wired connections from auditory periphery). However, even in these cases, sensory or motor activation may be necessary to maintain the circuits.

The location of primary and secondary cortical regions activated in processing the sensory and motor aspects of speech is largely determined genetically. The developmental basis of the organization of higher-level processing, however, is less clear. The location of experience-dependent circuits appears to be related to the nature of the stored information. For example, association cortex near visual regions often stores higher-level representations that include visual information and are connected to circuits in proximal primary and secondary visual cortex. However, association cortex can also be connected to distal regions (e.g., prefrontal cortex to occipital regions). Currently there are insufficient data describing the initial state (i.e., in newborns) of connectivity within and across association cortex.

A number of studies have also found sex differences in neurodevelopment, seen as hemispheric differences in processing speech and language, particularly for infants under 9 months of age (e.g., Shafer, Shucard, & Jaeger, 1999; Shucard & Shucard, 1990). These sex differences are another source of variability in studies of infants that can confound interpretation of hemispheric specialization for language.

In summary, lower levels of the nervous system mature earlier and are less dependent on sensory or motor input/activation than higher levels. Based on these observations, developmental studies of language should show less change across age in processing at lower levels and more change at higher levels, related to language input.

Neurodevelopment of Speech and Language

As revealed above, research over the past two decades has greatly increased our knowledge of neurobiology of language in the mature system. However, current knowledge of neurodevelopment is quite limited because the necessary studies are only beginning to be done. Even so, there are sufficient data to begin to address the three questions posed in the introduction, as will be illustrated below.

What is the developmental basis of adult language organization in the brain?

The first question of interest is how biological and environmental factors interact during development to lead to the neurobiological specialization for language found in the adult system. To address this question, we will focus on brain organization in semantic processing and morphosyntactic processing.

Semantics.   The description of organization of adult semantic processing revealed that activation of brain regions in processing a certain stimulus or in performing a semantic task was not random. For example, processing words that can be grasped activated anterior motor and premotor regions that are used in the motor activity of grasping. How does this organization develop?

Research by Mills and colleagues shows developmental changes in ERP activity, initially seen as broadly distributed negativity (over left and right hemispheres) to known words in infants with smaller vocabularies or to newly learned words (Mills, Prat, & Zangl, 2004). This negativity may reflect lexical-semantic processing indexed by the adult N400. This activity becomes left-lateralized with increasing vocabulary size. Mills and colleagues suggest that the developmental change in topography reflects rate of acquisition and number of exposures to a word (Mills & Conboy, 2005). The more focal left hemisphere activity may be related to increased specificity in neural firing. That is, synapses between neurons that do not fire in synchrony to a word will be weakened and lost, leaving a smaller, more focal population of neurons that is responsive to the word.

The claim that regions activated in learning are also activated in memory suggests a further interpretation of the data. Evidence from adult neurobiology indicates that right hemisphere activation is related to discourse aspects of processing, which include episodic memory, that is, memory for the situation and language context in which the word was used. Research has shown that first encounters with words lead to partial knowledge, which is typically context-bound (e.g., Wagovich & Newhoff, 2004). Thus, the right hemisphere activation seen in infants to newly learned words may reflect the same discourse-related functions as observed in adults.

Increasing exposure to a word will lead to more context-free knowledge, and less activation of right hemisphere structures for a word presented out of discourse. Networks activated in context-free representations of word meaning probably favor the left hemisphere as an indirect consequence of preferential processing of the phonetic features in the left hemisphere. Specifically, if more neural circuits for processing phonetic features are in the left superior temporal sulcus, then a greater number of connections can be made between semantic-representation circuits and phonetic-form circuits in this hemisphere. Dehaene-Lambertz and Gigla (2004) found evidence of greater left than right hemisphere activation in both speech and non-speech discrimination in infants, and suggested that left hemisphere lateralization for language in the mature system may arise from this developmental bias in auditory processing. Under this interpretation, the function/structure relationships found in adults are already present in toddlers.

In summary, these studies illustrate how neurodevelopmental data can be used to begin addressing the neurodevelopmental basis of semantic representation. These data are consistent with the claim that the structures involved in learning a particular type of information (in infancy or adulthood) are the same as those involved in memory for that information. Specifically, the pattern of activation of the right and left hemisphere to words in toddlers can be explained in terms of the adult system. Future studies will need to examine the neurodevelopment of different semantic categories (e.g., tools vs. animals) to further substantiate this claim.

Morphosyntax.   Brain structural studies indicate that the timecourse of maturation of anterior regions BA 44/45 is slow. Specifically, BA 45 (premotor cortex) does not reach adult structural asymmetry until age 5, and BA 44 (Broca's area) not until age 11 (Amunts, Schleicher, Ditterich, & Zilles, 2003). Behavioral studies also show subtle differences in processing syntax up to age 11 (see Hahne et al., 2004, for discussion).

The few studies that have examined ERPs to morphosyntax in young children also suggest slow maturation of function in these regions. Young children do not exhibit the typical eLAN and LAN observed in adults. Specifically, early positivities rather than negativities are elicited to violations in 2-year-old (Oberecker, Friedrich, & Friederici, 2005) and 6-year-old children (Hahne et al., 2004). In our laboratory, we also have observed this early positivity to structural violations in 4-year-old children, as shown in Figure 2.6. Following the early positivity, LAN and P600 are seen to violations in simple active sentences for 2-year-olds (31–34 months of age: Oberecker et al., 2005), and in passive sentences for 7- to 10-year-old children (Hahne et al., 2004). The early positivity is no longer present in these older children. The SAPs observed to the function word "the" in stories are also more posterior for children than adults, perhaps reflecting

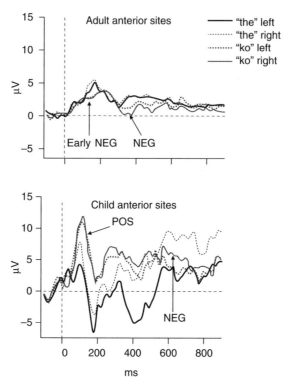

Figure 2.6 Four-year-old children show an early positivity and later negativity, unlike adults, to the nonsense syllable (ko) replacing the function word "the" in stories.

immaturity of anterior cortex (cf. Shafer, Schwartz, Morr, Kessler, & Kurtzberg, 2000, and Shafer, Kessler, et al., 2005).

In summary, the finding of LAN and P600 to structural violations in 2-year-old children suggests that brain structures activated in adult processing are sufficiently mature by the third year of life to support morphosyntactic learning. Differences between children and adults are found, particularly in the presence of an early positivity for the children under 7 years of age, and later latencies of the LAN and P600. The functional significance of the positive component to deviant patterns needs to be determined to allow further explanation of these developmental differences, although Oberecker et al. (2005) suggest that it reflects "heightened" sensitivity to acoustic cues. These data support the claim that structures involved in language processing in the adult are involved in learning in the child.

Which processes contributing to language are limited by sensitive/critical periods?

The second question posed in the introduction was which processes contributing to language are limited by sensitive/critical periods? There is reasonably good evidence from

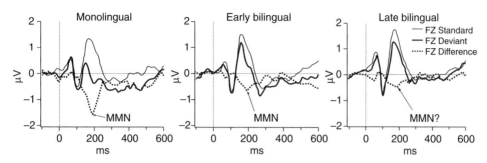

Figure 2.7 Mismatch negativities (MMNs) to the [I]/[ɛ] contrast for monolingual speakers of English (left), early bilinguals (center), and later learners of English with Spanish as a second language (from Garrido, Hisagi, & Shafer, 2005).

behavioral studies of late learners of a first language (L1) or second language (L2) indicating that there are sensitive periods for learning native speech categories and morphosyntactic patterns (Johnson & Newport, 1991; Strange & Shafer, in press). However, the complex nature of language processing makes it difficult to determine what underlying processes lead to these limitations. Neurophysiological data can inform this question by revealing which underlying processes and corresponding brain regions are the sources of these limitations. Developmental data are needed to reveal how age of exposure and amount of exposure interact in development of the brain circuits subserving language processing.

Event-related potential studies of adult L2 learners from our laboratory suggest that there may be an early sensitive period for learning of language-specific speech categories, which results in automatic selection of relevant speech cues. Specifically, early Spanish–English bilinguals with Spanish as L1 and who have learned English before age 5 have smaller-amplitude mismatch negativities than monolingual English listeners to the English phonemic contrast /I/ versus /ɛ/, as shown in Figure 2.7. This result contrasts with native-like identification and discrimination of these vowels in behavioral tasks by these early L2 learners. As expected, the MMN is absent for first-language (L1) Spanish speakers who know little English, because they have had little or no experience with these phonemes until late in life. These results suggest that early L2 learners need attention for native-like performance, and thus show less automaticity in processing. However, the larger MMNs to L2 contrasts for proficient compared with novice L2 users in this as well as other studies indicate that some improvement in automaticity of processing these L2 categories can occur with L2 experience (e.g., Winkler et al., 1999; Winkler, Kujala, Alku, & Naatanen, 2003).

A few ERP investigations of morphosyntactic processing in adults also suggest an early sensitive period for learning morphosyntactic patterns. Specifically, only early L2 learners of English showed an eLAN to morphosyntactic violations (Kessler et al., 2004) or left anterior negativity to function words (Weber-Fox & Neville, 1995). Note, however, that later-latency LANs may be a function of delayed phonological processing leading to delayed access to grammatical information.

These studies suggest that automatic, native-like processing requires learning of speech contrasts and morphosyntactic patterns in a narrow time-window, perhaps during

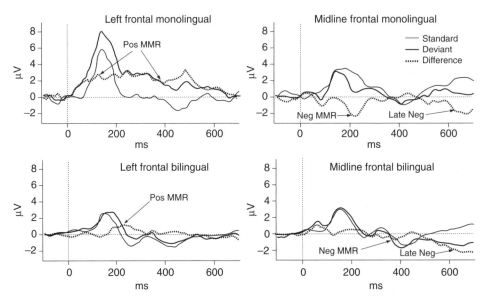

Figure 2.8   Event-related potentials to 250 ms [I]/[ɛ] contrast in 20- to 36-month-old monolingual and bilingual infants at left frontal (F3) and midline frontal (FZ) sites.

the first two or three years of life. However, data from children during this early period of development are necessary to determine how input changes processing in these circuits. Very little developmental data are available addressing this question and there are some uncertainties regarding the interpretation of infant ERP components. Even so, a number of recent studies are beginning to resolve the uncertainties in interpretation (e.g., Kushnerenko, Ceponiene, Balan, Fellman, & Naatanen, 2002; Morr, Shafer, Kreuzer, & Kurtzberg, 2002; Weber, Hahne, Friedrich, & Friederici, 2004) and two studies suggest that an MMN-like negativity can serve as an index of the development of speech categories, at least at 12 months of age (Cheour, Alho, & Ceponiene, 1998; Rivera-Gaxiola, Klarman, Garcia-Sierra, & Kuhl, 2005). Specifically, these two studies found a larger ERP negativity to native than non-native contrasts in 11- and 12-month-old infants. The results for 6-month-old infants in these studies are less easily interpreted because it appears that some infants showed positivities and others showed negativities. Preliminary data from our laboratory show smaller positive mismatch responses (MMRs) and later and smaller negative MMRs to an [I]/[ɛ] contrast in toddlers with bilingual exposure to English and Spanish compared with those with monolingual English exposure, as shown in Figure 2.8. However, we currently have data from twice as many bilingual toddlers, and will need more monolingual participants to determine whether this apparent difference is significant.

In summary, these studies illustrate that neurophysiological data can provide useful information regarding the sensitive periods for language development. Future studies need to examine how age of acquisition and amount of exposure affect the development of automaticity of speech processing. The infant ERP discriminative components also need further research to establish their functional significance and developmental timecourse.

What are the causes of developmental language disorders and delays?

Understanding of developmental language disorders is limited without knowledge of the internal mechanisms supporting language function, knowledge of which mechanisms are dysfunctional, and knowledge of how these mechanisms develop in typical and atypical cases. Researchers are beginning to identify neurobiological correlates of different types of developmental language disorder, such as specific language impairment (SLI), and a few studies have begun to examine the development of these processes in at-risk infant populations (e.g., Friedrich, Weber, & Friederici, 2004; Leppaanen, Pihko, Eklund, & Lyytinen, 1999; Molfese, 2000). This section will focus on SLI to illustrate how knowledge of typical versus atypical brain function and structure in processing language can help elucidate this disorder.

Specific language impairment is a developmental disorder specific to language in that language ability is significantly depressed compared with typical age-matched children, but non-language cognitive skills are within the normal range (see Rice, this volume). These children have particular difficulty with phonology and morphosyntax, and some may also have poor auditory processing. The causal nature of this disorder continues to be debated. As will be shown below, neurobiological data can aid in identifying possible causes.

Deficits in speech perception.   Event-related potential research on typical populations suggests that by 12 months of age the speech-sound memory representations that are accessed in the discriminative process indexed by MMN are weighted to reflect relevant cues of the ambient language. Studies of children with SLI have found absent and/or late MMNs to phonetically similar speech contrasts (Shafer, Morr, Datta, Kurtzberg, & Schwartz, 2005; Uwer, Albrecht, & von Suchodoletz, 2002). These findings, along with poor categorical perception in many of the SLI children, led to the suggestion that some children with SLI do not have correctly weighted phonological representations in auditory cortex. By contrast, the nature of the deficit for the children with SLI who showed late MMNs and good categorical perception may be one of less automatic processing (Shafer, Morr, et al., 2005).

Event-related potential evidence also supports the suggestion that poor phonological processing, for at least some children with SLI, is the consequence of poor auditory processing abilities. One study found immature obligatory components (P1, N1, P2 complex) in adolescent and teenage children with SLI (Bishop & McArthur, 2005). In another study, 6-month-old infants at risk for SLI were shown to have a reduced positive MMR to a pitch change in tone pairs with a short interstimulus interval (ISI) of 70 ms (Choudhury, Friedman, Realpe-Bonilla, Chojnowski, & Benasich, 2005).

In summary, these studies suggest that deficient processing of sounds in auditory cortex contributes to the types of language impairments found in some children with SLI. This knowledge will help determine the causes of SLI and remediate this disorder because it will be possible to explore how different factors, such as attention and training, affect processing at this level.

Morphosyntax.   Deficient learning of morphosyntax in SLI could be the consequence of a number of different causes, such as less salient phonetic substance of function words and inflections, limited cognitive resources (e.g., working memory) for learning complex patterns such as morphosyntax, or a specific deficit in learning hierarchical patterns (i.e., phrase structure). Knowledge of the brain structures and functions supporting processing of morphosyntactic information in typical and atypical development will help select among these various causes.

The few studies examining morphosyntactic processing in children with language impairment (some of whom are SLI) suggest deficient processing in left perisylvian cortex. Neville and colleagues found bilateral rather than the typical pattern of left-greater-than-right anterior negativity to function words in reading sentences in grade-school children with language learning impairments (Neville, Coffey, Holcomb, & Tallal, 1993). Shafer and colleagues observed reduced positivity to the function word "the" in stories or nonsense contexts at left temporal sites and increased positivity at right temporal sites in grade-school children with SLI compared with children with typical language (Shafer, Schwartz, et al., 2000). The increased right hemisphere positivity may reflect greater use of semantic/discourse processing to compensate for poor left hemisphere function.

The neural sources of these components may be left inferior frontal gyrus or left lateral temporal cortex. Evidence from structural neuroimaging studies (MRI) is consistent with these as possible sources. Specifically, adolescent children with SLI do not show the typical left-greater-than-right structural asymmetry in the planum temporale, pars triangularis, and premotor cortex (e.g., Gauger, Lombardino, & Leonard, 1997; Jernigan, Hesselink, Sowell, & Tallal, 1991; Plante, Swisher, Vance, & Rapcsak, 1991).

In summary, neurobiological studies suggest that deficits in left hemisphere processing underlie poor morphosyntactic processing. Although these studies do not definitively demonstrate the neural source of the deficit, they provide sufficient evidence to narrow the possible candidate structures. It is quite likely that neurobiological studies will show that there are several different patterns of deviant brain processing. For example, some children may show atypical processing in posterior auditory cortical regions and others in anterior cortex. These different patterns would suggest different causes contributing to SLI.

Conclusion

The goal of this chapter was to show how knowledge of the neurodevelopmental bases of language can advance our understanding of language organization in the mature system, and of the causes of developmental disorders of language. This area of study is relatively new, and there are considerable gaps in our knowledge. Even so, evidence from the available studies provides a starting point for examining these questions. These studies suggest that the precursors of adult brain organization can be found in infants. For example, right hemisphere processing of newly learned words in toddlers is consistent with the discourse function of right hemisphere structures in adults, and left hemisphere dysfunction in children with SLI suggests that this hemisphere plays a special role in language acquisition, as well as adult language functions. Neurobiological studies also are beginning to reveal which brain structures/functions have sensitive or critical periods. For example, failure to set up phonological representations in left auditory cortex in the first few years of life appears to limit automaticity of processing this information. Finally, neurobiological studies are helping to identify atypical brain function in developmental language disorders. In particular, atypical processing in left hemisphere structures were shown to contribute to deficits of phonological and morphosyntactic processing in children with SLI.

Future research needs to carefully trace the development of components found in adults back to their initial emergence during the first few years of life to help clarify the functional significance of infant ERP components. These studies are necessary to demonstrate that ERP indices of language processes seen in adults indeed have precursors early in development. The recent improvements in instrumentation and data analysis techniques should allow research on the neurodevelopment of language to flourish in the coming years. It is hoped that the increased ease of doing this research with infants and toddlers will encourage more laboratories to pursue these questions.

Notes

We thank Monica Wagner for providing thoughtful comments on the chapter. We are also indebted to the editors, Erika Hoff and Marilyn Shatz, for suggestions on how to approach this topic, which have made this chapter much more accessible to the prospective reader. The writing of this chapter was supported, in part, by NIH HD046193.

1   Electrical activity at a given site is always recorded with respect to activity at another active site called the reference. Thus the morphology of the waveform is dependent on activity at both sites (e.g., FZ relative to mastoid reference). However, the difference in amplitude between any pair of sites will be identical regardless of reference. For example, (FZ to mastoid ref.) − (CZ to mastoid ref.) = (FZ − CZ) + (mastoid ref. − mastoid ref.) = FZ − CZ, where FZ is fronto-central midline and CZ is central midline.

References

Amunts, K., Schleicher, A., Ditterich, A., & Zilles, K. (2003). Broca's region: Cytoarchitectonic asymmetry and developmental changes. *Journal of Comparative Neurology, 465*, 72–89.

Bishop, D. V. M., & McArthur, G. M. (2005). Individual differences in auditory processing in specific language impairment: A follow-up study using event-related potentials and behavioural thresholds. *Cortex, 41*, 327–341.

Bookheimer, S. (2002). Functional MRI of language: New approaches to understanding the cortical organization of semantic priming. *Annual Review of Neuroscience, 22*, 151–188.

Caplan, R., & Dapretto, M. (2001). Making sense during conversation: An fMRI study. *NeuroReport, 12*, 3625–3632.

Cheour, M., Alho, K., & Ceponiene, R. (1998). Maturation of mismatch negativity in infants. *International Journal of Psychophysiology, Special Issue: Event related potentials and information processing by infants, 29,* 217–226.

Choudhury, N., Friedman, J. T., Realpe-Bonilla, T., Chojnowski, C., & Benasich, A. (2005, April). *Difference in cortical responses to auditory stimuli in six-month-old infants with family history of specific language impairment and age-matched controls.* Poster session presented at the 12th Annual Meeting of the Cognitive Neuroscience Society, New York.

Coch, D., Maron, L., Wolf, M., & Holcomb, P. J. (2002). Word and picture processing in children: an event-related potential study. *Developmental Neuropsychology, 22,* 373–406.

Dehaene-Lambertz, G., & Gigla, T. (2004). Common neural basis for phoneme processing in *infants* and adults. *Journal of Cognitive Neuroscience, 16,* 1375–1387.

Friederici, A. D. (2002). Towards a neural basis of auditory sentence processing. *Trends in Cognitive Sciences, 6,* 78–84.

Friederici, A. D. (2004). Processing local transitions versus long-distance syntactic hierarchies. *Trends in Cognitive Sciences, 8,* 245–247.

Friederici, A. D., Kotz, S. A., Werheid, K., Hein, G., & von Cramon, D. (2003). Syntactic comprehension in Parkinson's disease: investigating early automatic and late integrational processes using event-related brain potentials. *Neuropsychology, 17,* 133–142.

Friederici, A. D., Ruschemeyer, S. A., Hahne, A., & Fiebach, C. J. (2003). The role of left inferior frontal and superior temporal cortex in sentence comprehension: Localizing syntactic and semantic processes. *Cerebral Cortex, 13,* 170–177.

Friedrich, M., & Friederici, A. D. (2004). N400 like semantic incongruity effect in 19-month olds: processing known words in picture contexts. *Journal of Cognitive Neuroscience, 16,* 1465–1477.

Friedrich, M., Weber, C., & Friederici, A. D. (2004). Electrophysiological evidence for delayed mismatch response in infants at risk for specific language impairment. *Psychophysiology, 41,* 772–782.

Frishkoff, G. A., Tucker, D. M., Davey, C., & Scherg, M. (2004). Frontal and posterior sources of event-related potentials in semantic comprehension. *Cognitive Brain Research, 20,* 329–354.

Garrido, K., Hisagi, M., & Shafer, V. L. (2005, April). *ERP indices of speech processing in Spanish–English bilinguals.* Poster presented at the 12th Annual Meeting of the Cognitive Neuroscience Society, New York.

Gauger, L., Lombardino, L. J., & Leonard, C. M. (1997). Brain morphology in children with specific language impairment. *Journal of Speech Language and Hearing Research, 40,* 1272–1284.

Greenough, W., Black, J., & Wallace, C. (1987). Experience and brain development. *Child Development, 58,* 539–559.

Hahne, A., Eckstein, K., & Friederici, A. D. (2004). Brain signatures of syntactic and semantic processes during children's language development. *Journal of Cognitive Neuroscience, 16,* 1302–1318.

Hebb, D. (1949). *The organization of behavior: A neurophysiological theory.* New York: Wiley.

Hestvik, A., Maxfield, N., Schwartz, R. G., & Shafer, V. L. (in press). Brain responses to filled gaps. *Brain and Language.*

Huttenlocher, P. R., & Dabholkar, A. S. (1997). Regional differences in synaptogenesis in human cerebral cortex. *Journal of Comparative Neurology, 387,* 167–178.

Jernigan, T. L., Hesselink, J. R., Sowell, E., & Tallal, P. A. (1991). Cerebral structure on magnetic resonance imaging in language and learning-impaired children. *Archives of Neurology, 48,* 539–545.

Johnson, J. S., & Newport, E. L. (1991). Critical period effects on universal properties of language: the status of subjacency in the acquisition of a second language. *Cognition, 39*, 215–258.

Kandel, E., Schwartz, J., & Jessell, T. (2000). Principles of neural science. New York: William Heinemann and Harvard University Press.

Kessler, K. L., Martaharjono, G., & Shafer, V. L. (2004). ERP evidence of grammatical processing in Spanish second language learners of English. In *Proceedings of the 28th Annual Boston University Conference on Language Development* (pp. 294–305). Somerville, MA: Cascadilla Press.

Knudsen, E. I. (2004). Sensitive periods in the development of the brain and behavior. *Journal of Cognitive Neuroscience, 16*, 1412–1425.

Kolb, B., & Whishaw, I. Q. (1996). *Fundamentals of human neuropsychology*. USA: W.H. Freeman and Company.

Kushnerenko, E., Ceponiene, R., Balan, P., Fellman, V., & Naatanen, R. (2002). Maturation of the auditory change detection response in infants: a longitudinal ERP study. *NeuroReport, 13*, 1843–1848.

Kutas, M., & Hillyard, S. (1980). Reading senseless sentences: Brain potentials reflect semantic incongruity. *Science, 207*, 203–205.

Leppaanen, P., Pihko, E., Eklund, K. M., & Lyytinen, H. (1999). Cortical responses of infants with and without a genetic risk for dyslexia: II group effects. *NeuroReport, 10*, 969–973.

Mills, D., & Conboy, B. T. (2005). Do changes in brain organization reflect shifts in symbolic functioning? In L. Namy (Ed.), *Symbol use and symbolic representation* (pp. 123–153). Mahwah, NJ: Lawrence Erlbaum Associates.

Mills, D. L., Prat, C., & Zangl, R. (2004). Language experience and the organization of brain activity to phonetically similar words: ERP evidence from 14- and 20-month-olds. *Journal of Cognitive Neuroscience, 16*, 1452–1464.

Molfese, D. L. (2000). Predicting dyslexia at 8 years of age using neonatal brain responses. *Brain and Language, 72*, 238–245.

Morr, M. L., Shafer, V. L., Kreuzer, J. A., & Kurtzberg, D. (2002). Maturation of Mismatch Negativity in typically-developing infants and pre-school children. *Ear and Hearing, 23*, 118–136.

Näätänen, R. (2001). The perception of speech sounds by the human brain as reflected by the mismatch negativity (MMN) and its magnetic equivalent (MMNm). *Psychophysiology, 38*, 1–21.

Näätänen, R., Lehtokoski, A., Lennes, M., Cheour, M., Huotilainen, M., Livonen, A., et al. (1997). Language-specific phoneme representations revealed by electric and magnetic brain responses. *Nature, 385*, 432–434.

Neville, H., Mills, D., & Lawson, D. (1992). Fractioning language: Different neural subsystems with different sensitive periods. *Cerebral Cortex, 2*, 244–258.

Neville, H. J., Coffey, S. A., Holcomb, P. J., & Tallal, P. (1993). The neurobiology of sensory and language processing in language impaired children. *Journal of Cognitive Neuroscience, 5*, 235–253.

Oberecker, R., Friedrich, M., & Friederici, A. D. (2005). Neural correlates of syntactic processing in two-year-olds. *Journal of Cognitive Neuroscience, 17*, 1667–1678.

Plante, E., Swisher, L., Vance, R., & Rapcsak, S. (1991). MRI findings in boys with specific language impairment. *Brain and Language, 41*, 52–66.

Ponton, C. W., Eggermont, J. J., Kwong, B., & Don, M. (2000). Maturation of human central auditory system activity: Evidence from multi-channel evoked potentials. *Clinical Neurophysiology, 111*, 220–236.

Praamstra, P., Meyer, A., & Levelt, W. (1994). Neurophysiological manifestations of phonological processing latency variation of a negative ERP component timelocked to phonological mismatch. *Journal of Cognitive Neuroscience, 6*, 204–219.

Pulvermüller, F. (1996). Hebb's concept of cell assemblies and the psychophysiology of word processing. *Psychophysiology, 33*, 317–333.

Rivera-Gaxiola, M., Klarman, L., Garcia-Sierra, A., & Kuhl, P. (2005). Neural patterns to speech and vocabulary growth in American infants. *NeuroReport, 16*, 494–498.

Scott, S., & Wise, R. (2004). The functional neuroanatomy of prelexical processing in speech perception. *Cognition, 92*, 13–45.

Shafer, V. L., Kessler, K. L., Morr, M. L., Schwartz, R. G., & Kurtzberg, D. (2005). Spatiotemporal brain activity to "the" in discourse. *Brain and Language, 93*, 277–297.

Shafer, V. L., Morr, M. L., Datta, H., Kurtzberg, D., & Schwartz, R. G. (2005). Neurophysiological indices of speech processing deficits in children with specific language impairment. *Journal of Cognitive Neuroscience, 17*, 1168–1180.

Shafer, V. L., Morr, M., Kreuzer, J., & Kurtzberg, D. (2000). Maturation of mismatch negativity in school-age children. *Ear and Hearing, 21*, 242–251.

Shafer, V. L., Schwartz, R. G., & Kessler, K. L. (2003). ERP indices of phonological and lexical processing in children and adults. In *Proceedings of the 27th Annual Boston University Conference on Language Development* (pp. 751–761). Somerville, MA: Cascadilla Press.

Shafer, V. L., Schwartz, R. G., & Kurtzberg, D. (2004). Language specific memory traces of consonants in the brain. *Cognitive Brain Research, 18*, 242–254.

Shafer, V. L., Schwartz, R. G., Morr, M. L., Kessler, K. L., & Kurtzberg, D. (2000). Deviant neurophysiological asymmetry in children with language impairment. *NeuroReport, 11*, 3715–3718.

Shafer, V. L., Shucard, D. W., & Jaeger, J. J. (1999). Cerebral specialization and the role of prosody in language acquisition in three-month-old infants. *Developmental Neuropsychology, 15*, 73–110.

Shucard, D., & Shucard, J. (1990). Auditory evoked potentials and hand preference in 6-month-old infants: Possible gender related differences in cerebral organization. *Developmental Psychology, 26*, 923–930.

Squire, L., & Kandel, E. (1999). *Memory: From mind and molecules.* New York: Scientific American Library/Scientific American Books.

Strange, W. S., & Shafer, V. L. (in press). *Speech perception in late second language learners: The re-education of selective perception.* Cambridge: Cambridge University Press.

Uwer, R., Albrecht, R., & von Suchodoletz, W. (2002). Automatic processing of tones and speech stimuli in children with specific language impairment. *Developmental Medicine and Child Neurology, 44*, 527–532.

Vaughan, H., & Kurtzberg, D. (1992). Electrophysiologic indices of human brain maturation and cognitive development. In M. R. Gunnar, & C. A. Nelson (Eds.), *Developmental behavioral neuroscience.* Hillsdale, NJ: Lawrence Erlbaum Associates.

Wagovich, S. A., & Newhoff, M. (2004). The single exposure: partial word knowledge growth through reading. *American Journal of Speech Language Pathology, 13*, 316–328.

Wassenaar, M., & Hagoort, P. (2005). Word-category violations in patients with Broca's aphasia: An ERP study. *Brain and Language, 92*, 117–137.

Weber, C., Hahne, A., Friedrich, M., & Friederici, A. (2004). Discrimination of word stress in early infant perception: electrophysiological evidence. *Cognitive Brain Research, 18*, 149–161.

Weber-Fox, C. M., & Neville, H. J. (1995). Maturational constraints on functional specializations for language processing: ERP and behavioral evidence in bilingual speakers. *Journal of Cognitive Neuroscience, 8*, 231–256.

Winkler, I., Kujala, T., Alku, P., & Naatanen, R. (2003). Language context and phonetic change detection. *Cognitive Brain Research, 17*, 833–844.

Winkler, I., Kujala, T., Tiitinen, H., Sivonen, P., Alku, P., Lehtokoski, A., et al. (1999). Brain responses reveal the learning of foreign language phonemes. *Psychophysiology, 36*, 638–642.

3

Formal and Computational Constraints on Language Development

Helen Goodluck

This chapter reviews approaches to change in children's grammatical abilities from the perspective of work in the framework of generative grammar. We will evaluate the idea that principles of grammar may mature over time, and look at the potential role of the mechanisms for language production and comprehension in explaining children's non-adult behaviors. Virtually all of the topics covered in this chapter are the subject of ongoing research and debate; my goal is simply to give a flavor of central issues, albeit with a bias toward my own interests.

Constraints on the Learner: Input Limitations and Universal Grammar

This section considers what type of situation the learner confronts when acquiring a first language, and how the learner's inbuilt knowledge of grammar may help him to cope with the limitations of the input he receives.

Input constraints

There are three major ways in which the linguistic input to the child is restricted. First, the child hears only a small subset of the infinite number of grammatical sentences in the ambient language. Second, the set of sentences the child hears may not fully represent the range of sentences that are grammatical in the adult language – some structures are grammatical but rare. Third, the child is not corrected if he or she produces a sentence that is not grammatical in the adult language. This restriction is generally called the no negative evidence constraint.

At least the third of these purported constraints on the input has been subject to a good deal of controversy from the 1970s onwards. However, I believe the state of current evidence indicates that the observation that children are not instructed – either explicitly or implicitly – is correct (see Valian, 1999, for a review).

Constraints on hypothesis formation: Universal Grammar

Despite the fact that the input to the learner is limited in the way just sketched, the sentences children are exposed to are in principle frequently amenable to multiple possible analyses, including analyses that do not conform to the patterns found in adult grammars. However, as we will see below, there is little evidence for children forming grammars that deviate substantially from the patterns attested in adult languages. In 1965 Noam Chomsky broke new ground, proposing a solution to the puzzle of how children achieve implicit knowledge of the grammar of their language in the face of input constraints. The first section of *Aspects of the theory of syntax* outlined the structure of a language acquisition device (LAD), proposing that the child tackled the task of analyzing the input with the use of an innate knowledge of the shape of human languages: Universal Grammar (UG). Universal Grammar comprises *formal* universals and *substantive* universals. Formal universals limit what types of rules are allowed in human languages. An elementary example is that no language uses linear order in the sentence as a basis for signaling the difference between sentence types. The difference between a declarative sentence and a yes–no question in English is signaled by inverting the subject of the sentence and the first verb, not by, for example, inverting the order of the first two words, as illustrated in (1) (an asterisk indicates ungrammaticality):

(1)   a.   This sentence is declarative.
       b.   Is this sentence declarative? (Inversion of subject and verb)
       c.   *Sentence this is declarative? (Inversion of the order of first two words)

Substantive universals are the "building blocks" of grammatical rules: the vocabulary out of which rules are constructed. Thus the categories Noun, Verb, Adjective, etc. (or a set of primitive features in terms of which these categories are defined) are substantive universals. Implicit knowledge of the formal and substantive universals that comprise UG will give the child a head-start in analyzing the input, steering her away from a multitude of logically possible, but grammatically impossible, hypotheses about the structure of her language.

Chomsky's 1981 book *Lectures on government and binding* put an important new spin on the concept of UG, by tackling language variation. Universal Grammar limits the range of possible human languages, but we don't all speak the same language or type of language. Not only are the vocabularies of different languages different, but so are the structures. Languages such as English have the basic word order subject–verb–object (SVO); languages such as Japanese have the basic word order SOV; and languages such as Irish have the basic word order VSO. Languages such as English do not allow the subject of a sentence to be omitted (2b); languages such as Italian permit the equivalent of such a sentence.

(2)   a.   She left in a huff.
       b.   *Left in a huff.

Although it is possible to question a position inside an embedded clause (3a), languages such as English do not allow questions such as (3b), in which the question word refers to a position inside a relative clause. By contrast, languages such as Japanese or Akan (spoken in Ghana) permit their equivalent.

(3)   a.   What did Jane think that the man had eaten?
       b.   *What did the man eat a veggieburger that contained?
             (cf. The man ate a veggieburger that contained tofu.)

Chomsky's basic proposal was that the *principles* of UG (formal universals) could be set to different values: the principles had *parameters* that needed to be fixed by the language learner on the basis of the evidence of the language she hears.[1]

Language Development: Continuity versus Maturation

In empirical work on language acquisition, the concepts of UG and principles and parameters were incorporated in the late 1970s onwards into hypotheses about the real-time course of language development. The most popular position was, and I believe continues to be, that of *continuity*. Under continuity, the child's developing grammar is hypothesized to be always a grammar that is a possible adult grammar, although it may not be the correct grammar for the target language. For continuity to be maintained, given the assumption of no negative evidence, the input must contain clues that will permit the child to deduce that she has not got the target grammar right, and hence that she must revise her grammar. In the terminology of principles and parameters, the input must be such that the child can reset a parameter to the correct value.

Another approach to child grammars is *maturation* (Borer & Wexler, 1987). The idea is that the child is equipped innately with knowledge of all properties of UG, but that some principles and/or substantive universals may kick in only after a period of time, in a manner similar to the biologically determined schedule for physical growth. A view of grammatical development that admits maturation is consistent with continuity, since the child may have enough in his arsenal of grammatical constructs to form a possible adult language, even if he doesn't have enough to construct the correct grammar of the language he is learning (Borer & Wexler, 1992; Clahsen, 1990/91; Wexler, 1999). A grammar that does not fit the target can be corrected by maturation of some principle(s). Such maturation may or may not be triggered by input, just as physical growth may be more or less dependent on diet and other external factors.

The continuity and maturation views of development differ in the source of non-adult grammars. Under maturation, the child forms a non-adult grammar because she doesn't have available yet the apparatus to form the adult rules; under continuity, the child may have all of the constructs of UG at her disposal, but she does not deploy some types of rule where the adult language does. The challenge for this view is to explain why the child eschews certain grammatical mechanisms. The maturation and continuity views also differ in that in principle maturation does allow for the child to form grammars that don't fall within the range of adult grammars, although as just noted this is not a necessary corollary of maturation.

Some Examples of Children's Grammatical Knowledge and Development

This section and the following one look at how the ideas just sketched fare in the face of studies of particular aspects of grammatical development. By about 18 months children are producing their first multiword utterances and there is substantial evidence that the parameter of basic word order is set very early, with consequences for other aspects of grammar (see, e.g., Hickey, 1990; Hirsh-Pasek & Golinkoff, 1991; Otsu, 1994), and with little evidence of experimentation or error. Other examples offer more evidence of development.

Example 1: Subjectless sentences

As mentioned above, languages vary as to whether they permit subjectless sentences such as (2b): Italian and Portuguese are among the languages that do, English is among the languages that do not. At early stages of language development, children learning English-type languages do produce subjectless sentences. Examples are given in (4) (taken from the speech of Adam (Brown, 1973), at age 27–29 months (cited in Pinker, 1995)):

(4)   play checkers
      screw part machine
      now put boots on

An early theory concerning such child utterances was that children learning English start off with an Italian-type grammar and then have to reset the parameter for subject-less sentences to block this possibility in English (Hyams, 1986). However, cross-linguistic work has largely discredited this hypothesis. For example, in a study of 2-year-old Portuguese-speaking children Valian and Eisenberg (1996) found that the children increased their use of subject pronouns over time. This argues that subject omission by English-speaking children does not reflect a mis-set grammatical parameter, but is more likely a reflection of error due to pressure on the immature language production system (see Bloom, 1990, and Valian & Aubry, 2005, for further discussion).

Example 2: Structural conditions on pronoun interpretation

Chomsky (1981) formulated a set of principles that govern the interpretation of definite and reflexive pronoun interpretation. The definite pronoun *her* in (5a) may not refer to *Sue*, but it may refer to *Mary* or to someone not mentioned in the sentence:

(5) a. Mary realized that Sue had e-mailed her.
     b. Mary realized that Sue had e-mailed herself.

By contrast, *herself* in (5b) must refer to *Sue*: it cannot refer to Mary. This basic contrast can be accounted for by requiring the reflexive pronoun to refer to a noun (phrase) that is structurally close to it. In the case of the English sentence (5b) "structurally close" means inside the lower, embedded sentence, not inside the main clause:

(6)

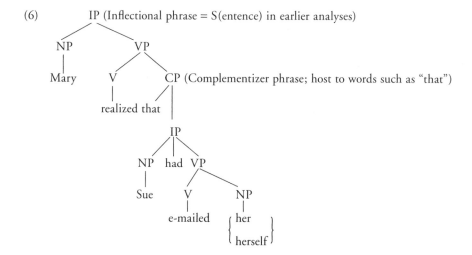

In the late 1970s and the 1980s, studies using a variety of experimental techniques showed that preschool children are sensitive to contrasts such as that in (5a) versus (5b), and that this sensitivity was based upon structural properties of the sentence, not upon surface order of words (see Kaufman, 1994, for a review). Lidz (this volume) gives details of the structural relationship on which the possibility of co-reference for pronouns and reflexives is determined, and other examples of the contrasts to which children are sensitive.

   However, children's performance is not error free. Many studies have shown that more mistakes are made with the interpretation of definite pronouns than with reflexives and this has spawned a rich discussion of factors which may affect children's behavior. Definite pronouns differ from reflexives in permitting extra-sentential (discourse) reference, and there are also discourse-related circumstances in which structural restrictions on definite pronoun interpretation may be overridden. For example, in the following discourse the pronoun in speaker B's utterance can be felicitously taken to refer to *Mary*, although this is not a permissible interpretation for the sentence taken in isolation:

(7)   Speaker A: I don't know anyone who likes Mary.
      Speaker B: Mary likes her.

One approach to children's errors with definite pronouns is to suggest that children may have trouble in executing such discourse-related conditions (see Chien & Wexler, 1990; Grodzinsky & Reinhart, 1993; Thornton & Wexler, 1999, among others).

A second approach to children's troubles with definite pronouns is to ask whether children know which lexical items are reflexive and which are definite. Some languages, such as Danish, have a more complex system of reflexive and non-reflexive pronouns, with a three-way distinction: reflexives and definite pronouns such as those in English, plus a reflexive that is "long distance," permitting the interpretation of sentences broadly equivalent to (5b) in which *herself* is taken to refer to *Mary*. Other languages have a "simpler" system in which there is just one pronominal form, used for both reflexive and non-reflexive meaning. An example is Maori. Given this cross-linguistic complexity, it is not unreasonable to suppose that the child might make errors that are rooted in mis-construing a definite pronoun in languages such as English as a reflexive lexical item that permits local reference (see Fodor, 1994, and Elbourne, 2005, for pertinent discussion).

Moreover, children's problems with pronouns are not restricted to definite pronouns. As just mentioned, Danish is a language that has a "long-distance" reflexive. Children learning such languages will have to use the input (sentences they hear) to work out that this is a grammatical option. That input may not be readily available. Jakubowicz (1994) shows that children learning Danish may be as old as 9 or 10 years before they master the fact that in a sentence such as (8) the long-distance reflexive *sig* cannot refer to the subject of the subordinate clause (*Ida*) but must refer to the subject of the main clause (*Minnie*). (This restriction is due to the nature of the verb in the embedded clause.) As Jakubowicz argues, the lengthy period of development for *sig* may be a reflex of the rarity of the *sig* construction in the input to the child.

(8)   Minnie beder Ida om at   pege på sig.
      Minnie asks   Ida   point at self.
      "Minnie asks Ida to point at herself (=Minnie)."

Example 3: Movement

We saw with examples (3a,b), repeated here as (9), that there are limits on the positions in a sentence that can be questioned, questioning from within a relative clause being blocked in English:

(9)   a.   What did Jane think that the man had eaten?
      b.   *What did the man eat a veggieburger that contained?

Such constraints are associated with a mechanism that moves the question word from its underlying position (as object of *eat/contain* in the examples) to the front of the sentence. The gist of the linguistic account of the difference between (9a) and (9b) is that there is an extra layer of structure in (9b), the noun phrase, and this prevents movement from within the relative clause:

(10) a. Partial structure for (9a)   (10) b. Partial structure for (9b)

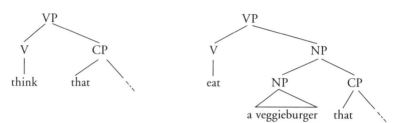

Nor can we question a position within an embedded question (11) or a temporal clause (12):

(11)   *What did Dave wonder who wrote __?
       (cf. Dave wondered who wrote that memo.)
(12)   *What did Dave write that memo after he read __?
       (cf. Dave wrote that memo after he read Jane's letter.)

As mentioned above, not all languages use a movement mechanism and its attendant constraints for question formation, presenting the learner with the challenge of working out which language type he is exposed to (movement or non-movement).

During the 1990s, several studies showed children to be sensitive to constraints on question formation in languages such as English. One of the clearest examples is de Villiers and Roeper (1995). They asked preschool children questions such as those in (13):

(13)   a.   How did the man who hurt his leg get home?
       b.   How did the man rescue the cat who broke her leg?

The questions were preceded by a short (two to three) sentence story that gave (for 13a) a manner of getting hurt and a manner of getting home and (for 13b) a manner of rescuing and a manner of breaking a leg. In a question such as (13a), where the verb *hurt* is embedded within a relative clause modifying *the man*, *how* was never interpreted as referring to the way in which the injury took place. By contrast, in a question such as (13b), where *rescue* is the main verb of the sentence, children freely construed the question word as referring to that verb (see also de Villiers, Roeper, & Vainikka, 1990, and Goodluck, Foley, & Sedivy, 1992, for evidence that children are sensitive to the impermissibility of questions such as (11) and (12), respectively).

While children have been shown to be sensitive to structural restrictions on question formation associated with a movement mechanism, there is some debate about the degree to which children's earliest grammars employ movement in questions (see, e.g., discussion in Thornton & Crain, 1994). In the case of relative clause formation, it is quite evident that children may go through a period of development before settling on the adult grammar. Just as in the case of question formation, there is cross-linguistic variation in the mechanisms used to form relative clauses. Some languages, such as English, use a movement mechanism and the internal structure of relative clauses is subject to the same structural constraints that govern question formation. Other languages, such as Akan, do not use a movement mechanism and relative clauses are not subject to structural constraints of the kind seen in English. In these languages, the noun phrase the relative clause modifies is linked to a position inside the relative via a mechanism of pronominal binding. Still other languages employ a dual mechanism for relative clauses, using both movement and binding. Such languages include Modern Irish and Modern Hebrew. Even in English there are pronominal structures that permit linkage of an element into a position from which movement is blocked. For example, in (14),

(14)   Bones, I know a dog that loves them.
        (cf. *What do I know a dog that loves?)

bones refers to the object *them* inside the relative clause *that loves them*. The difference between languages such as English and languages such as Akan, Irish, and Hebrew is that the latter type of language uses structures with pronominal binding much more freely than English does – allowing the equivalent of the starred question in (14), or the relative clause in (15):

(15)   *I met the man that everyone knows who betrayed (him).

Many studies have elicited relative clauses from preschool and young school-age children. Particularly pertinent to this discussion are studies of French (Labelle, 1990), Serbo-Croatian (Goodluck & Stojanović, 1996), and Modern Irish (Goodluck, Guilfoyle, & Harrington, 2006). Children's relatives do not always conform to the dictates of the adult grammar. A generalization that has emerged is that children produce relatives with the properties of a binding mechanism, even when the adult language uses only a movement mechanism. As we have seen in (14), one property of a binding mechanism is the use of pronouns. A pronoun occupies the site that the noun phrase the relative modifies refers to, as illustrated in the adult Irish examples in (16); such pronouns are known as resumptive pronouns.

(16)   a.   an carr a   dtiomáineann Nell ar scoil   gach lá   é
             the car COMP drives   Nell to school every day it
             "the car Nell drives to school every day"
        b.   an fear a   n-insíonn tú   an scéal do
             the man COMP told   you a story to-him
             "the man you told a story to"

Labelle (1990) found her French-speaking subjects innovated resumptive pronouns, although these are ungrammatical in the adult language. Examples from Labelle's data are given in (17):

(17) a. la petite fille qu'a   est assis sur la boîte
         the little girl COMP she is sat   on the box (NB: qu'a ([ka]) = que elle, "that
         she")
         "the little girl that is sitting on the box"
     b. sur la balle qu'i(l)   l'attrape
         on the ball COMP he it catches
         "on the ball that he catches"
     c. sur la boîte que le camion rentre dedans
         on the box that the truck goes   inside-it
         "on the box that the truck is going inside"

It might be supposed that the examples from child French in (17) are "slips of the tongue," rather than a genuine stage in grammatical development. In speech, resumptive pronouns are sometimes inserted in languages that do not permit resumptives, in order to "repair" an ungrammatical structure. Such repairs are found particularly when the distance between the resumptive and the element it refers to increases; compare (18a) with (18b,c):

(18) a. *What did Jane eat a veggieburger that contained it?
     b. ?*What did Sue claim that Jane had eaten a veggieburger that contained
         it?
     c. ??What did Ida believe that Sue had claimed that Jane had eaten a veggieburger
         that contained it?

The relatives in Labelle's study and other studies cited above were elicited from children in picture description tasks; perhaps the difficulty of this task prompts speech errors, including repair resumptive pronouns. The body of evidence from the various studies argues against this view as a complete account of the data. For example, another index of use of a binding as opposed to movement strategy for relative clause formation is the use of an invariant complementizer such as English *that* to introduce the relative clause. The children in Labelle's study used the invariant complementizer *que* to introduce their relatives, although the adult grammar requires a relative pronoun; children acquiring Serbo-Croatian produced relative clauses with an invariant complementizer (as opposed to a relative pronoun) more frequently than adults did (Goodluck & Stojanović, 1996). And children learning Irish innovated a structure that is plausibly the result of use of binding to form a relative clause in an environment where binding relatives are blocked in the adult grammar (Goodluck et al., 2006).

As in the case of subjectless sentences, we can appeal to pressure on the production mechanism to account for children's innovation of binding relatives. On the assumption that the movement operation adds an extra computational burden in producing a relative, we can say that children innovate binding relatives for ease of production. Note that in this case, production pressure leads to the temporary positing of a non-adult grammar, whereas in the case of subjectless sentences, production pressure leads to non-adult utterances that are in fact also ungrammatical for the child.

Summary

So far we have seen that from an early age children are sensitive to grammatical restrictions present in the ambient language, including whether their language permits subjectless sentences, and restrictions on reflexive and definite pronoun interpretation. When children do err, we have appealed to a variety of factors: pressure on the language production system (as in the case of English-speaking children's subjectless sentences and the innovation of a binding mechanism for forming relative clauses); the need to access discourse/real-world knowledge; the need to correctly identify grammatical categories (which elements are definite pronouns and which are reflexive); and the need to access input that is rare (Danish long-distance reflexive sentences). In each case it is possible to maintain continuity, in the sense that the child does not posit a grammar that deviates from what is permitted in adult languages. However, not all cases of non-adult behavior can easily be written off in a similar manner. In the next section, we will look at a case where children's grammar appears to be in violation of continuity.

A Problem for Continuity: Root Infinitives

One property of adult languages that is a candidate for an inviolable, non-parameterized constraint of Universal Grammar is the fact that (a small number of special cases aside) main clauses are always tensed – i.e. marked for past or present (or future in many languages). Thus it has generally been assumed that adult languages with sentences such as that in (19) are not attested (though this may be too strong; Borer & Rohrbacher, 2002):

(19)   *He (to) sleep.

But there is now abundant evidence that children produce such sentences. English has a relatively impoverished morphological system for marking tense, with the infinitive (non-tensed) form of the verb being identical in many cases to the tensed from. But in languages such as Dutch or French, in which the infinitive and tensed forms are clearly distinct, children's use of infinitives in main clauses is plain to see. Hoekstra and Hyams (1998) studied root (main clause) infinitives produced by children in the age range of approximately 18 to 36 months; (20) gives examples (taken from Hoekstra & Hyams, 1998, p. 83)[2]:

(20)   a.   Papa schoenen wassen
             Daddy shoes wash-inf.   (Dutch; Weverink, 1989)
       b.   Michel dormi
             Michel sleep-inf.   (French; Pierce, 1992)
       c.   Thorstn das haben
             Thorstn that have-inf.   (German; Poeppel & Wexler, 1993)
       d.   Jag också hoppa där å där
             I also hop-inf. there and there (Swedish; Santelmann, 1995)

If adult grammars impose the restriction that main clauses must be tensed, then such examples are a problem for continuity, which claims that children's grammars are always possible adult grammars, even if these child grammars do not always correspond to the grammar of the language at hand.

There is now a large literature on root infinitives, some of it advocating maturation and some continuity. Cross-linguistic comparisons have revealed consistent patterns in the distribution of children's root infinitives, leading the way for the development of an account of their distribution in which the deviation from adult grammars is not as large as it might at first appear. The following is based on Hoekstra and Hyams (1998).

Two major generalizations concerning child root infinitives in languages such as Dutch are the following:

(a)   Root infinitives are associated with eventive verbs (such as *wash* or *hop*) rather than stative verbs (such as *be* or *love*) (Ferdinand, 1996; Jordens, 1991). Eventive verbs basically denote actions or events, and stative verbs denote states/conditions.
(b)   Root infinitives are associated with modal interpretations – specifically, an interpretation of necessity or desire, as illustrated in the following child Dutch examples (based on Hoekstra & Hyams, p. 92).

(21)   a.   Eerst kaartje kopen!
              First ticket buy-inf.
              Intended meaning: "We must first buy a ticket"
        b.   Niekje buiten spelen
              Niekje outside play-inf.
              Intended meaning: "Niek (=speaker) wants to play outside"

Hoekstra and Hyams propose an analysis along the following lines. The infinitive in adult languages has a particular aspectual property: it "denotes an event not yet realized" (Hoekstra & Hyams, p. 102). Hoekstra and Hyams point out that this makes sense of the fact that in French, for example, the future tense is represented by an affix that is added to the infinitival form (*j'arriver-ai* "I shall arrive," where *arriver* is the infinitive and *ai* the future affix). Returning to the fact mentioned above, that adult languages do display root infinitives in a small number of special cases, we can see that these special cases also involve events not yet realized. The Dutch examples in (22) (from Wijnen, 1996, quoted in Hoekstra & Hyams, p. 103) illustrate this property:

(22)   a.   Hier geen fietsen plaatsen!
              Here no bicycles place-inf.
              "Don't put bicycles here!"
        b.   Jan met mijn zus trouwen?! Dat nooit.
              Jan my sister marry-inf. That never.

So now we are seeing a similarity between child root infinitives and adult grammars. But the fact that children produce so many such utterances in situations where the adult grammar requires other means of expressing the intended meaning (such as the use of a modal verb) still requires an explanation. Hoekstra and Hyams propose that where children and adults differ is in the degree of freedom they are allowed in interpreting a sentence with reference to the discourse. Roughly, they propose that adults are largely constrained to provide an interpretation of the sentence within its syntactic structure: the syntactic elements that represent tense must be fully interpreted inside the sentence. By contrast, children may use the discourse to "fill in" information about tense that is not computed internally to the syntax.

Processing Constraints

Thus far we have been concerned with constraints on children's hypothesis formation that derive from Universal Grammar, although we have seen that the outer course of development may be affected by the capacity of the sentence production mechanism. This section deals with another potential capacity limitation, that of sentence processing. There has been little intersection between research of language processing and language acquisition, despite the importance of the former for the latter – the child has to process the input to form a grammar (see Fodor, 1998, for one exception to this lack of intersection).

The sentence processor

The model of sentence processing that we assume for adults is one in which grammatical structure is built immediately as the sentence is input, and that much, if not all, of the detail that is justified in the theoretical literature is present in the syntactic structures assembled by the processor. In addition, we will assume the following: (a) small fragments of syntactic structure (phrasal chunks) are built immediately; (b) these chunks are subsequently assembled into larger structures, which may be partially determined in a top-down manner; (c) sentences (clauses) are important processing units, and sentence boundaries are the point at which material is recoded into a non-immediate memory representation, which may lose much of the fine-grained syntactic structure of first-stage processing; (d) the integration of sentential structure with a larger discourse-oriented representation takes place at a relatively late stage in the chain of processing operations; (e) the processor is a capacity-limited device that can overload. Figure 3.1 illustrates this view of sentence processing.

Some of these assumptions are more controversial than others. For example, (c) is supported by extensive experiments from the 1960s onwards, whereas (d) is the subject of considerable debate. See Fodor (1995), Tanenhaus and Trueswell (1995), and Treiman, Clifton, Meyer, and Wurm (2003) for useful reviews of the literature, and Frazier (1999) and Gibson (1998) for more technical discussions.

We will assume that the child's processing device has the same architecture as the adult's. Aside from a different stock of first language rules to draw on, the difference between children and adults with respect to processing will boil down to a difference in

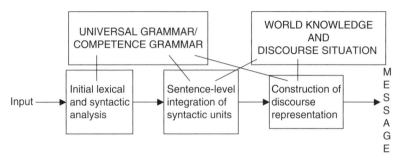

Figure 3.1   The human sentence processing mechanism.

processing capacity: the child's working memory and storage capacity will be less than the adult's.

What consequences will this lesser processing capacity have for language development? Newport (1988) has suggested that less may be more – if the child takes in only small chunks of language structure, this may allow her to analyze the details of the input, establishing morphological boundaries that may be crucial to cracking the language's syntactic system. On the other hand, lesser processing capacity may lead to error. Consider again the case of definite pronouns. Although preschool children show knowledge of structural restrictions on definite pronoun reference, errors are committed. One explanation we sketched above for this was that children may falter in their knowledge and/or execution of pragmatic, discourse-related principles that enter into definite pronoun interpretation, above and beyond structural restrictions. The model in Figure 3.1 is complementary to this account, and may be argued to explain children's difficulty with discourse-related operations: if children have lesser processing capacity and hence lesser ability to perform operations towards the end of the chain of operations in Figure 3.1, they will be more likely to make errors with definite pronouns than with reflexives (Goodluck, 1990; see also Avrutin, 2000), since the former but not the latter may require access to multiclause structures and discourse information. In favor of a processing account of some if not all errors with pronoun interpretation is the fact that there is evidence that children make errors with pronoun interpretation that can be linked to difficulty in accessing discourse, and which do not fall under other approaches to errors with pronouns (see, e.g., Goodluck & Solan, 2000; Goodluck, Terzi, & Chocano Díaz, 2001).

Another angle on the way in which the sentence processing mechanism may guide development concerns the issue of no negative evidence. It can be argued that the processor leads the child to conservative hypotheses, preventing her from positing incorrect grammars for which there will be no corrective input. Consider again the examples in (13). English is a language that does not permit a question word to refer inside a relative clause – hence *how* in (13a) cannot be taken to modify the verb *hurt*. De Villiers and Roeper (1995) showed that children categorically obeyed this restriction. However, there is another explanation for their findings. One of the properties of the sentence processing mechanism listed above is the importance of clausal units. Suppose the processor operates under the following constraint:

(23)   As the sentence is input, link a question word to a position in the incoming string only when the link results in a complete proposition.[3]

The fact that *hurt* is contained within a relative clause in (13a), whereas the verb *rescue* in (13b) is not, means that (23) will be violated if *how* is linked to the first verb in the sentence in the case of (13a), but not in the case of (13b):

(24)   a.   How did the man who hurt his leg . . . . (incomplete proposition)
        b.   How did the man rescue the cat . . . . (complete proposition)

It may seem that the processing constraint (23) simply reduces to knowledge of the grammatical constraint on questioning from within a relative clause: How can you know that the fragment in (24a) is not a complete proposition unless you have registered the fact that *hurt* is contained within a relative clause? However, these two accounts can be distinguished. If the constraint in (23) is a general constraint on processing, we predict that in a language which, unlike English, permits a question word to refer inside a relative clause, in sentence processing (23) will still block the location of the question word inside the relative clause in sentences equivalent to (13a). The relevant evidence has still to be gathered, but there are some preliminary data that suggest this may be the case (Saah & Goodluck, 1995).

Processing and learnability

During the 1980s, there was considerable discussion of the problem of *learnability*. It was reasoned that if the child receives no negative evidence, the language acquisition device must be structured in such a way as to prevent the child from hypothesizing grammars that were incorrect, and too permissive in terms of the range of grammatical sentence types sanctioned in the target language. Even if such a child grammar was permitted under the constraints of Universal Grammar, the child would have no input that allowed him to correct his erroneous hypothesis. One solution to this problem was the *subset principle* (Berwick, 1985). The subset principle proposes that the child posits the grammar that is (a) compatible with the input data (the speech he hears) and (b) generates the smallest set of output sentences. Thus, for example, suppose the child learner hears a sentence such as (the equivalent of) (13b), repeated here:

(25)   How did the man rescue the kitten who broke her leg?

Universal Grammar will tell him that there are two possibilities: either the question word *how* can refer only to the manner of rescuing (i.e., he is learning a language such as English, which blocks a question word from referring to a position inside a relative clause), or *how* can modify either verb (*rescue, break*). The subset principle will tell him to hypothesize that he is learning an English-type language, since that language type permits the smaller range of possible interpretations. If the child is in fact learning a language that permits both interpretations, he will eventually receive input that tells him that his grammar needs to be revised to allow a question word to refer inside a relative clause – such input would be, for example, the equivalent of a question such as (3/8b) (What did the man eat a veggieburger that contained?).

One criticism of the subset principle is that it is a principle for which there is little in the way of independent evidence that it is operative as a cognitive and/or grammatical principle. The proposal in the last section – that the processing mechanism may steer the hearer away from some logically possible (and in some languages grammatically permissible) interpretations – has the potential to explain cases where the child opts for a less liberal grammar than his language in fact allows, and to thus do away with the subset principle as a principle governing the language acquisition device.

More on Continuity versus Maturation

I have just suggested that an understanding of sentence processing limitations may help us do away with an otherwise stipulative principle guiding the child's hypothesis formation. In this section we will look again at root infinitives and also at passive sentences, and consider whether performance limitations – limitations on the child's ability to execute her knowledge in real-time production and comprehension – can replace the idea that grammatical principles may mature.

Root infinitives revisited

There is superficially a tension between the claim that children may have difficulty accessing discourse representations (contributing to their difficulties with definite pronoun interpretation) and the analysis of early root infinitives as a result of children's greater reliance on discourse to anchor the sentence in time relations. This is not necessarily a conflict. Notice that the difficulty children have with pronouns is to do with comprehension, whereas in the case of root infinitives we are dealing with production. We have already suggested that children's non-adult use of subjectless sentences and children's predilection for non-adult relative clauses formed by binding may be due to pressure on the production system. A similar kind of analysis can be proposed in the case of root infinitives. It is a fact that children's root infinitives exist side by side with correct tensed forms. Thus children at the stage of producing root infinitives cannot be said to lack knowledge of the realization of tense in their language.

Since the late 1980s inflectional phrase (IP) in Chomskyan generative grammar has been replaced by a series of "functional" categories, amongst which are categories that host the representation of tense and aspect, and number (singular, plural) of the subject. Such functional categories provide an infrastructure for the semantics of the sentence.[4] Thus a sentence such as "John is eating sushi" will have a structure roughly along the lines shown in (26):

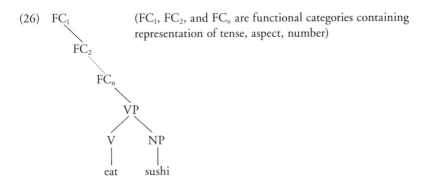

(26)   FC$_1$ (FC$_1$, FC$_2$, and FC$_n$ are functional categories containing
                        representation of tense, aspect, number)

This infrastructure of functional categories is critical to the representation of tense in adult languages. In Hoekstra and Hyams' (1998) analysis, there is an abstract tense operator (TO) in a complementizer phrase that binds the tense position (realized in TP = tense phrase):

(27)   TO$_i$ F$_1$ . . . . . F$_n$ Tense$_i$ VP

This binding operation is critical to the meaning of the sentence. Now consider the situation facing a child speaker of a language such as Dutch who wishes to express the proposition "We must first buy a ticket" (example 21a above). The child has an implicit choice – either she can compute the functional structure in the same way as adults do, or she can draw on her knowledge of the fact that infinitive forms denote events not yet realized, a fact that Hoekstra and Hyams argue is related to modal meaning, and produce a root infinitive. If the child takes the latter option, she is saved the "bother" of computing the tense operator structure for the sentence, but must rely on the discourse situation for the meaning of the sentence to be complete. Seen in this way, root infinitives may have their origin in a limitation in the capacity of the production mechanism, that is, at an early stage children may lack the computational power to consistently build higher levels of functional structure (cf. Rizzi, 1994) and tense operator representations. Thus in this case the child's lesser performance capacity in production may drive her into using discourse to complete the representation of the sentence, just as in the case of pronoun interpretation the structure of the processing device may deny her adequate access to discourse.[5] (See Borer & Rohrbacher, 2002, for a more recent analysis of root infinitives which draws on literature demonstrating reliance on discourse to specify tense in adult languages. Borer and Rohrbacher propose that children's root infinitives do involve the projection of (phonetically null) functional categories; however, their account is not incompatible with the account sketched above, given that the levels of functional category needed for discourse interpretation of tense are fewer than those needed for the sentence-internal specification of tense.)

Movement in passive sentences

Debate about whether children innovate a non-movement mechanism where the adult language uses a movement mechanism is not confined to the acquisition of relative clauses. In fact, the use of movement with respect to the development of passive sentences was a major impetus to the idea that some properties of grammar may mature in the course of childhood. In languages such as English, passive sentences are formed by moving the direct object of the sentence to subject position, as illustrated in (28):

(28)   a.   [e] was eaten the cake (by Billy) (structure before movement)
       b.   The cake$_i$ was eaten [e$_i$] (by Billy) (structure after movement)
          ([e] indicates an empty phrase, to which the object is moved.)

A number of studies have shown that preschool children have more trouble understanding passive sentences when they contain a non-action verb, such as *love*, than when they contain an action verb, such as *eat*. Borer and Wexler (1987) proposed that this asymmetry could be explained if children lacked the ability to perform movement to subject position (or whatever grammatical properties motivate that operation), but rather formed passives with the subject of the passive sentence always in subject position. They argued that the passive verb form (such as "eaten") in the passives produced by children was in fact an adjective, and that the difficulty children have with non-action passives is due to the fact that non-action verbs cannot readily be converted into adjectives. Borer and Wexler proposed that the capacity to perform movement to subject position matured in the course of development. A number of objections to this proposal were raised in the late 1980s and early 1990s (see Demuth, 1989; Pinker, Frost, & Lebeaux, 1987), and a significant experimental advance was made by Fox and Grodzinsky (1998). They found that performance on non-actional passive sentences improved when the passive sentence did not contain a *by* phrase. Thus sentences such as (29a) were found to be easier than sentences such as (29b), but the same was not true for (30a) versus (30b):

(29)   a.   The cake was eaten by Billy.
       b.   The thief was seen by Billy.
(30)   a.   The cake was eaten.
       b.   The thief was seen.

Fox and Grodzinsky argue that this result can be accounted for if children's difficulty with non-actional passives lies not with the operation of moving a direct object into subject position, but rather with the nature of the object of *by*. In (29a), *Billy* has the semantic role of agent, whereas in (29b), *Billy* has the role of experiencer (the person who undergoes the experience of seeing). They proposed that the agent role is the normal, "default" role conveyed by *by*, and that children's difficulties with non-agentive passives with a *by* phrase come from the need to transmit the non-canonical semantic role of experiencer via the *by* phrase. When this need is eliminated, as in (30b), performance on the non-agentive passives is improved. If this account is correct, then there is no need to propose that the ability to move to subject position matures.[6]

Can computational limitations replace maturation?

Maturational proposals have been made with respect to a number of areas of grammar in addition to the passive example just given, including movement in relative clauses (Guasti & Shlonsky, 1995) and the interpretation of adverbial clauses with missing subjects (Wexler, 1991; evaluated in Goodluck, 2001). Maturation handles non-adult behavior in a straightforward way: the child forms a non-adult grammar because she doesn't have the ability to do otherwise. One potential problem for maturation is that the age at which maturation is claimed to take place does not always jibe with evidence that children do command the relevant operation/property of grammar. For example, innovation of non-adult relative clauses can persist until the child is age 6 or older, yet there is evidence that younger children do have a movement operation for forming relative clauses (Goodluck et al., 2006; McKee & McDaniel, 2001). This problem is not serious. Wexler (1999) observes maturation can take place on a slightly different time schedule for different children; moreover, even after a grammatical property has matured the child may not be prompted to use it in her grammar immediately.

The challenge for advocates of continuity without maturation is to find a motivation for non-adult behaviors that does not deny children full access to Universal Grammar. I believe that performance limitations of the kind we have sketched above may provide some answers. We suggested that difficulty with definite pronoun interpretation may be rooted in relatively late access to discourse information by the sentence processing mechanism, and that a binding mechanism for relative clauses may be preferred because it is computationally simpler than movement. If it is the case that children use an adjectival structure for passives at early stages (modulo the reservations sketched above), then this also may result from the computational ease of a non-movement mechanism. Two objections, at least, can be made to the general idea that children's choice of a non-adult grammar may be rooted in performance limitations. First, it may be said that the idea provides no explanation of why a particular mechanism is used by the child in one circumstance but not another. For example, why do children avoid movement in relative clauses, but not in direct questions? Although the answer to such questions may not always be obvious, I feel this is just a call for more thought on the way in which the human sentence processing/production mechanisms shape grammar and influence the cross-linguistic frequency of structures. In the case of the asymmetry between questions and relative clauses, it appears that cross-linguistically a non-movement mechanism may have a special status for relative clauses, something that Goodluck et al. (2006) suggest may be rooted in pressure on the production device. The second objection is that we know too little about the structure and capacity of the performance mechanisms to evaluate the claim that children's ability is quantitatively less than adults'. It is certainly the case, as noted above, that the organization of the processing mechanism is highly controversial, and the idea that access to discourse takes place at a relatively late stage may not go down well in some research circles. However, progress is being made in evaluating children's processing capacity and its relation to the analysis of specific structures (Felser, Marinis, & Clahsen, 2003).

Summary and Conclusion

We can summarize the facts of development sketched in this chapter as follows:

- From early on, the child shows sensitivity to basic properties of the language-particular grammar he is learning (basic word order, subjectless sentences, structural constraints on pronominal reference).

- Some structures elude the child for a lesser or greater period: root infinitives disappear fairly rapidly, but complete mastery of, inter alia, adult-like relative clause structures and rare constructions such as the Danish *sig* reflexive may take into the school years.

It seems that the non-adult behaviors observed can be assimilated into a model of acquisition that assumes continuity (with full access to Universal Grammar), although this is a matter of ongoing debate. A promising avenue for an account of development is the integration of models of human sentence processing and production into models of language acquisition. Such an integration has the potential to supplant a previously proposed principle of language acquisition – the subset principle – as well as the construct of maturation, explaining changes in grammar over time in terms of an interaction between input, innate linguistic knowledge, and increased performance capacity.

Notes

Marilyn Shatz provided very helpful comments on both the form and content of earlier versions of this chapter.

1   Not touched on in this chapter is the influence on the study of language development of the Minimalist Program of Chomsky (1993, 1995) and subsequent work. This is because, to my understanding, this work has not to date had the impact on the study of language acquisition of the earlier frameworks (*Aspects of the theory of syntax* and *Lectures on government and binding*).
2   The sources are as cited in Hoekstra and Hyams (1998).
3   This general hypothesis may need to be modulated by capacity limitations (cf. J. Sedivy, unpublished master's thesis, University of Ottawa, 1991; Aoshima, Phillips, & Weinberg, 2004); however, it has a body of evidence in its favor (Goodluck, Finney, & Sedivy, 1992).
4   A large part of the continuity–maturation debate over the past 15 years has concerned whether functional categories mature. Guilfoyle and Noonan (1992) and Radford (1990) were early advocates of maturation; the more recent literature drawn on here is compatible with continuity.
5   The account just sketched does not in and of itself explain the fact that in Hoekstra and Hyams' (1998) survey root infinitives are confined to languages in which tense is realized by number (singular, plural) marking for subject on the verb.
6   Fox and Grodzinsky's (1998) interpretation of their data and the issue of the development of the passive is a matter of ongoing debate (Babyonshev, Ganger, Pesetsky, & Wexler, 2001; Wexler, 2004).

References

Aoshima, S., Phillips, C., & Weinberg, A. (2004). Processing filler-gap dependencies in a head-final language. *Journal of Memory and Language, 51*, 23–54.

Avrutin, S. (2000). Comprehension of discourse-linked and non-discourse-linked questions by children and Broca's aphasics. In Y. Grodzinsky, L. Shapiro, & D. Swinney (Eds.), *Language and brain: Representation and processing*. San Diego, CA: Academic Press.

Babyonshev, M., Ganger, J., Pesetsky, D., & Wexler, K. (2001). The maturation of grammatical principles. *Linguistic Inquiry, 32*, 1–44.

Berwick, R. (1985). *The acquisition of syntactic knowledge.* Cambridge, MA: MIT Press.

Bloom, P. (1990). Subjectless sentences in child language. *Linguistic Inquiry, 21*, 491–504.

Borer, H., & Wexler, K. (1987). The maturation of syntax. In T. Roeper & E. Williams (Eds.), *Parameter setting.* Dordrecht, The Netherlands: Reidel.

Borer, H., & Wexler, K. (1992). Bi-unique relations and the maturation of grammatical principles. *Natural Language and Linguistic Theory, 10*, 147–189.

Borer, H., & Rohrbacher, B. (2002). Minding the absent: Arguments for the full competence model. *Language Acquisition, 10*, 123–175.

Brown, R. (1973). *A first language.* Cambridge, MA: Harvard University Press.

Chien, Y.-C., & Wexler, K. (1990). Children's knowledge of locality conditions in binding as evidence for the modularity of syntax and pragmatics. *Language Acquisition, 1*, 225–295.

Chomsky, N. (1965). *Aspects of the theory of syntax.* Cambridge, MA: MIT Press.

Chomsky, N. (1981). *Lectures on government and binding.* Dordrecht, The Netherlands: Foris.

Chomsky, N. (1993). A minimalist program for linguistic theory. In K. Hale & S. J. Keyser (Eds.), *The view from Building 20.* Cambridge, MA: MIT Press.

Chomsky, N. (1995). *The minimalist program.* Cambridge, MA: MIT Press.

Clahsen, H. (1990/91). Constraints on parameter setting: A grammatical analysis of some acquisition stages in German child language. *Language Acquisition, 1*, 361–391.

De Villiers, J., & Roeper, T. (1995). Relative clauses are barriers to wh-movement in young children. *Journal of Child Language, 22*, 389–404.

De Villiers, J., Roeper, T., & Vainikka, A. (1990). The acquisition of long distance movement rules. In L. Frazier & J. de Villiers (Eds.), *Language acquisition and language processing.* Dordrecht, The Netherlands: Kluwer Academic Publishers.

Demuth, K. (1989). Maturation and the acquisition of the Sesotho passive. *Language, 65*, 56–80.

Elbourne, P. (2005). On the acquisition of principle B. *Linguistic Inquiry, 36*, 333–365.

Felser, C., Marinis, T., & Clahsen, H. (2003). Children's processing of ambiguous sentences: A study of relative clause attachment. *Language Acquisition, 11*, 127–163.

Ferdinand, A. (1996). *The acquisition of the subject in French.* PhD dissertation, HIL/Leiden University.

Fodor, J. D. (1994). How to obey the subset principle: Binding and locality. In B. Lust, G. Hermon, & J. Kornfilt (Eds.), *Syntactic theory and first language acquisition: Cross-linguistic perspectives. Vol. 2: Binding, dependencies and learnability.* Hillsdale, NJ: Lawrence Erlbaum Associates.

Fodor, J. D. (1995). Comprehending sentence structure. In L. Gleitman & M. Liberman (Eds.), *An invitation to cognitive science* (2nd ed.). *Vol. 1: Language.* Cambridge, MA: MIT Press.

Fodor, J. D. (1998). Parsing to learn. *Journal of Psycholinguistic Research, 27*, 339–374.

Fox, D., & Grodzinsky, Y. (1998). Children's passive: A view from the *by*-phrase. *Linguistic Inquiry, 29*, 311–332.

Frazier, L. (1999). *On sentence comprehension.* Dordrecht, The Netherlands: Kluwer Academic Publishers.

Gibson, E. (1998). Linguistic complexity: Locality of syntactic dependencies. *Cognition, 68*, 1–76.

Goodluck, H. (1990). Knowledge integration in processing and acquisition. In L. Frazier & J. de Villiers (Eds.), *Language acquisition and language processing.* Dordrecht, The Netherlands: Kluwer Academic Publishers.

Goodluck, H. (2001). The nominal analysis of children's interpretation of adjunct PRO clauses. *Language, 77*, 271–287.

Goodluck, H., Finney, M., & Sedivy, J. (1992). Completeness and filler-gap dependency parsing. In P. Coopmans, B. Schouten, & W. Zonneveld (Eds.), *The OTS Yearbook* (pp. 19–32). Utrecht, The Netherlands: Institute for Research in Language and Speech, University of Utrecht.

Goodluck, H., Foley, M., & Sedivy, J. (1992). Adjunct islands and acquisition. In H. Goodluck & M. Rochemont (Eds.), *Island constraints: Theory, acquisition and processing.* Dordrecht, The Netherlands: Kluwer Academic Publishers.

Goodluck, H., Guilfoyle, E., & Harrington, S. (2006). Merge and binding in child relative clauses: Evidence from Irish. *Journal of Linguistics, 42*, 629–661.

Goodluck, H., & Solan, L. (2000). Un effet du principe C chez l'enfant francophone. *Canadian Journal of Linguistics/Revue canadienne de linguistique, 45*, 49–62.

Goodluck, H., & Stojanović, D. (1996). The structure and acquisition of relative clauses in Serbo-Croatian. *Language Acquisition*, 5, 285–315.

Goodluck, H., Terzi, A., & Chocano Díaz, G. (2001). The acquisition of control cross-linguistically: lexical and structural factors in learning to license PRO. *Journal of Child Language, 28*, 158–172.

Grodzinsky, Y., & Reinhart, T. (1993). The innateness of binding and coreference. *Linguistic Inquiry, 24*, 69–101.

Guasti, T., & Shlonsky, U. (1995). The acquisition of French relative clauses reconsidered. *Language Acquisition*, 4, 257–276.

Guilfoyle, E., & Noonan, M. (1992). Functional categories and language acquisition. *Canadian Journal of Linguistics/Revue canadienne de linguistique*, 37, 241–272.

Hickey, T. (1990). The acquisition of Irish: A study of word order development. *Journal of Child Language, 17*, 17–41.

Hirsh-Pasek, K., & Golinkoff, R. (1991). Language comprehension: A new look at some old problems. In N. Krasnegor, D. Rumbaugh, R. Schiefelbusch, & M. Studdert-Kennedy (Eds.), *Biological and behavioral determinants of language development.* Hillsdale, NJ: Lawrence Erlbaum Associates.

Hoekstra, T., & Hyams, N. (1998). Aspects of root infinitives. *Lingua, 106*, 81–112.

Hyams, N. (1986). *Language acquisition and the theory of parameters.* Dordrecht, The Netherlands: Reidel.

Jakubowicz, C. (1994). Reflexives in French and Danish: Morphology, syntax and acquisition. In B. Lust, G. Hermon, & J. Kornfilt (Eds.), *Syntactic theory and first language acquisition: Cross-linguistic perspectives. Vol. 2: Binding, dependencies and learnability.* Hillsdale, NJ: Lawrence Erlbaum Associates.

Jordens, P. (1991). The acquisition of verb placement in Dutch and German. *Linguistics, 28*, 1407–1448.

Labelle, M. (1990). Predication, wh-movement and the development of relative clauses. *Language Acquisition, 1*, 95–119.

Kaufman, D. (1994). Grammatical or pragmatic: Will the real Principle B please stand up? In B. Lust, G. Hermon, & J. Kornfilt (Eds.), *Syntactic theory and first language acquisition: Cross-linguistic perspectives. Vol. 2: Binding, dependencies and learnability.* Hillsdale, NJ: Lawrence Erlbaum Associates.

McKee, C., & McDaniel, D. (2001). Resumptive pronouns in English relative clauses. *Language Acquisition, 9*, 113–156.

Newport, E. (1988). Constraints on learning and their role in language acquisition: Evidence from American Sign Language and language learning. In W. A. Collins (Ed.), *Aspects of the* development of competence. *Minnesota Symposia on Child Psychology: Vol. 14*. Hillsdale, NJ: Lawrence Erlbaum Associates.

Otsu, Y. (1994). Case marking particles and phrase structure in early Japanese acquisition. In B. Lust, M. Suñer, & J. Whitman (Eds.), *Syntactic theory and first language acquisition. Vol. 1: Heads, projections and learnability*. Hillsdale, NJ: Lawrence Erlbaum Associates.

Pierce, A. (1992). *Language acquisition and syntactic theory: A comparative analysis of French and English child grammars*. Dordrecht, The Netherlands: Kluwer Academic Publishers.

Pinker, S. (1995). Language acquisition. In L. Gleitman & M. Liberman (Eds.), *An invitation to cognitive science* (2nd ed.). *Vol. 1: Language*. Cambridge, MA: MIT Press.

Pinker, S., Frost, L., & Lebeaux, D. (1987). Productivity and constraints in the acquisition of the passive. *Cognition, 26*, 195–267.

Poeppel, D., & Wexler, K. (1993). The full competence hypothesis of clause structure in early German. *Language, 69*, 1–33.

Radford, A. (1990). *Syntactic theory and the acquisition of English syntax: The nature of early child grammars of English*. Oxford: Basil Blackwell.

Rizzi, L. (1994). Some notes on linguistic theory and language development: The case of root infinitives. *Language Acquisition, 3*, 371–393.

Saah, K., & Goodluck, H. (1995). Island effects in parsing and grammar: Evidence from Akan. *Linguistic Review, 12*, 381–409.

Santelmann, L. (1995). *The acquisition of verb second grammar in child Swedish*. PhD dissertation, Cornell University.

Tanenhaus, M., & Trueswell, J. (1995). Sentence comprehension. In J. Miller & P. Eimas (Eds.), *Speech, language and communication*: *Handbook of perception and cognition* (2nd ed.). San Diego, CA: Academic Press.

Thornton, R., & Crain, S. (1994). Successful cyclic movement. In T. Hoekstra & B. Schwartz (Eds.), *Language acquisition studies in generative grammar*. Amsterdam/Philadelphia: John Benjamins.

Thornton, R., & Wexler, K. (1999). *VP-ellipsis, binding theory and interpretation in child grammar*. Cambridge, MA: MIT Press.

Treiman, R., Clifton, C., Jr., Meyer, A., & Wurm, L. (2003). Language comprehension and production. In A. Healy & R. Proctor (Eds.), *Comprehensive handbook of psychology. Vol. 4: Experimental psychology*. New York: John Wiley & Sons.

Valian, V. (1999). Input and language acquisition. In W. Ritchie & T. Bhatia (Eds.), *Handbook of child language acquisition*. San Diego, CA: Academic Press.

Valian, V., & Aubry, S. (2005). When opportunity knocks twice: two-year-olds' repetition of sentence subjects. *Journal of Child Language, 32*, 617–641.

Valian, V., & Eisenberg, S. (1996). The development of syntactic subjects in Portuguese-speaking children. *Journal of Child Language, 23*, 103–128.

Weverink, M. (1989). *The subject in relation to inflection in child language*. MA thesis, University of Utrecht.

Wexler, K. (1999). Maturation and growth of grammar. In W. Ritchie & T. Bhatia (Eds.), *Handbook of child language acquisition*. San Diego, CA: Academic Press.

Wexler, K. (2004). Theory of phrasal development: Perfection in child grammar. *Plato's Problems: Papers on Language Acquisition, MIT Working Papers in Linguistics, 48*, 159–209.

Wijnen, F. (1996). Temporal reference and eventivity in root infinitives. *MIT Occasional Papers in Linguistics, 12*, 1–25.

4

Domain-General Learning Capacities

Jenny R. Saffran and Erik D. Thiessen

As far as acquisition of language is concerned, it seems clear that reinforcement, casual observation, and natural inquisitiveness (coupled with a strong tendency to imitate) are important factors, as is the remarkable capacity of the child to generalize, hypothesize, and "process information" in a variety of very special and apparently highly complex ways which we cannot yet describe or begin to understand, and which may be largely innate, or may develop through some sort of learning or through maturation of the nervous system. The manner in which such factors operate and interact in language acquisition is completely unknown. It is clear that what is necessary in such a case is research, not dogmatic and perfectly arbitrary claims, based on analogies to that small part of the experimental literature in which one happens to be interested.

Noam Chomsky (1959), *A review of Skinner's "Verbal Behavior"*

Language is arguably the most complex system acquired by humans. This fact, combined with the tender age at which language is typically learned, suggests that infants must come to the task of language acquisition already possessing the machinery required to master human language. What remains unknown is the nature of this machinery. Do infants possess dedicated domain-specific learning mechanisms, evolved for language acquisition? Or do infants take advantage of existing learning mechanisms that are not domain-specific to discover the structure of human language? In this chapter, we will consider the current state of the art in disentangling these views. While some progress has been made since Chomsky's (1959) quotation reprinted above, much still remains unknown.

It is important to note at the outset that the distinction between domain-specific and domain-general learning mechanisms is orthogonal to the nature/nurture issue (e.g., Peretz, in press). These two theoretical debates are often confounded; there is a tendency to assume that innateness entails domain-specific knowledge and/or learning mechanisms. However, all learning mechanisms presumably require innate structure, otherwise there would be no way to get learning off the ground. For example, connectionist networks – the paramount examples of domain-general learning devices – entail a great deal of "innate" structure, from input representations to learning rules to architectural constraints (e.g., Elman et al., 1996). Domain-general learning mechanisms can thus be innate, and domain-specificity can be learned (witness evidence for localized brain areas subserving learned tasks such as reading and writing).

Domain-specific learning mechanisms are traditionally invoked when learning phenomena are observed that are not seen in other domains. By contrast, domain-general learning mechanisms are invoked when parallel learning phenomena are observed across distinct domains. Importantly, identical learning mechanisms can render very different kinds of knowledge in different domains. This is due to the fact that different domains have different regularities, and infants face different constraints upon learning in different domains. Because of this, a detailed look at the structure of the to-be-learned domain, along with a close investigation of the operation of any potential learning mechanisms, is necessary before drawing conclusions about domain-generality or domain-specificity. To this end, this chapter will consider relevant empirical evidence and evaluate the extent to which domain-general learning capacities can account for the acquisition of natural languages. In particular, we will focus on the areas of speech perception, speech category learning, word segmentation, word learning, and syntax, aspects of language where domain-specificity has been an explicit focus of investigation.

Historical Issues: Chomsky versus Skinner

The conflict between domain-specific and domain-general views of language acquisition has its roots in an influential debate from the mid-twentieth century, with reverberations that extended far beyond the field of language. In 1957, B. F. Skinner published his classic volume, *Verbal Behavior*, which laid out his behaviorist theory of language acquisition. Skinner invoked equipotential mechanisms for language acquisition via operant conditioning: the detection of contingencies between observable entities. Language acquisition could thus be explained based on the organism's history of experiences and reinforcement, via the same mechanisms observed for learning in other domains and species.

In his devastating critique of Skinner's theory, Chomsky (1959) argued convincingly that internal representations are needed to explain language behavior. An internalized grammar allows learners to go beyond the particular sentences in the input, permitting generalization. By structuring the problem of language learning around the acquisition of a grammar, Chomsky radically altered the field's conceptualization of what language acquisition entails. This, in turn, suggested a need for more specialized learning mechanisms: "The fact that all normal children acquire essentially comparable grammars of great complexity with remarkable rapidity suggests that human beings are somehow specially designed to do this, with data-handling or 'hypothesis-formulating' ability of unknown character and complexity" (Chomsky, 1959). Subsequent theoretical innovations led to a proposed language acquisition device – innate linguistic knowledge in the form of a universal grammar, tied to dedicated language learning processes (Chomsky, 1965, 1968). Chomsky's early views continue to be extremely influential. In particular, there is no doubt that Skinner's central claims were incorrect; external reinforcement cannot explain child language acquisition. However, recent research has begun to examine other potentially general learning mechanisms that may play a role in language acquisition; these theoretical and empirical innovations will be the focus of the remainder of this chapter.

Speech Perception

Speech is a uniquely human capacity that is closely tied to language. As such, speech perception is often regarded as a likely domain in which to find evidence for domain-specific learning mechanisms. Many aspects of this investigation can be viewed as attempts to answer a deceptively simple question: Is speech special? That is, does speech perception invoke unique (and uniquely human) processes? One of the most compelling arguments advanced in favor of the claim that speech is special is based upon the phenomenon of categorical perception in speech perception. Categorical perception is said to occur when discrimination is determined by category identification: listeners discriminate between-category contrasts, but cannot discriminate between members of the same category. For example, in Liberman, Harris, Hoffman, and Griffith's (1957) classic experiment, listeners were able to discriminate more easily between /b/ and /d/ (a cross-category distinction) than between two different examples of /b/, even though the two examples of /b/ were as acoustically different as the cross-category pair. Other early experiments indicated that discrimination of non-speech stimuli was continuous, not categorical (Mattingly, Liberman, Syrdal, & Halwes, 1971), and that even very young infants show evidence of categorical perception for speech (Eimas, Siqueland, Jusczyk, & Vigorito, 1971). These results, and many others, were consistent with the theory that speech perception involves unique processes not seen in other domains (e.g., Eimas, 1974).

Later evidence was not consistent with this theory. Animal experiments demonstrated that a variety of non-human species perceive speech sounds categorically (e.g., Kuhl & Miller, 1975). Further, both adults and infants show categorical perception for many non-speech stimuli, including music-like sounds (e.g., Cutting & Rosner, 1974), faces (e.g., Etcoff & Magee, 1992), and color (e.g., Bornstein, Kessen, & Weiskopf, 1976). Categorical perception is more robust for stop consonants (e.g., /b/ and /k/) than it is for vowels (e.g., Pisoni, 1975). These differences have led to proposals that there are specialized memory systems for stop consonants and vowels (e.g., Schouten & van Hessen, 1992). However, categorical perception can also be observed to different degrees for *non-speech* sounds that differ in the extent to which they are characterized by rapidly changing acoustic dimensions – just as the acoustic information associated with stop consonants in speech changes more rapidly than vowels (Mirman, Holt, & McClelland, 2004). Considering the wide variety of domains in which categorical perception can be observed, recent theories and modeling work suggest that categorical perception may be an inherent byproduct of perception in any domain where sufficiently dense stimuli have a categorical structure, though of course categorical perception for speech is also influenced by the characteristics of the peripheral auditory system (e.g., Damper & Harnad, 2000).

In addition to categorical perception, a number of other phenomena were initially considered to support claims of unique processing/learning for speech stimuli. For example, duplex perception occurs when speech sounds, split into two streams and presented binaurally, simultaneously give rise to two distinct perceptual experiences (Fowler & Rosenblum, 1990). Initially, duplex perception was thought to occur only with speech; however, similar phenomena are seen with musical stimuli (e.g., Hall & Pastore, 1992). Similarly, the right ear advantage – in which sounds presented to the right ear can be detected at lower amplitudes than sounds presented to the left ear – was initially linked to the left hemisphere's specialization for language (e.g., Glanville, Best, & Levenson, 1977). However, the right ear advantage can also be demonstrated for non-linguistic stimuli such as tones or the "dot–dot–dashes" of Morse code in highly trained Morse operators (Brown, Fitch, & Tallal, 1999; Papçun, Krashen, Terbeek, Remington, & Harshman, 1974). Finally, the McGurk effect – an effect of visual information on the perception of an auditory stimulus (MacDonald & McGurk, 1978) – can also be found in the realm of music perception (Saldaña & Rosenblum, 1993). The fact that all of these phenomena also characterize non-linguistic perception suggests that the underlying mechanisms are domain-general, not specific to language.

While behavioral parallels between speech and non-speech domains are compelling, they fail to address an important question: Why are speech and language processing so consistently organized across individuals, tending to be centralized in the left hemisphere (e.g., Hickok, 2001)? Indeed, there are clear neurological differences between processing a sound when it is perceived as speech and when it is perceived as non-speech, even if the stimulus is identical (e.g., Dehaene-Lambertz et al., 2005). Further, event-related potential (ERP) data indicate that phoneme processing may invoke substantially similar neurological processes early in infancy and in adulthood (Dehaene-Lambertz & Baillet, 1998; Dehaene-Lambertz & Gliga, 2004). Given the behavioral similarities between processing speech and non-speech (e.g., categorical perception, duplex perception), it seems initially incongruous that there would be a brain region dedicated to speech processing, one that is at least partially consistent between infancy and adulthood.

Note, however, that different brain regions need not imply different domain-specific learning mechanisms. Zatorre and colleagues (Zatorre, 2001; Zatorre, Belin, & Penhune, 2002) have suggested that the left hemisphere may be better suited to processing transient stimuli that require high temporal resolution due to the nature of its neural connections. Further, regional specificity in the brain may be related to factors other than unique learning mechanisms. For example, many species preferentially attend to same-species vocalizations. This preference appears to be mediated by the activation of specific brain regions that represent or respond to same-species utterances (Wang & Kadia, 2001; Wang, Merzenich, Beitel, & Schreiner, 1995). If, in these species, neural specialization or specific recruitment is related to attentional biases toward conspecific vocalizations, the same may be true of human infants. Infants' brains may be geared to be particularly responsive to human speech. Consistent with this view, Vouloumanos and Werker

(2004) demonstrated that even 2-month-old infants have a reliable preference for human speech over a variety of other auditory stimuli.

Therefore, it may be that speech is special in one important way: infants appear to attend preferentially to speech, which may ensure that speech is a particularly important feature in their environment (Vouloumanos & Werker, 2004). The phenomena that appear unique to speech, or more frequently observed in speech, may in fact arise from an interaction between the acoustic characteristics of speech and our extensive experience listening to speech. This supposition is borne out by the fact that similar phenomena arise in other domains with comparable stimulus density (e.g., categorical perception in face recognition), acoustic characteristics (e.g., right ear advantage for tone discrimination, duplex perception of chords), and familiarity (e.g., right ear advantage in trained Morse code operators.). While early-developing or innate attentional biases favoring speech ensure that it is highly salient in a way few other stimuli are, there is mounting evidence to suggest that speech perception is influenced by the same learning mechanisms that are responsible for processing other types of stimuli. This parallel is most clearly seen in face perception: infants' early propensity to attend to face-like stimuli combines with subsequent experience to affect children's categorical perception of facial emotion displays (Pollak & Kistler, 2002).

Speech Categories

Across different languages, different acoustic contrasts are meaningful. For example, the distinction between /r/ and /l/ indicates different meanings in English (the difference is "phonemic," as in "*rock*" vs. "*lock*"), but not in Japanese. Infants must learn which acoustic distinctions are productive in their linguistic environment. This knowledge is acquired rapidly; infants adapt their responses to the phonemic categories of their language within the first year of life (see Polka, Rvachew, & Mattock, this volume). The mechanism that makes this learning possible may involve sensitivity to the statistical structure of the linguistic input, in the form of the distribution of speech sounds in the linguistic environment (see Gerken, this volume). A variety of non-human animals show similar attunement to particular acoustic contrasts in response to information about the distribution of speech sounds (e.g., Kluender, Lotto, Holt, & Bloedel, 1998). This suggests that learning about phonemic categories may arise from the same mechanisms as learning about any type of category.

Even newborns can categorize (Slater, 1995). Just as infants adapt to the speech sound categories of their native language in response to perceptual information, infants' early object categories are based on perceptual, rather than conceptual, information (e.g., Mandler, 2000; Quinn & Eimas, 2000). Also, just as distributional information plays an important role in infants' adaptation to phonemic categories, the frequency and distribution of infants' experience with different exemplars influences developing object categories. When presented with a set of exemplars with a highly variable distribution, infants form broad, inclusive categories. When familiarized with a more focused distribution of exemplars, infants form categories with tighter boundaries (e.g., Oakes &

Spalding, 1997). In a similar vein, Huttenlocher, Hedges, and Vevea (2000) demonstrated that adults' identification of exemplars is influenced by the previous distribution of category members they have experienced.

Huttenlocher, Hedges, Corrigan, and Crawford (2004) argue that a process critical to inductive categorization is the formation of categories that capture the distributional density of previously experienced exemplars. Ideally, categories should be formed with a prototypical member near the center of the distribution, the region of the highest density of exemplars. Category boundaries should be placed in regions with low exemplar density. Categories with these characteristics are efficient; placing category boundaries in sparsely populated regions means that there is less likelihood of misclassifying stimuli. Maye, Werker, and Gerken (2002) demonstrated that adults and infants place stimulus boundaries in regions of low density in response to different distributions of speech sounds. Therefore, it seems quite plausible that infants' ability to adapt to their language's categories of speech sounds may be a specific instance of a more general tendency to use distributional information as a cue to categorization. Note, however, that previous experience can prevent learners from forming efficient categories. Most famously, previous experience with a language that does not use a phonemic contrast (such as /r/ and /l/ in Japanese) can lead to difficulty acquiring the distinction in response to new acoustic distributions in a new linguistic environment. Similarly, perceptual biases can influence category formation. Japanese listeners find English /r/ to be more dissimilar to Japanese /r/ than English /l/, which has been proposed to explain why native Japanese speakers show more improvement in their use of /r/ than /l/ when learning English (Aoyama, Flege, Guion, Akahane-Yamada, & Yamada, 2004). Infants' and adults' discovery of speech categories is likely to be strongly influenced by the similarity of different speech sounds in their language.

Infants need not only to learn which acoustic distinctions are phonemic in their language. They must also learn how to appropriately produce the sounds comprising the phonemic inventory of their language. Perceptual input will, of course, play an important role in specifying infants' productive repertoire. Additional learning mechanisms must play a role, though. Goldstein, King, and West (2003) have demonstrated that social shaping plays an important role in allowing infants to converge upon language-appropriate verbal behavior, paralleling the development of birdsong. Sounds that receive more social response are more likely to recur, shaping the communicative inventory for future interactions, as demonstrated in the domain of infant babbling (Goldstein et al., 2003). Thus, humans and non-humans may share some learning mechanisms that support the development of productive communicative abilities.

Word Segmentation

Unlike the blank spaces between words in text, speakers do not consistently place pauses between words in fluent speech. This presents a challenge to young infants who must locate word boundaries. Despite the complexity of this task, infants are able to segment words from fluent speech by at least 7 months of age (Jusczyk & Aslin, 1995).

One cue that allows infants to discover words in fluent speech is sequential statistical information. Syllables within a word are more likely to occur together than syllables that are not part of the same word. Saffran, Aslin, and Newport (1996) provided evidence that both infants and adults are capable of using transitional probabilities between syllables to detect word boundaries in fluent speech. Statistical learning mechanisms are available across species (e.g., Hauser, Newport, & Aslin, 2001), and in a variety of domains. Adults and infants attend to transitional probabilities in visual stimuli and non-linguistic auditory stimuli (Fiser & Aslin, 2001; Saffran, Johnson, Aslin, & Newport, 1999).

Sequential statistical cues are available to infants from very early in life (Kirkham, Slemmer, & Johnson, 2002), and may play a role in infants' earliest segmentation of words from fluent speech (Thiessen & Saffran, 2003). However, infants also use another kind of cue to word segmentation: acoustic cues. For example, in English, stress is correlated with word beginnings, and between 8 and 9 months, infants begin to treat stressed syllables as word onsets (Jusczyk, Houston, & Newsome, 1999). While young infants favor transitional probabilities over stress cues, older infants rely more on stress cues (Johnson & Jusczyk, 2001). Infants may learn to use these acoustic cues to word boundaries via the same statistical learning abilities that allow infants to take advantage of transitional probabilities.

Statistical learning can be more broadly construed as attention to regularities in the environment. Attending to such regularities allows learners to discover which events predict other events (e.g., Canfield & Haith, 1991). On this interpretation, attention to transitional probabilities between elements in sequence is only one particular example of statistical learning. To discover acoustic regularities such as lexical stress, infants require experience to indicate which acoustic events have predicted word positions on previous occasions. To do so, infants must be familiar with at least a few words (possibly discovered via transitional probabilities in fluent speech, or heard in isolation). From these words, infants can detect which acoustic characteristics are correlated with word positions; for example, once infants are familiar with a few words, it is possible for them to discover that most of those words begin with a stressed syllable, and to begin to treat stress as a cue to word onsets (Swingley, 2005). Chambers, Onishi, and Fisher (2003) have suggested that similar learning mechanisms may allow infants to discover which sound combinations are permissible in their language. For example, in English, "fs" is not permitted in word-initial position; discovering these types of regularities can help infants segment fluent speech (Mattys, Jusczyk, Luce, & Morgan, 1999). With age and experience, infants become able to integrate multiple cues to word segmentation (e.g., Morgan & Saffran, 1995). A similar developmental progression – from reliance on single cues to weighting of multiple cues – is seen in object categorization (Younger & Cohen, 1986). Therefore, it seems likely that the developmental trajectory underlying infants' use and integration of multiple cues arises from domain-general processes.

Words and Meaning

Learning the meaning of words is one of the great milestones of early development. The majority of the research on infants' word learning has focused on nouns. In this context, "meaning" refers to the connection between a noun and the object to which it refers. This connection is often assessed via comprehension measures (such as looking), because infants comprehend far more words than they can produce (e.g., Benedict, 1979). Word learning is slow before the first birthday, but it does occur; for example, 6-month-olds look longer at a picture of their mother in response to the word "Mommy" (Tincoff & Jusczyk, 1999). Between their first and second birthday, children begin to learn words more easily (Bloom, 2000; Werker, Cohen, Lloyd, Casasola, & Stager, 1998). One of the most impressive abilities children demonstrate during this period is "fast-mapping," the ability to form a connection between words and referents with as little as one exposure (Heibeck & Markman, 1987). This seemingly unique phenomenon has prompted speculation that humans may possess a dedicated word-learning mechanism (e.g., Waxman & Booth, 2000).

To assess the claim that word learning is the result of a domain-specific mechanism, we must examine the processes that enable word learning. One process that is critical to word learning is the ability to detect correspondences between words and objects, and to form an association between them. Objects that are regularly present when a word occurs are likely candidates as referents for that word, at least for nouns (e.g., Plunkett & Schafer, 1999; Roy & Pentland, 2002). However, word learning is also influenced by a variety of adaptive biases and constraints. The shape bias, for example, refers to children's tendency to generalize names to novel objects on the basis of shape (Landau, Smith, & Jones, 1988). The principle of mutual exclusivity holds that any object has only one label (Markman & Wachtel, 1988). The whole object bias refers to children's preference to treat labels as referring to whole objects, rather than parts of objects (Soja, Carey, & Spelke, 1991). Finally, when children learn the name of an object, they tend to treat that label as a reference to a class of objects (such as dogs), rather than a single object; this is called the taxonomic bias (Markman & Hutchinson, 1984).

The origin of these biases is uncertain. One possibility is that they are both innate and specific to language, as has been argued for the whole object, taxonomic, and mutual exclusivity biases (e.g., Markman, 1991, but see Markman, 1992; for discussion, see Diesendruck, this volume). Alternatively, these biases could be specific to language, but arise from domain-general learning mechanisms. Infants' early experience with words may highlight linguistic regularities that facilitate subsequent word learning (e.g., Landau, Gershkoff-Stowe, & Samuelson, 2002; Samuelson, 2002). Finally, it may be the case that these biases are the result of domain-general constraints on the mechanisms that make word learning possible. For example, mutual exclusivity may arise from the fact that forming an association between two stimuli, X and Y, makes forming subsequent associations between one of those stimuli (X) and a new stimulus (Z) more difficult (e.g., Mackintosh, 1971). Many questions remain to be answered about the parallels between word learning and learning in other domains before it will be clear which of these positions is correct (e.g., Halberda, 2003; Sabbagh & Gelman, 2000).

A third source of information for word learning is social interaction. Infants are sensitive to the social intent of speakers in word-learning situations (see Baldwin & Meyer, this volume). An important direction for future research will be to examine the interactions between these sources of information. For example, there are likely to be several potential referents in the environment each time a word occurs. If an infant depends on statistical information alone, word learning will be extremely difficult (Bloom, 2000).

Social cues to referential intent can facilitate word learning. Similarly, the effect of constraints on word learning can be influenced by the pragmatic and perceptual context in which words are taught (Diesendruck, Gelman, & Lebowitz, 1998). As these examples illustrate, multiple domain-general learning mechanisms – such as statistical learning and social learning – can combine to create domain-specific knowledge (the meaning of words).

Any domain-general account of word learning, though, must account for fast-mapping, the signature phenomenon thought to demonstrate a unique mechanism for word learning. Critically, Markson and Bloom (1997) have demonstrated that children "fast-map" novel facts about objects as well as their names. These results suggest that fast-mapping is a specific realization of a general capacity. Evidence for fast-mapping in a dog (Kaminski, Call, & Fischer, 2004) has similar implications. However, the possibility that lexical learning arises from domain-general mechanisms does not imply that lexical learning proceeds in precisely the same manner as other types of learning. For example, whereas children extend names to other objects in the same category, children are more limited in their extensions of facts (e.g., Waxman & Booth, 2000). This difference may be due to the fact that general learning mechanisms render different knowledge as a function of the structure of the domain being acquired (Saffran, 2001a). When children learn the names of objects, those names frequently apply to all of the other objects in that category. Facts (such as "my uncle gave me this one") apply only to one individual object; they are like proper nouns (Bloom & Markson, 2001). The contrast between facts and words illustrates that learning mechanisms can give rise to very different knowledge based on children's experience.

Syntax

Along with speech perception, syntax is the aspect of language where domain-specificity has been most widely assumed. This domain-specificity takes two forms: innate linguistic knowledge (in the form of a universal grammar) and domain-specific learning mechanisms (e.g., triggering mechanisms in the principles and parameters framework; see Goodluck, this volume). Domain-specificity has been implicit in many of these theories for at least three reasons. First, syntax is typically abstract, and not transparently mirrored in the surface structure of the input, suggesting the need for dedicated machinery. Second, the languages of the world contain remarkably little syntactic variation, a fact that is readily explained by hypothesizing innate linguistic knowledge (e.g., Baker, 2001). Third, non-human animals have difficulty acquiring human syntactic structures; these species differences can be explained by hypothesizing dedicated human linguistic machinery.

However, evidence is mounting that at least some syntactic regularities may be learnable by domain-general mechanisms. For example, consider the acquisition of grammatical categories – determining which words are nouns, which are verbs, etc. Children are able to appropriately use grammatical category information by the middle of the second year (e.g., Bloom, 1970; Brown, 1973). Prominent semantic bootstrapping accounts of this phenomenon rely on innate linguistic knowledge concerning semantic–syntactic correspondences (e.g., Pinker, 1984). More recent accounts, however, building from an earlier proposal by Maratsos and Chalkley (1980), have argued that infants could discover which words cohere into grammatical categories by tracking patterns of co-occurrence of words in the input (e.g., Mintz, Newport, & Bever, 2002; Redington, Chater, & Finch, 1998). For example, one might discover the category Noun by determining that a certain set of words was typically preceded by "the." While there are many individual counterexamples (Pinker, 1985), computational analyses suggest that the information needed to cluster words into categories is available in child-directed speech, and adults learning artificial languages can discover grammatical categories using solely distributional information (Mintz, 2002). While these findings do not directly demonstrate domain-generality, as the materials are always linguistic, categorization via distributional information is unlikely to be limited to language learning.

Other lines of research have directly addressed the issue of domain-general versus domain-specific learning mechanisms by contrasting the use of linguistic and non-linguistic "grammars." Building on research by Morgan and Newport (1981; Morgan, Meier, & Newport, 1987, 1989), Saffran (2001b, 2002) investigated the use of distributional information for discovering linguistic phrase structure, a widespread aspect of syntactic structure cross-linguistically. Adults can use a statistical cue to phrasal units, predictive dependencies (e.g., the presence of "the" or "a" strongly predicts a noun somewhere downstream), to discover phrase boundaries (Saffran, 2001b). Moreover, adults and children are better at acquiring languages that contain predictive dependencies than those that do not (Saffran, 2002). Interestingly, the same constraint on learning emerges in tasks using non-linguistic materials, including both auditory non-linguistic grammars (in which the "words" were computer alert sounds) and visual non-linguistic grammars (simultaneously presented arrays of shapes). Saffran (2002, 2003a) hypothesized that this domain-general learning mechanism has played a role in shaping the structure of natural languages. On this view, languages contain predictive dependencies as cues to phrasal units because this information helps human learners to discover phrases in natural languages. A domain-general learning ability may have shaped the structure of something quite specific – language.

Challenges for Domain-General Accounts

How does one "prove" that a learning mechanism is domain-general? Even the clearest cases – where learners show equivalent performance when acquiring materials from two different domains, given the same patterns in the input – could equally well represent two parallel learning mechanisms in lieu of a single domain-general mechanism. Here we see a logical problem with demonstrations of domain-generality: while parsimony might suggest that one learning mechanism is better than two, the natural world is not always parsimonious. One approach to this problem would be to attempt to identify the neural basis of the learning mechanisms in question. In this attempt, though, it is important to remember that the use of distinct brain areas by expert users of a system (e.g., adults) does not necessarily signal the use of distinct learning mechanisms (for discussion, see McMullen & Saffran, 2004; Peretz, in press).

Other objections to claims of domain-generality arise from the empirical data themselves. Some mechanisms used for language learning, such as rule-pattern detection (Marcus, Vijayan, Rao, & Vishton, 1999), may not readily operate over all non-linguistic stimuli (Marcus, Johnson, & Fernandes, 2004). However, they are apparently usable by non-human primates (Hauser, Weiss, & Marcus, 2002), and do operate over at least some non-linguistic stimuli (Saffran, Pollak, Seibel, & Shkolnik, in press). More generally, debate continues over the degree to which complex syntactic structures require domain-specific innate knowledge, or whether they can instead be explained with reference to more general cognitive/social/pragmatic mechanisms (see Lidz, this volume). Evidence from circumstances in which children create their own languages, as in creolization (e.g., Senghas, Kita, & Ozyurek, 2004) and homesign (e.g., Goldin-Meadow, 2003), may help to resolve some of these issues. In such cases, there is a far greater divergence between the structure of the input and the child's eventual linguistic attainments, allowing for a careful parsing of the types of learning mechanisms in operation.

Other objections stem from the overall contour of the evidence concerning child language acquisition. For example, if children are relying on general learning mechanisms to acquire language, then why are they markedly more successful than non-human primates? That is, if language learning doesn't rely on anything special about language, why do only humans do it so well? The answer to such objections may well lie in the specifics of how the learning mechanisms work – as opposed to taking "language" and "cognition" as unitary constructs. For example, there are likely to be specific cognitive differences between humans and non-humans that may affect language learning, even if these differences did not evolve specifically to support language acquisition (e.g., Hauser, Chomsky, & Fitch, 2002). Recent evidence points to differences in the use of learning mechanisms across species that may affect language learning outcomes. For example, given transitional probabilities computed over non-adjacent syllables (with other syllables intervening between the target syllables), human and tamarin learners show quite different patterns of performance (Newport & Aslin, 2004; Newport, Hauser, Spaepen, & Aslin, 2004). Both species show limitations in the types of patterns they detect. Critically, however, the kinds of limitations observed in humans map onto natural language structures – segmental non-adjacency patterns that occur in languages are learnable by humans – whereas the tamarins' learning abilities appear to be unrelated to the structures observed in natural languages. The fact that humans also exhibit related constraints when acquiring non-linguistic sequences such as tones (Creel, Newport, & Aslin, 2004) supports the contention that non-linguistic limitations on what is learnable may have shaped the organization of human languages.

A related objection pertains to the contrast between child and adult learners. If language acquisition rests on general learning abilities, then wouldn't one expect adults to outperform children, when in fact the available evidence suggests that it is the other way around? Again, this sort of objection makes the assumption that there is some sort of overarching "general learning ability." This apparent paradox may be resolved by considering other features of cognition that distinguish children and adults. For example, Newport (1990) has argued that children's relatively constrained working memory capacities may in fact facilitate some aspects of language learning. Combinatorial systems like morphology and syntax require the discovery of small component pieces of language in order to discover the patterns that relate them. The sieve-like nature of children's memories might facilitate the discovery of these pieces, whereas adults are more likely to remember larger chunks of language, missing the underlying patterns. Consistent with this hypothesis, adults actually appear to learn certain aspects of novel languages more successfully when engaged in a concurrent capacity-limiting task (Cochran, McDonald, & Parault, 1999).

Evidence from atypical development is often raised in objections to domain-general accounts. The classic picture is that of a double dissociation, in which "language" is spared while "cognition" is disrupted as in Williams syndrome (WS) (e.g., Pinker, 1991; Rossen, Jones, Wang, & Klima, 1995), while the opposite pattern is obtained in specific language impairment (SLI) (Crago & Gopnik, 1994; Rice, 1999). These kinds of findings are taken as evidence for a distinction between abilities used to learn language and the rest of cognition; for example, Pinker (1999) contrasts individuals with SLI and WS by noting that "the genes of one group of children impair their grammar while sparing their intelligence; the genes of another group of children impair their intelligence while sparing their grammar" (p. 262). One reason that this picture of a clean double dissociation originally emerged is that language and cognition were each taken as unitary constructs. However, when the multiple interlocking subcomponents of language and cognition are considered, the picture of strengths and weaknesses within particular populations becomes more complex (e.g., Shatz, 1994). For example, individuals with WS show atypical language abilities in a number of subdomains, from word segmentation (Nazzi, Paterson, & Karmiloff-Smith, 2003) to morphosyntax (Karmiloff-Smith et al., 1997), suggesting that the intact language hypothesis in this population is a myth (for review, see Karmiloff-Smith, Brown, Grice, & Paterson, 2003). Similarly, individuals with SLI show impairments in non-"core" language abilities such as speech perception (Joanisse & Seidenberg, 1998), the use of symbolic representation (Johnston & Ramstad, 1983), and verbal working memory (Weismer, Evans, & Hesketh, 1999). This more complex picture of these disorders does not rule out the existence of specialized learning capacities. However, it does suggest that the classic double-dissociation argument is less clearly applicable than was previously believed.

Conclusions

"Domain-general" is a loaded term. It implies a set of generalized simple learning devices that can operate over any types of input, such as those espoused by Skinner. The literature that we have reviewed suggests that this is an overly simplistic view of the learning abilities that likely contribute to language learning. These learning mechanisms are constrained to operate over some types of input but not others, as a function of human perception and cognition. They may incorporate both innate and emergent properties. And much of the power of the mechanisms in question likely lies in the ways in which they mutually interact; for example, once learners perform distributional analyses that render categories, the input to learning changes, such that learners can begin to acquire patterns over categories (types) rather than over the raw input (tokens).

"Domain-specific" is also a loaded term, which usually implies an innate, modular, knowledge system. It is evident, however, that domain-specificity and innateness are rightly viewed as orthogonal variables. Modularity can emerge as a function of experience within a particular domain. While the adult state clearly involves some localization of cognitive and linguistic functions, this domain-specificity might be the end-result of domain-general mechanisms operating on material drawn from different input domains (e.g., McMullen & Saffran, 2004). The structure of the input-to-be-learned will influence the eventual outcome of learning, such that the same mechanism can obtain different results as a function of prior knowledge about the input domain (e.g., Saffran, 2001a, 2003b), the age of the learner (e.g., Saffran & Griepentrog, 2001), the structure of the input (Gerken, 2004; Saffran, Reeck, Niehbur, & Wilson, 2005), or the species of the learner (Newport et al., 2004). In addition, a developmental perspective is likely to be quite useful in disentangling initial states from eventual outcomes, for both typically and atypically developing populations (e.g., Karmiloff-Smith, 1998). Technological advances may also facilitate researchers' ability to ask whether distinct brain areas subserve the acquisition of distinct domains of knowledge early in infancy (e.g., Peña et al., 2003). Returning to the Chomsky (1959) quotation with which this chapter began, it is clear that continued research, rather than dogma, is needed in order to render the most significant progress on the question of domain-specificity and domain-generality in language acquisition.

Note

Preparation of this chapter was supported by grants to the first author from NICHD (R01HD37466) and NSF (BCS-9983630). We thank Katharine Graf Estes, Michael Kaschak, Erin McMullen, Isabelle Peretz, and David Rakison for helpful comments on a previous draft.

References

Aoyama, K., Flege, J. E., Guion, S. G., Akahane-Yamada, R., & Yamada, T. (2004). Perceived phonetic dissimilarity and L2 speech learning. *Journal of Phonetics, 32,* 233–250.

Baker, M. C. (2001). *The atoms of language.* New York: Basic Books.

Benedict, H. (1979). Early lexical development: Comprehension and production. *Journal of Child Language, 6,* 183–199.

Bloom, L. (1970). *Language development: Form and function in emerging grammars.* Cambridge, MA: MIT Press.

Bloom, P. (2000). *How children learn the meanings of words.* Cambridge, MA: MIT Press.

Bloom, P., & Markson, L. (2001). Are there principles that apply only to the acquisition of words? *Cognition, 78,* 89–90.

Bornstein, M. H., Kessen, W., & Weiskopf, S. (1976). The categories of hue in infancy. *Science, 191,* 201–202.

Brown, C. P., Fitch, H. R., & Tallal, P. (1999). Sex and hemispheric differences for rapid auditory processing in normal adults. *Lateralities: Asymmetries of Body, Brain, and Cognition, 4,* 39–50.

Brown, R. (1973). *A first language: The early stages.* London: George Allen & Unwin.

Canfield, R. L., & Haith, M. M. (1991). Young infants' visual expectations for symmetric and asymmetric stimulus sequences. *Developmental Psychology, 27,* 198–208.

Chambers, K. E., Onishi, K. H., & Fisher, C. (2003). Infants learn phonotactic regularities from brief auditory experiences. *Cognition, 87,* B69–B77.

Chomsky, N. (1959). A review of B.F. Skinner's "Verbal Behavior." *Language, 35,* 26–58.

Chomsky, N. (1965). *Aspects of the theory of syntax.* Cambridge, MA: MIT Press.

Chomsky, N. (1968). *Language and mind.* New York: Harcourt Brace Jovanovich.

Cochran, B. P., McDonald, J. L., & Parault, S. J. (1999). Too smart for their own good: The disadvantage of a superior processing capacity for adult language learners. *Journal of Memory and Language, 41,* 30–58.

Crago, M. B., & Gopnik, M. (1994). From families to phenotypes: Theoretical and clinical implications of research into the genetic basis of specific language impairment. In R. Watkins & M. Rice (Eds.), *Specific language impairments in children* (pp. 35–51). Baltimore, MD: Brookes.

Creel, S. C., Newport, E. L., & Aslin, R. N. (2004). Distant melodies: Statistical learning of non-adjacent dependencies in tone sequences. *Journal of Experimental Psychology: Learning, Memory, and Cognition, 30,* 1119–1130.

Cutting, J. E., & Rosner, B. S. (1974). Categories and boundaries in speech and music. *Perception and Psychophysics, 16,* 564–570.

Damper, R. I., & Harnad, S. R. (2000). Neural network models of categorical perception. *Perception and Psychophysics, 62,* 843–867.

Dehaene-Lambertz, G., & Baillet, S. (1998). A phonological representation in the infant brain. *NeuroReport, 9,* 1885–1888.

Dehaene-Lambertz, G., & Gliga, T. (2004). Common neural basis for phoneme processing in infants and adults. *Journal of Cognitive Neuroscience, 16,* 1375–1387.

Dehaene-Lambertz, G., Pallier, C., Serniclaes, W., Sprenger-Charolles, L., Jobert, A., & Dehaene, S. (2005). Neural correlates of switching from auditory to speech perception. *NeuroImage, 24,* 21–33.

Diesendruck, G., Gelman, S. A., & Lebowitz, K. (1998). Conceptual and linguistic biases in children's word learning. *Developmental Psychology, 34,* 823–839.

Eimas, P. D. (1974). Auditory and linguistic processing of cues for place of articulation by infants. *Perception and Psychophysics, 16,* 513–521.

Eimas, P. D., Siqueland, E. R., Jusczyk, P. W., & Vigorito, J. (1971). Speech perception in infants. *Science, 171,* 303–306.

Elman, J. L., Bates, E. A., Johnson, M. H., Karmiloff-Smith, A., Parisi, D., & Plunkett, K. (1996). *Rethinking innateness: A connectionist perspective on development.* Cambridge, MA: MIT Press.

Etcoff, N. L., & Magee, J. J. (1992). Categorical perception of facial expressions. *Cognition, 44,* 227–240.

Fiser, J., & Aslin, R. N. (2001). Unsupervised statistical learning of higher-order spatial structures from visual scenes. *Psychological Science, 12,* 499–504.

Fowler, C. A., & Rosenblum, L. D. (1990). Duplex perception: A comparison of monosyllables and slamming doors. *Journal of Experimental Psychology: Human Perception and Performance, 16,* 742–754.

Gerken, L. (2004, May). *Infants make different generalizations for the same formal system depending on the specifics of the input.* Paper presented at the 14th International Conference on Infant Studies, Chicago.

Glanville, B. B., Best, C. T., & Levenson, R. (1977). A cardiac measure of cerebral asymmetries in infant auditory speech perception. *Developmental Psychology, 13,* 54–59.

Goldin-Meadow, S. (2003). *The resilience of language: What gesture creation in deaf children can tell us about how all children learn language.* New York: Psychology Press.

Goldstein, M. H., King, A. P., & West, M. J. (2003). Social interaction shapes babbling: Testing parallels between birdsong and speech. *Proceedings of the National Academy of Sciences of the USA, 100,* 8030–8035.

Halberda, J. (2003). The development of a word-learning strategy. *Cognition, 87,* B23–B34.

Hall, M. D., & Pastore, R. E. (1992). Musical duplex perception: Perception of figurally good chords with subliminal distinguishing tones. *Journal of Experimental Psychology: Human Perception and Performance, 18,* 752–762.

Hauser, M. D., Chomsky, N., & Fitch, W. T. (2002). The faculty of language: What is it, who has it, and how did it evolve? *Science, 298,* 1569–1579.

Hauser, M. D., Newport, E. L., & Aslin, R. N. (2001). Segmentation of the speech stream in a non-human primate: Statistical learning in cotton-top tamarins. *Cognition, 78,* B53–B64.

Hauser, M. D., Weiss, D., & Marcus, G. (2002). Rule learning by cotton-top tamarins. *Cognition, 86,* B15–B22.

Heibeck, T. H., & Markman, E. M. (1987). Word learning in children: An examination of fast mapping. *Child Development, 58,* 1021–1034.

Hickok, G. (2001). Functional anatomy of speech perception and speech production: Psycholinguistic implications. *Journal of Psycholinguistic Research, 30,* 225–235.

Huttenlocher, J., Hedges, L. V., Corrigan, B., & Crawford, L. E. (2004). Spatial categories and the estimation of location. *Cognition, 93,* 75–97.

Huttenlocher, J., Hedges, L. V., & Vevea, J. L. (2000). Why do categories affect stimulus judgment? *Journal of Experimental Psychology: General, 129,* 220–241.

Joanisse, M., & Seidenberg, M. S. (1998). Specific language impairment: A deficit in grammar or processing? *Trends in Cognitive Sciences, 2,* 240–247.

Johnson, E. K., & Jusczyk, P. W. (2001). Word segmentation by 8-month-olds: When speech cues count more than statistics. *Journal of Memory and Language, 44,* 548–567.

Johnston, J. R., & Ramstad, V. (1983). Cognitive development in pre-adolescent language impaired children. *British Journal of Disorders of Communication, 18,* 49–55.

Jusczyk, P. W., & Aslin, R. N. (1995). Infants' detection of the sound patterns of words in fluent speech. *Cognitive Psychology, 29,* 1–23.

Jusczyk, P. W., Houston, D. M., & Newsome, M. (1999). The beginnings of word segmentation in English-learning infants. *Cognitive Psychology, 39,* 159–207.

Kaminski, J., Call, J., & Fischer, J. (2004). Word learning in a domestic dog: Evidence for fast mapping. *Science, 304,* 1682–1683.

Karmiloff-Smith, A. (1998). Development itself is the key to understanding developmental disorders. *Trends in Cognitive Sciences, 2,* 389–398.

Karmiloff-Smith, A., Brown, J. H., Grice, S., & Paterson, S. (2003). Dethroning the myth: Cognitive dissociations and innate modularity in Williams syndrome. *Developmental Neuropsychology, 23,* 229–244.

Karmiloff-Smith, A., Grant, J., Berthoud, I., Davies, M., Howlin, P., & Udwin, O. (1997) Language and Williams Syndrome: How intact is "Intact"? *Child Development, 68,* 246–262.

Kirkham, N. Z., Slemmer, J. A., & Johnson, S. P. (2002). Visual statistical learning in infancy: Evidence for a domain general learning mechanism. *Cognition, 83*, B35–B42.

Kluender, K. R., Lotto, A. J., Holt, L. L., & Bloedel, S. L. (1998). Role of experience for language-specific functional mappings of vowel sounds. *Journal of the Acoustical Society of America, 104*, 3568–3582.

Kuhl, P. K., & Miller, J. D. (1975). Speech perception by the chinchilla: Voiced–voiceless distinction in alveolar plosive consonants. *Science, 190*, 69–72.

Landau, B., Smith, L. B., & Jones, S. S. (1988). The importance of shape in early lexical learning. *Cognitive Development, 3*, 299–321.

Liberman, A. M., Harris, K. S., Hoffman, H., & Griffith, B. (1957). The discrimination of speech sounds within and across phoneme boundaries. *Journal of Experimental Psychology, 54*, 358–368.

MacDonald, J., & McGurk, H. (1978). Visual influences on speech perception processes. *Perception and Psychophysics, 24*, 253–257.

Mackintosh, N. J. (1971). An analysis of blocking and overshadowing. *Quarterly Journal of Experimental Psychology, 23*, 118–125.

Mandler, J. M. (2000). Perceptual and conceptual processes in infancy. *Journal of Cognition and Development, 1*, 3–36.

Maratsos, M., & Chalkley, M. A. (1980). The internal language of children's syntax: The ontogenesis and representation of syntactic categories. In K. Nelson (Ed.), *Children's language: Vol. 2* (pp. 127–214). New York: Gardner Press.

Marcus, G. F., Johnson, S. P., & Fernandes, K. (2004, November). *What's special about speech? Evidence from a contrast between rules and statistics.* Paper presented at the 29th Annual Boston University Conference on Language Development.

Marcus, G. F., Vijayan, S., Rao, S. B., & Vishton, P. M. (1999). Rule learning by seven-month-old infants. *Science, 283*, 77–80.

Markman, E. M. (1991). The whole-object, taxonomic, and mutual exclusivity assumptions as initial constraints on word meaning. In S. Gelman & J. Byrnes (Eds.), *Perspectives on language and thought: Interrelations in development* (pp. 72–106). Cambridge: Cambridge University Press.

Markman, E. M. (1992). Constraints on word learning: Speculations about their nature, origins, and domain specificity. In M. R. Gunnar & M. Maratsos (Eds.), *Modularity and constraints in language and cognition* (pp. 59–101). Hillsdale, NJ: Erlbaum.

Markman, E. M., & Hutchinson, J. E. (1984). Children's sensitivity to constraints on word meaning: Taxonomic versus thematic relations. *Cognitive Psychology, 16*, 1–27.

Markman, E. M., & Wachtel, G. F. (1988). Children's use of mutual exclusivity to constrain the meaning of words. *Cognitive Psychology, 20*, 121–157.

Markson, L., & Bloom, P. (1997). Evidence against a dedicated system for word learning in children. *Nature, 385*, 813–815.

Mattingly, I. G., Liberman, A. M., Syrdal, A. K., & Halwes, T. (1971). Discrimination in speech and nonspeech modes. *Cognitive Psychology, 2*, 131–157.

Mattys, S. L., Jusczyk, P. W., Luce, P. A., & Morgan, J. L. (1999). Phonotactic and prosodic effects on word segmentation in infants. *Cognitive Psychology, 38*, 465–494.

Maye, J., Werker, J. F., & Gerken, L. (2002). Infant sensitivity to distributional information can affect phonetic discrimination. *Cognition, 82*, B101–B111.

McMullen, E., & Saffran, J. R. (2004). Music and language: A developmental comparison. *Music Perception, 21*, 289–311.

Mintz, T. H. (2002). Category induction from distributional cues in an artificial language. *Memory and Cognition, 30*, 678–686.

Mintz, T. H., Newport, E. L., & Bever, T. G. (2002). The distributional structure of grammatical categories in speech to young children. *Cognitive Science, 26*, 393–424.

Mirman, D., Holt, L. L., & McClelland, J. L. (2004). Categorization and discrimination of nonspeech sounds: Differences between steady-state and rapidly-changing acoustic cues. *Journal of the Acoustical Society of America, 116*, 1198–1207.

Morgan, J. L., Meier, R. P., & Newport, E. L. (1987). Structural packaging in the input to language learning: Contributions of prosodic and morphological marking of phrases to the acquisition of language. *Cognitive Psychology, 19*, 498–550.

Morgan, J. L., Meier, R. P., & Newport, E. L. (1989). Facilitating the acquisition of syntax with cross-sentential cues to phrase structure. *Journal of Memory and Language, 28*, 360–374.

Morgan, J. L., & Newport, E. L. (1981). The role of constituent structure in the induction of an artificial language. *Journal of Verbal Learning and Verbal Behavior, 20*, 67–85.

Morgan, J. L., & Saffran, J. R. (1995). Emerging integration of sequential and suprasegmental information in preverbal speech segmentation. *Child Development, 66*, 911–936.

Nazzi, T., Paterson, S., & Karmiloff-Smith, A. (2003) Early word segmentation by infants and toddlers with Williams syndrome. *Infancy, 4*, 251–271.

Newport, E. L. (1990). Maturational constraints on language learning. *Cognitive Science, 14*, 11–28.

Newport, E. L., & Aslin, R. N. (2004). Learning at a distance: I. Statistical learning of non-adjacent dependencies. *Cognitive Psychology, 48*, 127–162.

Newport, E. L., Hauser, M. D., Spaepen, G., & Aslin, R. N. (2004). Learning at a distance: II. Statistical learning of non-adjacent dependencies in a non-human primate. *Cognitive Psychology, 49*, 85–117.

Oakes, L. M., & Spalding, T. L. (1997). The role of exemplar distribution in infants' differentiation of categories. *Infant Behavior and Development, 20*, 457–475.

Papçun, G., Krashen, D., Terbeek, D., Remington, R., & Harshman, R. (1974). Is the left hemisphere specialized for speech, language, and/or something else? *Journal of the Acoustical Society of America, 55*, 319–327.

Peña, M., Maki, A., Kovacic, D., Dehaene-Lambertz, G., Koizumi, H., Bouquet, F., & Mehler, J. (2003). Sounds and silence: an optical topography study of language recognition at birth. *Proceedings of the National Academy of Sciences of the USA, 100*, 11702–11705.

Peretz, I. (in press). Introduction to *The Nature of Music: A Special Issue of Cognition.*

Pinker, S. (1984). *Language learnability and language development.* Cambridge, MA: Harvard University Press.

Pinker, S. (1985). Language learnability and children's language: A multifaceted approach. In K. E. Nelson (Ed.), *Children's language: Vol. 5* (pp. 399–442). Hillsdale, NJ: Erlbaum.

Pinker, S. (1991). Rules of language. *Science, 253*, 530–535.

Pinker, S. (1999). *Words and rules.* London: Weidenfeld & Nicolson.

Pisoni, D. B. (1975). Auditory short-term memory and vowel perception. *Memory and Cognition, 3*, 7–18.

Plunkett, K., & Schafer, G. (1999). Early speech perception and word learning. In M. Barrett (Ed.), *The development of language* (pp. 51–71). Hove: Psychology Press.

Pollak, S. D., & Kistler, D. J. (2002). Early experience is associated with the development of categorical representations for facial expressions of emotion. *Proceedings of the National Academy of Sciences of the USA, 99*, 9072–9076.

Quinn, P. C., & Eimas, P. D. (2000). The emergence of category development during infancy: Are separate and conceptual processes required? *Journal of Cognition and Development, 1*, 55–61.

Redington, M., Chater, N., & Finch, S. (1998). Distributional information: A powerful cue for acquiring syntactic categories. *Cognitive Science, 22,* 425–469.

Rice, M. L. (1999). Specific grammatical limitations in children with specific language impairment. In H. Tager-Flusberg (Ed.), *Neurodevelopmental disorders* (pp. 331–359). Cambridge, MA: MIT Press.

Rossen, M. L., Jones, W., Wang, P. P., & Klima, E. S. (1995). Face processing: Remarkable sparing in Williams syndrome. *Genetic Counseling, 6,* 138–140.

Roy, D., & Pentland, A. (2002). Learning words from sights and sounds: A computational model. *Cognitive Science, 26,* 113–146.

Sabbagh, M. A., & Gelman, S. A. (2000). Buzzsaws and blueprints: What children need (or don't need) to learn language. *Journal of Child Language, 27,* 715–726.

Saffran, J. R. (2001a). Words in a sea of sounds: The output of statistical learning. *Cognition, 81,* 149–169.

Saffran, J. R. (2001b). The use of predictive dependencies in language learning. *Journal of Memory and Language, 44,* 493–515.

Saffran, J. R. (2002). Constraints on statistical language learning. *Journal of Memory and Language, 47,* 172–196.

Saffran, J. R. (2003a). Statistical language learning: Mechanisms and constraints. *Current Directions in Psychological Science, 12,* 110–114.

Saffran, J. R. (2003b). Absolute pitch in infancy and adulthood: The role of tonal structure. *Developmental Science, 6,* 37–45.

Saffran, J. R., Aslin, R. N., & Newport, E. L. (1996). Statistical learning by 8-month-old infants. *Science, 274,* 1926–1928.

Saffran, J. R., & Griepentrog, G. J. (2001). Absolute pitch in infant auditory learning: Evidence for developmental reorganization. *Developmental Psychology, 37,* 74–85.

Saffran, J. R., Johnson, E. K., Aslin, R. N., & Newport, E. L. (1999). Statistical learning of tone sequences by human infants and adults. *Cognition, 70,* 27–52.

Saffran, J. R., Pollak, S. D., Seibel, R. L., & Shkolnik, A. (in press). Dog is a dog is a dog: Infant rule learning is not specific to language. *Cognition.*

Saffran, J. R., Reeck, K., Niehbur, A., & Wilson, D. P. (2005). Changing the tune: Absolute and relative pitch processing by adults and infants. *Developmental Science, 8,* 1–7.

Saldaña, H. M., & Rosenblum, L. D. (1993). Visual influences on auditory pluck and bow judgments. *Perception and Psychophysics, 54,* 406–416.

Samuelson, L. K. (2002). Statistical regularities in vocabulary guide language acquisition in connectionist models and 15–20-month-olds. *Developmental Psychology, 38,* 1016–1037.

Schouten, M. E., & van Hessen, A. J. (1992). Modeling phoneme perception: I. Categorical perception. *Journal of the Acoustical Society of America, 92,* 1841–1855.

Shatz, M. (1994). Review of *Laura* and *First Verbs. Language, 70,* 789–796.

Senghas, A., Kita, S., & Ozyurek, A. (2004). Children creating core properties of language: Evidence from an emerging sign language in Nicaragua. *Science, 305,* 1779–1782.

Skinner, B. F. (1957). *Verbal Behavior.* New York: Appleton-Century-Crofts.

Slater, A. (1995). Visual perception and memory at birth. In C. Rovee-Collier & L. P. Lipsitt (Eds.), *Advances in infancy research: Vol. 9* (pp. 107–162). Norwood, NJ: Ables.

Soja, N. N., Carey, S., & Spelke, E. S. (1991). Ontological categories guide young children's inductions of word meaning: Object terms and substance terms. *Cognition, 38,* 179–211.

Swingley, D. (2005). Statistical clustering and the contents of the infant vocabulary. *Cognitive Psychology, 50,* 86–132.

Thiessen, E. D., & Saffran, J. R. (2003). When cues collide: Use of stress and statistical cues to word boundaries by 7- to 9-month-old infants. *Developmental Psychology, 39,* 706–716.

Tincoff, R., & Jusczyk, P. W. (1999). Some beginnings of word comprehension in 6-month-olds. *Psychological Science, 10,* 172–175.

Vouloumanos, A., & Werker, J. F. (2004). Tuned to the signal: The privileged status of speech for young infants. *Developmental Science, 7,* 270–276.

Wang, X., & Kadia, S. C. (2001). Differential representation of species-specific primate vocalizations in the auditory cortices of marmoset and cat. *Journal of Neurophysiology, 86,* 2616–2620.

Wang, X., Merzenich, M. M., Beitel, R., & Schreiner, C. E. (1995). Representations of species-specific vocalization in the primary auditory cortex of the common marmoset: Temporal and spectral characteristics. *Journal of Neurophysiology, 74,* 2685–2706.

Waxman, S. R., & Booth, A. E. (2000). Principles that are invoked in the acquisition of words, but not facts. *Cognition, 77,* B33–B43.

Weismer, S. E., Evans, J., & Hesketh, L. J. (1999). An examination of verbal working memory in children with specific language impairment. *Journal of Speech, Language, and Hearing Research, 42,* 1249–1260.

Werker, J. F., Cohen, L. B., Lloyd, V. L., Casasola, M., & Stager, C. L. (1998). Acquisition of word–object associations by 14-month-old infants. *Developmental Psychology, 34,* 1289–1309.

Younger, B. A., & Cohen, L. B. (1986). Developmental changes in infants' perception of correlations among attributes. *Child Development, 57,* 803–815.

Zatorre, R. J. (2001). The biological foundations of music (Eds. R. J. Zatorre & I. Peretz). *Annals of the New York Academy of Sciences, 930.*

Zatorre, R. J., Belin, P., & Penhune, V. B. (2002). Structure and function of auditory cortex: music and speech. *Trends in Cognitive Sciences, 6,* 37–46.

5

How Inherently Social is Language?

Dare Baldwin and Meredith Meyer

Paradoxically, the claim that social capacities are fundamental to language acquisition simply states the obvious and yet at one and the same time sparks considerable controversy. On the banal side, virtually no one would deny that language is inherently a social phenomenon, and thus that the acquisition of language rides in some form on social factors. Controversy arises, however, when social factors are broadly accorded a pivotal role in shaping language acquisition. That is, highly prominent accounts of certain aspects of language acquisition – most notably the acquisition of structural aspects of the language (e.g., grammar, phonology) – have traditionally concentrated on non-social mechanisms as core driving forces behind acquisition. Some have begun to question this view in recent years, however, proposing that social mechanisms are central to acquisition of structural aspects of language in addition to other components, such as the lexicon.

One way to conceptualize the history of research on language acquisition over the past four or five decades is in terms of a halting but inexorable thrust toward making a crucial role for social capacities increasingly explicit and rigorous. In this chapter we will pursue three specific goals: to trace the checkered history of researchers' attention to social factors in accounts of language acquisition, to elucidate some of the specific ways social capacities are now known to facilitate language acquisition, and to articulate how a socially based account of language acquisition has recently gained momentum to give rise to the high level of controversy that currently surrounds the topic.

Starting Distinctions

Gaining clarity on debates concerning the role of social factors in language acquisition requires distinguishing three kinds of social factors: social input, social responsiveness, and social understanding. Regarding social input, all agree that language learning takes place only in a social milieu; that is, language learning obviously depends on the presence of linguistic input, which, by definition, is social. However, precisely what form social and linguistic input must take for various aspects of language to emerge is not yet clear, and a range of interesting questions arises in this regard (see, e.g., Goldin-Meadow, 2003, for relevant discussion).

Another issue concerns infants' and children's responsiveness to social input. Language learning is a very different enterprise depending on what form such responsiveness takes. An example here is infants' responsiveness to "motherese" (or, more appropriately, infant-directed talk). This responsiveness benefits their acquisition, in that infant-directed talk provides exaggerated clues to meaning and structure now known to aid learning (e.g., Fernald, 1989; Jusczyk, 1997; Kuhl, 2004). Regarding the general topic of social responsiveness, it will be important to determine specifically what kinds of social responsiveness are key to language learning, as well as which specific aspects of language learning depend heavily on fundamental forms of social responsiveness.

Finally, social understanding (also known as social cognition) – skill at interpreting people's desires, intentions, and beliefs – also plays a role in language learning (e.g., Baldwin, 2000; Tomasello, 1999). Here the questions concern precisely what kind of social understanding language learners – characteristically infants and young children – must possess for language acquisition to progress normally, how advances in social understanding might in turn enhance (and, interestingly, in some cases perhaps complicate) language learning, and which aspects of language acquisition (e.g., word meanings vs. grammatical structure) hinge on early-emerging social understanding. In what follows we will consider the role played by each of these three kinds of social factors – properties of the input, responsiveness to the input, and use of "people smarts" to mine the input – in children's success at two of the basic tasks of language acquisition: discovering word meanings, and acquiring grammar.

Discovering Word Meanings

The meaning and reference components of language are social through and through, in the sense that words themselves don't actually mean or refer to anything; they mean or refer only by virtue of being used by people to mean or refer (e.g., Lyons, 1977; Quine, 1960). If we hear new words emitted by loudspeakers at random intervals we can't intuit their meanings; conversely, if we encounter new things in the world, no degree of careful inspection of the objects themselves will enable us to divine relevant labels for these things. We need to be around people using words meaningfully to discern reference and acquire word meanings. The discovery of meaning is thus inherently an extended process of social coordination. What form does this social coordination process take? All three dimensions delineated earlier – social input, social responsiveness, and social understanding – are directly relevant here.

Social input regarding word meaning

From birth infants are immersed in a social milieu rich with meaning-relevant information. The language they hear is rife with multimodal clues to meaning; this is especially true of the language that speakers in many cultures direct toward infants – now called infant-directed talk (IDT). Infant-directed talk is a meaning-rich stimulus along many dimensions. Among other things, when speaking to infants adults are more likely to utter content words (e.g., object labels, verbs, adjectives) in isolation (Brent & Siskind, 2001), to place content words in sentence-final position and at pitch peaks (Snow & Ferguson, 1977; Stern, Speiker, & MacKain, 1982), and to talk about things in the immediate, here-and-now context (Snow & Ferguson, 1977). These modifications have the potential to assist infants in extracting the relevant portion of the continuous sound stream (e.g., a specific word) and to link it with an object or event in the immediate surround.

Adults also tend to exaggerate intonation in ways that are correlated with emotional content and communicative intentions (e.g., Fernald, 1989). For example, mothers speaking languages quite diverse in typology (e.g., American English, Japanese, Hausa) all display a similar set of distinctive intonational patterns when attempting to convey specific emotion-laden messages to their infants (e.g., low-pitched, fluid intonation for soothing; low-pitched, staccato intonation for prohibiting; high-pitched, rapid-excursion intonation for attentional enhancement). By virtue of their use of these meaning-laden intonational contours, mothers are potentially providing infants with access to meaning long before infants have come to be able to interpret the conventional meanings of the specific words involved. Infants of course have access to prosodic/intonational properties of language well before they are born; hence even fetuses have the opportunity to begin processing this meaning-relevant, socially rich dimension of speech.

Adults – at least in Western, middle-class culture – also expend effort to achieve attentional coordination with infants in ways that ought to facilitate infants' discovery of meaning. For example, adults often follow in on infants' attentional focus and provide language relevant to that focus (e.g., Collis, 1977; Harris, Jones, & Grant, 1983; Tomasello & Todd, 1983). This is far from easy because infants' attention is mercurial, and not surprisingly such attempts at follow-in labeling meet with less than perfect success. As well, when not following infants' attentional lead, Western, middle-class adults show high rates of actively trying to direct infants' attention toward referents under discussion via gestures such as pointing and showing (e.g., Akhtar, Dunham, & Dunham, 1991; Kaye, 1982). Not surprisingly, adults' efforts at social coordination as they engage with infants clearly matter for meaning acquisition. Infants of mothers who engage in higher rates of follow-in labeling progress faster in vocabulary acquisition (e.g., Akhtar et al., 1991; Harris, Jones, Brookes, & Grant, 1986; Tomasello & Todd, 1983), and in experimental procedures infants often more readily learn to comprehend new object labels when the labels are introduced in the context of follow-in labeling (e.g., Baldwin, 1993; Dunham, Dunham, & Curwin, 1993; Tomasello & Farrar, 1986).

Adults also structure infants' lives and activities in ways that support the establishment of "scripts" or "formats": predictable patterns of action and interaction that enable infants to build expectations about which objects will be contacted and mentioned when

and for what purpose (e.g., Bruner, 1981; Nelson, 1985). Such scripted activity potentially helps to make transparent the meaning of any accompanying language. Put more
generally, responsive parenting reveals itself in the language domain as well as in other
domains of social interaction, and such responsiveness on parents' part benefits word
learning (e.g., Tamis-LeMonda, Bornstein, Baumwell, & Damast, 1996).

On many levels, then, infants are on the receiving end of linguistic input that is
riddled with social clues to meaning – one might be tempted to say that the words
themselves are the least of the meaning-relevant information available. Of course,
however, all this social richness would be of little value for meaning acquisition if infants
were insensitive to it, or if the modifications adults make were somehow incompatible
with the mechanisms infants deploy for acquiring meaning.

Meaning-relevant social responsiveness

While *in utero*, infants are already sensitive to a range of linguistic properties, including
at least some prosodic characteristics of their native language (e.g., Nazzi, Bertoncini, &
Mehler, 1998) and they can encode prosodic details of specific passages of speech (e.g.,
DeCaspar & Spence, 1986). Given this precocious sensitivity to prosodic aspects of
language, it is not surprising that infants adore IDT (e.g., Fernald, 1985; Fernald &
Kuhl, 1987; Werker & McLeod, 1989), which, among other things, exaggerates prosodic
characteristics of language. Evidence on many fronts now indicates that IDT benefits
language learning. For example, IDT facilitates infants' analysis of the phonological
properties of their native language (e.g., Burnham, Kitamura, & Vollmer-Conna, 2002;
Jusczyk, 1997; Kuhl et al., 1997; Liu, Kuhl, & Tsao, 2003), promoting their ability to
encode and recognize words within ambient speech. As well, IDT assists infants in
exploiting statistical regularities within continuous speech to identify word segments
(Thiessen, Hill, & Saffran, 2005). Other IDT modifications – such as placing relevant
content words at the ends of sentences or at pitch peaks – also dovetail nicely with infants'
processing strategies. For example, children learn words more readily when they occur
sentence final relative to sentence internal (Echols & Newport, 1992). Interestingly,
responsiveness to IDT is not universal. Where it is lacking, however, disruptions in language development also tend to be observed. Autism – associated strongly with disruptions in language development – is a case in point here. As a group, individuals with
autism prefer to listen to non-speech analogs of IDT rather than IDT itself, while normally developing children reliably prefer IDT (Kuhl, Coffey-Corina, Padden, & Dawson,
2005). Children with autism even prefer to hear many superimposed voices over their
own mother's IDT speech, in contrast to normally developing children and children with
non-autistic developmental delay (Klin, 1991, 1992).

Infants' learning about phonetic properties of speech plays a crucial role in word
learning, and recent evidence clarifies that phonetic learning is also modulated by social
responsiveness. For example, Kuhl, Tsao, and Liu (2003) found that 12 sessions of
exposure to Mandarin enabled English-learning American 9-month-olds to maintain
their sensitivity to a Mandarin phonetic contrast not found in English. However, this
occurred only if infants directly interacted with the Mandarin speaker. Infants who

watched a DVD of the Mandarin speaker (who was filmed while interacting with a different baby) did not maintain sensitivity to the Mandarin phonetic contrast. Contingent social interaction also increases the frequency and maturity of infants' own vocalizations (e.g., Goldstein, King, & West, 2003). Finally, Kuhl et al. (2005) report that a subset of children with autism who showed a preference for IDT over non-speech analogs also displayed brain electrical activity in response to a phonetic discrimination task that was significantly closer to the normal pattern than did autistic children who preferred non-speech analogs over IDT. Based on these and related findings, Kuhl (2004) suggests that social factors serve a "gating" function for neural computation of linguistic stimuli.

Fernald and others (e.g., Fernald, 1989; Bruner, 1983) have demonstrated that IDT is rich in emotional and intentional content as well as in phonetic information, and infants seem to be sensitive to the emotional correlates of distinct intonational contours within IDT. In one study (Fernald, 1993), for instance, infants showed higher rates of attention and smiling when hearing utterances couched in intonation characteristic of approval than when hearing utterances conveyed in intonation typical of prohibition. Strikingly, this effect generally held up even when infants were hearing IDT of mothers who spoke a different language than the one with which infants themselves were familiar (e.g., English-learning infants smiled and attended more to Italian mothers' approval statements than prohibitions). Infants' attunement to intonation potentially assists word learning in a variety of ways. In a very basic sense, infants seem to be pulling "meaning" – even if not conventional semantic meaning – out of the intonation itself; in Fernald's terms, "the melody carries the message" (1989, p. 1505). Infants' sensitivity to the specific emotional content of a particular utterance via its intonational properties can facilitate their interpretation of the utterance. For example, an infant who responds to attention-bid intonation accompanying an utterance like "It's a buzz-a-bee!" with increased attention to the relevant object is at an advantage for successfully mapping the new word (*buzz-a-bee*) to its appropriate referent. Along these lines, other research documents that such labeling utterances indeed enhance infants' attention to objects, and to object categories more specifically, adding to the plausibility of this story (Baldwin & Markman, 1989; Waxman, 2003).

Infants are also highly responsive to adults' attempts to coordinate attentional focus, which greatly expedites language learning. Infants start to reliably follow others' gaze and pointing gestures during the second half of the first year (e.g., Butterworth, 1991; Carpenter, Nagell, & Tomasello, 1998), and they appreciate the object-directedness of others' gaze and pointing gestures as early as 12 months of age (e.g., Woodward, 2003; Woodward & Guajardo, 2002). Interestingly, infants at 12 months will follow "gaze" or imitate a sequence of motions only if the entity involved appears to be animate, which they diagnose via a combination of surface characteristics such as eyes and fur and the entity's propensity to engage in contingent behavior (e.g., Johnson, 2000; Shimizu & Johnson, 2004). This is one indication that gaze following and attention to gestures as early as 12 months represents a genuine form of social responsiveness, rather than a non-social instance of reflexive orienting. In any case, responsiveness to others' gaze, gestures, and actions helps to ensure that infants are focused on relevant referents when objects and events are under discussion, helping them to link words with the correct things in the world.

Children with autism typically display significant deficits and/or delays in following others' gaze and attention-directing gestures, and in interpreting others' emotional displays and action (e.g., Baron-Cohen, Baldwin, & Crowson, 1997; Mundy, Sigman, Ungerer, & Sherman, 1986; Osterling, Dawson, & Munson, 2002). It is likely that these deficits in social responsiveness contribute significantly to the word-learning delay that is typical of this developmental disorder.

Discovering what people mean when they use words

If we think of meaning acquisition as an ongoing task of social coordination, one obvious question is whether, and to what degree, learners themselves actively pursue such social coordination in the service of meaning acquisition. In other words, is it correct to say that young children, or even infants, are *trying* to figure out what people use words to mean? Are they actively seeking to discover others' intentions and attentional focus in the service of drawing inferences about linguistic reference and meaning? And if so, how skillful are they at it? In an influential review, Shatz (1983) considered these (among other) questions at some length, concluding at the time that the available evidence provided no resolution. Inspired by Shatz' seminal analysis, several researchers embarked on research specifically to address such questions.

At the inception of such research, a relatively new body of work on children's developing theories of mind was revealing what appeared to be genuine conceptual deficits in infants' and young preschoolers' understanding of others' mental life. This work suggested that children younger than about 4 did not yet conceive of mentalistic notions such as beliefs, intentions, or attention (e.g., Moses & Flavell, 1990; Wellman, 1990; Wimmer & Perner, 1983). Such findings gave rise to general skepticism toward the idea that young children, or even infants, might be skilled contributors to the kind of social coordination that would promote language learning. If children couldn't yet understand notions such as intention, attention, or belief, for example, how could they possibly be skilled at tracking others' intentions and attentional focus to guide inferences about word meaning? On the other hand, language learning might provide an especially sensitive window on children's emerging mentalistic understanding, as it is a genuine, real-world task in which children are fully immersed on an ongoing basis.

Perhaps, then, children or even infants might display budding skills for mentalistic reasoning in the context of language learning tasks that would be more difficult to observe in other kinds of traditional experimental tasks. But what would constitute evidence that children make use of genuine social understanding in the service of language learning? The strategy researchers adopted was to identify language learning scenarios in which the relevant piece of mentalistic understanding would make all the difference for learning; in particular, scenarios in which a failure to understand (and make active use of the understanding) would put children at risk for making errors. In the first study of this kind, Baldwin (1991) presented infants in two age groups (16–17, and 18–19 months) with new labels for a novel toy in the context of "discrepant labeling" – a commonly occurring everyday phenomenon (e.g., Collis, 1977) in which a word is heard precisely when the learner is focused on a different object than the one to which the speaker intends to refer. In this context, infants might fall prey to a word-learning error – linking the new word with an inappropriate referent – because their attention was focused on the wrong object at the time they heard the new label. If, however, infants possess some skills for tracking others' referential intentions or attentional focus, they might be able to avoid an error. That is, errors needn't occur if infants understand that the speaker intends to label a specific object, and actively monitor the speaker for clues (e.g., gaze direction, body posture, voice direction) to the intended referent. In this study, infants in both age groups displayed high rates of checking the speaker's face in response to hearing novel labels, as though checking for clues to the speaker's referent. Their performance on a subsequent comprehension test confirmed that they made use of such clues: When asked to "Find the modi!" infants across the 16- to 19-month span rarely showed systematic selection of the toy they themselves had been focused on when they had heard the label. They did not make the word-learning error that the discrepant labeling scenario put them at risk for. This skill at avoiding errors was reliable in the younger group, but detectably more sophisticated in the older group. The younger group seemed to simply block a mapping between the novel label and the novel toy during discrepant labeling (they performed at chance levels to comprehension questions), while the older group went one better: they not only avoided the error, they actually succeeded in figuring out the correct referent of the novel label (they selected the toy that the speaker had been focused on in the discrepant labeling event). One might wonder whether the younger group's chance level performance was just an inability to establish new word–object links more generally, but an important control comparison revealed above-chance comprehension performance when the speaker labeled the toy infants were focused on. Thus their response to discrepant labeling seemed genuinely to be a case of blocking a potential error, whereas the 18- to 19-month-olds were able to exploit the available clues more fully not only to avoid an error but also to discover the correct referent of the new word.

All in all, the findings of this initial study confirmed that infants actively and spontaneously track clues to others' referential intentions, and use these clues to draw inferences about word meanings. This was among the first pieces of evidence suggesting the presence of some form of mentalistic understanding in infancy. These findings mesh nicely with Shatz' (1994) view that social understanding emerges early, but nevertheless undergoes gradual and extended development. The basic findings have since been replicated by others (e.g., Dunham et al., 1993; Hollich, Hirsh-Pasek, & Golinkoff, 2000), and elaborated in a number of ways (see Baldwin & Moses, 2001; Sabbagh & Baldwin, 2005; Tomasello, 1999 for reviews), indicating that infants (a) actively exploit an impressive array of intentional clues to guide inferences about word meaning, (b) can track these clues across time in the context of relatively novel and complex interactive scenarios, (c) frequently take social clues indicating referential intent as criterial for establishing new word–referent links (e.g., Baldwin et al., 1996), and (d) can mine input for social clues to meaning even when overhearing language addressed to others (e.g., Akhtar, 2005). Put another way, infants seem to track social clues to inform them about which word-to-world correspondences are worthy of registering and recalling; in this sense, social clues serve a "gating" function for establishing new word meanings, which is reminiscent of the role Kuhl suggests social responsiveness plays in phonological development.

Jaswal (2004) has also demonstrated that young children's intention detection skills not only guide their initial inferences about reference and meaning, but also facilitate their subsequent elaboration of word meaning. Finally, several recent studies have documented that language-related intention-monitoring processes are disrupted in children with autism. In particular, autistic children are prone to making word-learning errors specifically as a result of deficits in exploiting the social/intentional clues that speakers display (Baron-Cohen et al., 1997; Preissler & Carey, 2005).

This body of work on language-relevant social understanding has sparked controversy on a number of fronts. Two issues in particular have been the focus of considerable debate. The first of these was whether social understanding is really operating after all (e.g., Hoff & Naigles, 2002; Ruffman, 2003; Samuelson & Smith, 1998). At this juncture, the evidence is clear that infants nearing the end of their second year indeed spontaneously and actively monitor clues indicative of others' intentions, and use these clues to guide inferences about word meaning (e.g., Diesendruck, Markson, Akhtar, & Reudor, 2004; Hollich et al., 2000; Moore, Angelopoulos, & Bennett, 1999). On the other hand, there remains a real question whether this skill at capitalizing on social clues warrants the label "social understanding," or whether it is simply an impressive demonstration of infants' ability to exploit statistical regularities in others' behavior to guide learning (e.g., Ruffman, 2003; see also Perner & Ruffman, 2005, and Saffran & Thiessen, this volume, for related discussion). Disentangling the operation of genuine inferences about goals and intentions from sophisticated statistical learning is a challenging enterprise (Povinelli & Vonk, 2003) and remains a focus of current research. At present, however, it can safely be said that infants as young as 12 to 18 months are considerably more active in social coordination and more savvy in mining clues from others' behavior to guide language learning than anyone had previously imagined.

A second controversy hinged on the possibility that social understanding might actually be responsible for word-learning skills previously thought to arise from other mechanisms, such as word-learning constraints (e.g., Bloom, 2000; Saylor, Baldwin, & Sabbagh, 2004; Tomasello, 2000a; see Poulin-Dubois & Graham, this volume, regarding the constraints approach). The basic idea here is that word-learning constraints such as the whole object and mutual exclusivity assumptions (e.g., Markman, 1989) can readily be couched in terms of socially based assumptions on children's part. For example, the assumption that new words refer to whole objects rather than to parts, properties, or events (the whole object assumption) can readily be construed as the assumption that when speakers use words they intend to refer to whole objects rather than parts, properties, or events. Some recent data (a) indicate that parental input exhibits pragmatic regularities that would support children's adoption over time of constraints such as the mutual exclusivity assumption (Callanan & Sabbagh, 2004), and (b) point to pragmatic understanding providing a better account of children's inferences about meaning than constraints construed in non-pragmatic terms (e.g., Diesendruck & Markson, 2001; Saylor, Sabbagh, & Baldwin, 2002, but see Preissler & Carey, 2005, for potentially contradictory evidence from children with autism).

Summing up to this point, linguistic input is chock-full of clues to meaning; many of these clues are fundamentally social in that they reside in intonation, facial expression, gaze, gesture, ongoing action, and the history of social interaction. Children's social responsiveness and their growing ability to actively exploit such social sources of information contribute immensely to the smooth and speedy trajectory so characteristic of early word learning.

Acquiring Grammar

Given that word meanings are so obviously a product of social consensus, a central role for social processes in meaning acquisition seems entirely sensible. What of another domain equally important in acquiring language, namely the acquisition of syntax? Here there is substantial disagreement on how central a role social understanding can play. Specifically, a distinction in the syntactic domain can be drawn between formalist theories stressing pre-adapted acquisition mechanisms dedicated exclusively to grammar and socio-pragmatic accounts centering on grammar learning as a fundamentally social enterprise.

Nativist accounts background social input to linguistic structure

Children's ability to discover latent grammatical structure in the input they encounter has long been a source of inquiry. Formalist theories of syntax acquisition garnered widespread support soon after their introduction in the 1960s, offering an attractive alternative to the then-dominant, and clearly deficient, behaviorist version of "learned" language (e.g., Chomsky, 1959). Formalist proposals account for the acquisition of structural properties of language via universal constraints specific to syntax (see Lidz, this volume). On this view, syntactic competence is enabled by universal grammar (UG), an innate body of abstract, highly generalizable grammatical representations. This perspective necessitates a strongly nativist and modular account of syntax; consequently researchers allying themselves with a formalist position tend to question whether social capacities could play any sort of substantial role in syntax acquisition (e.g., Fisher, 2002; Lidz & Waxman, 2004). Such an outlook acknowledges social factors insofar as it recognizes that language acquisition depends crucially on the learner having access to a linguistic (thus, by definition, social) environment rich in positive evidence, but once such an environment is provided to the learner, the acquisition process is seen to rely most heavily on the operation of innate structural principles that are triggered by input. In other words, the formalist view gives little more than a reflexive nod in the direction of the social milieu within which language is acquired.

The formalist conception of a functionally independent, modular system of syntax leaves little room for investigation of social capacities in the domain of syntax acquisition. Indeed, a major reason that UG is considered the only plausible solution for syntactic competence is a belief that the input that children receive from the social world is incomplete; in particular, linguistic input is thought to lack clear evidence about the syntactic acceptability of utterances (e.g., Hyams, 1986; Pinker, 1994). Adults are less likely to provide negative feedback for syntactic errors than for violations of truth (Brown &

Hanlon, 1970); furthermore, the feedback that *is* provided for ungrammatical utterances is rarely consistent and is regarded by many to be insufficient as a source of reliable information about syntactic well-formedness (e.g., Marcus, 1993). Despite such an apparently impoverished stimulus, young children just beginning to combine words routinely avoid certain errors, and errors they do display seem principled, indicating the operation of an underlying system. For example, children rarely make errors in the use of auxiliaries that would be expected if they were simply generalizing from adult sentence patterns with main verbs (Stromswold, 1990, as cited in Pinker, 1994), and even 1-year-old children seem to operate with adult-like rules governing how adjectives may modify certain types of noun phrases (Bloom, 1990). Such patterns provide support for the formalist claim that even very early speech reflects underlying syntactic competence.

Initial socio-pragmatic alternatives emphasize social support for language acquisition

Soon after Chomsky articulated the first version of a generative grammar, a number of developmentalists sympathetic to pragmatic views of human behavior raised objections to what they viewed as a neglect of social factors on the part of formalist theories. According to the formalist position, a learner is already in possession of structural representations by virtue of UG, independent of any social experience in the world. Pragmatic developmentalists criticized what they believed to be an overly narrow focus on the innate aspects of structure, arguing that theories of language needed to incorporate social features and the ways in which children could respond to and learn from adults (Bruner, 1975; Halliday, 1975).

Bruner offered a particularly influential argument in this vein, proposing that grammatical knowledge emerged in the context of a child's linguistic interactions with an adult, particularly during communicative exchanges taking place during play (Bruner, 1975, 1981). He described a language assistance system (LAS), which encompassed a developmentally sequenced shift in communicative "initiative." Such initiative rested first with adults and was then progressively transferred to children via structured "formats" provided during play or other one-on-one interaction; children would gradually come to internalize the meaning and effect of a particular speech act, including the structural aspects of such an act. For example, Bruner proposed that children acquired basic order rules, at least in part, by observing repeated adult-narrated enactments of an agent–action–object–recipient relationship. In Bruner's conceptualization of syntactic development, then, basic social activities that jointly engage child and adult are crucial in providing the contextual support within which structure is acquired. Although LAS was not advanced as a mutually exclusive alternative to the Chomskyan language acquisition device (LAD), other theorists would later be influenced by Bruner's suggestion that LAS might play a large role in linking structure with the conceptual relationships expressed by grammar.

Bruner's ideas did much to encourage a deeper consideration of social factors when considering the task of language acquisition in general. An examination specific to grammatical development, however, rendered Bruner's account of syntax problematic for several reasons. First, interactions in the social sphere that Bruner proposed to be a source of grammatical understanding (such as the agent–action–object–recipient relationship) did not appear to provide a transparent way to directly map conceptual relationships onto meaningful word order (Shatz, 1981; Slobin, 1982). Second, contrary to what Bruner would predict, the course of syntactic development appeared largely uninfluenced by differences in available social support. For example, variability in maternal speech-style along dimensions such as mean length of utterance and propositional complexity was found to be largely unrelated to child language development (Newport, Gleitman, & Gleitman, 1977). Furthermore, studies of blind children lacking access to much of the social information available in such behavior as joint eye gaze and pointing neverthe-less evidenced a nearly normal progression of syntactic development (Gleitman & Newport, 1995; Landau & Gleitman, 1985). Similarly, examinations of the development of gestures in deaf children deprived of normal linguistic input from their hearing parents suggested a remarkable resiliency in the emergence of structured communication (e.g., Goldin-Meadow, 1985, 2003).

Contemporary socio-pragmatic accounts: Emphasizing children's social understanding

Bruner's writings endorsed the idea that linguistic support provided during one-on-one social contact with a parent or other adult is crucial to acquiring all aspects of language. The fact that substantial variability in the social context of language learning seemed to matter little in syntactic development thus posed difficulties for Bruner's account of how children come to understand and produce grammatical speech. More recent socio-pragmatic accounts of syntax acquisition address this problem by appealing more heavily to the ways in which children capitalize on their *own* social abilities in the service of acquisition – in other words, they focus more on the social knowledge that children bring to bear in the acquisition of language. By crediting the *learner* with an ability to capitalize on social knowledge from the very start, rather than positing the adult as the sole source of social support, contemporary accounts envision the child as an active and skilled participant in the language learning task. A child operating on the assumption that others intentionally use language to communicate has a substantial leg up on the classic Brunerian child, who is benefiting in a more passive sense from parental social support. This crucial difference lends current accounts considerably more strength and at the same time opens the door to an even more central role for social capacities in the acquisition of structure; social capacities are seen as a property of the child, and the information available to solve the acquisition task is considered to be the outcome of *both* the socially skilled child and the socially rich environment.

In rejecting the claim that children acquire syntax using innate, pre-specified gram-matical representations, socio-pragmatic theorists argue that children learn grammatical structure by observing and analyzing adults' usage (e.g., Tomasello, 2003, 2004). The acquisition of both structure and content is seen to rest fundamentally on children's ability to draw inferences about the adult's communicative intent to acquire meaning – crucially, meaning conveyed not just by words, but by grammatical structure itself. The process is not strictly imitative, however; in addition to capitalizing on their understanding of the function of any one particular speech act, children are believed to additionally recruit domain-general skills such as statistical learning and pattern recognition (e.g., Saffran, Aslin, & Newport, 1996) as well as structure mapping (e.g., Gentner, Holyoak, & Kokinov, 2001). Generativity, the feature of language that first prompted formalists to posit universal grammar, is thus explained not by a domain-specific language module, but rather by domain-general processes that operate in conjunction with an understanding of referential and communicative intent.

Current socio-pragmatic accounts thus incorporate social knowledge on the part of the young learners themselves, a shift from the early Brunerian focus on the external support that a parent offers. These contemporary accounts also differ from earlier socio-pragmatic work in that they explicitly describe syntax itself in very different terms from those of formalist theories. As a result, current socio-pragmatic accounts of syntax are more finely articulated than the original versions advanced by pragmatic developmentalists in the 1970s. They gain clarity by drawing heavily from theories of cognitive and usage-based grammars arising from a group of linguists skeptical of formalist claims of the logical necessity of UG (e.g., Bybee, 1985; Givón, 1993; Langacker, 1987; Van Valin, 1993). According to these theories, syntax reflects the tendency to regularize repeated patterns of word usage into grammatical structure. It is the tendency to regularize (grammaticize) that is universal across human cultures, not the syntactic representations themselves. As a consequence, socio-pragmatic accounts of language characterize competence as being in possession of an "inventory" of language-specific constructions rather than in possession of abstract knowledge of syntax.

Both formalist and socio-pragmatic accounts include explanations for many patterns observed in naturalistic speech data. As discussed above, the finding that children "play by the rules" of the syntax of their native language has traditionally been used to argue that humans come equipped with abstract grammatical representations to the language learning task. Socio-pragmatic accounts do not deny that children's speech often obeys grammatical convention (although see Tomasello, 2000b, for important counterexamples) or that children may show evidence of understanding structure before they can produce it, but they reject the claim that these findings are evidence of UG. If children indeed appreciate that language is used to communicate, then it is unsurprising that their own productions resemble adults'; they should naturally produce the forms that others use to fulfill specific communicative goals.

Empirical evidence for social capacities in syntax

Empirical investigations of syntax development shed additional light on the mechanisms involved in the acquisition of structure. Demonstrations of early syntactic understanding (e.g., Fisher, 2000; Hirsh-Pasek, Golinkoff, & Naigles, 1996) have traditionally been provided as strong support for theories of universal grammar. For example, children as young as 25 months are able to distinguish between transitive and intransitive sentence frames and can use this difference to infer the meaning of a novel verb (Naigles, 1990). This finding suggests both that children possess crucial syntactic knowledge (i.e., the transitive/intransitive distinction) at a remarkably early age and that they can use such syntactic knowledge to guide inferences about verb meaning. Socio-pragmatic theorists, however, explain these and similar data according to a model in which no universal grammar is necessary; rather, children are argued to possess such understanding because they have acquired the structure from adult examples through the same mechanisms used to acquire meaning, namely an understanding of communicative intent coupled with domain-general learning mechanisms that can allow for generalization to novel examples.

In a recent synthesis of both naturalistic speech production and experimental data, Tomasello (2000b) outlines a "verb-island" hypothesis, which stands in stark opposition to the formalist idea that children come equipped for syntax acquisition with abstract grammatical knowledge. This hypothesis states that very young children initially acquire verbs piecemeal by producing forms as they are received from the input. Later, once a body of verbs has been acquired, children can engage in off-line analysis of structural and semantic relationships across verbs, gradually constructing abstract syntactic usage rules over a period of months or years. Tomasello argues that an examination of young children's speech demonstrates a marked reluctance on children's part to go beyond examples provided in the input (e.g., Tomasello, 1992, 2000b). Such conservatism is taken as evidence counter to what a formalist account would predict: a theory of abstract syntactic knowledge predicts children will apply syntactic knowledge "across the board" to verbs as a category rather than on a case-by-case basis. Finally, Tomasello further notes that studies indicating *comprehension* of abstract grammatical structure, such as Naigles' (1990) study of transitive and intransitive verbs, tend to be conducted on populations of children who have been exposed to years of input. Without directly assessing the informativeness of this input, then, any ability evidenced by these children could plausibly be argued to have been acquired through social means.

In response to Tomasello's account that children acquire verbs piecemeal rather than by making use of an underlying innate grammar, Fisher (2002) counters that findings such as children's reluctance to innovate and uneven morphological marking are in no way problematic for formalist accounts. Although such theories do call for abstract knowledge that aids children in applying syntactic rules to novel instances, Fisher also reminds us that such theories fully recognize the importance of experiencing a language-specific pattern of verb usage. Tomasello's socio-pragmatic approach has also been criticized for relying too heavily on a unidirectional relationship between social capacities and linguistic competence. Shatz (1992), for example, encourages viewing the two abilities as mutually facilitative rather than positing social ability as the precursor and main contributor to language. Finally, socio-pragmatic theories are also sometimes believed to be hard-pressed to explain a large body of evidence describing dissociations between social abilities and grammatical competence (for a discussion of this and related issues see Shatz, 1992, and Tomasello, 1995).

For empirical evidence to be definitive in this debate, formalists and socio-pragmatic theorists will need to reach consensus on contrasting predictions that these accounts make (see Akhtar, 2004, for discussion on this topic). Lidz, Waxman, and Freedman (2003) argue that they have done exactly that. Their claims rest in part on a central difference between formalist and socio-pragmatic accounts, namely these theories' positions on the availability of evidence in the input. Children's acquisition of structure on a socio-pragmatic account depends crucially on the relevant evidence for that structure being available in the input. By contrast, the pre-specified abstract syntactic knowledge with which children are gifted on a formalist account could enable them to acquire some structures for which the input fails to provide sufficient evidence.

Lidz et al. (2003) found that young children possess abstract knowledge of hierarchically structured noun phrases despite minimal input demonstrating such structure. Specifically, 18-month-old children were shown to have an understanding that anaphoric *one* refers to a constituent consisting of an adjective and a noun rather than the noun alone. Infants possessed this understanding despite the fact that relevant examples of anaphoric *one* were rare in parental input (see Lidz, this volume). If Lidz and colleagues' analysis is correct in claiming that children possess syntactic knowledge despite a poverty of the stimulus, then evidence that children can acquire anaphoric *one* is tantamount to evidence of universal grammar in action. Debate has arisen regarding the viability of the poverty-of-the-stimulus argument here, however. Akhtar, Callanan, Pullum, and Scholz (2004) not only dispute the claim that positive examples of anaphoric *one* are rare, but also raise the possibility that pragmatic inference may aid a child in figuring out the correct referent of anaphoric *one* (see also Lidz & Waxman, 2004; Tomasello, 2004). It is exactly this type of ability – skill at inferring the communicative goals of others – that is crucial to a socio-pragmatic account of syntax acquisition.

Clearly, the findings as they currently stand invite future inquiry into processes underlying the acquisition of syntax. At present, evidence for innate structure guiding syntax acquisition is in dispute. Yet at the same time, no actual direct evidence documents the specific role of intention detection in children's processing of structural aspects of others' language use. Pursuing such evidence is one fruitful approach to resolving the current debate.

Wrapping Up: Social Factors Influence Language Learning at Many Levels of Analysis

To sum up our discussion, we now know that social processes play a multitude of roles in language learning. Regarding children's discovery of meaning, language input to children is infused with a rich array of social clues to meaning, and existing research indicates that infants and young children are highly responsive to a variety of these clues. Put another way, children – who, when developing normally, are highly attuned to social clues – are immersed from day one in a social context that shapes their experience in ways that make relevant referents salient and appropriate meanings transparent. At the same time, from as early as 12 months of age, children themselves actively monitor meaning-relevant social clues that others exhibit, and put these clues to work to guide inferences about reference and meaning. Powerful skills for statistical tracking available at least as early as 7 to 8 months likely play an important role in how children accomplish this, but at some point – quite possibly as early as 12 to 18 months – children spontaneously track others' social clues because they understand these clues offer them a useful window on others' referential intentions. Some of children's pragmatic inferences – those that are strongly supported across a wide range of contexts – may undergo a process of automatization that crystallizes them into default assumptions (constraints) that they can deploy to drive inferences about meaning even in the absence of available on-line social clues. All in all, children seem to approach the discovery of meaning as a social puzzle, and skillfully mine their social surroundings for clues to solve the puzzle.

Regarding meaning acquisition, few have ever doubted a central role for socio-pragmatic factors, although the precise nature of this role has generated controversy from time to time. By contrast, socio-pragmatic factors have frequently been dismissed as largely irrelevant to the acquisition of syntax. However, like the mythical phoenix, socio-pragmatic factors have recently re-emerged from the ashes of syntactic immolation. Early socio-pragmatic accounts emphasized the role that richly structured social input plays in grammar acquisition. Such accounts languished in the face of evidence showcasing the robustness of syntax acquisition despite substantial variability in the social context of language learning. Akhtar and Tomasello have recently breathed new life into a socio-pragmatic account for syntax acquisition. Their account emphasizes the new body of evidence documenting early-emerging social understanding; they propose that children actively work to discern the communicative purpose of structural patterns in the language. Children's skills for intention-processing, coupled with statistical learning, pattern recognition, and structure-mapping abilities, may be what enable them to discover latent structural principles underlying language use. Once again, socio-pragmatic factors are strong contenders for children's discovery of grammatical structure. This newly enlivened socio-pragmatic account presents a challenge to formalist accounts that is already receiving considerable attention. At the same time, the full power of this resurrected socio-pragmatic account is far from resolved. Whether it can account for the full range of complex syntactic structures that children acquire remains an important avenue for empirical investigation. At the very least, however, recent evidence makes it now safe to venture that social factors influence language learning at many levels of analysis – structural (phonological and syntactic) as well as content-related (word meaning). Language is inherently social to a very deep degree.

Note

We thank the volume editors for supporting our work on this chapter. The manuscript was prepared in part by means of funds provided by the National Science Foundation under Grant No. BCS-0214484.

References

Akhtar, N. (2004). Nativist versus constructivist goals in studying child language. *Journal of Child Language, 31*, 459–462.

Akhtar, N. (2005). The robustness of learning through overhearing. *Developmental Science, 8*, 199–209.

Akhtar, N., Callanan, M., Pullum, B., & Scholz, G. (2004). Learning antecedents for anaphoric *one. Cognition, 93*, 141–145.

Akhtar, N., Dunham, F., & Dunham, P. J. (1991). Directive interactions and early vocabulary development: The role of joint attentional focus. *Journal of Child Language, 18*, 41–49.

Baldwin, D. A. (1991). Infants' contribution to the achievement of joint reference. *Child Development, 62*, 875–890.

Baldwin, D. A. (1993). Infants' ability to consult the speaker for clues to word reference. *Journal of Child Language, 20*, 395–418.

Baldwin, D. A. (2000). Interpersonal understanding fuels knowledge acquisition. *Current Directions in Psychological Science, 9*, 40–45.

Baldwin, D. A., & Markman, E. M. (1989). Establishing word–object relations: A first step. *Child Development, 60*, 381–398.

Baldwin, D. A., Markman, E. M., Bill, B., Desjardins, R. N., Irwin, J., & Tidball, G. (1996). Infants' reliance on a social criterion for establishing word–object relations. *Child Development, 67*, 3135–3153.

Baldwin, D. A., & Moses, L. J. (2001). Links between social understanding and early word learning: Challenges to current accounts. *Social Development, 10*, 309–329.

Baron-Cohen, S., Baldwin, D. A., & Crowson, M. (1997). Do children with autism use the speaker's direction of gaze strategy to crack the code of language? *Child Development, 68*, 48–57.

Bloom, P. (1990). Syntactic distinctions in child language. *Journal of Child Language, 17*, 343–355.

Bloom, P. (2000). *How children learn the meanings of words.* Cambridge, MA: MIT Press.

Brent, M. R., & Siskind, J. M. (2001). The role of exposure to isolated words in early vocabulary development. *Cognition, 81*, B33–B44.

Brown, R., & Hanlon, C. (1970). Derivational complexity and the order of acquisition in child speech. In J. R. Hayes (Ed.), *Cognition and the development of language* (pp. 11–54). New York: Wiley.

Bruner, J. S. (1975). The ontogenesis of speech acts. *Journal of Child Language, 2*, 1–19.

Bruner, J. S. (1981). The social context of language acquisition. *Language and Communication, 1*, 155–178.

Bruner, J. S. (1983). *Child's talk: Learning to use language.* New York: W. W. Norton.

Burnham, D., Kitamura, C., & Vollmer-Conna, U. (2002). What's new, pussycat? On talking to babies and animals. *Science, 296*, 1435.

Butterworth, G. (1991). The ontogeny and phylogeny of joint visual attention. In A. Whiten (Ed.), *Natural theories of mind* (pp. 223–232). Oxford: Basil Blackwell.

Bybee, J. (1985). *Morphology.* Amsterdam: Benjamins.

Callanan, M. A., & Sabbagh, M. A. (2004). Multiple labels for objects in conversations with young children: Parents' language and children's developing expectations about word meanings. *Developmental Psychology, 40*, 746–763.

Carpenter, M., Nagell, K., & Tomasello, M. (1998). Social cognition, joint attention, and communicative competence from 9–15 months of age. *Monographs of the Society for Research in Child Development, 63* (4, Serial No. 255).

Chomsky, N. (1959). A review of B. F. Skinner's "Verbal Behavior." *Language, 35*, 26–58.

Collis, G. M. (1977). Visual co-orientation and maternal speech. In H. R. Schaffer (Ed.), *Studies in mother–infant interaction* (pp. 355–375). New York: Academic Press.

DeCaspar, A. J., & Spence, M. J. (1986). Prenatal maternal speech influences newborns' perception of speech sounds. *Infant Behavior and Development, 9*, 133–150.

Diesendruck, G., & Markson, L. (2001). Children's avoidance of lexical overlap: A pragmatic account. *Developmental Psychology, 37*, 630–641.

Diesendruck, G., Markson, L., Akhtar, N., & Reudor, A. (2004). Two-year-olds' sensitivity to speakers' intention: An alternative account of Samuelson and Smith. *Developmental Science, 7*, 33–41.

Dunham, P. J., Dunham, F., & Curwin, A. (1993). Joint attentional states and lexical acquisition at 18 months. *Developmental Psychology, 29*, 827–831.

Echols, C. H., & Newport, E. L. (1992). The role of stress and position in determining first words. *Language Acquisition, 2*, 189–220.

Fernald, A. (1985). Four-month-old infants prefer to listen to motherese. *Infant Behavior and Development, 8*, 181–195.

Fernald, A. (1989). Intonation and communicative intent in mother's speech to infants: Is the melody the message? *Child Development, 60*, 1497–1510.

Fernald, A. (1993). Approval and disapproval: Infant responsiveness to vocal affect in familiar and unfamiliar languages. *Child Development, 64*, 657–674.

Fernald, A., & Kuhl, P. K. (1987). Acoustic determinants of infant preference for parentese speech. *Infant Behavior and Development, 10*, 279–293.

Fisher, C. (2000, July). *Who's blicking whom? Word order in early verb learning.* Poster session presented at the 11th International Conference on Infant Studies, Brighton, England.

Fisher, C. (2002). The role of abstract syntactic knowledge in language acquisition: A reply to Tomasello (2000). *Cognition, 82*, 259–278.

Gentner, D., Holyoak, K., & Kokinov, B. (Eds.). (2001). *The analogical mind.* Cambridge, MA: MIT Press.

Givón, T. (1993). *English grammar: A function-based introduction.* Amsterdam: Benjamins.

Gleitman, L. R., & Newport, E. L. (1995). The invention of language by children: Environmental and biological influences on the acquisition of language. In L. R. Gleitman & M. Liberman (Eds.), *An invitation to cognitive science: Vol. 2. Language* (2nd ed., pp. 1–24). Cambridge, MA: MIT Press.

Goldin-Meadow, S. (1985). Language development under atypical learning conditions: Replication and implications of a study of deaf children of hearing parents. In K. Nelson (Ed.), *Children's language: Vol. 5* (pp. 197–245). Hillsdale, NJ: Lawrence Erlbaum Associates.

Goldin-Meadow, S. (2003). *The resilience of language: What gesture creation in deaf children can tell us about how all children learn language.* New York: Psychology Press.

Goldstein, M., King, A., & West, M. (2003). Social interaction shapes babbling: Testing parallels between birdsong and speech. *Proceedings of the National Academy of Sciences, 100*, 8030–8035.

Halliday, M. A. K. (1975). *Learning how to mean.* London: Edward Arnold.

Harris, M., Jones, D., Brookes, S., & Grant, J. (1986). Relations between the non-verbal context of maternal speech and rate of language development. *British Journal of Developmental Psychology, 4*, 261–268.

Harris, M., Jones, D., & Grant, J. (1983). The nonverbal context of mothers' speech to infants. *First Language, 4*, 21–30.

Hirsh-Pasek, K., Golinkoff, R., & Naigles, L. (1996). Young children's use of syntactic frames to derive meaning. In K. Hirsh-Pasek & R. Golinkoff (Eds.), *The origins of grammar* (pp. 123–158). Cambridge, MA: MIT Press.

Hoff, E., & Naigles, L. (2002). How children use input to acquire a lexicon. *Child Development, 73*, 418–433.

Hollich, G. J., Hirsh-Pasek, K., & Golinkoff, R. M. (2000). Breaking the language barrier: An emergentist coalition model for the origins of word learning. *Monographs of the Society for Research in Child Development, 65* (3, Serial No. 262).

Hyams, N. (1986). *Language acquisition and the theory of parameters.* Dordrecht, The Netherlands: Reidel.

Jaswal, V. K. (2004). Don't believe everything you hear: Preschoolers' sensitivity to speaker intent in category induction. *Child Development, 75,* 1871–1885.

Johnson, S. C. (2000). The recognition of mentalistic agents in infancy. *Trends in Cognitive Sciences, 4,* 22–28.

Jusczyk, P. (1997). *The discovery of spoken language.* Cambridge, MA: MIT Press.

Kaye, K. (1982). *The mental and social life of babies: How parents create persons.* Chicago: University of Chicago Press.

Klin, A. (1991). Young autistic children's listening preferences in regard to speech: a possible characterization of the symptom of social withdrawal. *Journal of Autism and Developmental Disorders, 21,* 29–42.

Klin, A. (1992). Listening preferences in regard to speech in four children with developmental disabilities. *Journal of Child Psychology and Psychiatry, 33,* 763–776.

Kuhl, P. K. (2004). Early language acquisition: Cracking the speech code. *Nature Reviews Neuroscience, 5,* 831–843.

Kuhl, P. K., Andruski, J. E., Chistovich, I. A., Chistovich, L. A., Kozhevnikova, E. V., Ryskina, V. L., et al. (1997). Cross language analysis of phonetic units in language addressed to infants. *Science, 277,* 684–686.

Kuhl, P. K., Coffey-Corina, S., Padden, D., & Dawson, G. (2005). Links between social and linguistic processing of speech in preschool children with autism: Behavioral and electrophysiological evidence. *Developmental Science, 8,* F1–F12.

Kuhl, P. K., Tsao, F.-M., & Liu, H.-M. (2003). Foreign-language experience in infancy: Effects of short-term exposure and social interaction on phonetic learning. *Proceedings of the National Academy of Sciences, 100,* 9096–9101.

Landau, B., & Gleitman, L. R. (1985). *Language and experience: Evidence from the blind child.* Cambridge, MA: MIT Press.

Langacker, R. W. (1987). *Foundations of cognitive grammar: Vol. 1.* Stanford, CA: Stanford University Press.

Lidz, J., & Waxman, S. (2004). Reaffirming the poverty of the stimulus argument: a reply to the replies. *Cognition, 93,* 157–165.

Lidz, J., Waxman, S., & Freedman, J. (2003). What infants know about syntax but couldn't have learned: Evidence for syntactic structure at 18 months. *Cognition, 89,* B65–B73.

Liu, H.-M., Kuhl, P. K., & Tsao, F.-M. (2003). An association between mothers' speech clarity and infants' speech discrimination skills. *Developmental Science, 6,* F1–F10.

Lyons, J. (1977). *Semantics: Vol. 1.* Cambridge: Cambridge University Press.

Marcus, G. F. (1993). Negative evidence in language acquisition. *Cognition, 46,* 53–85.

Markman, E. M. (1989). *The development of categories and category names: Problems of induction.* Cambridge, MA: MIT Press.

Moore, C., Angelopoulos, M., & Bennett, P. (1999). Word learning in the context of referential and salience cues. *Developmental Psychology, 35,* 60–68.

Moses, L. J., & Flavell, J. H. (1990). Inferring false beliefs from actions and reactions. *Child Development, 61,* 929–945.

Mundy, P., Sigman, M., Ungerer, J., & Sherman, T. (1986). Defining the social deficits of autism: The contribution of nonverbal communication measures. *Journal of Child Psychology and Psychiatry, 27,* 657–669.

Naigles, L. (1990). Children use syntax to learn verb meaning. *Journal of Child Language, 17,* 357–374.

Nazzi, T., Bertoncini, J., & Mehler, J. (1998). Language discrimination by newborns: Toward an understanding of the role of rhythm. *Journal of Experimental Psychology: Human Perception and Performance, 24,* 756–766.

Nelson, K. (1985). *Making sense: The acquisition of shared meaning.* New York: Academic Press.

Newport, E., Gleitman, H., & Gleitman, L. R. (1977). Mother, I'd rather do it myself: Some effects and noneffects of maternal speech style. In C. E. Snow & C. A. Ferguson (Eds.), *Talking to children: Language input and acquisition* (pp. 109–150). Cambridge: Cambridge University Press.

Osterling, J., Dawson, G., & Munson, J. (2002). Early recognition of 1-year-old infants with autism spectrum disorder versus mental retardation. *Development and Psychopathology, 14,* 239–251.

Perner, J., & Ruffman, T. (2005). Infants' insight into the mind: How deep? *Science, 308,* 214–216.

Pinker, S. (1994). *The language instinct.* London: Allen Lane.

Povinelli, D. J., & Vonk, J. (2003). Chimpanzee minds: Suspiciously human? *Trends in Cognitive Sciences, 7,* 157–160.

Preissler, M. A., & Carey, S. (2005). The role of inferences about referential intent in word learning: Evidence from autism. *Cognition, 97,* B13–B23.

Quine, W. V. O. (1960). *Word and object.* Cambridge, MA: MIT Press.

Ruffman, T. (2003). *Does the infant have a theory of mind?* New Zealand: University of Otago.

Sabbagh, M., & Baldwin, D. A. (2005). Understanding the role of communicative intentions in word learning. In N. Eilan, C. Hoerl, T. McCormack, & J. Roessler (Eds.), *Joint attention: Communication and others' minds* (pp. 165–184). Oxford: Oxford University Press.

Saffran, J. R., Aslin, R. N., & Newport, E. L. (1996). Statistical learning by 8-month-old infants. *Science, 274,* 1926–1928.

Samuelson, L. K., & Smith, L. B. (1998). Memory and attention make smart word learning: An alternative account of Akhtar, Carpenter, and Tomasello. *Child Development, 69,* 94–104.

Saylor, M., Sabbagh, M. A., & Baldwin, D. A. (2002). Children use whole-part juxtaposition as a pragmatic cue to word meaning. *Developmental Psychology, 38,* 993–1003.

Saylor, M. M., Baldwin, D. A., & Sabbagh, M. A. (2004). Converging on word meaning. In D. G. Hall & S. R. Waxman (Eds.), *Weaving a lexicon* (pp. 509–531). Cambridge, MA: MIT Press.

Shatz, M. (1981). Learning the rules of the game: Four views of the relation between grammar acquisition and social interaction. In W. Deutsch (Ed.), *The child's construction of language* (pp. 17–38). London: Academic Press.

Shatz, M. (1983). Communication. In J. H. Flavell & E. M. Markman (Eds.), *Handbook of child psychology: Vol. 3. Cognitive development* (3rd ed., pp. 841–890). New York: Wiley.

Shatz, M. (1992). A forward or backward step in the search for an adequate theory of language acquisition. *Social Development, 1,* 151–154.

Shatz, M. (1994). Theory of mind and the development of social-linguistic intelligence in early childhood. In C. Lewis & P. Mitchell (Eds.), *Children's early understanding of mind: origins and development* (pp. 311–329). Hillsdale, NJ: Lawrence Erlbaum Associates.

Shimizu, Y. A., & Johnson, S. C. (2004). Infants' attribution of a goal to a morphologically unfamiliar agent. *Developmental Science, 7,* 425–430.

Slobin, D. I. (1982). Universal and particular in the acquisition of language. In E. Wanner & L. R. Gleitman (Eds.), *Language acquisition: The state of the art* (pp. 128–170). Cambridge: Cambridge University Press.

Snow, C. E., & Ferguson, C. A. (Eds.). (1977). *Talking to children: Language input and acquisition*. Cambridge: Cambridge University Press.

Stern, D. N., Speiker, S., & MacKain, K. (1982). Intonational contours as signals in maternal speech to prelinguistic infants. *Developmental Psychology, 18*, 727–735.

Tamis-LeMonda, C. S., Bornstein, M. H., Baumwell, L., & Damast, A. M. (1996). Responsive parenting in the second year: Specific influences on children's language and play. In C. S. Tamis-LeMonda (Ed.), *Parenting sensitivity: Individual, contextual and cultural factors in recent conceptualizations: Thematic issue of Early Development and Parenting, 5*, 173–183.

Thiessen, E. D., Hill, E., & Saffran, J. R. (2005). Infant-directed speech facilitates word segmentation. *Infancy, 7*, 53–71.

Tomasello, M. (1992). *First verbs: A case study in early grammatical development*. Cambridge: Cambridge University Press.

Tomasello, M. (1995). Language is not an instinct. *Cognitive Development, 10*, 131–156.

Tomasello, M. (1999). *The cultural origins of human cognition*. Cambridge, MA: Harvard University Press.

Tomasello, M. (2000a). Perceiving intentions and learning words in the second year of life. In M. Bowerman & S. Levinson (Eds.), *Language acquisition and conceptual development* (pp. 132–158). Cambridge: Cambridge University Press.

Tomasello, M. (2000b). Do young children have adult syntactic competence? *Cognition, 74*, 209–253.

Tomasello, M. (2003). *Constructing a language*. Cambridge, MA: Harvard University Press.

Tomasello, M. (2004). Syntax or semantics? Response to Lidz et al. *Cognition, 93*, 139–140.

Tomasello, M., & Farrar, J. (1986). Joint attention and early language. *Child Development, 57*, 1454–1463.

Tomasello, M., & Todd, J. (1983). Joint attention and lexical acquisition style. *First Language, 4*, 197–212.

Van Valin, R. (1993). A synopsis of role and reference grammar. In R. Van Valin (Ed.), *Advances in role and reference grammar* (pp. 1–164). Amsterdam: Benjamins.

Waxman, S. R. (2003). Links between object categorization and naming: Origins and emergence in human infants. In D. H. Rakison & L. M. Oakes (Eds.), *Early category and concept development: Making sense of the blooming buzzing confusion* (pp. 213–241). New York: Oxford University Press.

Wellman, H. J. (1990). *The child's theory of mind*. Cambridge, MA: MIT Press.

Werker, J. F., & McLeod, P. J. (1989). Infant preference for both male and female infant-directed talk: A developmental study of attentional and affective responsiveness. *Canadian Journal of Psychology, 43*, 230–246.

Wimmer, H., & Perner, J. (1983). Beliefs about beliefs: representation and constraining function of wrong beliefs in young children's understanding of deception. *Cognition, 13*, 103–128.

Woodward, A. L. (2003). Infants' developing understanding of the link between looker and object. *Developmental Science, 6*, 297–311.

Woodward, A. L., & Guajardo, J. J. (2002). Infants' understanding of the point gesture as an object-directed action. *Cognitive Development, 83*, 1–24.

6

Input and the Acquisition of Language: Three Questions

Virginia C. Mueller Gathercole and Erika Hoff

What is the role of input in the language acquisition process? Obviously, infants spoken to in a given language reliably become children who speak that language, demonstrating in a general way that input must affect language development. But questions concerning the role of input go beyond this obvious level and lie ultimately at the heart of the language acquisition process itself. Three central questions are: (1) What is the nature of the input, and what information about the grammar can the child extract from it? (2) Does input control either the sequence in which or the speed with which children construct the grammar? (3) Is the input alone sufficient to explain the child's construction of the grammar, or do other factors contribute to the process of acquisition; if so, how do these interact with the input? The aim of this chapter is to review the theoretical positions on these questions and to examine the available evidence. We focus on the role of input in the acquisition of language structure, the subject of the most long-standing and vigorous debates.

Q1: What is the nature of the input, and what information about the grammar can the child extract from it?

Theories of the role of input

The nativist view: Input plays a minor role.   One of the staunchest positions on the input is that taken by many nativists. In response to the three questions above they have argued (1) that the input to the child is an inadequate database from which to induce language structure, (2) that children need relatively little exposure to the input to induce the structure of the language, and input has little to do with sequence or speed of acquisition, and (3) that children must be attributed with innate linguistic knowledge for them to be able to construct language.

The nativist position is grounded in Chomsky's (e.g., 1965, 1968, 1975) description of language as a system of marvelous complexity, his assertion that a description of that system is a description of linguistic knowledge represented in the human mind, and the corollary assertion that studying the acquisition of language is thus to study how the language-specific system "flowers" from that knowledge. With this, Chomsky also claimed that children acquire language "on relatively slight exposure and without specific training" (Chomsky, 1975, p. 4). Furthermore, he argued, the input could not be very important because it is an inadequate database from which to induce language structure. This "poverty of the stimulus" assertion has two component claims: (1) that the speech children hear is full of errors, and (2) that any set of sentences in a language is, in principle, inadequate as a database because the underlying structure of language is not fully revealed in surface structures of sentences. Chomsky also asserted that general-purpose learning mechanisms operating on input alone would be insufficient to construct the grammar of any language. These claims that the knowledge acquired is complex, that the available data are insufficient, and that the learning mechanisms are inadequate together have been termed "the logical problem of language acquisition" (Baker & McCarthy, 1981). The nativist solution to this problem has been to attribute innate linguistic knowledge of the universal properties of language to the child. That universal knowledge is then said to guide the child in constructing the language-particular instantiation of those universals from the input (see also Lidz, this volume).

Since the original formulation of this problem, proposals concerning exactly what is innate and how children manage to learn the particulars of the language they hear have been refined (see, e.g., Crain & Thornton, 1998; Pinker, 1994; discussions in MacWhinney, 2004, and Sabbagh & Gelman, 2000, and commentaries). Among the proposals is the parameter setting model of acquisition (e.g., Hyams, 1986; Roeper & Williams, 1987), which attributes complex sets of parameters to the innate endowment of the child. Each parameter may give the child a choice of two or three "settings," and the child's job as an acquirer of the language is to determine from the input which setting fits the language s/he is hearing. (For example, the "*pro*-drop" parameter specifies that a language can have either obligatory overt subjects, like English (*he was walking*), or optional overt subjects, like Spanish (_*caminaba*).) Determining the correct parameter setting might be complicated because it may involve several correlated features of the grammar. (For example, whether or not a language allows *pro*-drop is correlated with whether that language allows expletive subjects (as in *it is raining*), or has "real" auxiliaries (*may*, *can*), without person, tense, and number marking; see Hyams, 1987.) Critically, the theory explicitly holds that the innate parameters are designed in such a way that the child can set each parameter on the basis of very minimal information in the input, according to a "subset principle" (Berwick, 1985; Wexler & Manzini, 1987; but see Atkinson, 2001; Lust, 1999). The role of the input is simply to act as a "trigger" for setting parameters. This view has engendered many debates and proposed alternatives (see Goodluck, this volume; Drozd, 2004; Sabbagh & Gelman, 2000; and commentaries for recent discussions).

It may even be possible, under the nativist position, to acquire language in the absence of input. Nativists point to the development of fully complex creoles from grammatically simpler pidgins as children acquire pidgins as their native language (see, e.g., Bickerton's (1981, 1984) bioprogram hypothesis). A recent case in point is the development of the Idioma de Señas Nicaragüense/Nicaraguan Sign Language (ISN). Kegl and colleagues have documented the rise of ISN from the 1970s, when a Nicaraguan school for the deaf was opened (Kegl, 2002, 2004; Kegl, Senghas, & Coppola, 1999; Senghas, Kita, & Özyürek, 2004). This new full language grew out of disparate – and very basic – "home sign" and gesturing systems used in individual families before the families' coming together in the school. Proponents of the nativist position argue that the complexification of the gesturing systems into ISN occurred within a single generation and was possible because the children learning the sign system as their native language contributed aspects of their innate linguistic knowledge to develop a more abstract, more complex system. Some have counter-argued, however, that the creolization process does not reflect the contribution of Universal Grammar to pidgins but inter-borrowing of linguistic patterns from the native languages of the adults into the creoles children create (e.g., Goodman, 1985; Maratsos, 1984; Lightfoot, 1984). Furthermore, the complexification process in the case of both oral creoles and ISN may be a result of shortcuts typical of grammaticization (Slobin, 1997), which is also not necessarily dependent on innate knowledge. It is of note as well that the development of ISN occurred over more than one generation (Senghas & Coppola, 2001), which one might argue is counter to the expectation if the complexification arose out of the individual children's access to Universal Grammar.

Alternative views: Input plays a major role.   The nativist position has been challenged on a number of general grounds. Alternative linguistic theories have challenged the Chomskyan position on the nature of adult grammar. Cognitive and functionalist theories ground language structure in general properties of human cognition and in the communicative functions of language (Culicover & Jackendoff, 2005; Foley & Van Valin, 1984; Tomasello, 1995, 2003). Theories of acquisition based on these descriptions of the grammar argue that children achieve grammar via its basis in communicative function (Bates & MacWhinney, 1989; Budwig, 1995). Construction grammars (Croft, 2001; Goldberg, 1995) posit that grammars consist of networks of constructions, based to a degree on meaning and existing at multiple levels of concreteness and abstraction. Language, in these alternative views, is not less complex, but it is less abstract than in the Chomskyan descriptions. In addition, universals of language are posited to lie not in innate linguistic structures, but in universal cognitive structures and universals of the human condition (Croft, 2001; Tomasello, 1995, 2003). Under these theories, language acquisition is more plausibly achievable without innate language-specific knowledge. The less abstract constructs posited make language more accessible through the input, and the child's task can be taken as one of induction from the input (MacWhinney, 2004).

Other challenges to Chomskyan nativism have focused more directly on the role of input and have argued against the claims that input is deficient and that children rely only minimally on input to construct a grammar. This work is of two sorts: (1) illustrations that the input is more well-formed and revealing of linguistic structure than nativists had argued, and (2) evidence that patterns in the input are associated with patterns in children's developing language, suggesting that language acquisition makes direct use of distributional patterns in the input. We will examine these in turn.

Descriptions of the input

Motherese.   In response to the claim that input is deficient, early research first took a closer look at the nature of the input. The initial work asked whether, in fact, input to children is errorful and therefore a deficient database from which to derive the regularities of language. The clear finding was that, when talking to children, adults produce speech that is slow and highly grammatical and that has a higher pitch and broader pitch range than speech among adults (Fernald et al., 1989; see Gerken, 1994). Furthermore, adults adjust the complexity of their speech, at least grossly, to the child's level of comprehension (Snow & Ferguson, 1977). Beyond simplifying their speech, adults also tend to follow the child's attentional focus, produce multiple utterances on the same topic, ask questions, and provide contingent replies; these may have their own consequences for language learning beyond those posited as contingent on the simplification processes. This special register for talking to children was dubbed "motherese" (Newport, Gleitman, & Gleitman, 1977). Subsequent work revealed that the high pitch and exaggerated intonation contour of motherese made it especially interesting to infants (Cooper & Aslin, 1994; Fernald, 1985). One hypothesis was that the correspondence between intonation contour and grammatical structure might make this special register helpful to children's learning of language structure; this was supported by the finding that infants preferred to listen to exaggerated contours that corresponded to phrase boundaries over equally varied patterns that did not (Hirsh-Pasek et al., 1987).

   Another suggestion was that motherese supported language development by providing a simpler model of language than does adult-directed speech and, by extension, that within the variability in child-directed speech that exists, simpler is better. That latter hypothesis finds little support in the evidence. There is one finding in the literature that shorter maternal mean lengths of utterance are positively related to children's syntactic development (Furrow, Nelson, & Benedict, 1979), but that finding has never been replicated despite multiple attempts to do so (Pine, 1994). To the contrary, several studies have found that children who hear longer utterances in input are more advanced in syntactic development (Harkness, 1977; Hoff-Ginsberg, 1998; Huttenlocher, Vasilyeva, Cymerman, & Levine, 2002). Additionally, some input features that are positively associated with children's syntactic development, such as adult question-asking, involve grammatically complex forms. (Despite such findings, it may still be the case that the average degree of simplification in child-directed speech benefits language acquisition. All of the observed benefits of complexity in mothers' speech have been obtained within a range of complexity that was more limited than in speech directed to adults.)

   One recent hypothesis has suggested that the *child*, not the caregiver, may be the source of simplification of input. Newport (1990) and her colleagues have suggested that the limited perceptual and memory capacities of young children give the child an advantage. If the child can process and store only "pieces" of the input, this facilitates analysis, because it minimizes the logically possible combinatorial hypotheses the child will have to consider. Thus, "less is more." The child will access more complex forms when ready to take in larger chunks of input.

Another argument against a critical role for motherese draws on the considerable variation that exists across cultures in the extent to which parents modify their speech to children, or even speak directly to children (Lieven, 1994). Despite a wide range in patterns (e.g., Ochs, 1985; Schieffelin, 1985), children still learn language. It is argued, therefore, that because motherese is not universal, language development cannot be contingent on the child hearing motherese (see Hoff, 2006).

Input as a source of corrective feedback?   A second potential characteristic of input that research addressed early on is the provision of corrective feedback for error. If input provided corrective feedback, this would contradict Chomsky's claim that children receive no training in language. An early study found that mothers did not correct their children's ungrammatical utterances (Brown & Hanlon, 1970). Furthermore, children seem remarkably resistant even when parents do make occasional corrections. On the basis of these findings, the consensus in the field has long been that children do not generally receive corrective feedback.

More recent work has explored whether adults may provide more subtle feedback. Some have found that when children produce well-formed utterances, adults are more likely to repeat them verbatim, whereas when children produce ungrammatical forms, adults are more likely to modify them, to provide correct forms, or to ask for clarification (Bohannon & Stanowicz, 1988; Chouinard & Clark, 2003; Demetras, Post, & Snow, 1986; Saxton, 1997; Saxton, Backley, & Gallaway, 2005). Just how useful this feedback is to the child is a matter of debate. Chouinard and Clark (2003) argue that children do frequently recognize reformulations as corrections; Saxton et al. (2005) report that contrastive use of correct forms by adults predicts changes in children's error rates. Countering this view, Atkinson (2001) notes that demonstrations of occasional feedback do not necessarily mean that the adult *reliably* signals the grammaticality of children's utterances, nor that such feedback is a *necessary* element of acquisition. Given the probabilistic nature of feedback, Marcus (1993) estimated that a child would have to say the same ungrammatical sentence 85 times in order to have enough data to determine that the sentence was ungrammatical. Any feedback the child is receiving, therefore, can be seen, at best, only as an aid to language development; language development cannot be seen as contingent on such feedback. Moreover, Shatz and Ebeling (1991) argued that children actually revise their own utterances syntactically more than their parents do.

Input as data for distributional learning.   The theoretical importance of feedback declines if structural properties of the language can be induced directly from distributional patterns in the input, as argued first by Maratsos and Chalkley (1980). Several sources of evidence support this possibility, ranging from computer simulations of language development, to analyses of distributions of forms in parental input, to evidence of children's attention to frequency distributions in the input.

Computational models have demonstrated clearly that computers can induce grammatical features of language and syntax–semantics mappings. Redington and Chater (1997), for example, have shown that given a large sample of speech (including adult-to-adult and adult-to-child speech) as input, computer models can extract word classes (nouns, verbs, etc.), often posited as innate, from distributional patterns in that input. Smith and colleagues (Colunga & Smith, 2005; Gasser & Smith, 1998) have shown similarly that nouns can be distinguished from adjectives based on characteristics of the input, and that the association of nouns with solids and non-solids can emerge through associative learning. Landauer and Dumais (1997) have demonstrated that a computer can "learn" semantic associations among words using simple associationist mechanisms. Such demonstrations confirm that, in principle, structure-relevant patterns are available in the input language.

In direct examinations of speech addressed to children, Mintz (2003) found that frequently occurring word frames reliably surround words of the same grammatical category, and Naigles and Hoff-Ginsberg (1995) found that verbs in different semantic categories (e.g., internal state verbs, motion verbs) appeared in different syntactic environments. These findings make plausible the argument that children could induce form classes from the input. Pine and his colleagues (Gobet, Freudenthal, & Pine, 2004) have gone one step further: in computer simulations of children's language development using real parental speech to children as input, they have successfully simulated a number of phenomena observed in children's language, including the emergence of optional infinitive phenomena, verb-island phenomena, subject omissions, and case marking errors.

These studies examining patterns in the input and simulations of learning based on input data are complemented by behavioral studies showing that children can and do extract patterns of language from the input. Recent research has provided an explosion of evidence that human infants are powerful learners, able to extract information about the perceptual properties of language from the distributional properties of the speech they hear. Jusczyk and colleagues (e.g., Jusczyk, 1997) have demonstrated that infants have keen abilities to attend to stress, prosody, syllable, and lexical patterns in speech, and these aid in the infants' extraction of patterns in the input. Saffran and colleagues have found reliable effects showing that infants carry out rapid learning of statistical probabilities in language – whether those have to do with phonological patterns, lexical items, or phrase structure patterns (see, e.g., Saffran, 2003). These abilities to track statistical probabilities are not limited to language but extend also to tones and visual patterns as well as to rhythmic patterns (Hannon & Trehub, 2005; Kirkham, Slemmer, & Johnson, 2002; Saffran & Thiessen, this volume). However, infants do favor certain patterns over others, in particular, patterns consistent with those found in the world's languages (Saffran, 2003). But, importantly, since these abilities at tracking statistical probabilities are present in other species as well, Saffran (2003) argues that "the similarities across languages . . . are not the result of innate linguistic knowledge. Instead, human languages have been shaped by human learning mechanisms" (p. 110). (See also Gerken; Saffran & Thiessen, this volume.)

A rich body of research with toddlers has suggested how this early sensitivity to form in the input provides the basis for language-specific morphosyntactic and semantic inductions. For example, English-speaking children learn early that a word following *a* probably refers to an object, while the same new word following *some* (*some blicket*) probably refers to a substance (Bloom, 1994; Carey, 1994; Gathercole, Cramer, Somerville, & Jansen op de Haar, 1995; Gordon, 1988; Soja, 1992; Soja, Carey, & Spelke, 1991). English-speaking children also use the correspondences between the semantics of verbs and the structures in which they appear as clues to verb meaning (Naigles & Hoff-Ginsberg, 1998; Naigles & Swensen, this volume). Similarly, English-speaking children who hear a new word ending in *-ish* (*foppish*) learn to infer that that word refers to a property of an object, not the object itself, while Spanish-speaking children treat adjective-like forms in their language as if they refer to objects, because of the structure of Spanish (Waxman, Senghas, & Benveniste, 1997). Welsh-speaking children learn that if they hear a new word in a noun slot, that word might refer to either a single object or to a collection, while English- and Spanish-speaking children learn that a new noun in their language is likely to refer to a single whole object (Gathercole, Thomas, & Evans, 2000). In a similar vein, Spanish-speaking children learn that a new verb referring to a motion is likely to incorporate the direction of motion (as in *Juan subió la colina corriendo*, "Juan <u>ascended</u> the hill running"), while English-speaking children learn that a new verb referring to a motion is likely to incorporate the manner of motion (as in *John <u>ran</u> up the hill*) (Hohenstein, 2001).

In addition, the distribution of forms in children's speech often reflects the distributional frequencies in the adult language, indicating that children are highly sensitive to those distributions. Theakston, Lieven, Pine, and Rowland (2002) reported that children's early use of the verb *go* in English involves several isolated structures linking syntactic form with semantics, and that these correspond highly with the structural forms of *go* in the input. De Villiers (1985) found that the structures in which young children used particular verbs corresponded to the structures in which their mothers used those verbs. Henry (2003) reported on children's use of past forms in Ulster English, which allows both irregular and regularized forms for many verbs. She found that the children's patterns of usage closely followed those of the adults around them. Gobet et al. (2004) demonstrated that English-, Dutch-, and Spanish-speaking children's use of bare infinitives versus finite verb forms – which has figured prominently in nativist arguments (Wexler, 1994, 1998) – can be successfully mimicked in computer simulations that combine simple distributional analyses with a well-known child strategy (Slobin, 1973) of focusing on the ends of input utterances.

Together these studies support the position that the speech children hear contains structure-revealing information and that children have the capacity to find that information and use it to induce structural properties of their language. Further, the evidence argues that children are sensitive to the form–meaning correspondences of their language and use these to predict and infer linguistic properties of new forms when they encounter them (see also Choi, 2006; Gathercole, 2006; and see Lidz, this volume, on children's recovery from incorrect inferences). Whether these abilities rely solely on the child's attention to the input or involve other factors will be considered when we address question 3. We turn now to our second question.

Q2: Does input control either the sequence in which or the speed with which children construct the grammar?

We begin with evidence indicating that input – or more properly, frequency of input – does not control the *sequence* in which forms are acquired (except in the limited case in which sufficient input is not available); we follow with evidence showing that input does affect *speed* of acquisition.

Input and sequence of acquisition

If the acquisition of language were a simple process of storing and mimicking the input, one might expect that the sequence in which forms develop would correspond directly with their relative input frequency. It is clear that this is not the case. First, the forms that often are the most frequent in the input, such as function words (like *a*, *the*, and *of*), are rarely those that appear first in children's speech. Second, if children simply copied patterns available in the input, one would not expect them to make errors, at least not frequently. Again, this is not the case. Third, examinations of developmental sequences (e.g., for grammatical morphemes) make it clear that, assuming some minimal input level, other factors such as linguistic complexity and perceptual salience (see below) are more influential in determining order of acquisition than frequency in the input (Brown, 1973; de Villiers & de Villiers, 1973).

Even though input does not largely control the order in which children acquire the forms of language, input is relevant to order of acquisition in at least two ways. First, input affects order of acquisition in the extreme, in that children cannot acquire what they do not hear in the input. Several researchers have proposed, in fact, the need for a "critical mass" of input for acquisition or abstraction to occur (Conti-Ramsden & Jones, 1997; Elman, 2003; Gathercole, 2002b, 2002c; Marchman & Bates, 1994). If such a critical mass is not available to a child, the relevant structure may not be acquired, may be acquired late, or may not be acquired fully.

Two cases in point are the passive in English and the present perfect in American English. English-speaking children learn the passive (e.g., *he was beaten by his opponent*) quite late. Some nativists have posited that this is due to the late maturation of certain relevant innate linguistic principles (Borer & Wexler, 1987; see Goodluck, this volume). However, the passive is used infrequently in English. Children learning languages in which the passive is more frequent have been observed to use the passive early (Allen & Crago, 1996; Demuth, 1989; Pye & Quixtan Poz, 1988). Furthermore, if the frequency of passive forms is increased in speech to English-speaking children, children can learn some aspects of the passive earlier (de Villiers, 1980). Another telling case is the acquisition of the present perfect in American versus British English. While these two dialects share the same syntactic and semantic forms for the present perfect, American English uses the present perfect much less frequently than British English (optionally substituting, for some uses of the present perfect, the regular past: *Did you eat yet?* for *Have you eaten yet?*). This difference in frequency affects timing of acquisition, with British children using present perfect constructs by 3 years, and American children not until much later (Gathercole, 1986).

The exact quantity that constitutes the "critical mass" for the acquisition of a structure may be debatable, but appears to be linked with the relative transparency/opacity of the structure. Structures that are transparent appear to require a lower critical mass than opaque structures for abstraction of the relevant patterns. For example, grammatical gender in Spanish, which is very transparent, is acquired at an early age (Cain, Weber-Olsen, & Smith, 1987; Hernández Pina, 1984); grammatical gender in Welsh, which is very opaque, involving multiple overlapping form–function correspondences, is not learned until after age 9 (Gathercole & Thomas, 2005; Gathercole, Thomas, & Laporte, 2001; Thomas, 2001). Similarly, *that*-trace structures (e.g., ¿Quién piensas *que* tiene ojos verdes?/Who do you think (*that* omitted) has green eyes?) and the overall use of complementizer *que* in Spanish are transparent and are learned early, whereas *that*-trace structures and the overall use of complementizer *that* in English are opaque and learned late (Gathercole, 2002c; Gathercole & Montes, 1997).

A second way in which frequency of input might affect sequence of acquisition, or, rather, the nature of acquisition in that sequence, has to do with the extent to which children generalize beyond learned instances. If children construct language from patterns in the input, one theoretical question is how they arrive at appropriate levels of productivity for structures. Productivity is essential to linguistic knowledge, for it allows the use of language beyond learned instances. We know that at certain points in development children can extend their grammatical knowledge to novel forms (e.g., Berko, 1958), and they generalize and overgeneralize to novel instances – for example, using regularized forms in place of irregular items (e.g., *falled* instead of *fell*; *I disappeared it* instead of *I made it disappear*). Two critical questions regarding (over)generalizations concern (1) when these forms occur and (2) how the child manages to eventually eliminate incorrect forms from his/her speech. Tomasello (2000) has recently argued that input frequency plays a role in determining when overgeneralizations occur in child speech. He argues that specific items that are frequently heard become entrenched, and such items are less likely to be overgeneralized than items that are less frequent in input. For example, the high-frequency verb *laugh* becomes entrenched as an intransitive verb and is not likely to be overgeneralized to a transitive use, *I laughed him*. Overgeneralizations are also constrained by presence in input of alternative forms, which preempt overgeneralization. In this way, hearing the construction *made X disappear* blocks the overgeneralization of *disappear* to a transitive use, *I disappeared it* (Brooks & Tomasello, 1999). Items of an intermediate level of frequency (e.g., *giggle*) are the most susceptible to overgeneralization (*You giggled me*), according to this argument, because the appropriate forms are not heard frequently enough to become entrenched, yet are likely to be learned before the system is fully worked out. There is empirical support for some postulates of this account (Brooks, Tomasello, Dodson, & Lewis, 1999), although the issue of how children manage to be productive language users without being wildly overproductive has not been fully resolved (see Maratsos, 2000, and Elman, 2003, for related arguments).

Concerning the sequence in which constructs develop, then, frequency of input *per se* does not control order of acquisition. Something else does. However, frequency of input does affect the availability of a structure, and for each structure, the child must accumulate enough experience to be able to draw the relevant generalizations when ready to do so. If the structures in question are quite transparent, that critical mass will be smaller than if the structures in question are quite opaque. In addition, as the child is accumulating that critical mass, s/he is not likely to make errors of overgeneralization on entrenched items (learned early and heard frequently), only on items that are less entrenched, and only before the system is fully worked out.

Input and speed of acquisition

While relative frequency of input does not affect sequence of acquisition, it can influence speed of acquisition. One "natural laboratory" source of evidence is in comparisons of bilingual and monolingual groups learning the same pair of languages. Comparisons of children growing up in contexts in which the relative proportion of input in languages A and B varies yield consistent differences in the timing of acquisition of structures. Gathercole (2002a, 2002b, 2002c) found this to be the case for Spanish–English bilinguals learning mass/count structures in English, grammatical gender in Spanish, and *that*-trace structures in English and Spanish: Bilinguals who had the greatest amount of English input had an earlier command of the English constructs than their peers, while bilinguals who had the greatest amount of Spanish input had an earlier command of the Spanish constructs than their peers. (This also meant that English and Spanish monolinguals gained command of these structures before their bilingual peers.) Gathercole and Thomas (2005) found this also to be the case for Welsh–English bilinguals learning grammatical gender and verb-argument structures in Welsh: Those with a greater amount of Welsh input on a daily basis showed an earlier command of the Welsh constructs than their peers with less Welsh input. (See also Rieckborn (2006) and Kupisch (2003) for similar effects in bilinguals' development of tense/aspect and determiners, respectively.)

Monolingual children also differ in how much they hear the language or particular structures in the language they are acquiring, and this affects their rate of grammatical development. The total quantity of speech addressed to children at home and in day care relates to children's linguistic development (Bradley & Caldwell, 1976; Clarke-Stewart, 1973; McCartney, 1984; National Institute of Child Health and Human Development, 2000). The talkativeness of English-speaking mothers in interaction with young children relates to the children's syntactic and semantic development (Barnes, Gutfreund, Satterly, & Wells, 1983). Kindergarten children whose teachers use more complex sentences grow more rapidly in their use of complex sentences than those whose teachers produce fewer complex sentences (Huttenlocher et al., 2002). The more frequently children hear questions with auxiliary inversion, the more rapidly they grow in their own use of auxiliary verbs (Hoff-Ginsberg, 1985; Newport et al., 1977; Shatz, Hoff-Ginsberg, & MacIver, 1989). The variety of syntactic frames in which children hear verbs used predicts the syntactic flexibility of children's verb use (Naigles & Hoff-Ginsberg, 1998). The discourse environment of forms in input also affects language development. Expansions and recasts by adults may positively predict syntactic development (Newport et al., 1977), as may mothers' inexact self-repetitions (Cross, 1978; Hoff-Ginsberg, 1985, 1986).

Besides amount of input, other properties of children's conversational experience have also been shown to affect rates of grammatical development, including the amount of time spent in joint attention (Carpenter, Nagell, & Tomasello, 1998; Laakso, Poikkeus, Katajamaki, & Lyytinen, 1999; Mundy & Gomes, 1998), maternal responsivity to child verbalizations (Tamis-LeMonda, Bornstein, & Baumwell, 2001), and contingency of maternal speech (Snow, Perlmann, & Nathan, 1987). The benefits of these features of conversational experience might in the end reflect the amount of input provided the child. That is, when mothers and children are more engaged in conversation, children receive more language-advancing data. It may also be, however, that having a responsive conversational partner motivates language acquisition by demonstrating to children that communication is both possible and interesting (Hoff, 2003, 2006); alternatively, the partner who shares focus with the child may be more likely to provide input in line with the child's cognitive abilities (see below).

The upshot of all of this research is that (a) frequency of input *per se* does not control the sequence of acquisition across forms, but (b) input does affect rapidity of acquisition. More input means more rapid development – through a course of development whose sequence appears to be largely dictated by other factors.

Why might the quantity of input affect the rapidity of acquisition of forms in language? There are a number of possibilities:

1   With more input, there is greater frequency of the tokens of any form, which may contribute to the better storage and retention of tokens (e.g., *walked* heard 30 times is more likely to be retained than *walked* heard twice). Token frequency may be particularly important for the acquisition of isolated irregular forms (*drank, flew*) (Maratsos, 2000).

2   More input may also entail more distinct contexts (linguistic and non-linguistic) in which tokens are heard. This may facilitate the mapping problem of a form with its sense.

3   Greater input frequency likely entails greater frequency of lexical types participating in a given morphological or syntactic structure (e.g., hearing not only *walked*, but also *talked, laughed*, etc.). Frequency of types provides the "grist" for the language development mill that will help the child to construct morphosyntactic structures (here, use of *-ed* for past tense).

4   Greater input frequency is likely to provide richer information on relations across tokens and types, thus enabling a faster and stronger construction of networks of forms in the child's repertoire. That is, not only will the child be hearing each token (*talked, flew*) more often and in more non-linguistic contexts (e.g., *flew* in relation to a bird at the pond last week, in relation to a bug that has just flown in the window, etc.), but s/he will be hearing other types used with similar morphological forms (*walked, laughed, threw, drew*) in similar non-linguistic contexts (in reference to past time, in reference to time immediately preceding the utterance, etc.).

It is likely that all of these factors contribute to success in the child's ability to construct the language being learned from the available input. They constitute the elements that will make up the "critical mass" of data that will eventually allow the child to abstract out the common structures that link them.

Q3: Is the input alone sufficient to explain the child's construction of the grammar, or do other factors contribute to the process of acquisition; if so, how do these interact with the input?

Let us turn now to the third question, regarding what might be needed in addition to input for the child to construct a language. We have already seen above that input alone cannot explain the order of acquisition across structures. So what contributes to acquisition besides input to explain the order?

Influences other than input

A strong nativist position might explain the sequence of development across structures as controlled by the innate Universal Grammar. Some have posited that innate knowledge comes on line according to a maturational program, which controls the sequence of development and helps explain why children's knowledge does not necessarily match what might predominate in the input. Thus, for example, the late acquisition of functional categories (e.g., determiners and prepositions) relative to lexical categories (e.g., nouns and verbs), or the later acquisition of tense marking relative to person marking, might well be explained according to different maturational schedules for distinct elements of Universal Grammar (e.g., Grinstead, 2000; Radford, 1990, 1996). However, this is not the only possibility. Another possibility, one that does not rely on innate knowledge, is that what children can take from the input is dependent on their own "readiness" for attending to, noticing, or understanding what the input has to offer. That readiness might be, at least in part, in the form of cognitive understanding or of the child's linguistic development up to that point.

Cognitive understanding and language acquisition.   Input clearly interacts with cognition in determining what the child acquires when. Some demonstrations of the role of cognitive preparedness come from the acquisition of lexical items (see, e.g., Rice's (1980) classic study of children's acquisition of color terms), but grammatical examples, the focus of this chapter, are also in evidence. Some of these come from children's early misuses of terms that involve, in adult usage, complex cognitive knowledge. For example, children's early uses of comparative forms (which in their adult-like use demand some understanding of seriation or scalarity) often involve incorrect applications in contexts where intensification ("very X"), a simpler concept, would be appropriate (Gathercole, 1983); early uses of relative clauses may be for compounding instead of relativization (Tavakolian, 1981). In a recent study, Shirai and Miyata (2006) demonstrated that Japanese-speaking children use past tense morphology productively long before they use it appropriately for deictic past reference. In children's use of object labels, the greater difficulty of understanding functions related to substances than to shape seems to make children's extension of word categories based on material function harder (Gathercole & Whitfield, 2001). These examples show that if what is frequent in the input corresponds to complex cognitive concepts, the forms may be learned early with a simpler meaning (as in the case of the comparative in English or the past in Japanese), or may wait for the child's cognitive understanding to advance to a certain level (as in the case of word categories based on substance functions).

This is not to say, however, that cognition always drives language acquisition; the reverse is also possible, that language can help "push" the child to attend to aspects of referents and to develop certain cognitive concepts earlier (e.g., Bowerman, 1996; Choi, 2006; Gopnik & Choi, 1990). (However, the cognitive options open for such manipulation by language may be within a certain available cognitive range: Gathercole, 2006; McCune, 2006.) But ultimately, input alone cannot control order of acquisition because it must interact with, among other things, the child's cognitive understanding of the world to which language is referring.

Linguistic complexity and language acquisition.   The order in which children acquire forms also depends to some extent on linguistic complexity. Take, for example, the acquisition of the third person singular form of verbs. In Spanish, this is the first finite form that becomes productive; in English, it is a relatively late development. In Spanish, this form can be considered the unmarked, least complex, form of the verb, while in English, the third person singular can be considered a marked, complex, form (Gathercole, Sebastián, & Soto, 1999, 2002). Similarly, children typically acquire simple sentences before complex ones (involving more than one clause). Likewise, as noted above, constructions that involve opaque form–function mappings (e.g., Welsh grammatical gender, English *that*-trace) take longer to acquire than similar constructions involving more transparent form–function mappings (e.g., Spanish gender, Spanish *que*) (see Smoczynska, 1985). Another example, from Morgan, Barrière, and Woll (2006), comes from the acquisition of British Sign Language, in which agreement morphology is learned late; they attribute this to the difficulty of segmenting the relevant signs into morphemes and to the complexity of semantically and syntactically conditioned agreement rules which must be mastered.

It should be noted that complexity may depend not only on the structure in question but also on the relationships between the given construct and others in the linguistic system. Researchers have long noted that acquisition of a form may hinge on the prior acquisition of simpler related forms (e.g., Brown's (1973) "law of cumulative complexity"), a notion that has returned recently in the shape of "construction conspiracies" (Abbot-Smith & Behrens, 2002; Morris, Cottrell, & Elman, 2000). Abbot-Smith and Behrens, for example, demonstrate that their German subject learned stative passives before eventive passives because he had already acquired the "source constructions" for the former. Similarly, Rice (1980) found that all of the children in her color study took much longer to learn the first two-color-word contrast than to add a third color term to their system once they had acquired the first contrast. Children clearly build on previously acquired knowledge to move forward in the development of their linguistic system. The knowledge they have already acquired can ultimately serve to help them make more efficient use of new, related information in the input.

Conclusion

The questions addressed in this chapter concern the degree to which the input children receive can explain the course that language development follows. When the modern field of child language began in the 1960s, the dominant linguistic view was that language was an innate faculty of the human mind and that the complex structure of language is only faintly evident in the surface forms; thus the child's achievement of that complex structure could only be explained by positing innate linguistic knowledge. The evidence reviewed in this chapter suggests that the role of input in accounting for the fact of language acquisition is much greater than this early view allowed. Studies suggest that input does more than faintly reveal language's abstract structure, and that human infants and children have the capacity to induce language structure from surface regularities. We have seen that not only is an input-dependent account of language acquisition plausible, but that there is strong support for its validity. Variation in the amount and nature of the input children receive correlates with variation in the rate at which they acquire language. This evidence suggests that input provides the database for language induction.

The evidence reviewed in this chapter also suggests, at the same time, that the language acquisition mechanism is not solely input driven. The sequence in which the structures of language are acquired does not directly reflect the frequency with which structures occur in the input. Cognitive preparedness on the part of the child, and the linguistic complexity of the forms to be acquired, also play key roles. The fact that children's cognitive understanding can influence the acquisition of language structures makes the point that language is not a completely isolable domain, and the influence of linguistic complexity brings us full circle to input. Linguistically complex structures are, in part, those for which it is difficult to discern consistent patterns in the input. Thus, the effects of linguistic complexity serve to underline the fact that the child's extraction of regularities in the input must ultimately play a key role in the final analysis of how language acquisition takes place.

References

Abbot-Smith, K., & Behrens, H. (2002, July). *Construction conspiracies in the acquisition of the German passive*. Paper presented at the 10th Conference of the International Association for the Study of Child Language, Madison, WI.

Allen, S. E. M., & Crago, M. B. (1996). Early passive acquisition in Inuktitut. *Journal of Child Language, 23*, 129–155.

Atkinson, M. (2001). Learnability and the acquisition of syntax. In S. Bertolo (Ed.), *Language acquisition and learnability* (pp. 15–80). Cambridge: Cambridge University Press.

Baker, C. L., & McCarthy, J. J. (Eds.). (1981). *The logical problem of language acquisition*. Cambridge, MA: MIT Press.

Barnes, S., Gutfreund, M., Satterly, D., & Wells, G. (1983). Characteristics of adult speech which predict children's language development. *Journal of Child Language, 10*, 65–84.

Bates, E., & MacWhinney, B. (1989). Functionalism and the competition model. In B. MacWhinney & E. Bates (Eds.), *The crosslinguistic study of sentence processing* (pp. 3–73). Cambridge: Cambridge University Press.

Berko, J. (1958). The child's learning of English morphology. *Word, 14,* 50–77.

Berwick, R. (1985). *The acquisition of syntactic knowledge.* Cambridge, MA: MIT Press.

Bickerton, D. (1981). *Roots of language.* Ann Arbor, MI: Karoma.

Bickerton, D. (1984). The language bioprogram hypothesis. *Behavioral and Brain Sciences, 7,* 173–222.

Bloom, P. (1994). Semantic competence as an explanation for some transitions in language development. In Y. Levy (Ed.), *Other children, other languages: Theoretical issues in language development* (pp. 41–75). Hillsdale, NJ: Erlbaum.

Bohannon, J. S., & Stanowicz, L. (1988). The issue of negative evidence: Adult responses to children's language errors. *Developmental Psychology, 24,* 684–689.

Borer, H., & Wexler, K. (1987). The maturation of syntax. In T. Roeper & E. Williams (Eds.), *Parameter setting* (pp. 123–172). Dordrecht: D. Reidel Publishing Company.

Bowerman, M. (1996). The origins of children's spatial semantic categories: Cognitive versus linguistic determinants. In J. J. Gumperz & S. C. Levinson (Eds.), *Rethinking linguistic relativity* (pp. 145–176). Cambridge: Cambridge University Press.

Bradley, R. H., & Caldwell, B. M. (1976). The relation of infants' home environments to mental test performance at fifty-four months: a follow-up study. *Child Development, 47,* 1172–1174.

Brooks, P. J., & Tomasello, M. (1999). How children constrain their argument structure constructions. *Language, 75,* 720–738.

Brown, R. (1973). *A first language: The early stages.* Cambridge, MA: Harvard University Press.

Brown, R., & Hanlon, C. (1970). Derivational complexity and order of acquisition in child speech. In R. Brown (Ed.), *Psycholinguistics* (pp. 155–207). New York: Free Press.

Budwig, N. (1995). *A developmental-functionalist approach to child language.* Mahwah, NJ: Erlbaum.

Cain, J., Weber-Olsen, M., & Smith, R. (1987). Acquisition strategies in a first and second language: Are they the same? *Journal of Child Language, 14,* 333–352.

Carey, S. (1994). Does learning a language require the child to reconceptualize the world? In L. Gleitman & B. Landau (Eds.), *The acquisition of the lexicon* (pp. 143–167). Cambridge, MA: MIT Press.

Carpenter, M., Nagell, K., & Tomasello, M. (1998). Social cognition, joint attention, and communicative competence from 9 to 15 months of age. *Monographs of the Society for Research in Child Development, 63* (4, Serial No. 255).

Choi, S. (2006). Influence of language-specific input on spatial cognition: Categories of containment. *First Language, 26,* 207–232.

Chomsky, N. (1965). *Aspects of the theory of syntax.* Cambridge, MA: MIT Press.

Chomsky, N. (1968). *Language and mind.* New York: Harcourt Brace & World, Inc.

Chomsky, N. (1975). *Reflections on language.* New York: Pantheon Books.

Chouinard, M. M., & Clark, E. V. (2003). Adult reformulations of child errors as negative evidence. *Journal of Child Language, 30,* 637–669.

Clarke-Stewart, K. A. (1973). Interactions between mothers and their young children: characteristics and consequences. *Monographs of the Society for Research in Child Development, 38* (6–7, Serial No. 153).

Colunga, E., & Smith, L. B. (2005). From the lexicon to expectations about kinds: A role for associative learning. *Psychological Review, 112,* 347–382.

Conti-Ramsden, G., & Jones, M. (1997). Verb use in specific language impairment. *Journal of Speech, Language and Hearing Research, 40,* 1298–1313.

Cooper, R. P., & Aslin, R. N. (1994). Developmental differences in infant attention to the spectral properties of infant-directed speech. *Child Development, 65,* 1663–1667.

Crain, S., & Thornton, R. (1998). *Investigations in Universal Grammar: A guide to experiments on the acquisition of syntax and semantics.* Cambridge, MA: MIT Press.

Croft, W. (2001). *Radical construction grammar: Syntactic theory in typological perspective.* Oxford: Oxford University Press.

Cross, T. (1978). Mothers' speech and its association with linguistic development in young children. In N. Waterson & C. Snow (Eds.), *The development of communication* (pp. 199–216). Chichester, England: Wiley.

Culicover, P., & Jackendoff, R. (2005). *Simpler syntax.* Oxford: Oxford University Press.

De Villiers, J. G. (1980). The process of rule learning in child speech: A new look. In K. E. Nelson (Ed.), *Children's language: Vol. 2* (pp. 1–44). New York: Gardner Press.

De Villiers, J. G. (1985). Learning how to use verbs: lexical coding and the influence of the input. *Journal of Child Language, 12,* 587–595.

De Villiers, J. G., & de Villiers, P. A. (1973). A cross-sectional study of the acquisition of grammatical morphemes in child speech. *Journal of Psycholinguistic Research, 2,* 267–278.

Demetras, M. J., Post, K. N., & Snow, C. E. (1986). Feedback to first language learners: The role of repetitions and clarification questions. *Journal of Child Language, 13,* 275–292.

Demuth, K. (1989). Maturation, continuity and the acquisition of Sesotho passive. *Language, 65,* 56–80.

Drozd, K. (2004). Learnability and linguistic performance. *Journal of Child Language, 31,* 431–457.

Elman, J. (2003). Generalization from sparse input. *Proceedings of the 38th Annual Meeting of the Chicago Linguistic Society.*

Fernald, A. (1985). Four-month-old infants prefer to listen to motherese. *Infant Behavior and Development, 8,* 181–195.

Fernald, A., Taeschner, T., Dunn, J., Papousek, M., De Boyson-Bardies, B., & Fukui, I. (1989). A cross-language study of prosodic modifications in mothers' and fathers' speech to preverbal infants. *Journal of Child Language, 16,* 477–501.

Foley, W., & Van Valin, R. (1984). *Functional syntax and universal grammar.* Cambridge: Cambridge University Press.

Furrow, D., Nelson, K., & Benedict, H. (1979). Mothers' speech to children and syntactic development: some simple relationships. *Journal of Child Language, 6,* 423–442.

Gasser, M., & Smith, L. B. (1998). Learning nouns and adjectives: A connectionist account. In K. Plunkett (Ed.), *Language acquisition and connectionism* (pp. 269–306). Hove: Psychology Press.

Gathercole, V. C. (1983). Haphazard examples, prototype theory, and the acquisition of comparatives. *First Language, 4,* 169–196.

Gathercole, V. C. (1986). The acquisition of the present perfect: Explaining differences in the speech of Scottish and American children. *Journal of Child Language, 13,* 537–560.

Gathercole, V. C. M. (2002a). Command of the mass/count distinction in bilingual and monolingual children: An English morphosyntactic distinction. In D. K. Oller & R. E. Eilers (Eds.), *Language and literacy in bilingual children* (pp. 175–206). Multilingual Matters.

Gathercole, V. C. M. (2002b). Grammatical gender in bilingual and monolingual children: A Spanish morphosyntactic distinction. In D. K. Oller & R. E. Eilers (Eds.), *Language and literacy in bilingual children* (pp. 207–219). Multilingual Matters.

Gathercole, V. C. M. (2002c). Monolingual and bilingual acquisition: Learning different treatments of *that*-trace phenomena in English and Spanish. In D. K. Oller & R. E. Eilers (Eds.), *Language and literacy in bilingual children* (pp. 220–254). Multilingual Matters.

Gathercole, V. C. M. (2006). Introduction to Special Issue: Language-specific influences on acquisition and cognition. *First Language, 26,* 5–17.

Gathercole, V. C. M., Cramer, L., Somerville, S., & Jansen op de Haar, M. (1995). Ontological categories and function: Acquisition of new names. *Cognitive Development, 10,* 225–251.

Gathercole, V. C. M., & Montes, C. (1997). *That*-trace effects in Spanish- and English-speaking monolinguals and bilinguals. In A. T. Pérez-Leroux & W. R. Glass (Eds.), *Contemporary perspectives on the acquisition of Spanish: Vol. 1. Developing grammars* (pp. 75–95). Somerville, MA: Cascadilla Press.

Gathercole, V. C. M., Sebastián, E., & Soto, P. (1999). The early acquisition of Spanish verbal morphology: Across-the-board or piecemeal knowledge? *International Journal of Bilingualism, 3,* 133–182.

Gathercole, V. C. M., Sebastián, E., & Soto, P. (2002). The emergence of linguistic Person in Spanish-speaking children. *Language Learning, 52,* 679–722.

Gathercole, V. C. M., & Thomas, E. M. (2005). Minority language survival: Input factors influencing the acquisition of Welsh. In J. Cohen, K. McAlister, K. Rolstad, & J. MacSwan (Eds.), *ISB4: Proceedings of the 4th International Symposium on Bilingualism.* Somerville, MA: Cascadilla Press.

Gathercole, V. C. M., Thomas, E. M., & Evans, D. (2000). What's in a noun? Welsh-, English-, and Spanish-speaking children see it differently. *First Language, 20,* 55–90.

Gathercole, V. C. M., Thomas, E. M., & Laporte, N. (2001). The acquisition of grammatical gender in Welsh. *Journal of Celtic Language Learning, 6,* 53–87.

Gathercole, V. C. M., & Whitfield, L. (2001). Function as a criterion for the extension of new words. *Journal of Child Language, 28,* 87–125.

Gerken, L. (1994). Child phonology: Past research, present questions, future direction. In M. A. Gernsbacher (Ed.), *Handbook of psycholinguistics* (pp. 781–820). New York: Academic Press.

Gobet, F., Freudenthal, D., & Pine, J. M. (2004). Modelling syntactic development in a cross-linguistic context. In W. G. Sakas (Ed.), *Proceedings of the First COLING Workshop on Psycho-Computational Models of Human Language Acquisition.*

Goldberg, A. (1995). *Constructions: A Construction Grammar approach to argument structure.* Chicago: University of Chicago Press.

Goodman, M. (1985). Roots of languages (Review article). *International Journal of American Linguistics, 51,* 109–137.

Gopnik, A., & Choi, S. (1990). Do linguistic differences lead to cognitive differences: A cross-linguistic study of semantic and cognitive development. *First Language, 10,* 199–215.

Gordon, P. (1988). Count/mass category acquisition: Distributional distinctions in children's speech. *Journal of Child Language, 15,* 109–128.

Grinstead, J. (2000). Case, inflection and subject licensing in child Catalan and Spanish. *Journal of Child Language, 27,* 119–155.

Hannon, E. E., & Trehub, S. E. (2005). Tuning in to musical rhythms: Infants learn more readily than adults. *Proceedings of the National Academy of Sciences, 102,* 12639–12643.

Harkness, S. (1977). Aspects of the social environment and first language acquisition in rural Africa. In C. E. Snow & C. A. Ferguson (Eds.), *Talking to children: Language input and acquisition* (pp. 309–318). Cambridge: Cambridge University Press.

Henry, A. (2003, April). *Acquiring past tenses from variable input.* Keynote speech, Fifth Annual Gregynog Conference on Child Language, Powys, Wales.

Hernández Pina, F. (1984). *Teorías psicosociolingüísticas y su aplicación a la adquisición del español como lengua materna.* Madrid: Siglo XXI de España Editores, S.A.

Hirsh-Pasek, K., Kemler Nelson, D. G., Jusczyk, P. W., Wright Cassidy, K., Druss, B., & Kennedy, L. (1987). Clauses are perceptual units for young infants. *Cognition, 26,* 269–286.

Hoff, E. (2003). The specificity of environmental influence: Socioeconomic status affects early vocabulary development via maternal speech. *Child Development, 74,* 1368–1378.

Hoff, E. (2006). How social contexts support and shape language development. *Developmental Review, 26,* 55–88.

Hoff-Ginsberg, E. (1985). Some contributions of mothers' speech to their children's syntactic growth. *Journal of Child Language, 12,* 367–386.

Hoff-Ginsberg, E. (1986). Function and structure in maternal speech: Their relation to the child's development of syntax. *Developmental Psychology, 22,* 155–163.

Hoff-Ginsberg, E. (1998). The relation of birth order and socioeconomic status to children's language experience and language development. *Applied Psycholinguistics, 19,* 603–629.

Hohenstein, J. (2001). *Motion event similarities in English- and Spanish-speaking children.* Unpublished doctoral dissertation, Yale University.

Huttenlocher, J., Vasilyeva, M., Cymerman, E., & Levine, S. (2002). Language input at home and at school: Relation to child syntax. *Cognitive Psychology, 45,* 337–374.

Hyams, N. M. (1986). *Language acquisition and the theory of parameters.* Dordrecht: D. Reidel Publishing Company.

Hyams, N. M. (1987). The theory of parameters and syntactic development. In T. Roeper & E. Williams (Eds.), *Parameter setting* (pp. 1–22). Dordrecht: D. Reidel Publishing Company.

Jusczyk, P. W. (1997). *The discovery of spoken language.* Cambridge, MA: MIT Press.

Kegl, J. (2002). Language emergence in a language-ready brain: Acquisition issues. In G. Morgan & B. Woll (Eds.), *Language acquisition in signed languages* (pp. 207–254). Cambridge: Cambridge University Press.

Kegl, J. (2004). Language emergence in a language-ready brain: Acquisition issues. In L. Jenkins (Ed.), *Biolinguistics and the evolution of language.* Amsterdam: John Benjamins.

Kegl, J., Senghas, A., & Coppola, M. (1999). Creation through contact: Sign language emergence and sign language change in Nicaragua. In M. DeGraff (Ed.), *Comparative grammatical change: The intersection of language acquisition, creole genesis, and diachronic syntax* (pp. 179–237). Cambridge, MA: MIT Press.

Kirkham, N. Z., Slemmer, J. A., & Johnson, S. P. (2002). Visual statistical learning in infancy: Evidence of a domain general learning mechanism. *Cognition, 83,* B35–B42.

Kupisch, T. (2003). On the relation between input frequency and acquisition patterns from a cross-linguistic perspective. In J. van Kampen & S. Baauw (Eds.), *Proceedings of GALA 2003.* LOT Occasional Series.

Laakso, M.-L., Poikkeus, A.-M., Katajamaki, J., & Lyytinen, P. (1999). Early intentional communication as a predictor of language development in young toddlers. *First Language, 19,* 207–231.

Landauer, T. K., & Dumais, S. T. (1997). A solution to Plato's problem: The latent semantic analysis theory of acquisition, induction, and representation of knowledge. *Psychological Review, 104,* 211–240.

Lieven, E. V. M. (1994). Cross-linguistic and cross-cultural aspects of language addressed to children. In C. Gallaway & B. J. Richards (Eds.), *Input and interaction in language acquisition* (pp. 56–73). Cambridge: Cambridge University Press.

Lightfoot, D. (1984). The relative richness of triggers and the bioprogram. *Behavioral and Brain Sciences, 7,* 198–199.

Lust, B. (1999). Universal grammar: The strong continuity hypothesis in first language acquisition. In W. C. Ritchie & T. K. Bhatia (Eds.), *Handbook of child language acquisition* (pp. 111–153). San Diego, CA: Academic Press.

MacWhinney, B. (2004). A multiple process solution to the logical problem of language acquisition. *Journal of Child Language, 31,* 963–968.

Maratsos, M. (1984). How degenerate is the input to creoles and where do its biases come from? *Behavioral and Brain Sciences, 7,* 199–200.

Maratsos, M. (2000). More overregularizations after all: New data and discussion on Marcus, Pinker, Ullman, Hollander, Rosen & Xu. *Journal of Child Language, 27,* 183–212.

Maratsos, M., & Chalkley, M. A. (1980). The internal language of children's syntax: The ontogenesis and representation of syntactic categories. In K. Nelson (Ed.), *Children's language: Vol. 2* (pp. 127–214). New York: Gardner Press.

Marchman, V. A., & Bates, E. (1994). Continuity in lexical and morphological development: A test of the critical mass hypothesis. *Journal of Child Language, 21,* 339–365.

Marcus, G. F. (1993). Negative evidence in language acquisition. *Cognition, 46,* 53–85.

McCartney, K. (1984). Effect of quality of day care environment on children's language development. *Developmental Psychology, 20,* 244–260.

McCune, L. (2006). Dynamic event words: From common cognition to varied linguistic expression. *First Language, 26,* 233–255.

Mintz, T. (2003). Frequent frames as a cue for grammatical categories in child directed speech. *Cognition, 90,* 91–117.

Morgan, G., Barrière, I., & Woll, B. (2006). The influence of typology and modality on the acquisition of verb agreement morphology in British Sign Language. *First Language, 26,* 19–43.

Morris, W. C., Cottrell, G. W., & Elman, J. L. (2000). A connectionist simulation of the empirical acquisition of grammatical relations. In S. Wermter & R. Sun (Eds.), *Hybrid neural symbolic integration* (pp. 175–193). Berlin: Springer-Verlag.

Mundy, P., & Gomes, A. (1998). Individual differences in joint attention skill development in the second year. *Infant Behavior and Development, 21,* 469–482.

Naigles, L., & Hoff-Ginsberg, E. (1995). Input to verb learning: Evidence for the plausibility of syntactic bootstrapping. *Developmental Psychology, 31,* 827–837.

Naigles, L., & Hoff-Ginsberg, E. (1998). Why are some verbs learned before other verbs? Effects of input frequency and structure on children's early verb use. *Journal of Child Language, 25,* 95–120.

National Institute of Child Health and Human Development Early Child Care Research Network (2000). The relation of child care to cognitive and language development. *Child Development, 71,* 960–980.

Newport, E. L. (1990). Maturational constraints on language learning. *Cognitive Science, 14,* 11–28.

Newport, E. L., Gleitman, H., & Gleitman, L. R. (1977). Mother, I'd rather do it myself: Some effects and non-effects of maternal speech style. In C. E. Snow & C. A. Ferguson (Eds.), *Talking to children: Language input and acquisition* (pp. 109–150). Cambridge: Cambridge University Press.

Ochs, E. (1985). Variation and error: A sociolinguistic approach to language acquisition in Samoa. In D. I. Slobin (Ed.), *The cross-linguistic study of language acquisition: Vol. 1* (pp. 783–838). Hillsdale, NJ: Erlbaum.

Pine, J. M. (1994). The language of primary caregivers. In C. Gallaway & B. J. Richards (Eds.), *Input and interaction in language acquisition* (pp. 15–37). Cambridge: Cambridge University Press.

Pinker, S. (1994). *The language instinct: How the mind creates language.* New York: William Morrow.

Pye, C., & Quixtan Poz, P. (1988). Precocious passives (and antipassives) in Quiché Mayan. *Papers and Reports on Child Language Development, 27,* 71–80.

Radford, A. (1990). *Syntactic theory and the acquisition of English syntax.* Oxford: Blackwell.

Radford, A. (1996). Towards a structure-building model of acquisition. In H. Clahsen (Ed.), *Generative perspectives on language acquisition* (pp. 43–89). Amsterdam: John Benjamins.

Redington, M., & Chater, N. (1997). Probabilistic and distributional approaches to language acquisition. *Trends in Cognitive Sciences, 1,* 273–281.

Rice, M. (1980). *Cognition to language: Categories, word meaning, and training.* Baltimore, MD: University Park Press.

Rieckborn, S. (2006). The development of forms and functions in the acquisition of tense and aspect in German–French bilingual children. In C. Lleó (Ed.), *Interfaces in multilingualism: Acquisition and representation* (pp. 61–89). Amsterdam: John Benjamins.

Roeper, T., & Williams, E. (Eds.). (1987). *Parameter setting.* Dordrecht: D. Reidel Publishing Company.

Sabbagh, M. A., & Gelman, S. A. (2000) Buzzsaws and blueprints: What children need (or don't need) to learn about language. *Journal of Child Language, 27,* 715–726.

Saffran, J. R. (2003). Statistical language learning: Mechanisms and constraints. *Current Directions in Psychological Science, 12,* 110–114.

Saxton, M. (1997). The contrast theory of negative input. *Journal of Child Language, 24,* 139–161.

Saxton, M., Backley, P., & Gallaway, C. (2005). Negative input for grammatical errors: Effects after a lag of 12 weeks. *Journal of Child Language, 32,* 643–672.

Schieffelin, B. B. (1985). The acquisition of Kaluli. In D. I. Slobin (Ed.), *The cross-linguistic study of language acquisition: Vol. 1* (pp. 525–593). Hillsdale, NJ: Erlbaum.

Senghas, A., & Coppola, M. (2001). Children creating language: How Nicaraguan Sign Language acquired a spatial grammar. *Psychological Science, 12,* 323–328.

Senghas, A., Kita, S., & Özyürek, A. (2004). Children creating core properties of language: Evidence from an emerging sign language in Nicaragua. *Science, 305,* 1779–1782.

Shatz, M., & Ebeling, K. (1991). Patterns of language learning-related behaviours: evidence for self-help in acquiring grammar. *Journal of Child Language, 18,* 295–313.

Shatz, M., Hoff-Ginsberg, E., & MacIver, D. (1989). Induction and the acquisition of English auxiliaries: The effects of differentially enriched input. *Journal of Child Language, 16,* 121–140.

Shirai, Y., & Miyata, S. (2006). Does past tense marking indicate the acquisition of the concept of temporal displacement in children's cognitive development? *First Language, 26,* 45–66.

Slobin, D. I. (1973). Cognitive prerequisites for the development of grammar. In C. A. Ferguson & D. I. Slobin (Eds.), *Studies of child language development* (pp. 175–208). New York: Holt, Reinhart and Winston.

Slobin, D. I. (1997). The origins of grammaticizable notions: Beyond the individual mind. In D. I. Slobin (Ed.), *The cross-linguistic study of language acquisition: Vol. 5. Expanding the contexts* (pp. 265–323). Mahwah, NJ: Erlbaum.

Smoczynska, M. (1985). Acquisition of Polish. In D. I. Slobin (Ed.), *The cross-linguistic study of language acquisition: Vol. 1* (pp. 595–686). Hillsdale, NJ: Erlbaum.

Snow, C. E., Perlmann, R., & Nathan, D. (1987). Why routines are different: Toward a multiple-factors model of the relation between input and language acquisition. In K. Nelson & A. van Kleeck (Eds.), *Children's language: Vol. 6* (pp. 65–98). Hillsdale, NJ: Erlbaum.

Snow, C. E., & Ferguson, C. A. (Eds.). (1977). *Talking to children: Language input and acquisition*. Cambridge: Cambridge University Press.

Soja, N. N. (1992). Inferences about the meanings of nouns: The relationship between perception and syntax. *Cognitive Development, 7*, 29–45.

Soja, N. N., Carey, S., & Spelke, E. S. (1991). Ontological categories guide young children's inductions of word meaning: Object terms and substances terms. *Cognition, 38*, 179–211.

Tamis-LeMonda, C. S., Bornstein, M. H., & Baumwell, L. (2001). Maternal responsiveness and children's achievement of language milestones. *Child Development, 72*, 748–767.

Tavakolian, S. (1981). The conjoined clause analysis of relative clauses. In S. Tavakolian (Ed.), *Language acquisition and linguistic theory* (pp. 167–187). Cambridge, MA: MIT Press.

Theakston, A. L., Lieven, E. V. M., Pine, J. M., & Rowland, C. F. (2002). Going, going, gone: the acquisition of the verb 'Go'. *Journal of Child Language, 29*, 783–811.

Thomas, E. (2001). *Aspects of gender mutation in Welsh*. Unpublished PhD thesis, University of Wales Bangor.

Tomasello, M. (1995). Language is not an instinct. Review of Pinker's (1994) *The language instinct: How the mind creates language* (New York: William Morrow). *Cognitive Development, 10*, 131–156.

Tomasello, M. (2000). Do young children have adult syntactic competence? *Cognition, 74*, 209–253.

Tomasello, M. (2003). *Constructing a language: A usage-based theory of language acquisition*. Cambridge, MA: Harvard University Press.

Waxman, S. R., Senghas, A., & Benveniste, S. (1997). A cross-linguistic examination of the noun-category bias: Its existence and specificity in French- and Spanish-speaking preschool-aged children. *Cognitive Psychology, 32*, 183–218.

Wexler, K. (1994). Optional infinitives, head movement and the economy of derivation in child grammar. In N. Hornstein & D. Lightfoot (Eds.), *Verb movement* (pp. 305–350). Cambridge: Cambridge University Press.

Wexler, K. (1998). Very early parameter setting and the unique checking constraint: a new explanation of the optional infinitive stage. *Lingua, 106*, 23–79.

Wexler, K., & Manzini, M. R. (1987). Parameters and learnability in binding theory. In T. Roeper & E. Williams (Eds.), *Parameter setting* (pp. 41–76). Dordrecht: D. Reidel Publishing Company.

7

The Emergence of Language: A Dynamical Systems Account

Julia L. Evans

The process by which children's language abilities emerge and the beliefs of a research community regarding the nature of language and its representation in the brain often are conflated in child language research. Since the late 1950s the dominant metaphor for language and cognition has been the digital computer and the belief that human intelligence is a process of computations on symbolic representations – rule-based manipulation of symbols. Language, from this perspective, is a symbolic system that is innate, residing in the human genetic code. As a result, the focus of child language research has been on the universal, stable, orderly, stage-like patterns in children's language and the discovery of these innate abstract linguistic structures.

The emphasis of child language researchers has shifted recently to highlighting the flexible, transient, dynamic aspects of the emergence of language abilities. In this endeavor, researchers are extending principles of dynamic systems theory (DST) and the self-organization of complex systems to study this process. From this perspective, language is no longer a static, abstract, symbolic system, but language patterns that emerge over time as a property of the self-organization of a complex system. Language development is no longer seen as a process of acquiring abstract rules, but as the *emergence* of language abilities in *real time*, where changes over days, months, and years and moment-to-moment changes in language "processing" are the same phenomena, differing only in their timescales. Extending principles of DST and its emphasis on the fluid, transient, contextually sensitive nature of behavior, the goal of this approach is to identify the mechanisms and states of the child's emerging language abilities that engender developmental change at all levels of real-time continuous processing.

The purpose of this chapter is to introduce the principles of DST and their application to language development. To set the stage, a brief overview of current theories of language development is provided, along with a brief discussion of aspects of language development not accounted for by these theories. The fundamental concepts of DST are introduced and different modeling approaches to the study of language development within DST are presented.

Historical Overview

Several viable accounts of language development currently exist. These accounts all endeavor to explain language development, yet they differ along several dimensions including the emphasis placed on the structural versus functional aspects of children's language development and on children's competence (their knowledge of language) versus performance (actual language use). These accounts also differ with respect to the degree to which posited mechanisms of language development are believed to reside solely in the child, the environment, or some combination of the two.

Behaviorist accounts were introduced in the late 1950s, and highlight the observable and measurable aspects of language behavior. Language is viewed as a behavior like any other behavior. Behaviorists eschew any account of language development that relies on implicit knowledge or language competence (Mowrer, 1960; Osgood, 1963; Skinner, 1957; Staats, 1971). Social-interaction accounts argue that the functional use of language within the social-communicative contexts drives language development. Social-interactionist accounts argue that the unique form of talk directed to children by caregivers (i.e., child directed speech) is a critical part of the developmental process, with parents providing a tailored learning environment for the child (e.g., Bates, Beeghly-Smith, Bretherton, & McNew, 1983; Bohannon & Warren-Leubecker, 1988; Gleason, 1977; Snow, 1979, 1989). Cognitive theories acknowledge the influence of social-communicative interactions, but include an additional caveat – that the child also brings innate cognitive categories such as agents, patients, actions, and locations to the language learning processes (Bates, Begnigni, Bretherton, Camaioni, & Volterra, 1979; Bates & Snyder, 1987). These domain-general innate forms are semantic in nature and aid the child in interpreting her environment (Bowerman, 1982). Only later do abstract grammatical classes such as noun and verb phrases emerge because of the reorganization of the innate semantic categories. Nativist accounts view language as a species-specific, innate ability, where the child is endowed with the grammatical structures of language, not semantic categories, which are domain-specific, genetically predetermined forms (e.g., Chomsky, 1982, 1988). In the nativist accounts, emphasis is placed on identifying commonalities of linguistic forms both across children and across cultures as evidence of linguistic universals (Pinker, 1984).

Cognitivism: The Mind-as-Computer Metaphor

The social-interactionist, cognitive, and nativist theories are strongly influenced by the assumptions of cognitive science introduced in the 1950s known as cognitivism (see Verela, Thompson, & Rosch, 1996). Cognitivism views human intelligence as being so similar to digital computation in its essence that intelligence should be viewed as computations on symbolic representations. Cognitive behavior from this perspective is viewed as actions on representations that are physically realized in the form of a symbolic code in the brain or a machine, and where representations are viewed as static structures of discrete symbols.

Information processing from this perspective is symbolic computations – the rule-based manipulation of symbols – where the system interacts only with the form of the symbols, not their meaning. Language, from the cognitivist perspective, is comprised of discrete symbols, where it is the computations performed on the symbols that represent the meanings they stand for (see Chomsky, 1982, 1988). This abstract language knowledge is a symbolic code that is believed to be species-specific, and determined by human evolution.

The mind-as-computer metaphor comes with its own problems. The first is that a distinction is made between the disembodied computational mechanisms of "pure cognition" and the physical implementation of behavior by the brain. This distinction results in a dualism between competence – the abstract, stable, enduring mental symbols that are modular and time-independent – and performance – the "vagaries" of real-time language use. In the same way that the full range of a computer program's power is not manifested in individual operations, it is believed that the child's language competence is not always displayed in real-time processing. Extracting these "essential" rules from the messy language performance in children has been problematic for researchers, since these "core abilities" seem sensitive to even the smallest changes in experimental contexts. Methodologically, this requires the construction of experimental tasks or observational contexts that reveal a child's core language competence at the earliest ages possible, through the careful control of performance demands.

The mind-as-computer metaphor is an excellent means to study the stable, universal aspects of development, but it does not provide a framework to address certain key questions. These include: Where does competence reside? If competence is genetic as Chomsky suggests (1988), how is it specified in the brain? Or as Oyama (1985) cogently argues, starting with the assumption that the code resides either in the genes or in the environment inevitably leads to a logic trap – who or what turns on the genes or decides what information stays and what goes? Experimentally, why should small changes in experimental methodologies (e.g., preferential looking versus enactment paradigms) result in vastly different outcomes? What are the mechanisms that account for accurate performance under some circumstances and incorrect performance under others? Shouldn't these innate competences be more robust? Finally, if infants appear to have a particular language skill, why is it that often this same language knowledge appears lacking in older toddlers?

The cognitivist approach also does not provide a framework for child language researchers to study language acquisition as a process of continuous change over time. It specifies discrete steps in the sequence of acquisition of different language skills at different stages in development that occur in arbitrary timesteps. The problem is, while language development often looks like a discrete stage-like progression toward more complex language forms, it is often characterized by times where progress stops and even reverts to earlier stages in development. This shifting, nonincremental nature of language development gives rise to questions such as how does one predict a trajectory of language development if change over time is left out of the picture? How do the moment-to-moment aspects of language learning map onto the longer timescales of development (Elman, 2003)? Where do novel language behaviors come from? How does the child move from one stage to the next in language development?

Finally, with the mind-as-computer metaphor, how are abstract symbols connected to real-word meanings? (the symbol-grounding problem). In defining symbol representations independent of their physical realizations it is not possible to know the meanings of abstract symbols that are themselves manipulated solely on the basis of their (arbitrary) shapes, unless they are grounded in something other than more abstract symbols (Barsalou, 1999; Harnad, 1990; Searle, 1980). If the goal is to describe the underlying mechanisms, states, and processes that engender language learning as a real-time continuous process, then one needs to start at a different point conceptually. Or as Port and van Gelder (1995, p. 2) argue, in the same way that "astronomy could only make progress by displacing the earth from the center of the universe, so must developmental science also displace the inner computer from the center of cognitive performance" to understand language development as a continuous process.

An alternative is to view language development as change over time – to assume that the emergence of language abilities and real-time language processing are the same phenomenon differing only in the timescale with which they are observed. This view assumes that language is not abstract symbols, but embodied in real life experiences (Ford & Lerner, 1992; Thelen & Smith, 1994; Verela et al., 1996). It holds that language is softly assembled, unfolding in real time as a process of continuous, simultaneous changes in the interactions between the environment, the body, and the nervous system – where time is always part of the equation (Elman, 2003; Port & van Gelder, 1995). Dynamic systems theory provides such a framework.

Dynamic Systems Theory

Dynamic systems theory (DST) is grounded in recent advances in the fields of complex, nonlinear, dynamic systems in physics and mathematics, and a longstanding tradition of systems thinking in biology and psychology. The term *dynamic systems* refers both to complex, nonlinear systems that change over time and to the formal class of mathematical equations used to describe these systems. Inherent in DST are assumptions of self-organization, complexity, and emergentism. Dynamic systems theory assumes that novel, complex forms of behavior emerge from the interaction of the components of the system and the environment. The goal in extending this approach to the study of language development is to explain how observable language abilities evolve over time. The target of study in this approach is the change in the behavior of complex systems, in particular, the trajectory of behaviors across different timescales. Knowledge within DST is embodied; it is derived from, and inextricably bound to, actions and perceptions. The defining property of development from DST is the occurrence of increasingly complex novel forms of behavior.

Three assumptions characterize a DST approach to the study of development. First, developmental outcomes can be explained through the spontaneous emergence of more complex forms of behavior due to the cooperation of the multiple heterogeneous parts of the system that produce coherent complex patterned behavior. This process is known as *self-organization*. It occurs without pre-specification from internal rules or genetic code. Rather, development is truly self-organizing because it occurs through the recursive interactions of the components of the system. This process depends both on the organism itself and on the constraints put on the organism by the environment in which it resides. This self-organization results in the emergence of novel, complex forms of behavior. Thus, developmental scientists, working within DST, see language development as a process of emergence, as opposed to growth, learning, or construction (see Lewis, 2000). Second, a DST approach assumes that self-organization is continuous in time – a *dynamic* process. Development is the simultaneous continuity across multiple levels and multiple timescales. Key to this alternative view is the idea that developmental processes are both nested as well as coupled across different timescales. For detailed discussion of DST of development, see work by Thelen, Smith, and colleagues (Corbetta & Thelen, 1996; Fogel & Thelen, 1987; Gershkoff-Stowe & Thelen, 2004; Kelso, Ding, & Schöner, 1986a; Muchisky, Gershkoff-Stowe, Cole, & Thelen, 1996; Smith & Thelen, 1993; Thelen, 1989; Thelen, Corbetta, & Spencer, 1996; Thelen & Fischer, 1982; Thelen, Schöner, Scheier, & Smith, 2001; Thelen & Smith, 1994; Thelen & Ulrich, 1991).

Stability and *instability* are central to how behavioral patterns are conceptualized within DST. Stability is the "persistence of behavioral or neural states in the face of systematic or random perturbations" to the system (Spencer & Schöner, 2003, p. 394). We see examples throughout all of child language development, where children come to acquire stable language forms in the face of extreme variability in the input. For example, children are able to learn the phonemic contrasts of their language in the context of extreme within and across speaker variability. While achieving behavioral stability is critical in development, so is the need for flexibility and dissolution of old forms. With the emergence of novel, more complex forms, stable patterns must become unstable for change to occur. This instability itself allows the components of the system to reorganize in novel ways. From a DST perspective *variability* is not simply "noise" in the system but instead provides valuable insights into the nature of language development and may in fact be the actual mechanism of change in development (Gershkoff-Stowe & Thelen, 2004, p. 13).

In DST the *emergence* of behaviors is synonymous with developmental change. This notion of emergence is in fundamental contrast to nativist accounts, in that it refers to the coming into existence of new forms or properties through the ongoing processes intrinsic to the system itself. Emergence is not a metaphor but is a general principle underlying self-organization. Moreover, the application of the concept of emergence of self-organization to development may inherently provide a vehicle for the unification of ideas and thinking about the process of development across multiple domains (Lewis, 2000).

Dynamic Models of Language Development

Dynamic systems theory models of language and cognitive development derive from nonequilibrium thermodynamics (Nicolis & Priogogine, 1989), catastrophe theory (Thom, 1975), synergetics (Haken, 1983, 1993, 1996), chaos theory (Ott, 1993), Hebbian learning (Hebb, 1949), and entrainment of complex systems (Kelso, 1984; Kelso et al., 1986a). These models include van der Maas and Molenaar's use of catastrophe theory to model cognitive development (van der Maas, 1998; van der Maas & Molenaar, 1992), van Geert's use of ecological growth models to model language development (van Geert, 1991, 1993, 1994, 1998), connectionist models (e.g., Bates & Elman, 2000; Elman, 2001, 2003; Elman et al., 1996; Rumelhart, McClelland, & Group, 1986), and Thelen and colleagues' use of Haken's principles of synergetics (Haken, 1983, 1993, 1996) and Waddington's epigenetic landscape (Waddington, 1954, 1957, 1977) to describe the spontaneous emergence of novel motor, cognitive, and language skills as well as to conceptualize real-time language processing and the longer timescale of language development as integrated phenomena. Finally, both Fogel and Buder and their colleagues have used coupled logistics equations and principles of entrainment of complex systems to model speaker behaviors in mother–child dyadic interactions (Buder, 1986, 1991, 1996; Buder & Eriksson, 1997; Fogel & Thelen, 1987; Hsu & Fogel, 2003). Each of these models is discussed below.

Catastrophe models

Catastrophe models of stage-wise cognitive development employ key concepts such as attractor states, stable attractors, and equilibrium (e.g., van der Maas, 1998; van der Maas & Molenaar, 1992). Van der Maas, Molenaar, and colleagues argue that principles of self-organization are the only solution to answer the question of the origins of novel forms. In their work, they show how discontinuous jumps in development can be formally predicted by catastrophe theory. In these models, "cognitive strategies" are defined as coherent behavioral attractors – preferred organizational states of the system. These attractors each have their own inherent stability, and can, with perturbations to the system, be brought so far out of equilibrium that the system falls apart or "transforms" into a different behavioral strategy in a discontinuous manner. Reaction time is a measure of equilibrium in these models, with shorter reaction times reflecting greater stability of the system.

In catastrophe models, children will shift suddenly from one developmental state to another when two different cognitive strategies are highly active and competing. This competition between two behavioral attractors is what causes disequilibrium of the system, manifesting as behavioral instability, forcing the child to reorganize into a novel, more stable state space. The onset of developmental transitions is signaled by "catastrophe flags". These "flags" are characterized by a sudden increase in behavioral variability, bimodality (e.g., shifting between two behavioral states), and slower recovery from perturbations to the system (e.g., slower reaction times).

Van der Maas and Molenaar focus primarily on the shifts in cognitive development; however, their work extends to language development. In their models, syntax is no longer an abstract structure but is instead coherent behavioral attractors (Elman, 1995; Tabor, Juliano, & Tanenhaus, 1997). Accordingly, the emergence of new developmental language abilities is marked by a sudden increase in behavioral variability, such as the simultaneous use of multiple language forms from different stages in development (e.g., "I runded, I randed, I ran from the doggie!"), and slower reaction times for processing of novel information, which is precisely what we see in children's language development (Gershkoff-Stowe & Thelen, 2004).

Logistic growth models

Van Geert's (1991, 1994) pioneering work adapting growth models and ecological systems to model language development employs different aspects of DST. In this work, language growth is modeled using the same logistic equations that model competing resources in ecosystems. Language, in these models, is comparable to an ecosystem comprised of various subsystems that are in a complex relationship with each other, each vying for the finite resources that it requires to grow and change. Importantly, the carrying capacity of the system varies with changes in the demands made by each of the subsystems.

These models show the competition and trade-offs between the demands of different language forms, such as lexical and syntactic growth in children's language development. Van Geert's models also demonstrate tight interrelationships between phonological, lexical, and syntactic growth, as well as the continuous competition between lexical and syntactic growth, and/or phonological and lexical growth (van Geert, 1991, 1993, 1994). These models show how logistic growth models exhibit the same stage-like behavioral transitions in development we see in children's emerging language abilities. Finally, van Geert's models show "bootstrapping" effects between phonological, lexical, and syntactic subsystems, and "competition" for cognitive resources between subsystems, all in the absence of abstract rules.

Connectionist models

The focus of connectionist models is on the emergence of complex behavior in real time (Elman et al., 1996; O'Reilly & Munakata, 2000; Rumelhart & McClelland, 1986; Rumelhart et al., 1986). Using principles of neuroscience and computer simulations, connectionist accounts of language development demonstrate that seemingly rule-governed language forms emerge spontaneously from locally distributed information (e.g., Elman, 1995). From the connectionist perspective, what the child brings to the process of language development is neurological in nature (e.g., neurons with different structures found in different parts of the brain with differing firing thresholds and refractory periods), and this constrains the child's processing of information in the language learning environment.

The traditional, innately determined symbolic grammars are instead represented in a distributed manner through the local connections that vary in degree of connection weights – the micro-circuitry of the brain. Connectionist models show that the seemingly distinct "modular" aspects of language instead simply emerge from the intrinsic properties of language input. For example, children's over-regularization of regular past tense inflections as seen in their production of *goed* instead of *went* has been seen as evidence of a rule-based system. However, connectionist models show that these grammatical contrasts can arise from the same neural network's sensitivity to both the systematicity and frequency with which regular and irregular past tense forms occur in the extant language environment (e.g., Plunkett & Marchman, 1993).

Synergetics

The work of Thelen and colleagues has its roots in synergetics and its principles of self-organization of complex systems (Haken, 1983). Synergetics focuses on the most striking feature of biological systems – the emergence of behavior at the macroscopic level, behavior absent in the individual components of the system (Haken, 1993; Nicolis & Priogogine, 1989). This is known as *pattern complexity*, where the collective impact of the aggregation of interconnected components of the system is greater than the sum of the individual parts. This relationship between the components of a system is viewed as a synergetic one where they are temporally assembled in a functional, task-specific manner when under the influence of some external variable (Haken, 1996; Kelso, 1984; Kelso et al., 1986a; Kelso, Scholz, & Schöner, 1986b; Sadovsky, 1983).

Since principles of complexity hold across all levels of complexity; the "heuristic" value of the approach taken by Thelen and colleagues is such that the same principles of complexity can be extended to discussions of all conventional "stages" in children's language development. Development, from DST, is the emergence of "softly assembled" patterns due to the interaction between the intrinsic dynamics of the child and external conditions. To date, Thelen, Smith and colleagues have investigated two phenomena in language development – the sudden nonlinear change in the rate of children's developmental trajectories of the acquisition of object labels, and U-shaped patterns in language skills where children initially demonstrate mastery of a given language form and then suddenly seem to lose this mastery at points in development (e.g., Plunkett & Marchman, 1991).

Children produce their first words around their first birthday. Initially word learning is slow, with children requiring multiple exposures to learn the names of objects and often needing many exemplars of a category of words before they are able to extend the name of the object to other like kinds. As children become more efficient word learners, however, the rate at which they are able to learn new words increases substantially to the point that they need only hear the name of a novel object once to learn its label (Mervis & Bertrand, 1994). Children also begin to correctly extend the label to other objects sharing the same physical features at this same time (Jones, Smith, & Landau, 1991; Landau, Smith, & Jones, 1988; Markman, 1989; Smith, Jones, Landau, & Gershkoff-Stowe, 2002; Waxman & Hall, 1993).

What is curious is that when children have acquired about 75 words, their learning of nouns based upon their shape increases their attention to shape properties of other objects, which subsequently leads to an increase in learning names for new objects having the same shape and so on. This sudden attention to shapes of objects results in the acceleration of children's learning of object names based upon their shape (Smith, 2000). One question is whether this attention to shape is an innate tendency, a "shape bias" at this point in language development, or whether some other phenomenon is contributing to this sudden "snowball" effect. Research suggests that while this occurs naturally, children's prior history of word learning can be manipulated experimentally to examine whether the "language learning history" children bring to the word-learning task affects their learning of new words (Samuelson, 2002; Samuelson & Smith, 1999, 2000; Smith, 2000; Smith et al., 2002). In a series of studies, Smith and her colleagues showed that by training children to attend to shape (i.e., artificially creating a shape bias) before the point at which the shape bias typically occurs in development, the rate of children's noun learning outside the laboratory was accelerated by 300% in an 8-week period. This finding indicates that, at least for word learning, children's attention to different properties of objects may not be an innate feature but instead the collective representation of the child's prior language learning history, which influences all future aspects of language acquisition.

While children's language learning can appear stage-like when viewed globally, progressing toward ever-increasing complexity, when observed in detail it is marked not only by the sudden regression back to earlier developmental stages, but often by a sudden increase in errors before the acquisition of novel forms. While this often occurs as children begin to learn regular and irregular past tense verb forms (e.g., Plunkett & Marchman, 1991), another point where this occurs is when children mistakenly use the wrong name for an object for which they already know the name. This typically occurs when children suddenly start acquiring words at an accelerated rate. These naming errors continue and even increase after this vocabulary spurt (Dromi, 1987).

These instances when children "revert" back to performance characteristic of younger, less mature children have been interpreted in several ways: (1) the loss or abandonment of behavior (Bever, 1982), (2) the result of experimental methods which affect performance (Klahr, 1982), or (3) as behavioral changes, which give the appearance of U-shaped growth, but which are distinct from true representational changes (Karmiloff-Smith, 1992). Gershkoff-Stowe and Thelen argue that U-shaped patterns in development "are special cases of the nonlinearity that are the inevitable product of complex systems, composed of many, often heterogeneous parts which assemble themselves in different configurations depending on the status of the components, the environment, and the task" (Gershkoff-Stowe & Thelen, 2004, p. 12).

Gershkoff-Stowe and Smith (1997) investigated the naming skills of children before, during, and after the vocabulary spurt. Their analysis revealed a sudden substantial increase followed by an equally rapid decline in naming errors when children's word-learning rate was at its peak, when children had approximately 75 words in their productive vocabulary. The types of errors children made were in using the wrong word to name a familiar object. In particular, children would call the familiar object by a word they had just said which indicates that they had difficulty retrieving words from lexical memory. Gershkoff-Stowe and Smith suggest that these naming errors were the result of the weakening of access of familiar words in children's lexicons because of the rapid expansion of the lexicon.

In a second study Gershkoff-Stowe (2001) intentionally strengthened children's representations of specific words through practice to determine if this made them less vulnerable to interference from newly acquired words. From a DST perspective, the representations for newly emerging object labels are too weak to prevent the child from being "sucked" into older, more stable lexical states (Gershkoff-Stowe, 2001; Gershkoff-Stowe & Smith, 1997). This work suggests that word frequency may be one of the critical factors in accounting for naming errors at this point in development, with low-frequency, newly acquired words being more vulnerable to processing demands. Moreover, Gershkoff-Stowe's (2001) work shows that the child's prior history of use of certain words (e.g., more practiced) reduces their vulnerability to interference from other words as compared with less practiced words.

These studies show how the types of words children learn in the first stages of development create an attractor for those types of words (e.g., shape-based categories of words) that subsequently narrows their attention, shifting it away from learning other types of words. The emphasis of Thelen, Smith, and colleagues' approach is on how prior learning states influence future language learning – the *developmental language trajectory*. This work demonstrates that at any point in time, children's emerging language is the instantaneous, functional, organization of the components of the child's system to meet the demands of real-time communication. This emergence of language is a reflection not only of the intrinsic dynamics of the child, but also of the child's entire language learning history, current preferred states, and the extrinsic dynamics of the immediate context (Corbetta & Thelen, 1996; Fischer, Rotenberg, Bullock, & Raya, 1993; Smith & Thelen, 1993; Thelen & Ulrich, 1991).

An epigenetic landscape: From babbling to first words

Thelen and colleagues often use Waddington's epigenetic landscape to conceptualize moment-to-moment language processing and language development as integrated phenomena (Waddington, 1954, 1957, 1977). Figure 7.1 shows such a landscape. In the landscape, three dimensions are represented: (1) time, (2) emergent behavior, and (3) the relative stability of the system at any point in time (e.g., depth of the attractors – preferred organizational states of a system). Starting at the back and working forward, the surface of the landscape represents the irreversible process of development – the evolving attractor landscape. The cross-section is the likelihood of an attractor state occurring at a given moment in time. Each of the cross-lines in the figure represents the multi-attractor character of development at that point in time. The depth of the attractor landscape visually represents the stability of the system when in that self-organized state. The height of the surface is the sensitivity of the system when in that self-organized state to external perturbations from the environment. All of the levels are completely co-dependent. As a result, the landscape is self-organizing through the entire developmental process.

"Learning" in biological complex systems is synonymous with changes in the underlying attractor landscape due to input to the system (Haken, 1996). The accumulated

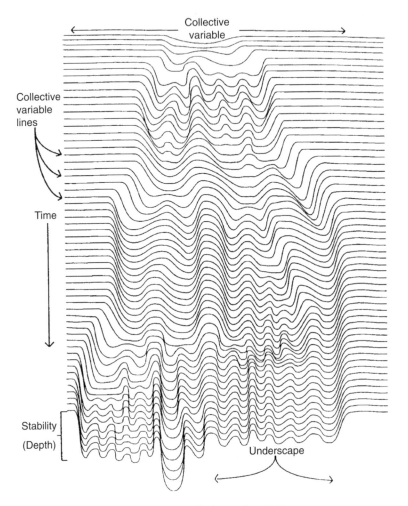

Figure 7.1 Dynamic attractor landscape (Muchisky et al., 1996).

effect of repeated real-time ordered states gives rise to the emergence of new collective behavioral states and the disappearance of developmentally older states (Haken, 1996). These ordered states will be more or less stable and coherent, and will always be a reflection of the underlying architecture of an individual's representational multi-attractor landscape (van der Maas, 1998).

Muchisky et al. (1996) use this landscape to characterize the transition from babbling to first words. In this approach, the changing landscape for speech development reflects the interplay between the infant's changing articulatory system (intrinsic dynamics), the impact of continuous language input to the infant on the infant's underlying speech attractor landscape, and moment-to-moment extrinsic dynamics of the surrounding context (Figure 7.2).

The infant's attractor landscape is initially comprised of three attractors: nonreflexive sounds, crying sounds, and the reflexive sounds that the infant can produce at birth.

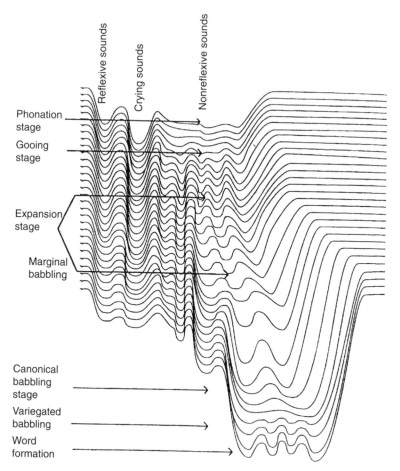

Figure 7.2   Evolving speech attractor landscape (Muchisky et al., 1996).

The infant's prior state includes all the exposure to speech up to that point in time, as well as all prior instances of sound production by the infant, all of which are continuously altering the properties of the underlying speech landscape. Changes in external conditions shift the infant into and out of reflexive, nonreflexive, and crying states. As the infant's vocal tract changes, vocal activity expands to include cooing and gooing, and variations in pitch and amplitude of vocalizations. New sounds appear on the speech landscape as multi-dimensional attractors, with rhythmic stereotypic sequences occurring at transitions to more coordinated activity at each stage. The infants' increasingly detailed phonological attractor landscape eventually begins to mirror the frequency of occurrence of speech sounds in the language environment.

Distinct phonological representational states gradually emerge in the attractor landscape due to the accumulating vocalizing experience, resulting in the emergence of more detailed and skilled speech production. The underlying "language" attractor landscape mirrors the properties of the language learning environment. Dynamic systems theory simultaneously predicts global similarities in the pattern of development across children, mirroring the global consistency of a given language, as well as individual differences across children reflecting the unique, idiosyncratic, language learning environment of each child.

Dyadic interactions and coupled dynamic complex systems

Language is social behavior that occurs within a communicative context (Searle, 1980). During dyadic interactions, individuals continuously alter their verbal behavior to converge to that of their speaking partners during ongoing discourse (Beebe, Jaffe, Feldstein, Mays, & Alson, 1985; Capella, 1988; Street, 1981). One critical dimension along which speakers converge is *timing* parameters such as response duration, and speaking rates (Capella, 1988; Street, 1981). Speakers' attempts to converge often result in individuals shifting from their preferred speaking rates to a third rate, that of the dyad. Developmental differences exist in the degree to which children shift to the adult's rate, with children as young as 5 attempting to match an adult's turn durations, response latencies, internal pauses, and speech rates (Welkowitz, Cariffe, & Feldstein, 1976).

In nature, complex systems constantly interact with each other. When the elements of one complex system influence the state of another system, we can talk about coupling of complex systems. Two systems are "coupled" if changes in the value of a parameter in one system influence the value of the same parameter in a second system. This is known as entrainment. Nonlinear dynamic models of the dyadic interactions of two independent complex systems show that (1) biological systems have a strong tendency to converge or coordinate at many different behavioral levels (Kelso et al., 1986a), and (2) changes in the behavior of one system can result in instability in the behavior of the second system (Buder, 1991). Research on the coupling or entrainment of two systems indicates that the problem of convergence is solved adaptively, whereby two systems alter temporal features to reach mutual relative coordination. Thus, entrained systems should be expected to match only along some dimensions, but not all dimensions.

Buder's (1991) logistic model of dyadic discourse interactions shows how the impact of changes in one speaker's behavior on another changes over time. The model captures how speakers converge on a range of discourse parameters such as degree of desire to participate and degree of other relatedness. When both speakers in the dyad have the same desire to participate in the interaction, the model converges easily. However, the model also shows that when the behavior of one speaker is altered continuously along a dimension (e.g., lack of willingness to participate, or no response on the listener's part) to the point where it reaches a critical threshold, the behavior of the second speaker becomes erratic and neither speaker in the dyad is able to converge. The instability and chaotic behavior of the dyad generated by the Buder (1991) model has been observed in the phase portraits of turn-by-turn behavior of children with specific language impairments who fail to meet the timing demands of dyadic interactions with an adult speaking partner. The result is the continuous breakdown in turn-taking between the adult examiner and the child when in conversation with children with language disorders (Evans, 1998, 2002).

These techniques, which capture the behavior of coupled complex systems, also provide the means to mathematically capture the state of the individual child's verbal system as it is shifted out of its preferred processing "state space" due to changes in the "external" discourse demands. They also show the degree to which caregivers and infants can converge along verbal and nonverbal dimensions during dyadic interactions (e.g., Fogel & Thelen, 1987; Hsu & Fogel, 2003; Newtson, 1998). These studies have important methodological implications. One common method of studying language development is to record children's spontaneous language during examiner–child, or parent–child, dyads and then study only the child's language productions in isolation. However, nonlinear dynamic models clearly show that there is no point at which children's language can be studied independent of the context within which the data are collected.

Each of the lines of work discussed so far demonstrate how, at any point in development, the emergence of language is the instantaneous, functional, organization of the components of the child's language system to meet the real-time communicative demands. Language abilities are a reflection not only of the intrinsic dynamics of the child, but also of the child's prior language learning history, current preferred states, and the extrinsic dynamics of the immediate context.

Mental Representations: Dynamic Field Theory and Connectionism

Any study of language development has to address the mind's representation of language. Earlier work in DST assumed that representations, if they even existed, were unlikely to play the kind of role in the brain that they play in the structure of computational systems (see Port & van Gelder, 1995). In contrast to connectionism, earlier DST approaches did not have a formalized theory of mental representations and learning. Dynamic field theory (DFT) addresses the issue of representational states (Erlhagen, Bastian, Jancke, Riehle, & Schöner, 1999; Erlhagen & Schöner, 2002; Schöner, Kopecz, & Erlhagen, 1997; Schutte & Spencer, 2002; Schutte, Spencer, & Schöner, 2003; Thelen et al., 2001).

In DFT, stability is a central tenet, allowing representational states to emerge from sensory-motor origins. Dynamic field theory makes a critical distinction between representations and representational states, however, invoking the time-dependent concept of activation consistent with mathematical psychology, connectionism, and theoretical neuroscience (Bates & Elman, 2000; Churchland & Sejnowski, 1992; Williams, 1986). Dynamic field theory grounds the representational states in the pre-cognitive era of the 1940s and 1950s where representational states were seen as actually re-presenting events of the environment in the nervous system. In DFT, representational states are activation fields that are mathematically defined across the dimensions being represented. To date, DFT has been extended primarily to the study of infant and children's spatial working memory for location (Schutte & Spencer, 2002; Schutte et al., 2003) and infant's perseverative reaching (e.g., Thelen et al., 2001). However, the use of a model that relies both on distributed representations while simultaneously incorporating changes in representational states via working memory stands to integrate connectionist modeling and classical DST into a more complete DST account of language development.

Conclusion

The predominant cognitivist approaches provide little guidance to the study of language competence and performance as an integrate phenomenon which emerges in real time as a continual process of change. In DST, moment-to-moment language processing and the longer timecourse of development are the same phenomenon simply viewed on different timescales. Real-time language processing is the spontaneous self-organization of the system as it moves into and out of different meaning attractors, whereas language development is the change in this same underlying attractor language landscape due to input to the system. There is no distinction between "competence" and "performance" in DST. Instead, language is always and only performance within context. As Thelen (1995) notes, "even though some preferred states of the system will be so stable that they may 'look' like they are the result of symbolic rules, or stages in development, the stability of the child's multi-attractor language landscape is a function of the child-in-context, always. In other words, development looks stage-like only because in the immediate assembly of the activity within context, certain patterns are strongly preferred" (p. 77).

Dynamic systems theory is the study of self-organized, emerging patterns of complex systems. Its strength is its focus on the stability and the variability of emerging language abilities. Dynamic systems theory provides a set of assumptions regarding how language is organized and changes over time. It provides an approach to empirically unlock the nature of these patterns as they change in real time as well as a framework to integrate the study of development from the neurophysiology of embodied representations as intentional communication grounded within the socially communicative context. It does not tell researchers which language patterns to study, the nature of the interaction between the child and the observational context, nor the key features of the child's prior learning history that influence later language learning. These must be discovered. Dynamic systems theory does provide a clear starting point, however. It is at points of instability – the noisy, messy, unpredictable points in the emergence of language – that the underlying dynamics of the emergence of language in children will be revealed. By not holding experimental conditions constant, but instead intentionally changing experimental conditions in clearly specified ways, researchers will be able to understand more fully the process of the emergence of language in children.

References

Barsalou, L. W. (1999). Perceptual symbol systems. *Behavioral and Brain Sciences, 22*, 577–660.

Bates, E., Beeghly-Smith, L., Bretherton, I., & McNew, S. (1983). Social basis of language development: A reassessment. In H. Reese & L. P. Lipsitt (Eds.), *Advances in child development and behavior: Vol. 16* (pp. 8–75). New York: Academic Press.

Bates, E., Begnigni, L., Bretherton, I., Camaioni, L., & Volterra, V. (1979). *The emergence of symbols: Cognitive and communication in infancy.* New York: Academic Press.

Bates, E., & Elman, J. (2000). The ontogeny and phylogeny of language: A neural network perspective. In S. T. Parker & J. Langer (Eds.), *Biology, brains, and behavior: The evolution of human development* (pp. 89–130). Santa Fe, NM: School of American Research Press.

Bates, E., & Snyder, L. (1987). The cognitive hypothesis in language development. In I. Uzgiris & J. McV. Hunt (Eds.), *Research with scales of psychological development in infancy* (pp. 168–206). Champaign, IL: University of Illinois Press.

Beebe, B., Jaffe, J., Feldstein, S., Mays, K., & Alson, D. (1985). Interpersonal timing: The applications of an adult dialogue model to mother–infant vocal and kinesthetic interactions. In T. Field & N. Fox (Eds.), *Social perception in infants* (pp. 217–247). Norwood, NJ: Ablex.

Bever, T. G. (1982). *Regressions in mental development: Basic phenomena and theories.* Hillsdale, NJ: Lawrence Erlbaum Associates.

Bohannon, J. N., & Warren-Leubecker, A. (1988). Recent development in child-directed speech: You've come a long way, baby-talk. *Language Sciences, 10*, 89–110.

Bowerman, M. (1982). Re-organizational processes in lexical and syntactic development. In E. Wanner & I. Gleitman (Eds.), *Language acquisition: The state of the art.* Cambridge: Cambridge University Press.

Buder, E. H. (1986). Coherence of speech rhythms in conversations: Autocorrelation analysis of fundamental voice frequency. *Toronto Semiotic Circle Monograph.*

Buder, E. H. (1991). A nonlinear dynamic model of social interaction. *Communication Research, 18*, 174–198.

Buder, E. H. (1996). Dynamics of speech processes in dyadic interactions. In J. H. Watt & C. A. VanLear (Eds.), *Dynamic patterns in communication processes* (pp. 301–325). Thousand Oaks, CA: Sage.

Buder, E. H., & Eriksson, A. (1997). Prosodic cycles and interpersonal synchrony in American English and Swedish. *Proc. Eurospeech, 1*, 235–238.

Capella, J. (1988). Interaction patterns and social interpersonal relationships. In S. Duck (Ed.), *Handbook of social and personal relationships.* New York: Guildford Press.

Chomsky, N. (1982). *Lectures on government and binding.* New York: Foris.

Chomsky, N. (1988). *Language and the problems of knowledge.* Cambridge, MA: MIT Press.

Churchland, P. S., & Sejnowski, T. J. (1992). *The computational brain.* Cambridge, MA: Bradford Book/MIT Press.

Corbetta, D., & Thelen, E. (1996). The developmental origins of bimanual coordination: A dynamic systems perspective. *Journal of Experimental Psychology: Human Perception and Performance, 22*, 502–522.

Dromi, E. (1987). *Early lexical development.* Cambridge: Cambridge University Press.

Elman, J. (1995). Language as a dynamical system. In R. F. Port & T. van Gelder (Eds.), *Mind as motion.* Cambridge, MA: MIT Press.

Elman, J. (2001). Connectionism and language acquisition. In M. Tomasello & E. Bates (Eds.), *Language development: The essential readings* (pp. 295–306). Malden, MA: Blackwell Publishers.

Elman, J. (2003). Development: It's about time. *Developmental Science, 6*, 430–433.

Elman, J., Bates, E., Johnson, M., Karmiloff-Smith, A., Parisi, D., & Plunkett, K. (1996). *Rethinking innateness: A connectionist perspective on development.* Cambridge, MA: MIT Press.

Erlhagen, W., Bastian, A., Jancke, D., Riehle, A., & Schöner, G. (1999). The distribution of neuronal population activation (dpa) as a tool to study interactions and integration in cortical representations. *Journal of Neural-science Methods, 94*, 53–66.

Erlhagen, W., & Schöner, G. (2002). Dynamic field theory of movement preparation. *Psychological Review, 109*, 545–572.

Evans, J. L. (1998). *Verbal and nonverbal discourse cues in nonlinear dynamic models of discourse.* American Psychological Associate Annual Meeting, Washington, DC.

Evans, J. L. (2002). Variability in comprehension strategy use in children with SLI: A dynamical systems account. *International Journal of Language and Communication Disorders, 37,* 95–116.

Fischer, K. W., Rotenberg, E. J., Bullock, D. H., & Raya, P. (1993). The dynamics of competence: How context contributes directly to skill. In R. H. Wozniak & K. W. Fischer (Eds.), *Development in context: Acting and thinking in specific environments* (pp. 93–117). Hillsdale, NJ: Lawrence Erlbaum Associates.

Fogel, A., & Thelen, E. (1987). Development of early expressive and communicative action: Reinterpreting the evidence from a dynamic systems perspective. *Developmental Psychology, 23,* 747–761.

Ford, D. H., & Lerner, R. M. (1992). *Developmental systems theory: An integrative approach.* Newbury Park, CA: Sage.

Gershkoff-Stowe, L. (2001). The course of children's naming errors in early word learning. *Journal of Cognition and Development, 2,* 131–155.

Gershkoff-Stowe, L., & Smith, L. B. (1997). A curvilinear trend in naming errors as a function of early vocabulary growth. *Cognitive Psychology, 34,* 37–71.

Gershkoff-Stowe, L., & Thelen, E. (2004). U-shaped changes in behavior: A dynamic systems approach. *Journal of Cognition and Development, 5,* 11–36.

Gleason, J. B. (1977). Some notes on feedback. In C. E. Snow & C. A. Ferguson (Eds.), *Talking to children: Language input and acquisition.* Cambridge: Cambridge University Press.

Haken, H. (1983). *Synergetics, an introduction.* New York: Springer-Verlag.

Haken, H. (1993). *Advance synergetics: Instability hierarchies of self-organizing systems and devices.* New York: Springer-Verlag.

Haken, H. (1996). *Principles of brain functioning: A synergetic approach to brain activity, behavior and cognition.* Berlin, Germany: Springer-Verlag.

Harnad, S. (1990). The symbol grounding problem. *Physica, D, 42,* 335–346.

Hebb, D. O. (1949). *The organization of behavior.* New York: Wiley.

Hsu, H. C., & Fogel, A. (2003). Stability and transitions in mother–infant face-to-face communication during the first 6 months: A micro-historical approach. *Developmental Psychology, 39,* 1061–1082.

Jones, S. S., Smith, L. B., & Landau, B. (1991). Object properties and knowledge in early lexical learning. *Child Development, 62,* 499–516.

Karmiloff-Smith, A. (1992). *Beyond modularity: A developmental perspective on cognitive science.* Cambridge, MA: MIT Press.

Kelso, J. A. S. (1984). Phase transitions and critical behavior in human bimanual coordination. *American Journal of Physiology: Regulatory, Integrative, and Comparative Physiology, 15,* 1000–1004.

Kelso, J. A. S., Ding, M., & Schöner, G. (1986a). Dynamic pattern formation: A tutorial. In L. B. Smith & E. Thelen (Eds.), *A dynamic systems approach to development: Applications* (pp. 13–50). Boston, MA: MIT Press.

Kelso, J. A. S., Scholz, J. P., & Schöner, G. (1986b). Non-equilibrium phase transitions in coordinated biological motion: Critical fluctuations. *Physic Letters A, 118,* 279–284.

Klahr, D. (1982). Non-monotone assessment of monotone development: An information processing analysis. In S. Strauss (Ed.), *U-shaped behavioral growth* (pp. 63–86). New York: Academic Press.

Landau, B., Smith, L. B., & Jones, S. S. (1988). The importance of shape in early lexical learning. *Cognitive Development, 3,* 299–321.

Lewis, M. D. (2000). The promise of dynamic systems approaches for an integrated account of human development. *Child Development, 71,* 36–43.

Markman, E. M. (1989). *Categorization and naming in children*. Cambridge, MA: MIT Press.

Mervis, C. D., & Bertrand, J. (1994). Acquisition of the novel name–nameless category principle. *Child Development, 65*, 1646–1662.

Mowrer, O. H. (1960). *Learning theory and the symbolic process*. New York: Wiley.

Muchisky, M., Gershkoff-Stowe, L., Cole, E., & Thelen, E. (Eds.). (1996). *The epigenetic landscape revisited: A dynamic interpretation: Vol. 10*. Greenwood Publishing.

Newtson, D. (1998). Dynamical systems and the structure of behavior. In K. M. Newell & P. C. Molenaar (Eds.), *Applications of nonlinear dynamics to developmental process modeling* (pp. 199–220). Mahwah, NJ: Lawrence Erlbaum Associates.

Nicolis, G., & Priogogine, I. (1989). *Exploring complexity: An introduction*. New York: W. H. Freeman & Company.

O'Reilly, R. C., & Munakata, Y. (2000). *Computational explorations in cognitive neuroscience: Understanding the mind by simulating the brain*. Cambridge, MA: MIT Press.

Osgood, C. (1963). *Method and theory in experimental psychology*. New York: Oxford University Press.

Ott, E. (1993). *Chaos in dynamical systems*. Cambridge: Cambridge University Press.

Oyama, S. (1985). *The ontogeny of information: Developmental systems and evolution*. Cambridge, MA: Cambridge University Press.

Pinker, S. (1984). *Language learnability and language development*. Cambridge, MA: Harvard University Press.

Plunkett, K., & Marchman, V. (1991). U-shaped learning and frequency effects in a multi-layered perceptron: Implications for child language acquisition. *Cognition, 38*, 43–102.

Plunkett, K., & Marchman, V. (1993). From rote learning to system building: Acquiring verb morphology in children and connectionist nets. *Cognition, 48*, 21–69.

Port, R. F., & van Gelder, T. (1995). *Mind as motion*. Cambridge, MA: MIT Press.

Rumelhart, D. E., & McClelland, R. J. (1986). On learning the past tenses of English verbs. In R. J. McClelland & D. E. Rumelhart (Eds.), *Parallel distributed processing: Explorations in the microstructure of cognition: Vol. 2*. Cambridge, MA: MIT Press.

Rumelhart, D. E., McClelland, R. J., & Group, T. P. R. (Eds.). (1986). *Parallel distributed processing: Explorations in the microstructure of cognition: Vol. 1. Foundations*. Cambridge, MA: MIT Press.

Sadovsky, N. N. (1983). Systems theory. In R. Harré & R. Lamb (Eds.), *The encyclopedic dictionary of psychology* (pp. 623–625). Oxford: Blackwell.

Samuelson, L. K. (2002). Statistical regularities in vocabulary guide language acquisition in connectionist models and 15–20-month-olds. *Developmental Psychology, 36*, 1016–1037.

Samuelson, L. K., & Smith, L. B. (1999). Early noun vocabularies: Do ontology, category, organization and syntax correspond? *Cognition, 73*, 1–33.

Samuelson, L. K., & Smith, L. B. (2000). Children's attention to rigid and deformable shape in naming and non-naming tasks. *Child Development, 71*, 1555–1570.

Schöner, G., Kopecz, K., & Erlhagen, W. (1997). The dynamic neural field theory of motor programming: Arm and eye movements. In P. G. Morasso & V. Sanguineti (Eds.), *Self-organization, computational maps and motor control: Vol. 119* (pp. 271–310). Amsterdam: Elsevier-North Holland.

Schutte, A. R., & Spencer, J. (2002). Generalizing the dynamic field theory of the a-not-b error beyond infancy: Three-year-olds' delay- and experience-dependent location memory biases. *Child Development, 73*, 377–404.

Schutte, A. R., Spencer, J., & Schöner, G. (2003). Testing the dynamic field theory: Working memory for locations becomes more spatially precise over development. *Child Development, 74*, 1393–1417.

Searle, J. R. (1980). Minds, brains and programs. *Behavioral and Brain Sciences, 3*, 417–457.

Skinner, B. F. (1957). *Verbal behavior.* Englewood Cliffs, NJ: Prentice-Hall.

Smith, L. B. (2000). Learning how to learn words: An associative crane. In K. Hirsh-Pasek (Ed.), *Becoming a word learner: A debate on lexical acquisition* (pp. 51–80). New York: Oxford University Press.

Smith, L. B., Jones, S. S., Landau, B., & Gershkoff-Stowe, L. (2002). Object naming learning provides on-the-job training for attention. *Psychological Science, 13*, 13–19.

Smith, L. B., & Thelen, E. (Eds.). (1993). *A dynamic systems approach to development: Applications.* Cambridge, MA: MIT Press.

Snow, C. E. (1979). The role of social interaction in language acquisition. In W. A. Collins (Ed.), *Minnesota symposia on child psychology: Vol. 12.* Hillsdale, NJ: Lawrence Erlbaum Associates.

Snow, C. E. (1989). Understanding social interaction and language acquisition: Sentences are not enough. In M. Bornstein & J. Brunner (Eds.), *Interactions in human development* (pp. 83–104). Hillsdale, NJ: Lawrence Erlbaum Associates.

Spencer, J., & Schöner, G. (2003). Bridging the representational gap in the dynamic systems approach to development. *Developmental Science, 6*, 392–412.

Staats, A. (1971). Linguistic-mentalistic theory versus an explanatory s-r learning theory of language development. In D. I. Slobin (Ed.), *The ontogenesis of grammar.* New York: Academic Press.

Street, R. L. (1981). Evaluation of convergence in mother–child conversations. *Social Communication, 36*, 87–95.

Tabor, W., Juliano, C., & Tanenhaus, M. (1997). Parsing in dynamical systems: An attractor-based account of the interaction of lexical and structural constraints in sentence processing. *Language and Cognitive Processes, 12*, 211–271.

Thelen, E. (1989). Self-organization in developmental processes: Can systems approaches work? In M. Gunnar & E. Thelen (Eds.), *Systems and development: Minnesota symposia on child psychology: Vol. 22* (pp. 77–117). Hillsdale, NJ: Lawrence Erlbaum Associates.

Thelen, E. (1995). Time-scale dynamics and the development of an embodied cognition. In R. F. Port & T. van Gelder (Eds.), *Mind in motion.* Cambridge, MA: MIT Press.

Thelen, E., Corbetta, D., & Spencer, J. (1996). The development of reaching during the first year: The role of movement speed. *Journal of Experimental Psychology: Human Perception and Performance, 22*, 1059–1076.

Thelen, E., & Fischer, D. M. (1982). Newborn stepping: An explanation for a "disappearing reflex." *Developmental Psychology, 18*, 760–770.

Thelen, E., Schöner, G., Scheier, C., & Smith, L. B. (2001). The dynamics of embodiment: A field theory of infant perseverative reaching. *Behavioral and Brain Sciences, 24*, 1–86.

Thelen, E., & Smith, L. B. (1994). *A dynamic systems approach to the development of cognition and action.* Cambridge, MA: MIT Press.

Thelen, E., & Ulrich, B. D. (1991). Hidden skills: A dynamical systems analysis of treadmill stepping during the first year. *Monographs of the Society for Research in Child Development, 56* (233).

Thom, R. (1975). *Structural stability and morphogenesis.* Reading: Benjamin.

Van der Maas, H. L. J. (1998). The dynamical and statistical properties of cognitive strategies: Relations between strategies, attractors, and latent classes. In K. M. Newell & P. C. M. Molenaar (Eds.), *Applications of nonlinear dynamics to developmental process modeling* (pp. 161–176). Mahwah, NJ: Lawrence Erlbaum Associates.

Van der Maas, H. L. J., & Molenaar, P. C. (1992). Stage-wise cognitive development: An application of catastrophe theory. *Psychological Review, 99*, 395–417.

Van Geert, P. (1991). A dynamic systems model of cognitive and language growth. *Psychological Review*, *98*, 3–53.

Van Geert, P. (1993). A dynamic systems model of cognitive growth: Competition and support under limited resources conditions. In L. B. Smith & E. Thelen (Eds.), *A dynamic systems approach to development: Applications*. Cambridge, MA: MIT Press.

Van Geert, P. (1994). *Dynamic systems of development*. London: Harvester Wheatsheaf.

Van Geert, P. (1998). A dynamic systems model of cognitive and language growth. *Psychological Review*, *98*, 3–53.

Verela, F. J., Thompson, E., & Rosch, E. (1996). *The embodied mind*. Cambridge, MA: MIT Press.

Waddington, C. H. (1954). The integration of gene-controlled processes and its bearing on evolution. *Proceedings of the 9th International Conference of Genetics*, *9*, 232–245.

Waddington, C. H. (1957). *The strategy of the genes*. London: Allen & Unwin.

Waddington, C. H. (1977). *Tools for thought*. London: Allen & Unwin.

Waxman, S. R., & Hall, D. G. (1993). The development of a linkage between count nouns and object categories: Evidence from fifteen- to twenty-one-month-old infants. *Child Development*, *64*, 1224–1241.

Welkowitz, J., Cariffe, G., & Feldstein, S. (1976). Conversational congruence as a criterion of socialization in children. *Child Development*, *47*, 296–272.

Williams, R. J. (1986). The logic of activation functions. In D. E. Rumelhart, R. J. McClelland & T. P. R. Group (Eds.), *Parallel distributed processing: Explorations in the microstructure of cognition: Vol. 1. Foundations* (pp. 423–443). Cambridge, MA: MIT Press.

PART II

Language Development in Infancy

Introduction

The ingredients that produce language acquisition, when combined, are a human infant and exposure to speech. The chapters in this Part ask what in human infants, what in the speech they hear, and what internal processes produce this reliably obtained result. Four chapters address these questions, describing the infant's starting state and the processes and outcomes of the language learning that takes place in the first years of life. Polka, Rvachew, and Mattock describe the development of speech perception and production as resulting from the interaction of three factors: infants' initial perceptual capacities and biases, the language(s) to which infants are exposed, and infants' perceptions of the sounds they themselves produce. On the perception side, intake capacities and input properties tune an "emerging language filter" with the result that infants become less sensitive to some contrasts the language does not use and more sensitive to some the language does use. The full developmental pattern is more complex than this, however, and Polka et al. also set out for us the phenomena that, at this point, await an explanatory framework. On the production side, Polka et al. describe a process in which infants use adult input to form representations of the target sounds and use their perceptions of self-produced speech to adapt their articulatory gestures to produce those targets.

Gerken describes infants as bringing to the language learning task the capacity to detect patterns in input and to generalize from these detected patterns, given sufficient evidence. As a result of applying these capacities to the input they receive, infants know about the sound sequences that make possible words in their language and something about the word sequences that make possible sentences in their language well before they produce these forms or understand their meanings.

Whereas the chapters by Polka et al. and Gerken describe the infant's acquisition of language form, the chapters by Poulin-Dubois and Graham and by Naigles and Swensen address how infants (and toddlers) learn the mappings from language forms to meaning.

Poulin-Dubois and Graham review evidence regarding the cognitive understandings that infants bring to the task of learning words. Before acquiring language, infants organize their world into individuated objects and they parse the ongoing flow of activity into separable events. This cognitive organization supports, but does not explain, lexical development. Poulin-Dubois and Graham also describe effects of language on categorization and developmental changes in how children bring nonlinguistic processes to bear as they acquire the vocabulary of their language.

Naigles and Swensen make the argument that very young children approach the word learning task already knowing something about syntax and the correspondences between syntax and semantics. Some syntax/semantics correspondences might be universal and available to children before 18 months; others are language specific and must be learned, but even these are operating at 24 months. For the child who can make use of syntax/ semantics correspondences, the task of figuring out the meaning of newly encountered words is not just a matter of finding the referent in the world. There are clues to word meaning in the syntactic frame that surrounds the word.

Together these chapters describe a very competent infant who enters the world with perceptual and learning capacities that bias the infant to attend to speech, to extract patterns from that to which they attend, and to generalize these patterns. As a result, very young children have the ability to segment the speech stream and to recognize the recurring sequences that are the words and sentences of their language. As they begin the task of finding the meanings of the words they encounter, infants rely on both their cognitive organization of the world and the information provided by the structures in which words appear.

8

Experiential Influences on Speech Perception and Speech Production in Infancy

Linda Polka, Susan Rvachew, and Karen Mattock

Mature language users are highly specialized, expert, and efficient perceivers and producers of their native language. This expertise begins to develop in infancy, a time when the infant acquires language-specific perception of native language phonetic categories and learns to produce speech-like syllables in the form of canonical babble. The emergence of these skills is well described by past research but the precise mechanisms by which these foundational abilities develop have not been identified.

This chapter provides an overview of what is currently known about the impact of language experience on the development of speech perception and production during infancy. Throughout we affirm that experiential influences on phonetic development cannot be understood without considering the interaction between the constraints that the child brings to the task and the nature of the environmental input. In the perception and production domains our current understanding of this interaction is incomplete and tends to focus on the child as a passive receiver of input. In our review, we signal a recent shift in research attention to the infant's role in actively selecting and learning from the input.

We begin this chapter by describing what is currently known about the determinants of speech perception and speech production development during infancy while highlighting important gaps to be filled within each domain. We close by emphasizing the need to integrate research across the perception and production domains.

Speech Perception Development

Speech perception development involves a complex interaction between the child and his/her language environment(s). In this section we discuss when and how language input begins to shape speech perception and then consider how speech intake is directed and constrained from the infant side of the interaction. This discussion focuses on the development of speech perception at the segmental or phonetic level, that is, the perception of consonants, vowels, and tones.

Effects of age and language input

Developmental cross-linguistic research has shown that from the first few months of life the ambient language begins to guide the infant toward the goal of language-specific speech perception. Werker and collaborators conducted the first systematic investigations of the effects of age and language experience on phonetic perception. In a series of studies, they found that 6- to 8-month-old English infants and native adult speakers discriminated Hindi and Salish contrasts equally well, but discrimination declined with age for infants tested at 8 to 10 and at 10 to 12 months and was poor for English adults; no decline in discrimination over age was reported for Hindi and Salish infants (Werker, Gilbert, Humphrey, & Tees, 1981; Werker & Tees, 1983, 1984a). These findings showed that infants initially respond to phonetic differences in a language-neutral way but their perception becomes more language-specific by the end of the first year of life.

Werker's findings were initially interpreted as showing that the absence of language experience results in a "loss" of perceptual function. This meshed well with the idea that language experience sets up a perceptual filter for speech, an idea that first emerged to explain poor perception of non-native phonetic contrasts by adults (e.g., Miyawaki et al., 1975). Subsequent developmental cross-linguistic research expanded to include a wider variety of phonetic contrasts from many languages, including consonants, vowels, and tones, as well as more varied infant groups, including infants acquiring languages other than English and infants learning more than one language simultaneously. Now that we have a more detailed picture of the changes in phonetic perception that are shaped by experience with a specific language during infancy, it is time to reassess the filter analogy. For this reason, we will summarize developmental and cross-linguistic research by considering what this work tells us about the functional properties of the native language filter that is emerging in infancy. In the current literature it is clear that the process by which infants arrive at language-specific phonetic perception is more complex than the original interpretation of the early studies by Werker and colleagues. The diverse developmental patterns of speech perception that we describe show that the emerging filter is active and can operate to facilitate as well as to attenuate access to phonetic differences. Furthermore, these patterns reflect an emerging native language filter that is sensitive to the demands of the perceptual task (discrimination vs. labeling), the stimulus domain of the test materials (speech vs. non-speech), and the functional status of the phonetic elements in the native language (phonemic vs. non-phonemic; segmental vs. non-segmental).

Developmental patterns in non-native phonetic perception.   The initial view of a "loss" of non-native phonetic perception was re-interpreted when it was found that adult perception of native and non-native contrasts is comparable when task demands are reduced (e.g., Werker & Logan, 1985; Werker & Tees, 1984b), therefore confirming that the perceptual filter established by language experience is not absolute. Similarly, infant speech perception patterns are not so simple. Research clearly indicated that the native language filter emerging in infancy is *domain-specific* and does not impact how infants perceive sounds that are not recognized as speech. The first cross-linguistic evidence to support this claim was provided by Best, McRoberts, and Sithole (1988). They found that English infants failed to show a decline in discrimination of a non-native consonant contrast (lateral–apical clicks) from the Zulu language. The domain-specificity of the native language filter in infants is also confirmed by a study of tone perception in infants. In this study 6- and 9-month-old non-tone (English) and tone language infants (Chinese: Cantonese or Mandarin) were tested on discrimination of lexical tone contrasts cued mostly by fundamental frequency (F0: perceived as speakers' pitch) and non-speech tone analogs with the same F0 differences (Mattock & Burnham, 2006). There was a decline in discrimination over age for lexical tone contrasts in English but not Chinese infants. Discrimination level for non-speech tone was maintained over age for both language groups.

Mattock and Burnham's work (2006) shows that the native language filter operates in a *functionally specific* way – the ability to interpret F0 as a segmental cue was maintained only by infants acquiring a language in which F0 has a segmental (as opposed to a suprasegmental) function. Functional specificity of the native language filter is also supported by findings of Pegg and Werker (1997) showing that infants also fail to maintain perception of an allophonic difference, a phonetic difference that occurs regularly in the ambient language but is not used to signal differences in word meaning. They found that English infants' perception of two allophones of English /p/ – a voiceless aspirated bilabial stop (e.g., the first consonant in "pie") and a voiceless unaspirated bilabial stop (e.g., the second consonant in "spy") – declined between 6–8 and 10–12 months of age despite their exposure to each phone in different phonological contexts.

Cross-linguistic research on the perception of segmental contrasts reveals differences in the timing of the perceptual decline across different non-native contrasts – 6 to 12 months for consonant contrasts (Best, 1995; Best et al., 1990; Best, McRoberts, LaFleur, & Silver-Isenstadt, 1995; Bosch & Sebastián-Gallés, 2003b; Eilers, Gavin, & Oller, 1982; Tsao, Liu, Kuhl, & Tseng, 2000; Tsushima et al., 1994), 6 to 8 months for vowel contrasts (Best et al., 1997; Bosch & Sebastián-Gallés, 2003a; Polka & Werker, 1994), and 6 to 9 months for lexical tone[1] (Mattock & Burnham, 2006).

Although attenuation with age is often observed for perception of non-native contrasts, this is not the only reported developmental pattern. Some non-native contrasts remain discriminable through the native language filter, including certain consonant (see Best, 1991, 1995; Best et al., 1990; Polka, Colantonio, & Sundara, 2001) and vowel contrasts (see Polka & Bohn, 1996). In these studies discrimination levels are consistently quite high across development.[2] It is not yet clear what these findings tell us about the emerging native language filter.

Developmental patterns in native phonetic perception.   There is increasing evidence that varied developmental patterns are also observed for *native* language phonetic perception. We observed a facilitative effect of native language experience in our lab when we compared monolingual English and monolingual French listeners in four age groups (6–8 months; 10–12 months; 4 years; adults) on their perception of English /d/ versus /ð/, a contrast that is not phonemic in French. English perceivers showed significant improvement in discrimination of the English /d–ð/ contrast between 10–12 months and 4 years, and further improvement between 4 years and adulthood; French perceivers showed no change with age (Polka et al., 2001; Sundara, Polka, & Genesee, 2006). Tsao et al. (2000) also found evidence for native language facilitation in Chinese-learning infants' perception of a native fricative–affricate contrast. These findings challenge the long established view that language experience serves *only* to prevent a developmental decline in perceptual discrimination of some contrasts. The evidence for facilitation as well as maintenance demonstrates that the language filter is *active*: it can enhance as well as reduce accessibility to phonetic contrasts.

An age-related decline in discrimination in infancy has also been found for a native phonetic contrast, specifically English-learning infants' discrimination of the native /s–z/ fricative voicing contrast (Best & McRoberts, 2003). This finding indicates that some phonetic differences are less salient than others irrespective of language experience, leading to different developmental patterns within the native language. Moreover, findings also show that infant perception of native contrasts also depends on the task at hand. For example, Stager and Werker (1997) observed that 14-month-old English-learning infants were unable to detect a native /bI–dI/ contrast when each syllable was paired with a moving object, but they succeeded when the syllables were paired with a static checkerboard pattern. The authors argue that differences in the task demands and overall processing load in these two tasks are important in understanding these differences in perception within the native language.

Research on infants being raised bilingually also suggests a complex pattern for native phonetic development. Bosch and Sebastián-Gallés (2003a) studied infants at different ages from three language groups (Spanish, Catalan, and bilingual Spanish/ Catalan). They examined their perception of the /ɛ–e/ vowel contrast which is phonemic in Catalan but not in Spanish and is difficult for monolingual speakers of Spanish to discriminate (Pallier, Bosch, & Sebastián, 1997). All three infant groups discriminated this contrast at 4 months of age. As expected, an attenuation of perception with age was observed for the Spanish infants but not for the Catalan infants. The bilingual group showed a U-shaped developmental pattern whereby discrimination declined between 4 and 8 months of age, but then improved to the level of native monolingual Catalan infants at 12 months. A U-shape developmental pattern was reported in two subsequent studies that examined consonant perception in bilingual and monolingual infants (Bosch & Sebastián-Gallés, 2003b; Burns, Werker, & McVie, 2003).

Note that this U-shape pattern was observed when bilingual infants were tested on contrasts that have a conflicting status across their two languages – native in one of the languages and non-native in the other. At present it is not known why perception of such contrasts reveals a temporary weak spot in the bilingual infant's emerging native language filter(s). The conflicting functional status, reduced exposure to such contrasts in the bilingual input, or both factors, may contribute to the U-shape pattern. Alternatively, the bilingual infant may construe the perceptual task differently than the monolingual infant. (See Werker, Hall, & Fais, 2004, for a discussion of U-shape developmental functions.) For now, these data pose a challenge and an opportunity for future research.

Overall, the developmental course that unfolds as infants begin tuning into the phonetic structure of their native language is not uniform. Diverse developmental patterns evident in perception of native and non-native phonetic categories reveal an emerging native language filter that operates in an active, task-specific, domain-specific, and functionally specific way to facilitate as well as to attenuate access to phonetic differences. To retain the filter analogy to conceptualize these assorted effects of language experience, our notion of a filter must be more sophisticated than a passive sieve. The filter evident in the existing data is more akin to a resonator, a filtering device that can selectively enhance as well as selectively attenuate an input signal. Even with a more appropriate analogy, there is no current conceptual framework that can predict when and explain how these diverse developmental patterns arise. (See Best & McRoberts, 2003, for a detailed discussion of hypotheses proposed to explain varied developmental patterns.) A better understanding of how language input is tied to developmental patterns is needed. There is little doubt that phonetic contrasts vary in perceptual salience in ways that are independent of linguistic function and impact perceptual development. One challenge for future research is to provide an acceptable metric to gauge this variation in perceptual salience and determine how it interacts with age and language experience. We must also understand other factors that impact speech intake in infants and explain how these factors interact with language input.

Variables influencing speech intake in infancy

To understand how language input shapes developmental changes in phonetic perception, we must identify factors that constrain and direct the infant's intake of speech information. Typically, researchers present stimuli in very quiet testing environments using test paradigms that tap a perceptual function defined by the experimenter, for example discrimination or categorization. This approach is informative yet it tells us very little about what happens when infants encounter speech in their everyday lives. Learning through exposure to the ambient language requires the infant to selectively attend to speech and detect relevant patterns in the speech stream. Outside the speech lab, infants encounter speech in presence of noise and other competing auditory and visual signals and are not explicitly reinforced for responding to specific phonetic elements. Unlike the speech presented in many laboratory studies, real language input consists of connected speech in which a critical feature or property of the language has not been isolated. Although very little is known about how infants gain access to relevant speech information "in the wild," some studies have explored this question by assessing what infants learn from a brief exposure to a corpus of speech that has been carefully structured by the researcher. Findings obtained using this artificial language approach to study phonetic and phonological development are described in Gerken (this volume). Our discussion will focus on two other lines of research that have explored speech intake in infants.

Effects of noise and hearing loss.   Infant speech perception is impacted by conditions that alter the amount or quality of language input available, such as the presence of hearing loss or the presence of background noise. Although hearing loss clearly impacts speech perception development, few systematic studies of its specific effects have been conducted with infants. Houston, Pisoni, Iler Kirk, Ying, and Miyamoto (2003) compared attention to a visual pattern, either paired with an auditory speech signal or with silence, by normal hearing and hearing impaired infants before and after cochlear implantation (CI). Their results demonstrate a strong impact of hearing loss on infant attention to speech. Normal hearing infants showed a strong preference for the stimulus trials with a speech signal. Hearing impaired infants showed no difference in looking time across speech and silent trials before CI; a preference for speech began to emerge in some infants 6 months after CI but was significantly weaker compared with normal hearing infants. Despite their poor selective attention to speech, the hearing impaired infants were able to discriminate an obvious vowel versus syllable difference ("ah" vs. "hop") in a laboratory test situation. However, poor attention to speech is likely to impact their processing of more subtle speech patterns in less optimal listening conditions.

We found that experience with otitis media with effusion (OME) also impacts infant responses to speech in the first year of life (Polka & Rvachew, 2005). Otitis media with effusion causes fluid to accumulate in the middle ear and can create a mild to moderate fluctuating conductive hearing loss. To assess effects of OME on phonetic discrimination, we tested 6- to 8-month-olds on a native phonetic contrast, /bu–gu/, using the conditioned headturn procedure. Tympanometry, performed after discrimination testing, revealed three groups of infants: (a) infants with middle ear effusion on test day, (b) infants who had received medical treatment for OM in the past but showing no middle ear effusion on test day, and (c) infants with no history of OM and no effusion on test day. Discrimination performance was best for infants with no history of OME and worst for infants with middle ear effusion on the day of testing. Infants with a history of OME but normal middle ear function on test day showed an intermediate level of discrimination performance, suggesting that OME negatively impacts phonetic perception even after the middle ear fluid is gone. Furthermore, the poorer performance in the history-only group (b above) cannot be explained as an effect of reduced audibility and suggests that experience with OME affects infant attention to speech.

Background noise present in many natural listening environments can also impede access to relevant speech patterns. When tested in presence of noise, infants can detect phonetic differences (Nozza, Miller, Rossman, & Bond, 1991), segment words from fluent speech (Newman & Jusczyk, 1996), and recognize their name (Newman, 2005) and their mother's voice (Barker & Newman, 2004). However, infants need substantially higher signal-to-noise ratios than adults to succeed at these tasks.

Noise acts to block access to relevant sensory information and pull attention away from the speech signal or critical parts of the speech signal. Although these effects are typically inseparable in the real world, it is informative to explore how each impacts infant perceptual processing. Moreover, as infants mature, their ability to control attention will improve whereas the sensory impact of noise is unlikely to change. In our lab, we tested infant phonetic perception using a distraction masker paradigm to assess the role of selective attention independently of sensory effects of noise (Polka, Rvachew, & Molnar, submitted). We tested infant discrimination of /bu/ versus /gu/ using a habituation procedure. To create a distractor condition a high frequency noise was added to the sound file of each syllable so that it gated on and off with the onset and offset of the syllable. The distractor noise was a recording of bird and cricket songs whose frequencies do not overlap with the test syllables; this added signal does not make it harder to hear the syllables but it can distract infants if they cannot focus their attention well. Infants (6–8 months) tested in quiet (i.e., unmodified syllables) performed significantly better than infants tested in the distractor condition; discrimination scores showed little overlap between the two groups. These findings indicate that perceiving auditory phonetic patterns in the presence of noise poses a substantial cognitive challenge for young infants. Recent findings suggest that the availability of multi-modal speech information – an auditory-visual speech stimulus – may provide the critical support that makes speech perception in noise possible for infants (Hollich, Newman, & Jusczyk, 2005).

Infant perceptual biases.   A second way that researchers have explored how infants access speech information is by observing their listening preferences in test paradigms that allow infants to control their access to speech samples. Infant listening preferences are evidence of perceptual biases that guide speech intake. Research has focused on biases related to suprasegmental or indexical properties of speech such as speaker's voice, affect, or stress (see Werker & Curtin, 2005). Recent research in our lab shows that infants display strong biases at the phonetic level as well. Our earlier cross-language studies of infant vowel discrimination revealed very robust and predictable directional asymmetries (see Polka & Bohn, 2003). For example, Polka and Werker (1994) found that infants who were presented with one direction of change, /y/ to /u/, found discrimination easier than infants presented with the same vowel pair in the reverse direction, that is, a change from /u/ to /y/. In this and other examples, we observed that vowel discrimination was consistently easier when infants were tested on a change from a less-peripheral to a more-peripheral vowel within the vowel space, suggesting that infant perception is sensitive to the structure of the vowel space. Subsequent research using a preferential listening task has confirmed that these directional asymmetries reflect a strong perceptual bias for peripheral vowels (i.e., vowels closer to the corners of the F1/F2 vowel space, /i/, /a/, /u/) – the same vowels that are strongly favored in vowel inventories across languages. Vowel biases measured in young infants are similar across infants learning different languages but change as language acquisition unfolds. Experiments with adults also show that the vowel biases observed in infancy have been shaped by language experience, toward optimizing vowel processing in a specific language. We can gain many insights into speech perception from the study of infant perceptual biases because they show us where the infants' perceptual priorities lie and point to the information that they are actively extracting from their input. Perceptual biases can also provide a relative index of perceptual salience and thus potentially help explain the variability in phonetic perception observed in the cross-language research described above.

In an effort to account for different aspects of speech perception development Werker and Curtin (2005) recently outlined a framework that integrates a wide range of speech perception phenomena (e.g., input effects, perceptual biases, word learning) within the broader context of language acquisition. The child's active intake of speech information is a prominent feature of their model, called PRIMIR (Processing Rich Information from Multidimensional Interactive Representations). According to PRIMIR three variables – initial biases, developmental level of the child, and task demands – act as dynamic filters and work together to direct the infant's attention to speech. Further research investigating speech intake processes is needed to test the merits of the PRIMIR model and to advance our overall knowledge of speech perception development.

We have outlined some functional properties of the native language filter that is emerging in early infancy and have discussed a recent shift in research focus toward factors that modulate speech intake in the developing infant. However, the story of infant speech perception is incomplete until we also understand how these perceptual processes interact with and are shaped by emerging speech production skills.

Speech Production Development

Recent developments in the study of infant speech production rest on the pioneering efforts of Oller (1980), Stark (1980), and Koopmans-van Beinum and van der Stelt (1986) to describe the course of infant speech development using metrics specially adapted to the infant context. Oller's (2000) comprehensive overview of this literature can be briefly summarized as follows: Normally developing infants universally progress through a series of stages of vocal development that culminate in the production of canonical babble, typically by 7 months of age; canonical babble is characterized by the production of speech-like consonant–vowel syllables, often produced as rhythmic strings of reduplicated syllables containing stop consonants and front or central vowels; and there is considerable continuity in the phonetic content of babble and early meaningful speech. More recent research has been directed at understanding the biological and experiential influences on the form of infant vocalizations.

Biological influences on early speech production

Vocal tract anatomy.   Major developmental changes in vocal tract shape occur shortly after birth, including the descent of the larynx and a sharper angle between the oral and pharyngeal cavities. A significant increase in the length of the vocal tract also occurs during the first year, with growth of the pharyngeal cavity being disproportionately large relative to oral cavity growth throughout development (Fitch & Giedd, 1999; Kent & Vorperian, 1995; Kent, Vorperian, Gentry, & Yandell, 1999).

The constraints that vocal tract morphology might place on infant speech output have been investigated through computer modeling by Ménard, Schwartz, and Boë (2002, 2004). Although infant vocal tract anatomy does partially explain the preference for low and front vowels, they demonstrated that the infant's vocal tract anatomy does not prevent the production of the full range of vowels used in the ambient language. However, while it is possible to produce vowels with an infant vocal tract that are perceptually equivalent to adult vowel categories, in many cases the infant would need to employ different articulatory gestures than the adult to achieve the same perceptual outcome. Ménard et al. (2002) also identified acoustic cues to vowel identity that are valid for the full range of vocal tract sizes. Therefore, infants can potentially perceive equivalency between their own vowel productions and those of adult models using the same normalization algorithms for speech-like vocalizations produced by talkers of all ages.

Speech motor control.   Infant speech production is clearly limited by immature speech motor control abilities although the exact nature of these limitations has not been fully determined. Indirect investigations of the infant's ability to control the vocal tract have been conducted within the context of the frame/content theory. MacNeilage (1998) proposed that the "frame" for speech production is the repeated opening and closing of the vocal tract. The ability to modulate the "frame" to produce varied "content" is hypothesized to emerge quite late in development, with "frame dominance" persisting through the early word learning stage. Consequently, very little individual variation in the phonetic content of babble or even early words is expected during infancy, within or across language groups. MacNeilage and Davis (2000) summarized a number of studies that provide support for this hypothesis in the form of apparently universal patterns of consonant and vowel co-occurrence. However, these results are based on phonetic transcriptions that are of questionable reliability and validity for infant speech.

Kinematic studies of infants' articulatory movements and acoustic analyses of infants' speech output have provided a more direct and reliable picture of physiological con-straints on infant speech production (Green, Moore, Higashikawa, & Steeve, 2000; Green, Moore, & Reilly, 2002; Sussman, Duder, Dalston, & Caciatore, 1999; Sussman, Minifie, Buder, Stoel-Gammon, & Smith, 1996). Overall these data are consistent with an initial dominance of the "mandibular frame," followed by a progressive differentiation of articulator movements. At the same time, rapid changes in speech motor control appear to be occurring during the first 4 months of the child's babbling experience, and limitations on infant control of the articulatory system do not prevent the infant from producing a wide variety of consonant–vowel combinations even during the first year. This leads to questions about how the infant achieves this ability, given a continuously changing vocal tract anatomy and limited speech motor control.

Guenther (1995) proposed a solution to the infant's problem in the form of a com-putational model (Directions in Articulatory space to Velocities in Articulator space; DIVA). A fundamental characteristic of this self-organizing model is that the goal of speaking is considered to be the production of certain acoustic products that will be perceived by the listener as the intended target sounds. Auditory perceptual feedback is used to develop the mapping between the acoustic target and the required vocal tract constrictions (Guenther, Hampson, & Johnson, 1998). Callan, Kent, Guenther, and Vorperian (2000) demonstrated that this model adapts well to developmental changes in vocal tract size and shape. This model predicts that access to both adult and self-produced speech is critical to the development of speech motor control. Adult input allows the infant to develop representations for language-specific acoustic–phonetic targets (as described above). Access to the infant's own speech allows the child to use auditory feedback to flexibly adapt articulatory gestures to achieve the production of those targets.

Experiential influences on speech production

Empirical investigations have demonstrated that auditory input is crucial for normal speech development during infancy. The emergence of the canonical babble stage is delayed in infants with sensory–neural hearing loss (Oller & Eilers, 1988) but canonical babble appears in the vocalizations of hearing impaired children shortly after they receive cochlear implants (Ertmer & Mellon, 2001). These studies do not, however, illuminate the exact nature of experiential influences on the course of prelinguistic vocal development. Oller (2000) suggests that a certain amount of auditory experience is required for "triggering the events that lead to well-formed syllable production" (p. 132). It is not clear that the specific phonetic content of the adult input is important to the process and indeed, no direct link between underlying perceptual representations and the characteristics of infant speech has been established. The dominant view posits that babbling is a strongly canalized motor behavior in which feedback of self-produced sounds serves to help the infant coordinate articulation and phonation (Koopmans-van Beinum, Clement, & van den Dikkenberg-Pot, 2001) or regulate the temporal rhythm of babble, in a manner similar to the way in which audible rattles seem to facilitate rhythmic hand-banging (Ejiri & Masataka, 2001).

By contrast, the DIVA model emphasizes the role of speech input in the formation of auditory–perceptual targets for speech output as well as the importance of auditory feedback of the infant's own speech for the achievement of speech motor control. This model predicts that the speech environment will influence the acoustic-phonetic characteristics of the infant's speech output from at least the beginning of the canonical babbling stage. Investigations of this hypothesis sometimes employ laboratory induced variations in speech input to the infant but more frequently examine the impact of natural variations in the auditory environment associated with different language groups.

Laboratory investigations of the impact of speech input on speech production.   Two developmental changes in infant vowels occur during the first year: first, more vowels with full oral resonance are produced in comparison to vowels with nasal resonance; subsequently, the infant's vowel repertoire expands to include the point vowels (/i/, /a/, /u/) in addition to the predominant low and central vowels. Two laboratory studies have shown that auditory input plays a role in these developments.

An elegant series of studies was conducted by Bloom (Bloom, 1988; Bloom, Russell, & Wassenberg, 1987) in which both the timing and content of speech input to 3-month-old infants were varied systematically in the laboratory. Infants produced a higher proportion of more speech-like utterances involving full resonance when they received speech input (compared with non-speech vocal input), and this effect was enhanced when the input was provided contingent upon the infants' vocalizations.

In a study focused on the specific phonetic content of the adult input and the infant speech output, Kuhl and Meltzoff (1996) presented one of three point vowels to infants aged 12, 16, and 20 weeks. Perceptual and acoustic analyses showed that the infants shifted their vowel production to better match the target vowel category, even at the youngest age. Kuhl and Meltzoff speculated that this matching-to-target phenomenon, combined with the shift to language-specific perceptual processing, underlies developmental changes in acoustic characteristics of infant vowel production.

Cross-linguistic investigations of the impact of speech input on speech production.   Descriptions of the prosodic characteristics of infant speech also suggest that environmental input impacts infant speech output. For example, French-learning infants' babble can be differentiated from the babble of infants learning other languages with respect to intonational contours, syllable structure, and number of syllables per utterance (Hallé, de Boysson-Bardies, & Vihman, 1991; Levitt & Utman, 1992; Whalen, Levitt, & Wang, 1992). Maneva and Genesee (2002) recently reported similar findings for a single child learning both English and French, recorded separately with his English-speaking mother or his French-speaking father. Unfortunately, these studies involved very small samples and are largely based on phonetic transcriptions of the infants' speech; therefore the existence of "babbling drift," in which infant babble "drifts" toward the ambient language in its sound properties, is not universally accepted (Oller, 2000).

In our lab, we have been describing the acoustic characteristics of vowels produced by infants learning Canadian English or Canadian French in a cross-sectional study (Rvachew, Mattock, Polka, & Ménard, 2006). Figure 8.1 shows the mean first (F1) and second (F2) formant frequencies of vowels produced by the 42 infants that we have recorded thus far. The language groups do not differ with respect to F1 or F2 frequency at 8 months of age. At 10 months of age the groups differ in a manner similar to that reported by de Boysson-Bardies, Hallé, Sagart, and Durand (1989), with the mean F2 being significantly lower for French-learning than for English-learning infants. Between 10 and 18 months of age, the mean F2 for the English-learning group falls below that of the French-learning group which shows a rising F2 during this period. The result is a significant interaction between age and language group for F2 [$F_{(3,42)} = 3.68$, $p = .02$].

These data do not represent a pattern of initial overlap of the vowel spaces followed by a linear divergence of the two groups' "average vowel" with advancing age, as we had expected. Rather, the patterns of developmental change and cross-linguistic differences suggest a more complex and dynamic situation in which the child's ability to attend to and reproduce specific features of the native language vowel space shifts with age. However, it is difficult to interpret these findings because it is not clear what the language-specific targets are for the infant vowel space. The vowels produced by infants are necessarily described in terms of the mean and dispersion of formant values for the entire vowel space while the adult input is universally presented as formant values for specific vowels produced in an adult-directed fashion. For example, Escudero and Polka (2003) have shown that there are acoustic differences among Canadian English and Canadian French vowels in adult speech, even for shared point vowels. However, these data cannot be used to predict developmental changes in the infant's mean vowels because the adult vowel space is not described using the same method that is used for the description of

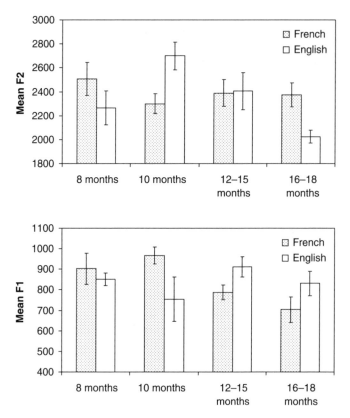

Figure 8.1   Mean second formant frequencies (F2; top panel) and first formant frequencies (F1; bottom panel) for infants learning Canadian English (white bars) or Canadian French (speckled bars), by age group. Error bars represent standard error of the mean.

infant vowels. Furthermore, it is clear that adult-directed speech is significantly different from infant-directed speech and this is likely to have implications for the acoustics of the vowels that infants hear (e.g., see Kuhl et al., 1997). Studies in which the speech addressed to the infant and the speech produced by the infant are recorded in the same context and described using the same procedures are required.

In addition to establishing the characteristics of the input vowel space from the infant's perspective, we need to have a better understanding of how the infant processes that input if we are to predict patterns of developmental change in speech production. For example, the non-linear changes in infant vowel characteristics that are shown in Figure 8.1 might be explained by age-related changes in infant attention to specific properties of the adult input and the infant's own speech. As an example, one characteristic of the French vowel space is the presence of rounded vowels that are cued by a complex integration of the relatively low amplitude second, third, and fourth formant frequencies (Ménard et al., 2004). It is possible that the cue for lip rounding has diminished salience in the child's own speech at a young age. This cue may become available to the child later in the infant period, as a function of increased exposure, changes in vocal tract and laryngeal anatomy, and improved control of lip movements. If the infant then begins to try to manipulate the cue in his or her own speech output, this could cause a non-linear shift in the child's vowel space. However, this hypothesis cannot be tested without more information about the child's ability to attend to and process different acoustic cues in infant and adult speech. This brings us to the issue of infant intake of speech input.

The impact of variations in speech intake.   The infant's ability to receive speech input is obviously impacted by the integrity of the child's auditory system, and hearing impairment has a clear impact on infant speech production as described above. To date, almost no research has considered the potential role of the infant's active efforts to listen to the speech input and select the relevant information.

It is now well known that infants listen preferentially to certain types of speech but the developmental implications of variations in selective attention are not clear. Vihman and Nakai (2003) reported a negative correlation between listening preferences for and productive use of a given consonant. The results are interpreted within the context of the articulatory filter hypothesis in which the physical act of producing a given speech sound impacts on the child's perception of speech and helps the child to develop "more robust lexical and phonological representations" (p. 1017). Vihman (2002) further speculates that articulation of adult-like syllables activates neurons that are active when performing or observing an action (i.e., mirror neurons; see Vihman for more detail). This hypothesis presumes that speech perception and speech production development are independent during the first year of life. The onset of canonical babble is attributed to "maturation" and "rhythmic motoric advances" while the child's implicit perceptual knowledge of native language sound categories is attributed to "passive intake"; when the mirror neurons are activated and perception and production become integrated the infants "lay down phonological representations at a new level" (p. 1017; Vihman & Nakai, 2003).

Note that this account of early phonetic development is based upon a correlational study in which it is impossible to determine the direction of causality. The finding that the infants preferred to listen to consonants that they were *less* likely to produce is difficult to interpret. However, the focus on the child's active intake of information from the language environment is extremely important, and there is a clear need for more studies in which the relationship between selective attention and speech production is explored.

Interactions between the integrity of the auditory mechanism and the development of selective attention have been proposed, as discussed above in relation to the reduced attention to speech observed in recipients of cochlear implants (Houston et al., 2003). In particular, selective attending deficits may explain the impact of otitis media on language development. The impact is small and the clinical significance of otitis media-related language delay has been questioned (e.g., Paradise et al., 2000). However, the hearing loss associated with otitis media is so subtle and transitory that any measurable impact on language development is surprising. And yet these impacts can be observed even during the first year of life in the form of slower emergence of the canonical babble stage and a restricted vowel space (Rvachew, Slawinski, Williams, & Green, 1996, 1999). Current hypotheses about the way in which otitis media impacts on speech development recognize that the issue is not simply one of signal audibility. The fluctuating nature of the hearing deficit may make it difficult for the child to discover regularities in the speech input and lead the child to become less attentive to speech (Feagans, 1986; Mody, Schwartz, Gravel, & Ruben, 1999). Furthermore, 12-month-olds with chronic otitis media experience fewer episodes of joint attention with their parents than children with normal hearing (Yont, Snow, & Vernon-Feagans, 2003). Thus it appears that the early vocalizations of children with early-onset otitis media are determined by a complex interaction of biological factors (integrity of the peripheral auditory system), input factors (quality of input provided by parents), and intake factors (child attention to speech and ability to engage in joint attention routines).

Speech Perception and Speech Production Development: Challenges for the Future

The study of infant phonetic development has been marked by tension between competing perspectives about the goal of the enterprise itself, the purported basis for developmental change during infancy, and the significance of these changes for later language acquisition. Specifically, some researchers have focused on the universal characteristics of the infant's phonetic abilities while others have investigated individual variation in phonetic development. Developmental changes in language acquisition are assumed by some to emerge directly from the maturation of certain neurological, physiological, and anatomical structures, while others privilege the infant's active efforts to learn from the input. Although phonetic development during infancy is considered to be an important foundation for later language learning, the nature of its relation to later phonological, lexical, and syntactic development remains a question of debate.

Competing perspectives on the relation between perception and production processes in early development were labeled by de Boysson-Bardies et al. (1989) as the *independence hypothesis* and the *interactional hypothesis*. From the independence perspective, speech perception and production skills develop independently during the first year, with any continuity between infant phonetic skills and later language development viewed as a function of common biological constraints on perceptual and articulatory performance during the prelinguistic and early linguistic stages. For example, Kent and Miolo (1994) suggested that speech perception and speech production "may have somewhat different courses of development, but they are ultimately integrated in spoken language competence" (p. 304). Locke (1994) proposed independent neurological mechanisms and maturational timecourses to account for early phonetic development and phonological development after the first 50 word stage.

From the interactional perspective, the child's developing knowledge of the perceptual and articulatory characteristics of native language phonetic categories is seen as integrated from the beginning. For example, de Boysson-Bardies et al. (1989) stated that "articulatory procedures that are mastered step by step are oriented by auditory configurations" (p. 2). This perspective is associated with strong claims for continuity between phonetic development during this first year and language development during the second year, as exemplified by Tsao, Liu, and Kuhl's (2004) assertion that "phonetic perception plays a critical role in the early phases of language acquisition" (p. 1082).

While the research reviewed here has not yet provided a resolution to this debate, recent changes in theoretical perspectives, methodological tools, and research approaches promise considerable advances in our understanding of how perception and production might interact during the first year to produce the emergence of language in the second year of life. The DIVA model provides a theoretical account of how these domains influence each other throughout the lifespan. The PRIMIR model suggests that apparent discontinuities in infant performance may actually be indicative of a fundamental underlying continuity from the prelinguistic to the linguistic phases of development. New research tools provide us with the opportunity to assess the merits of these theories. Investigation of individual differences in babbling after taking into account universal biomechanical constraints has been facilitated by a number of new technologies (e.g., magnetic resonance imaging of the vocal tract, computational modeling of the impact of vocal tract development on speech output, and kinematic and acoustic descriptions of infant speech production). Infant speech perception research has in the past tapped into natural variation in language input via cross-linguistic comparisons to explore linguistic influences. Researchers are beginning to actively control and manipulate language experience. For example, Kuhl, Tsao, and Liu (2003) manipulated different components of a natural language setting to show the impact of a live social context on phonetic learning. Given the wide acceptance of highly controlled artificial language paradigms, cross-linguistic studies implementing this approach will soon provide insights into the language-specificity (or lack thereof) of infant on-line speech processing. Along with these new methods there is a growing interest in examining individual differences in perceptual responding under conditions that are more akin to the infant's natural environment.

Together these new technologies make it possible for researchers, currently working separately in the domains of speech perception or speech production, to come together to investigate the relationship between individual variations in speech perception and production performance in the same infants. The DIVA and PRIMIR models suggest some specific directions for future research. The PRIMIR model predicts that there will be individual differences and developmental changes in the intake of specific aspects of the rich and multidimensional input available to the infant. Ongoing efforts to understand the infant's role in the selection of input are extremely important. The DIVA model shows that a critical but as yet unexplored aspect of this input is the infant's own speech. Collaborative and interdisciplinary research is needed to focus research on the interplay between perception and production processes within the developing child. The results will have a profound impact on our understanding of early language development.

Notes

1   Note that no studies of lexical tone perception have been conducted with infants younger than 6 or older than 9 months so it is not known whether the perceptual decline actually occurs earlier in development or continues later.
2   The lower discrimination levels in the Polka et al. study are an exception.

References

Barker, B. A., & Newman, R. S. (2004). Listen to your mother! The role of talker familiarity in infant streaming. *Cognition, 94,* B45–B53.

Best, C. T. (1991, April). *Phonetic influences on the perception of non-native speech contrasts by 6–8 and 10–12-month-olds.* Paper presented at the Meeting of Society for Research in Child Development, Seattle, WA.

Best, C. T. (1995). A direct-realist view of cross-language speech perception. In W. Strange (Ed.), *Speech perception and early linguistic experience* (pp. 171–206). Baltimore, MD: York Press.

Best, C., & McRoberts, G. W. (2003). Infant perception of non-native consonant contrasts that adults assimilate in different ways. *Language and Speech, 46,* 183–216.

Best, C. T., McRoberts, G. W., Goodell, E., Wormer, J. S., Insabella, G., Kim, P., et al. (1990, April). *Infant and adult perception of non-native speech contrasts differing in relation to the listener's native phonology.* Paper presented at the Meeting of the International Conference on Infant Studies, Montreal.

Best, C. T., McRoberts, G., LaFleur, R., & Silver-Isenstadt, J. (1995). Divergent developmental patterns for infants' perception of two nonnative consonant contrasts. *Infant Behavior and Development, 18,* 339–350.

Best, C. T., McRoberts, G. W., & Sithole, N. M. (1988). Examination of perceptual reorganization for nonnative speech contrasts: Zulu click discrimination by English-speaking adults and infants. *Journal of Experimental Psychology: Human Perception and Performance, 14,* 345–360.

Best, C., Singh, L., Bouchard, J., Connelly, G., Cook, A., & Faber, A. (1997, April). *Developmental changes in infants' discrimination of non-native vowels that assimilate to two native categories.* Paper presented at the Meeting of Society of Research in Child Development.

Bloom, K. (1988). Quality of adult vocalizations affects the quality of infant vocalizations. *Journal of Child Language, 15,* 469–480.

Bloom, K., Russell, A., & Wassenberg, K. (1987). Turn taking affects the quality of infant vocalizations. *Journal of Child Language, 14,* 211–227.

Bosch, L., & Sebastián-Gallés, N. (2003a). Simultaneous bilingualism and the perception of a language-specific vowel contrast in the first year of life. *Language and Speech, 46,* 217–243.

Bosch, L., & Sebastián-Gallés, N. (2003b). *Language experience and the perception of a voicing contrast in fricatives: Infant and adult data.* Paper presented at the 15th International Conference of the Phonetic Sciences, Barcelona, Spain.

Burns, T. C., Werker, J. F., & McVie, K. (2003). Development of phonetic categories in infants raised in bilingual and monolingual environments. In B. Beachley, A. Brown, & F. Conlin (Eds.), *Proceedings of the 27th Annual Boston University Conference on Language Development.* Somerville, MA: Cascadilla Press.

Callan, D. E., Kent, R. D., Guenther, F. H., & Vorperian, H. K. (2000). An auditory-feedback-based neural network model of speech production that is robust to developmental changes in the size and shape of the articulatory system. *Journal of Speech, Language, and Hearing Research, 43,* 721–738.

De Boysson-Bardies, B., Hallé, P., Sagart, L., & Durand, C. (1989). A crosslinguistic investigation of vowel formants in babbling. *Journal of Child Language, 16,* 1–17.

Eilers, R. E., Gavin, W. J., & Oller, D. K. (1982). Cross-linguistic perception in infancy: Early effects of linguistic experience. *Journal of Child Language, 9,* 289–302.

Ejiri, K., & Masataka, N. (2001). Co-occurrence of preverbal vocal behavior and motor action in early infancy. *Developmental Science, 4,* 40–48.

Ertmer, D. J., & Mellon, J. A. (2001). Beginning to talk at 20 months: Early vocal development in a young cochlear implant recipient. *Journal of Speech, Language, and Hearing Research, 44,* 192–206.

Escudero, P., & Polka, L. (2003). *A cross-language study of vowel categorization and vowel acoustics: Canadian English versus Canadian French.* Paper presented at Paper presented at the 15th International Conference of the Phonetic Sciences, Barcelona, Spain.

Feagans, L. (1986). Otitis media: A model for long-term effects with implications for intervention. In J. F. Kavanagh (Ed.), *Otitis media and child development* (pp. 192–208). Parkton, MD: York Press.

Fitch, W. T., & Giedd, J. (1999). Morphology and development of the human vocal tract: A study using magnetic resonance imaging. *Journal of the Acoustical Society of America, 106,* 1511–1522.

Green, J. R., Moore, C. A., Higashikawa, M., & Steeve, R. W. (2000). The physiologic development of speech motor control: Lip and jaw coordination. *Journal of Speech, Language, and Hearing Research, 43,* 239–255.

Green, J. R., Moore, C. A., & Reilly, K. J. (2002). The sequential development of jaw and lip control for speech. *Journal of Speech, Language, and Hearing Research, 45,* 66–79.

Guenther, F. H. (1995). Speech sound acquisition, coarticulation, and rate effects in a neural network model of speech production. *Psychological Review, 102,* 594–621.

Guenther, F. H., Hampson, M., & Johnson, D. (1998). A theoretical investigation of reference frames for the planning of speech movements. *Psychological Review, 105,* 611–633.

Hallé, P. A., de Boysson-Bardies, B., & Vihman, M. M. (1991). Beginnings of prosodic organization: Intonation and duration patterns of disyllables produced by Japanese and French infants. *Language and Speech, 34,* 299–318.

Hollich, G., Newman, R. S., & Jusczyk, P. W. (2005). Infant's use of synchronized visual information to separate streams of speech. *Child Development, 76,* 1–16.

Houston, D. M., Pisoni, D., Iler Kirk, K., Ying, E. A., & Miyamoto, R. T. (2003). Speech perception skills of deaf infants following cochlear implantation: a first report. *International Journal of Pediatric Otorhinolaryngology, 67,* 479–495.

Kent, R. D., & Miolo, G. (1994). Phonetic abilities in the first year of life. In P. Fletcher & B. MacWhinney (Eds.), *Handbook of child language* (pp. 303–334). Oxford: Blackwell.

Kent, R. D., & Vorperian, H. K. (1995). Anatomic development of the craniofacial-oral laryngeal systems: A review. *Journal of Medical Speech-Language Pathology, 3,* 145–190.

Kent, R. D., Vorperian, H. K., Gentry, L. R., & Yandell, B. S. (1999). Magnetic resonance imaging procedures to study the concurrent anatomic development of vocal tract structures: preliminary results. *International Journal of Pediatric Otorhinolaryngology, 49,* 197–206.

Koopmans-van Beinum, F. J., Clement, C. J., & van den Dikkenberg-Pot, I. (2001). Babbling and the lack of auditory speech perception: a matter of coordination? *Developmental Science, 4,* 61–70.

Koopmans-van Beinum, F. J., & van der Stelt, J. M. (1986). Early stages in the development of speech movements. In B. Lindblom & R. Zetterstrom (Eds.), *Precursors of early speech* (pp. 37–50). New York: Stockton Press, Inc.

Kuhl, P. K., Andruski, J. E., Chistovich, I. A., Kozhevnikova, E. V., Ryskina, V. L., Stolyarova, E. I., et al. (1997). Cross-language analysis of phonetic units in language addressed to infants. *Science, 277,* 684–686.

Kuhl, P. K., & Meltzoff, A. N. (1996). Infant vocalizations in response to speech: Vocal imitation and developmental change. *Journal of the Acoustical Society of America, 100,* 2425–2438.

Kuhl, P. K., Tsao, F.-M., & Liu, H.-M. (2003). Foreign-language experience in infancy: Effects of short-term exposure and social interaction on phonetic learning. *Proceedings of the National Academy of Sciences, 100*, 9096–9101.

Levitt, A. G., & Utman, J. A. (1992). From babbling towards the sound systems of English and French: A longitudinal two-case study. *Journal of Child Language, 19*, 19–49.

Locke, J. L. (1994). Development of the capacity for spoken language. In P. Fletcher & B. MacWhinney (Eds.), *Handbook of child language* (pp. 278–302). Oxford: Blackwell.

MacNeilage, P. F. (1998). The frame/content theory of evolution of speech production. *Behavioral and Brain Sciences, 21*, 499–546.

MacNeilage, P. F., & Davis, B. L. (2000). On the origin of internal structure of word forms. *Science, 288*, 527–531.

Maneva, B., & Genesee, F. (2002). Bilingual babbling: Evidence for language differentiation in dual language acquisition. In B. Skarbela et al. (Eds.), *Boston University Conference on Language Development 26 Proceedings* (pp. 383–392). Somerville, MA: Cascadilla Press.

Mattock, K., & Burnham, D. (2006). Chinese and English infants' tone perception: Evidence for perceptual reorganization. *Infancy, 10.*

Ménard, L., Schwartz, J., & Boë, L. (2002). Auditory normalization of French vowels synthesized by an articulatory model simulating growth from birth to adulthood. *Journal of the Acoustical Society of America, 111*, 1892–1905.

Ménard, L., Schwartz, J., & Boë, L. (2004). Role of vocal tract morphology in speech development: Perceptual targets and sensorimotor maps for synthesized vowels from birth to adulthood. *Journal of Speech, Language, and Hearing Research, 47*, 1059–1080.

Miyawaki, K., Strange, W., Verbrugge, R., Liberman, A., Jenkins, J., & Fujimura, O. (1975). An effect of language experience: The discrimination of /r/ and /l/ by native speakers of Japanese and English. *Perception and Psychophysics, 18*, 331–340.

Mody, M., Schwartz, R. G., Gravel, J. S., & Ruben, R. J. (1999). Speech perception and verbal memory in children with and without histories of otitis media. *Journal of Speech, Language, and Hearing Research, 42*, 1069–1079.

Newman, R. S. (2005). The cocktail party effect revisited: Listening to one's own name in noise. *Developmental Psychology, 41*, 352–362.

Newman, R. S., & Jusczyk, P. W. (1996). The cocktail party effect in infants. *Perception and Psychophysics, 58*, 1145–1156.

Nozza, R. J., Miller, S. L., Rossman, R. N. F., & Bond, L. C. (1991). Reliability and validity of infant speech-sound discrimination-in-noise thresholds. *Journal of Speech and Hearing Research, 34*, 643–650.

Oller, D. K. (1980). The emergence of the sounds of speech in infancy. In G. H. Yeni-Komshian, J. F. Kavanagh, & C. A. Ferguson (Eds.), *Child phonology: Vol. 1* (pp. 93–112). New York: Academic Press.

Oller, D. K. (2000). *The emergence of the speech capacity.* Mahwah, NJ: Lawrence Erlbaum Associates.

Oller, D. K., & Eilers, R. E. (1988). The role of audition in infant babbling. *Child Development, 59*, 441–449.

Pallier, C., Bosch, L., & Sebastián, N. (1997). A limit on behavioral plasticity in vowel acquisition. *Cognition, 64*, B9–B17.

Paradise, J. L., Dollaghan, C. A., Campbell, T. F., Feldman, H. M., Bernard, B. S., Colborn, K., et al. (2000). Language, speech sound production, and cognition in three-year-old children in relation to otitis media in their first three years of life. *Pediatrics, 105*, 1119–1130.

Pegg, J. E., & Werker, J. F. (1997). Adult and infant perception of two English phones. *Journal of the Acoustical Society of America, 102*, 3742–3753.

Polka, L., & Bohn, O. S. (1996). A cross-language comparison of vowel perception in English-learning and German-learning infants. *Journal of the Acoustical Society of America, 100,* 577–592.

Polka, L., & Bohn, O.-S. (2003). Asymmetries in vowel perception. *Speech Communication, 41,* 221–231.

Polka, L., Colantonio, C., & Sundara, M. (2001). A cross-language comparison of /d/–/ð/ perception: Evidence for a new developmental pattern. *Journal of the Acoustical Society of America, 109,* 2190–2201.

Polka, L., & Rvachew, S. (2005). The impact of otitis media with effusion on infant phonetic perception. *Infancy, 8,* 101–117.

Polka, L., Rvachew, S., & Molnar, M. (submitted). The role of attention in infant speech perception. *Cognition.*

Polka, L., & Werker, J. F. (1994). Developmental changes in perception of nonnative vowel contrasts. *Journal of Experimental Psychology: Human Perception and Performance, 20,* 421–435.

Rvachew, S., Mattock, K., Polka, L., & Ménard, L. (2006). Developmental and cross-linguistic variation in the infant vowel space: the case of Canadian English and Canadian French. *Journal of the Acoustical Society of America, 120.*

Rvachew, S., Slawinski, E. B., Williams, M., & Green, C. (1996). Formant frequencies of vowels produced by infants with and without early onset otitis media. *Canadian Acoustics, 24,* 19–28.

Rvachew, S., Slawinski, E. B., Williams, M., & Green, C. L. (1999). The impact of early onset otitis media on babbling and early language development. *Journal of the Acoustical Society of America, 105,* 467–475.

Stager, C. L., & Werker, J. (1997). Infants listen for more phonetic detail in speech perception than in word-learning tasks. *Nature, 388,* 381–382.

Stark, R. (1980). Stages of speech development in the first year of life. In G. H. Yeni-Komshian, J. F. Kavanagh, & C. A. Ferguson (Eds.), *Child phonology: Vol. 1* (pp. 73–92). New York: Academic Press.

Sundara, M., Polka, L., & Genesee, G. (2006). Language experience facilitates discrimination of /d–ð/ in monolingual and bilingual acquisition of English. *Cognition, 100,* 369–388.

Sussman, H. M., Duder, C., Dalston, E., & Caciatore, A. (1999). An acoustic analysis of the development of CV coarticulation: A case study. *Journal of Speech, Language, and Hearing Research, 42,* 1080–1096.

Sussman, H. M., Minifie, F. D., Buder, E. H., Stoel-Gammon, C., & Smith, J. (1996). Consonant–vowel interdependencies in babbling and early words: Preliminary examination of a locus equation approach. *Journal of Speech, Language, and Hearing Research, 39,* 424–433.

Tsao, F., Liu, H.-M., & Kuhl, P. K. (2004). Speech perception in infancy predicts language development in the second year of life: A longitudinal study. *Child Development, 75,* 1067–1084.

Tsao, F., Liu, H., Kuhl, P. K., & Tseng, C. (2000). *Perceptual discrimination of Mandarin fricative–affricate contrast by English-learning and Mandarin-learning infants.* Paper presented at the International Conference on Infant Studies, Brighton, UK.

Tsushima, T., Takizawa, O., Sasaki, M., Shiraki, S., Nishi, K., Kohno, M., et al. (1994). *Discrimination of English /r–l/ and /w–y/ by Japanese infants at 6–12 months: Language-specific developmental changes in speech perception abilities.* Paper presented at the International Conference on Spoken Language Processing.

Vihman, M. M. (2002). The role of mirror neurons in the ontogeny of speech. In M. I. Stamenov & V. Gallese (Eds.), *Mirror neurons and the evolution of brain and language* (pp. 305–314). Advances in Consciousness Research: Vol. 42. Amsterdam: John Benjamins Publishing Company.

Vihman, M. M., & Nakai, S. (2003). Experimental evidence for an effect of vocal experience on infant speech perception. In M. J. Sole, D. Recasens, & J. Romero (Eds.), *Proceedings of the 15th International Congress of Phonetic Science, Barcelona* (pp. 1017–1020). Universitat Autonoma de Barcelona.

Werker, J. F., & Curtin, S. (2005). PRIMIR: A developmental framework of infant speech processing. *Language Development and Learning, 1,* 197–234.

Werker, J. F., Gilbert, J. H. V., Humphrey, K., & Tees, R. C. (1981). Developmental aspects of cross-language speech perception. *Child Development, 52,* 349–355.

Werker, J. F., Hall, G., & Fais, L. (2004). Reconstructing U-shaped functions. *Journal of Cognition and Development, 5,* 147–151.

Werker, J. F., & Logan, J. (1985). Cross-language evidence for three factors in speech perception. *Perception and Psychophysics, 37,* 35–44.

Werker, J. F., & Tees, R. C. (1983). Developmental changes across childhood in the perception of nonnative speech sounds. *Canadian Journal of Psychology, 37,* 278–286.

Werker, J. F., & Tees, R. C. (1984a). Cross-language speech perception: Evidence for perceptual reorganisation in the first year of life. *Infant Behavior and Development, 7,* 49–63.

Werker, J. F., & Tees, R. C. (1984b). Phonemic and phonetic factors in adult cross-language speech perception. *Journal of the Acoustical Society of America, 75,* 1866–1878.

Whalen, D. H., Levitt, A. G., & Wang, Q. (1992). Intonational differences between the reduplicative babbling of French- and English-learning infants. *Journal of Child Language, 18,* 501–516.

Yont, K. M., Snow, C. E., & Vernon-Feagans, L. (2003). Is chronic otitis media associated with differences in parental input at 12 months of age? An analysis of joint attention and directives. *Applied Psycholinguistics, 24,* 581–602.

9

Acquiring Linguistic Structure

LouAnn Gerken

This chapter is an overview of what scientists currently know about human sensitivity to linguistic form during infancy. We can think of language form at two levels: a sub-meaning level that includes the sounds that combine to make words in a spoken language, and a meaning level that includes words and phrases that combine to make sentences. The ability to generate new combinations at both of these levels is what gives human language its infinite creativity. It is standard when discussing linguistic form to subdivide the territory into linguistic categories of various sorts (e.g., the phonological category "stop consonants" or the syntactic category "nouns") and rules, principles, or statistical regularities describing the typical ways in which these categories are combined (e.g., a stop cannot follow a liquid in word initial position in English).

The inclusion of such a chapter in a book on language development would probably not even have been considered 20 years ago. Why has the topic of infants' sensitivity to linguistic form become one of so much interest? I can identify two reasons, one methodological and one theoretical. The first is that, largely for technological reasons, the earliest studies of infant sensitivity to language asked questions about young learners' ability to discriminate acoustic–phonetic forms without any reference field (e.g., Eimas, Siqueland, Jusczyk, & Vigorrito, 1971; Werker & Tees, 1984). Later studies examining infants' sensitivity to linguistic units larger than individual speech sound or syllables continued to use discrimination, not association with reference, as the method of choice (e.g., Hirsh-Pasek et al., 1987; Jusczyk & Aslin, 1995). As the questions asked of infants using form discrimination measures became more and more linguistically sophisticated, it became clear that sensitivity to form may precede in many respects the ability to map forms to meanings (Gómez & Gerken, 2000; Naigles, 2002; see Naigles & Swensen, this volume).

A second reason for the field's interest in infants' sensitivity to linguistic form concerns the debate about whether language is learnable using a set of general purpose learning mechanisms, or whether we must posit strong innate constraints on the language acquisition process (e.g., Chomsky, 1981; see Saffran & Thiessen, this volume). This debate has often focused on linguistic form, particularly syntactic form. An argument favoring nativist views of language development is that any set of data can potentially give rise to an infinite number of generalizations. How can a learner be sure that she is making the correct generalization, given the data? The nativist solution to this question is to posit that learners are born strongly constrained to consider only a very restricted set of possible generalizations. In the limit, a single input datum might trigger the correct generalization in a particular linguistic domain (e.g., whether sentences require overt subjects; Hyams, 1986).

Contrary to such views, the recent research on infants' sensitivity to linguistic form hints at the possibility that, given a reasonable subset of the input data, infants are capable of converging on the appropriate linguistic generalizations, possibly using general purpose learning mechanisms coupled with general purpose perceptual/conceptual constraints. The logical observation that any set of input admits multiple possible generalizations which somehow must be constrained can be kept distinct from an empirical claim about the nature of the input – the "poverty of the stimulus" argument. This argument states that certain critical types of linguistic data are so rare that learners are not exposed to them early in language development (see Pullum & Scholz, 2002 and responses). Nevertheless, nativists argue, children have knowledge of the formal principles underlying the putatively unheard data. I return briefly to the poverty of the stimulus argument in the final section.

The data that I present in this chapter all come from experiments in which 6- to 18-month-old infants are tested on their preference for one auditory stimulus type versus another, with preference defined as greater attention to one stimulus type than the other over multiple trials in a controlled setting. In some studies, infants are tested on their ability to discriminate two types of stimuli based on existing knowledge they had when entering the laboratory. In other studies, infants are familiarized with new auditory stimuli and then tested to determine whether they can discriminate the newly familiarized stimuli from very similar stimuli. The question each researcher is asking is whether infants can discriminate two types of stimuli based on form alone, without assessing their interpretation of utterances. The careful reader will note that in some studies discrimination is reflected in greater attention to familiar forms, while in other studies there is greater attention to novel forms. Which type of preference is observed in which type of experiment may be related to how well infants were able to encode the relevant properties of the stimulus before testing, which itself is probably affected by the age of the infant, the length of exposure before testing, the complexity of the stimulus, and the complexity of the testing environment. At this point in the development of the field, researchers focus on whether or not infants demonstrate significant discrimination, regardless of the direction.

The next two sections address what is known about infants' sensitivity to phonological and syntactic form, in terms of categories and combinatorial regularities. The final section addresses what, if anything, the findings of infant sensitivity to linguistic form tell us about the nature of language development.

Sensitivity to Phonological Form

Languages of the world demonstrate a variety of patterns in the sounds that they use. For example, they select a subset of all possible humanly producible and perceivable sounds, and they do so in such a way that the sounds can be organized along a small number of dimensions (i.e., phonetic features such as voicing). Languages also restrict which sounds can occur in sequence, and again, they do so based not on particular sounds, but on featurally defined sound classes. Finally, languages assign stress to syllables of multi-syllabic words based on certain abstract properties, such as syllable shape (e.g., consonant–vowel–consonant) and position in a word (e.g., second to last). Below, we will consider what is known about infants' sensitivity to information in the speech signal relevant in each of these three areas.

Sensitivity to phonetic features

Let us begin this section by considering how infants determine what acoustic differences are relevant in their language and which are not. We might naïvely assume that infants lose their ability to discriminate sounds that are not in the input. However, such an assumption misses the point that many acoustic differences that are phonemic in one language appear in another language as allophones (contextually conditioned variants) of a single phoneme. For example, English-speakers have the option of releasing or not releasing and aspirating word final stops. Thus, English-learning infants may be exposed to both released and unreleased stops, but this phonetic difference does not affect meaning in English. The same acoustic difference does affect meaning in Hindi. What causes the English-learning infant and the Hindi-learning infant, both of whom hear variation in aspiration in their input, to treat aspiration differently?

One class of hypotheses is based on the observation that infants show a decline in non-native consonant discrimination at roughly the period of development that they begin to recognize and produce first words (e.g., Best, 1995; Jusczyk, 1985; MacKain, 1982; Werker & Pegg, 1992). Perhaps associating word forms with meanings as part of building a lexicon causes learners to focus on which aspects of form are relevant to meaning and which are not. A potential problem with this view is that infants' ability to discriminate non-native vowel sounds declines at about 6 months, a time at which word learning is not obviously underway (Kuhl et al., 1992; Polka & Werker, 1994). If a non-lexical mechanism for perceptual change exists for vowels, the same mechanism may explain developmental change in consonant perception as well. Another problem with views that depend on word learning for change in speech sound discrimination is that infants appear to have difficulty discriminating minimal word pairs at the early stage of word learning (Stager & Werker, 1997; Werker, Fennell, Corcoran, & Stager, 2002; see Polka, Rvachew, & Mattock, this volume). For example, an infant who easily discriminates *ba* from *pa* might have difficulty discriminating *bear* from *pear* in the early stages of word learning. It is difficult to see how such an infant could use word–meaning pairs to focus on voicing as an important feature of English words. Finally, even if a learner were able to use the meaning distinction between "bear" and "pear" to determine that /b/ and /p/ are distinct, this realization by itself does nothing to help them determine that the feature voicing is distinctive in English. In other words, do learners need to encounter a minimal pair that contrasts each possible pair of English phonemes (e.g., /b/ vs. /p/, /d/ vs. /t/, /z/ vs. /s/, etc.)? Or does determining that the phonetic feature voicing is important for distinguishing one pair of phonemes "buy" the infant a whole set of distinctions that depend on the feature voicing? The question of infants' sensitivity to phonetic features is important in the discussion in this and the following two sections.

Another hypothesis about the mechanism that underlies infants' focus on the phonetic features that are relevant in the target language concerns their attention to the statistical properties of their input (e.g., Guenther & Gjaja, 1996; Maye, Werker, & Gerken, 2002). On this view, an English-learning infant might hear a continuum of different degrees of aspiration on word final stops, with most of the values clustering around a particular point in the acoustic distribution. That is, English-learning infants are likely to hear a unimodal distribution of aspiration. Hindi-learning infants are also likely to hear a range of aspiration values; however, the values should cluster around two points in the distribution – one for segments in which the speaker intends aspiration and the other for intentionally unaspirated segments. Thus, the Hindi-learner is exposed to a bimodal distribution of this acoustic variable.

Research by Maye and colleagues suggests that even 6-month-olds respond differently to uni- versus bimodal distributions of speech sounds (Maye et al., 2002). Six- and 8-month-old infants were exposed for about two minutes to syllables that varied along the acoustic dimension represented by the endpoints of [d] as in *day* and the unaspirated [t] in *stay* along with filler stimuli (adult English-speakers perceive both endpoints as /d/). All infants heard all of the stimuli from an eight-token continuum. However, half of the infants heard a stimulus set in which most tokens came from the middle of the continuum (tokens 4 & 5, unimodal group), while the other half heard a set in which most tokens came from near the endpoints (tokens 2 & 7, bimodal group). During test, infants' listening times were measured as they were exposed to trials comprising either an ongoing alternation between the two endpoints (tokens 1 & 8, alternating trials) or a single stimulus from the continuum repeated (tokens 1 or 8, non-alternating trials). Each trial ended when the infant stopped fixating the visual target for a predetermined time. Only infants from the bimodal group responded differentially to the alternating versus non-alternating trials.

One interpretation of these findings is that exposure to a bimodal distribution helped infants determine that the acoustic dimension in question was potentially relevant. By contrast, exposure to a unimodal distribution made it more likely that infants would ignore the same acoustic difference. These results suggest that infants are able to perform some sort of tacit descriptive statistics on acoustic input. Does this statistical analysis reveal which speech sounds are distinct from each other in a pair-by-pair fashion (e.g., /pa/ vs. /ba/, /ta/ vs. /da/, etc.), or does it also reveal more abstract ways in which speech sounds might differ from each other (i.e., phonetic features)? Maye and Weiss (2003) found that 8-month-olds familiarized with a bimodal [d]–[t] continuum like that described in the preceding paragraph were able to discriminate a different, [g]~[k], continuum, which is based on the same phonetic feature. By contrast, infants exposed to a unimodal [d]~[t] continuum were not able to discriminate the [g]~[k] continuum. These data indicate that infants are able to generalize a contrast discovered via the statistics over one pair of sounds to another pair of sounds differing on the same featural dimension. It is interesting to note that adults exposed to stimuli similar to those employed by Maye and Weiss failed to generalize (Maye & Gerken, 2001). However, Maye and Weiss used multiple versions of each token in the continuum, while the study with adults did not. Therefore, we cannot determine at this point whether infants are more adept at featural generalization than adults, or if infants in the existing experiments were presented with stimuli that better promoted feature-based generalization.

Sensitivity to segment sequences

Two lines of research suggest that infants are sensitive to segment sequences in the speech stream. The first line was begun by Peter Jusczyk and colleagues, and it demonstrates that infants are able to discriminate words composed of sequences of segments that occur frequently in the infants' native language from less frequent (or entirely absent) sequences (Gerken & Zamuner, in press; Jusczyk, Friederici, Wessels, Svenkerud, & Jusczyk, 1993; Jusczyk, Luce, & Charles-Luce, 1994; Sebastián Gallés & Bosch, 2002). The second line of research demonstrates that infants are able to learn new segment-sequencing patterns in a brief laboratory exposure. In one study of the latter sort, Chambers, Onishi, and Fisher (2003) familiarized 16.5-month-old infants with consonant–vowel–consonant (CVC) syllables in which particular consonants were artificially restricted to either initial or final position (e.g., /bæp/ not /pæb/). During test, infants listened significantly longer to new syllables that violated the familiarized positional constraints than to new syllables that obeyed them. In this study, infants could have responded based on familiar segment-by-syllable position correlations (e.g., b first, p last). That is, there is no evidence that they encoded the sequence constraints in terms of features.

Two similar studies suggest that infants are able to encode segment sequences in terms of featural relations. Saffran and Thiessen (2003) familiarized 9-month-olds with words with a consistent word-shape template. For example, in one condition of their second experiment, infants were familiarized with CVCCVC words which had the pattern +V, −V, +V, −V on the four consonants (e.g., /gutbap/). Infants were then tested to determine if they were able to segment from fluent speech new words that fit versus did not fit the familiarized pattern. The familiarization and test words were designed so that no particular sequence of consonants occurred in both familiarization and test (e.g., g_tb_p occurred in familiarization but not in test, and g_kb_p occurred in test but not in familiarization). Therefore, the influence of the familiarization phase on infants' preference during test was probably due to word templates specified in terms of features, not specific phonemes.

A similar point is made by Seidl and Buckley (2005), who demonstrated that 9-month-olds exposed to a phonological pattern instantiated with one set of segments could recognize the pattern instantiated in another set of segments. In one condition of one experiment, infants were familiarized with stimuli that exhibited the restriction that fricatives and affricates occurred only between two vowels, and no stops occurred in that position (e.g., [pasat nodʒɛt mitʃa]). During test, infants discriminated stimuli that adhered to the restriction from stimuli that did not, even though the set of fricatives, stops, and vowels used in the test stimuli were different from those used during familiarization. These data, like those of Maye and Weiss (2003) and Saffran and Thiessen (2003), suggest that infants generalize about the sound properties of their language based on phonetic features.

Sensitivity to properties affecting stress assignment

As for infants' sensitivity to stress assignment principles, research has followed a trajectory similar to that of explorations of sensitivity to segment sequences. Early studies asked whether infants are sensitive to the canonical stress pattern of their language, while later studies asked what infants can learn about stress assignment principles in a brief laboratory exposure. Beginning with what infants know about the stress properties of their own language, Jusczyk, Cutler, and Redanz (1993) demonstrated that 9-month-old American infants listen longer to disyllabic words exhibiting a trochaic pattern (strong–weak) than an iambic pattern (weak–strong). The vast majority of disyllabic words in English exhibit a trochaic pattern (Cutler & Carter, 1987), and it appears that English-learning infants have noticed this statistical bias in their language (also see Echols, Crowhurst, & Childers, 1997; Thiessen & Saffran, 2003).

The trochaic bias in English words can be seen to stem from a set of stress assignment principles such as those in (1a–d), below (e.g., Hogg & McCully, 1987).

(1)   a.   Stress penultimate (second to last) syllables
      b.   Stress heavy syllables (CV with long vowel or CVC(C)(C))
      c.   Avoid two stressed syllables in sequence
      d.   Alternate stress from right to left.

Turk, Jusczyk, and Gerken (1995) asked whether infants were sensitive to the principle that heavy syllables should receive stress, examining infants' listening time to trochaic versus iambic words in which the strong syllable was light (a CVC with a short vowel). They found that syllable weight is not a necessary component of the strong–weak preference observed by Jusczyk, Cutler, et al. (1993). However, the third experiment in the published series, plus additional unpublished experiments, make it clear that infants are sensitive to syllable weight and to the typical patterns of heavy and light syllables that occur in English words.

Gerken (2004) further explored infants' sensitivity to stress assignment principles, utilizing principles and stimuli created by Guest, Dell, and Cole (2000) for a study with adults. In the infant study, 6- and 9-month-olds were familiarized with five types of three- to five-syllable words from one of two artificial languages that differed in most of their stress assignment principles. No single familiarization word type exhibited all of the stress assignment principles for the language. During test, infants heard new words with different stress patterns from the ones heard during familiarization, although the test words of each language were consistent with the stress assignment principles of that language. Importantly, Language 1 and Language 2 test words had the same stress patterns, and differed only in the placement of a heavy (CVC) syllable. For example, *do-TON-re-MI-fa* was a test word from Language 1, and *do-RE-mi-TON-fa* was a test word from Language 2 (capital letters indicate stressed syllables). Nine-month-olds discriminated the test words, suggesting that they were able to generalize to new words by combining information from the different types of words encountered during familiarization. Six-month-olds did not discriminate the test words.

Can we conclude from this study that infants infer stress assignment principles like (1a–d)? One barrier to drawing such a conclusion is that the only heavy syllable used by Gerken (2004) was *TON*. Therefore, infants might have determined that *TON* should be stressed, while not drawing the more abstract conclusion that heavy syllables should be stressed. Unpublished follow-up studies suggest a more complicated story. Infants failed to generalize to test stimuli with a different heavy syllable than the one heard during familiarization. However, if multiple heavy syllables were heard during familiarization, infants were able to generalize to a new heavy syllable at test. These data suggest that infants are not prepared to infer a principle like "stress heavy syllables" from encountering a single heavy syllable. However, they do appear to generalize based on categories like "heavy syllable" if they hear a small number of exemplars from that category.

Summary of sensitivity to phonological form

The studies of infants' sensitivity to phonological form reveal at least two properties common across phonological domains. First, infants demonstrate sensitivity to the segment inventory, segment sequences, and stress properties of their native language at about 9 months of age, although sensitivity to the vowel inventory appears somewhat earlier. Second, infants are remarkably skilled at detecting phonological patterns in stimuli presented in brief laboratory visits, and they appear to be able to generalize beyond the particular stimuli that they have encountered when given appropriate evidence. In the domain of segment inventories, appropriate evidence for the existence of a featurally based segment category may be a bimodal distribution of acoustic–phonetic tokens along a particular acoustic dimension, and perhaps multiple instances of each token. In the domain of segment sequences, there has not been a systematic exploration of what evidence is required for featurally based generalization. For example, although it seems unlikely that infants familiarized with a set of pVsVC tokens would show evidence of having induced a stop–V–fricative–VC pattern, we do not yet know the limits on infants' generalization in this domain. In the domain of stress assignment, we have some preliminary evidence that multiple instances of a category (e.g., heavy syllable) are needed for generalization.

One question raised by the work on infants' sensitivity to phonological form is whether infants are in any sense biologically prepared to entertain certain categories of sound experience, or whether any readily perceivable acoustic dimension can serve as a basis for a category. Another way of framing the question is whether segments, segment sequences, or stress assignment principles that are found among the world's languages can be learned more readily by human infants than other equally complex categories that are not found in natural language. Researchers are just beginning to address this question. At the present time, the answer appears to be that arbitrary patterns are learnable (Chambers et al., 2003; Seidl & Buckley, 2005), although patterns that are characterizable in terms of disjunctions (e.g., words begin with /p/ or /s/) may suffer a disadvantage in generalization (Saffran & Thiessen, 2003). Much more research is needed on the sound stimulus properties required for generalization.

Sensitivity to Syntactic Form

Although the mantra of generative linguists over the past 50 years has been that syntax is logically distinct from meaning (e.g., Chomsky, 1965), many diagnostics of syntactic structure involve assessing meaning. For example, the fact that *him* in (2), below, cannot refer to Bill is taken as evidence about the structural constraints on coreference. Surely it makes little sense to assess learners' sensitivity to such constraints before they can understand sentences like (2).

(2)   *Bill$_i$ likes him$_i$.

Nevertheless, there are at least two aspects of syntactic sensitivity that can, in principle, be assessed in the absence of sentence interpretation: word order and syntactic categories. Although both of these components of syntax ultimately influence sentence interpretation, they can also be assessed to some extent on their own. For example, regardless of what meaning is intended, (3a) is not a possible sentence of English, because it violates English word order. Similarly, you may not know what *zig, rif,* or *nug* mean, but if you hear these words used in sentence (3b), you can feel confident that (3c) is a grammatical sentence. Researchers studying infants' sensitivity to syntactic form have taken advantage of these non-interpretational aspects of syntax to study early sensitivity to the orders of word-like units and to syntactic categories.

(3)   a.   *Dog the cat the chased.
      b.   The zigs were riffing the nugs.
      c.   Look at those zigs rif.

Sensitivity to the order of word-like units

As in the studies of sensitivity to phonological form, the first studies examining infants' sensitivity to the syntactic form involved the form of language the infant was already learning. Shady, Gerken, and Jusczyk (1995) presented 10.5-month-olds with normal English sentences as well as sentences in which determiners and nouns were reversed, resulting in phrases like *kitten the*. The stimuli were recorded using a speech synthesizer to avoid disruptions in prosody that are likely to occur when a human talker produces ungrammatical sentences. Infants listened longer to the unmodified sentences, suggesting that they were able to tell the difference between the two types of stimuli. Similar studies presented 10- to 12-month-old infants with normal English sentences versus sentences in which a subset of grammatical morphemes was replaced by nonsense syllables. Infants could discriminate the grammatical and ungrammatical stimuli (4a vs. 4b, below), but not stimuli in which nonsense words replaced content words (4a vs. 4c; Shady, 1996; Shafer, Shucard, Shucard, & Gerken, 1998).

(4)   a.   There was once a little kitten who was born in a dark, cozy closet.
      b.   There [ki] once [gu] little kitten who [ki] born in [gu] dark, cozy closet.
      c.   There was once a little [mafIt] who was [tɛk] in a dark, cozy closet.

This pattern of results suggests that the information carried by grammatical morphemes was more salient to infants than particular content words, which they may or may not have recognized. Santelmann and Jusczyk (1998) showed that 18-month-olds, but not 15-month-olds, are able to detect violations in dependencies between English morphemes, such as auxiliary *is* and progressive suffix *-ing* (e.g., *Grandma is singing* vs. *Grandma can singing*), only when the distance between the two morphemes was between one and three syllables.

Although these studies indicate that infants are sensitive to aspects of their input that might serve as "cues" to an aspect of adult syntax, we cannot take such cue sensitivity to indicate that these infants have knowledge of English phrase structure. Rather, cue sensitivity merely indicates that infants have encoded frequently occurring patterns in their native language. For example, in the Shady et al. (1995) study, many of the ungrammatical sentences contained two grammatical morphemes in sequence (e.g., *a that*). Such sequences are virtually non-existent in English, and infants were probably responding to this and similar aspects of the stimuli, as opposed to any tacit expectation for determiners to precede nouns.

Because it is difficult to separate sensitivity to syntactic structure and frequency of occurrence in the native language, researchers studying infants' generalizations over sentence-like stimuli have turned to familiarization studies like those discussed in the section on infants' sensitivity to phonological form. In one such study, Gómez and Gerken (1999) presented 12-month-olds with a subset of strings produced by one of two finite state grammars. The two grammars began and ended in the same CVC nonsense words, with the only difference being the string-internal sequences of words allowed. In one study, half of the infants were familiarized for about two minutes with strings from Grammar 1 and half with strings from Grammar 2. For example, *VOT PEL* was a legal sequence in strings of Grammar 1, but not Grammar 2. During test, both groups of infants heard new strings from the two grammars. Infants showed a significant preference for the new strings generated by their familiarization grammar. This study showed that infants learned about the sequential dependencies of the words in their familiarization grammar and applied this knowledge to new strings during test.

Table 9.1   AAB familiarization stimuli used by Marcus et al. (1999)

A	B			
	di	*je*	*li*	*we*
le	leledi	leleje	leleli	lelewe
wi	wiwidi	wiwije	wiwili	wiwiwe
ji	jijidi	jijije	jijili	jijiwe
de	dededi	dedeje	dedeli	dedewe

One important property of Grammar 1, and not Grammar 2, was that certain words were allowed to repeat in sequence. For example, *VOT PEL PEL JIC* was a legal string in Grammar 1. By contrast, Grammar 2 contained strings in which the same word occurred in multiple string positions with other words intervening (e.g., *PEL RUD JIC VOT RUD*). These repetitions and alternations might allow learners to recognize the abstract form of some of the strings in their familiarization language, even if the test items contained new vocabulary. To test this possibility, Gómez and Gerken (1999) paired each word from the familiarization vocabulary with a new word in the test vocabulary (e.g., JED, FIM, TUP, DAK, SOG were matched with VOT, PEL, JIC, RUD, TAM, respectively). Thus, an infant who heard a string like JED-FIM-FIM-TUP in training might hear a string like VOT-PEL-PEL-JIC in test (both strings were generated by Grammar 1). Again, infants showed a preference for strings that were consistent with their familiarization grammar, suggesting that they had discerned the pattern of repetitions and alternations of the two grammars (also see Gómez & Gerken, 1998).

In a similar series of studies, Marcus, Vijayan, Rao, and Vishton (1999) exposed 7-month-olds to three-minute speech samples of strings with ABA (*wi-di-wi* and *de-li-de*) or ABB (*wi-di-di* and *de-li-li*) patterns. During test, infants heard strings with the same pattern they had heard during training as well as the other pattern, both instantiated in new vocabulary (e.g., *ba-po-ba* vs. *ba-po-po*). Infants trained on ABA stimuli preferred ABB stimuli at test, while infants trained on ABB stimuli preferred ABA stimuli at test (i.e., a novelty preference). These results, coupled with those of Gómez and Gerken (1999), make clear that infants can generalize beyond specific word order based on patterns of repeating or alternating elements.

A follow-up study using a subset of the stimuli used by Marcus et al. (1999) sheds some light on the conditions under which infants do and do not generalize beyond the specifics of their input (Gerken, 2006). The stimuli from the AAB condition of the Marcus et al. study are shown in Table 9.1. If one considers all of the information in the table, a succinct generalization is that all strings have an AAB form. The same is true if one considers just the four stimuli on the diagonal. However, if one considers the stimuli in the first column, all of the strings not only have an AAB form but also end in the syllable *di*. Which generalization is correct? Recall, the observation that a set of input data can give rise to multiple generalizations has been used as an argument that learners are innately constrained to make some generalizations and not others (see above).

To determine which generalization infants made, Gerken (2006) familiarized 9-month-olds with one of four sets of stimuli: AAB stimuli from the diagonal of Table 9.1, ABA stimuli from the diagonal (ledile, wijewi, jiliji, dewede), AAB stimuli from the first column of Table 9.1, and ABA stimuli from the first column (ledile, widiwi, jidiji, dedide). At test, infants heard new AAB and ABA strings. The rationale was if infants discerned either an AAB or ABA pattern in the familiarization stimuli, they would be able to discriminate the new AAB and ABA test strings, replicating Marcus et al. (1999). In fact, only infants who were familiarized with stimuli from the diagonal discriminated the test strings, suggesting that infants familiarized with the first column made the more local "contains *di*" generalization. This interpretation was confirmed in a second study, in which infants familiarized with the first column (either the AAB or ABA version) were tested on new strings in which the B element was the syllable *di*. In this study, infants were able to discriminate AAB from ABA test stimuli. These studies suggest that the type of form-based generalization learners make is very much dependent on the specific properties of the input they encounter. Although we cannot yet determine how infants select one generalization out of a number of possibilities, the answer to that question will help us to compare nativist versus learning accounts of language development.

The input required for infants to make a particular generalization has been explored in another set of studies that focus on the conditions under which infants discern long distance dependency relations. Gómez (2002) familiarized 18-month-olds with an artificial grammar of the form AXB and CXD, in which there is a dependency between the A and B elements and between the C and D elements. Importantly, she found that it was only when the middle element was selected from a large pool (24) that infants could detect the relation between the first and third elements in the grammar. Gómez interprets her result to mean that infants attempt to process the strings in terms of sequential dependencies (A–X, X–B) until some point at which doing so becomes unfeasible. Thus, the processing resources required to encode stimuli in one manner versus another may be one factor driving the particular generalizations that learners make.

Sensitivity to syntactic categories

Researchers have begun to examine, in addition to word order, infants' sensitivity to the distributional correlates of syntactic categories. The basic research strategy is to test infants' sensitivity to morpho-phonemic paradigms, as exemplified for Russian noun gender in Table 9.2 (Gerken, Wilson, & Lewis, 2005). Seventeen-month-old infants were familiarized for two minutes with the non-emboldened words in Table 9.2. Note that if infants were able to detect that the case endings *u* and *oj* occurred on one set of words and *ya* and *yem* occurred on another set, they might be tacitly able to predict the withheld emboldened words. During test, infants heard on alternate trials the grammatical emboldened words and ungrammatical words created by combining masculine nouns with feminine case endings and vice versa. Infants were able to discriminate the

Table 9.2   Russian feminine and masculine nouns, each with two case endings

Feminine nouns					
polkoj	rubashkoj	ruchkoj	**vannoj**	knigoj	korovoj
polku	rubashku	ruchku	vannu	knigu	**korovu**
Masculine nouns					
uchitel'ya	stroitel'ya	zhitel'ya	**medved'ya**	korn'ya	pisar'ya
uchitel'yem	stroitel'yem	zhitel'yem	medved'yem	korn'yem	**pisar'yem**

Words in bold were withheld during familiarization and comprised the grammatical test items. An apostrophe after a consonant indicates that the consonant is palatalized in Russian. Ungrammatical words were *vannya, korovyem, medevedoj, pisaru*.

grammatical from ungrammatical items, suggesting that they had discerned the paradigm (Gerken et al., 2005). It is important to note that 12-month-old infants were unable to discern the Russian gender paradigm shown in Table 9.2. However, infants at that age demonstrate a potential precursor to the categorization ability shown by 17-month-olds (for details see Gómez & LaKusta, 2004).

It is also important to note, however, that infants, like adults, were able to discriminate grammatical from ungrammatical items only when a subset of the words contained a second cue to category membership. Note that a subset of the feminine words in Table 9.2 end in *k* and a subset of the masculine words end in *tel*. Studies with adults and children tested in a paradigm completion format suggest that they too are unable to discern the structure of a morpho-phonological paradigm unless morphological markers to categories are supplemented with semantics, phonology, or additional morphology (Braine, 1987; Frigo & McDonald, 1998; Mintz, 2002; Wilson, 2000). Gerken et al. (2005) suggest that requiring multiple cues to syntactic categories protects learners from overgeneralizing category structure.

Other researchers have investigated infants' sensitivity to morpho-phonological paradigms in their native language (Höhle, Weissenborn, Kiefer, Schulz, & Schmitz, 2004). Researchers familiarized 14- to 16-month-old German learners with two nonsense words in either a noun context (preceded by a determiner) or a verb context (preceded by a pronoun). The infants then heard passages in which the new words were used as nouns or verbs. Infants who were familiarized with phrases in which the novel word was used as a noun preferred passages in which it was used as a verb. These results suggest that infants track the morphological contexts that occur with particular nouns. When they hear a new word in a noun context, they expect that the new word will also appear in other noun contexts. This expectation may be a sign of infants' having formed proto-syntactic categories.

Summary of infants' sensitivity to syntactic form

The studies of infants' sensitivity to syntactic form, like the studies examining sensitivity to phonological form, indicate that infants are skilled at detecting patterns in language and are able to generalize beyond the particular stimuli that they have encountered when given appropriate evidence. The age at which sensitivity to possible precursors of syntax appears varies considerably from 7 months (Marcus et al., 1999) to the middle of the second year (Gerken et al., 2005; Gómez, 2002; Höhle et al., 2004).

As in the case of the studies on infants' sensitivity to phonological form, we can ask how the data on infants' sensitivity to syntactic form is related to what we know about syntactic structures and categories in human language. The studies on word order suggest that infants are sensitive to the order of particular elements in a string, to patterns of repeating and alternating elements, and to correlations between non-adjacent items. Although languages make some limited use of repeated morphemes (i.e., reduplication), repetition of the same word or morpheme is not typically viewed as central to morpho-syntax. Similarly, long distance dependencies in natural languages occur across constituents without a fixed length (e.g., Arielle <u>called</u> her soccer-playing friend, Sara, <u>up</u>). The studies on infants' sensitivity to morpho-phonological paradigms may better reflect processes that occur in the acquisition of natural language syntax (e.g., Braine, 1987). However, it is important to note that the syntactic categories derived via morpho-phonological cues are simply groups of words that appear in similar morpho-syntactic contexts. That is, they are not labeled for the learner as *noun*, *verb*, etc. Therefore, in theories that hold labeled syntactic categories to be crucial (e.g., Baker, 2001), categories created based on morpho-phonological cues alone may be of limited use (see Pinker, 1984).

What Early Sensitivity to Linguistic Form Tells Us about Language Development

Throughout the chapter, hints about developmental sequence can be found in statements like "17-month-olds, but not 12-month-olds discriminated . . .". The reader is cautioned that almost none of these developmental differences is statistically reliable, thereby making it very difficult in most of the research reported to determine a developmental timeline or developmental mechanisms. Nevertheless, we can attempt to construct a rough timeline for the infant abilities discussed in this chapter.

The studies on phonological form presented in this chapter suggest that 9-month-old infants are sensitive to the basic categories of phonology, including phonetic features and syllable shapes, and to at least some of the principles by which these categories are combined. The studies on syntactic form suggest that infants are sensitive to the ordering of word-like units by 7 months, and perhaps before. However, infants' ability to track the information required to infer syntactic categories has not been shown in infants younger than 14 months.

What do these studies, which demonstrate infants' sensitivity to linguistic form in the absence of meaning, tell us about language development? The ability to generalize beyond our linguistic experience to produce and comprehend new utterances based on an arbitrary, multi-leveled, system has been taken as the great mystery of human language. The studies presented in this chapter demonstrate that infants have a remarkable ability to keep track of the specifics of the form of their input and, importantly, to generalize to new forms given sufficient evidence that generalization is warranted. Does this mean that the abilities documented in the studies presented here reflect the beginnings of language development?

In considering the answer to that question, we must keep in mind that the ability to generalize across fairly complex patterns is not the unique domain of human language but rather can be seen in a host of non-humans. For example, the types of generalization by infants reported by Marcus et al. (1999) and Gerken (2006) can be seen in honey bees, pigeons, and cotton-top tamarins (Cumming & Berryman, 1961; Giurfa, Zhang, Jenett, Menzel, & Srinivasan, 2001; Hauser, Weiss, & Marcus, 2002). By contrast, other human linguistic abilities may have no parallel in non-humans (e.g., Fitch & Hauser, 2004; Hauser, Chomsky, & Fitch, 2002; Hauser, Newport, & Aslin, 2001). For example, humans, but not cotton-top tamarins, can learn a grammar of the form A^nB^n, which generates strings like (AB, AABB, AAABBB, etc.). Because only humans have communication systems with the power of human language, should we consider only abilities seen in humans and not other animals when we contemplate the mechanisms of language development? If so, many of the studies reported here will ultimately be dismissed as irrelevant to language development, although they may inform us about human learning more generally.

Alternatively, we can view the process of language development as one in which learners must use their pattern detection and categorization skills to discern the patterns and categories employed by human language. On this view, some of these skills may well be shared by other species. A similar argument has been made about categorical perception for speech sounds, which can be seen in species other than humans (e.g., Kuhl & Miller, 1975). It is now generally accepted that human speech perception has taken advantage of a general auditory property also found in other animals (Aslin, Pisoni, & Jusczyk, 1983). One barrier to the view that language develops from the application of general, but powerful, learning mechanisms to linguistic data is the argument of "poverty of the stimulus," which states that children are not exposed to linguistic structures of certain types that nevertheless appear to be part of their early knowledge of language (e.g., Chomsky, 1980). If relevant input from which patterns and categories can be detected does not exist, even the most computationally skilled learner cannot acquire a language. Although there is growing skepticism about the degree to which the input is truly impoverished (e.g., Elman, 2003; Lewis & Elman, 2001; Pullum & Scholz, 2002), much more work needs to be done to determine if there are indeed critical gaps in the infants' experience.

In the mean time, however, explorations of infants' sensitivity to linguistic form provide us with a potentially important view of the infant's world. They have the potential to inform us about what abstract structures are relatively easy and difficult to detect. Further, as infant studies come systematically to examine sensitivity to forms like those found in languages of the world, they have the potential to change how we view human language and its development.

References

Aslin, R. N., Pisoni, D. B., & Jusczyk, P. W. (1983). Auditory development and speech perception in infancy. In M. M. Haith & J. J. Campos (Eds.), *Handbook of child psychology: Infant development.* New York: Wiley.

Baker, M. C. (2001). *The atoms of language.* New York: Basic Books.

Best, C. T. (1995). Learning to perceive the sound pattern of English. In C. Rovee-Collier & L. Lipsitt (Eds.), *Advances in infancy research* (pp. 217–304). Norwood, NJ: Ablex Publishing Co.

Braine, M. D. S. (1987). What is learned in acquiring word classes – a step toward an acquisition theory. In B. MacWhinney (Ed.), *Mechanisms of language acquisition* (pp. 65–87). Hillsdale, NJ: Lawrence Erlbaum Associates.

Chambers, K. E., Onishi, K. H., & Fisher, C. L. (2003). Infants learn phonotactic regularities from brief auditory experience. *Cognition, 87,* B69–B77.

Chomsky, N. (1965). *Aspects of the theory of syntax.* Cambridge, MA: MIT Press.

Chomsky, N. (1980). The linguistic approach. In M. Piattelli-Palmarini (Ed.), *Language and learning* (pp. 109–116). Cambridge, MA: Harvard University Press.

Chomsky, N. (1981). *Lectures on government and binding.* Dordrecht: Foris.

Cumming, W. W., & Berryman, R. (1961). Some data on matching behavior in the pigeon. *Journal of the Experimental Analysis of Behavior, 4,* 281–284.

Cutler, A., & Carter, D. (1987). The predominance of strong initial syllables in the English vocabulary. *Computer Speech and Language, 2,* 133–142.

Echols, C., Crowhurst, M., & Childers, J. B. (1997). The perception of rhythmic units in speech by infants and adults. *Journal of Memory and Language, 36,* 202–225.

Eimas, P., Siqueland, E., Jusczyk, P. W., & Vigorrito, K. (1971). Speech perception in infants. *Science, 171,* 303–306.

Elman, J. (2003). Generalization from sparse input. In *Proceedings of the 38th Annual Meeting of the Chicago Linguistic Society.* Chicago: University of Chicago Press.

Fitch, W. T., & Hauser, M. D. (2004). Computational constraints on syntactic processing in a nonhuman primate. *Science, 303,* 377–380.

Frigo, L., & McDonald, J. (1998). Properties of phonological markers that affect the acquisition of gender-like subclasses. *Journal of Memory and Language, 39,* 218–245.

Gerken, L. A. (2004). Nine-month-olds extract structural principles required for natural language. *Cognition, 93,* B89–B96.

Gerken, L. A. (2006). Decisions, decisions: Infant language learning when multiple generalizations are possible. *Cognition, 98,* B67–B74.

Gerken, L. A., Wilson, R., & Lewis, W. (2005). 17-month-olds can use distributional cues to form syntactic categories. *Journal of Child Language, 32,* 249–268.

Gerken, L. A., & Zamuner, T. (in press). Exploring the basis for generalization in language acquisition. In J. Cole & J. Hualde (Eds.), *LabPhon IX: Change in phonology.* The Hague: Mouton de Gruyter.

Giurfa, M., Zhang, S. W., Jenett, A., Menzel, R., & Srinivasan, M. V. (2001). The concepts of "sameness" and "difference" in an insect. *Nature, 410,* 930–933.

Gómez, R. L. (2002). Variability and detection of invariant structure. *Psychological Science, 13,* 431–436.

Gómez, R. L., & Gerken, L. A. (1998, April). *Determining the basis of abstraction in artificial language acquisition.* Paper presented at the International Society on Infant Studies, Atlanta, GA.

Gómez, R. L., & Gerken, L. A. (1999). Artificial grammar learning by 1-year-olds leads to specific and abstract knowledge. *Cognition, 70*, 109–135.

Gómez, R. L., & Gerken, L. A. (2000). Infant artificial language learning and language acquisition. *Trends in Cognitive Sciences, 4*, 178–186.

Gómez, R. L., & LaKusta, L. (2004). A first step in form-based category abstraction by 12-month-old infants. *Developmental Science, 7*, 567–580.

Guenther, F. H., & Gjaja, M. N. (1996). The perceptual magnet effect as an emergent property of neural map formation. *Journal of the Acoustical Society of America, 100*, 1111–1121.

Guest, D. J., Dell, G. S., & Cole, J. S. (2000). Violable constraints in language production: Testing the transitivity assumption of Optimal Theory. *Journal of Memory and Language, 42*, 272–299.

Hauser, M. D., Chomsky, N., & Fitch, T. (2002). The faculty of language: what is it, who has it, and how did it evolve? *Science, 298*, 1569–1579.

Hauser, M. D., Newport, E. L., & Aslin, R. N. (2001). Segmentation of the speech stream in a non-human primate: Statistical learning in cotton-top tamarins. *Cognition, 78*, B53–B64.

Hauser, M. D., Weiss, D., & Marcus, G. F. (2002). Rule learning by cotton-top tamarins. *Cognition, 86*, B15–B22.

Hirsh-Pasek, K., Kemler Nelson, D., Jusczyk, P. W., Wright Cassidy, K., Druss, B., & Kennedy, L. (1987). Clauses are perceptual units for prelinguistic infants. *Cognition, 26*, 269–286.

Hogg, R., & McCully, C. B. (1987). *Metrical phonology*. Cambridge: Cambridge University Press.

Höhle, B., Weissenborn, J., Kiefer, D., Schulz, A., & Schmitz, M. (2004). Functional elements in infants' speech processing: The role of determiners in segmentation and categorization of lexical elements. *Infancy, 5*, 341–353.

Hyams, N. (1986). *Language acquisition and the theory of parameters*. Dordrecht: Reidel.

Jusczyk, P. W. (1985). On characterizing the development of speech perception. In J. Mehler & R. Fox (Eds.), *Neonate cognition: Beyond the blooming buzzing confusion*. Hillsdale, NJ: Lawrence Erlbaum Associates.

Jusczyk, P. W., & Aslin, R. N. (1995). Infants' detection of the sound patterns of words in fluent speech. *Cognitive Psychology, 29*, 1–23.

Jusczyk, P. W., Cutler, A., & Redanz, N. (1993). Infants' sensitivity to predominant word stress patterns in English. *Child Development, 64*, 675–687.

Jusczyk, P. W., Friederici, A. D., Wessels, J. M., Svenkerud, V. Y., & Jusczyk, A. M. (1993). Infants' sensitivity to the sound patterns of native language words. *Journal of Memory and Language, 32*, 402–420.

Jusczyk, P. W., Luce, P. A., & Charles-Luce, J. (1994). Infants' sensitivity to phonotactic patterns in the native language. *Journal of Memory and Language, 33*, 630–645.

Kuhl, P. K., & Miller, J. D. (1975). Speech perception in the chinchilla: Voiced–voiceless distinction in alveolar plosive consonants. *Science, 190*, 69–72.

Kuhl, P. K., Williams, K. A., Lacerda, F., Stevens, K. N., & Lindblom, B. (1992). Linguistic experience alters phonetic perception in infants by 6 months of age. *Science, 255*, 606–608.

Lewis, J. D., & Elman, J. L. (2001). A connectionist investigation of linguistic arguments from the poverty of the stimulus: Learning the unlearnable. In J. D. Moore & K. Stenning (Eds.), *Proceedings of the Twenty-Third Annual Conference of the Cognitive Science Society* (pp. 552–557). Mahwah, NJ: Erlbaum.

MacKain, C. (1982). Assessing the role of experience in infant speech discrimination. *Journal of Child Language, 9*, 527–542.

Marcus, G. F., Vijayan, S., Rao, S. B., & Vishton, P. M. (1999). Rule learning by seven-month-old infants. *Science, 283*, 77–80.

Maye, J., & Gerken, L. A. (2001). Learning phonemes: How far can the input take us? In H.-J. Do, L. Domínguez, & A. Johansen (Eds.), *Proceedings of the 25th Annual Boston University Conference on Language Development* (pp. 480–490). Somerville, MA: Cascadilla Press.

Maye, J., & Weiss, D. J. (2003). Statistical cues facilitate infants' discrimination of difficult phonetic contrasts. In B. Beachley, A. Brown, & F. Conlin (Eds.), *Proceedings of the 27th Annual Boston University Conference on Language Development* (pp. 508–518). Somerville, MA: Cascadilla Press.

Maye, J., Werker, J. F., & Gerken, L. A. (2002). Infant sensitivity to distributional information can affect phonetic discrimination. *Cognition, 82*, B101–B111.

Mintz, T. (2002). Category induction from distributional cues in an artificial language. *Memory and Cognition, 30*, 678–686.

Naigles, L. R. (2002). Form is easy, meaning is hard: Resolving a paradox in early child language. *Cognition, 86*, 157–199.

Pinker, S. (1984). *Language learnability and language development.* Cambridge, MA: Harvard University Press.

Polka, L., & Werker, J. F. (1994). Developmental changes in perception of nonnative vowel contrasts. *Journal of Experimental Psychology: Human Perception and Performance, 20*, 421–435.

Pullum, G. K., & Scholz, B. C. (2002). Empirical assessment of stimulus poverty arguments. *Linguistic Review, 19*, 9–50.

Saffran, J. R., & Thiessen, E. D. (2003). Pattern induction by infant language learners. *Developmental Psychology, 39*, 484–494.

Santelmann, L. M., & Jusczyk, P. W. (1998). Sensitivity to discontinuous dependencies in language learners: Evidence for limitations in processing space. *Cognition, 69*, 105–134.

Sebastián Gallés, N., & Bosch, L. (2002). The building of phonotactic knowledge in bilinguals: The role of early exposure. *Perception and Psychophysics, 28*, 974–989.

Seidl, A., & Buckley, E. (2005). On the learning of arbitrary phonological rules. *Language Learning and Development, 3–4*, 289–316.

Shady, M. E. (1996). *Infants' sensitivity to function morphemes.* Unpublished PhD dissertation, State University of New York at Buffalo, Buffalo, NY.

Shady, M. E., Gerken, L. A., & Jusczyk, P. W. (1995). Some evidence of sensitivity to prosody and word order in ten-month-olds. In D. MacLaughlin & S. McEwan (Eds.), *Proceedings of the 19th Boston University Conference on Language Development: Vol. 2.* Somerville, MA: Cascadilla Press.

Shafer, V. L., Shucard, D. W., Shucard, J. L., & Gerken, L. A. (1998). An electrophysiological study of infants' sensitivity to the sound patterns of English speech. *Journal of Speech, Language, and Hearing Research, 41*, 874–886.

Stager, C. L., & Werker, J. F. (1997). Infants listen for more phonetic detail in speech perception than in word-learning tasks. *Nature, 388*, 381–382.

Thiessen, E. D., & Saffran, J. R. (2003). When cues collide: Use of stress and statistical cues to word boundaries by 7- to 9-month-old infants. *Developmental Psychology, 39*, 706–716.

Turk, A., Jusczyk, P. W., & Gerken, L. A. (1995). Infants' sensitivity to syllable weight as a determinant of English stress. *Language and Speech, 38*, 143–158.

Werker, J. F., Fennell, C., Corcoran, K., & Stager, C. L. (2002). Infants' ability to learn phonetically similar words: Effects of age and vocabulary size. *Infancy, 3*, 1–30.

Werker, J. F., & Pegg, J. E. (1992). Infant speech perception and phonological acquisition. In C. A. Ferguson, L. Menn, & C. Stoel-Gammon (Eds.), *Phonological development: Models, research, implications* (pp. 285–311). Timonium, MD: York Press.

Werker, J. F., & Tees, R. C. (1984). Cross-language speech perception: Evidence for perceptual reorganization during the first year of life. *Infant Behavior and Development, 7,* 49–63.

Wilson, R. (2000). *Category learning in second language acquisition: What artificial grammars can tell us.* Unpublished Masters thesis, University of Arizona, Tucson, AZ.

10

Cognitive Processes in Early Word Learning

Diane Poulin-Dubois and Susan A. Graham

In this chapter, we examine the challenging issue of how children learn their first words and become master word learners before they can tie their shoes. By the end of the first year, infants have acquired sophisticated speech perception skills and have started to utter conventional words. They are also budding scientists, having developed some primitive "theories" about human psychology and object physics. The next challenge facing the child is to bridge the gap between words and concepts in order to establish what words mean. There are many questions surrounding this important milestone: What words do children learn first and why are some words easier to learn than others? What do children know about the meanings of words? What are the cognitive mechanisms involved in learning words? We address these questions by reviewing research on early lexical development and cognitive development in order to uncover the tools infants have at their disposal to acquire a lexicon. We review research on how cognitive skills, both domain-general and domain-specific (those skills tailored to process only certain kinds of information), are instrumental in helping children solve the formidable induction problem posed by word learning, including research on object and event representations and categories, as well as precursors to a theory of mind.

A Brief Historical Review

The notion that the development of cognitive abilities provides a foundation for the acquisition of language has been unanimously shared by developmentalists interested in early semantic development for many years (e.g., Clark, 1983; Dromi, 1993). One of the most influential proponents of this view was Jean Piaget. An important contribution of Piaget's work was to demonstrate first, that infants develop concepts and problem-solving skills during the first 18 to 24 months of life (the sensorimotor period). Piaget further demonstrated that these cognitive abilities provide the foundations for the emergence of symbolic representations, as expressed in language, pretend play, and other symbols. Piaget's perspective on the relationship between language and cognition contrasted sharply with the nativist view on language that also emerged at that time (Piatelli-Palmarini, 1980).

Despite the fact that Piaget's theory did not address directly the task of word learning, his theory contributed to the emergence of a strong cognitive hypothesis. According to this proposal, conceptual notions serve as the prerequisites for acquiring the linguistic forms that encode them (e.g., MacNamara, 1972). This proposal was soon followed, in the 1970s and 1980s, by a flurry of studies on the relations between linguistic and cognitive developments in infancy (e.g., Bates, Benigni, Bretherton, Camaioni, & Volterra, 1979; Gopnik, 1984). Many of these studies examined the relationship between infants' general sensorimotor development and general measures of early language such as mean length of utterance, age of acquisition of first words, or vocabulary size. In general, the results of these studies indicated a weak correspondence between language and cognition, although the predictive value of conceptual skills increased significantly when specific linguistic and conceptual milestones were considered. This finding led some researchers to propose that language and cognition are interrelated only when specific tasks are considered, a proposal that has been referred to as the specificity hypothesis (Gopnik & Meltzoff, 1986). An often-cited piece of evidence for this hypothesis concerns the link between the naming explosion typically observed around 18 months of age and a new milestone in the ability to categorize objects (Gopnik & Meltzoff, 1987; Poulin-Dubois, Graham, & Sippola, 1995, but see Gershkoff-Stowe, Thal, Smith, & Namy, 1997).

Over the last two decades, the issue of how language acquisition builds on cognitive development has taken new directions. One direction has been to specify the constraints that children honor when learning a new word (e.g., Markman, 1994; Woodward & Markman, 1998). The purely linguistic nature of these constraints is a topic of controversy (Bloom, 2000). Another line of research has examined the cognitive prerequisites for acquiring specific word forms. That is, it has been proposed that the acquisition of the meanings of nouns will be much more dependent on cognitive than linguistic factors relative to the acquisition of other words (Gentner & Boroditsky, 2001). A third research area concerns the cognitive factors that influence how infants generalize words to new referents. In particular, research on infant categorization has provided new information regarding the basis for children's word usage in the second year of life. Finally, the role of social cognitive abilities in assisting infants in some stages of lexical development has received a great deal of empirical attention (e.g., Baldwin & Meyer, this volume; Tomasello, 2001).

Types of Words in Infants' Lexicon

While infants' vocabularies contain a variety of words, the early vocabulary of young word learners has often been characterized as biased toward nouns. Nouns form the majority of children's early receptive and productive vocabulary and are typically acquired earlier than other word classes in many languages (Bates et al., 1994; Bloom, 1998; Fenson et al., 1994). As infants acquire more vocabulary, the gap between nouns and other word forms begins to close.

The main theoretical argument for the early dominance of nouns emphasizes conceptual factors, positing that it is easier to acquire labels for objects than labels for verbs. That is, it is proposed that nouns are easier to learn because they refer to perceptually distinct and coherent units that are stable and consistent across time and context (Gentner, 1982). By contrast, the task involved in learning a label for an action is a cognitively more complex one, as the child needs to abstract the constant elements across a variety of contexts labeled by the verb, and understand the particular relationship between subject and object (Gentner, 1981; MacNamara, 1972). In a recent paper, Gentner and Boroditsky (2001) have developed and expanded upon Gentner's (1982) original position by proposing the "division of dominance" hypothesis, which posits that words vary along a continuum of cognitive versus linguistic dominance. On the cognitive end of the continuum lie words that refer to perceptually "individuated" items (i.e., concrete nouns). Words that cannot "exist independently of language" are at the linguistic end of the continuum (i.e., determiners and conjunctions). Verbs lie somewhere in the middle of this continuum, as languages vary in the way they choose to lexicalize and package the same event. Consequently, it is argued that verbs are acquired later, and previously learned lexical items, such as noun–object pairs, influence verb learning (Gentner & Boroditsky, 2001).

Despite the empirical evidence and theoretical support for dominance of nouns in early vocabulary, it has been argued that the noun bias might simply be an artifact of the linguistic structure of English, rather than a universal in infants' vocabularies (Choi & Gopnik, 1995; Tardif, Gelman, & Xu, 1999). Proponents of this view have argued that infants' early lexicon reflects the linguistic input to which they are exposed, calling attention to the fact that the structural properties of languages differ in their emphasis on nouns. For example, in English, names for objects are most likely to be the loudest element of a sentence and they are often found in sentence final position (Tardif, Shatz, & Naigles, 1997). These characteristics of English may make nouns the most salient part of the sentence, making it easier for children to attend to them (Slobin, 1973). This is in sharp contrast to SOV (Subject–Object–Verb) languages like Korean and Japanese. Despite this debate, it remains that the "noun bias" has been reported in a wide range of languages other than English, including French, Italian, Spanish, Hebrew, Dutch, Korean, and Mandarin (Au, Dapretto, & Song, 1994; Bornstein et al., 2004; Caselli et al., 1995; Dromi, 1987; Gentner, 1982; Jackson-Maldonado, Thal, Marchman, Bates, & Gutierrez-Clellen, 1993; Poulin-Dubois et al., 1995; Tardif et al., 1999).

In sum, the universal presence of many different word types in the early lexicon suggests that children create meaning to map onto different word forms at the very first stages of lexical development. To do so, they have to draw on the repertoire of conceptual knowledge that they have built over their first year of life, such as knowledge about objects, actions, and properties and how they map to different linguistic categories like nouns, verbs, and adjectives (Clark, 1993). In the next sections, we review the domain-general as well as domain-specific cognitive processes that are utilized by children to learn each of these word forms.

Domain-General Processes in Learning Words

There is a large literature that indicates that domain-general cognitive mechanisms (e.g., learning processes, memory, attention, social-cognitive skills, etc.) facilitate all aspects of language learning, including speech segmentation, phonetic and grammatical categorization, and word learning (see Baldwin & Meyer, this volume; Saffran & Thiessen, this volume). With regard to word learning, researchers have proposed that many word learning skills are domain-general processes that are recruited in a wide range of learning contexts (e.g., Bloom, 2000; Samuelson & Smith, 2000). For example, mechanisms of learning, memory, and retrieval, which are well known in the adult verbal learning literature, also apply to the early stages of word learning. This is well demonstrated by overextension errors which occur when the child knows the correct word but accesses the wrong word by mistake (e.g., dog for horse). These errors appear to reflect a difficulty in retrieving a known word from the lexicon and are more frequent at the time of rapid vocabulary growth (Gershkoff-Stowe, 2002; Huttenlocher, 1974). Sensitivity to attentional cues, such as gaze direction, is another case of a domain-general mechanism which can be instrumental in establishing the reference of a new word and in distinguishing between accidental and intentional actions (Baldwin, 1993; Woodward, 2004). In fact, some researchers have argued that specialized developmental mechanisms for learning words are the product of language development, with general and dumb processes initially driving word generalizations (Smith, 2001). In this chapter, we presume that children do bring a powerful set of domain-general learning processes to the task of learning words, including memory capabilities, categorization skills, selective attention, and a sensitivity to the intentions of others. In the sections that follow, we review how specific cognitive accomplishments assist infants in acquiring specific types of words.

Cognitive Processes in Learning Nouns

As described earlier, words for objects, or nouns, occupy a privileged position in the early lexicon. Not surprisingly, a great deal of research has been devoted to understanding the processes that underlie the acquisition of nouns (see Bloom, 2000; Hall & Waxman, 2004, for reviews). In this section, we review the cognitive processes that underlie object word learning, focusing on infants' understanding of objects and object categories.

Object representations

One of the initial steps in learning an object word is to identify the referent of a word amongst the many possible candidates present in any given situation. The word learner must then make a link between that word and the object. In order to make a reliable mapping between a word and an object, infants must build a representation of the object that is the referent of the new word. This process of building an object representation rests upon infants' ability to view an object as a solid body that continues to exist when occluded and that maintains its identity over time. In this section, we review evidence indicating that well before they reach their first birthdays, infants have developed an impressive understanding of objects.

In order to determine which object is the intended referent of the new word, infants must be able to identify the often numerous objects present in the scene. Thus, they first must parse the surfaces present into distinct entities, a task referred to as object segregation. For example, they must appreciate that the dog partially hidden behind a tree is one dog, rather than multiple objects. Second, they must be able to determine the number of distinct entities present in any given scene and must track the identity of these objects through space and time, a task referred to as object individuation. For example, they must recognize that the dog they saw behind the tree is the same dog that is now running across the field. Research has demonstrated that already before 12 months of age infants are highly skilled at both of these tasks. That is, they can use a variety of perceptual cues for object segregation, including motion of visible surfaces and edge alignment (e.g., Johnson, 2004). Similarly, infants can utilize several types of information when individuating objects, including spatiotemporal information, featural information, and kind information (see Wilcox, Schweinle, & Chapa, 2003; Xu, 2003).

In addition to the ability to segregate and individuate objects, infants need to appreciate some fundamental aspects of objects, such as object permanence. Seminal research by Baillargeon and her colleagues with procedures based on visual attention has demonstrated that infants as young as 2.5 months of age can appreciate that objects continue to exist when hidden (e.g., Baillargeon, 2004). Furthermore, infants can represent the locations of hidden objects and they view objects as cohesive, three-dimensional bodies that trace continuous paths in space and time (Spelke & Van de Walle, 1993). Finally, infants appear to have a basic understanding of physical properties of objects, including gravity, and causality (Cohen & Oakes, 1993; Leslie & Keeble, 1987). In sum, research indicates that infants in the first year of life can segregate, individuate, and represent objects.

Object categories

Another important step in the word learning process involves generalizing a newly learnt word to other appropriate instances of the referent when encountered in the future. To accomplish this task, infants require some understanding of the category or concept that is marked by that word. How early in their word learning career infants can do so is the subject of debate. Some researchers believe that some early word learners can learn only context-bound words whereas others argue that infants can extend linguistic knowledge to new contexts as soon as they comprehend their first words around 9 months (Barrett, 1995; Schafer, 2005). In this section, first, we review evidence indicating that preverbal infants have well-developed categorization abilities; second, we review research describing the developmental path that infants follow when attaching words to categories, and third, we describe the nature of early lexical object categories.

Well before they utter their first word, infants are already highly skilled at object categorization. For a young child to engage in categorization, he or she must perceive entities as alike, thereby employing some type of similarity rule to group them together. Studies have demonstrated that by 2 to 3 months of age, infants can learn global category representations, such as a category of furniture that includes novel furniture items but excludes mammals. By 3 to 4 months of age, infants can also form basic-level category representations, such as a category that includes novel cats but excludes birds, dogs, and horses. By 6 to 7 months of age, infants can form more specific, subordinate-like categories, such as a category of tabby cats that excluded Siamese cats (see Quinn, 2004, for a review). Of course, these early perceptual categories demonstrate only that infants are adept at extracting common properties across a wide range of objects. Infants' object categories undergo further development during the second year of life with basic-level categories developing after global categories as shown by more "conservative" categorization tasks, such as object examination and sequential touching (e.g., Mandler, 2003).

Infants not only have well-developed categorization abilities, but they can also use the categories they form to guide their inductive inferences. Inductive inferences typically involve the following line of reasoning: first, observing that X has the property Y (e.g., a robin can fly); second, deciding that X and Z are the same kind of thing (e.g., a robin and a sparrow are both birds); and third, inferring that Z also has the property Y (e.g., therefore a sparrow can fly). Following from Susan Gelman's seminal research on preschoolers' inductive abilities (see Diesendruck, this volume), studies have demonstrated that infants as young as 9 months of age possess basic inductive reasoning abilities. For example, Baldwin, Markman, and Melartin (1993) found that 9- to 16-month-old infants generalized nonobvious object properties to objects that were perceptually similar to a target object (see also Graham, Kilbreath, & Welder, 2004; Welder & Graham, 2001). Recent research has focused on the nature of the categories that guide infants' inductive generalizations. For example, infants as young as 9 months can generalize "animal" properties (e.g., drinking) to other animals and "vehicle" properties (e.g., being keyed) to other vehicles (Mandler & McDonough, 1996, 1998). Furthermore, infants will not cross category boundaries and imitate actions appropriate for animals on vehicles and vice versa.

Linking words to objects

As infants cross the word learning threshold, they appear to begin with a broad expectation linking words to commonalities among objects, rather than with a specific expectation that words link to category-based commonalities (Waxman, 2004; Waxman & Lidz, 2006). That is, infants begin with the notion that words highlight many different types of commonalities amongst objects including category-based commonalities (e.g., dogs, cats), event-based commonalities (jumping, rolling), and property-based commonalities (e.g., rough things, smooth things). In support of this proposal, Waxman and Booth (2003) found that 11-month-old infants construed the same set of objects (e.g., four purple animals) as either members of the same category (e.g., animals) or as all possessing a salient property (e.g., purple things). Moreover, infants linked novel words, presented either as nouns or as adjectives, to either construal. Waxman and her colleagues have argued that this initial broad link serves a number of critical functions including facilitating the formation of many different concepts and assisting the infant in discovering more specific mappings between specific types of words (e.g., nouns, adjectives) and specific types of relations they mark (e.g., noun–object categories, adjectives–object properties).

This broad expectation that words map to a variety of commonalities becomes more precise as infants establish their lexicon (Waxman, 2004; Waxman & Lidz, 2006). That is, around 13 to 14 months of age, infants begin to map novel nouns to category-based commonalities amongst objects. Waxman and Booth (2001) demonstrated that 14-month-olds map novel nouns to category-based commonalities amongst objects (e.g., horses) and not to property-based commonalities (e.g., purple things). Interestingly, infants mapped novel adjectives to either property-based or category-based commonalities. Thus, their expectations for novel nouns are more precise than their expectations for novel adjectives at 14 months of age.

Nature of Early Lexical Categories

In recent years, a great deal of empirical attention has been devoted to investigating the nature of infants' categories with specific focus on the characteristics of the similarity rules that are used to guide categorization (see Rakison & Oakes, 2003, for a review). In this section, we focus only on a particular type of lexical category, namely, categories that are labeled by nouns, and we describe several conclusions regarding the nature of this particular type of lexical category during infancy.

First, perceptual features, in particular shape similarity, can play an important role in the organization of infants' lexical categories about objects. Several studies have demonstrated that infants tend to privilege shape information over other types of perceptual information such as color and size when extending novel words (e.g., Gershkoff-Stowe & Smith, 2004; Graham & Poulin-Dubois, 1999). Although there is little controversy around the finding that infants' lexical categories can be organized by shape, there is significant debate regarding why children attend to shape when extending novel words. Some researchers suggest that children attend to shape similarity when categorizing objects as their categories reflect primarily their attention to salient perceptual features (e.g., Jones & Smith, 1993). By contrast, other researchers suggest that children attend to shape information when categorizing objects because it serves as a perceptually available cue to the kind to which an object belongs (e.g., Bloom, 2000; Gelman & Diesendruck, 1999). In support of the latter position, research has demonstrated that infants expect objects that share a high degree of shape similarity also to share nonobvious properties, suggesting that they appreciate that shape similarity is a reliable cue to category membership (e.g., Graham et al., 2004; Welder & Graham, 2001).

Second, and importantly, infants are not limited to grouping objects together on the basis of perceptual features when forming lexical categories of objects. For example, studies have demonstrated that when objects are named, 14-month-old infants will categorize objects that share less perceptually obvious features such as function (e.g., Booth & Waxman, 2002; Welder & Graham, 2006). Similarly, Waxman and her colleagues have demonstrated that naming objects with the same label will aid infants in forming superordinate categories of objects that may share minimal perceptual similarity (Waxman & Markow, 1995). Finally, when 13- and 18-month-old infants are provided with information about category membership in the form of shared object names, they assume that two perceptually dissimilar objects belong to the same category and therefore share a nonobvious property (Graham et al., 2004; Welder & Graham, 2001). Thus, when forming a lexical category, infants will treat object names as marking category membership and will use that information to group together objects that may not share perceptual similarity. Importantly, sound tones and emotional expressions (e.g., "Ah") do not appear to have the same facilitative effect on categorization as words (Balaban & Waxman, 1997; Xu, 2002). In support of the integration of both perceptual and categorical knowledge in early word meaning, toddlers appear to make many overextension errors in production (e.g., referring to a pomegranate as an apple) that are not always errors of use but also reflect underlying broad word meanings based on shape and taxonomic relatedness (Gelman, Croft, Fu, Clausner, & Gottfried, 1998).

Finally, recent research has demonstrated that the associations children make between a word and its referent in early word learning may be explained by a prototype framework (Barrett, 1995). For example, around 12 months of age, infants may first map a word to a typical member of a category (e.g., a golden retriever) and not to an atypical member of the category (e.g., a pug). By 18 months, however, infants broaden their extensions to include less typical category members (Meints, Plunkett, & Harris, 1999). Similarly, infants as young as 18 months are flexible in their object word extension in that they will consider intact (e.g., a dog) and incomplete objects (e.g., a dog without a tail and legs) as equally acceptable referents for familiar labels (Poulin-Dubois & Sissons, 2002).

In sum, there is a great deal of evidence indicating that infants are highly skilled at building object representations and forming object categories. These abilities set the stage for the rapid acquisition of object words that takes place during infancy.

Cognitive Processes in Verb Learning

Although some verbs appear early in the lexicon, verbs seem to be universally harder to learn than nouns (Bornstein et al., 2004). The problem in verb learning seems to be about mapping a verb onto an action or event rather than about learning the underlying concepts that verbs encode (Maguire, Hirsch-Pasek, & Golinkoff, 2006). To learn a verb, children have to determine which aspect of an ongoing event is being referred to, or to solve what Tomasello (1995) has called the "packaging problem." One source of the difficulty naïve learners encounter in solving the verb packaging problem is that verbs can be interpreted in terms of numerous semantic elements such as manner of motion (e.g., walk vs. run), direction relative to the speaker (e.g., come vs. go), the instrument involved (spoon vs. pedal), or by the result achieved (e.g., fill vs. empty) to name but a

few (Gentner, 1982; Talmy, 1985). In addition to learning which aspects of a verb's referent become conflated with meaning, children must also interpret actors' behavioral
intentions and speakers' semantic intentions, as well as relying on their own semantic
and syntactic understanding to overcome the referential obstacles to acquiring verb
meaning (Forbes & Farrar, 1995). In this section, we discuss how early action verbs are
represented as well as the recent studies on infants' understanding of human action and
object motion.

Infants' representations of verbs

The few studies that have focused on young children's initial representation of verb
meaning indicate that verbs are initially narrowly defined and context-specific (Forbes
& Farrar, 1993; Forbes & Poulin-Dubois, 1997). Children initially represent action verb
meaning in terms of event appearance, that is, the overall configuration of an action. By
the end of the third year, children's representation of verb meaning includes proportion-
ally more defining elements of semantic meaning, including the actor's intentions
(Poulin-Dubois & Forbes, 2002, 2006), speaker's semantic intentions (e.g., Forbes,
Ashley, & Martin, 2003), as well as syntactic form and function relationships (e.g.,
Naigles & Terrazas, 1998; Slobin, 2001).

Recent experimental research has demonstrated that children seem to take more time
to learn labels for actions than for objects. For example, when 2.5-year-olds are taught
novel labels for novel objects and novel actions, children learn the noun–object association more easily than the verb–action association (Childers & Tomasello, 2002). A
similar advantage of nouns over verbs is observed in studies that have examined how
well children generalize newly learned nouns and verbs to new instances. Both English-
and Japanese-speaking preschoolers fail to extend a new verb to other similar actions
when the object that is acted on is changed. By contrast, they extend nouns on the basis
of similarity of objects independent of the action in which the object is used (Imai,
Haryu, & Okada, 2005; Kersten & Smith, 2002). In a recent direct test of the word–
object versus word–action association, 18- to 20-month-old infants were first familiarized with novel labels (e.g., fep) for computer-animated motion events and then shown
test events in which either the motion or the object were switched in the presence of the
original label (Katerelos, Poulin-Dubois, & Oshima-Takane, submitted). The results
indicated that French-, English-, and Japanese-speaking infants mapped the novel label
preferentially to the object. Because the linguistic properties of Japanese (e.g., argument-
dropping, SOV language) would predict that verb learning would precede noun learning,
these findings provide strong evidence for the universal noun advantage.

Furthermore, young children tend to rely on general-purpose verbs at the early stages
of verb acquisition (e.g., go, get). These findings may be due to the fact that categories
of actions are less coherent than categories of objects. That is, action categories differ
from object categories in that first, actions involve a relation between at least one agent
and some activity, and second, action categories are not as well defined as object categories. For example, it is not clear when the action of picking up an object begins. Does
it begin when the hand starts to move toward the object, when the object is grasped, or

when it is lifted off the floor? Finally, the "glue" that holds exemplars of an action category together is less binding than in the case of object categories. For example, in the case of transitive actions, there is great diversity in the objects involved in actions sharing the same label, as illustrated by activities labeled "holding," including a vase holding flowers, a mother holding a child, and a barrette holding hair (Clark, 1993).

Infants' understanding of motion events

While some of the conceptual foundations for verb learning do overlap with those for noun learning, there is knowledge that will be uniquely recruited for verb learning. In particular, in addition to the ability to attend to, individuate, and categorize actions, infants also have to determine which elements of meanings are encoded in a verb to successfully map words to actions (Golinkoff et al., 2002).

Since most early verbs denote concrete events, the processing of object motion and human action is required in order to learn verbs efficiently. A large body of research indicates that preverbal infants can discriminate and conceptualize motion events. First, motion attracts the attention of very young infants. For example, infants of 2 to 3 months of age prefer to look at moving rather than stationary objects (Kellman & Banks, 1998; Slater, 1989). Infants as young as 3 months of age can extract motion commonalities when presented with point-light displays of the pendular motion of animals walking in place or the rotary motion of vehicles rolling in place (Arterberry & Bornstein, 2001, 2002). During the first year, infants also show sensitivity to a wide range of motion properties, such as trajectory and onset of motion. For instance, infants as young as 3 months discriminate between a point-light display representing a walking person and an incoherent display (Fox & McDaniel, 1982). Movement is also instrumental in the development of infants' understanding of objects' properties (see Baillargeon, 2004, for a review) and is critical in the perception of object unity (Johnson & Aslin, 1995; Smith, Johnson, & Spelke, 2003). By 6 months of age, infants can discriminate subtle differences between action events, such as causal versus noncausal launching events and contingent versus noncontingent motion (Bahrick, Gogate, & Ruiz, 2002; Cohen & Amsel, 1998). Infants of this age also discriminate manner and path in a motion event (Casasola, Bhagwat, & Ferguson, 2006) and can categorize dynamic point-light displays of the motion patterns of animals and vehicles (Arterberry & Bornstein, 2002). Using geometric figures as stimuli, studies have demonstrated that by the end of the first year, infants can categorize events based on path across varying manners and based on manner across varying paths (Pulverman, Hirsh-Pasek, Golinkoff, Pruden, & Salkind, 2006).

Not only do infants make fine discriminations of motion patterns, but infants are adept at generalizing motion across a wide range of agents, paving the way for action word extension (Poulin-Dubois & Vyncke, 2005). In one study, we tested 14- and 18-month-olds' ability to associate animals and people with animate motions (e.g., climbing stairs, jumping over a block) and vehicles with inanimate motions (e.g., jumping across a gap, sliding along a U-shaped block). An experimenter modeled each action three times with an appropriate target exemplar with each demonstration accompanied by a specific vocalization (e.g., making a dog walk up the stairs while saying "Tum, tum, tum").

Infants were then given two test exemplars to imitate the action (e.g., a horse and a car). Infants as young as 14 months generalized motion trajectory from one category exemplar to a member of the same object kind. Interestingly, in another experiment, infants were also able to generalize the actions modeled with an animal to both a person and another animal, showing a broad concept of agents. Another recent series of experiments using similar stimuli with the infant-controlled habituation paradigm provides converging evidence that the ability to generalize motion properties across objects emerges during the second year (Baker, Demke, & Poulin-Dubois, submitted). For example, when habituated to films featuring a dog jumping over a wall and a car bouncing off the wall, infants as young as 12 months dishabituated to incongruent test events (e.g., bus jumping over the wall) but not to congruent events (e.g., cat jumping over the wall).

In sum, by the beginning of the second year infants are not only competent in discriminating human actions and object motion, but they also understand that many different agents are capable of performing the same actions. This knowledge makes possible the extension of action verbs to many different agents at a very early stage in lexical development, analogous to the way nouns are extended to object categories.

Infants' understanding of the intentional nature of actions

Although motion and action processing constitute the building blocks from which infants can learn the meaning of many concrete action verbs (e.g., run, jump), other cognitive abilities are required to establish the reference of other verbs, such as spill and pour. To learn these verbs, infants must be able to represent human actions not only as physical motion through space but also as having an intentional structure. Although the lexicons of very young infants do not contain many instances of this type of verb, there is evidence that children can learn verbs like spill and pour toward the end of the second year (Poulin-Dubois & Forbes, 2002, 2006). Furthermore, by the beginning of the second year, children have begun to produce mental terms, more specifically terms that refer to desires (e.g., want, like), with other mental verbs emerging around the third birthday (Bartsch & Wellman, 1995; Shatz, Wellman, & Silber, 1983).

A number of recent studies have examined when infants represent actions in terms of intentional relations (see Buresh, Woodward, & Brune, 2006, for a review). By 5 or 6 months of age, infants are attentive to grasping events and represent them as object-directed events (Woodward, 1998, 1999). Interestingly, the same object-grasping actions are not interpreted as object-directed if an inanimate object is the agent or if the hand only touches the object (Woodward, 1999; Woodward & Somerville, 2000). A few months later, infants can infer goals from gaze or pointing alone, without physical contact with the object (Sodian & Thoermer, 2004; Woodward, 2003). By 10 or 11 months of age, infants can parse an ongoing stream of action by using the beginning and end of intention-in-actions as boundaries. For example, when pauses are inserted in videos of everyday events (e.g., cleaning the kitchen), infants show more interest when the pauses occur in the middle of an intentional action than if they are inserted after or before the action (Baldwin, Baird, Saylor, & Clark, 2001). When asked to imitate the actions of other people, infants are also sensitive to behavioral cues that mark the underlying goals of people's action. For example, after observing an actor who tried, but failed, to complete an action, 18-month-olds (but not 12-month-olds) are as likely to produce the target action as those who had seen a demonstration in which the actor achieved his goal (Bellagamba & Tomasello, 1999; Meltzoff, 1995). When infants ranging from 14 to 18 months of age are requested to imitate an actor's actions on objects, they are more likely to imitate actions accompanied by behavioral cues that suggest intentional actions (i.e., actor said "There!" and looking at the object while completing the action) than actions that appear accidental (i.e., actor said "Whoops!" while looking away as she completes the action) (Carpenter, Nagell, & Tomasello, 1998; Olineck & Poulin-Dubois, 2005). Finally, it has recently been shown that in a toy request task, infants as young as 9 months react with more frustration if a person appears to refuse to hand a toy to the child than if she seems to fail to hand the toy because she is clumsy (Behne, Carpenter, Call, & Tomasello, 2005). Taken together, this research suggests that infants possess the necessary cognitive skills to represent actions in terms of their intentional structures by the time that action words enter their receptive vocabulary.

Although infants' early vocabularies are composed mainly of nouns and verbs, other types of words are present as well. Moreover, these other words can account for a substantial portion of the vocabulary by the end of the infancy period. Although there is relatively little research on word meanings other than nouns and verbs, researchers have started to examine the cognitive foundations for these words. We review some of the available evidence in the next section, focusing on recent studies on spatial prepositions (see Waxman & Lidz, 2006, for a review of the processes underlying adjective acquisition).

Learning Spatial Words

In many languages, including English, Italian, Turkish, and Hebrew, the spatial prepositions "in," "on," and "under" are the first to be understood and produced by very young children, with the preposition "in" understood before the other two (Bowerman, 1996; Clark, 1973). Recent research with the preferential looking paradigm has demonstrated that infants as young as 15 months understand these prepositions when shown typical situations, as defined by the centrality of the object relative to the reference object. By 18 months of age, children have broadened the scope of the meaning of spatial prepositions to include less typical locations (Meints, Plunkett, Harris, & Dimmock, 2002).

As we have seen, children's earliest representations of objects, relations, and events provide the universal foundations for linguistic categories. What is the universal conceptual knowledge that infants possess about space? In order to map spatial terms to the appropriate referents, infants must attend to one type of relation while ignoring other possible relations that may be present in an event. Research over the last several years has yielded strong evidence that infants possess sophisticated nonlinguistic knowledge about space. As young as 2.5 months, infants understand the basics of the concept of containment, such as the fact that a container must have an opening. By 5 or 6 months, infants also discriminate between the action of placing an object in a tight-fit containment relation and the action of placing an object fitting loosely into a container. They also appreciate that a wide object cannot be placed into a narrower container (Aguiar & Baillargeon, 1998; Spelke & Hespos, 2002). Infants of this age can easily habituate to a container seen from different angles and holding different objects (Casasola, Cohen, & Chiarello, 2003). A few months later, infants as young as 9 months can form a spatial category of tight-fit containment events that are different from another category of loose-fit containment events, even if such a distinction is not lexically encoded in their own language (McDonough, Choi, & Mandler, 2003). However, if familiarized with both types of containment, infants can form a more inclusive category of containment (Casasola & Cohen, 2002). This precocious understanding of containment explains the results of earlier studies that tested the comprehension of spatial prepositions with act-out tasks. These studies demonstrated that children will put objects in a container if there is one available, even if the linguistic instructions require the child to put the object on or under a container.

In addition to the concepts of support and containment, infants also develop knowledge about other spatial relations. For example, they possess the categorical representation of "above" versus "below" as early as 3 months of age, though this knowledge does become more robust by 6 months of age (Quinn, Polly, Furer, Dobson, & Narter, 2002). Similarly, infants first demonstrate the ability to discriminate the relation of "between" from a different relation at 6 months of age (Quinn, Adams, Kennedy, Shettler, & Wasnik, 2003).

In accord with the proposal that the mapping of spatial terms is not uniquely driven by cognitive development, a number of recent studies have documented that languages conflate information about space in different ways into distinct lexical items. For example, English, Spanish, and Dutch use from one to three prepositions to express containment, support, and attachment (Clark, 2004). Studies of the spontaneous speech of children have reported language-related differences as early as 17 to 20 months (see Bowerman & Choi, 2003, for a review). For example, learners of English distinguish between actions involving containment (in) and those involving contact/support (on) while learners of Korean ignored this distinction in favor of a categorization of spatial events in terms of loose versus tight fitting (kkita vs. nehta). In other words, when the children talked about spatial events, they showed sensitivity to language-specific distinctions. This illustrates well the fact that although language acquisition builds on cognitive development, linguistic representations capture only certain aspects of universal cognitive representations as well as emphasizing specific cognitive distinctions not yet represented by the infant.

Conclusions

Word learning is a linguistic problem that, unlike many other language acquisition tasks, requires as many tools from the conceptual domain as from the linguistic domain. As we have reviewed, infants possess impressive knowledge about object categories and properties as well as knowledge about relations between entities. They also have developed sophisticated social-cognitive and learning skills that will allow them to establish reference for many types of words. Thus, by the time first words are understood or produced, infants have built up strong cognitive functions that they can recruit in the process of mapping words to the objects and events. This knowledge base sets the stage for the prodigious word learning that occurs during the second year of life and beyond.

Throughout the chapter, we have focused on the cognitive underpinnings of word learning. At the same time, we must emphasize the critical role that language plays in cognition. Over the past decade, numerous studies have demonstrated how linguistic input shapes cognition. For example, hearing a common name to refer to distinct objects promotes the formation of object categories in infancy (e.g., Graham et al., 2004; Waxman & Markow, 1995) while hearing distinct names promotes individuation (Xu, 2002). Furthermore, the specific language that children are exposed to will also shape the way they conceptualize the world. For example, researchers have started to examine how learning language-specific spatial semantic categories influences early spatial semantic development (Bowerman & Choi, 2003). In turn, language-specific categories of space lead the adult speaker to become increasingly skilled at detecting spatial distinctions that are mapped in her mother tongue and less skilled at others (McDonough et al., 2003). When in development this language-specific influence exerts its impact on spatial cognition remains to be determined.

The research reviewed in this chapter suggests that infants come well equipped to acquire word meanings, but also that their limited cognitive abilities impact their early lexical development. That is, recent experimental research on word learning has demonstrated that early in their word learning career, 12- to 13-month-old infants are immature word learners in many ways. With regard to word reference, infants of that age tend to be initially biased by superficial cues such as the perceptual salience of objects or actions instead of following the perspective of the speaker (Hollich, Hirsh-Pasek, & Golinkoff, 2000). They also need more exposure and more cues from the speaker to map a novel word to a referent relative to more experienced word learners (Hirsh-Pasek et al., 2000; Woodward, 2004). Furthermore, at the very early stages of word learning, children have not yet figured out the ways in which words are different from other symbols (Namy, 2001; Woodward & Hoyne, 1999). With regard to word extension, although infants extend words readily from the beginning, the research that we have reviewed in this chapter indicates that unexperienced word learners are more conservative as well as more liberal than more experienced word learners in their use of words, regardless of the linguistic form class (e.g., Forbes & Farrar, 1993; Meints et al., 1999; Theakston, Lieven, Pine, & Rowland, 2002; Tomasello, 1992). Understanding how these patterns change over the second year of life and how these changes may be related to cognitive changes will offer important insights into word learning and contribute to a better understanding of language development in general.

Note

This research was supported by operating grants awarded to both authors by the Natural Sciences and Engineering Research Council of Canada. Susan Graham also acknowledges support from the Canada Research Chairs program.

References

Aguiar, A., & Baillargeon, R. (1998). Eight-and-a-half-month-old infants' reasoning about containment events. *Child Development, 69,* 636–653.

Arterberry, M. E., & Bornstein, M. H. (2001). Three-month-old infants' categorization of animals and vehicles based on static and dynamic attributes. *Journal of Experimental Child Psychology, 80,* 333–346.

Arterberry, M. E., & Bornstein, M. H. (2002). Infant perceptual and conceptual categorization: The roles of static and dynamic stimulus attributes. *Cognition, 86,* 1–24.

Au, T. K. F., Dapretto, M., & Song, Y. K. (1994). Input versus constraints: Early word acquisition in Korean and English. *Journal of Memory and Language, 33,* 567–582.

Bahrick, L. E., Gogate, L. J., & Ruiz, I. (2002). Attention and memory for faces and actions in infancy: The salience of actions over faces in dynamic events. *Child Development, 73,* 1629–1643.

Baillargeon, R. (2004). Infants' reasoning about hidden objects: Evidence for event-general and event-specific expectations. *Developmental Science, 7,* 391–424.

Baker, R. K., Demke, T. L., & Poulin-Dubois, D. (submitted). Infants' ability to associate motion trajectories with object kinds.

Balaban, M. T., & Waxman, S. R. (1997). Do words facilitate object categorization in 9-month-old infants? *Journal of Experimental Child Psychology, 64,* 3–26.

Baldwin, D. A. (1993). Early referential understanding: Infants' ability to recognize referential acts for what they are. *Developmental Psychology, 29,* 832–843.

Baldwin, D. A., Baird, J. A., Saylor, M. M., & Clark, M. A. (2001). Infants parse dynamic action. *Child Development, 72,* 708–717.

Baldwin, D. A., Markman, E. M., & Melartin, R. L. (1993). Infants' ability to draw inferences about nonobvious object properties: Evidence from exploratory play. *Child Development, 64,* 711–728.

Barrett, M. D. (1995). Early lexical development. In P. Fletcher & B. MacWhinney (Eds.), *Handbook of child language* (pp. 362–392). Oxford: Blackwell.

Bartsch, K., & Wellman, H. M. (1995). *Children talk about the mind.* New York: Oxford University Press.

Bates, E., Benigni, L., Bretherton, I., Camaioni, L., & Volterra, V. (1979). *The emergence of symbols: Cognition and communication in infancy.* New York: Academic Press.

Bates, E., Marchman, V. A., Thal, D., Fenson, L., Dale, P., & Reznick, S. (1994). Developmental and stylistic variation in the composition of early vocabulary. *Journal of Child Language, 21,* 85–123.

Behne, T., Carpenter, M., Call, J., & Tomasello, M. (2005). Unwilling versus unable: Infants' understanding of intentional action. *Developmental Psychology, 41,* 328–337.

Bellagamba, F., & Tomasello, M. (1999). Re-enacting intended acts: Comparing 12- and 18-month-olds. *Infant Behavior and Development, 22,* 277–282.

Bloom, P. (1998). Theories of artefact categorization. *Cognition, 66,* 87–93.

Bloom, P. (2000). *How children learn the meanings of words.* Cambridge, MA: MIT Press.

Booth, A. E., & Waxman, S. R. (2002). Object names and object functions serve as cues to categories for infants. *Developmental Psychology, 38,* 948–957.

Bornstein, M. H., Coté, L. R., Maital, S., Painter, K., Park, S. Y., Pascual, L., et al. (2004). Cross-linguistic analysis of vocabulary in young children: Spanish, Dutch, French, Hebrew, Italian, Korean, and American English. *Child Development, 75,* 1115–1139.

Bowerman, M. (1996). The origins of children's spatial semantic categories: Cognitive versus linguistic determinants. In J. J. Gumperz & S. C. Levinson (Eds.), *Rethinking linguistic relativity* (pp. 145–176). New York: Cambridge University Press.

Bowerman, M., & Choi, S. (2003). Space under construction: Language-specific spatial categorization in first language acquisition. In D. Gentner & S. Goldin-Meadow (Eds.), *Language in mind: Advances in the study of language and thought* (pp. 387–427). Cambridge, MA: MIT Press.

Buresh, J. S., Woodward, A., & Brune, C. W. (2006). The roots of verbs in prelinguisitic action knowledge. In K. Hirsh-Pasek & R. M. Golinkoff (Eds.), *Action meets word: How children learn verbs* (pp. 208–227). New York: Oxford University Press.

Carpenter, M., Nagell, K., & Tomasello, M. (1998). Social cognition, joint attention, and communicative competence from 9 to 15 months of age. *Monographs of the Society for Research in Child Development, 63* (4, Serial No. 255).

Casasola, M., Bhagwat, J., & Ferguson, K. T. (2006). Precursors to verb learning: Infants' understanding of motion events. In K. Hirsh-Pasek & R. M. Golinkoff (Eds.), *Action meets word: How children learn verbs* (pp. 160–190). New York: Oxford University Press.

Casasola, M., & Cohen, L. (2002). Infant categorization of containment, support and tight-fit spatial relationships. *Developmental Science, 5,* 247–264.

Casasola, M., Cohen, L. B., & Chiarello, E. (2003). Six-month-old infants' categorization of containment spatial relations. *Child Development, 74,* 679–693.

Caselli, M. C., Bates, E., Casadio, P., Fenson, J., Fenson, L., & Sanderl, L. (1995). A cross-linguistic study of early lexical development. *Cognitive Development, 10,* 159–199.

Childers, J. B., & Tomasello, M. (2002). Two-year-olds learn novel nouns, verbs, and conventional actions from massed or spaced exposures. *Developmental Psychology, 38,* 967–978.

Choi, S., & Gopnik, A. (1995). Early acquisition of verbs in Korean: A cross-linguistic study. *Journal of Child Language, 22,* 497–529.

Clark, E. V. (1973). What's in a word? On the child's acquisition of semantics in his first language. In T. E. Moore (Ed.), *Cognitive development and the acquisition of language*. New York: Academic Press.

Clark, E. V. (1983). Meanings and concepts. In J. H. Flavell & E. M. Markman (Eds.), *Handbook of child development* (pp. 787–840). New York: Wiley.

Clark, E. V. (1993). *The lexicon in acquisition.* Cambridge: Cambridge University Press.

Clark, E. V. (2004). How language acquisition builds on cognitive development. *Trends in Cognitive Sciences, 8,* 472–478.

Cohen, L. B., & Amsel, G. (1998). Precursors to infants' perception of the causality of a simple event. *Infant Behavior and Development, 21,* 713–731.

Cohen, L. B., & Oakes, L. M. (1993). How infants perceive a simple causal event. *Developmental Psychology, 29,* 421–433.

Dromi, E. (1987). *Early lexical development.* Cambridge: Cambridge University Press.

Dromi, E. (1993). The mysteries of early lexical development: Underlying cognitive and linguistic processes in meaning acquisition. In E. Dromi (Ed.), *Language and cognition: A developmental perspective* (pp. 32–60). Norwood, NJ: Ablex Publishing Co.

Fenson, L., Dale, P. S., Reznick, J. S., Bates, E., Thal, D., & Pethick, S. (1994). Variability in early communicative development. *Monographs of the Society for Research in Child Development, 59* (Serial No. 242).

Forbes, J. N., Ashley, T., & Martin, A. (2003). *Interpreting others' intentions facilitates toddlers' verb learning.* Paper presented at the meeting of the American Psychological Association, Atlanta, GA.

Forbes, J. N., & Farrar, M. J. (1993). Children's initial assumptions about the meaning of novel motion verbs: Biased and conservative? *Cognitive Development, 8,* 273–290.

Forbes, J. N., & Farrar, M. J. (1995). Learning to represent word meaning: What initial training events reveal about children's developing action verb concepts. *Cognitive Development, 10,* 1–20.

Forbes, J. N., & Poulin-Dubois, D. (1997). Representational changes in infants' interpretation of familiar action word meaning. *Journal of Child Language, 24,* 389–406.

Fox, R., & McDaniel, C. (1982). The perception of biological motion by human infants. *Science, 218,* 486–487.

Gelman, S. A., Croft, W., Fu, P., Clausner, T., & Gottfried, G. (1998). Why is a pomegranate an apple? The role of shape, taxonomic relatedness, and prior lexical knowledge in children's overextensions of apple and dog. *Journal of Child Language, 25,* 267–291.

Gelman, S. A., & Diesendruck, G. (1999). What's in a concept? Context, variability, and psychological essentialism. In I. E. Sigel (Ed.), *Development of mental representation: Theories and applications* (pp. 87–111). Mahwah, NJ: Erlbaum.

Gentner, D. (1981). Some interesting differences between verbs and nouns. *Cognition and Brain Theory, 4,* 161–178.

Gentner, D. (1982). Why nouns are learned before verbs: Linguistic relativity versus natural partitioning. In S. Kuczaj (Ed.), *Language development: Language, thought and culture.* Hillsdale, NJ: Erlbaum.

Gentner, D., & Boroditsky, L. (2001). Individuation, relativity and early word learning. In M. Bowerman & S. C. Levinson (Eds.), *Language acquisition and conceptual development* (pp. 215–256). Cambridge: Cambridge University Press.

Gershkoff-Stowe, L. (2002). Object naming, vocabulary growth, and the development of word retrieval abilities. *Journal of Memory and Language, 46,* 665–687.

Gershkoff-Stowe, L., & Smith, L. B. (2004). Shape and the first hundred nouns. *Child Development, 75,* 1098–1114.

Gershkoff-Stowe, L., Thal, D. J., Smith, L. B., & Namy, L. L. (1997). Categorization and its developmental relation to early language. *Child Development, 69,* 843–859.

Golinkoff, R. M., Chung, H. L., Hirsh-Pasek, K., Liu, J., Bertenthal, B. I., Brand, R., et al. (2002). Young children can extend motion verbs to point-light displays. *Developmental Psychology, 38,* 604–614.

Gopnik, A. (1984). The acquisition of gone and the development of the object concept. *Journal of Child Language, 11,* 273–292.

Gopnik, A., & Meltzoff, A. N. (1986). Relations between semantic and cognitive development in the one-word stage: The specificity hypothesis. *Child Development, 57,* 1040–1053.

Gopnik, A., & Meltzoff, A. (1987). The development of categorization in the second year and its relation to other cognitive and linguistic developments. *Child Development, 58,* 1523–1531.

Graham, S. A., Kilbreath, C. S., & Welder, A. N. (2004). 13-month-olds rely on shared labels and shape similarity for inductive inferences. *Child Development, 75,* 409–427.

Graham, S. A., & Poulin-Dubois, D. (1999). Infants' use of shape to extend novel labels to animate and inanimate objects. *Journal of Child Language, 26,* 295–320.

Hall, D. G., & Waxman, S. R. (Eds.). (2004). *Weaving a lexicon.* Cambridge, MA: MIT Press.

Hirsh-Pasek, K., Golinkoff, R. M., & Hollich, G. (2000). An emergentist coalition model for word learning: Mapping words to objects is a product of the interaction of multiple cues. In

R. M. Golinkoff, K. Hirsh-Pasek, L. Bloom, L. B. Smith, A. L. Woodward, N. Akhtar, et al. (Eds.), *Becoming a word learner: A debate on lexical acquisition* (pp. 136–164). Oxford: Oxford University Press.

Hollich, G. J., Hirsh-Pasek, K., & Golinkoff, R. M. (2000). Breaking the language barrier: An emergent coalition model for the origins of word learning. *Monographs of the Society for Research in Child Development, 65* (3, Serial No. 262).

Huttenlocher, J. (1974). The origin of language comprehension. In R. L. Solso (Ed.), *Theories of cognitive psychology: The Loyola Symposium* (pp. 331–368). New York: Halsted Press, Winston-Wiley.

Imai, M., Haryu, E., & Okada, H. (2005). Mapping novel nouns and verbs onto dynamic action events: Are verb meanings easier to learn than noun meanings for Japanese children? *Child Development, 76,* 340–355.

Jackson-Maldonado, D., Thal, D., Marchman, V., Bates, E., & Gutierrez-Clellen, V. (1993). Early lexical development in Spanish-speaking infants and toddlers. *Journal of Child Language, 20,* 523–549.

Johnson, S. P. (2004). Development of perceptual completion in infancy. *Psychological Science, 15,* 769–775.

Johnson, S. P., & Aslin, R. N. (1995). Perception of object unity in 2-month-old infants. *Developmental Psychology, 31,* 739–745.

Jones, S. S., & Smith, L. B. (1993). The place of perception in children's concepts. *Cognitive Development, 8,* 113–139.

Katerelos, M., Poulin-Dubois, D., & Oshima-Takane, Y. (submitted). A cross-linguistic study of word mapping in 18- to 20-month-old infants.

Kellman, P. J., & Banks, M. S. (1998). Infant visual perception. In W. Damon (Series Ed.) and D. Kuhn & R. S. Siegler (Vol. Eds.), *Handbook of child psychology: Vol. 2. Cognition, perception, and language* (5th ed., pp. 103–146). New York: Wiley.

Kersten, A. W., & Smith, L. (2002). Attention to novel objects during verb learning. *Child Development, 73,* 93–109.

Leslie, A. M., & Keeble, S. (1987). Do six-month-old infants perceive causality? *Cognition, 25,* 265–288.

MacNamara, J. (1972). Cognitive basis of language learning in infants. *Psychological Review, 79,* 1–13.

Maguire, M. J., Hirsch-Pasek, K., & Golinkoff, R. M. (2006). A unified theory of word learning: Putting verb acquisition in context. In K. Hirsh-Pasek & R. M. Golinkoff (Eds.), *Action meets word: How children learn verbs* (pp. 364–391). New York: Oxford University Press.

Mandler, J. M. (2003). Conceptual categorization. In D. H. Rakison & L. M. Oakes (Eds.), *Early category and concept development.* Oxford: Oxford University Press.

Mandler, J. M., & McDonough, L. (1996). Drinking and driving don't mix: Inductive generalization in infancy. *Cognition, 59,* 307–335.

Mandler, J. M., & McDonough, L. (1998). Studies in inductive inference in infancy. *Cognitive Psychology, 37,* 60–96.

Markman, E. M. (1994). Constraints on word meaning in early language acquisition. In L. Gleitman & B. Landau (Eds.), *The acquisition of the lexicon.* Cambridge, MA: MIT Press.

McDonough, L., Choi, S., & Mandler, J. M. (2003). Understanding spatial relations: Flexible infants, lexical adults. *Cognitive Psychology, 46,* 229–259.

Meints, K., Plunkett, K., & Harris, P. L. (1999). When does an ostrich become a bird? The role of typicality in early word comprehension. *Developmental Psychology, 35,* 1072–1078.

Meints, K., Plunkett, K., Harris, P. L., & Dimmock, D. (2002). What is 'on' and 'under' for 15-, 18-, and 24-month-olds? Typicality effects in early comprehension of spatial prepositions. *British Journal of Developmental Psychology, 20*, 113–120.

Meltzoff, A. N. (1995). Understanding the intentions of others: Re-enactment of intended acts by 18-month-old children. *Developmental Psychology, 31*, 838–850.

Naigles, L. R., & Terrazas, P. (1998). Motion-verb generalizations in English and Spanish: Influences of language and syntax. *Psychological Science, 9*, 363–369.

Namy, L. L. (2001). What's in a name when it isn't a word? 17-month-olds' mapping of nonverbal symbols to object categories. *Infancy, 2*, 73–86.

Olineck, K. M., & Poulin-Dubois, D. (2005). Infants' ability to distinguish between accidental and intentional actions and its relation to internal state language. *Infancy, 8*, 91–100.

Piatelli-Palmarini, M. (Ed.). (1980). *Language and learning: The debate between Jean Piaget and Noam Chomsky.* Cambridge, MA: Harvard University Press.

Poulin-Dubois, D., & Forbes, J. N. (2002). Toddlers' attention to intentions-in-action in learning novel action words. *Developmental Psychology, 38*, 104–114.

Poulin-Dubois, D., & Forbes, J. N. (2006). Word, intention and action: A two-tiered model of action word learning. In K. Hirsh-Pasek & R. M. Golinkoff (Eds.), *Action meets word: How children learn verbs* (pp. 262–285). New York: Oxford University Press.

Poulin-Dubois, D., Graham, S. A., & Sippola, L. (1995). Parental labeling, categorization, and early lexical development. *Journal of Child Language, 22*, 325–343.

Poulin-Dubois, D., & Sissons, M. E. (2002). Is this still called a dog? 18-month-olds' generalization of familiar labels to unusual objects. *Infant and Child Development, 11*, 57–67.

Poulin-Dubois, D., & Vyncke, J. (2005). *The cow jumped over the moon: Infants' inductive generalization of motion properties.* Unpublished manuscript, Concordia University, Montreal, Quebec, Canada.

Pulverman, R., Hirsh-Pasek, K., Golinkoff, R. M., Pruden, S., & Salkind, S. J. (2006). Conceptual foundations for verb learning: Celebrating the event. In K. Hirsh-Pasek & R. M. Golinkoff (Eds.), *Action meets word: How children learn verbs* (pp. 134–159). New York: Oxford University Press.

Quinn, P. (2004). Early categorization: A new synthesis. In U. Goswami (Ed.), *Blackwell handbook of childhood cognitive development* (pp. 84–101). Oxford: Blackwell Publishing.

Quinn, P. C., Adams, A., Kennedy, E., Shettler, L., & Wasnik, A. (2003). Development of an abstract category representation for the spatial relation between in 6- to 10-month-old infants. *Developmental Psychology, 39*, 151–163.

Quinn, P. C., Polly, J. L., Furer, M. J., Dobson, V., & Narter, D. B. (2002). Young infants' performance in the object-variation version of the above–below categorization task: A result of perceptual distraction or conceptual limitation? *Infancy, 3*, 323–348.

Rakison, D. H., & Oakes, L. M. (Eds.). (2003). *Early category and concept development.* Oxford: Oxford University Press.

Samuelson, L. K., & Smith, L. B. (2000). Grounding development in cognitive processes. *Child Development, 71*, 98–106.

Schafer, G. (2005). Infants can learn decontextualized words before their first birthday. *Child Development, 76*, 87–96.

Shatz, M., Wellman, H. M., & Silber, S. (1983). The acquisition of mental verbs: a systematic investigation of the first reference to mental state. *Cognition, 14*, 301–321.

Slater, A. (1989). Visual memory and perception in early infancy. In G. Bremner & A. Slater (Eds.), *Infant development* (pp. 43–71). Hillsdale, NJ: Erlbaum.

Slobin, D. I. (1973). Cognitive prerequisites for the development of grammar. In C. Ferguson & D. I. Slobin (Eds.), *Studies of child language development* (pp. 173–208). New York: Holt, Rinehart, & Winston.

Slobin, D. I. (2001). Form–function relations: How do children find out what they are? In M. Bowerman & S. C. Levinson (Eds.), *Language acquisition and conceptual development* (pp. 406–449). Cambridge: Cambridge University Press.

Smith, L. B. (2001). How domain-general processes may create domain-specific biases. In M. Bowerman & S. C. Levinson (Eds.), *Language acquisition and conceptual development* (pp. 101–131). Cambridge: Cambridge University Press.

Smith, W. C., Johnson, S. P., & Spelke, E. S. (2003). Motion and edge sensitivity in perception of object unity. *Cognitive Psychology, 46,* 31–64.

Sodian, B., & Thoermer, C. (2004). Infants' understanding of looking, pointing, and reaching as cues to goal-directed action. *Journal of Cognition and Development, 5,* 289–316.

Spelke, E. S., & Hespos, S. J. (2002). Conceptual development in infancy: The case of containment. In P. J. Bauer & N. L. Stein (Eds.), *Representation, memory, and development: Essays in honor of Jean Mandler* (pp. 223–246). Mahwah, NJ: Erlbaum.

Spelke, E. S., & Van de Walle, G. (1993). Perceiving and reasoning about objects: Insights from infants. In N. Eilan, R. McCarthy, & W. Brewer (Eds.), *Spatial representation* (pp. 132–161). Malden, MA: Blackwell Publishers.

Talmy, L. (1985). Lexicalization patterns: semantic structure in lexical forms. In T. Shopen (Ed.), *Language typology and syntactic description: Vol. 3* (pp. 57–149). Cambridge: Cambridge University Press.

Tardif, T., Gelman, S. A., & Xu, F. (1999). Putting the "noun-bias" in context: a comparison of English and Mandarin. *Child Development, 70,* 620–635.

Tardif, T., Shatz, M., & Naigles, L. (1997). Caregiver speech and children's use of nouns versus verbs: A comparison of English, Italian, and Mandarin. *Journal of Child Language, 24,* 535–565.

Theakston, A. L., Lieven, E., Pine, J. M., & Rowland, C. F. (2002). Going, going, gone: The acquisition of the verb 'go'. *Journal of Child Language, 29,* 273–290.

Tomasello, M. (1992). *First verbs.* Cambridge: Cambridge University Press.

Tomasello, M. (1995). Pragmatic contexts for early verb learning. In M. Tomasello & W. E. Merriman (Eds.), *Beyond names for things: Young children's acquisition of verbs* (pp. 115–146). Hillsdale, NJ: Erlbaum.

Tomasello, M. (2001). Perceiving intentions and learning words in the second year of life. In E. Bates & M. Tomasello (Eds.), *Language development: The essential readings* (pp. 111–128). Malden, MA: Blackwell Publishers.

Waxman, S. R. (2004). Everything had a name, and each name gave birth to a new thought: Links between early word learning and conceptual organization. In D. G. Hall & S. R. Waxman (Eds.), *Weaving a lexicon* (pp. 295–335). Cambridge, MA: MIT Press.

Waxman, S. R., & Booth, A. (2001). Seeing pink elephants: Fourteen-month-olds' interpretations of novel nouns and adjectives. *Cognitive Psychology, 43,* 217–242.

Waxman, S., & Booth, A. (2003). The origins and evolution of links between word learning and conceptual organization: New evidence from 11-month-olds. *Developmental Science, 6,* 128–135.

Waxman, S. R., & Lidz, J. (2006). Early word learning. In D. Kuhn & R. Siegler (Eds.), *Handbook of child psychology: Vol. 2* (6th ed., pp. 299–335). Hoboken, NJ: Wiley.

Waxman, S. R., & Markow, D. B. (1995). Words as invitations to form categories: Evidence from 12- to 13-month-old infants. *Cognitive Psychology, 29,* 257–302.

Welder, A. N., & Graham, S. A. (2001). The influence of shape similarity and shared labels on infants' inductive inferences about nonobvious object properties. *Child Development, 72,* 1653–1673.

Welder, A. N., & Graham, S. A. (2006). Infants' categorization of objects with more or less obvious features. *Cognitive Psychology, 52,* 57–91.

Wilcox, T., Schweinle, A., & Chapa, C. (2003). Object individuation in infancy. In F. Fagan & H. Hayne (Eds.), *Progress in infancy research: Vol. 3* (pp. 193–243). Mahwah, NJ: Erlbaum.

Woodward, A. L. (1998). Infants selectively encode the goal object of an actor's reach. *Cognition, 69,* 1–34.

Woodward, A. L. (1999). Infants' ability to distinguish between purposeful and non-purposeful behaviors. *Infant Behavior and Development, 22,* 145–160.

Woodward, A. L. (2003). Infants' developing understanding of the link between looker and object. *Developmental Science, 6,* 297–311.

Woodward, A. L. (2004). Infants' use of action knowledge to get a grasp on words. In D. G. Hall & S. R. Waxman (Eds.), *Weaving a lexicon* (pp. 149–171). Cambridge, MA: MIT Press.

Woodward, A. L., & Hoyne, K. L. (1999). Infants' learning about words and sounds in relation to objects. *Child Development, 70,* 65–77.

Woodward, A., & Markman, E. (1998). Early word learning. In W. Damon (Series Ed.) and D. Kuhn & R. S. Siegler (Vol. Eds.), *Handbook of child psychology: Vol. 2. Cognition, perception, and language* (5th ed., pp. 371–420). New York: Wiley.

Woodward, A. L., & Somerville, J. A. (2000). Twelve-month-old infants interpret action in context. *Psychological Science, 11,* 73–77.

Xu, F. (2002). The role of language in acquiring object kind concepts in infancy. *Cognition, 85,* 223–250.

Xu, F. (2003). The development of object individuation in infancy. In J. Fagen & H. Haynes (Eds.), *Progress in infancy research: Vol. 3* (pp. 159–192). Mahwah, NJ: Erlbaum.

11

Syntactic Supports for Word Learning

Letitia R. Naigles and Lauren D. Swensen

TAMARIAN CAPTAIN:	Rye and Jirry at Lunga . . . Jirry and Umbaya; Umbaya of Crossroads at Lunga. Lunga, her sky grey.
ENTERPRISE CAPTAIN PICARD:	Analysis, Mr. Data?
COMMANDER DATA:	The Tamarian seems to be stating the proper names of individuals and locations.

Star Trek: The Next Generation, "Darmok"

Syntactic bootstrapping is the procedure by which children use the syntax in which a newly encountered word is placed to narrow down or constrain the meanings hypothesized for that word. For example, in the epigraph above, Commander Data knew that *Umbaya* was the name of an individual and *Lunga* the name of a location because "Umbaya" appeared in subject position without a determiner and "Lunga" appeared following the preposition "at." The main question we address in this chapter is to what extent do children exploit this procedure during vocabulary acquisition? While the actual phenomenon of syntactic bootstrapping is not in doubt for preschool-aged children, the questions that currently drive this research area concern how pervasively it is used developmentally (i.e., how early in word learning?), cross-linguistically (i.e., for which languages?), and in the real world (i.e., outside of laboratory settings). In this chapter, we explain both why syntactic bootstrapping is needed as a procedure for word learning, and how and why it works for young word learners.

A History of Syntactic Bootstrapping

In 1957, Roger Brown published a paper entitled "Linguistic determinism and the part of speech," in which he showed that preschool-aged children selected different aspects of a picture as the meaning of the novel word *zup* depending on whether he had told them "this is a zup," "this is some zup," or "this is zupping." No one, least of all Brown himself, realized that this was the first empirical demonstration of the phenomenon of syntactic bootstrapping. A subsequent paper by Katz, Baker, and Macnamara (1974) extended the phenomenon to the contrast between proper and count nouns – that "Zup" refers to an individual whereas "a zup" refers to a category – still apparently with little realization of the true scope of the phenomenon. The 1980s saw the rise of two scientific developments, which together provided the basis for the emergence of syntactic bootstrapping as a theory. First, theoretical linguists published numerous detailed analyses demonstrating correspondences between verb syntax (i.e., subcategorization frames; see below for definitions) and verb semantics (e.g., Jackendoff, 1983; Levin, 1993) and researchers in language acquisition conjectured that children who had learned the meanings of verbs could use the correspondences to project each verb's syntax – so-called *semantic bootstrapping* (e.g., Grimshaw, 1981; Pinker, 1989). Second, two psycholinguists studied the verb development of a blind child, and arrived at the complementary conclusion, that she had used subcategorization frames to distinguish the meanings of the perception verbs *look* and *see*, which involved haptic exploration for this child, from action-oriented haptic verbs such as *hold* and *put* (Landau & Gleitman, 1985). This procedure has been dubbed *syntactic bootstrapping* (Gleitman, 1990; see also Lasnik, 1989). The subsequent 20 years have seen a plethora of studies exploring and demonstrating how and when young children use syntax to learn about word meanings. Before presenting these demonstrations, though, we explore just what syntactic bootstrapping is.

What is Syntactic Bootstrapping?

Syntactic bootstrapping is a procedure by which children use the syntax in which a word is placed to narrow down or constrain the meaning of that word (strictly speaking, children use both the morphology and the syntax in which the word is placed; however, *syntactic* bootstrapping is the conventional term). It is based on strong correspondences between lexical syntax and lexical semantics. It relies on differences between verbs in the number and arrangement of noun phrases (NPs) that appear with the verb (i.e., the frame), and on differences between both nouns and verbs in the sheer presence and specific type of co-occurring closed-class item(s). Moreover, syntactic bootstrapping operates across utterances, revealing aspects of a word's meaning via the diverse structures in which it appears. And syntactic bootstrapping operates in concert with the observed visual–spatial scene, semantic or conceptual constraints or biases, and pragmatic information, to reveal the totality of a word's meaning.

Syntactic bootstrapping is a procedure for constraining or focusing the meanings of words

The procedure of syntactic bootstrapping serves as a partial solution to a word learning problem described in detail by Quine (1960), Wittgenstein (1953), and others (see also

Baldwin & Meyer; Diesendruck, this volume). In brief, children learn most of their words – especially while preliterate – via their experience with the visual–spatial world. However, for any given pairing of the world and a word, the world supports a plethora of possible meanings for that word. For example, consider the scene in which a child is carrying her new stuffed animal to Grandma and hears an older speaker of the language say "blick." A completely open-minded child could map "blick" onto one of a number of object, property, or action referents; however, as discussed in more detail in other chapters (e.g., Baldwin & Meyer; Diesendruck; Poulin-Dubois & Graham), actual child word learners do not behave as if they are completely open-minded. The inescapable conclusion is that the child word learner approaches her new words with additional information to that presented in the visual–spatial world. The theory of syntactic bootstrapping proposes that one such source of information – not the only one, but a crucial one nonetheless – is the syntactic frame in which the word is placed (Gleitman, 1990). After all, children actually *hear* their words in sentences, not in isolation as was presented above.

Syntactic bootstrapping is based on correspondences between syntax and semantics

Why should a word's syntax be so informative? Consider again the scene presented above, and how different syntactic frames lead to different meanings for the word:

- You're carrying the blick to Grandma → kind of animal/doggie
- You're carrying Blick to Grandma → name of animal
- You're carrying the blickish doggie to Grandma → property of animal
- You're blicking the doggie to Grandma → *carry* or *bring*
- Grandma's gonna blick the doggie → *take* or *get*
- The doggie's blicking to Grandma → *go* or *move*
- Grandma blicks that the doggie is gonna love her → *think*

These syntactically dependent inferences about word meaning are not random, but are instead predictable from facts about English syntax (in some cases, possibly, universal syntax).

Syntactic bootstrapping works because of observed correspondences between words and the types of phrases and sentences in which they appear. Just what these correspondences are is the topic of much research in linguistics and psycholinguistics (e.g., Fisher, Gleitman, & Gleitman, 1991; Goldberg, 1995; Kako, 2004; Levin, 1993; Lyons, 1977; Talmy, 2000). For example, transitive frames, which include direct objects, co-occur with verbs involving causation (e.g., *He dropped the ball*) whereas intransitive frames, which exclude direct objects, appear with verbs not involving causation (e.g., *The ball fell*). Furthermore, verbs that involve motion usually appear with prepositional phrases (PPs: *She walked to the store*) whereas verbs that involve mental states or communication appear with sentence complements (SComps: *He thought that it was raining*). Grammatical forms also typically distinguish nouns from verbs; for example, words preceded by "the" are nouns (*the play*) whereas words ending in "-ing" are usually verbs (*walking*). Within the NP, nouns preceded by "a" usually designate countable things (*a box, an idea*), those preceded by "some" usually indicate things considered en masse (*some spaghetti*), and those that appear alone usually indicate specific individuals (*Spot, Canada*). Words with suffixes such as "-ish" or "-y" usually designate properties of the nouns they modify (*a devilish grin*).

None of these correspondences between morphosyntactic forms and word meanings are categorical; that is, there exist transitive verbs that do not imply causality (e.g., *see*), mental verb utterances that do not include SComps (*I'm thinking about the rain*), utterances with "some" that refer to countable things (*some ideas*), verbs that appear without "-ing" (*We want to play*), and nouns that appear with "-ing" (*pudding*). Recent psycholinguistic work has demonstrated, however, that these and other correspondences are pervasive and regular, even if not absolute. For example, Fisher et al. (1991) found that the verbs that one group of adults rate as fitting well into PP and SComp frames were the same verbs that another group of adults clustered tightly together (clusters which they labeled as motion and mental). Further studies have replicated these findings with Italian speakers and extended them to more specific frames and smaller semantic clusters. Moreover, analyses of maternal speech have demonstrated that these correspondences hold in children's actual input. Naigles and Hoff-Ginsberg (1995) parsed maternal child-directed utterances containing 25 common verbs and found that mental verbs appeared with SComps significantly more frequently than did motion verbs; analogously, motion verbs appeared with PPs significantly more frequently than did mental verbs (see also Lederer, Gleitman, & Gleitman, 1995). In sum, adult intuitions and maternal speech agree: the correspondences between the syntactic frames in which verbs appear and their semantic categories are pervasive; moreover, the frames themselves – as manifested in children's input – provide very reliable cues to semantic categories of verbs.

Several points from the preceding discussion warrant further elaboration. First, notice that some syntactic differences are purely on the level of the frame, such as the presence of a direct object, PP, determiner, or SComp. Other differences turn on variations within the frame, that is, between different grammatical or "closed-class" words – for example, different types of determiners ("the" can be used for most nouns, "a" only for count nouns, "some" for mass nouns), prepositions (e.g., "into"), and suffixes ("-ing" for verbs, "-ish" for adjectives). This means that a child syntactic bootstrapper must ultimately be able to distinguish both fairly broad differences in sentence configuration, such as the number and arrangement of arguments, and fairly subtle differences in NP-internal or VP-internal phrasal configuration that turn on the appearance of specific lexical items. As we will see in the section *How Pervasive is Syntactic Bootstrapping*, children's ability to bootstrap syntactically depends, at least partially, on their ability to analyze a sentence in terms of these components.

Second, most verbs can appear in multiple sentence frames and will belong to multiple semantic classes (Grimshaw, 1994). For example, perception verbs such as *see* appear with PPs (*Can you see <u>around that corner?</u>*) as well as with SComps (*Can you see <u>if the principal is back from lunch?</u>*), thereby indicating that they belong to both the class of motion verbs and the class of mental/communication verbs. Some transitive verbs also have intransitive instantiations (*She dropped the ball/The ball dropped*) whereas others do not (*She brought the ball/ *The ball brought*). As discussed in detail by Levin (1993), these different sets of verbs have different semantic implications (e.g., involving causation vs. activity). And verbs can differ in ways that are not realized syntactically, such as the differences between *run, walk,* and *skip*, or between *bring* and *carry*.

Third, the input data tell us that children cannot count on hearing the necessary frames for bootstrapping the meanings of verbs 100% of the time. Some instances of usually transitive verbs will appear without direct objects, some instances of intransitive verbs will appear with what seems to be direct objects (e.g., "There goes the train"), some instances of motion verbs will appear without PPs ("Are you coming?") and so on. These latter two points, taken together, lead to two further characteristics of the procedure of syntactic bootstrapping.

Syntactic bootstrapping occurs over multiple trials and frames

Because verbs belong to multiple syntactic and semantic classes, and because children's input sometimes omits or truncates the relevant frames, the procedure of syntactic bootstrapping must be a probabilistic one. Children will need to listen to *multiple* instances of a given word before arriving at a good approximation of its meaning. Thus, syntactic bootstrapping is not a procedure for one-trial learning, in which a child hears a new word in a given frame and immediately knows everything about that word. Instead, syntactic bootstrapping (probably, like all of word learning) is a long-term procedure in which children use the multiple syntactic frames in which words are placed to build up or accrue the full meanings of words. Moreover, children will need to pay attention to the statistical probabilities with which various words appear with various frames. For example, if verb X appears in a transitive frame 90% of the time, it probably *is* transitive, those few intransitive instances notwithstanding. Whereas if verb Y appears with SComps 40% of the time and PPs 60% of the time, both of these frames should be considered well attested in the input and should impact the constructed meaning of the verb (Cartwright & Brent, 1997; Saffran & Thiessen, this volume). We consider in the section *How Pervasive is Syntactic Bootstrapping* the extent to which – or ages at which – children seem capable of performing such analyses. We also take up yet another reason why children need multiple frames to learn words: the existence of cross-linguistic variation in the syntax/semantics correspondences.

Syntactic bootstrapping operates in concert with the visual–spatial world, lexical constraints, and/or pragmatic information

When children encounter a new word, numerous kinds of information are available to them. That is, while children are listening to words in sentences produced by adults or older children around them, they are also observing the objects, actions, and relations within their purview. They then use the syntax embedded in those sentences to figure out which aspect of the scene the word refers to. Thus, the meaning that a noun, verb, or adjective might have is only partly a function of the frame(s) in which it is placed;

different scenes could yield different meanings for words placed in identical frames. So, for example, in the sentence *The doggie is blicking to Grandma* coupled with the scene described earlier, "blick" probably means *move* or *come*; however, if the child was holding the doggie high above her head and swaying it back and forth, then "blick" – in the same frame – might mean something closer to *fly*. What the syntax enables the child to do is to focus on a single or narrower aspect of the given scene – it confines the child's apperception to one part of the scene – but the scene itself also provides crucial specific semantic information (Fisher, Hall, Rakowitz, & Gleitman, 1994; Gleitman, 1990). Furthermore, syntactic bootstrapping must also operate in concert with the other kinds of information that children use in learning words, such as lexical biases and pragmatic knowledge (see other chapters, this volume). Nothing about the syntactic bootstrapping procedure presupposes that it is the only game in town; in the section *How Pervasive is Syntactic Bootstrapping* we consider how syntactic bootstrapping might be weighted in relation to these other kinds of information.

Preschoolers: Syntactic Bootstrappers *Par Excellence*

We begin with relatively "old" word learners – those of 3 to 5 years of age – to demonstrate the myriad ways in which they have been shown to exploit syntactic bootstrapping in their lexical acquisition. The canonical method for demonstrating syntactic bootstrapping in preschoolers derives from Brown (1957): Children are shown a novel visual stimulus that enables multiple mappings between word and meaning; for example, an object of shape S (e.g., a honey dipper) covered with design D (e.g., polka dots). The visual scene is then described with a novel or nonsense word, presented in at least two different syntactic contexts. In this way, the children are taught some aspect of the meaning of the novel word by the pairing of visual stimulus and syntactic context. Finally, the children are shown several new visual stimuli, each of which differs from the original along a relevant conceptual/relational dimension. For example, an object with the original shape covered with a new design might be compared with an object with a new shape covered with the original design. The children are asked to choose which new stimulus can be called by the taught word. The key question concerns whether the children's extension – and so by inference their meaning of the new word – fits the interpretation given by the syntactic context of the new word.

Syntactic variations within the NP lead preschoolers to a wide range of conjectures about objects and their properties. Count nouns elicit basic- and superordinate-level category interpretations; for example, labeling a novel object "a blick" leads preschoolers to conjecture that other objects from the same basic level category (e.g., the same shape but varying in size and coloration) are also blicks. Moreover, labeling a pear "a blick" leads preschoolers learning English to conjecture that bananas and strawberries, but not phones and trucks, are also blicks; this is also true for preschoolers learning French or Spanish (Waxman, 1994). Proper nouns, in contrast, elicit individual rather than category interpretations, and apply more readily to animate than inanimate objects (e.g., Markman & Jaswal, 2004). Furthermore, the use of the determiner *some* rather than *a* (e.g., "some dax" vs. "a dax") leads preschoolers to infer that "dax" refers to a non-solid substance (such as some spaghetti) rather than to a solid object (such as the bowl holding the spaghetti; Brown, 1957; see also Soja, Carey, & Spelke, 1991). And numerous studies have demonstrated that adjectives lead preschoolers to deduce a material or property interpretation (Mintz & Gleitman, 2002; Waxman, 1994, 2004). In sum, the presence, absence, and type of determiner within the NP each has differing ramifications for the child in conjecturing the meaning – or at least the referent – of a novel word.

Structural properties also influence children's inference that a word refers to a verb rather than a noun. Brown's (1957) study also included a condition where the novel word was presented as a verb: "He's daxing." Preschoolers hearing this sentence chose neither the bowl nor the spaghetti as their referent of "dax," but instead the picture of the hands. Thus, the presence of the "-ing" form at the end of a word is taken as an indication that the word refers to an event or action rather than to an object or substance. Behrend, Harris, and Cartwright (1995) further demonstrated that morphological variations on the *verb* could lead children to different conjectures about that verb's meaning by exploiting the tendency across languages for verbs describing processes or actions to be used primarily with progressive aspect ("-ing" in English) whereas verbs describing results are used more frequently with completive aspect ("-ed" in English; see Shirai & Anderson, 1995, for a review). And indeed, preschoolers who were taught novel verbs with the -ing suffix extended them best to events of similar manners whereas those taught verbs with the -ed suffix extended them best to events of similar results.

The lion's share of research on syntactic bootstrapping with verbs, though, has focused on their argument structure rather than their morphology. Two methods have been prevalent with preschoolers. In the *verb interpretation* paradigm, children are shown a dynamic action paired with a novel verb (e.g., *dax*). The verb is taught in at least two sentence contexts (between subjects). Children are then asked "What does daxing mean?" The key question concerns whether the children's interpretation of the verb varies by the type of sentence in which it was placed. In the *act-out* paradigm, children are asked to enact sentences containing familiar verbs, using toy animals as props. While most of the sentences are grammatical, some present the verb with too many or too few arguments. The key question concerns whether the children enact the sentence according to the demands of the frame; that is, do they systematically adjust the meaning of the verb now that it has appeared in this new frame?

Syntactic variations within the VP lead preschoolers to make differing conjectures about verb meanings. Fisher et al. (1994) used the verb interpretation paradigm to show that syntactic context affects preschoolers' perspectives on the action pairs *give/receive* and *chase/flee*. For example, when viewing a give/receive scene (e.g., Jazz giving a book to George/George receiving the book from Jazz), the children's default interpretation of the novel verb was agentive (*give*), but when they were told "George is blicking the book from Jazz," they changed their interpretation to *receive*. Thus, the appearance of the named characters in the subject versus the predicate, plus the presence of specific prepositions (*to* vs. *from*), successfully altered the children's interpretation of the novel verb. This finding has been replicated with Mandarin Chinese-speaking preschoolers (Cheung, 1998).

Preschoolers also alter the meanings of familiar verbs depending on whether they appear in transitive versus intransitive frames. Using the act-out paradigm, Naigles,

Gleitman, and Gleitman (1993) asked preschoolers to enact sentences in which usually transitive verbs were presented in intransitive frames (e.g., "The zebra brings to Noah"), and usually intransitive verbs were presented in transitive frames (e.g., "The zebra goes the lion"). The children consistently enacted sentences of the latter type causatively (e.g., by making the zebra make the lion go) and sentences of the former type non-causatively (e.g., by making the zebra move alone to Noah), showing that they could extend the meanings of *go* to include, and *bring* to exclude, a causative component. The generality of this finding can be seen in the replications that have been published, for languages both similar (e.g., French: Naigles & Lehrer, 2002) and dissimilar (e.g., Kannada: Lidz, Gleitman, & Gleitman, 2003) to the original American English.

Finally, verbs in SComp constructions can lead children to infer mental state or communication interpretations. When preschoolers were asked to enact ungrammatical sentences in which motion verbs were presented in SComp constructions (e.g., "the zebra brings that the giraffe jumps"), almost half of the children produced similar enactments as for the grammatical *the zebra thinks that the giraffe jumps* (Lidz, Gleitman, & Gleitman, 2004). And preschoolers can determine whether a *novel* verb refers to a mental/communication relation versus a transfer relation by the syntax in which it is placed (Johnson, de Villiers, D'Amato, Deschamps, & Huneke, 2002). In particular, the SComp *The clown meeped the woman to send the apple* led them to make a communication/mental interpretation whereas the ditransitive *The woman meeped the apple to the clown* led them to make a transfer interpretation.

How Pervasive is Syntactic Bootstrapping in Development, across Languages, and in the Real World?

The previous section illustrated how the *existence* of syntactic bootstrapping cannot be disputed – preschool-aged children use syntactic structure to learn about the meanings of a wide range of words. Given its existence, much recent research has begun to examine how *pervasive* this procedure might be. Such pervasiveness can be questioned along several dimensions: First, how pervasive is syntactic bootstrapping *in development*? That is, how early in development does it, or could it, operate? Second, how pervasive is syntactic bootstrapping *across languages*? For example, how might a procedure that relies on the presence of nominal arguments or morphological markers operate in languages that allow for nominal and/or morphological ellipsis? Third, how pervasive is syntactic bootstrapping in the *"usual" course of lexical development*? That is, how much do children *really* rely on grammatical information when they are learning the meanings of conventional words in their input language? We will consider each dimension separately but they inevitably interact.

Developmental issues

As seen in the previous section, 3- to 5-year-old children have the syntactic wherewithal to parse their input and determine the morphosyntactic frames of the relevant words, they can extract and/or recognize the relevant semantics instantiated in their apprehension of experience, they know which morphosyntactic structures implicate which semantic instantiations, and they use these structures to make conjectures about the meanings of newly encountered words. The developmental question, then, is when do these abilities emerge? Researchers have addressed this question by investigating whether children younger than 3 years of age can make syntactically based conjectures about word meaning. We describe here the findings from toddlers learning (a) about the causativity of verbs from transitive frames, and (b) about the properties of objects from adjectival frames.

Using the act-out paradigm, Naigles et al. (1993) had also asked 2.5-year-olds to enact ungrammatical sentences, and found even more pronounced frame compliance than with older preschool children: these children enacted the novel transitive sentences primarily causatively and the novel intransitive sentences primarily non-causatively. However, children younger than 2.5 years do not easily participate in act-out tasks; therefore, to investigate whether even younger children could learn verbs via syntactic bootstrapping, Naigles and her colleagues switched to the intermodal preferential looking paradigm (IPL) (Hirsh-Pasek & Golinkoff, 1996).

In a series of studies, 2-year-olds were taught novel verbs in different syntactic frames. Typically, children would be presented with a multiple-action scene, displaying both a causative and a non-causative/synchronous action. The scene was paired with a novel verb, either in a transitive ("The duck is gorping the bunny") or intransitive ("The duck and the bunny are gorping") frame. After several such presentations, the two actions were separated and the child was asked to "find gorping." Children as young as 24 months of age consistently looked longer at the causative action when they had been taught the verb in the transitive frame, and at the non-causative action when taught the verb in the intransitive frame (Naigles, 1998; see also Bavin & Kidd, 2000; Fisher & Gleitman, 2002). Hirsh-Pasek, Golinkoff, and Naigles (1996) further demonstrated that 2-year-olds matched the non-causative action with the intransitive frame even when this frame included a single-NP subject instead of coordinate-NP subject ("The duck is gorping with the bunny"). However, they found little difference by syntactic frame in 18-month-olds' novel verb mapping preferences. Thus, whereas syntactic bootstrapping to distinguish types of verbs seems quite robust in 2-year-olds, it has yet to be definitively demonstrated in younger children.

This is not to say that 1-year-olds cannot exploit grammar at all with reference to verb learning. Echols and Marti (2004) recently replicated Brown's (1957) noun/verb distinction using the IPL with 18-month-olds. Children who were taught "That's a gep, it's a gep" looked significantly longer at the scene with the original object whereas the children who were taught "It's gepping. See? It geps" looked significantly longer at the scene with the original action. Thus, the children were able to exploit the morphosyntactic differences between noun and verb presentations to determine whether the word referred to an object or an action (see also Naigles, 1998).

With respect to syntactic bootstrapping within the NP, toddlers distinguish proper from count nouns when making conjectures about noun meaning. Children as young as 17 months of age consistently extend a taught count noun ("a dax" compared with "Dax") to label new animals similar in shape to the original referent (Jaswal & Markman,

2001; Katz et al., 1974). Two-year-olds also deduce property interpretations for novel adjectives (Mintz & Gleitman, 2002); however, 1-year-olds have more difficulty with this frame. For example, 21-month-olds select new objects of the same color when the original is labeled "this one is blickish," but only when the new objects are of the same basic-level kind as the original (e.g., all dogs) (Waxman & Markow, 1998). Still younger infants (11 and 14 months of age) treat count nouns and adjectives similarly in all contexts, consistently extending a new word to objects of the same category as the original. Thus, Waxman (2004) traced a developmental path for syntactic bootstrapping within the NP in which 10- to 14-month-olds typically link a new word – regardless of its syntactic presentation – to object categories. She proposed that, later in the second year, infants begin to notice distinct patterns of grammatical frames and so then use these to subdivide the object categories by property and by individual status, with grammatical patterns then operational by age 2.

In sum, the developmental evidence demonstrates that children can use syntax to make conjectures about word meanings by the age of 24 months. But of course, they are learning words at age 12 months (or even earlier), and the evidence for syntactic bootstrapping during the second year of life is as yet slim. One possible conclusion from the current evidence is that children don't use syntax to learn their first words because they don't yet have the grammatical means to do so (e.g., Fisher & Gleitman, 2002; Gillette, Gleitman, Gleitman, & Lederer, 1999; Waxman, 2004). However, there is reason to believe that the absence of syntactic bootstrapping in the second year, if real, cannot be purely or even primarily attributed to a deficit in syntactic knowledge. That is, there is mounting evidence that infants under 24 months of age do possess considerable syntactic knowledge (Gerken, this volume; Weissenborn & Hohle, 2001). The evidence from Gerken (see also Naigles, 2002) indicates that the 1-year-old has many tools in his or her grammatical toolkit, including sensitivity to the order of both open-class and closed-class words, the positioning of specific morphemes, and the distinction between at least some English versus non-English syntactic forms, and the ability to recognize language-like patterns instantiated in novel items. But then why are these children not using their syntactic abilities, if real, for learning word meanings? Possibly, research has not yet been successful in revealing such usage; easier tasks and/or better stimuli might be needed. Alternatively, children may be in possession of the necessary syntactic structures but not yet clear on what these mean – that is, they may not yet have learned the syntax/semantics correspondences necessary to do syntactic bootstrapping. And one reason for their lag in learning the correspondences may arise because at least some of these are language-specific. Therefore, we turn next to such cross-linguistic issues.

Cross-linguistic issues

If all syntax/semantics correspondences were universal, then children should be able to bootstrap syntactically as soon as they can parse their input sufficiently to determine what the frames are. Gleitman (1990; see also Fisher & Gleitman, 2002; Fisher et al., 1991; Pinker, 1989) has proposed that correspondences related to the theta criterion (Chomsky, 1981) are innately given; for example, that those actions/relations involving only one participant surface as intransitive verbs, those actions/relations involving two participants surface as transitive verbs, those events involving motion surface as verbs with accompanying prepositional (or oblique) phrases, and those relations involving mental states or communication surface as verbs with accompanying SComps. As described in the section *What is Syntactic Bootstrapping?*, these and other syntax/semantics correspondences have emerged from a variety of scientific paradigms (i.e., linguistic analysis, psycholinguistic experimentation with adults, and analysis of children's input). However, these correspondences have also been subjected to three major challenges pertaining to their cross-linguistic validity (e.g., Bowerman & Brown, in press).

The challenge of null arguments.   The first challenge involves ellipsis: many languages of the world permit null arguments; that is, utterances in which the arguments of a verb are routinely omitted. So whereas the presence or absence of the direct object distinguishes transitive from intransitive verbs in English, languages such as Mandarin Chinese or Japanese may not make such information about verb meaning consistently available to the child learner (Rispoli, 1995). Recall the example used earlier, of the child carrying the puppy to Grandma. In Mandarin Chinese, one can simply describe this scene with the verb alone, *bei1* "carry," without mentioning either what is to be carried or who is to do the carrying (Li & Thompson, 1981). Worse, the same scene can be described with transitive (e.g., *carry*) and intransitive (e.g., *walk*) verbs *in practically the same syntactic frame*:

(1) *Bei1*dao4 po2po nar4
     Carry **arrive Grandma there**
     Carry (it to) Grandma (who is over there)
(2) *Zou3* **qu4 po2po nar4**
     Walk **go Grandma there**
     Walk (over to) Grandma there

Utterances such as (1) and (2) indeed present a potential challenge to the use of syntactic bootstrapping, because this procedure is predicated on the notion that verbs that vary in their meanings also vary in their syntactic expressions. However, the mere existence of these utterances need not be regarded as proof that syntactic bootstrapping could not operate in Mandarin, because, as discussed in the section *What is Syntactic Bootstrapping?*, syntactic bootstrapping is a probabilistic, rather than categorical, procedure. It need not be the case that transitive verbs appear 100% of the time with their direct objects, but instead that the presence of the direct object be a *reliable* cue to transitivity – for example, that post-verbal NPs appear more frequently with transitive verbs than with intransitive ones (e.g., Fernald & McRoberts, 1996).

Lee and Naigles (2005) have demonstrated that such is the case for Mandarin. They parsed some 6000+ adult utterances to children from the Beijing corpus on CHILDES (MacWhinney, 2000; Tardif, 1993) and performed the same analyses as in Naigles and Hoff-Ginsberg (1995). Very similar results were found, in that Mandarin caregivers used post-verbal NPs significantly more frequently with transitive verbs (involving two participants) than intransitive ones (involving only one participant). Furthermore, verbs describing motion events appeared more frequently with prepositions and locatives than did verbs describing mental states whereas the latter verbs appeared significantly more frequently with SComps than did verbs describing motion. Lee and Naigles' (2005) analyses thus support the cross-linguistic stability and universality of some of the most basic syntax/semantics correspondences (see also Bowerman & Brown, in press).

The challenge of language-specific correspondences between syntax and semantics: A case study of the transitive frame.   The second cross-linguistic challenge concerns the specificity of meaning that is implicated by a particular frame. Again, the problem emerges most obviously with the transitive frame. Previous experimental demonstrations of the meaning that this frame enables have been quite specific; for the most part, children seem to treat a transitive frame as encoding causative meaning, such as change-of-state or change-of-position. Yet as several researchers have pointed out, the semantic implications of the transitive frame may vary cross-linguistically (Bowerman & Brown, in press; Hohenstein, Naigles, & Eisenberg, 2004), especially in that many verbs not directly indicating causality may appear under the transitive banner. The problem is thus that a verb in a transitive frame could be referring to a causal action, a motion event (e.g., *entrar/enter* in Spanish), and/or a contacting activity (e.g., *sweep, stroke, pat*). Because children's earliest verbs include both those that refer to causal actions (e.g., *break*) and those that refer to contacting activities (e.g., *pat*), it is not likely that one type of meaning develops earlier than the other (Goldin-Meadow, Seligman, & Gelman, 1976; Tomasello, 1992). How then do the children choose? Two types of solutions to this challenge have adduced some experimental evidence.

Solution 1: General meanings.   The first type of solution allows a much more general meaning to be inferred from the transitive frame. That is, rather than assuming that "transitive means causative," transitive frames could instead indicate a general notion that the action involves an actor plus some kind of *affected object* (e.g., Pinker, 1989). The way(s) that the object is affected can vary, and are probably open to the child's observation, such as when the affected object changes its state or position, is the source or goal of the action, or is the recipient of the action. In support of this more general interpretation, Naigles and her colleagues have demonstrated using the IPL that young 2-year-old English learners mapped novel transitive verbs onto contacting activities rather than synchronous actions (Naigles, 1998). Moreover, Hohenstein et al. (2004) have shown that 3-year-olds, learning either English or Spanish, mapped novel verbs in the transitive frame onto the *path* aspects of motion events. For example, "She's kradding the tree/Está mecando al árbol" was conjectured to refer to *approaching* rather than *skipping*. Thus, both English and Spanish learners were able to use the transitive frame to focus on a specific aspect of the observed scene that in no way involved causation.

When only one affected object action or relation is present, then, the transitive frame targets this action or relation. But of course, the world doesn't obligingly restrict its events to just one affected-object relation at a time. For example, consider the scene when a child is stroking a cat, and the cat arches its back in response. This scene could involve two types of affected-object relations: the first one, which English calls *stroking*, just includes the activity the child is doing, and the second one, which has been dubbed *cataltituding* (Hall, 1984), includes also the result of the child's activity, namely, the cat arching its back. The first affected-object relation is a contacting one, the second is a causative one. How could a child determine which is the target of the sentence "You are blicking the cat"? Clearly, the single transitive frame – even if generally construed – is insufficient.

Solution 2: Multiple frames.   Possibly, children store both available meanings in their lexicons until such a time when "blick" is heard but only one of the possible meanings is present (perhaps the child is stroking an *unresponsive* cat) (Pinker, 1994). Plausible as this strategy is, there is as yet little empirical evidence with children to support it or to distinguish it from a raw frequency effect. Alternatively, as noted by Landau and Gleitman (1985), children need to hear verbs in multiple frames in order to more fully specify or target their meaning (see also the section *What is Syntactic Bootstrapping?*). Thus, while a single frame might not suffice to identify or target the intended action in a given scene, multiple frames would provide additional relevant information. For example, when causative and contacting actions are presented simultaneously to young 2-year-olds, paired with only a single novel verb in a transitive frame, the toddlers prefer to map the verb onto the causative action rather than the contacting one (Naigles, 1998). However, when presented with the novel verb in one specific *set* of frames, their mapping preferences change. In particular, Naigles (1998) taught 2-year-olds novel verbs in two types of transitive/intransitive alternation patterns (Levin, 1993). One pattern was more closely linked with causative verbs such as *move*: (*The duck krads the frog/The frog krads*), and the second was more closely associated with activities such as *pat*: (*The duck krads the frog/The duck krads*). The second pattern of alternation was found to direct 2-year-olds' attention successfully to the contacting activity over the causative action. Interestingly, this success has been positively correlated with reported vocabulary size; however, it is not clear whether larger vocabularies enable the use of multiple frames, the use of multiple frames enables larger vocabularies, or, what is most likely, large vocabularies and multiple-frame syntactic bootstrapping assist each other simultaneously.

In sum, this second cross-linguistic challenge to syntactic bootstrapping, that the meaning a given syntactic frame implicates might vary across or within languages, might achieve resolution in two ways. First, the meaning corresponding to such a frame might be general rather than specific, and as such could be cross-linguistically stable. More specific meanings attached to a given verb would then be a function of specifics of the scene in which the verb-in-frame was used. Second, specificity of meaning could be attained via the use of multiple syntactic frames. Whereas a single frame might be insufficient to specify a new verb's meaning in the observed scene, the combination of frames in which the verb appears may frequently be sufficient to do so (see also Bowerman & Brown, in press). These resolutions, however, do not yet impact a third, related, cross-linguistic challenge faced by syntactic bootstrapping accounts of word learning.

The challenge of learning the meanings of language-specific morphosyntactic patterns.   Regardless of the universality of argument structure and certain facts about verb meaning, more specific syntax/semantics correlations, which depend on language-specific morphological patterns, most definitely have to be learned. For example, the facts that words preceded by "a" are count nouns and so likely to refer to objects, words followed by "-ish" or "-y" are likely to be adjectives referring to properties, and words followed by "-ing" are likely to be verbs referring to actions are all particular to English and the results of learning (Grimshaw, 1994). There has been little detailed discussion of this process, as most researchers have been content to state the general point that children probably use their initial knowledge of words to develop their syntax and induce such specific syntax/semantics correspondences (e.g., Fisher & Gleitman, 2002; Naigles, 2002; Pinker, 1989; Shatz, 1987; Waxman, 2004).

Markman and Jaswal (2004), in contrast, have proposed a more detailed account of how one specific syntax/semantics correspondence could be acquired, namely, the linkage between proper nouns and names for individuals. Markman and Jaswal begin with the (possibly innate or else very early learned) correspondence between words – any words – and object categories (see also Waxman, 1994, 2004). Recall that Waxman's (2004) investigations of preverbal and barely verbal infants showed that these learners map new words of any stripe onto novel object categories. Given this initial bias, children might begin to notice that some already-learned words (mapped already onto object categories) appear with determiners and plurals whereas other words – perhaps not well mapped yet – do not. Children's attempts to make something of the meanings of these other kinds of words could involve statistical, pragmatic, and constraint-based analyses such as the following: Statistically, infants might calculate the range of entities labeled by words, and notice that these vary widely but systematically; for example, words referring to object categories apply to a wider range of entities than words referring to individuals. Infants might also use constraints such as the taxonomic assumption, that words extend to things of the same kind, to assume that all objects of the same kind *should* receive the same label. When it happens that one does not (e.g., when a dog is called "Spot" instead of "doggie"), this violation might provide a clue that the label refers to individuals rather than kinds. Pragmatic principles might work similarly. Children would then observe that when a word is presented that does *not* extend to a range of entities and is *not* used for all objects of its kind, such a word also has the distinct morphosyntactic properties of appearing (a) in the singular but (b) without a determiner. Eventually, children would arrive at the realization that *all* such words implicate meanings that are restricted to individuals rather than inclusive of categories (Markman & Jaswal, 2004).

Summary. In this section, we have discussed three challenges to the cross-linguistic validity of syntactic bootstrapping as a procedure for word learning. The first challenge asked how syntactic bootstrapping could work in languages that permit the omission of arguments. Our resolution, based on analyses of Mandarin Chinese, suggested that the crucial arguments appear to be present with sufficient frequency to distinguish success-fully between verb classes in similar patterns to that observed for English. Similar analyses of other null-argument languages are, of course, needed. The second challenge asked how syntactic bootstrapping could work when a given frame might correspond to a range of meanings. Our resolutions here suggested that some such frames might carry general, possibly innate, meanings that would be stable across languages. Further specificity for a given verb could be gleaned from the accompanying scenes and/or the multiple frames in which the verb was used. The third challenge asked how the meanings of language-specific morphosyntactic patterns might be acquired. Resolutions here rely on children's abilities to learn some words without the syntactic information, to compare the statistical and/or pragmatic patterns of use of different types of words, and so to induce some syntax/semantics correspondences by matching these words with specific morphosyntactic patterns.

The role of syntax in real-world word learning

How pervasive is syntactic bootstrapping during the acquisition of words in children's input language (as opposed to those nonsense words taught in the laboratory)? It is important to reiterate the statement from the section *What is Syntactic Bootstrapping?*, that no one claims that children use only syntactic information in their acquisition of word meanings. Syntax is a clearly vital source of information for children, but as noted earlier it is not the only source of information. An obvious next question is: What is the *relative weight* of syntactic information for children as they learn the meanings of words?

Some of the most interesting data pertaining to this question come, not from studies with children, but from studies – "human simulations," they are called – with adults. Gleitman and her colleagues (Gillette et al., 1999; Kako, 2004; Snedeker & Gleitman, 2004) have demonstrated that, when adults are shown scenes of mother–child interaction and asked to guess which word the mother produces at a specific time, the adults' guessing accuracy varied with the type of information presented with the scenes. In particular, with just the scene information, the adults performed much better guessing nouns (45% correct) than guessing verbs (15% correct) (Gillette et al., 1999). Only when *syntactic* information was given did the adults guess the verbs correctly; simple presentation of co-occurring nouns was not sufficient. Thus, one might conjecture that overall, nouns require less syntactic information for their acquisition than do verbs. Moreover, adults performed better with only scene information when guessing action verbs and basic-level nouns; their performance when guessing mental verbs and non-basic-level nouns showed the greatest improvement when the scene information was paired with syntactic information (Kako, 2004; Snedeker & Gleitman, 2004). Thus, one might conjecture that syntax is more useful – and/or used – for children while they are learning less concrete verbs and nouns not drawn from the basic level.

Replicating such stringently controlled research with toddlers, who are in the thick of word learning but notoriously resistant to following directions, would be difficult. However, two studies have investigated the relative weights of syntactic versus other information in toddlers' development of conventional (English) words. First, Naigles and Hoff-Ginsberg (1998) extended their analyses of maternal input, described in the section *What is Syntactic Bootstrapping?*, to include analyses of the children's current and subsequent speech. That is, they investigated whether the ways that mothers used verbs at Time 1, when the children's mean length of utterance (MLU) was around 1.5, predicted how the children used those same verbs at Time 2, 10 weeks later. Two factors in maternal speech significantly predicted subsequent child speech, namely, verb frequency and syntactic diversity. Frequency exerted the stronger effect: verbs that were used more frequently by mothers were also used more frequently by children. Still, verbs used in more diverse syntactic frames by mothers – controlling for frequency – were also used more frequently, and in more diverse syntactic frames (but with different co-occurring words and usually in shorter sentences), by the children. This study provided the first evidence that syntactic bootstrapping was used by children in their real-world verb learning, as opposed just to their nonsense verb learning in laboratory tasks. More recently, these findings have been replicated to some extent in Mandarin Chinese, using the Beijing corpus described earlier (Lee, Nelson, & Naigles, 2003).

Subsequently, Hoff and Naigles (2002) compared the roles of maternal use of joint attention and maternal MLU on children's overall vocabulary development (MLU may be considered a proxy for syntactic complexity as mothers with higher MLUs might be considered to provide more syntactic information). They found that maternal MLU accounted for significantly more of the variance among children than amounts of joint attention, suggesting that, at least during this developmental period, syntactic information is weighted relatively heavily for vocabulary growth. Thus, syntactic information has been shown to play a significant role in children's acquisition of the conventional words of their language; however, it is important to point out that such correlational studies provide relatively weaker evidence for syntactic bootstrapping than the experimental studies discussed earlier.

Unfortunately, we do not have similar studies that have investigated noun development in the real world; most analyses of input have compared children's vocabulary growth in nouns versus verbs, and the input analyses have focused on frequency and pragmatic information rather than syntactic information (see Baldwin & Meyer; Poulin-Dubois & Graham, this volume). Thus, what is still needed are (a) analyses of the grammatical ways that adults use nouns in speaking to children, and (b) investigations that address how much noun development varies – both by nouns and by children – according to grammatical factors in the input. In an ideal world, one would have a large enough corpus to include a wide range of nouns and a wide range of verbs produced by caregivers, as well as a dense enough corpus to be confident in both the uses and non-uses of the nouns and verbs by their children. The corpus would make available the social/pragmatic (of various kinds, not just joint attention) and syntactic information accessible to the children each time the word was produced. And crucially, the outcome measure would involve an assessment of the children's knowledge of the words' meanings and not just the frequency of the words' production. Then, perhaps, one could perform an analysis to determine how much of each type of information accounts for the variance in the children's subsequent vocabulary development. Moreover, such a dataset could be revealing concerning whether syntactic bootstrapping is more important for verb learning than for noun learning, as we have suggested based on the available data, or whether morphosyntactic information is actually equally important for both, but perhaps at different points in development.

Conclusions

Preschool-aged children can use syntactic information to learn about a wide variety of words, including nouns, verbs, and adjectives. The evidence concerning the development of syntactic bootstrapping suggests that the use of syntax to learn novel words is fragile between 18 and 24 months of age and fully operational at 24 months. Moreover, the cross-linguistic data suggest that some syntax/semantics correspondences, if couched generally, could be universal and so available before 18 months whereas other correspondences, obviously language-specific, must be learned and so are not readily available to 1-year-olds. Waxman's (2004) developmental timecourse for syntactic bootstrapping within the noun phrase is consistent with the current evidence: the syntax/semantics correspondences relevant to the noun phrase are language-specific, they seem to emerge after some nouns have been learned, and the first evidence of syntactic bootstrapping within the noun phrase has been found from children around 18 months of age. By contrast, the developmental timecourse of syntactic bootstrapping within the verb phrase is less clear: if syntax/semantics correspondences such as transitive/affected-object are universal and innate (e.g., Lidz et al., 2003), then 1-year-olds might be expected to use syntax to distinguish between verbs. Yet the empirical evidence for this is weak and sparse (compare Hirsh-Pasek et al., 1996, and Naigles & Hoff-Ginsberg, 1998). Clearly, more research with verb learning in 1-year-olds is needed.

Children's ability to use syntactic supports for word learning contributes to the explanation of both semantic and syntactic development in early childhood, because some syntactic development is obviously a requirement for syntactic bootstrapping to proceed, and semantic development is clearly one result of the syntactic bootstrapping procedure. As such, syntactic bootstrapping is a good example of how different areas of language are intertwined in children's development.

Note

This chapter was written while the first author was on sabbatical leave; she thanks the University of Connecticut for providing the leave and Koç University in Istanbul, Turkey, for providing such a stimulating place to spend the sabbatical. We thank Aylin Küntay, Erika Hoff, and Marilyn Shatz for their helpful comments on earlier versions.

References

Bavin, E. L., & Kidd, E. (2000). Learning new verbs: Beyond the input. In C. Davis & R. Wales (Eds.), *Cognitive science in Australia* (pp. 113–125). Adelaide: Causal Press.

Behrend, D., Harris, L., & Cartwright, K. (1995). Morphological cues to verb meaning: verb inflections and the initial mapping of verb meanings. *Journal of Child Language, 22,* 89–106.

Bowerman, M., & Brown, P. (in press). *Crosslinguistic perspectives on argument structure: Implications for learnability.* Hillsdale, NJ: Erlbaum.

Brown, R. (1957). Linguistic determinism and the part of speech. *Journal of Abnormal and Social Psychology, 55,* 1–5.

Cartwright, T., & Brent, M. (1997). Syntactic categorization in early language acquisition: formalizing the role of distributional analysis. *Cognition, 63,* 121–170.

Cheung, H. (1998). The use of syntactic information in learning Chinese verbs. *National Taiwan University Working Papers in Linguistics, 1.*

Chomsky, N. (1981). *Lectures on government and binding.* Berlin: Mouton de Gruyter.

Echols, C. H., & Marti, C. N. (2004). The identification of words and their meanings: From perceptual biases to language-specific cues. In D. G. Hall & S. R. Waxman (Eds.), *Weaving a lexicon* (pp. 3–40). Cambridge, MA: MIT Press.

Fernald, A., & McRoberts, G. (1996). Prosodic bootstrapping: A critical analysis of the argument and the evidence. In J. L. Morgan & K. Demuth (Eds.), *Signal to syntax: Bootstrapping from speech to syntax in early acquisition* (pp. 365–388). Hillsdale, NJ: Erlbaum.

Fisher, C., & Gleitman, L. (2002). Language acquisition. In H. Pashler & R. Gallistel (Eds.), *Steven's handbook of experimental psychology: Vol. 3. Learning, motivation, and emotion* (3rd ed., pp. 445–496). New York: John Wiley & Sons.

Fisher, C., Gleitman, H., & Gleitman, L. (1991). On the semantic content of subcategorization frames. *Cognitive Psychology, 23*, 331–392.

Fisher, C., Hall, D. G., Rakowitz, S., & Gleitman, L. R. (1994). When it is better to receive than to give: Syntactic and conceptual constraints on vocabulary growth. *Lingua, 92*, 333–376.

Gillette, J., Gleitman, H., Gleitman, L., & Lederer, A. (1999). Human simulation of vocabulary learning. *Cognition, 73*, 135–176.

Gleitman, L. (1990). The structural sources of verb meanings. *Language Acquisition, 1*, 3–55.

Goldberg, A. (1995). *Constructions: A construction grammar approach to argument structure.* Chicago: University of Chicago Press.

Goldin-Meadow, S., Seligman, M., & Gelman, R. (1976). Language in the two-year-old. *Cognition, 5*, 189–202.

Grimshaw, J. (1981). Form, function, and the language acquisition device. In C. Baker & J. McCarthy (Eds.), *The logical problem of language acquisition.* Cambridge, MA: MIT Press.

Grimshaw, J. (1994). Lexical reconciliation. In L. Gleitman & B. Landau (Eds.), *The acquisition of the lexicon.* Cambridge, MA: MIT Press.

Hall, R., & friends. (1984). *Sniglets (snig'let): Any word that doesn't appear in the dictionary but should.* New York: Macmillan.

Hirsh-Pasek, K., & Golinkoff, R. (1996). *The origins of grammar: Evidence from early language comprehension.* Cambridge, MA: MIT Press.

Hirsh-Pasek, K., Golinkoff, R., & Naigles, L. (1996). Young children's ability to use syntactic frames to derive meaning. In K. Hirsh-Pasek & R. Golinkoff (Eds.), *The origins of grammar: Evidence from early language comprehension* (pp. 123–158). Cambridge, MA: MIT Press.

Hoff, E., & Naigles, L. (2002). How children use input to acquire a lexicon. *Child Development, 73*, 418–433.

Hohenstein, J., Naigles, L., & Eisenberg, A. (2004). Keeping verb acquisition in motion: A comparison of English and Spanish. In G. Hall & S. Waxman (Eds.), *Weaving a lexicon* (pp. 569–602). Cambridge, MA: MIT Press.

Jackendoff, R. (1983). *Semantics and cognition.* Cambridge, MA: MIT Press.

Jaswal, V. K., & Markman, E. M. (2001). Learning proper and common names in inferential versus ostensive contexts. *Child Development, 72*, 768–786.

Johnson, V., de Villiers, J. G., D'Amato, K., Deschamps, C., & Huneke, S. (2002, July). *Can syntax give you complements?* Paper presented at the Meeting of the International Association for the Study of Child Language, Madison, WI.

Kako, E. (2004). Information sources for noun learning. *Cognitive Science, 29*, 223–260.

Katz, N., Baker, E., & Macnamara, J. (1974). What's in a name? A study of how children learn common and proper names. *Child Development, 45*, 469–473.

Landau, B., & Gleitman, L. (1985). *Language and experience.* Cambridge, MA: Harvard University Press.

Lasnik, H. (1989). On certain substitutes for negative data. In R. Matthews & W. Demonpoulos (Eds.), *Learnability and linguistic theory* (pp. 89–105). Dordrecht: D. Reidel Publishing Company.

Lederer, A., Gleitman, L., & Gleitman, H. (1995). Input to a deductive verb acquisition procedure. In M. Tomasello & W. Merriman (Eds.), *Beyond names for things: Young children's acquisition of verbs* (pp. 277–297). Hillsdale, NJ: Erlbaum.

Lee, J., & Naigles, L. R. (2005). Input to verb learning in Mandarin Chinese: A role for syntactic bootstrapping. *Developmental Psychology, 41*, 529–540.

Lee, J., Nelson, J., & Naigles, L. (2003, November). *Syntactic bootstrapping: A viable learning strategy for children learning Mandarin.* Paper presented at the Boston University Conference on Language Development, Boston, MA.

Levin, B. (1993). *English verb classes and alternations: A preliminary investigation.* Chicago: University of Chicago Press.

Li, C., & Thompson, S. (1981). *Mandarin Chinese: A functional reference grammar.* Berkeley, CA: University of California Press.

Lidz, J., Gleitman, H., & Gleitman, L. (2003). Understanding how input matters: verb learning and the footprint of universal grammar. *Cognition, 87*, 151–178.

Lidz, J., Gleitman, H., & Gleitman, L. R. (2004). Kidz in the 'hood: Syntactic bootstrapping and the mental lexicon. In D. G. Hall & S. R. Waxman (Eds.), *Weaving a lexicon* (pp. 603–636). Cambridge, MA: MIT Press.

Lyons, J. (1977). *Semantics.* New York: Cambridge University Press.

MacWhinney, B. (2000). *The CHILDES project: Tools for analyzing talk* (3rd ed.). Mahwah, NJ: Erlbaum.

Markman, E. M., & Jaswal, V. K. (2004). Acquiring and using a grammatical form class: Lessons from proper-count distinction. In D. G. Hall & S. R. Waxman (Eds.), *Weaving a lexicon* (pp. 371–410). Cambridge, MA: MIT Press.

Mintz, T. H., & Gleitman, L. (2002). Adjectives really do modify nouns: The incremental and restricted nature of early adjective acquisition. *Cognition, 84*, 267–293.

Naigles, L. (1998). Developmental changes in the use of structure in verb learning. In C. Rovee-Collier, L. Lipsitt, & H. Haynes (Eds.), *Advances in infancy research: Vol. 12* (pp. 298–318). London: Ablex.

Naigles, L. R. (2002). Form is easy, meaning is hard: Resolving a paradox in early child language. *Cognition, 86*, 157–199.

Naigles, L., Gleitman, L. R., & Gleitman, H. (1993). Children acquire word meaning components from syntactic evidence. In E. Dromi (Ed.), *Language and cognition: A developmental perspective* (pp. 104–140). Norwood, NJ: Ablex.

Naigles, L., & Hoff-Ginsberg, E. (1995). Input to verb learning: Evidence for the plausibility of syntactic bootstrapping. *Developmental Psychology, 31*, 827–837.

Naigles, L., & Hoff-Ginsberg, E. (1998). Why are some verbs learned before other verbs? Effects of input frequency and structure on children's early verb use. *Journal of Child Language, 25*, 95–120.

Naigles, L., & Lehrer, N. (2002). Language-general and language-specific influences on children's acquisition of argument structure: A comparison of French and English. *Journal of Child Language, 29*, 545–566.

Pinker, S. (1989). *Learnability and cognition: The acquisition of argument structure.* Cambridge, MA: MIT Press.

Pinker, S. (1994). How could a child use verb syntax to learn verb semantics? In L. Gleitman & B. Landau (Eds.), *The acquisition of the lexicon.* Cambridge, MA: MIT Press.

Quine, W. V. O. (1960). *Word and object*. Cambridge, MA: Harvard University Press.

Rispoli, M. (1995). Missing arguments and the acquisition of predicate meanings. In M. Tomasello & W. E. Merriman (Eds.), *Beyond names for things: Young children's acquisition of verbs* (pp. 331–352). Hillsdale, NJ: Erlbaum.

Shatz, M. (1987). Bootstrapping operations in child language. In K. E. Nelson & A. van Kleek (Eds.), *Children's language: Vol. 6* (pp. 1–22). Hillsdale, NJ: Erlbaum.

Shirai, Y., & Anderson, R. (1995). The acquisition of tense-aspect morphology: a prototype account. *Language, 71*, 743–762.

Snedeker, J., & Gleitman, L. (2004). Why is it hard to label our concepts? In D. G. Hall & S. R. Waxman (Eds.), *Weaving a lexicon* (pp. 257–294). Cambridge, MA: MIT Press.

Soja, N., Carey, S., & Spelke, E. S. (1991). Ontological categories guide young children's inductions of word meaning: Object terms and substance terms. *Cognition, 38*, 179–211.

Talmy, L. (2000). *Toward a cognitive semantics: Vol. 1. Concept structuring systems*. Cambridge, MA: MIT Press.

Tardif, T. (1993). *Adult-to-child speech and language acquisition in Mandarin Chinese*. Unpublished doctoral dissertation, Yale University, CT.

Tomasello, M. (1992). *First verbs: A case study of early grammatical development*. Cambridge: Cambridge University Press.

Waxman, S. R. (1994). The development of an appreciation of specific linkages between linguistic and conceptual organization. In L. Gleitman & B. Landau (Eds.), *The acquisition of the lexicon*. Cambridge, MA: MIT Press.

Waxman, S. R. (2004). Everything had a name, and each name gave birth to a new thought: Links between early word learning and conceptual organization. In D. G. Hall & S. R. Waxman (Eds.), *Weaving a lexicon* (pp. 295–335). Cambridge, MA: MIT Press.

Waxman, S. R., & Markow, D. B. (1998). Object properties and object kind: Twenty-one-month-old infants' extension of novel adjectives. *Child Development, 69*, 1313–1329.

Weissenborn, J., & Hohle, B. (Eds.). (2001). *Approaches to bootstrapping: Phonological, lexical, syntactic and neurophysiological aspects of early language acquisition: Vol. 1*. Amsterdam: John Benjamins Publishing Co.

Wittgenstein, L. (1953). *Philosophical investigations*. New York: Macmillan.

PART III

Language Development in Early Childhood

Introduction

Early childhood is the period during which language development is most obvious. Although infants are very busy at language learning, as the chapters in the previous Part have shown, the outward signs of their accomplishments are subtle. Not so, once productive language begins. In the years from 1 to 4, the child as communicator changes rapidly and dramatically. The five chapters in this Part describe and seek to explain these changes.

Stoel-Gammon and Sosa describe changes in the sounds children produce, and they describe mutual influences between children's developing sound systems and growing lexicons. They present a picture in which children's early phonetic inventories do not include all the sound contrasts in the target language, and this limits lexical development because children initially are selective in the words they produce – avoiding words outside their phonetic inventories. As vocabulary grows, however, lexical development becomes a driving force in phonological development as children expand their phonetic inventories to maintain distinctions among their increasingly large repertoire of lexical items. In addition to the descriptive facts about phonological development and the empirical evidence regarding the relation between phonology and the lexicon in development, Stoel-Gammon and Sosa provide a theoretical survey of the field of phonological development. They lay out for us the facts that a theory of phonological development must explain (e.g., developmental changes in children's productions, individual differences in patterns of acquisition, and the facts of adult phonology), and they review historical and current theories of phonological development, evaluating each against those criteria.

The basic descriptive fact that is the focus of Diesendruck's chapter on word learning is that children are prodigious word learners, acquiring a vocabulary of up to 10,000 words by the age of 6 years. The basic theoretical challenge is the Quinean problem that in any situation, a newly encountered word has multiple plausible interpretations. How then does the child ever figure out its meaning? Diesendruck provides a schema for organizing the many current proposals regarding what helps the child narrow the inferential possibilities and successfully discover the meanings of newly encountered words. His schema organizes proposals on two dimensions: from endogenous sources to exogenous sources of constraint and from lexically specific to general cognitive learning mechanisms and procedures. Diesendruck reviews the evidence in support of each view and the empirical challenges to each, concluding that no single mechanism is an adequate explanation of how children learn words and calling for an approach that integrates multiple mechanisms.

The phenomenon requiring explanation in Lidz's chapter is easily stated, if not easily explained: Children acquire the ability to produce and understand sentences that they have never heard before. Lidz takes as his starting point the generative grammar description of the knowledge that underlies this ability in adults and proceeds through the empirical evidence on when children's language use and language comprehension indicate that they too have these representations of the linguistic system. He marshals evidence that, from the beginning of language development, children represent language in terms of abstract relations defined over hierarchical structures – the hallmark of adult syntactic knowledge. However, Lidz notes that such evidence is insufficient to answer the question of how acquisition of a particular language is accomplished because even the most nativist position, which attributes abstract representations to innate knowledge, must explain how the learner identifies which forms in input correspond to which innate syntactic representations. That is, language experience must be linkable to language representations. Further bridging what has historically been a great divide between generative and input accounts of acquisition, Lidz offers an example of how an abstract hypothesis space might be elaborated for a particular language with the use of input cues that increase in salience or probabilistic value with experience. He goes on to argue that an account of the nature of early syntactic representations provides a basis for discovering how they change on the basis of experience, and he concludes that the field is now primed to do such work.

Young children who have acquired a substantial vocabulary and who have become proficient in the grammar of their language may, nonetheless, lack proficiency as conversationalists. Siegel and Surian illustrate how children may misinterpret (that is, from the adult point of view) questions that are posed to them. The result of children's misinterpretations is that their answers to questions may not reveal the knowledge the question was designed to probe. Siegel and Surian use evidence from studies of children's conceptual development to describe systematic misinterpretations children make. Their review makes an important point for students of language development: pragmatic competence does not automatically fall out of competence in other domains of language, but must itself be acquired. Their review also makes an important point for those who would use language to tap the minds of immature conversationalists: the question the child answers may not be the question you thought you were asking.

In the last chapter in this Part, Genesee and Nicoladis consider the not-so-rare circumstance in which language development is the development of more than one language. Bilingualism (and multilingualism, for that matter) has probably existed for as long as multiple languages have existed. Nonetheless, the field of child language restricted its inquiry to monolingual development for a long time. In recent years, however, the study of bilingual development has burgeoned both because growing numbers of bilingual children in schools have brought attention to the topic and because researchers have seen that the study of bilingualism can address basic questions about the nature of the human language capacity. Genesee and Nicoladis review the evidence that bilingual children reach the basic milestones of language development in both their languages within the same time frame as monolingual children, indicating that the language acquisition capacity is equipped for the task of bilingual development. On the other hand, they also present evidence that vocabulary building may progress less rapidly in each language than it does for children building only one lexicon and that the phonological representations built from bilingual input may differ from those built from monolingual input. Genesee and Nicoladis also review the evidence on codeswitching, concluding that when children shift from one language to another it reflects a pragmatic choice rather than a linguistic confusion, and, in fact, bilingual children reveal communicative competence that monolingual children have no way to reveal, as bilingual children switch from one of their languages to the other to accommodate other speakers.

Together, the chapters in this Part represent what has been the core of the field of language development, spanning the ages from approximately 1 to 5 years and covering the accomplishments of phonological, lexical, syntactic, and pragmatic development. These chapters present a picture of a field that incorporates internal and external factors in explaining development and of a field that makes contact with research on cognitive and social development to illuminate influences on both the process and the consequences of gains in linguistic knowledge.

12

Phonological Development

Carol Stoel-Gammon and Anna Vogel Sosa

In learning to talk, children must gain knowledge of the phonological forms of words and phrases of their native language and must learn the articulatory and phonatory movements needed to produce these words and phrases in an adult-like manner. Thus, phonological acquisition has two basic components: a cognitive–linguistic component associated with learning the phonological system of the ambient language and the development of speech–motor skills needed for adult-like productions. A full understanding of phonological development, then, must be broad-based, including an understanding of the motor and auditory skills underlying speech production and of processes of memory and pattern recognition associated with storage and retrieval of words in a child's lexicon. This chapter addresses these issues by providing a summary of phonological development in typically developing children, a discussion of the relationship between phonological and lexical acquisition, and a summary of theoretical approaches to the study of child phonology.

In the discussion of phonological development in children, descriptions of some speech sounds contain terms with which readers may not be familiar. The following provides brief definitions of some of these terms. In the field of phonetics and phonology, consonants are often grouped together into classes on the basis of "features" denoting *place* of articulation (where in the mouth the sound is produced) and *manner* of articulation (how the sound is produced). The places of articulation frequently referred to in the following discussion of phonological development are *labial*, that is, consonants produced with the lips (e.g., [p,b,m]), *alveolar*, that is, consonants produced with the front of the tongue (e.g., [d,n,s]), and *velar*, that is, consonants produced with the back of the tongue (e.g., [k,g]). The manners of articulation referred to in the following sections are *stop*, that is, consonants produced with full blockage of the airstream (e.g., [p,b,t,d]), *fricative*, that is, consonants produced with frication of the airstream (e.g., [f,s,z]), *nasal*, that is, consonants produced with the airstream passing through the nasal cavity (e.g., [m,n]), *liquid*, that is, consonants produced with little blockage of the airstream (e.g., [l,r]), and *glide*, that is, "vowel-like" consonants produced with no blockage of the airstream (e.g., [w,j]; the consonant [j] is the first sound of the word "you"). More complete phonetic descriptions of the *segments* of English (i.e., the consonants and vowels) are available in texts by Chomsky and Halle (1968), Stoel-Gammon and Dunn (1985), and Bernhardt and Stemberger (1998).

Typical Phonological Development

Prelinguistic development

Prior to the onset of meaningful speech, infants produce a wide range of utterance types. In the first month of life, the output is not very "speech-like": common utterance types include cries, coughs, burps, or wheezes. Around 2 to 3 months of age, however, vowel-like vocalizations occur, and by 6 to 7 months, most infants produce consonant–vowel (CV) syllables that, although non-meaningful, resemble syllables, or words, of adult languages. The repertoire of speech sounds changes dramatically during the first year of life. In the first 6 months, vowel articulations tend to predominate and most consonantal sounds are produced in the back of the mouth. With the onset of CV babbling (also referred to as canonical babbling), consonants produced in the front of the mouth, articulated with the lips or front of the tongue, are frequent, particularly [m], [b], and [d]. Thus babies produce many one- and two-syllable utterances like [baba] or [di]. Between 6 and 12 months, the consonantal repertoire expands considerably, but claims that babies produce all the sounds of all languages of the world have not been substantiated (see the discussion of Jakobson, 1968, below). In fact, a limited set of consonants, primarily stops, nasals, and glides, accounts for the great majority of consonant productions (Locke, 1983). Although some language-specific features are present in late babble (10–12 months), analyses of prelinguistic vocalizations from infants raised in many different linguistic communities have shown a predominance of these consonant classes in all infants (Locke, 1983).

During the prelinguistic period, babies are exposed to adult input and begin to form representations that will allow them to understand and produce words of their language. In addition, they hear their own babbled productions, which serve as the basis for linking their own articulatory movements with the resulting acoustic signal (Vihman, 1996). This link is important for the production of words: The baby who repeatedly produces the non-meaningful syllable [ma] at 7 months becomes aware of the tactual and kinesthetic sensations associated with this syllable and hears the acoustic output associated with the production, creating an articulatory–auditory "feedback loop" that is fundamental to speech production throughout life (Fry, 1966; Stoel-Gammon, 1998a). Furthermore, in the case of a word-like form such as [ma], the match between the babble [ma] and the real word [mama] means that the child's non-meaningful vocalization can be transformed into meaningful speech with relative ease (Locke, 1993).

From babble to words

Babies typically produce the first words around their first birthday, and words and babble co-exist for several months thereafter. The phonetic properties of babble and early words are highly similar, with the same consonants and syllable types occurring in both (Stoel-Gammon, 1998a). Developmentally, babble productions serve as the building blocks for the articulation of adult-based words. Comprehension and production of words require the presence of "underlying representations" and thus add an important element to the child's developing phonological system. Although the precise nature of underlying representations is not well understood, even in adult speech, it is generally agreed that these "stored" representations contain information that allows a speaker to understand and produce words. It is particularly difficult to determine the form of underlying representations for children in the early stages of acquisition. On the one hand, it is possible that their representations are very similar to those of adults; on the other, because of their limited lexicon, their representations may contain much less detail than those of an adult. In addition, it is possible that a child's mispronunciation of a word influences the underlying representation for that word.

Longitudinal studies of babbling and early words show that individual production patterns in terms of sounds, syllable shapes, and vocalization length are often "carried forward" to a child's first words (Stoel-Gammon & Cooper, 1984; Vihman, 1996; Vihman, Elbert, & Ferguson, 1987). Experimental evidence of this type of continuity comes from a study of the acquisition of nonsense words. Messick (1984) exposed children in the very early stages of word learning to nonsense words that were either phonetically similar or dissimilar to their own babbles; she found that the children produced a significantly greater number of words that were phonetically similar to their own babbled productions, but that they showed no differences in their ability to understand the two types of nonsense forms.

Although children vary extensively in the age of onset of meaningful speech and in the rate at which they add new words to their developing lexicon, common tendencies in the phonological patterns of first word productions are quite striking. The period from the onset of meaningful speech to acquisition of a 50-word vocabulary is characterized by a "phonetic inventory" of simple syllabic structures and a small repertoire of consonants and vowels. (The term "phonetic inventory" is used here to describe the elements occurring in a child's productions and does not take into account accuracy of production.) In English, syllable types predominating in the first-word period include CV (consonant–vowel) as in *go*, CVC as in *sit*, and CVCV as in *baby*; in terms of consonantal repertoire, productions are composed primarily of stops, nasals, and glides. Consonants missing from the inventories of young children tend to be those that occur infrequently in the language, such as [v], and/or require more articulatory precision, such as the initial consonants of the words *chew*, *shy*, *red*, *juice*, *think*, *they* (note that two letters in written forms, e.g., *ch*, represent a single sound in the spoken form).

Research on first word production in languages other than English reveals the same general properties in terms of sound types and syllable structure: in all languages, CV syllables tend to predominate, and stops, nasals, and glides occur frequently. Language-specific influences are apparent, however, in the frequency of occurrence of particular sound classes, syllable types, and stress patterns. For example, children acquiring English produce many CVC words (e.g., *ball, book*) and disyllables with stress on the first syllable (e.g., *mommy, bottle, cracker*); French-learning children, by comparison, produce a greater proportion of two-syllable words, more words with stress on the last syllable, and more nasal consonants, all features of the French language (de Boysson-Bardies et al., 1992).

Phonological development beyond the first-word stage

The end of the first-word stage, around 18 months, is signaled by a rapid increase in vocabulary size, an expansion of the repertoire of segments and syllable shapes, and the onset of two-word utterances. By 24 months, the typically developing child learning English has acquired a productive vocabulary of 250 to 350 words and can produce multiword sentences. At this period, a child's phonological system can be described in two ways: through an "independent" analysis, with a focus on the child's productions without reference to the adult model, or via a "relational" analysis, comparing the child's production to the adult model. Each type of analysis provides important information. An independent analysis includes a summary of the child's phonetic inventory, that is, a list of segments, sound classes, syllable and word structures, and suprasegmental patterns in the child's speech. A relational analysis, in contrast, focuses on similarities and differences between the child's pronunciation of a word and the adult form.

Phonetic inventories.   Independent analyses of the speech of 2-year-old children without reference to the adult model show that the basic elements of the adult system are present, although the child's system is not complete; the phonetic inventory (i.e., the sounds and syllable structures produced) of a typically developing 2-year-old child includes stops (as in *pie, bee, toe, doe, key, go*), labial and alveolar nasals (as in *me* and *no*), and glides (as in *we* and *you*) (Stoel-Gammon, 1985). In terms of syllable structures, the repertoire includes CV and CVC syllables that can combine to form disyllabic words. In addition, the average 2-year-old can produce some words with consonant clusters (i.e., two adjacent consonants) as in *twin* or *milk*. The vowel repertoire is more complete than the consonantal system (Stoel-Gammon & Herrington, 1990). By age 36 months, the typical phonetic inventory has expanded to include consonants from nearly all place and manner classes of English as well as a range of syllable and word types.

Adult–child comparisons.   Relational analyses of children's productions are based on a comparison of the adult form and the child's production and are used to examine accuracy of production and to determine the types of errors that occur. Such analyses reveal that accuracy of consonantal production improves markedly between 24 and 36 months, as a majority of children acquiring English can accurately produce all stops, nasals, and glides, as well as some fricatives, during this period. By 42 months, the repertoire of accurate segments, at least in some word positions, has increased to include liquids, fricatives, and affricates as in *church* and *judge*.

Study of the differences between the adult target and the child's production show that, in some cases, the two forms differ to such an extent that it is impossible to determine what the child was trying to say; in this case, the child's form is classified as "unintelligible." At the age of 2 years, about half of a child's utterances are intelligible (i.e., can be understood by an adult who is not familiar with the child). By the age of 3 years, the level of intelligibility increases to 75% and by age 4, it is 100% (Coplan & Gleason, 1988). This does not mean that the child's productions are fully adult-like by age 4, rather that the errors do not interfere with intelligibility.

Comparisons of adult targets and child productions of intelligible words reveal that differences in the two forms are quite systematic; these differences have been described in terms of phonological "processes" (Stampe, 1969) that modify the target by omitting sounds or syllables, or by substituting one sound class for another. In terms of omissions, children often simplify a word by omitting the final consonant, producing a CV rather than a CVC syllable (e.g., omitting the [r] of *car*), or by producing a single consonant rather than a sequence of consonants (e.g., omitting the [l] of *blue*). Both of these patterns yield CV syllables, the basic syllable type from the babble period. Stress patterns within a word also play a role in children's omissions: unstressed syllables are often omitted from the child's form. Thus the first syllable in *spaghetti* or *banana* may be omitted (or the second syllable in *telephone* or *crocodile*).

Errors involving substitutions can also be related to patterns of late babble. In particular, fricatives and affricates in the target word, which are rare in babble, may be produced as stops; thus *very* is produced with an initial [b]; *shoe* and *sip* with initial [t], and *Joe* and *zoo* with initial [d]. Other common substitution patterns include velar stops (/k/ and /g/) produced as alveolar stops ([t] and [d]), as in the word *go* produced with a [d], and target liquids (/l/ and /r/) produced as glides ([w] and [j]), as in *red* and *light* produced with initial [w]. Works by Ingram (1976), Grunwell (1981), and Stoel-Gammon and Dunn (1985), among others, include more complete descriptions of common error patterns in children's speech.

This summary has provided a brief description of phonological development from birth to 3 years, with emphasis on production and examples primarily from English. Basic production patterns that first appear in the prelinguistic period, that is, CV syllable structures with stop, nasal, and glide consonants, tend to predominate in the first-word period. With increasing age and an expanding vocabulary, children begin to move beyond the basic repertoire and learn to produce a wider range of features of the target language. The following section explores the relationships between phonology and acquisition of the lexicon.

The Relationship between Phonological and Lexical Development

Lexical selection in early words

As noted above, the individual sound pattern preferences in babble have been found to carry over into meaningful speech, forming the building blocks for the child's early lexical items. Research focusing on phonology and the lexicon shows that individual children exhibit patterns of lexical selection and avoidance based on their own phonological abilities and preferences. Ferguson and Farwell (1975), for example, described a child who showed a marked preference for words with sibilant consonants (e.g., *ice*, *shoes*). Another child, described by Stoel-Gammon and Cooper (1984), had a preference for words ending with a velar stop; his very early vocabulary included many velar-final words such as *milk*, *clock*, *talk*, *walk*, *frog*, *block*, *quack*, *whack*, *sock*, and *yuk*, all pronounced as [gak]. These findings indicate that the specific words in a child's early vocabulary are determined not only by semantic and pragmatic influences, but also by a child's productive phonological ability.

Experimental evidence for the phenomenon of lexical selection and avoidance comes from a set of studies of novel word learning by Leonard and colleagues (Leonard, Schwartz, Morris, & Chapman, 1981; Schwartz & Leonard, 1982). The studies show that young children are more likely to produce novel words whose phonological characteristics are consistent with their own phonologies (IN words) than words with phonological features not present in the children's phonologies (OUT words). These studies provide additional evidence of the influence of phonology on lexical acquisition during the period of the first 50 to 100 words.

Lexical–phonological patterns beyond the early-word period

The relationship between phonology and lexical development continues to exist beyond the first 50-word period. Stoel-Gammon (1998b) investigated the phonological characteristics of earlier- and later-acquired words based on age-of-acquisition data taken from the MacArthur Communicative Development Inventory, a parental checklist of receptive and productive vocabulary for infants and toddlers up to 30 months of age. Words acquired between 11 and 19 months of age showed considerable effects of lexical selection; in initial position, words with stops and bilabial consonants (e.g., /p,b,m/) were predominant; in contrast, words acquired between 20 and 30 months displayed a greater variety of phonetic characteristics, indicating reduced phonological influence on the selection of new words.

The relationship between lexical and phonological development is not unique to English. Using normative data from a Cantonese version of the Communicative Development Inventory, Fletcher and colleagues (Fletcher et al., 2004) compared the phonological characteristics of words acquired between 16 and 22 months with characteristics of words acquired between 23 and 30 months. The results of this study were very similar to those found by Stoel-Gammon (1998b): target words with initial bilabials, nasals, glides, and stops are highly preferred for the early-acquired words in Cantonese. The authors conclude that lexical selection based on the initial consonant of the target word was evident for early-acquired words, but that this effect weakened for the later-acquired words. The authors note that their results indicate a pattern of lexical selection beyond the first 50-word stage because the average productive vocabulary size of the younger group was 98 words.

As the child acquires a larger vocabulary, the influence of lexical selection appears to decline; the relationship between phonological and lexical acquisition does not disappear, but takes on a different form. Beyond the first 50 words, a strong relationship between the number of words in the child's productive vocabulary and the complexity of the child's phonological inventory is observed; children with larger vocabularies tend to have larger inventories of speech sounds and syllable structures than children who produce fewer words (Stoel-Gammon, 1998a). At this point of development, it appears that the increasing size of the lexicon becomes a driving force in the acquisition of phonology, a view supported by the work of Lindblom (1992) and Walley (1993), among others.

Thus far, this chapter has focused on the "what" of phonological development, including the ages and stages of typical development; the sounds and syllable structures acquired; the types of errors that occur; the nature of individual differences; and the relationship between phonological and lexical acquisition. The following section explores the "why" of phonological development, by providing a summary of theoretical accounts that have been proposed to account for this aspect of language learning.

Theoretical Approaches to Phonological Development

This section presents a brief outline of the field of developmental phonology and a more detailed discussion of some of the most influential theories and of the major works that reflect each theoretical framework. The dividing line between theories is not always easy to determine, as many of the most influential works reflect the dynamic nature of the field, with individuals borrowing one feature of a theory and incorporating it into another, as the knowledge of the facts of phonological development evolves over time. The description of each theory includes a summary of its strengths and weaknesses.

Developing a theory

Menn (1980) stated that there are, in general, three stages that unfold when an existing "central" theory is extended to encompass a new, related area. In this case, the existing theory is that of adult phonology and the related area is the study of child phonology. The first phase is the extension phase, during which time the existing theory is simply applied, without modification, to the new area of study. The second phase is the comparison phase, when researchers use new data to test the existing theories and begin to discover the pitfalls and problems of a simple extension of the existing theory. The final stage consists of the creation of a new theory, either specialized for the new area or a modification of the existing general theory to encompass the related field.

In child phonology, the extension phase began with Jakobson's (1941) monograph *Child language, aphasia and phonological universals* (translated from German in 1968), as he applied unmodified, structuralist phonological principles to the process of phonological acquisition. The extension phase continued with the generative accounts of phonological development, most notably Neil Smith's (1973) description of his son's development, and to a lesser extent with David Stampe's natural phonology (Donegan & Stampe, 1979). As more information regarding the facts of phonological acquisition became available in the 1970s, people began to test the ideas of the earlier theorists against the growing body of data. During this period, work of Charles Ferguson and his colleagues and students introduced new child-centered theories of phonological development. Since then, we continue to be in Menn's third stage of the development of a theory, the creation of a new theory, and numerous potential theories have been proposed. The following sections summarize the requirements of a theory and describe major theories that have been proposed.

The field of phonology has traditionally been distinguished from phonetics, with phonology describing the abstract, linguistically meaningful properties of the sound system and phonetics describing the concrete, redundant, and physical characteristics of speech production and perception. Approaches to the study of speech development are often divided along these same lines: Phonological approaches tend to analyze development in terms of its relationship to the endpoint (a mature, symbolic linguistic system), while phonetic approaches address the acquisition of speech from the initial state, a motorically and cognitively immature organism.

Requirements of a theory of phonological development

Three different publications (Bernhardt & Stemberger, 1998; Ferguson & Garnica, 1975; Stoel-Gammon & Dunn, 1985), spanning a period of more than 20 years, offer remarkably similar descriptions of what a theory of phonological development must account for. A combined summary of the necessary components reveals the following: A theory must: (1) account for the facts of adult phonology; (2) account for the facts of child phonology, including: (a) general patterns of development, including common error patterns as noted in the first section of this chapter; (b) individual differences in patterns of acquisition; (c) within-child variability in the production of individual sounds and words; (d) continuity between prelinguistic and linguistic development; and (e) the fact that child productions change over time; (3) be able to explain the role of input; (4) be able to account for the discrepancy between perception and production; (5) account for both phonetic (i.e., articulatory) and phonological learning; (6) be compatible with other theories of linguistic and non-linguistic learning; and (7) must make testable predictions regarding patterns of acquisition and error types. It is clear from the descriptions below that some of these "requirements" were not considered at all in some theories; at the same time, fundamental constructs of a particular theory may not have been included in the list above.

Structuralist theories

Roman Jakobson's (1941) monograph is probably the best-known and most influential account of phonological development, and is grounded in the framework of structural linguistics, which was dominant at the time. Structuralism is rooted in the empiricist tradition, with an emphasis on establishing structural grammatical laws based on analysis of spoken language. The proposals put forth by Jakobson were the motivation for dozens of researchers who set out to test the theories against a growing body of child data.

Eventually, many of Jakobson's proposals would be discredited, paving the way for the development of new theories that would better account for the facts of child phonology.

One of Jakobson's major claims is that there is a discontinuity between prelinguistic and linguistic vocal development. He describes the babbling period as a "purposeless egocentric soliloquy" and a "biologically oriented period of 'tongue-delirium'" (1968, p. 24), and states that babies produce a wide variety of different speech sounds, representing all conceivable sounds of the languages of the world. Given the strong relationships between babbling and speech cited in the earlier sections, this view is no longer tenable.

The emergence of phonological development, according to Jakobson, represents the beginnings of true speech. During this period, the "phonetic abundance" of the babbling period (i.e., the large number of different sounds) is replaced by the "phonemic poverty" of early word productions (i.e., the small number of different sounds); acquisition of phonemic contrasts is said to adhere to a universal order, subject to laws of "irreversible solidarity" that dictate the relative order of acquisition of individual phonemic contrasts in all children and all languages. The order is based on structural principles and implicational hierarchies regarding the nature of phonemic inventories in adult languages. For example, the presence of fricatives (e.g., /f,s/) in a language implies the presence of the more "basic" stops (e.g., /p,t/), just as the acquisition of fricatives by the child implies that stops have been acquired.

Jakobson did not gather developmental data, but rather relied on a few published diary accounts and anecdotal claims. Given his interest in linguistic universals and the minimal data the conclusions are based on, the strengths of this theory lie in its ability to explain the general patterns of the appearance of individual sounds that are often observed in children. The widely observed pattern of consonants produced with the lips or front of the tongue (e.g., [b,d]) appearing before consonants produced with the back of the tongue (e.g., [k,g]), for example, is readily accounted for by Jakobson's rules of "irreversible solidarity." While we know now that there is an enormous amount of individual variability, Jakobson's universal order of acquisition is still considered important, especially in the field of speech language pathology for the diagnosis and treatment of phonological disorders. Children are identified as disordered or delayed based on these principles, and treatment is typically grounded in the notion of a universal order (and timetable) of acquisition.

While some of Jakobson's conclusions are still accepted, numerous criticisms of his theory have been cited. The major criticisms, as presented by Ferguson and Garnica (1975), focus on the inability to account for many of the facts of child phonology. For example, inter- and intra-child variability, now well documented, is ignored, and the strict discontinuity between babble and speech has been found to be false, as noted in the description of development provided above.

Rule- and constraint-based theories

Generative phonology.   While the structuralist tradition emphasized the importance of analyzing overt speech to identify structural laws and linguistic universals, linguists within the generative tradition took a position that stressed the difference between what speakers produce and what they actually know about their language, thus distinguishing performance from competence, and taking competence as the focus of study. Noting the structural similarities among the languages of the world, Chomsky (1972) proposed the existence of a Universal Grammar, a set of restrictions on the possible structure of language based on an innate, hard-wired language device. The ability to acquire language, according to his view, involves "an innate mental endowment" that allows children to discover the structure of their language with relatively little data from the adult language. The primary generative influence for both adult and child phonology comes from a seminal work by Chomsky and Halle (1968), *The sound pattern of English*. In this work, underlying phonological representations are taken to be abstract, encompassing only that information that is not predictable from the system of phonological and phonetic rules that operate on-line in the generation of spoken words. Thus, phonology consists of an abstract underlying representation together with a system of ordered rules that transform the representation into the surface form we actually say.

In 1973, Neil Smith published a detailed account of his son Amahl's language development, rooted in the generative tradition. Smith provided a complete formal description of the phonological rules active at each stage of Amahl's speech development, using data obtained between the ages of 2;2 and 4;0. Smith assumes (1) that the child's underlying representations are adult-like; (2) that there is a set of strictly ordered, obligatory realization rules that produce the child's phonological form; and (3) that the phonological form is then subject to phonetic rules that create the child's output. According to Smith, phonological development can be described as a process of rule modification applied to stable, adult-like representations, and there is no evidence for an independent, child-based phonological system. His basic argument for adult-like mental representations is the assertion that sound change is an "across-the-board" phenomenon, by which a newly acquired sound is immediately used in all relevant words. Interestingly, Smith's data provide multiple examples of change that is not, in fact, across-the-board. In the longitudinal description, many, if not most, of the rules are described as becoming optional before disappearing.

A major strength of all rule-based theories of child phonology is the ability to account for the regular correspondences between adult targets and child productions. If final consonants are never present, then a rule deleting consonants in final position can capture this pattern. Furthermore, the central role of features (subunits of phonemes) in generative theory allows for these generalizations to be stated parsimoniously; it is a fact of child language that certain types of speech sounds tend to pattern together (e.g., fricatives are produced as stops). Another fact of child phonology, however, is that development includes variability, non-linearities, and exceptions, especially in the earliest stages. Generative theory, however, does not have an adequate mechanism for accounting for these now well-known facts. Smith's study of his son's development does not start until 26 months of age; an attempt to use a set of realization rules to describe the productions of a younger child in the very earliest stages of language acquisition would not be an easy task. Just how phonological representations come to exist is not specified, and the assumption that perceptual abilities are fully developed at the onset of linguistic production is problematic. The question of continuity between prelinguistic and linguistic development is an interesting one for generative theory. While the assumption of innate, hard-wired language structures implies at least implicit continuity, there is no treatment of the role of prelinguistic vocalizations in the major generative works. Lastly, not only does the theory not account for the role of input in acquisition, it downplays the importance of language input, making it difficult to account for the early appearance of language-specific phonological patterns in child speech. According to generative theory, language, by definition, is not learnable so must therefore be innate.

Natural phonology.   Another important work within the rule-based approaches to child phonology, Stampe's theory of natural phonology (Stampe, 1969), shares a number of important characteristics with traditional generative theory. First, the child is assumed to be operating with adult-like representations from the very earliest stages of language acquisition; in addition, a certain amount of linguistic knowledge is presumed to be innate. In the case of natural phonology, the child is born with a predetermined, universal set of phonological processes that dictate the form of his productions. The basic thesis of natural phonology is that "the living sound patterns of language, in their development in each individual as well as in their evolution over the centuries, are governed by forces implicit in human vocalization and perception" (Donegan & Stampe, 1979, p. 126). According to Donegan and Stampe, every child is born with the same set of innate processes, and the act of acquiring a language-specific phonology consists of learning the constraints a language imposes on these natural processes. Children must learn to suppress, limit, and reorder the processes in accordance with the phonology of their native language.

   Natural phonology has some advantages over traditional generative theory: it specifies clearly what is considered to be innate, and by positing the universal existence of these natural processes accounts for the structuralist observations of the congruencies between child processes and phonological patterns in adults. The processes, by definition, may apply variably, accounting for variability in the production of individual sounds within a child. Input is granted a somewhat more important role in the process of learning, and the fact that the processes are assumed to be grounded in the physical attributes of the child's speech mechanism begins to provide some explanation for the nature of child productions. The most enduring influence of Stampe's theory, however, is probably the role that phonological processes continue to play in the description of the systematic errors that occur both in typical development and in children with phonological disorders (see the section *Typical Phonological Development* above for examples of these processes). As with previous theories, however, no attention is given to the role of prelinguistic vocal development or to individual differences across children.

Constraint-based approaches.   Stampe modified generative phonology to incorporate the notion of natural processes; he did not, however, completely reject the generative notion of rules that transform underlying representations into surface (i.e., spoken) forms, but distinguished between innate processes and learned rules. Another approach to both child and adult phonology is a constraint-based approach referred to as "optimality theory" (Prince & Smolensky, 1997). Constraint-based approaches to child phonology, as outlined by Bernhardt and Stemberger (1998), maintain many of the fundamental characteristics of generative phonology; the feature (a subunit of the phoneme) is maintained as the basic unit of phonological representation and underlying representations are thought to consist only of unpredictable phonological information, with redundant and predictable information stored in the child's grammar. Instead of strictly ordered rules, however, output is governed by a set of constraints that are ranked and determine the optimal production of a word. The two basic types of constraints are faithfulness constraints, which dictate that the output should be as similar to the adult form as possible, and output constraints, which are based on articulatory and perceptual abilities. Constraints, unlike rules, can be violated, and output forms are generated by constraints and violations of constraints. Phonological acquisition is a process of re-ranking constraints so that the output matches the adult form. The initial state of the system, however, is not clearly specified and the question of the origin of the individual constraints is left unanswered.

A constraint-based system has many similarities with traditional generative theory in its description of child phonology. Underlying representations remain the same; however, ordered rules are replaced by ranked constraints. Because they are more recent, however, constraint-based theories do not ignore many of the facts of child phonology that are now known. Thus, the concept of prelinguistic to linguistic continuity is accommodated by positing constraints that operate during the babbling period and are then carried over to the beginning of meaningful speech, accounting for the similarities between babble and early word productions. Furthermore, individual differences are ascribed to a certain amount of randomness in the initial ranking of constraints; while some constraints may be universally ranked high or low, others are random and ranked differently by individual children. Other applications of constraint-based approaches to phonological developmental can be found in the works of Dinnsen and colleagues (e.g., Dinnsen & O'Connor, 2001) and Gierut and colleagues (e.g., Gierut, 2001; Gierut, Morrisette, & Champion, 1999).

Child-centered theories

Child-centered theories reflect the beginnings of the third phase in the development of a theory of child phonology with the realization that the facts of child phonology, having been tested against the existing theories, necessitate a more radical departure from adult theory than had previously been attempted. According to these theories, child phonology must be addressed on its own terms, rather than in relation to the adult system.

Prosodic theory.   Waterson's (1971) prosodic approach to phonological development differed dramatically from traditional structuralist and generative accounts. In particular, it questioned the idea that the phoneme or the feature was the basic unit of representation for the child, as it was assumed to be for the adult. Furthermore, the role of perception and the specific nature of the input were elevated to primary status in the theory. According to Waterson, perception develops gradually in conjunction with production. Underlying representations are not assumed to be adult-like, since perception is not adult-like in the earliest stages. In the analysis of the speech of her young son, P, she

used a non-segmental approach, incorporating articulatory features as well as suprasegmental features such as syllable structure and stress patterns, and established five different
structure types to describe P's productions. According to Waterson, the child perceives
a schema for a set of words with a particular structure and then reproduces the salient
characteristics in his own output. Thus, the words *fish*, *fetch*, *brush*, and *dish* form a
"sibilant" schema in that the final consonant of each of these words is a sibilant consonant
in the adult form; P's productions of these words also contained a sibilant consonant.
The features that appear in the child's spoken form are determined by the child's perception, by the child's own output system, and by the "strength" and "salience" of articulation in the adult form.

Obviously, not all children base their early productions on these same schemas, a fact
accounted for by the role Waterson gives to the input: Each child hears a different set
of words with enough frequency for them to be recorded, and extracts schemas from
this input. The strengths of this theory include the explicit treatment of the role of perception and input in phonological development, the recognition of individual patterns
of development (in the form of different schemas), and the variable stability of sounds
in different contexts. It is, however, quite limited in scope as it is based on a small dataset
from one young child, and does not address the systematic error patterns that occur or
the typical order of acquisition of individual sounds.

Cognitive theory.   One of the basic principles of the cognitive theory of phonological
development is that children play an active role in acquiring the phonology of their language; they choose words to say based on their own articulatory abilities, and then formulate, test, and revise hypotheses regarding phonology based on linguistic experience.
Because of this, a major strength of the theory is its attention to the phenomenon of
individual patterns of acquisition. It is, by definition, designed to account for observed
phenomena such as lexical selection, regression, and the use of phonological strategies,
which are generally characteristic of the very earliest stages of development. It does not,
however, have much to say about the systematic correspondences observed between adult
forms and child productions that appear later in development.

Ferguson and Farwell (1975) provide a detailed account of the longitudinal development of initial consonant categories in three children, a paper now considered a seminal
work illustrating the cognitive theory of phonological development. One important
observation from this study is the frequent occurrence of intra-word variability, that is,
the fact that some words are pronounced in different ways by the same child at the same
point in time. Ferguson and Farwell claim that this variability "makes it difficult to
make statements about either phonological contrasts or unique underlying forms and
systematic rules" (1975, p. 425). Other observations include the presence of regressive
and progressive phonological idioms (words that are either more or less advanced than
the current phonological system would suggest) and the selectivity of the child in choosing individual words to try to produce. The authors highlight the importance of the
lexicon in phonological acquisition (as described in a previous section); phonological
development is not just a matter of change in the system (rules), but may take place
on a word-by-word basis, reflecting the individual experiences and preferences of
the child.

Ferguson and Farwell (1975) offered an outline of the essential characteristics for any phonological theory, based on their observations. The model should: (1) de-emphasize the separation of phonetic and phonemic development; (2) emphasize individual variation, but incorporate the notion of "universal phonetic tendencies"; (3) emphasize the importance of lexical items in phonological development; and (4) allow for the gradual development of a phonological system, based on generalizations from the child's own "phonic core" of words and the articulations needed to produce them.

Biological theories

Biological models for the development of early speech (e.g., Kent, 1992) are based on an approach that emphasizes the importance of general principles of developmental biology and the role of anatomical and motor development in the development of a phonological system. In Kent's model for early phonological acquisition (1992), audition and speech motor function are viewed as genetically determined. Early productions are limited by motor ability, especially by jaw-tongue synergy and by the inability to move the tongue in a precise manner. Universal patterns in terms of order of acquisition are described in relation to the development of specific motor capacities. Little attention is given to the role of perception in the acquisition of phonology; however, other biological theorists have suggested that substitution errors in child speech are at least partly predicted by acoustic similarity, and Thelen (1991) highlights the importance of multimodal mapping (including acoustic, sensory, and visual) in the production of canonical babble and later speech.

Kent described the production of early words as holistic "motor scores" that become more reliable as coordination improves. These motor scores may be compared to the vocal motor schemes described by Vihman (1992) and to Browman and Goldstein's (1992) "gestural phonology." In this view, segmental consistency is rooted in the developing precision of motor performance. Phonemic organization emerges through global mapping between sensory and motor routines. A fundamental difference between this view and the approaches described above is that in the biological approach, "development is a process in which the child progressively applies available resources in attempting to emulate the mature behavior" as opposed to the view that development is "a process in which the child simplifies a fully comprehended version of the mature behavior" (Kent, 1992, p. 85).

The strengths of this approach include the emphasis on continuity between phonetic and phonological learning and prelinguistic and linguistic production as well as the integration with other types of non-linguistic learning and development. Variability in production can also be accounted for in terms of the use of motor scores and the gradual increase in coordinative ability. Furthermore, this approach allows for the simultaneous development of production and perception skills, by not attributing adult-like phonemic representations to young children. Although not specified completely, systematic correspondences between child and adult forms are potentially accounted for by motoric and perceptual limitations. One criticism of biological models that has been noted, however, is that the infant is often portrayed as a passive learner, rather than an active participant in the acquisition process, and that little attention is given to individual patterns of development.

Usage-based phonology

A relatively new linguistic theory, "usage-based linguistics" (Kemmer & Barlow, 2000), assumes a close relationship between language use and language structure, with structure seen as both a generator and a product of language use. With specific reference to phonology, a usage-based account emphasizes the role that language use plays in shaping a linguistic sound system (Bybee, 2001), while a usage-based approach to phonological acquisition highlights the important role of language input and use in the instantiation and ongoing modification of the child's phonological system. From this perspective, phonology is not acquired independently of other aspects of grammar, but is intimately linked to the individual words that are present in the lexicon and the characteristics of use of those words. Thus, a usage-based account predicts that lexical effects will be detected in children's productions of non-words. Two lexical characteristics that have been investigated are word frequency and neighborhood density of individual words.

It is well documented that word frequency influences adults' speech. In particular, high frequency words display an advantage in both perception and production tasks (summary in Ellis, 2002); in addition, word frequency has also been shown to have an important effect on processes of historical sound change. It is reasonable, then, to suspect that word frequency plays a role in the development of a linguistic sound system. A few researchers have investigated this hypothesis, with mixed results. For example, studies by Leonard and Ritterman (1971) and Tyler and Edwards (1993) showed facilitative effects of word frequency on accuracy of children's productions. By contrast, Velten (1943) observed that his daughter's high frequency words were the last to change when a new contrast entered her phonological system.

Effects of "neighborhood density," which refers to the phonological relationships between words in an individual's lexicon, are also well known in the adult perception and production literature. Phonological "neighbors" are defined as words that differ from one another by a one phoneme addition, deletion, or substitution (Luce & Pisoni, 1998); for example, the words *bat, mat, pit, pet, past, spat, at*, among others, would be neighbors of the word *pat*. For children acquiring language, neighborhood density may influence the ongoing reorganization of phonological representations during development. For instance, words that reside in dense neighborhoods (i.e., have many neighbors) may need more detailed phonological representations due to potential confusability with other similar sounding words. Charles-Luce and Luce (1990) conducted a computational analysis of the lexicons of children aged 5;0 and 7;0 and found that they are less dense than adult lexicons, suggesting that children may be able to function with less detailed phonological representations. In an experimental test of this hypothesis, Metsala (1997) found effects of both word frequency and neighborhood density on the ability of children in first grade to recognize spoken words in a gating task, a task in which successively more acoustic–phonetic information is provided to the listener until the word is identified. The children performed best on high frequency, high density words, suggesting that these words may be more specified phonetically.

The role of neighborhood density has also been investigated in relation to children's production abilities. Gierut and Storkel (2002) and Morrisette (1999) found mixed results of the effect of neighborhood density on accurate production of fricatives. In a study of imitative productions of non-words by typically developing 2-year-olds, Zamuner, Gerken, and Hammond (2004) found that high phonotactic probability (which was correlated with high neighborhood density) consistently facilitated accurate production of coda consonants. Beckman and Edwards (2000) found similar results with somewhat older children.

While the research that exists regarding the role of lexical factors in phonological development sometimes presents conflicting results, there is substantial evidence that young children are sensitive to many of the same lexical factors as adults and that these lexical characteristics may play an important role in the acquisition of phonology. Future research will let us know if this is indeed a promising framework for contributing to our understanding of critical parameters of phonological development.

Summary: Theories of phonological development

This section has provided a historical overview of the various linguistic theories that have been used in the description of the acquisition of a phonological system. Each theory was shown to have its individual strengths and weaknesses in terms of the ability to account for what were presented as the basic requirements for any theory of child phonology. Notable differences were found in views of underlying representations and in the amount of attention given to the phonological–cognitive aspects of development compared with the phonetic–biological aspects. No single theory was able to account for all phenomena that have been documented in studies of phonological acquisition, yet each was good at accounting for particular aspects of the data. The most recent theory, a "usage-based" approach, lacks sufficient child data from children under the age of 4 years to be fully evaluated at this point.

Conclusion

This chapter has provided a review of three interrelated aspects of the study of phonological development. In the first section, a brief outline of patterns of development was presented, beginning with the prelinguistic period and continuing to the age of 42 months. Similarities between babble and early speech were highlighted and cross-linguistic patterns were discussed. The second section focused on the link between phonological and lexical development in young children. Research in this area makes it clear that phonological acquisition affects, and is affected by, the acquisition of words. The third section provided a historical overview and evaluation of theories of phonological development. A complete theory should account for a wide range of phenomena related to development, including the links between perception and production, the presence of both common patterns and individual differences, the formation of underlying representations, and the mechanisms underlying change in a child's phonology from first words to adult-like productions. At present, no single theory accounts for all of these; however, as the body of research in this field increases, we should be able to formulate new theories, or modify existing ones, to reach a goal of a full understanding of this area of study.

References

Beckman, M. E., & Edwards, J. (2000). Lexical frequency effects on young children's imitative productions. In M. B. Broe & J. B. Pierrehumbert (Eds.), *Papers in laboratory phonology V* (pp. 208–218). Cambridge: Cambridge University Press.

Bernhardt, B., & Stemberger, J. (1998). *Handbook of phonological development: From the perspective of constraint-based non-linear phonology.* San Diego, CA: Academic Press.

Boysson-Bardies, B. de, Vihman, M., Roug-Hellichius, L., Durand, C., Landberg, I., & Arao, F. (1992). Material evidence of infant selection from the target language: A cross-linguistic study. In C. A. Ferguson, L. Menn, & C. Stoel-Gammon (Eds.), *Phonological development: Models, research, implications* (pp. 369–391). Timonium, MD: York Press, Inc.

Browman, C., & Goldstein, L. (1992). Articulatory phonology: An overview. *Phonetica, 49,* 155–180.

Bybee, J. (2001). *Phonology and language use.* Cambridge: Cambridge University Press.

Charles-Luce, J., & Luce, P. A. (1990). Similarity neighbourhoods of words in young children's lexicons. *Journal of Child Language, 17,* 205–215.

Chomsky, N. (1972). *Language and mind.* New York: Harcourt, Brace & World, Inc.

Chomsky, N., & Halle, M. (1968). *The sound pattern of English.* New York: Harper & Row.

Coplan, J., & Gleason, J. (1988). Unclear speech: recognition and significance of unintelligible speech in preschool children. *Pediatrics, 82,* 447–452.

Dinnsen, D. (2001). Typological predictions in developmental phonology. *Journal of Child Language, 28,* 597–628.

Donegan, P. J., & Stampe, D. (1979). The study of natural phonology. In D. A. Dinnsen (Ed.), *Current approaches to phonological theory* (pp. 126–173). Bloomington, IN: Indiana University Press.

Ellis, N. (2002). Frequency effects in language processing: a review with implications of implicit and explicit theories of language acquisition. *Studies in Second Language Acquisition, 24,* 143–188.

Ferguson, C. A., & Farwell, C. B. (1975). Words and sounds in early language acquisition. *Language, 51,* 419–439.

Ferguson, C. A., & Garnica, O. (1975). Theories of phonological development. In E. H. Lenneberg & E. Lenneberg (Eds.), *Foundations of language development: A multidisciplinary approach* (pp. 153–180). New York: Academic Press.

Fletcher, P., Chan, C., Wong, P., Stokes, S., Tardif, T., & Leung, S. (2004). The interface between phonetic and lexical abilities in early Cantonese language development. *Clinical Linguistics and Phonetics, 18,* 1–11.

Fry, D. B. (1966). The development of the phonological system in the normal and deaf child. In F. Smith & G. A. Miller (Eds.), *The genesis of language* (pp. 187–216). Cambridge, MA: MIT Press.

Gierut, J. (2001). A model of lexical diffusion in phonological acquisition. *Clinical Linguistics and Phonetics, 15*, 19–22.

Gierut, J., Morrisette, M., & Champion, A. (1999). Lexical constraints in phonological acquisition. *Journal of Child Language, 26*, 261–294.

Gierut, J., & Storkel, H. (2002). Markedness and the grammar in lexical diffusion of fricatives. *Clinical Linguistics and Phonetics, 16*, 115–134.

Grunwell, P. (1981). The development of phonology: A descriptive profile. *First Language, 3*, 161–191.

Ingram, D. (1976). *Phonological disability in children*. London: Edward Arnold.

Jakobson, R. (1941/1968). *Child language, aphasia and phonological universals* (A. R. Keiler, Trans.). The Hague, The Netherlands: Mouton.

Kemmer, S., & Barlow, M. (2000). Introduction: A usage-based conception of language. In M. Barlow & S. Kemmer (Eds.), *Usage-based models of language* (pp. vii–xxvii). Stanford, CA: CSLI Publications.

Kent, R. (1992). The biology of phonological development. In C. A. Ferguson, L. Menn, & C. Stoel-Gammon (Eds.), *Phonological development: Models, research, implications* (pp. 65–90). Timonium, MD: York Press, Inc.

Leonard, L., & Ritterman, S. (1971). Articulation of /s/ as a function of cluster and word frequency of occurrence. *Journal of Speech and Hearing Research, 14*, 476–485.

Leonard, L., Schwartz, R. G., Morris, B., & Chapman, K. (1981). Factors influencing early lexical acquisition: Lexical orientation and phonological composition. *Child Development, 52*, 882–887.

Lindblom, B. (1992). Phonological units as adaptive emergents of lexical development. In C. A. Ferguson, L. Menn, & C. Stoel-Gammon (Eds.), *Phonological development: Models, research, implications* (pp. 131–163). Timonium, MD: York Press, Inc.

Locke, J. (1983). *Phonological acquisition and change*. New York: Academic Press.

Locke, J. (1993). *The child's path to spoken language*. Cambridge, MA: Harvard University Press.

Luce, P. A., & Pisoni, D. B. (1998). Recognizing spoken words: The neighborhood activation model. *Ear and Hearing, 19*, 1–36.

Menn, L. (1980). Phonological theory and child phonology. In G. Yeni-Komshian, J. Kavanagh, & C. Ferguson (Eds.), *Child phonology: Vol. 1. Production* (pp. 23–41). New York: Academic Press.

Messick, C. (1984). *Phonetic and contextual aspects of the transition to early words*. Unpublished doctoral dissertation, Purdue University, West Lafayette, IN.

Metsala, J. L. (1997). An examination of word frequency and neighborhood density in the development of spoken-word recognition. *Memory and Cognition, 25*, 47–56.

Morrisette, M. (1999). Lexical characteristics of sound change. *Clinical Linguistics and Phonetics, 13*, 219–238.

Prince, A., & Smolensky, P. (1997). From neural networks to universal grammar. *Science, 275*, 1604–1610.

Schwartz, R. G., & Leonard, L. B. (1982). Do children pick and choose? An examination of phonological selection and avoidance in early lexical acquisition. *Journal of Child Language, 9*, 319–336.

Smith, N. V. (1973). *The acquisition of phonology: A case study*. Cambridge: Cambridge University Press.

Stampe, D. (1969). *The acquisition of phonetic representation*. Paper presented at the Fifth Regional Meeting of the Chicago Linguistic Society, Chicago.

Stoel-Gammon, C. (1985). Phonetic inventories: 15–24 months: A longitudinal study. *Journal of Speech and Hearing Research, 28*, 505–512.

Stoel-Gammon, C. (1998a). The role of babbling and phonology in early linguistic development. In A. M. Wetherby, S. F. Warren, & J. Reichle (Eds.), *Transitions in prelinguistic communication* (pp. 87–110). Baltimore, MD: Paul H. Brookes Publishing Co.

Stoel-Gammon, C. (1998b). Sounds and words in early language acquisition. In R. Paul (Ed.), *Exploring the speech–language connection* (pp. 25–52). Baltimore, MD: Paul H. Brookes Publishing Co.

Stoel-Gammon, C., & Cooper, J. (1984). Patterns of early lexical and phonological development. *Journal of Child Language, 11*, 247–271.

Stoel-Gammon, C., & Dunn, C. (1985). *Normal and disordered phonology in children*. Baltimore, MD: University Park Press.

Stoel-Gammon, C., & Herrington, P. (1990). Vowel systems of normally developing and phonologically disordered children. *Clinical Linguistics and Phonetics, 4*, 145–160.

Thelen, E. (1991). Motor aspects of emergent speech: A dynamic approach. In N. Krasnegor, D. Rumbaugh, R. Schiefelbusch, & M. Studdert-Kennedy (Eds.), *Biological and behavioral determinants of language development* (pp. 339–362). Hillsdale, NJ: Lawrence Erlbaum Associates.

Tyler, A., & Edwards, M. L. (1993). Lexical acquisition and acquisition of initial voiceless stops. *Journal of Child Language, 20*, 253–273.

Velten, H. V. (1943). The growth of phonemic and lexical patterns in infant language. *Language, 19*, 231–292.

Vihman, M. (1992). Early syllables and the construction of phonology. In C. A. Ferguson, L. Menn, & C. Stoel-Gammon (Eds.), *Phonological development: Models, research, implications* (pp. 393–422). Timonium, MD: York Press, Inc.

Vihman, M. M. (1996). *Phonological development: The origins of language in the child*. Cambridge, MA: Blackwell.

Vihman, M., Elbert, M., & Ferguson, C. (1987). Phonological development from babbling to speech: Common tendencies and individual differences. *Applied Psycholinguistics, 7*, 3–40.

Walley, A. (1993). The role of vocabulary development in children's spoken word recognition and segmentation ability. *Developmental Review, 13*, 286–350.

Waterson, N. (1971). Child phonology: a prosodic view. *Journal of Linguistics, 7*, 179–211.

Zamuner, T. S., Gerken, L., & Hammond, M. (2004). Phonotactic probabilities in young children's speech production. *Journal of Child Language, 31*, 515–536.

13

Mechanisms of Word Learning

Gil Diesendruck

Words are conventional arbitrary symbols used to communicate concepts. By school age, children have thousands of these. What are the mechanisms that allow children to accomplish this feat?

In answering this question, I will start with an introduction of the phenomenon, emphasizing the most puzzling question word-learning theorists attempt to explain: What allows children to limit the possible meanings of words? I will describe six mechanisms proposed to answer this question, and discuss empirical challenges facing them. My goal is to define the narrower fields in which particular theoretical debates are being contested, and describe some of the most recent discoveries about word learning that any general theory needs to explain. Reflecting a bias in the literature, I will focus primarily on the learning of count nouns.

I will characterize the proposals as differing on two broad dimensions. The main one is the *degree of specificity* of the mechanism, that is, whether it is specific to the acquisition of words, or instead applicable to a variety of cognitive problems. A secondary dimension has to do with the *source of the constraints*, specifically, whether the constraints are endogenous or exogenous to the child. Figure 13.1 presents the placement of the six mechanisms on this two-dimensional grid.

The review of the mechanisms and challenges will lead to the conclusion that no single mechanism suffices to account for word learning, and that instead, the field needs approaches that critically integrate multiple mechanisms. Two such approaches will then be discussed. I will end with some general conclusions about where the field stands theoretically, and what are the empirical directions towards which the field should move.

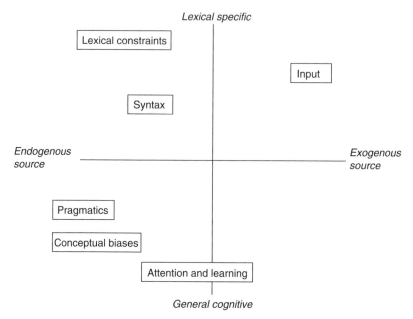

Figure 13.1   Position of the various word learning mechanisms in relation to the dimensions of "specificity" and "source."

The Phenomenon

Word learning is fast

It is commonly assumed that children start producing words by their first birthday. By 16 to 18 months of age, children are believed to have an average vocabulary size of 50 words. Most theorists of lexical development believe that around this time, children go through a "vocabulary spurt," acquiring words at a much faster pace (Dromi, 1987). Recently, Bloom (2004) challenged this notion of a vocabulary spurt, arguing instead that lexical acquisition is a continuous process with a relatively stable rate of change. This debate notwithstanding, all word-learning researchers agree in their amazement regarding the move from the 50 words average vocabulary children have at 18 months of age to the estimated 10,000 words they have by age 6 (Anglin, 1993).

Part of the explanation for how children manage to acquire so many words is that they have good learning and memory capacities. Children can learn a new word associated with an object after a few exposures to the word, and can remember the word for a long period of time – a phenomenon dubbed "fast mapping" (Carey & Bartlett, 1978). Recent studies have further defined this phenomenon, showing that even 13-month-olds are capable of fast mapping (Woodward, Markman, & Fitzsimmons, 1994), and 3-year-olds are just as good as adults in remembering such mappings (Markson & Bloom, 1997).

Word learning is universal

Prototypical North American middle-class children are to some extent directly bombarded with linguistic information. Parents tend to talk to their prelinguistic infants frequently, and in a particularly simplified, high frequency, and accentuated manner – often called motherese or baby-talk. Once children start talking, parents often engage them in language games, especially games that invite children to extend or express their emerging knowledge of the language.

The linguistic input children in other cultures receive differs from this prototypical North American middle-class speech. Specifically, cultures differ in the extent, manner, and emphasis of adults' direct talk to children (Gathercole & Hoff, this volume; Hoff, 2006). As I shall review later, some of these differences in input do correlate with specific differences in children's eventual linguistic knowledge. Nonetheless, the important conclusion for the present purpose is that despite these differences, children in all cultures studied acquire language at around the same ages, and with relatively similar efficacy.

Word learning is inductive

A popular belief is that word learning is one of the easiest aspects of language acquisition, because, presumably, all that children have to do is imitate adults. This belief implies that children are exposed to words in communicatively optimal contexts, in which an adult and the child are jointly focused on the same object or event, and the adult repeatedly utters the new word associated with the object or event. Fast mapping would then do the rest of the job.

The first major problem with this assumption is that most of the words children learn they encounter in much less optimal communicative contexts than the one just described. This is the case not only in non-Western cultures but also in typical Western middle-class families (Harris, Jones, & Grant, 1983). For instance, it is often the case that when children hear a word, its intended referent is not even visually available.

The second major problem with the popular notion is that even if the typical communicative context in which children encountered new words were optimal in the sense described earlier, there still would not be enough information in the input to allow a definite determination of the meaning of a word. This problem, first noted by Quine (1960), has to do with the fact that any word can have an infinite number of meanings (Poulin-Dubois & Graham, this volume). For instance, upon hearing a bottle of milk being labeled "bottle," what in the situation can lead the child to rule out the color of the object, its material, its contents, the event itself, and a myriad of other possible concepts, as the referents of the word "bottle"? What would lead the child to necessarily infer that "bottle" refers to that specific kind of object? How does the child even establish what "specific kind of object" that thing is?

What these two problems highlight is that the information available to children in typical communicative interactions underdetermines the possible meanings of words. Thus, children have to do a lot of inductive work to figure out what it is that they are supposed to imitate in adults' speech. In what follows, I will describe some of the mechanisms arguably used by children in this inductive process.

Mechanisms of Word Learning

Input

While differences across cultures in children's exposure to language do not seem to have a substantial impact in whether or not children acquire language, they do affect how and what exactly children acquire. One relatively robust finding in this regard is that across cultures, parents from higher socio-economic standing talk more to their children, and children from higher socio-economic standing have larger vocabularies (Gathercole & Hoff, this volume; Hoff, 2006). Longitudinal studies suggest that it is indeed properties of maternal speech to children – such as number of words – that most strongly predict children's vocabulary size. In fact, it has been found that the frequency of specific words in maternal speech to children correlates with the frequency of these words in children's vocabulary (Huttenlocher, Haight, Bryk, Seltzer, & Lyons, 1991).

Arguably, the most investigated issue regarding links between input and child language has to do with the composition of children's vocabularies. Gentner (1982) found that the proportion of nouns was higher than the proportion of any other word class (e.g., verbs) in the vocabulary of children speakers of various languages. Based on this universal similarity, Gentner argued that this "noun bias" is a result of the relative conceptual simplicity of nouns over verbs. Since then, Gentner's original findings and conclusions have been tested and challenged (Poulin-Dubois & Graham, this volume). On the one hand, countering Gentner's conclusion, studies of the vocabulary composition of children speaking Korean and Mandarin Chinese have not found a noun bias. On the other hand, consistent with Gentner's claim, investigations of the vocabulary composition of children speaking various Western languages have confirmed a prevalence of nouns. This debate notwithstanding, the studies on the noun bias reinforce the notion that the linguistic input children receive can explain certain individual differences in children's vocabulary acquisition.

The remaining question on this matter is whether linguistic input can constrain how children infer word meanings. The argument underlying this possibility is that by being cooperative communicators, parents simplify the induction problem by providing children with numerous cues about the meanings of words, and the relationship between words (Clark & Wong, 2002; Nelson, 1988). One common labeling pattern found in parents' speech to children is to refer to objects first and foremost by using basic-level count nouns (Callanan, 1985). It is possible that this type of exposure explains children's tendency to map new words onto objects of similar kind (Waxman, 1991). A further example is that parents rarely use multiple labels to refer to the same object, and when they do it is usually qualified by clarifying expressions (Callanan & Sabbagh, 2004). Callanan and Sabbagh concluded that parents' labeling tendencies seemed to endorse the development of an expectation in children that there is a "best" name for each object, if not an assumption that each object can have only one name. Consistent with this latter possibility, studies found that how parents introduce nouns depends on the familiarity of the nouns to the child (Masur, 1997). Specifically, mothers typically question children about the referents of familiar names, but directly provide the names of novel objects. This parental strategy might encourage the development in children of an assumption that novel words refer to novel objects.

In sum, the "input proposal" suggests that not only the rate but also the manner by which children acquire words are significantly affected by the way their parents talk to them. The emphasis on parents as the source of the constraints makes this an exogenous mechanism, even if, eventually, children internalize the biases detected in the input. The fact that the constraining factor is linguistic input makes this a highly lexical-specific account.

Syntax

Another language-specific mechanism argued to help children figure out the meanings of words is their knowledge of syntax. The argument is that via an awareness of the different characteristic meanings associated with particular grammatical classes of words, children can substantially narrow down the meanings of words. For instance, by recognizing that a novel word they hear is a *count noun*, children can then search for the possible *kind of object* the word refers to. Similarly, children should search for the *characteristic of an object* when hearing a novel *adjective*, the *particular individual* referred to by a *proper noun*, or the unique *action* portrayed by a novel *verb*.

Evidently, for this mechanism to be effective, children need to be able to distinguish among the syntactic frames in which the different types of words appear. There is mounting evidence that, even before their second birthday, children indeed do make these distinctions, differentially extending words based on whether the words are syntactically framed as proper nouns, count nouns, or adjectives (Brown, 1957; Gelman & Taylor, 1984; Hall, 1994; see also Naigles & Swensen, this volume).

In a striking demonstration of children's sensitivity to lexical form, Hall and colleagues showed 4-year-olds animate-looking novel entities, and described the entities either with a salient familiar adjective (e.g., "This is a red one") or with a descriptive proper noun (e.g., "This is Mr. Red") (Hall, Waxman, Bredart, & Nicolay, 2003). Children were told a story about an entity that lost its salient characteristic (e.g., it became blue). Children were then asked if the same entity, now with a different characteristic, or a different entity but with the same original salient characteristic, was the referent of the adjective or proper noun. Hall et al. found that children in the proper noun condition selected the same entity with a different characteristic, but children in the adjective condition selected the different entity with the same characteristic.

Extending this line of work, Hall and Graham (1999) examined whether children make different kinds of inferences about the relationship between two words depending on the lexical class to which they belong. The experimenter showed children pairs of familiar animals, and taught them either a novel proper name ("This dog is named Daxy") or a novel adjective ("This dog is very daxy") for one of the animals. Children were then asked for the referent of a second novel proper name or adjective. Hall and Graham found that while children in the proper name–proper name condition tended to select the animal that lacked a proper name, children in the adjective–adjective condition tended to pick randomly between the two animals. The authors concluded that children seem to recognize that because proper names designate individuals, it is probable that two different proper names designate two different individuals. In turn, given that adjectives describe characteristics of individuals, it is plausible that two different adjectives nonetheless apply to the same individual.

Lexical constraints

Arguably, the most direct solution to the word-learning induction problem is that children are equipped with lexical constraints. Markman (1989) suggested that children have a set of three constraints that help limit the possible meanings of a word: a whole object bias (words refer to whole objects, not parts or features), a taxonomic bias (words refer to kinds of things, not individuals), and a mutual exclusivity bias (every object can have only one name). These three constraints work together and help children infer the meanings of words. For instance, if children are shown a familiar object, and an adult labels it with a novel name, mutual exclusivity leads children to overcome the whole object bias and to infer that the label probably refers to an unknown part or characteristic of the object (Markman & Wachtel, 1988).

Although Markman (1992) discusses the possibility that the origins of these biases are in general cognitive mechanisms, most of the studies attempt to show that the biases are unique to word-learning contexts. For instance, in traditional tests of the taxonomic bias the experimenter presents children a familiar object (e.g., a banana), labels it with a novel name, and then asks children to extend the name to either a taxonomically (e.g., an apple) or a thematically (e.g., a monkey) related object. Children typically extend the name based on taxonomic similarity. However, if asked to pick an object that "goes with" the target object, children pick based on thematic similarity (Imai, Gentner, & Uchida, 1994; Waxman & Namy, 1997). Furthermore, in line with the idea that these biases are especially dedicated for word acquisition, Markman and colleagues found that children respond in ways consistent with these biases from very early on in development (Liittschwager & Markman, 1994; Markman, Wasow, & Hansen, 2003; see also Halberda, 2003).

In an attempt to capture more precisely the dynamic interactions among various biases, Golinkoff, Mervis, and Hirsh-Pasek (1994) proposed a system of six lexical principles, divided into two developmental tiers. One of the basic differences from Markman's proposal is that some of the principles were themselves the results of word learning which, once developed, helped children further narrow the meanings of words. The first tier of principles consists of biases that get word learning started. They are: reference (words stand for objects), extendibility (words extend beyond the individual item labeled), and object scope (words refer to objects). The second tier consists of principles that evolve from the first tier principles. They are: conventionality (there are standard/expected words used to refer to things), categorical scope (words are extended on the basis of taxonomic similarity), and novel-name nameless-category (new words refer to nameless objects). Despite the differences, this "developmental principles" approach shares with Markman's proposal the emphasis on the lexical specificity of the principles, and the fact that the primary source of the constraints rests within the child rather than explicitly in the input (see also Merriman & Bowman, 1989; Waxman, 1991, for other proposals).

A final point regarding the lexical constraints account is that the constraints are not viewed as fully deterministic and encapsulated (Behrend, 1990; Woodward & Markman, 1998) but rather as default assumptions that can be overcome in the presence of contradictory evidence (for examples see Au & Glusman, 1990; Diesendruck & Shatz, 1997, 2001).

Attention and learning mechanisms

The least lexical-specific account of word learning stipulates that it can be explained by the general mechanisms of associative learning coupled with the operations of attention and memory. Indirect support for this account comes from studies revealing the sophisticated capacities of young infants to detect patterns in streams of linguistic signs (Gerken; Saffran & Thiessen, this volume).

The word-learning phenomenon addressed in most detail by such an account is children's "shape bias," that is, the tendency to favor extending object names based on shape similarity over similarity on any other dimension (e.g., color, material, size) (Jones, Smith, & Landau, 1991; Landau, Smith, & Jones, 1988). According to the attention and learning account, most object names to which English-speaking children are exposed are count nouns describing shape-based categories (Samuelson & Smith, 1999). Given this regular association between a count noun construction (e.g., "This is an X") and the physical dimension of shape, every time children hear a novel count noun their attention automatically turns towards the shape of objects. In other words, general learning mechanisms pick out a regularity in the linguistic input to children, thus establishing a firm lexical-specific bias. Consistent with this account, a shape bias is manifested when 3-year-olds are asked to extend names, but not when asked to pick objects that go together (Landau et al., 1988). Furthermore, longitudinal studies show a relationship between children's acquisition of a vocabulary of shape-based object names and their shape bias (Gershkoff-Stowe & Smith, 2004), and training studies reveal that as 2-year-olds get taught shape-based object names so their shape bias increases (Smith, Jones, Landau, Gershkoff-Stowe, & Samuelson, 2002). Also, connectionist networks develop a shape bias similar to that of children as a result of being trained in an input corpus of words similar to the ones children are exposed to (Samuelson, 2002). Importantly, while children's initial word-learning bias is directed at shape – presumably reflecting the distributional frequency in the input – as children develop they come to notice further regular associations between different types of words in the input and their respective referents, thus developing biases tuned to these finer distinctions (Smith, 1999).

The importance of attention and memory in driving children's learning of words was further illustrated in a study by Samuelson and Smith (1998). In that study, an experimenter showed 2-year-olds three novel objects while sitting on the floor. The experimenter then invited children to move to a table, where she showed children a fourth novel object. The experimenter and the child returned to the floor, the experimenter placed all four objects on a tray, and then asked the child to find the referent of a novel word. Samuelson and Smith found that 2-year-olds tended to select the object seen at the table in response to the experimenter's request. The authors argued that given the distinctiveness of the "table" context, the object seen in that context stood out in children's memory, and was consequently the most attention-grabbing.

In sum, this account builds on general cognitive mechanisms that are not specific to word learning, but which, in interaction with regularities in the linguistic input children are exposed to, may give rise to lexical biases.

Conceptual biases

The problem of inducing word meanings is massively underdetermined because a word can refer to any *logically* plausible concept. *Psychologically*, however, the problem could be more constrained if we were a priori biased to entertain only certain concepts. Specifically, children might have sufficient knowledge about the kinds of things that exist in the world so as to elaborate narrow hypotheses about the possible meanings of new words they encounter (Carey, 2001; Spelke, 1994). Among this knowledge are distinctions between individuated and non-individuated entities, between objects and actions, between animate and inanimate beings, and even between within-domain categories (e.g., between cats and dogs). Given this rich prelinguistic knowledge, upon encountering a novel word applied to a novel entity the child first decides upon the most likely conceptual category to which the potential referent belongs, and then maps the word onto that category.

In an investigation of this kind of bias, Soja, Carey, and Spelke (1991) showed 2-year-olds either novel solid objects or novel piles of stuff. The experimenter applied a novel word to such a target entity, and then asked children to generalize the word to either an entity of similar shape but made of different material, or an entity of different shape but made of the same material. It was found that when the word was applied to a solid object, children extended the word based on similarity of shape; when the word was applied to a pile of stuff, children extended the word based on similarity of material. Importantly, this pattern was found irrespective of whether children understood the syntactic difference between count nouns and mass nouns. The authors concluded that children's conceptual differentiation of countable and non-countable entities predates the acquisition of the linguistic distinction, and in fact guides the acquisition of word meanings (see also Prasada, Ferenz, & Haskell, 2002).

Another type of conceptual knowledge children rely on has to do with the conceptual category to which the referent of a noun belongs. For instance, Diesendruck, Gelman, and Lebowitz (1998) found that the same type of information about two entities differentially affected 3- and 4-year-olds' pattern of name extension depending on whether the entities were animals or artifacts. In particular, telling children that two animals had the same internal properties led children to accept the same name for the animals, but the same type of information applied to two artifacts did not have the same effect.

Finally, a number of studies show that young children are more likely to interpret a novel word applied to an object as a proper name if the object is animate rather than inanimate (Imai & Haryu, 2001; Sorrentino, 2001).

All these studies illustrate how the way in which children construe the world may influence the kinds of hypotheses they entertain about the meaning of a word. These are endogenous constraining factors, but they are not specific to lexical acquisition: children's concepts also constrain how they categorize and reason about objects and events.

Pragmatics

According to the social–pragmatic account, when children hear a new word they are primarily interested in figuring out what is in the speaker's mind (Akhtar & Tomasello, 2000; Baldwin & Moses, 2001; L. Bloom, 1998; P. Bloom, 2000). The argument is that by being sensitive to the communicative context, cues about the speaker's behaviors, and a speaker's state of knowledge and dispositions, children can substantially narrow down the plausible referential intents of a speaker and consequently the possible meaning of a word.

This social–pragmatic account presumes that by the time children start acquiring words they have some sensitivity to people's mental states. Indeed, there is a growing body of research suggesting that by their second birthday children interpret people's behaviors in psychological terms (Baldwin & Meyer, this volume). As Baldwin and Meyer review, the empirical evidence that children recruit this understanding of minds for word learning is also substantial. For instance, by 2 years of age children learn words primarily in communicative contexts, following and keeping track of speakers' referential intents, and attending to the intentionality in speakers' interactions with objects.

Various studies also show that from a young age children are sensitive to a speaker's state of knowledge when inferring his/her referential intent. Akhtar, Carpenter, and Tomasello (1996) found that 2-year-olds interpret a speaker's novel word as referring to an object that was novel *to the speaker* in a communicative context. This attentiveness to speakers' knowledge is also manifested in children's sensitivity to different types of words and speakers. For instance, 3-year-olds are aware that speakers might know the common names of novel objects even if they have never been exposed to them, but will not know the proper names of objects under the same circumstances (Birch & Bloom, 2002; Diesendruck, 2005). Moreover, children monitor speakers' expressed knowledge of language. Thus, even before their second birthday (Koenig & Echols, 2003), but also after that (Sabbagh & Baldwin, 2001; Sabbagh, Wdowiak, & Ottaway, 2003), children infer that speakers who have been unreliable in their knowledge of words are likely not good sources for learning new words. By 4 years of age children draw the same kind of inference about speakers who speak a different language (Diesendruck, 2005).

These sensitivities to speakers' intents and knowledge states have encouraged the development of pragmatic accounts of phenomena originally presented as examples of the operation of other mechanisms. One example has to do with the mutual exclusivity bias or novel-name nameless-category principle described before. These lexical constraints explain why it is that children tend to select an object without a known label – as opposed to an also available familiar object – in response to an experimenter's request for the referent of a novel label. The pragmatic account of this phenomenon is that children might reason that if the experimenter had wanted the familiar object, she could have simply asked for it by using its conventionally known name. The experimenter's use of a different name probably indicates that she intended to refer to the other object (Clark, 1988, 1990). A series of studies now support this pragmatic account (Diesendruck, 2005; Diesendruck, Hall, & Graham, 2006; Diesendruck & Markson, 2001). First, children respond in the same way when asked for the referent of a novel fact – thus the inference is not about count nouns only, but about referential acts in general. Second, children respond in this way only if they are certain that the experimenter knows the information associated with one of the objects – thus the inference is not based only on what children know, but instead is modulated by what the speakers know. And finally, children respond in this way only if the linguistic information attached to the objects is clearly referentially constraining – thus the inference is not about all communicative acts.

Altogether, the emphasis on children's understanding of speakers' minds makes this an endogenous, not lexical-specific, account.

Empirical Challenges

In this section, I will describe some of the empirical challenges to certain conceptualizations of the mechanisms, particularly with respect to the specificity of various word-learning phenomena, and the precise nature of the endogenous mechanisms.

How specific is word learning?

A number of proposals argue that children's inferences of word meanings are driven by lexical-specific biases or constraints. Recent findings challenge this contention. For instance, according to the attention and learning account, children's initial shape bias is specific to naming because it derives from the interaction of these general mechanisms with specific linguistic input (Smith, 1999). Contrary to this position, Diesendruck and Bloom (2003) found that 2- and 3-year-olds were as likely to favor shape over color or material when asked to pick objects "of the same kind" as a target object as they were when asked to pick objects with the same name as the target. In fact, this preference for shape when categorizing objects seems to precede children's word learning, intimating that the bias may not derive from exposure to a lexical-specific regularity (Diesendruck, Graham, & Onysyk, 2004; Samuelson & Smith, 2005).

A second example regards lexical constraints. On the one hand, words more efficaciously facilitate object categorization by infants than do other auditory stimuli (Balaban & Waxman, 1997), 2-year-olds are more likely to accept a word as a referential symbol than they are to accept a gesture (Namy & Waxman, 1998), and 3-year-olds are more likely to extend a word to taxonomically related objects than they are to extend a fact (Behrend, Scofield, & Kleinknecht, 2001; Waxman & Booth, 2000). On the other hand, when words are compared with other intentional acts, some of these advantages of words disappear (e.g., Childers & Tomasello, 2003; Markson & Bloom, 1997). Similarly, with regards to the mutual exclusivity bias or the novel-name nameless-category principle, Diesendruck and Markson (2001) found that 3-year-olds were as likely to select an object without a label in response to a request for the referent of a different novel label as they were to select an object without a *fact* in response to the request for the referent of a different novel fact.

The crucial questions coming out of this mixed pattern of comparative advantages of labels are to what extent, in which respects, and why are labels special? We have some clues for answers to these questions. For instance, sounds seem to function as referential signs only when paired with extensive intentional cues (Campbell & Namy, 2003). This raises the questions of the age at which and why labels are treated as intentional acts. A further example is that while facts might not be readily extended to other referents, certain novel actions clearly performed intentionally on objects are (Childers & Tomasello, 2003). Thus, what is the relationship between intentionality and extendibility? Finally, there are differences in how easily children learn to map certain kinds of facts to objects (Markson & Bloom, 1997), and in the kinds of assumptions children make about people's knowledge of facts and words (Diesendruck & Markson, 2001). This raises the question of how is it that children come to develop distinct expectations about these various types of information.

More broadly, these challenges to the specificity of word-learning phenomena emphasize the need to better define the cognitive capacities responsible for children's inferences of word meanings.

What does the child bring to word learning?

While speech directed to children can influence what words children acquire, and how they do so (see *Input* above), studies reveal that children are quite capable of going far beyond this type of input. For instance, studies reveal that 2-year-olds manage to learn the referents of labels by monitoring naming events in third-party conversations (Akhtar, Jipson, & Callanan, 2001), even if they are engaged in a distracting activity at the time the naming occurs, or if the label is embedded in a non-salient sentence position (Akhtar, 2005). In fact, children are as likely to map a word to its correct referent when directly taught the mapping as when only indirectly exposed to it (Jaswal & Markman, 2001).

What are the cognitive capacities that allow children to make these indirect mappings? For one, children's rich conceptual beliefs certainly modulate their attention, such as to help them make adequate inferences. One example of such modulation has to do with the shape bias. Specifically, Jones et al. (1991) found that the addition of eyes to novel objects led 3-year-olds to extend names based not only on objects' shape but also their texture. Jones et al. explained this finding by arguing that, in the input children are naturally exposed to, objects with eyes are regularly associated with commonality in both shape and texture, thus leading to the development of this biased association. An alternative interpretation of this finding is that the presence of eyes indicated to children that the objects in question were animate beings, about which children have particular conceptual beliefs. Booth and Waxman (2002) showed 3-year-olds novel objects (with or without eyes), taught children novel names for the objects, and then asked them to extend the names to other objects. The critical manipulation was that, via stories, the experimenter conveyed to children that the objects were either animate or inanimate. Booth and Waxman found that what determined children's pattern of extension was not the presence or absence of eyes, but rather whether the objects were conceived of as animate or inanimate. Children extended the names of inanimate objects based solely on shape similarity, and the names of animate objects based on both shape and texture. A recent study revealed a similar pattern of findings with 18-month-olds, indicating that from very early on children's name extensions are grounded in conceptual knowledge (Booth, Waxman, & Huang, 2005).

A second type of cognitive capacity that helps modulate children's inferences is their burgeoning understanding of minds. Recent studies suggest that what might seem like modulation via other mechanisms, such as *attention and memory* or *syntax*, might in fact be hiding an understanding of intentions. For instance, Samuelson and Smith (1998) argued that children's choice of a particular object presented to them at a table – rather than at the floor – as the referent of a novel label derives from the relative contextual salience of the object in the children's memory. Diesendruck, Markson, Akhtar, and Reudor (2004) addressed an alternative interpretation of their findings, namely, that children's choice of the object derived from their interpretation of the experimenter's move to the table as a *deliberate* act reflecting the special status of that object *to the experimenter*. To test this hypothesis, we introduced a condition in which the change in context (i.e., from the floor to the table) was evidently accidental, as opposed to a condition in which it seemed intentional; and we introduced another condition in which the speaker asking the child for the referent of a novel name was not the experimenter but rather a different speaker who had no previous interaction with the objects. We found that in these two additional conditions, 2-year-olds did not associate the novel name with the object they were exposed to at the table. Thus, children's inference of the referent of the new name did not derive solely from the fact that an object was seen in a novel context, but rather from children's inferences about the intent underlying a speaker's interaction with the object.

An understanding of intentions also seems to modulate the role of syntax in driving children's inferences about word meanings (Diesendruck et al., 2006). In this study, children were taught either a novel prenominal (e.g., "This is a very daxy dog") or a predicate adjective (e.g., "This dog is very daxy") about one of two identical looking familiar animals. Children were then asked for the referent of a different novel prenominal or predicate adjective. Prenominal adjectives differ from predicate adjectives in that they restrict the reference of the noun attached to them. The question was whether children would respect this difference, and thus infer that the use of a different noun-restricting prenominal adjective likely indicated that the speaker had a different referent in mind. Or instead, whether children would treat both kinds of adjectives as describing characteristics of individuals, and thus conclude that the speaker in both conditions could be referring to either animal (as Hall & Graham, 1999, had found using only predicate adjectives). The results supported the first possibility: children in the prenominal condition selected the unlabeled animal, and children in the predicate condition selected randomly. That is, children selectively applied an inference of contrast based on their understanding of the semantic implications of different adjectival syntactic frames.

These studies indicate that children's inferences about the meanings of words are informed not only by their sensitivity to syntactic cues or their basic attentional tendencies, but also by their conceptual beliefs and assumptions about speakers' communicative intents given particular linguistic and behavioral contexts.

Integrative Approaches

The review of the six different mechanisms and the empirical challenges makes it apparent that no single mechanism can fully account for the relevant phenomena. One possible conclusion to be drawn from this review is that all these mechanisms contribute to word learning. However, in an attempt to maximize parsimony and explanatory power, a number of integrative proposals have been put forth. Each proposal highlights a different subset of the mechanisms that, in combination, are sufficient to account for the range of phenomena. The theoretical benefit of these approaches is that they make specific explanations and predictions about how children learn words in various contexts, based on the postulated relative weights of the different mechanisms at play. I will focus on two prominent such approaches.

Emergentist model

One of the most detailed integrative accounts of word learning is the so-called "emergentist coalition model" (Hollich, Hirsh-Pasek, & Golinkoff, 2000). The model postulates three basic assumptions about the word-learning process. The first assumption is that children rely on multiple mechanisms, such as their knowledge of syntax, their sensitivity to attention-grabbing salient aspects of the context, and their understanding of speakers' intentions. The second assumption is that children differentially weight these mechanisms, and that the weights actually change with children's development. For instance, early on in development, perceptual salience may be more heavily weighted than intentional cues. The final assumption is that as a consequence of development, children's word-learning tendencies might become automatized. That is, word-learning principles emerge as a result of word learning, rather than being present from the outset. Once in place, however, these lexical principles enhance and expand children's word learning.

Much of the evidence in support of the emergentist model comes from studies tracking how children's attention to various cues changes with development (Hollich et al., 2000). For instance, while 12-month-olds seem to rely primarily on object salience over the direction of a speaker's eye gaze to determine the referent of a novel word, 20-

month-olds are sensitive to speakers' eye gaze but are still attracted by object salience, and it is only by 24 months of age that eye gaze determines children's referent choice. Arguably, as children's understanding of intentions and of the symbolic nature of words develops, social cues become more heavily weighted among all the cues driving word learning. Further evidence for the model comes from studies showing that certain lexical principles appear to become active only after a substantial amount of vocabulary has been acquired. In particular, the tendency to apply novel names to nameless categories (Mervis & Bertrand, 1994), and to link names onto categories more generally (Nazzi & Bertoncini, 2003), arguably emerges only after a vocabulary spurt. A similar case can be made for the role of syntax in word learning. Evidently, syntax can only become a factor after children have acquired a significant number of words. That is, syntax probably cannot help children in the earliest stages of acquisition.

Theory of mind, concepts, and syntax

P. Bloom (2000) argues that children learn words by relying on three basic capacities: an understanding of mental states, an understanding of the kinds of things that exist in the world, and knowledge of syntax. In Bloom's view, children's learning of words is not driven by specially dedicated mechanisms such as lexical constraints but rather results from mechanisms children rely on for understanding a variety of their experiences, particularly social ones.

Evidence in support of Bloom's position comes from a number of studies already reviewed, for instance that word-learning responses presumably driven by lexical constraints or attentional mechanisms might actually be a product of intentional inference (Diesendruck & Markson, 2001) or conceptual understanding (Diesendruck & Bloom, 2003). Importantly, there is also evidence consistent with the idea that these basic capacities indeed interact so as to sufficiently account for word learning. For instance, Birch and Bloom (2002) demonstrated that 2-year-olds can (1) identify proper nouns based on syntactic information, and (2) draw pragmatically appropriate inferences about a speaker's referential intent when using a proper noun – namely, speakers use proper names to refer to familiar objects.

Concluding Remarks

Most students of word learning agree that in order to account for the range of pertinent phenomena we need some integrative approach (see Hall & Waxman, 2004, for further proposals). One of the major challenges to such integrative approaches, however, is to provide a sufficiently detailed mechanistic account of how the various factors interact (see, e.g., Shatz, in press). How are the relative weights of the different mechanisms defined? Are they context-specific? Are they age-sensitive? If the answer to all these questions is affirmative, as they might turn out to be, then we may have to compromise with a fairly piece-meal "theory" of word learning. I want to end with a more optimistic perspective.

The common theme underlying integrative approaches is that multiple mechanisms, with varying weights, are involved in word learning. This idea opens the possibility that there are various ways in which these mechanisms can be combined for the task of word learning. In principle, nobody denies this possibility. De facto, however, it is still part of the mainstream research agenda to attempt to rule out mechanisms by demonstrating their irrelevance in specific contexts. What such an "eliminativist" agenda might end up revealing, however, is the *relative* weight of a mechanism in a specific context, or the degree of attunement of the mechanism.

Take for instance the research on the variety of word-learning populations. Parrots (Pepperberg & Wilcox, 2000), chimpanzees (Savage-Rumbaugh et al., 1993), and dogs (Kaminsky, Call, & Fischer, 2004) have been shown to understand, and some even produce, word-like symbols. Rico the dog, for instance, not only understands over 200 words, but also seems to map novel words onto objects for which he does not have a name. Recent work shows that infants as young as 14 months of age also can learn word-to-object pairings (Schafer & Plunkett, 1998; Werker, Cohen, Lloyd, Casasola, & Stager, 1998), and even 12-month-olds seem to honor mutual exclusivity (Halberda, 2003; Markman et al., 2003; Xu, Cote, & Baker, 2005). Last but not least, studies have found that differently from typically developing 18-month-olds, children with autism do not rely on the direction of eye gaze of a speaker to determine the referent of a word (Baron-Cohen, Baldwin, & Crowson, 1997). That is, they do not seem to recruit an understanding of intentions to acquire words. Nonetheless, despite this impairment, children with autism map novel words onto novel objects (Preissler & Carey, 2005). All these findings are taken to challenge the idea that typically developing children's mapping of novel names to novel objects derives from their sensitivity to speakers' intents.

There are two logically possible responses to this type of challenge. One is that all these populations have the basic understanding of minds presumed to be necessary for word learning. In fact, there are suggestions that this might indeed be the case (e.g., Onishi & Baillargeon, 2005; Tomasello, Call, & Hare, 2003); but these are all highly contentious claims (see Perner & Ruffman, 2005; Povinelli & Vonk, 2003).

A second type of defense – and the one I want to stress here – is that the cocktail of underlying mechanisms driving word learning in animals, infants, and children with autism might be different from the one used by typically developing children. For instance, it is possible that while Rico's selection of novel objects derives from novelty preference, and that children with autism's word learning is driven by associative training, typically developing children solve these problems by inferring speakers' intents. An implication of this interpretation of the data is that instead of stopping at documenting the similarity on some outcome measure we should look at finer-grained consequences of such distinctive types of word learning. For instance, what kind of word-*teaching* paradigm works best for children with autism compared with for typically developing children? Can we find traces of differential acquisition processes in children's *uses* of words? What are the assumptions that typically developing children, as opposed to other word-learning populations, make about words?

Another example of this eliminativist agenda is manifested in attempts to systematically trace when certain mechanisms are important for word learning. The rationale there is that if children are not sensitive to a certain type of cue (e.g., speakers' eye gaze), then the underlying mechanism implicated by the cue (e.g., understanding intentions) is probably irrelevant – and vice versa. This equivalence between "contextual cues" and "mechanisms," however, requires caution. For instance, children might over-attribute intentionality in contexts where none was presumed to be involved. An example of this kind of dynamics can be found in studies reviewed earlier. Specifically, what Akhtar et al. (1996) interpreted as sensitivity to speakers' knowledge state, Samuelson and Smith (1998) viewed as attention to novelty. What Samuelson and Smith then manipulated to test their hypothesis, Diesendruck et al. (2004) deemed as a manipulation of intentionality. This has important implications for how we interpret the developmental data, and how we design our studies. Lack of sensitivity to a cue might not mean that the capacity is unavailable, but rather that it is not tuned to that cue yet.

Addressing all these issues will bring us closer not only to a theory of word learning, but to an appreciation of the intricate links between this skill and the various other cognitive capacities that so uniquely characterize the human mind. That is the promise, and the appeal, of the study of word learning in children.

References

Akhtar, N. (2005). The robustness of learning through overhearing. *Developmental Science, 8*, 199–209.

Akhtar, N., Carpenter, M., & Tomasello, M. (1996). The role of discourse novelty in early word learning. *Child Development, 67*, 635–645.

Akhtar, N., Jipson, J., & Callanan, M. (2001). Learning words through overhearing. *Child Development, 72*, 416–430.

Akhtar, N., & Tomasello, M. (2000). The social nature of words and word learning. In R. M. Golinkoff & K. Hirsh-Pasek (Eds.), *Becoming a word learner: A debate on lexical acquisition* (pp. 115–135). Oxford: Oxford University Press.

Anglin, J. M. (1993). Vocabulary development: A morphological analysis. *Monographs of the Society for Research in Child Development, 58* (10, Serial No. 238).

Au, T. K., & Glusman, M. (1990). The principle of mutual exclusivity in word learning: To honor or not to honor? *Child Development, 61*, 1474–1490.

Balaban, M. T., & Waxman, S. R. (1997). Do words facilitate object categorization in 9-month-old infants? *Journal of Experimental Child Psychology, 64*, 3–26.

Baldwin, D. A., & Moses, L. J. (2001). Links between social understanding and early word learning: Challenges to current accounts. *Social Development, 10*, 309–329.

Baron-Cohen, S., Baldwin, D. A., & Crowson, M. (1997). Do children with autism use the direction of gaze strategy to crack the code of language? *Child Development, 68*, 48–57.

Behrend, D. A. (1990). Constraints and development: A reply to Nelson (1988). *Cognitive Development, 5*, 313–330.

Behrend, D. A., Scofield, J., & Kleinknecht, E. E. (2001). Beyond fast mapping: Young children's extensions of novel words and novel facts. *Developmental Psychology, 37*, 698–705.

Birch, S. A. J., & Bloom, P. (2002). Preschoolers are sensitive to the speaker's knowledge when learning proper names. *Child Development, 73*, 434–444.

Bloom, L. (1998). Language acquisition in its developmental context. In W. Damon (Series Ed.) and D. Kuhn & R. S. Siegler (Vol. Eds.), *Handbook of child psychology: Vol. 2. Cognition, perception, and language* (5th ed., pp. 309–370). New York: Wiley.

Bloom, P. (2000). *How children learn the meanings of words.* Cambridge, MA: MIT Press.

Bloom, P. (2004). Myths of word learning. In D. G. Hall & S. R. Waxman (Eds.), *Weaving a lexicon* (pp. 205–224). Cambridge, MA: MIT Press.

Booth, A. E., & Waxman, S. R. (2002). Word learning is 'smart': Evidence that conceptual information affects preschoolers' extension of novel words. *Cognition*, *84*, B11–B22.

Booth, A. E., Waxman, S. R., & Huang, Y. T. (2005). Conceptual information permeates word learning in infancy. *Developmental Psychology*, *41*, 491–505.

Brown, R. (1957). Linguistic determinism and the part of speech. *Journal of Abnormal and Social Psychology*, *55*, 1–5.

Callanan, M. A. (1985). How parents name objects for young children: The role of input in the acquisition of category hierarchies. *Child Development*, *56*, 508–523.

Callanan, M. A., & Sabbagh, M. A. (2004). Multiple labels for objects in conversations with young children: Parents' language and children's developing expectations about word meanings. *Developmental Psychology*, *40*, 746–763.

Campbell, A. L., & Namy, L. L. (2003). The role of social-referential context in verbal and nonverbal symbol learning. *Child Development*, *74*, 549–563.

Carey, S. (2001). Whorf vs. Continuity theorists: Bringing data to bear on the debate. In M. Bowerman & S. C. Levinson (Eds.), *Language acquisition and conceptual development* (pp. 185–214). Cambridge: Cambridge University Press.

Carey, S., & Bartlett, E. (1978). Acquiring a single new word. *Proceedings of the Stanford Child Language Conference*, *15*, 17–29.

Childers, J. B., & Tomasello, M. (2003). Children extend both words and non-verbal actions to novel exemplars. *Developmental Science*, *6*, 185–190.

Clark, E. V. (1988). On the logic of contrast. *Journal of Child Language*, *15*, 317–335.

Clark, E. V. (1990). On the pragmatics of contrast. *Journal of Child Language*, *17*, 417–431.

Clark, E. V., & Wong, A. D. W. (2002). Pragmatic directions about language use: Offers of words and relations. *Language and Society*, *31*, 181–212.

Diesendruck, G. (2005). The principles of conventionality and contrast in word learning: An empirical examination. *Developmental Psychology*, *41*, 451–463.

Diesendruck, G., & Bloom, P. (2003). How specific is the shape bias? *Child Development*, *74*, 168–178.

Diesendruck, G., Gelman, S. A., & Lebowitz, K. (1998). Conceptual and linguistic biases in children's word learning. *Developmental Psychology*, *34*, 823–839.

Diesendruck, G., Graham, S., & Onysyk, S. (2004). *A non-lexical shape bias in 15-month-olds.* Paper presented at the International Conference on Infant Studies, Chicago.

Diesendruck, G., Hall, D. G., & Graham, S. (2006). Children's use of syntactic and pragmatic knowledge in the interpretation of novel adjectives. *Child Development*, *77*, 16–30.

Diesendruck, G., & Markson, L. (2001). Children's avoidance of lexical overlap: A pragmatic account. *Developmental Psychology*, *37*, 630–641.

Diesendruck, G., Markson, L., Akhtar, N., & Reudor, A. (2004). Two-year-olds' sensitivity to speakers' intent: An alternative account of Samuelson and Smith. *Developmental Science*, *7*, 33–41.

Diesendruck, G., & Shatz, M. (1997). The effect of perceptual similarity and linguistic input on children's acquisition of object labels. *Journal of Child Language*, *24*, 695–717.

Diesendruck, G., & Shatz, M. (2001). Two-year-olds' recognition of hierarchies: Evidence from their interpretation of the semantic relation between object labels. *Cognitive Development*, *16*, 577–594.

Dromi, E. (1987). *Early lexical development.* Cambridge: Cambridge University Press.

Gelman, S. A., & Taylor, M. (1984). How two-year-old children interpret proper and common names for unfamiliar objects. *Child Development*, *55*, 1535–1540.

Gentner, D. (1982). Why nouns are learned before verbs: Linguistic relativity versus natural partitioning. In S. Kuczaj (Ed.), *Language development: Language, thought, and culture* (pp. 301–334). Hillsdale, NJ: Erlbaum.

Gershkoff-Stowe, L., & Smith, L. B. (2004). Shape and the first hundred nouns. *Child Development, 75,* 1098–1114.

Golinkoff, R. M., Mervis, C. B., & Hirsh-Pasek, K. (1994). Early object labels: The case for a developmental lexical principles framework. *Journal of Child Language, 21,* 125–156.

Halberda, J. (2003). The development of a word-learning strategy. *Cognition, 87,* B23–B34.

Hall, D. G. (1994). Semantic constraints on word learning: Proper names and adjectives. *Child Development, 65,* 1299–1317.

Hall, D. G., & Graham, S. A. (1999). Lexical form class information guides word-to-object mapping in preschoolers. *Child Development, 70,* 78–91.

Hall, D. G., & Waxman, S. R. (Eds.). (2004). *Weaving a lexicon.* Cambridge, MA: MIT Press.

Hall, D. G., Waxman, S. R., Bredart, S., & Nicolay, A. C. (2003). Preschoolers' use of form class cues to learn descriptive proper names. *Child Development, 74,* 1547–1560.

Harris, M., Jones, D., & Grant, J. (1983). The nonverbal context of mothers' speech to infants. *First Language, 4,* 21–31.

Hoff, E. (2006). How social contexts support and shape language development. *Developmental Review, 26,* 55–88.

Hollich, G. J., Hirsh-Pasek, K., & Golinkoff, R. M. (2000). Breaking the language barrier: An emergentist coalition model for the origins of word learning. *Monographs of the Society for Research in Child Development, 65* (3, Serial No. 262).

Huttenlocher, J., Haight, W., Bryk, A., Seltzer, M., & Lyons, T. (1991). Early vocabulary growth: Relation to language input and gender. *Developmental Psychology, 27,* 236–248.

Imai, M., Gentner, D., & Uchida, N. (1994). Children's theories of word meaning: The role of shape similarity in early acquisition. *Cognitive Development, 9,* 45–75.

Imai, M., & Haryu, E. (2001). Learning proper nouns and common nouns without clues from syntax. *Child Development, 72,* 787–802.

Jaswal, V. K., & Markman, E. M. (2001). Learning proper and common names in inferential versus ostensive contexts. *Child Development, 72,* 768–786.

Jones, S. S., Smith, L. B., & Landau, B. (1991). Object properties and knowledge in early lexical learning. *Child Development, 62,* 499–512.

Kaminsky, J., Call, J., & Fischer, J. (2004). Word learning in a domestic dog: Evidence for "fast mapping". *Science, 304,* 1682–1683.

Koenig, M. A., & Echols, C. H. (2003). Infants' understanding of false labeling events: The referential roles of words and the speakers who use them. *Cognition, 87,* 179–208.

Landau, B., Smith, L. B., & Jones, S. S. (1988). The importance of shape in early lexical learning. *Cognitive Development, 3,* 299–321.

Liittschwager, J. C., & Markman, E. M. (1994). Sixteen- and 24-month-olds' use of mutual exclusivity as a default assumption in second-label learning. *Developmental Psychology, 30,* 955–968.

Markman, E. M. (1989). *Categorization and naming in young children.* Cambridge, MA: MIT Press.

Markman, E. M. (1992). Constraints on word learning: Speculations about their nature, origins, and domain specificity. In M. R. Gunnar & M. Maratsos (Eds.), *Modularity and constraints in language and cognition* (pp. 59–101). Hillsdale, NJ: Erlbaum.

Markman, E. M., & Wachtel, G. F. (1988). Children's use of mutual exclusivity to constrain the meaning of words. *Cognitive Psychology, 20,* 121–157.

Markman, E. M., Wasow, J. L., & Hansen, M. B. (2003). Use of the mutual exclusivity assumption by young word learners. *Cognitive Psychology, 47*, 241–275.

Markson, L., & Bloom, P. (1997). Evidence against a dedicated system for word learning in children. *Nature, 385*, 813–815.

Masur, E. F. (1997). Maternal labeling of novel and familiar objects: Implications for children's development of lexical constraints. *Journal of Child Language, 24*, 427–439.

Merriman, W. E., & Bowman, L. L. (1989). The mutual exclusivity bias in children's word learning. *Monographs of the Society for Research in Child Development, 54* (3–4, Serial No. 220).

Mervis, C. B., & Bertrand, J. (1994). Acquisition of the novel name nameless category (N3C) principle. *Child Development, 65*, 1646–1662.

Namy, L. L., & Waxman, S. R. (1998). Words and symbolic gestures: Infants' interpretations of different forms of symbolic reference. *Child Development, 69*, 295–308.

Nazzi, T., & Bertoncini, J. (2003). Before and after the vocabulary spurt: Two modes of word acquisition? *Developmental Science, 6*, 136–142.

Nelson, K. (1988). Constraints on word meaning? *Cognitive Development, 3*, 221–246.

Onishi, K., & Baillargeon, R. (2005). Do 15-month-old infants understand false beliefs? *Science, 308*, 255–258.

Pepperberg, I. M., & Wilcox, S. E. (2000). Evidence for a form of mutual exclusivity during label acquisition by grey parrots. *Journal of Comparative Psychology, 114*, 219–231.

Perner, J., & Ruffman, T. (2005). Infants' insight in to the mind: How deep? *Science, 308*, 214–216.

Povinelli, D. J., & Vonk, J. (2003). Chimpanzee minds: Suspiciously human? *Trends in Cognitive Sciences, 7*, 157–160.

Prasada, S., Ferenz, K., & Haskell, T. (2002). Conceiving of entities as objects and as stuff. *Cognition, 83*, 141–165.

Preissler, M. A., & Carey, S. (2005). The role of inferences about referential intent in word learning: Evidence from autism. *Cognition, 97*, B13–B23.

Quine, W. V. O. (1960). *Word and object: An inquiry into the linguistic mechanisms of objective reference*. New York: Wiley.

Sabbagh, M. A., & Baldwin, D. A. (2001). Learning words from knowledgeable versus ignorant speakers: Links between preschoolers' theory of mind and semantic development. *Child Development, 72*, 1054–1070.

Sabbagh, M. A., Wdowiak, S. D., & Ottaway, J. M. (2003). Do word learners ignore ignorant speakers? *Journal of Child Language, 30*, 905–924.

Samuelson, L. K. (2002). Statistical regularities in vocabulary guide language acquisition in connectionist models and 15–20-months-olds. *Developmental Psychology, 38*, 1016–1037.

Samuelson, L. K., & Smith, L. B. (1998). Memory and attention make smart word learning: An alternative account of Akhtar, Carpenter, and Tomasello. *Child Development, 69*, 94–104.

Samuelson, L. K., & Smith, L. B. (1999). Early noun vocabularies: Do ontology, category structure and syntax correspond? *Cognition, 73*, 1–33.

Samuelson, L. K., & Smith, L. B. (2005). They call it like they see it: Spontaneous naming and attention to shape. *Developmental Science, 8*, 182–198.

Savage-Rumbaugh, E., Murphy, J., Sevcik, R. A., Brakke, K. E., Williams, S. L., & Rumbaugh, D. M. (1993). Language comprehension in ape and child. *Monographs of the Society for Research in Child Development, 58* (3–4, Serial No. 233).

Schafer, G., & Plunkett, K. (1998). Rapid word learning by fifteen-month-olds under tightly controlled conditions. *Child Development, 69*, 309–320.

Shatz, M. (in press). Revisiting *A Toddler's Life* for *The Toddler Years*: Conversational participation as a tool for learning across knowledge domains. In A. Brownell & C. B. Kopp (Eds.), *Transitions in early socioemotional development: The toddler years*. New York: Guilford.

Smith, L. B. (1999). Children's noun learning: How general learning processes make specialized learning mechanisms. In B. MacWhinney (Ed.), *The emergence of language* (pp. 277–303). Mahwah, NJ: Erlbaum.

Smith, L. B., Jones, S. S., Landau, B., Gershkoff-Stowe, L., & Samuelson, L. (2002). Object name learning provides on-the-job training for attention. *Psychological Science, 13*, 13–19.

Soja, N., Carey, S., & Spelke, E. S. (1991). Ontological categories guide young children's inductions of word meaning: Object terms and substance terms. *Cognition, 38*, 179–211.

Sorrentino, C. (2001). Individuation, identity, and proper names in cognitive development. *Developmental Science, 4*, 399–407.

Spelke, E. S. (1994). Initial knowledge: Six suggestions. *Cognition, 50*, 431–445.

Tomasello, M., Call, J., & Hare, B. (2003). Chimpanzees understand psychological states – the question is which ones and to what extent. *Trends in Cognitive Sciences, 7*, 153–156.

Waxman, S. R. (1991). Convergences between semantic and conceptual organization in the preschool years. In S. A. Gelman & J. P. Byrnes (Eds.), *Perspectives on language and cognition: Interrelations in development* (pp. 107–145). Cambridge: Cambridge University Press.

Waxman, S. R., & Booth, A. E. (2000). Principles that are invoked in the acquisition of words, but not facts. *Cognition, 77*, B45–B57.

Waxman, S. R., & Namy, L. L. (1997). Challenging the notion of a thematic preference in young children. *Developmental Psychology, 33*, 555–567.

Werker, J. F., Cohen, L. B., Lloyd, V. L., Casasola, M., & Stager, C. L. (1998). Acquisition of word–object associations by 14-month-olds infants. *Developmental Psychology, 34*, 1289–1309.

Woodward, A. L., & Markman, E. M. (1998). Early word learning. In W. Damon (Series Ed.) and D. Kuhn & R. S. Siegler (Vol. Eds.), *Handbook of child psychology: Vol. 2. Cognition, perception, and language* (5th ed., pp. 371–420). New York: Wiley.

Woodward, A. L., Markman, E. M., & Fitzsimmons, C. M. (1994). Rapid word learning in 13- and 18-month-olds. *Developmental Psychology, 30*, 553–566.

Xu, F., Cote, M., & Baker, A. (2005). Labeling guides object individuation in 12-month-old infants. *Psychological Science, 16*, 372–377.

14

The Abstract Nature of Syntactic Representations: Consequences for a Theory of Learning

Jeffrey Lidz

The modern study of syntax begins with the observation that people can produce and understand sentences that they have never heard before (Chomsky, 1957). From this observation, we conclude that linguistic knowledge must be in the form of a generative symbol system. The term *generative*, in this context, refers to the property that a finite number of symbols describes a potentially infinite set of sentences. When someone knows a language he possesses a system of mental representations and computations that allows for the generation of an unbounded number of novel expressions. Of course, not any novel arrangement of words counts as a sentence and so the system must be constrained to distinguish the possible from the impossible. In short, syntactic knowledge consists of a system of rules and representations that allows for the generation of all and only the sentences that are possible in a given language.

The field of generative syntax aims to identify the nature of this symbol system. Lurking behind this agenda, however, lies the more fundamental problem of determining how such a symbol system is acquired. How does a learner exposed to sentences acquire a symbol system? In order to gain traction on this problem, we require an understanding of the kinds of representations and computations that undergird adult languages. But even before turning to syntactic representations, I would like to discuss the nature of symbol systems in general, so as to provide a framework from which to view syntactic systems in particular.

A symbol system consists of three components: the symbols, rules for manipulating these symbols, and a way to interpret these symbols. To take a simple example, in the domain of fourth grade mathematics the numbers and the operators ($+$, $-$, $\times$, $\div$, $=$) are the symbols, the rules for manipulating these symbols are the rules of arithmetic, and the interpretation of the symbols is the relation between the symbols and what they represent. We take the computation in (1) to be a valid computation because (a) it follows the rules for manipulating the symbols and (b) the conclusion drawn from manipulating the symbols is in accord with the conclusion drawn from performing the addition with real quantities.

(1) $3 + 4 = 7$

Conversely, we do not take the computations in (2) to be valid because, there, the rules for manipulating the symbols are not followed.

(2)   a. $+ 3 = 4\ 7$
      b. $3 + 4 = 9$

We believe that we understand addition because the results of manipulating the symbols are identical to the results of adding actual quantities.

Turning now to the symbol systems that describe human syntactic competence, the symbols are the linguistic representations that are proposed to explain syntactic structure. The rules for manipulating these symbols are the principles that determine how sentences are built and related to sound and meaning. The interpretation of the symbols is the relation between these symbols and the sentences of a language.

Consider, for example, the grammar fragment in (3). This fragment generates only the sentences in (4). The sentences in (5) are predicted to be impossible.

(3)   a. $S \rightarrow NP\ VP$
      b. $VP \rightarrow V\ NP$
      c. $NP \rightarrow Det\ N$
      d. N = cat, dog
      e. V = chased, caught
      f.   Det = the
(4)   The cat chased the dog; The cat chased the cat; The dog chased the dog; The dog chased the cat; The cat caught the dog; The cat caught the cat; The dog caught the dog; The dog caught the cat
(5)   The dog chased; Chased the cat the dog; Caught; Cat chased dog, . . .

This isomorphism between the consequences of the operations of the symbol system and the sentences of the language is what is meant by the psychological reality of linguistic theory. We take the symbol system to be a valid representation of syntactic knowledge because manipulations of the symbols yield results that are identical to the results of trying to make the relevant sentences. If it is true that the sentences in (4) are possible and that the sentences in (5) are not, then we take the grammar fragment in (3) to be an accurate representation of (a portion of) the knowledge underlying the ability to speak English.

That said, two points are obvious. First, we understand the symbol system of simple arithmetic considerably better than we understand the symbol systems that underlie human languages. Second, the symbol systems underlying human languages are enormously more complex than the grammar fragment in (3). Consequently, questions about how syntactic systems are acquired lead to the dual challenge of, first, ensuring that the representations that the researcher assumes must be acquired are the right ones, and, second, determining how these representations are actually acquired. Given the general uncertainty and widespread disagreement about precisely what representations and computations characterize syntactic systems, one might conclude that it is pointless to ask about language acquisition. After all, if we don't have a full understanding of *what* is to be acquired, how could we possibly build a theory of *how* it is acquired?

The difficulty of building a theory of how syntactic symbol systems change across development is directly reflected in research on children's syntax. This research has largely focused on the character of children's representations and only rarely has addressed questions of development (see Guasti, 2001). Speaking broadly, this research generally finds that children's representations do not differ in kind from those of adults and that in cases where children behave differently from adults, it is rarely because they have the wrong representations. Instead, differences between children and adults are often attributed to task demands (Crain & Thornton, 1998), computational limitations (Bloom, 1990; Grodzinsky & Reinhart, 1993), and the problems of pragmatic integration (Thornton & Wexler, 1999) but only rarely to representational differences between children and adults (Radford, 1995; see also Goodluck, this volume). Even in the cases where differences between children's and adults' syntactic representations have been found, very little work has examined the transition to maturity (Wexler, 1990).

One clear example of these trends in the literature can be seen in the study of children's subjectless sentences. Bloom (1970) observed that 2- and 3-year-old children learning English produce sentences lacking overt subjects, as shown in (6), despite the fact that the adult language requires a subject in all sentences.

(6) a. play it (Bloom, 1970, p. 108)
     b. eating cereal
     c. shake hands
     d. see window

This difference between children and adults has been attributed to a wide range of factors, with debates centering around two questions. First, do children's errors derive from their having nonadult representations or from a difficulty in expressing these representations through their behavior? Second, if the problem is representational in nature, what are the erroneous representations like? Similarly, if the problem is based in linguistic performance, which performance factors stand in the way of adult-like production?

Among those who argue for a representational account of children's errors, we find several distinct hypotheses. One kind of approach takes the typology of natural language syntax as a framework in which to view the errors that children make in acquiring a particular language (Crain & Thornton, 1998; Hyams, 1986). For example, Hyams (1986) proposes that children drop subjects because their grammars contain features that are appropriate for languages like Italian, but not for English. Others propose similar explanations, but make the child grammar more like Chinese than Italian or English (Hyams, 1992; Rizzi, 1993/1994; Valian, 1991). This style of proposal attributes to children what would be the correct grammatical representations for some language, but not for the language they happen to be learning.

Alternative representational approaches attribute to children incomplete phrase structure representations (Radford, 1990; Vainikka, 1994). Radford (1990) proposes that subjectless sentences derive from children having built only partial syntactic representations. They have learned how to construct some phrases of their language, but are lacking the feature of syntactic representation that makes subjects obligatory.

Performance accounts, on the other hand, propose that children have the same representations as adults, but that other factors, for example prosodic properties of pronouns (Gerken, 1991) or processing difficulties at the beginnings of long sentences (Bloom, 1990), are responsible for the lack of subjects in children's productions.

Because the jury is still out on how these various factors might contribute, singly or in combination, to the production of subjectless sentences, very little research has been able to ask how the transition to maturity takes place. Explanations of the course of development will have a different character depending on what the starting place is, and so it is vital to understand the grammatical and extragrammatical contributors to children's errors as a first step in building an explicit model of development.

With these points in mind, it should now be clear that a theory of syntactic development begins with an understanding of children's syntactic representations and the degree to which they are like those of adults. In this paper, I discuss three features of syntactic symbol systems that are shared across all languages. I will show not only that adult grammars exhibit these properties but also that children's grammars do. First, syntactic representations are hierarchically structured. Second, rules of grammar make reference to abstract relations defined over these hierarchically structured representations. Third, certain abstract properties of syntactic representations contribute to the behavior of wide ranges of syntactic phenomena.

Accepting these observations as valid, I argue, places limits on models of the learning systems that drive the acquisition of syntax. Any learning system must, at the very least, yield as its output these abstract syntactic representations. Theories of syntactic development must also be structured in a way that allows for children both to come to the wrong representations and to explain how these errors can be overcome. While children may have syntactic representations that differ from those of the adults around them, in many cases these representations are constrained to conform to the abstract nature described herein.

The chapter proceeds as follows. I begin by reviewing evidence showing that sentences are represented as hierarchical structures and that 18-month-old infants are sensitive to this kind of structure. We then move on to a higher level of abstraction showing that the rules of natural language syntax are stated in terms of relations defined over hierarchical representations. Children also show evidence of a sensitivity to these abstract relations. Moreover, children show a sensitivity to abstract hierarchical relations even in constructions for which these relations are not used by adults, suggesting that children are biased to encode syntactic structure in these terms. We then proceed to an even higher level of abstraction, showing that certain abstract features of grammatical representation contribute to wide ranges of syntactic phenomena that do not appear to be alike on the surface. In this domain, we find significant correlations in the acquisition of superficially distinct syntactic constructions, suggesting that abstract features drive the acquisition of syntax.

Taken together these three kinds of results indicate that children's knowledge of syntax must be stated in abstract terms from the beginning of development. Abstract symbolic representations are not just the output of syntactic learning but rather form the core out of which knowledge of a particular syntactic symbol system is built. Finally, I briefly discuss how these conclusions about children's syntactic representations can guide future research into syntactic development. To preview this discussion, a theory of syntactic development, which traces the evolution of syntactic knowledge throughout infancy and childhood, must begin with the question of how children map their linguistic experience onto the kinds of abstract representations that appear to drive the acquisition of language.

Syntactic Representations are Hierarchical

Perhaps the most fundamental property of linguistic representations is their hierarchical nature. In this section, I review evidence showing first that this is the correct characterization of adult syntactic systems and second that at the earliest stages of syntactic development, this is also the correct characterization of children's syntactic representations.

A sentence like (7) is not just a string of words, but rather can be represented as a hierarchical tree structure in which words combine to form phrases and these phrases combine to form larger phrases, as in (8).

(7)　The lion chased the zebra

(8)

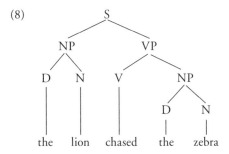

Two kinds of evidence support the claim that sentences have internal hierarchical structure. First, a wide range of phenomena treat the subparts of sentences as units. Either of the phrases labeled NP (noun phrase) above can be pronominalized, moved, or coordinated with another phrase of the same type:

(9)　a.　<u>He</u> chased the zebra
　　　b.　The lion chased <u>him</u>
(10)　a.　<u>The lion</u> is what chased the zebra
　　　b.　<u>The zebra</u> is what the lion chased

(11)   a.   <u>The lion and the tiger</u> chased the zebra
       b.   The lion chased <u>the zebra and the tiger</u>

Second, the hierarchical nature of syntactic structures can be detected by examining ambiguous expressions like (12):

(12)   John saw the man with binoculars

This sentence has two possible interpretations. On the instrumental interpretation, John used binoculars in order to see the man. On the modificational interpretation, what John saw was a man who had binoculars. Given that the sentence has only one set of words, it must be that the arrangement of the words into subgroups (i.e., the sentence's hierarchical structure) explains the ambiguity. In this case, each of the interpretations arises from a unique syntactic representation. The instrumental interpretation of the prepositional phrase in (12) derives from the structure in (13a) whereas the modificational interpretation of the prepositional phrase derives from the structure in (13b).

(13)

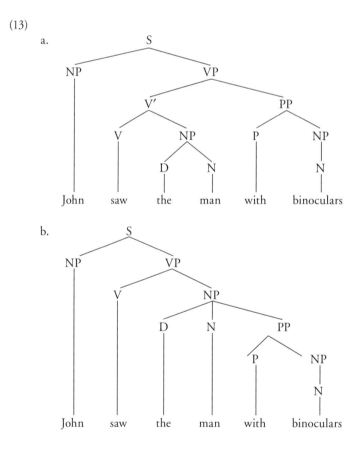

These analyses are supported by the diagnostics we observed above.

(14)   a.   John saw <u>him</u> with binoculars
       b.   <u>the man</u> is what John saw with binoculars
       c.   <u>the man with binoculars</u> is what John saw

Only in (13a) is the string *the man* a constituent and so only the corresponding instru-mental interpretation is available when we pronominalize that string as in (14a) or front it, as in (14b). Similarly, when we front *the man with binoculars*, as in (14c), only the modificational interpretation is available since only that interpretation treats that string as a constituent.

Children's knowledge of hierarchical structure

Hierarchical syntactic structure has been observed experimentally in children as young as 18 months of age (Lidz, Waxman, & Freedman, 2003). Consider two hypotheses for the structure of NP, given in (15). Both would, in principle, be consistent with the input that children receive.

(15)   a.   Flat structure hypothesis   b.   Hierarchical structure hypothesis

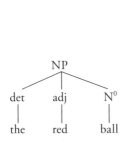
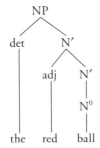

We know, on the basis of anaphoric substitution, that for adults (15b) is the correct representation. In (16), the element *one* refers anaphorically to the constituent [*red ball*].

(16)   I'll play with this red ball and you can play with that one

Since anaphoric elements substitute only for constituents and since it is only under the nested structure hypothesis that the string *red ball* is represented as a constituent (i.e., a single node containing only that string), it follows that (15b) is the correct structure.

Lidz et al. (2003) tested 18-month-old infants in a preferential looking study (Hirsh-Pasek & Golinkoff, 1996) in order to determine whether children represent strings like *the red ball* as containing hierarchical structure. Each infant participated in four trials, each consisting of two phases. During the familiarization phase, an image of a single object (e.g., a yellow bottle) was presented three times, appearing in alternating fashion on either the left or right side of the television monitor. Each presentation was accompanied by a recorded voice that named the object with a phrase consisting of a determiner, adjective, and noun (e.g., "Look! A yellow bottle."). During the test phase, two new objects appeared simultaneously on opposite sides of the television monitor (e.g., a yellow bottle and a blue bottle). Both objects were from the same category as the familiarization object, but only one was the same color. Infants were randomly assigned to one of two conditions which differed only in the linguistic stimulus. In the control condition, subjects heard a neutral phrase ("Now look. What do you see now?"). In the anaphoric condition, subjects heard a phrase containing the anaphoric expression *one* ("Now look. Do you see another one?").

The assumption guiding the preferential looking method is that infants prefer to look at an image that matches the linguistic stimulus, if one is available. Given this methodological assumption, the predictions were as follows. In the control condition, where the linguistic stimulus does not favor one image over the other, infants were expected to prefer the novel image (the blue bottle), as compared with the now-familiar image (the yellow bottle). In the anaphoric condition, infants' performance should reveal their representation of the NP. Here, there were two possible outcomes. If infants represent the NP with a flat structure, and therefore interpret *one* as anaphoric to the category N^0, then both images would be potential referents of the noun (*bottle*). In this case, the linguistic stimulus is uninformative with regard to the test images, and so infants should reveal the same pattern of performance as in the control condition. However, if infants represent the NP with a nested structure, and interpret *one* as anaphoric to N', then they should reveal a preference for the (only) image that is picked out by N' (the yellow bottle).

Subjects in the control condition revealed the predicted preference for the novel image, devoting more attention to it than to the familiar image. This preference was reversed in the anaphoric condition, where infants devoted more attention to the familiar than to the novel image. This constitutes clear evidence for the hypothesis that by 18 months, infants interpret *one* as anaphoric to the category N' and thus that they represent the NP with a nested, hierarchical, structure. More generally, we learn from this study, among others (e.g., Golinkoff, Hirsh-Pasek, Cauley, & Gordon, 1987; Hamburger & Crain, 1984; Valian, 1986), that at the earliest stages of syntactic development, children's syntactic representations are hierarchically structured, just like those of adults.

Syntactic Relations are Defined over Hierarchical Representations

At this point, we have seen that linguistic representations in adults and infants are hierarchically structured. In this section, I show that the rules and constraints that apply to linguistic expressions also make reference to this structure. Moreover, I show that both adults and children make use of abstract relations defined over hierarchical structures. In addition, we will see that children sometimes apply these relations more liberally than adults, suggesting that their use of these abstract relations is not a consequence of acquisition but rather acts as a guiding force in syntactic development.

As we have seen, various rules of grammar target constituents, indicating that the structural representation of a sentence contains internal hierarchical structure. More abstractly, however, many rules of grammar are defined in terms of relations that are defined over these hierarchical structures. Consider the following:

(17)   a.   *Hillary* decided that *she* will run for president
       b.   **She decided that *Hillary* will run for president
       c.   After *she* moved to New York, *Hillary* decided to run for president

The contrast between (17a) and (17b) illustrates that there are constraints determining when a pronoun, like *she*, and a referential expression, like *Hillary*, can refer to the same entity. This constraint is not based on precedence, as can be seen from examining (17c) in which the pronoun precedes the referential expression. The appropriate generalization becomes clear when we examine the structure underlying (17a) and (17b).

(18)

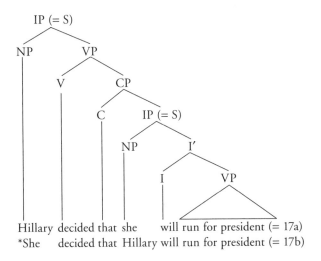

Hillary decided that she   will run for president (= 17a)
*She   decided that Hillary will run for president (= 17b)

Informally, what rules out (17b) is a constraint barring a pronoun from being interpreted as identical in reference to an expression that is contained in the smallest (nontrivial) constituent containing the pronoun itself. Here, the smallest constituent containing the subject of the sentence is the entire sentence and so a pronoun in that position cannot be interpreted as coreferential with anything else in the sentence. In the structure underlying (17a), the smallest constituent containing the pronoun is the embedded sentence (IP). Since *Hillary* is not contained within this constituent, coreference with the pronoun is allowed.

This generalization is supported by the observation that if we put the pronoun inside a branching constituent in subject position, coreference is allowed:

(19)   *Her* husband thinks *Hillary* will run for president

(20)

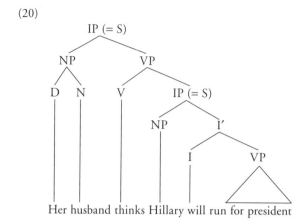

Her husband thinks Hillary will run for president

Here, the smallest constituent containing the pronoun is the subject NP. Since there is no coreferential expression within this constituent, the pronoun can corefer with anything else in the sentence.

The relation expressed in the previous discussion has been formalized under the notions of *c-command* and *binding* (Chomsky, 1981; Reinhart, 1976).

(21)   *x* <u>c-commands</u> *y* iff
     a.   the first branching node dominating *x* also dominates *y*
     b.   *x* does not dominate *y*
     c. $x \neq y$
(22)   *x* <u>binds</u> *y* iff
     a.   *x* c-commands *y*
     b.   *x* and *y* are coreferential

The constraint on coreference, called Principle C by Chomsky (1981), can now be stated as (23):

(23)   Principle C: A referring expression cannot be bound

Because the expression *Hillary* is c-commanded by and coreferential with the pronoun in (17b), coreference is blocked by (23). The crucial observation for our purposes is that the explanatory predicate "bind" is based on a relation defined over hierarchical representations, namely c-command. It is only in defining relations over hierarchical representations that we find an explanation for the observed phenomenon, and so we have evidence that these representations exist as part of adults' implicit knowledge of syntax. Importantly, the c-command relation has been found to bear a significant explanatory burden in a wide range of seemingly unrelated phenomena including the interpretation of pronouns (Chomsky, 1981; Reinhart, 1976), the placement of question words (Fiengo, 1977), the computation of syntactic locality (Rizzi, 1990), the scope of syntactic operators (May, 1985), and the assignment of thematic roles (Chomsky, 1981), among others. The prevalence of the c-command relation in syntactic explanation suggests that this relation plays a primitive role in defining syntactic competence (Frank & Vijay-Shanker, 2001; Kayne, 1995).

Children's knowledge of c-command

We can now ask whether children's grammars include relations that are defined over abstract hierarchical representations. A wide range of evidence reveals children's knowledge of the c-command relation across different constructions and in different languages (Chien & Wexler, 1990; Crain & McKee, 1985; McDaniel, Cairns, & Hsu, 1991; McKee, 1992). In this section, I review two kinds of evidence showing that preschool-aged children represent relations defined over hierarchical structures as part of their syntactic knowledge.

Children correctly apply the c-command relation: Backwards anaphora and Principle C. Crain and McKee (1985) examined English-learning preschoolers' knowledge of Principle C (23), asking whether children know that a pronoun can precede its antecedent but cannot c-command it. We refer to cases in which a pronoun precedes its antecedent as "backwards anaphora." In a truth-value judgment experiment, children were presented with sentences like (24a) and (24b):

(24)   a.   While he was dancing, the Ninja Turtle ate pizza
     b.   He ate pizza while the Ninja Turtle was dancing

In this task, participants observe a story acted out by the experimenter with toys and props. At the end of the story a puppet makes a statement about the story. The participant's task is to tell the puppet whether he was right or wrong. Crain and McKee (1985) presented children with these sentences following stories with two crucial features. First, the Ninja Turtle ate pizza while dancing. This makes the interpretation in which the pronoun (*he*) and the referring expression (*the Ninja Turtle*) are coreferential true. Second, there was an additional salient character who did not eat pizza while the Ninja Turtle danced. This aspect of the story makes the interpretation in which the pronoun refers to a character not named in the test sentence false. Thus, if children allow coreference in these sentences, they should accept them as true, but if children disallow coreference, then they should reject them as false. The reasoning behind this manipulation is as follows. If children reject the coreference interpretation, then they must search for an additional extrasentential antecedent for the pronoun. Doing so, however, makes the sentence false. The theoretical question is whether children know that backwards anaphora is possible in sentences like (24a) but not (24b).

Crain and McKee found that, in these contexts, children as young as 3 years old accepted sentences like (24a), but overwhelmingly rejected sentences like (24b). The fact that they treated the two sentence types differently, rejecting coreference only in those sentences that violate Principle C, indicates that by 3 years of age, English-learning children respect Principle C, and therefore that they use the c-command relation in their syntactic computations.

The observation that children use the c-command relation in determining whether two noun phrases are coreferential illustrates that this relation plays a role in defining their syntactic representations. This conclusion raises the question of the origin of the c-command relation and the rules and constraints that make reference to it. The fact that children as young as 3 years of age behave at adult-like levels in rejecting sentences that violate Principle C is often taken as strong evidence not just for the role of c-command in children's representations, but also for the innateness of Principle C itself (Crain, 1991). The reasoning behind the argument is that Principle C is a constraint on what is possible in language. It says that a given pairing between certain sentences and certain meanings is *im*possible. But, given that children do not have access to explicit evidence regarding what is *not* a possible form–meaning pairing in their language (see Marcus, 1993, for a review), their acquisition of Principle C must be driven by internally generated constraints and not by experience alone (see Gelman & Williams, 1998).

In recent years, however, the possibility that children can learn in an indirect fashion on the basis of Bayesian learning algorithms has gained some prominence (Regier & Gahl, 2003; Tenenbaum & Griffiths, 2001; among others). On this view, the absence of a given form–meaning pairing might be informative about the structure of the grammar. In the particular case under discussion, the learner might observe that she has never seen a situation in which a pronoun c-commands its antecedent and thus remove from the hypothesis space any grammar in which pronouns are allowed to c-command their antecedents. Now, it is important to observe that this kind of approach would have to assume that the learner is representing sentences in hierarchical terms and that she is keeping track of c-command relations among possibly coreferential expressions. Without this assumption, the indirect learner could not even begin. Nonetheless, it does bring up the possibility that the existence of a constraint against certain form–meaning pairings is not by itself evidence of the innateness of that constraint.

Kazanina and Phillips (2001) addressed this issue by looking at the acquisition of backwards anaphora in Russian. Like every language, Russian obeys Principle C. Importantly, however, Russian exhibits a further constraint against backwards anaphora when the pronoun is contained in certain adverbial clauses but not others. These facts are illustrated in (25):

(25)　a.　Pux$_i$ s"el　jabloko, poka on$_i$ čital　knigu
　　　　　Pooh ate.PERF apple　while he read.IMP book
　　　　　Pooh ate an apple while he was reading a book

　　　b.　Poka Pux$_i$ čital　knigu, on$_i$ s"el　jabloko
　　　　　while Pooh read.IMP book　he ate.PERF apple
　　　　　While Pooh was reading a book, he ate an apple

　　　c.　*On$_i$ s"el　jabloko, poka Pux$_i$ čital　knigu
　　　　　he ate.PERF apple　while Pooh read.IMP book
　　　　　He ate an apple while Pooh was reading a book

　　　d.　*Poka on$_i$ čital　knigu, Pux$_i$ s"el　jabloko
　　　　　while he read.IMP book　Pooh ate.PERF apple
　　　　　While he was reading a book, Pooh ate an apple

In (25) we see that forwards anaphora is completely free, as in English, but that backwards anaphora is more restricted than in English. In (25c), the pronoun both precedes and c-commands its antecedent and so the sentence is ruled out by Principle C. But, in (25d), the pronoun does not c-command its antecedent, but still the sentence is ungrammatical, unlike its English counterpart. The restriction on backwards anaphora appears to be tied to certain adverbial clauses, as illustrated above with the temporal adverbial *poka*, "while." With different temporal adverbials, backwards anaphora is possible, as shown in (26):

(26)   Do togo kak ona pereehala   v Rossiyu, Masha zhila   vo Fancii
       before   she moved.PERF to Russia,   Masha was living.IMP in France
       Before she moved to Russia, Masha lived in France

However the restriction on backwards anaphora in *poka*-clauses is to be formulated, it is clear that it is a Russian-specific constraint, since it does not hold in English (see Kazanina, 2005, for details). The existence of two kinds of constraint against backwards anaphora allows us to ask about the origins of Principle C. In particular, the existence of language-particular constraints undermines the argument that Principle C must be innate simply because it is a constraint. The existence of constraints like the Russian *poka*-constraint, therefore, makes a Bayesian approach to constraint learning more plausible. Nonetheless, Kazanina and Phillips asked whether children learning Russian demonstrate the same knowledge of Principle C as their English-learning counterparts and whether they also demonstrate knowledge of the *poka*-constraint.

These researchers found a developmental dissociation between Principle C and the *poka*-constraint in Russian. While 3-year-olds demonstrated adult-like knowledge for Principle C violating sentences, children at this age appeared not to know the *poka*-constraint. By 5 years of age, however, the Russian children had acquired the *poka*-constraint (Figure 14.1).

Because Principle C is a universal constraint but the constraint against backwards anaphora in Russian *poka*-clauses is specific to that language, Kazanina and Phillips suggest that their dissociation in acquisition derives from how they are learned. Principle C is a universal, innate, constraint on possible grammars and so does not need to be learned. Consequently, the effects of this constraint are visible in children at the earliest possible experimental observations. The *poka*-constraint, on the other hand, is specific to Russian and so must be learned from experience, perhaps on the basis of indirect negative evidence, as discussed above.

If the learning of both constraints were based on indirect negative evidence, then we would expect prima facie that both would be acquired concurrently. That is, children's experience with sentences that fail to obey either of these constraints is equal: they have encountered no such sentences. Consequently, a learner using indirect negative evidence should acquire both constructions at the same rate, contrary to fact. However, a proponent of the indirect learning approach might argue that the base rate of relevant observations is higher for Principle C configurations than for *poka*-constraint configurations and so acquisition of Principle C precedes acquisition of the *poka*-constraint. Testing this variant of the indirect learning hypothesis would require a measure of

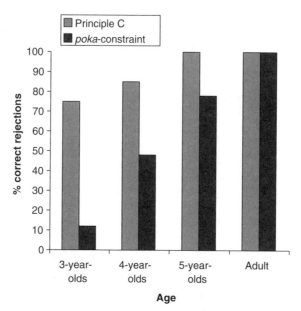

Figure 14.1   Backwards anaphora in Russian (from Kazanina & Phillips, 2001).

the relative frequency of the two kinds of configurations, a project that has yet to be carried out.

However these constraints are learned, the data on the acquisition of backwards anaphora minimally lead us to conclude that children keep track of abstract relations defined over hierarchical structures, one of the hallmarks of adult syntactic knowledge.

Children over-apply the c-command relation: Quantifier scope.   While the data from young children's adherence to Principle C cross-linguistically provide compelling evidence that their grammars make use of abstract relations defined over hierarchical structures, we have yet to determine whether this sensitivity to the c-command relation is due to a responsiveness to the data they have been exposed to or whether it derives from a more basic representational constraint on syntactic relations. In this light, Lidz and Musolino (2002) examined children's errors in scope assignment preferences in order to ask whether their errors are driven by an attention to c-command where none is called for in the adult language. This study illustrates that children use the c-command relation as a constraint on syntax even when adults do not, suggesting that the c-command relation plays a role in defining how children interpret their linguistic experience. While children's adherence to Principle C shows that they can acquire a constraint that is based on the c-command relation, Lidz and Musolino show that children sometimes build erroneous constraints based on this relation. This observation leads to the conclusion that children's sensitivity to c-command does not derive from their experience, but rather guides them through it. Before we can describe the study motivating this conclusion, however, we must first review the background context.

Musolino, Crain, and Thornton (2000) examined children's interpretations of ambiguous sentences containing quantifiers and negation. Such sentences permit readings which do not directly follow from an isomorphic mapping of surface form to semantic interpretation (Büring, 1997; Horn, 1989; Jackendoff, 1972; among others). Consider the following.

(27)   Every horse didn't jump over the fence
    a. $\forall x$ [horse (x) $\rightarrow \neg$ jump over the fence (x)]
        every horse is such that it didn't jump over the fence (i.e., none jumped)
    b. $\neg \forall x$ [horse (x) $\rightarrow$ jump over the fence (x)]
        not every horse jumped over the fence (i.e., some jumped and some didn't)

Sentences like (27) are scopally ambiguous. On one interpretation, (27) means that none of the horses jumped over the fence. Here, the universally quantified subject takes scope over negation (abbreviated every > not), as illustrated by the logical representation given in (27a). We call this an *isomorphic* interpretation because in this case the scope relation between the universally quantified NP and negation coincides with their surface positions. Another possible interpretation of (27) is that not all of the horses jumped over the fence. In this case, negation takes scope over the quantified subject (abbreviated not > every), as shown in the logical representation given in (27b). We call this a *nonisomorphic* interpretation because here, negation takes scope over the whole sentence, that is, in a position different from the one it occupies in surface syntax.

Musolino et al. (2000) tested children's comprehension of quantificationally ambiguous sentences. They found that while adults can easily access the nonisomorphic interpretations of such sentences, 4-year-olds systematically assign such sentences an isomorphic interpretation only. This was true also for sentences like (28) in which the isomorphic reading is the opposite from that of (27). While 4-year-olds do not assign sentences like (27) a not > every interpretation, they do assign that interpretation to (28).

(28)   The smurf didn't buy every orange

The finding that children systematically assign examples like (27) and (28) isomorphic interpretations leads us to conclude that young children, unlike adults, systematically interpret negation and quantified NPs on the basis of their position in overt syntax.

Musolino et al.'s findings, however, do not tell us the nature of the constraint underlying children's resistance to nonisomorphic interpretations. One possibility is that children's overly isomorphic interpretations reflect the linear arrangement between the quantified NPs and negation. Alternatively, children's interpretations may be constrained by the surface c-command relations holding between these elements. These alternatives arise because c-command and linear order are systematically confounded in the materials used by Musolino et al. As can be seen in the tree diagrams below, the subject position always precedes and falls outside the c-command domain of negation while the object position always follows and falls within the c-command domain of negation.

(29)

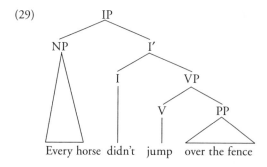

Every horse didn't jump over the fence

(30)

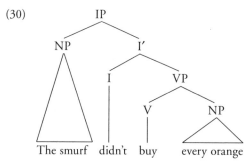

The smurf didn't buy every orange

Thus, there is no way to know from these data whether children's behavior is driven by linear order or hierarchical relations.

In order to tease these possibilities apart, Lidz and Musolino (2002) examined English- and Kannada-learning children's understanding of sentences like (31).

(31)   The smurf didn't catch two guys

Kannada is a Dravidian language spoken by approximately 40 million people in the state of Karnataka in south-western India. The canonical word order in Kannada is Subject–Object–Verb (SOV) and Kannada displays the same kind of scope ambiguities as English with respect to negation and quantified NPs (Lidz, 2006a). These properties are illustrated in (32), which can be interpreted as meaning that it is not the case that I read two books, a narrow scope interpretation of the numeral, or that there are two books that I didn't read, a wide scope interpretation of the numeral.

(32)   naanu eraDu pustaka ood-al-illa
       I-NOM two   book   read-INF-NEG
       I didn't read two books

The crucial difference between Kannada and English is that in Kannada, linear order and c-command are not confounded. Consider the representations in (33). In English, negation both precedes and c-commands the object position. In Kannada, however, negation c-commands the object but *does not* precede it.

(33)

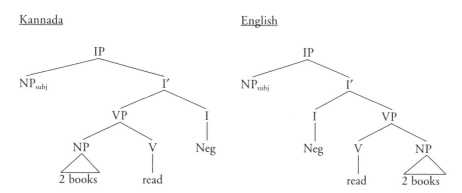

Kannada therefore provides the ideal language to tease apart the contribution of linear and hierarchical relations in children's assignment of scope. To the extent that Kannada-speaking children are restricted to one of the two possible interpretations of sentences like (32) in the way that English-speaking children are, linear order and hierarchical relations make opposite predictions. If children's interpretations of scope relations are constrained by linear order, then Kannada-learning children will display a preference for the wide scope reading of the quantified object with respect to negation. On the other hand, if children's interpretations of scope relations are constrained by c-command relations between negation and the quantified object, then Kannada-learning children will display a preference for the narrow scope reading of the object with respect to negation.

Lidz and Musolino found that children assigned a narrow scope reading to the numeral independent of the language being acquired (Figure 14.2). This finding illustrates that children's scope assignment preferences are determined by the hierarchical

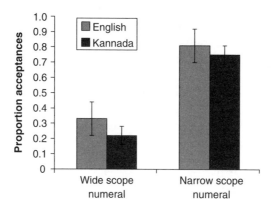

Figure 14.2 Scope interpretations of Kannada- and English-learning 4-year-olds (from Lidz & Musolino, 2002).

relation of c-command and not by linear order. Crucially, it is children's nonadult behavior that allows us to see that their representations are of the same character as adults'. The fact that children's scope interpretations differ from adults' enabled us to determine that their limitations derive from the same kinds of representations as we find in mature linguistic systems. Children use the c-command relation defined over hierarchical representations in determining scope, even though adult grammars are more flexible in this regard.

More broadly, we have determined that relations defined over hierarchical structures play an explanatory role not only in the characterization of adult knowledge but also in the characterization of children's knowledge. The fact that children apply the c-command relation in structures to which they shouldn't suggests that children prioritize this relation in their syntactic representations, using it to guide their acquisition.

Links between Cross-Linguistic Variability and Syntactic Acquisition

Although there is great diversity in human languages, languages do not vary at random (Greenberg, 1963). Certain surface features of a language are predictive of other features. For example, if verbs precede their objects in some language, then auxiliary verbs precede main verbs in that language. Likewise, if main verbs follow their objects, then auxiliary verbs follow main verbs (Baker, 2003). These kinds of typological generalizations point toward abstract principles of grammar that unify constructions with apparently unrelated surface properties. These principles are stated in terms of abstract properties of syntactic representations, so that one point of variability in the representations can lead to a wide range of surface differences (Chomsky, 1986; Baker, 2003).

If this perspective on cross-linguistic variation is correct, then it makes a strong prediction about language acquisition: if two superficially distinct constructions share a certain piece of representational structure, then the acquisition of those two constructions should be significantly correlated (Snyder, 1995, 2001; Snyder & Stromswold, 1997; Baker, 2005b). Importantly, if this prediction is borne out, then it supports a view of children's syntactic knowledge as being stated over abstract properties of representations.

The prediction has been tested in a range of studies conducted by William Snyder and his colleagues. Snyder and Stromswold (1997) examined the acquisition of a wide range of "complex predicate" constructions, given in (34):

(34) a. John painted the house red.   (resultative)
      b. Mary lifted up the box/lifted the box up.   (verb-particle)
      c. Fred made Barney leave.   (*make*-causative)
      d. Fred saw Barney leave.   (perceptual report)
      e. Bob put the book on the table.   (*put*-locative)
      f. Alice sent the letter to Sue.   (*to*-dative)
      g. Alice sent Sue the letter.   (double-object dative)

These constructions are all alike in that they involve multiple predications but only a single tense specification. For example, (34a) contains the predicates *paint* and *red*, (34b) contains the predicates *lift* and *up*, etc. Languages differ with respect to whether they exhibit this set of "complex predicate" constructions. English and other Germanic languages typically exhibit all of these constructions, whereas the Romance languages lack direct counterparts of them.

The possibility that these constructions form a family related by an abstract syntactic property, and that this property plays an explanatory role in the acquisition of these constructions, was examined by Snyder and Stromswold (1997). These researchers examined longitudinal transcripts of the spontaneous speech of 12 children from the CHILDES database (MacWhinney & Snow, 1985). For each of the constructions in (34b–g), Snyder and Stromswold determined the first clear use of that construction and used that as a measure of acquisition. By this measure, every child in the sample acquired all of these constructions as a group. In addition, Snyder and Stromswold showed that the tight correlations between age of acquisition of these constructions were not a consequence of general syntactic ability, mean length of utterance, or specific lexical properties. These results suggest that the unit of acquisition in syntax is not the construction, but rather a more abstract component of representation that ties together constructions with different surface properties.

Snyder (2001) argues that these constructions share the property of involving syntactic compounding of the two predicates at an abstract level of representation. On this view, (34a) is syntactically represented as in (35), although the tight relation between the two predicates is ultimately obscured in the word order (Larson, 1991).

(35)   [john [[painted red] [the house]]]

As support for this view, Snyder notes that only languages with productive noun–noun compounding exhibit complex predicate constructions. English has productive compounding, as in (36), whereas Spanish does not, as in (37). In languages like Spanish, noun–noun compounds are formed only through conscious coinage.

(36)   English:
      a.   banana box (= a box for bananas, a banana shaped box, etc.)
      b.   box banana (= a banana shaped like a box, a banana that came from a box, etc.)

(37)   Spanish:
      a.   *platano caja
          banana box
      b.   *caja platano
          box banana

Similarly, English but not Spanish has complex predicate constructions like those in (38).

(38)   a.   John <u>hammered</u> the iron <u>flat</u>
       b.   Juan <u>golpeò</u> el hierro (*<u>plano</u>)
       c.   John <u>lifted</u> the box <u>up</u>
       d.   Juan <u>levantò</u> la caja (*<u>arriba</u>)

In a typological survey drawing from 12 language families, Snyder (2001) found that only languages that allow productive noun–noun compounding also allow resultatives and separable particle constructions. This pattern indicates that noun–noun compounding is a necessary condition for complex predication. The abstract feature of syntactic representations that licenses noun–noun compounding is therefore implicitly tied to the possibility of complex predicate constructions, explaining why these constructions co-occur cross-linguistically.

Snyder (2001) also showed that the acquisition of complex predicate constructions, like resultatives and separable particle constructions, is directly tied to the acquisition of noun–noun compounding. Looking again at first clear use, the age of acquisition of compounding and complex predicate constructions was shown to be nearly identical in almost all children, ranging from 1.8 to 2.6 years of age. Putting this together with the typological data, we have strong evidence that there is a representational link between compounding and complex predicate constructions.

An additional test of the relation between compounding and complex predicates was performed by Sugisaki and Isobe (2000). These authors observe that in Japanese, novel compounding is acquired later than in English, between 3 and 4 years of age. This relative delay in acquisition allowed them to test experimentally for a relationship between resultatives and compounding in 3- and 4-year-old children. As a test of the compounding parameter, these authors asked whether only Japanese children who can produce novel noun–noun compounds can also understand resultatives in an adult-like fashion.

Each child received an elicited production test of novel compounds (as in 39), and a comprehension test of transitive resultatives (as in 40b) as compared to transitive sentences with attributive adjectives (40a).

(39)   *kame pan* "turtle bread" (i.e., bread in the shape of a turtle)
(40)   a.   Pikachu-wa aka-i isu-o nutte-imasu.   (attributive)
            "Pikachu is painting the red chair."
       b.   Pikachu-wa aka-ku isu-o nutteiru.   (resultative)
            "Pikachu is painting the chair red."

As illustrated in Table 14.1, there was a significant contingency between passing the test on resultatives and passing the test on compounding. Performance on one test predicted performance on the other.

These results lend further support to the hypothesis that compounding and complex predicate constructions share a certain piece of representational structure. Learning that abstract piece of syntactic structure leads to the concurrent acquisition of superficially distinct constructions.

More generally, this kind of data points toward a theory of children's syntactic knowledge that is stated in terms of abstract syntactic representations. Such a theory entails

Table 14.1 Contingency between understanding of resultatives and producing compounds (adapted from Sugisaki & Isobe, 2000)

		Resultatives	
		Pass	*Fail*
Compounding	*Pass*	10	2
	Fail	2	6

that the object of acquisition for a syntactic learner is this kind of abstract representation and not something more closely tied to surface forms. This kind of data also invites more thorough integration of work in comparative syntax with work in syntactic acquisition. Identifying the range and limits of cross-linguistic variation can provide useful hypotheses about children's representations and can thereby restrict the class of learning theories that are consistent with a given phenomenon (Lidz, 2006b).

Consequences for Learning

In the preceding sections, we have identified three properties of syntactic representations that are continuous across children and adults. First, children's syntactic representations are hierarchical from the earliest stages of acquisition. Second, children compute and keep track of abstract relations defined over hierarchical structures, like the c-command relation, and use such relations in building their grammatical knowledge. Third, children's syntactic representations contain abstract features that lead to concurrent acquisition of superficially distinct constructions.

Having identified these properties puts us in position to ask about syntactic learning. At least three possible explanations for this continuity can be developed. First, the strong nativist position would hold that the reason we find this kind of representational continuity is that this is simply the vocabulary over which the learning algorithm is defined. On this view, when children hear sentences they automatically encode them in terms of abstract hierarchical representations with consequences for wide ranges of surface phenomena (Baker, 2003; Chomsky, 1975; Wexler, 1996). A second, more weakly nativist, position would hold that this kind of representational continuity results from constraints on computations. The representations themselves are not innate, but rather they are the only possible output of a certain kind of learning algorithm (Newport, 1990; Newport & Aslin, 2000). A third option would be even less nativist in its orientation, taking the unity of linguistic representations across children and adults to be a consequence of the kinds of information that can be extracted from linguistic experience by a general purpose learning mechanism across time (Elman, 1993; Thomas & Karmiloff-Smith, 2005). On this view, certain features of a grammar are unable to be noticed by the learner until other features are already in place. Moreover, the nature of what can be learned at a given stage of development constrains the kinds of representations that are built at later stages of development. On this view, the uniformity of syntactic representations across languages and across populations results from a cascading learning procedure that becomes more constrained as it develops.

Various combinations of these proposals can and have been put together. For example, some of the mathematically inspired language learnability work (Lightfoot, 1991; Wexler & Culicover, 1980) proposes that limited computational resources guide the learner through an innate space of possible representations. Similarly, proposals concerning parameter setting (Baker, 2005a; Dresher & Kaye, 1990) and experimental work on vocabulary acquisition (Gleitman, Cassidy, Nappa, Papafragou, & Trueswell, 2005; Waxman & Lidz, 2006) argue that learning is guided through an innate hypothesis space on the basis of the degree to which prior representational commitments must be made before some feature of the language can be learned. On this view, the order of acquisition of certain features is driven by changes in the learner's representational space. Once a given feature is acquired, it makes available new resources for the acquisition of subsequent features.

Whatever the appropriate learning theory for syntax is, understanding the kinds of representations that make up adult languages and the kinds of representations children have at a given stage of development places limits on hypotheses concerning this theory. At a minimum, a researcher asking about the acquisition of some syntactic phenomenon must ask three questions. First, what is the representation that is acquired for that phenomenon? Second, how is this phenomenon expressed in speech to children? Third, how could the representation be acquired on the basis of experience?

Notice that even the most staunch nativist must provide an answer to the last question. Even if we view learning as triggering (i.e., the representations are fully specified at birth but need only to be activated by experience), the learner faces the problem of identifying which forms in the input correspond to her innate syntactic representations. Simply having a representational vocabulary is insufficient for acquisition. Rather, the learner must be able to link data from experience with those representations (Pinker, 1989; Tomasello, 2000).

A clear example of how experience could play a role in identifying innate representations comes from recent work by Misha Becker (2006), which examines the acquisition of raising and control structures like those in (41).

(41) a. Chris seems to be happy. (raising)
      b. Chris wants to be happy. (control)

The problem presented by these kinds of sentences is that although their structural representations are distinct, their surface properties are identical. In both sentences the main clause has an overt subject and the embedded infinitival clause does not. Despite these similarities, a number of syntactic tests illustrate that these kinds of sentences have distinct structural descriptions. For example, only the subject of raising verbs can be a pleonastic:

(42) a. It seems to rain every time I go to Paris
      b. *It wants to rain every time I go to Paris

    c.   There seems to be a riot every time I go to Paris
    d.   *There wants to be a riot every time I go to Paris

Similarly, phrasal idioms can be separated by raising verbs but not by control verbs:

(43)   a.   The shit seems to hit the fan every time I go to Paris
        b.   *The shit wants to hit the fan every time I go to Paris

These differences (among others) derive from the fact that the subject of a control verb is a participant in the event denoted by that verb (in addition to the event denoted by the embedded verb) whereas the subject of a raising verb is a participant only in the event denoted by the embedded verb. If learners knew the meanings of the relevant verbs upon hearing a sentence like (41a) or (41b), then they would know what structure to assign. However, it is unlikely that learners could identify the relevant meanings independent of the syntactic structures they encounter the verb in (see Gleitman, 1990). Consequently, upon hearing these kinds of sentences with previously unknown verbs, the learner is provided with no information about whether to assign a raising or a control structure, since the surface realizations of these structures are alike.

With these surface similarities in mind, Becker (2006) proposes that there are certain probabilistic cues to these structures that derive from, but are not entailed by, the structural differences between raising and control. For example, because control verbs exert selectional restrictions (typically having to do with animacy or volitionality) on their subjects but raising verbs do not, Becker proposes that learners should treat the animacy of the subject as a probabilistic cue to the control analysis of a sentence with an infinitival complement. She goes on to show that adults and 5-year-old children do treat the animacy of the subject as a cue to the control structure, despite the fact that it is only probabilistically present across the whole language. Interestingly, 3- and 4-year-old children were less sensitive to animacy as a cue to control than were 5-year-olds, suggesting that the initial analysis of a novel infinitival complement taking verb is the raising analysis and that this analysis is overcome over time on the basis of experience with the relevant probabilistic cues.

This kind of analysis is important because it reveals that learners who are equipped with a set of possible syntactic structures might be able to predict what kinds of sentences are likely to instantiate those structures. Crucially, these predictions need not be entailments of the structure. In Becker's example, animacy is not a trigger for control, since animate subjects are possible with both raising and control verbs, but it is a cue for control since control verbs are more likely to insist that their subjects be animate. This cue-based theory of learning illustrates how learners with rich innate structures might go about identifying the strings that realize those structures (see Dresher & Kaye, 1990; Fodor, 1998; Lightfoot, 1999; Yang, 2002, for related proposals).

Speaking more generally, the solution to the problem of how a grammatical system becomes increasingly specified on the basis of experience will require an understanding of how the sentences falling outside of the current representational space are encoded and how the existing representations can be updated on the basis of that experience (Valian & Casey, 2003). Experience, not surprisingly, plays a critical role in understanding syntax acquisition. But, the learner's reliance on the input may be most successful when learners are constrained in the kinds of representations they consider. In sum, an emphasis on syntactic representations as both the target of acquisition and a contributor to syntactic development will allow us to more precisely formulate the significant role of input in syntactic acquisition.

The general framework outlined here, with its emphasis on children's representational systems for syntax across time, makes it possible to bridge developmental and theoretical research in language acquisition. As noted above, very little work in syntactic acquisition, if any, has attempted to ask what drives syntactic change in actual learners. This dearth of research is probably explained in part by the difficulty of formulating hypotheses about representational change. As noted by Fodor (1998), there is an inherent paradox in syntactic development. The problem is that learners can only parse strings for which they have representations. For those sentences there is nothing to be learned. On the other hand, if the parser can't assign a structure to a sentence, then how could the learner possibly learn from it? A cue-based learning approach like that described above gives one possible solution to this paradox since a sensitivity to the surface cues that point to a structure could aid parsing even for those sentences that fall outside of the learner's current grammar.

A second contributor to the scarcity of developmental hypotheses in language acquisition is the problem of identifying the child's representations at a given stage, as noted in the introduction to this chapter. Only when we have some understanding of the successive representational systems built by children over time can we begin to ask about the mechanisms that drive the elaboration of syntactic knowledge. I believe we have now reached a stage where we have a great deal of information about the character of children's syntactic representations. As we have seen in this chapter, these representations are highly abstract, with rules and relations defined over hierarchical structures playing a critical role in a wide range of superficially distinct constructions. Future work in the field must take advantage of these conclusions in order to ask both how these representations are learned and how they contribute to learning.

Note

This paper was supported in part by grants from the National Science Foundation (BCS-0418309) and the National Institutes of Health (R03-DC006829). Thanks also to Marilyn Shatz, Sandy Waxman, Colin Phillips, Tonia Bleam, Kristen Syrett, Ann Bunger, Misha Becker, Justin Halberda, Rebecca Baier, and the students in Child Language at Northwestern University in Winter 2005 for helpful input.

References

Baker, M. (2003). *The atoms of language*. New York: Basic Books.
Baker, M. (2005a). Mapping the terrain of language acquisition. *Language Learning and Development*, *1*, 93–129.

Baker, M. (2005b). *Lexical categories: verbs, nouns and adjectives*. Cambridge, MA: Cambridge University Press.

Becker, M. (2006). There began to be a learnability puzzle. *Linguistic Inquiry, 37*, 441–456.

Bloom, L. (1970). *Language development: Form and function in emerging grammars*. Cambridge, MA: MIT Press.

Bloom, P. (1990). Subjectless sentences in child language. *Linguistic Inquiry, 21*, 491–504.

Büring, D. (1997). The great scope inversion conspiracy. *Linguistics and Philosophy, 20*, 175–194.

Chien, Y. C., & Wexler, K. (1990). Children's knowledge of locality conditions in binding as evidence for the modularity of syntax and pragmatics. *Language Acquisition, 1*, 225–295.

Chomsky, N. (1957). *Syntactic structures*. Mouton.

Chomsky, N. (1975). *Reflections on language*. New York: Pantheon.

Chomsky, N. (1981). *Lectures on government and binding*. Dordrecht: Foris.

Chomsky, N. (1986). *Knowledge of language*. Praeger.

Crain, S. (1991). Language acquisition in the absence of experience. *Behavioral and Brain Science, 14*, 597–650.

Crain, S., & McKee, C. (1985). The acquisition of structural restrictions on anaphora. *Proceedings of NELS, 15*, 94–110.

Crain, S., & Thornton, R. (1998). *Investigations in Universal Grammar: A guide to research on the acquisition of syntax and semantics*. Cambridge, MA: MIT Press.

Dresher, B. E., & Kaye, J. D. (1990). A computational learning model for metrical phonology. *Cognition, 34*, 137–195.

Elman, J. L. (1993). Learning and development in neural networks: The importance of starting small. *Cognition, 48*, 71–99.

Fiengo, R. (1977). On trace theory. *Linguistic Inquiry, 8*, 35–61.

Fodor, J. D. (1998). Unambiguous triggers. *Linguistic Inquiry, 29*, 1–36.

Frank, R., & Vijay-Shanker, K. (2001). Primitive C-command. *Syntax, 4*, 164–204.

Gelman, R., & Williams, E. (1998). Enabling constraints for cognitive development and learning: Domain specificity and epigenesis. In D. Kuhn & R. Siegler (Eds.), *Handbook of child psychology: Vol. 2. Cognition, perception and language* (5th ed., pp. 575–630). New York: Wiley.

Gerken, L. A. (1991). The metrical basis for children's subjectless sentences. *Journal of Memory and Language, 30*, 431–451.

Gleitman, L. (1990). Structural sources of verb learning. *Language Acquisition, 1*, 1–63.

Gleitman L. R., Cassidy, K., Nappa, R., Papafragou, A., & Trueswell, J. C. (2005). Hard words. *Language Learning and Development, 1*, 23–64.

Golinkoff, R., Hirsh-Pasek, K., Cauley, K. M., & Gordon, L. (1987). The eyes have it: Lexical and syntactical comprehension in a new paradigm. *Journal of Child Language, 14*, 23–45.

Greenberg, J. (1963). Some universals of grammar with special reference to the order of words. In J. Greenberg (Ed.), *Universals of language*. Cambridge, MA: MIT Press.

Grodzinsky, Y., & Reinhart, T. (1993). The innateness of binding and coreference. *Linguistic Inquiry, 24*, 69–101.

Guasti, M. T. (2001). *Language acquisition: The growth of grammar*. Cambridge, MA: MIT Press.

Hamburger, H., & Crain, S. (1984). Acquisition of cognitive compiling. *Cognition, 17*, 85–136.

Hirsh-Pasek, K., & Golinkoff, R. M. (1996). *The origins of grammar*. Cambridge, MA: MIT Press.

Horn, L. R. (1989). *A natural history of negation*. Chicago: University of Chicago Press.

Hyams, N. (1986). *Language acquisition and the theory of parameters*. Dordrecht: Reidel.

Hyams, N. (1992). A reanalysis of null subjects in child language. In J. Weissenborn, H. Goodluck, & T. Roeper (Eds.), *Theoretical issues in language acquisition*. Hillsdale, NJ: Lawrence Erlbaum.

Jackendoff, R. (1972). *Semantic interpretation in generative grammar*. Cambridge, MA: MIT Press.

Kayne, R. (1995). *The antisymmetry of syntax*. Cambridge, MA: MIT Press.

Kazanina, N. (2005). *The acquisition and processing of backwards anaphora*. PhD dissertation, University of Maryland.

Kazanina, N., & Phillips, C. (2001). Coreference in child Russian: Distinguishing syntactic and discourse constraints. In A. H.-J. Do, L. Domínguez, & A. Johansen (Eds.), *Proceedings of the 25th Annual Boston University Conference for Language Development* (pp. 413–424). Somerville, MA: Cascadilla Press.

Larson, R. (1991). Some issues in verb serialization. In C. Lefebvre (Ed.), *Serial verbs*. Benjamins: Philadelphia.

Lidz, J. (2006a). The grammar of accusative case in Kannada. *Language, 82*, 1–23.

Lidz, J. (2006b). Verb learning as a probe for children's grammars. In K. Hirsh-Pasek & R. Golinkoff (Eds.), *Action meets word* (pp. 429–449). Oxford: Oxford University Press.

Lidz, J., & Musolino, J. (2002). Children's command of quantification. *Cognition, 84*, 113–154.

Lidz, J., Waxman, S., & Freedman, J. (2003). What infants know about syntax but couldn't have learned. *Cognition, 89*, B65–B73.

Lightfoot, D. (1991). *How to set parameters: Arguments from language change*. Cambridge, MA: MIT Press.

Lightfoot, D. (1999). *The development of language: acquisition, change and evolution*. Oxford: Blackwell.

MacWhinney, B., & Snow, C. (1985). The Child Language Data Exchange System. *Journal of Child Language, 12*, 271–296.

Marcus, G. F. (1993). Negative evidence in language acquisition. *Cognition, 46*, 53–85.

May, R. (1985). *Logical form: Its structure and derivation*. Cambridge, MA: MIT Press.

McDaniel, D., Cairns, H. S., & Hsu, J. R. (1991). Control principles in the grammars of young children. *Language Acquisition, 1*, 297–335.

McKee, C. (1992). A comparison of pronouns and anaphors in Italian and English acquisition. *Language Acquisition, 1*, 21–55.

Musolino, J., Crain, S., & Thornton, R. (2000). Navigating negative quantificational space. *Linguistics, 38*, 1–32.

Newport, E. L. (1990). Maturational constraints on language learning. *Cognitive Science, 14*, 11–28.

Newport, E., & Aslin, R. (2000). Innately constrained learning: Blending old and new approaches to language acquisition. In S. C. Howell, S. A. Fish, & T. Keith-Lucas (Eds.), *Proceedings of the 24th Annual Boston University Conference on Language Development*. Somerville, MA: Cascadilla Press.

Pinker, S. (1989). *Learnability and cognition: the acquisition of argument structure*. Cambridge, MA: MIT Press.

Radford, A. (1990). *Syntactic theory and the acquisition of English syntax: The nature of early child grammars in English*. Oxford: Blackwell.

Radford, A. (1995). Phrase structure and functional categories. In P. Fletcher & B. MacWhinney (Eds.), *The handbook of child language*. Oxford: Blackwell.

Regier, T., & Gahl, S. (2003). Learning the unlearnable: the role of missing evidence. *Cognition*, 93, 147–155.

Reinhart, T. (1976). *The syntactic domain of anaphora*. Doctoral dissertation, MIT, Cambridge, MA.

Rizzi, L. (1990). *Relativized minimality*. Cambridge, MA: MIT Press.

Rizzi, L. (1993/1994). Some notes on linguistic theory and language development: The case of root infinitives. *Language Acquisition*, 3, 371–393.

Snyder, W. (1995). *Language acquisition and language variation*. PhD dissertation, MIT, Cambridge, MA.

Snyder, W. (2001). On the nature of syntactic variation: evidence from complex predicates and complex word formation. *Language*, 77, 324–342.

Snyder, W., & Stromswold, K. (1997). The structure and acquisition of English dative constructions. *Linguistic Inquiry*, 28, 281–317.

Sugisaki, K., & Isobe, M. (2000). Resultatives result from the compounding parameter. *Proceedings of West Coast Conference of Formal Linguistics*. Cambridge, MA: Cascadilla Press.

Tenenbaum, J., & Griffiths, T. (2001). Generalization, similarity and Bayesian inference. *Behavioral and Brain Sciences*, 24, 629–640.

Thomas, M., & Karmiloff-Smith, A. (2005). Can developmental disorders reveal the component parts of the human language faculty? *Language Learning and Development*, 1, 65–93.

Thornton, R., & Wexler, K. (1999). *Principle B, VP ellipsis, and interpretation in child grammar*. Cambridge, MA: MIT Press.

Tomasello, M. (2000). Do children have adult syntactic competence? *Cognition*, 74, 209–253.

Vainikka, A. (1994). Case in the development of English syntax. *Language Acquisition*, 3, 257–325.

Valian, V. (1986). Syntactic categories in the speech of young children. *Developmental Psychology*, 22, 562–579.

Valian, V. (1991). Syntactic subjects in the early speech of American and Italian children. *Cognition*, 40, 21–81.

Valian, V., & Casey, L. (2003). Young children's acquisition of wh-questions: the role of structured input. *Journal of Child Language*, 30, 117–143.

Waxman, S. R., & Lidz, J. (2006). Early word learning. In D. Kuhn & R. Siegler (Eds.), *Handbook of child psychology: Cognition, perception and language* (6th ed., pp. 299–335). New York: Wiley.

Wexler, K. (1990). Innateness and maturation in linguistic development. *Developmental Psychobiology*, 23, 645–660.

Wexler, K. (1996). Very early parameter setting and the unique checking constraint. *Lingua*, 106, 23–79.

Wexler, K., & Culicover, P. W. (1980). *Formal principles of language acquisition*. Cambridge, MA: MIT Press.

Yang, C. (2002). *Knowledge and learning in natural language*. Oxford: Oxford University Press.

15

Conversational Understanding in Young Children

Michael Siegal and Luca Surian

Suppose a messy little boy hears his mother exclaim, "Thanks for putting away your toys again neatly like you always do." To understand the intended meaning of her remark, the boy is required to draw the implication that his mother is making a sarcastic comment since he has done precisely the opposite. How children recognize such implications is the key issue in studies of the development of conversational pragmatics. When adults interpret language, they go well beyond what is said, enriching, and sometimes even reversing, what is encoded linguistically. They commonly add a wealth of implicit information that, when all goes well, enables the speaker's intended meaning to be retrieved – a special challenge for children who are inexperienced in conversation.

The processes by which children interpret language are important to an accurate characterization of both their conversational competence and their competence in various areas of their conceptual development. Children's conversational competence is based on their developing sensitivity to linguistic and extra-linguistic contexts. At the same time, the gap between the conversational experience of adults and children gives rise to the important methodological problem of how adults should pose questions to children to determine the nature of conceptual knowledge. Although studies of children's cognitive development require that they interpret test questions as intended by investigators, there is an ever present chance that their lack of success on tests used to determine what they know does not in fact reflect genuine cognitive deficits but rather their developing conversational understanding. By the age of 3 years, children are fluent speakers insofar as they display mastery of the lexicon and grammar of their native language. Nevertheless, as Berman (this volume) points out, children and even adolescents may have a long way to go before this fluency leads to an adult-like proficiency in how language is used in making sense of conversation.

It has been generally acknowledged that an analysis of conversational competence needs to explain how listeners identify and take communicative context into account in the assignment of reference and the resolution of ambiguity, for example, in humor, irony, metaphors, and sarcasm (Carston, 1998, 2002; Clark, 1996; Gazdar, 1979; Glucksberg, 2003; Horn, 1989; Levinson, 2000; Ninio & Snow, 1996; Sperber & Wilson, 1995, 2002; Wilson & Sperber, 2004; Winner, 1988). Central to the history of research on conversational understanding is the analysis introduced by Grice (1975, 1989) who proposed that the expectations of participants in conversation are characterized by maxims which enjoin speakers to "say no more or no less than is required for the purpose of the exchange" (maxims of *quantity*), "to tell the truth and avoid statements for which there is insufficient evidence (maxims of *quality*)", "be relevant (maxim of *relation*)", and "avoid ambiguity, confusion and obscurity (maxims of *manner*)."

According to Grice's account, violations of these maxims necessarily occur in that, for example, to follow one maxim may mean that another is violated. This process creates a "logic in conversation" that allows listeners to follow the implications contained in natural language. For example, if a person complains that she has a headache, a friend may respond that there is a drugstore around the corner. The implications are that the walk to the drugstore is short, that the drugstore is open at the time, that it sells tablets to alleviate headaches, and that these tablets are publicly available to be sold to the sufferer. To state all this explicitly would be to violate the maxims of quantity since the implications are likely to be mutually understood among conversationally experienced speakers. If the speaker appears to violate one or more of these maxims but the hearer has reason to believe that the speaker is cooperative, then the hearer needs to generate pragmatic inferences (termed by Grice "conversational implicatures") to ensure that the speaker's contribution to the conversation is adequate at the level of intended meaning. For example, if a professor violates the quantity rule by stating in a letter of recommendation only that "This student speaks English well and has been present all the time," the inference would be that the student is not particularly brilliant since if he was the professor would have written much more.

Limitations in children's understanding of how language is used in terms of a Gricean analysis are of particular interest as these may mask the nature of conceptual knowledge in a number of ways. In particular, young children, who are unskilled in understanding why, when, and how conversational maxims are violated, may often fail to interpret speakers' meanings and reveal the nature of their conceptual competence as intended. For example, an adult experimenter may inadvertently depart from the maxims of relation and manner. In such instances, children, particularly those aged 3 years, may be asked questions that they do not interpret as distinct and new. Thus they answer these questions repeatedly in the same way amounting to a form of response bias. Alternatively, children may not follow why an adult experimenter in studies of conceptual development departs from the maxims of quantity and seems to say more than is required, using repeated questioning, for the purpose of determining the certainty of what they know. This concern has arisen, for example, in characterizing children's performance on Piagetian conservation tasks, where they are asked to indicate whether the number of objects in front of them remains the same or changes after these undergo a perceptual transformation. In the face of such repeated questioning, it has often been maintained that children, particularly those aged 4, 5, and 6 years, may inappropriately abandon their original correct answer for a different one in the hope of finding the answer that is intended by the experimenter (Donaldson, 1978; Siegal, 1997). Some children may engage in answer switching if they are uncertain of the correctness of their original answer. However, even if certain, children may switch should they come to believe that an adult experimenter expects them to offer a different reply – an issue that often arises in situations where children are required to resist suggestive questions in reporting accurately on the characteristics of persons, objects, and events that they have previously witnessed (Bright-Paul, Jarrold, & Wright, 2005; Howie, Sheehan, Mojarrad, & Wrzesinska, 2004; Pipe, Lamb, Orbach, & Esplin, 2004).

Nevertheless, despite what children say under such conditions, they can still demonstrate a wealth of conceptual knowledge in tasks that reduce the requirement for them to follow the implications of questions (German & Leslie, 2001; Surian & Leslie, 1999; Yazdi, German, Defeyer, & Siegal, 2006). As Gelman, Meck, and Merkin (1986) observed some time ago, children's incorrect answers on tasks designed to examine their conceptual development might truly reflect limitations in their conceptual competence in a particular domain of knowledge. However, quite separately from the issue of conceptual competence, their performance on the same tasks may require a type of planning or procedural competence that is not yet within the child's grasp. But even if children have both a conceptual and planning competence, they may still not display the depth of their understanding owing to difficulties in correctly interpreting instructions through sharing the speaker's conversational implications (Siegal, 1999).

According to one longstanding interpretation, children as old as 7 years do not easily understand contradictions and tautologies in language (Osherson & Markman, 1975). Their increasing accuracy in interpreting utterances itself requires conceptual development as is made possible by the acquisition of a distinction between literal meaning and speaker's meaning (Beal & Flavell, 1984; Robinson, Goelman, & Olson, 1983). According to this account, young children have yet to understand that the literal meaning of a message may differ from that intended by the speaker and that such messages may be ambiguous. For example, they do not recognize the inadequacy of a description of one of two red balls as "the red one" and that the literal meaning in such instances is not sufficient to convey the speaker's meaning. By contrast, older children recognize that messages can be ambiguous and have more than one meaning that differs from that intended by the speaker.

However, recent findings suggest that a number of mechanisms underwrite the development of conversational understanding that involve an increasing sensitivity with age to conversational conventions and to linguistic and extra-linguistic contexts for the interpretation of meaning. In this chapter, we examine several new research directions that contribute to illuminating the relationship between conversational understanding and conceptual competence in children's cognitive development. These concern studies of (1) children's knowledge of the distinction between reality and the phenomenal world of appearances, (2) their knowledge of certain scientific concepts such as, for example, those used in cosmology, (3) their ability to compute the implications of statements that include quantifiers or logical connectives, and (4) their ability to process sentences as intended by interpreting extra-linguistic contexts appropriately.

Finding Appropriate Questions and Contexts to Determine Children's Conceptual Competence: Research on Knowledge of the Appearance–Reality Distinction

One of the most profound areas in which children's limitations in conversational under-standing may mask their conceptual development involves the ability to distinguish between reality and the phenomenal world of appearances. Flavell, Green, and Flavell (1986) devised tests to determine whether children aged 3 and 4 years can distinguish between the true color of a substance, or the true category membership of a living thing, and its appearance under, for example, colored filters or masks and costumes. For example, in one task, children are shown milk in a glass with a red filter wrapped around it. The children were asked, "What color is the milk really and truly? Is it really and truly red or really and truly white? Now here is the second question. When you look at the milk with your eyes right now, does it look white or does it look red?" In contrast to most of the 4-year-olds who succeeded on this task, less than half of the 3-year-olds correctly identified the milk to *look red* but to *be white* really and truly. Many 3-year-olds make "phenomenism" errors in giving the same answer to both appearance and reality questions. In saying that the milk is really and truly red, they indicate that the red appearance of the milk is a genuine reflection of reality.

Although such results have been taken to reveal a conceptual deficit in development, children as young as 2 years do display a grasp of the appearance–reality distinction. In a show-and-tell game, for example, they can describe the appearance and show the real function of objects (Gauvain & Greene, 1994; Rice, Koinis, Sullivan, Tager-Flusberg, & Winner 1997). Moreover, children aged 3 years prefer a candle that looks like a crayon to a real crayon when asked "to draw with something that *looks like* a crayon," and they prefer a real sponge to a sponge that looks like a rock when asked to clean up some spilled water (Sapp, Lee, & Muir, 2000). They often use more than one label for the same object depending on the context of a speaker's request (Deák, Yen, & Pettit, 2001; Gelman & Bloom, 2000; Gelman & Ebeling, 1998). In adapting their terminology to context, they are not limited to a single label that exclusively refers to appearance or reality. As Clark (1997) suggests, in the process of acquiring a lexicon, children from the start readily apply multiple terms from alternative perspectives to the same objects or events. Children do sometimes fail to learn new words but these are in cases when they lack adequate pragmatic directions from adults. From the age of 2 years, children work hard to use a wide variety of cues (including mention of action, intonation, and form of question) to guide their responses in conversation (Shatz, 1978; Shatz & McCloskey, 1984). They use their understanding of language to increase their know-ledge of the world of people and objects and they use their knowledge of the world to increase their understanding of language (Shatz, 1994).

Why then would children show a type of response bias on appearance–reality tasks in giving the same answer to questions about both appearance and reality? Deák, Ray, and Brenneman (2003) have shown that the lack of success by 3-year-olds on appearance–

reality tasks reflects a difficulty in identifying the point of the conversation initiated by the interviewer. They found that there is a strong relation between answers on the appearance–reality questions and "overlapping" control tasks in which children were asked parallel questions about the properties of a single item. For example, children were shown a picture of a bear holding a key and asked two test questions, "What does this look like? Does it look like a key or does it look like a bear? What does it have? Does it have a key or does it have a bear?" Children who "perseverated" on control tasks choosing the same answer on both test questions often did so on the "standard" appearance–reality tasks (e.g., in providing a "phenomenism" pattern of responses). According to this analysis, if asked two questions about appearance and reality that involve deciding between choices of appearance and reality, children may be unclear whether each of the two questions requires a distinct, newly reasoned answer – one that does not depend on the other. If this is the case, then they may stick with their first answer until provided with feedback or until asked a question that they recognize as altogether new. As Hansen and Markman (2005) point out, the term "looks like" in everyday conversation can refer both to outward appearance and likely reality. For this reason, children may take "looks like" to refer to reality when asked about appearance in appearance–reality tasks. In this sense, appearance questions posed to children are liable to depart from Grice's maxims of relation and manner.

In instances where the relation or relevance of questions is not readily comprehensible such as in the case of questions about their knowledge of the distinction between appearance and reality, children's consistent answers may reflect a response bias pattern that may be characterized in terms of phenomenism. This pattern in which children consistently stick to their first answer may extend to yes–no questions. Fritzley and Lee (2003) investigated whether yes–no questions would lead to a yes bias in young children's answers to questions. They asked 2- to 5-year-olds comprehensible and incomprehensible yes–no questions about familiar and unfamiliar objects. The 2-year-olds displayed a consistent yes bias whereas 4- and 5-year-olds varied their answers and showed no response bias toward comprehensible questions and a negative response bias toward incomprehensible questions. Results for 3-year-olds were mixed, suggesting that the age of 3 years is a period of developmental transition in their response tendencies toward answering yes–no questions. Fritzley and Lee concluded that yes–no questions are suitable for older children, providing these are made to be comprehensible (and do not involve meaningless terms), but that such questioning may result in biased results when used with younger children and when incomprehensible.

As shown by Fritzley and Lee, young children can be reluctant to say that they don't know the answer to closed-ended questions even when they are explicitly told that such a response is acceptable. This is particularly the case when children are asked closed-ended questions that require either a yes or no answer compared with open-ended questions that require children to generate their own responses (Waterman, Blades, & Spencer, 2001, 2004). At least for children in Western cultures, there may be a cooperative norm to strive toward providing an answer rather than admitting ignorance. In general, how children interpret task instructions and their attentiveness to the range of available alternatives underscores their performance on tasks that require flexibility in meaning (Deák & Narasimham, 2003; Deák, Ray, & Pick, 2004; Merriman, Jarvis, & Marazita, 1995).

In other research on children's knowledge of the distinction between appearance and reality, both the timing and the extent to which children have gained access to language and participate in conversations seems critical. Compared with typically developing hearing children, late signing deaf children from hearing families who gain access to a sign language only once they come into contact with deaf signers outside their home appear to be impaired in their performance on appearance–reality tasks (Courtin & Melot, 2005), possibly because they are less aware of the experimenter's purpose and relevance in asking test questions about the appearance and reality of objects. At the same time, compared with monolingual children, children who acquire two languages early perform better on appearance–reality tasks, possibly because they are adept at inhibiting incorrect answers by switching appropriately from one dimension of an object to another (Bialystok & Senman, 2004). Alternatively, bilingual children may be pragmatically more skilled since they are exposed to a greater wealth of linguistic information and conversational experience than are monolingual children (Goetz, 2003).

Conversational Understanding and Conceptual Competence: The Case of Cosmology

The appearance–reality distinction is fundamental to knowledge in any causal domain, from biology to psychology and from physics to cosmology. To take one example, children need to learn that, though the earth looks flat, in reality it is a spherical body that revolves around the sun in a heliocentric solar system. In this respect, Vosniadou and her colleagues (Vosniadou & Brewer 1992; Vosniadou, Skopeliti, & Ikospentaki, 2004) have proposed that young children are constrained to confuse appearance with reality in believing that the outward appearance of a flat earth that they see is a genuine reflection of the earth's real shape. They can be seen to possess a naïve cosmology founded on the "entrenched presuppositions" that the earth is a flat plane (the "flatness" constraint) and that unsupported objects fall "down" (the "support" constraint). Thus, in Vosniadou's account, young children believe that the earth is in some sense flat (for example, forming a hemisphere topped by a platform on which people live), consistent with the everyday observation of the earth as a physically flat plane, and that it has an edge from which people could fall off, consistent with the everyday observation that unsupported objects fall down.

As children grow older, their naïve theory of the shape of the earth is said to come into contact with the culturally received view such as the accepted scientific case in Western countries that the earth is a spherically shaped body. When children are told that the earth is round, they are said to form "synthetic" mental models that guide their reasoning about the earth's shape. These mental models are an amalgam of the child's naïve theory based on entrenched presuppositions and the culturally received view.

Yet there persist a number of reservations concerning how children interpret the task and implications of test questions that prompt a reconsideration of this position. First, evidence is based largely on children's expertise in drawing and in constructing clay models. As children's art often does not correspond to their choice of representation of objects as these actually are (Ingram & Butterworth, 1989; Jolley, Knox, & Foster, 2000), their responses may reflect a lack of planning competence that underestimates their conceptual development. In this regard, a Gricean analysis suggests that children can interpret test questions like "Is there an edge or an end to the earth?" as "Is there an edge to the circle that you have drawn to represent the earth?" If so, they may offer an apparent flat earth response to an unintentionally ambiguous question when they actually hold no such belief. Second, as the children were repeatedly questioned on a theme ("Would you ever reach the edge of the earth? Say we kept on walking and walking and had plenty of food with us? Could you fall off the edge of the earth?"), they may vary their responses simply in an attempt to provide what the experimenter may consider to be the right answer. Children aged 4 years and older may believe, for example, that they have already answered a question about the edge of the earth that the experimenter had not accepted because she proceeded to rephrase and ask the question once again in the hope of soliciting a different answer. A third reservation is that children in many cultures may initially not detect the relevance of questions asked about cosmological concepts in that they have no models, beliefs or theories about the shape of the earth and the day–night cycle prior to scientific instruction. If so, they do not strive for empirical feedback on the accuracy of their beliefs for they may not have turned their minds to issues of cosmology and their answers to cosmological questions may reflect these post-hoc rationalizations rather than mental models based on entrenched presuppositions. An exception is Australia where, in contrast to countries such as England, children are given systematic instruction on cosmology at an early age and are aware that they are living on a large distinctively shaped land mass that is remote from other parts of the world that, nevertheless, share similarities in history, language, and culture.

In a recent comparison of Australian and English children's knowledge of the shape of the earth and the day–night cycle (Siegal, Butterworth, & Newcombe, 2004), Australian children were nearly always significantly in advance of their English counterparts. In response to explicit questioning designed to overcome the need to follow the implications of conversation, children often produced answers compatible with a conception of a round earth that rotates around the sun on which people can live all over without falling off. However, their level of performance was achieved only on tasks involving explicit, rather than open-ended, questioning for which children were often provided with a range of alternative answers. These answers were sometimes given to questions that referred to an array of 3D models (Figure 15.1) that in comparison with drawings and clay models provided unambiguous reference points. Panagiotaki, Nobes, and Banerjee (2006) report a study that corroborates these findings, further demonstrating the importance of both the form of questioning and the context in which the questions are posed on children's responses to measures of their cosmological understanding.

Therefore the questioning methods used in previous research may have underestimated children's competence in understanding certain key cosmological concepts (Schoultz, Saljo, & Wyndhamn, 2001). Indeed, "entrenched presuppositions" notwithstanding, children can be easily trained on factual aspects of cosmology (Hayes, Goodhew, Heit, & Gillan, 2003; Nobes, Martin, & Panagiotaki, 2005), in keeping with the results of recent studies showing that children at a very young age have knowledge of the

Figure 15.1 Choice of models to represent the shape of the earth (from Siegal et al., 2004).

distinction between appearance and reality – a knowledge that extends to an appreciation of the hidden non-obvious essence of objects and events despite their outward appearances (Gelman, 2003). As even adults may have trouble identifying explanatory cosmological concepts such as gravity (Hayes et al., 2003), research to date does not attribute to children a sophisticated understanding of cosmology but points to the existence of a grasp of factual information that serves as a "placeholder" until such an understanding is achieved – if it is to be at all – in adolescence and adulthood (Gelman, 2000; Medin, 1989).

Scalar Implicatures and the Development of Conversational Understanding

Conversational understanding, as shown on tasks designed to examine children's understanding of the appearance–reality distinction or certain scientific concepts, reflects a broad development in conversational competence that continues throughout childhood. Of particular concern is the ability to draw "scalar implicatures" that arise when a speaker uses a weak member of a scale (e.g., *some, or, might*) to imply that the stronger term of the scale (*all, and, must*) does not hold. For example, the utterance:

(1)   Some of the dwarfs loved Snow White

implies

(2)   Not every dwarf loved Snow White

Analysis of scalar implicatures can be traced back to J. S. Mill (1867, p. 501) who noticed that if I say to someone "I saw some of your children today" the hearer is induced to infer that I did not see them all, "not because the words mean it, but because, if I had seen them all, it is most likely that I should have said so...". According to Grice (1975), scalar implicatures exploit the quantity maxim to make one's contribution to the conversation as informative as possible since the speaker could have chosen an informationally more powerful term *all* but yet chose the weaker term *some*. In recognizing that the

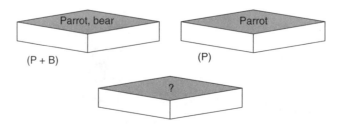

Figure 15.2   Design of a scalar implicature task (adapted from Noveck, 2001).

speaker declined the option to use *all*, the hearer draws the implication that the stronger statement (e.g., "All of the dwarfs loved Snow White") does not hold. Following Mill and Grice, systematic investigations have now been carried out on children's understanding of scalar implicatures in tasks involving the quantifiers *some* and *all*.

Noveck (2001) tested the proposal that the semantic or "logical" meaning of *some*, as compatible with *all*, appears earlier in development than its pragmatic, "some, but not all" meaning. He gave children aged 7 to 9 years and adults sentences such as "Some giraffes have long necks." Children assigned a logical meaning to *some* as compatible with *all* whereas adults often provided a pragmatic interpretation in rejecting this proposition. Similar patterns of results were obtained in tasks involving connectives (*and*, *or*) and epistemic modals (*might*, *must*). In the latter case (see Figure 15.2), the experimenter tells the children that there are two boxes (one that contains a parrot and bear and another that contains only a parrot) and says, "All I know is that whatever is inside this (lower) box looks like what's inside this box (P+B) or this box (P)." The children are then asked to evaluate the following statements as right or wrong: There has to be a parrot in the box (correct response: right). There doesn't have to be a parrot in the box (correct response: wrong). There cannot be a parrot in the box (correct response: wrong). There might be a parrot in the box (right on a semantic or logical interpretation but wrong on a pragmatic interpretation). Children's answers were consistent with earlier findings (Braine & Rumain, 1981; Smith, 1980) showing that young children prefer logical interpretations of connectives and modals (with *or* viewed as compatible with *and*, as well as *might* viewed as compatible with *must*).

However, when the goal of scalar implicature tasks is made more salient, even 5-year-olds can be prompted to choose a pragmatic rather than a logical interpretation. Papafragou and Musolino (2003) examined how 5-year-olds and adults judge the appropriateness of utterances that include the terms *start*, *some*, or *two* when used in contexts that would have justified the use of stronger terms (i.e., *finish*, *all*, and *three*, respectively). For example, participants were first shown three toy horses on a table and all of the horses jumped over a toy fence. Then a puppet said "Some horses jumped over the fence" and participants were asked to say whether "the puppet answered well." Adults overwhelmingly rejected such infelicitous, pragmatically deviant statements. By contrast, children performed less well in that they often accepted such infelicitous utterances, but their response depended on the type of statement and the clarity of the instructions. Their success was enhanced when the instructions and the procedure made it clear that they were expected to evaluate the felicity of utterances, rather than their truthfulness.

In a follow-up study, Papafragou and Tantalou (2004) gave 5-year-olds situations such as one involving an elephant described as having been told to color a set of four paper stars. When asked about what he had colored, the elephant is said to reply, "I colored some." In this situation, 5-year-olds often said that the elephant should not be given a prize, choosing the pragmatic interpretation, rather than the logical–semantic one.

As shown by research on the understanding of scalar implicatures, children at 5 to 6 years of age are not very skillful at detecting violations of conversational maxims. By comparison, older children and adults are proficient conversationalists who are sensitive to conventions and contexts – both linguistic and extra-linguistic – that serve to guide the interpretation of speakers' meanings. However, in certain contexts, young children are nevertheless able to draw the appropriate pragmatic inferences following violations of conversational maxims, particularly when they are aware of the goal of the task and when task demands and hence computational effort are reduced (Gualmini, Crain, & Meroni, 2001; Surian, 1995; Surian & Job, 1987). Further research is needed to individuate the crucial factors affecting children's ability to interpret scalar terms and to constrain future computational and developmental models of scalar and other related forms of implicatures.

Currently, there are two main models that aim to account for how scalar implicatures are processed. According to the position adopted by Levinson (2000), scalar implicatures are often automatically and effortlessly computed whenever a particular form occurs in an utterance. For example, in hearing "Some students are bright" we automatically infer that not all of them are bright. Contextual consideration only comes into play to replace the default interpretation with a more appropriate one (as in "My diet allows me to eat 2000 calories per day" which implies "at most," rather than the default "at least" or "exactly"). By contrast, relevance theory (Sperber & Wilson, 1995; Wilson & Sperber, 2004) proposes that all scalar implicatures are effortful as these are derived when the hearer is trying to compute an optimally relevant interpretation of the utterance.

The development of scalar implicatures in children would seem to support the effortful interpretation from relevance theory in that children, with increasing age, come to expend the effort required to detect the implications of quantifiers such as *some* apart from their semantic meaning (Pouscoulous & Noveck, 2004). Research with adults would also seem to support this position. For example, Bott and Noveck (2004; see also Breheny, Katsos, & Williams, 2006; Noveck & Posada, 2003) asked adult subjects to comprehend and evaluate infelicitous sentences such as "Some elephants are mammals." Those who rejected them (i.e., they interpreted the items by assigning the meaning "Some but not all elephants are mammals") took significantly longer to answer, indicating that those who were interpreting these items pragmatically were engaged in effortful inferential processing aimed at deriving an implicature.

Attention to Context in Research on Children's Sentence Processing

Disparities between the conversational understanding of 5-year-olds and adults are also apparent in research on attention to extra-linguistic contexts in experiments on sentence

Figure 15.3   Scene for a two-referent sentence processing task "Put the frog on the napkin into the box" (adapted from Trueswell et al., 1999, and Meroni & Crain, 2003).

processing. Trueswell, Sekerina, Hill, and Logrip (1999) showed 5-year-olds and adults two toy frogs, one resting on a napkin and one on a tray (see Figure 15.3). Next to the frogs there was another napkin with nothing resting on it. The experimenter's request was to "Put the frog on the napkin into the box." This request is processed far less efficiently by 5-year-olds than by adults. Whereas adults moved the frog on the napkin directly into the box, many children moved the frog that was on the tray onto the blank napkin and then put it into the box.

According to Trueswell et al., children are unlike adults in that they are easily led down the "garden path" in their use of extra-linguistic context to process sentences. The context may provide a distraction that leads them to believe, following the maxim of relation or relevance, that the presence of an empty napkin implies that it should be used in interpreting the experimenter's request or else it would be absent. However, children are capable of acknowledging ambiguity in the meaning of utterances that accompany such extra-linguistic contexts as shown by the pattern of their eye gaze (Sekerina, Stromswold, & Hestvik, 2004). The nature of the communicative setting can be such that even adults may not avoid distractions that preclude taking account of the listener's perspective whereas if these distractions are reduced even young children can communicate effectively (Keysar & Henly, 2002; Nadig & Sedivy, 2002).

Recently, Meroni and Crain (2003) have proposed that, for adults, the process of acting out instructions like "Put the frog on the napkin into the box" is based on a plan that is completely formed and compiled before it is executed. By contrast, a child listener might start to plan and even act while the instructions are still being uttered. According to Meroni and Crain (2003), should children's planning be less compiled or "automated" than adults, they may act out the meanings of sentences such as "Put the frog on the napkin into the box" in an order-of-mention fashion, whereas adults act them out in the order that is conceptually correct (e.g., using the "given" information first). As children interleave planning and execution, they may start to act out parts of the plan before all the planning that is necessary to interpret the sentence as intended has been completed. For example, children aged 4 to 6 years and adults can be asked to consider a row of six balls in an array where the second, third, and fifth balls from the left are striped:

When asked, "Point to the second striped ball," adults pointed to the third ball from the left, that is, the second striped one. By contrast, children often point to the second ball from the left, that happens to be striped (Matthei, 1981). However, if children's attention is drawn to the whole sentence before they are to act out the request, they are able to compile a plan that enables them to respond in an adult manner (Hamburger & Crain, 1984).

Following this analysis, Meroni and Crain (2003) report an experiment designed to enable children to respond as adults in "frog garden path" situations. The methodology involved two innovations. First, to prompt children to "inhibit" the pragmatic inference that the empty napkin was present in order that it should accommodate a frog, children aged 4 to 5 years were shown both frogs already sitting on a napkin. One frog sat on a blue napkin and the other on a red napkin. Second, to allow the children to formulate a plan without being overly distracted by salient features of the frogs, napkins, and box, the children were asked to turn away from the display while they listened to the target sentence, "Put the frog on the red napkin into the box." Meroni and Crain report that, under these conditions, there was a 93% correct performance rate. They suggest that children's failure to use referential information in previous research was due to their tendency to make a reasonable pragmatic inference and to execute action plans on the fly. Meroni and Crain maintain that, when steps are taken to block this inference and to prevent a premature execution of a plan for action, children demonstrate that they can parse sentences in the same way as adults by using referential information.

It is noteworthy that children's persistent difficulties with problems in which they are required to identify tautological and contradictory statements as illogical also have been viewed to reflect at least in part an incomplete problem solving strategy that is confined to the first part of a statement – an "order-of-mention" reaction that overlooks logical connectives and the second part of the statement (Fay & Klahr, 1996; Morris & Sloutsky, 2002). For example, they seek empirical verification for a tautological statement such as "It will rain today or it will not rain today" by responding only to the first part of the statement in terms of the current weather conditions, and to a tautological statement that refers to the outcome of a ball dropping game such as "The ball will land on red or will not land on red" by claiming that the ball has to be dropped on red to show that this statement is true. In the case of contradictory statements, preschoolers will often use local conversational concerns in an attempt to extract meaning rather than claim that such are simply nonsensical (Scholnick & Wing, 1991; Sharpe, Eakin, Saragovi, &

Macnamara, 1996). For example, they will interpret a statement such as "The dinner was good and wasn't good" as "The salad was good but the dessert was not." The extent to which young children can be trained to interpret tautological and contradictory statements in terms of logic rather than in terms of empirical verification remains in need of further study.

Characterizing Children's Conceptual Knowledge and Conversational Competence

Age differences in performance on scalar implicature and garden path sentence processing tasks illustrate how young children who are fluent conversationalists in their native language are yet to be proficient conversationalists. Young children may not follow conversational conventions that require pragmatic, rather than logical, interpretations of speakers' assertions and requests. Even in attempting a pragmatic interpretation, as shown in sentence processing tasks, they may process sentences by interpreting the extra-linguistic contexts of situations in a manner differently than those that speakers intend.

A lack of proficiency in interpreting speakers' messages as intended and in considering extra-linguistic contexts appropriately in compiling plans for action influences children's performance on measures of their conceptual competence. This is evident, for example, in their answers to test questions that concern their knowledge of the distinction between reality and the phenomenal world of appearances and their knowledge of certain scientific concepts such as those used in cosmology. Without proficiency in conversational competence, children and adults may not agree on the purpose and relevance of test questions to determine what children can and do know. For very young children, particularly at the age of 2 to 3 years, there may be a mismatch between what adults assume is a new question and what the child assumes to be simply a variant on the same theme. Thus as in their responses to appearance–reality tasks, children may persist with the same answer, creating a response bias, rather than varying their answer to fit the test questions as intended. Alternatively, adults may assume that they are asking questions on a single line of questioning that simply require confirmatory answers but the child does not recognize that the questioning amounts to a variation that they should ignore. Thus, for example, in response to questions about cosmological concepts such as the shape of the earth that may invoke different extra-linguistic contexts (e.g., circles to represent spheres and references to edges of shapes) children aged 4 years and older may vary their answer rather than persist with the same answer as intended.

Even so, as we have illustrated, children may be questioned under conditions in which the Gricean maxims are less likely to be put aside and in which the extra-linguistic context is less likely to require them to inhibit an inappropriate pragmatic inference. Under such conditions, children seem more likely to demonstrate the extent of their conceptual knowledge. It is important, however, to recognize that conceptual competence often remains to be achieved irrespective of children's conversational understanding. In the area of number, for example, children's concepts of fractions as shown in their responses to interviews and on number understanding tasks may reflect their representations of the minuteness of matter (Smith, Solomon, & Carey, 2005) – responses that might be seen in terms of children's conceptual development rather than their degree of sophistication in conversational pragmatics.

Children's sensitivity with age to conventions and contexts of conversations and the intended meaning of speakers can be considered to be an outgrowth of a mechanism that facilitates the expression of "theory of mind" (ToM) reasoning. According to Leslie's influential account, ToM reasoning involves metarepresentational abilities that concern the mental world of others – their beliefs, feelings, interests, intentions, and other mental states and how others' beliefs may differ from one's own beliefs and from reality. Metarepresentation can be seen to require both a rich innate core competence (Leslie, 1987) and, as shown in work with deaf children, early exposure to conversation (Woolfe, Want, & Siegal, 2002). During conversation, speakers are required to constantly update their representations of their interlocutors' mind and to infer their informative and communicative intentions (Grice, 1989). This process requires increasing accuracy in planning and executing responses to linguistic and extra-linguistic contexts in conversation. As noted elsewhere (Harris, 1996; Harris, de Rosnay, & Pons, 2005; Siegal & Surian, in press; Siegal & Varley, 2002), it is not grammatical understanding in language that permits ToM reasoning based on propositions about others' beliefs. Rather, early access to language and immersion in conversation acts as a spur for attentional development that enables children to gain insight into speakers' beliefs and other mental states.

In this sense, one mechanism that underpins improvements in conversational understanding with age can be seen as similar to Leslie's Selection Processor (SP) that enables children to express ToM reasoning accurately. The SP can be defined as a mechanism of attention – an "executive functioning" process – that permits children to compute the true or false contents of others' beliefs correctly (Friedman & Leslie, 2004; Leslie, Friedman, & German, 2004; Leslie, German, & Polizzi, 2005). For example, ToM reasoning measures often take the form of a "Sally-Anne" task (Baron-Cohen, Leslie, & Frith, 1985) in which children are told about Sally, a story character with a false belief about the location of a ball. Sally is described as having placed the ball in a box but, when she is away, another story character called Anne moves it into a different location. The test question concerns where Sally – who has not witnessed the deception and therefore has a false belief – will look for the ball. Whereas most 3-year-olds have difficulty with the Sally-Anne task in this form, most 4-year-olds succeed. According to Leslie, this transition occurs not because children are undergoing a conceptual change that leads to the understanding that beliefs may be true or false but because the SP comes on-line. The SP enables 4-year-olds to recognize that the question refers not to the straightforward issue of where Sally will have to look or must look for the ball but instead carries that implication that it refers to where Sally will look first. Asking the more explicit question "Where will Sally look first for her ball?" enables most 3-year-olds children to "inhibit" the interpretation that the question refers to where Sally will have to look or must look for the ball and instead to interpret the question as intended to refer to the consequences of Sally holding an initial false belief about the location of an object (Joseph, 1998; Nelson et al., 2003; Siegal & Beattie, 1991; Surian & Leslie, 1999; Yazdi et al., 2006). Put somewhat differently, the standard test question "Where will

Sally look for her ball?" conveys less information than is needed for effective communication and hence departs from Grice's quality maxim whereas the simple addition of "first" to the question now enables the child to interpret the test question as intended.

Executive functioning mechanisms, similar to that of a ToM-SP, may serve to underpin the development of conversational understanding by ensuring that both speakers and listeners are communicating cooperatively on the basis of mutually held beliefs. Here we suggest that three mechanisms of executive functioning delineated by Miyake, Friedman, Emerson, Witzki, and Howerter (2000) are particularly relevant. First, there is the process of "shifting" between tasks involving the ability to perform another operation without distraction. Second is the "updating" function that requires monitoring and coding incoming information for relevance to the task at hand and then revising working memory by replacing older irrelevant information with new relevant information. Then there is a third executive function that involves the "inhibition" of prepotent responses. Clearly, proficiency in conversational understanding requires skill in all three functions. Children need to shift back and forth between alternative interpretations of utterances, to update representations of the linguistic and extra-linguistic contexts of utterances, and to inhibit prepotent responses. In the latter case, for example, children need to recognize the possibility that speakers who according to a Gricean framework are usually assumed to abide by the quality maxim and not to deceive can be sarcastic or utter falsehoods. A direction for further research is to specify the exact nature of these mechanisms in terms of the range of information required to interpret speakers' messages as these are intended. In this respect, research on selective impairments in children's pragmatic abilities (e.g., Bishop & Baird, 2001; Bishop & Norbury, 2002; Martin & McDonald, 2003; Whalen, Talbot, Eskritt, & Lee, 2002) is especially likely to illuminate the role of diverse executive functions in the development of conversational understanding.

Conclusion

Links between children's conversational understanding and responses to tasks designed to evaluate their conceptual development are clearly evident. The gap between the conversational experience of adults and children requires a consideration of developmental processes that characterize children's conversational understanding, together with the important methodological problem of how adults should pose questions to children with the aim of determining their conceptual competence. Research on children's knowledge of the appearance–reality distinction and their appreciation of basic cosmological concepts provides illustrations of how children may misinterpret the linguistic and extra-linguistic contexts of questions designed to determine what they know. Studies of children's responses to scalar implicature and sentence processing tasks demonstrate the extent to which task success demands sophistication in planning and attending to the relevant criteria for interpreting an utterance. From the research reviewed here, it can be seen that experimental tasks and test questions can often be framed in a way that circumvents the gap between the conversational experience of children and adults in order to draw out more clearly the nature of children's conceptual competence.

In the light of recent research, the need to acquire a conceptual distinction between literal meaning and speaker's meaning that was viewed as central to conversational understanding more than 20 years ago can now be seen in terms of another explanation that involves an emphasis on attentional development rather than conceptual change. When a mother says to her messy child, "you are really tidy now and your toys are put away nicely," the child – who already knows that messages can have more than one interpretation – needs to attend to the intended sarcastic meaning that, in fact, is the opposite of its literal interpretation. Systematically taking issues of conversational understanding into account promises to lead to a richer, more complete account of conceptual development and conceptual competence.

Note

This chapter was prepared with the support of a Leverhulme Trust Research Interchange Grant, and has been adapted in part from *Trends in Cognitive Sciences, 7*, 534–538 (2004).

References

Baron-Cohen, S., Leslie, A. M., & Frith, U. (1985). Does the autistic child have a theory of mind? *Cognition, 21*, 37–46.

Beal, C. R., & Flavell, J. H. (1984). Development of the ability to distinguish communicative intention and literal message meaning. *Child Development, 55*, 920–928.

Bialystok, E., & Senman, L. (2004). Executive processes in appearance–reality tasks: The role of inhibition of attention and symbolic representation. *Child Development, 75*, 562–579.

Bishop, D. V. M., & Baird, G. (2001). Parent and teacher report of pragmatic aspects of communication: Use of the children's communication checklist in a clinical setting. *Developmental Medicine and Child Neurology, 43*, 809–818.

Bishop, D. V. M., & Norbury, C. F. (2002). Exploring the borderlands of autistic disorder and specific language impairment: A study using standardised diagnostic instruments. *Journal of Child Psychology and Psychiatry, 43*, 917–929.

Bott, L., & Noveck, I. A. (2004). Some utterances are underinformative: The onset and time course of scalar implicatures. *Journal of Memory and Language, 51*, 437–457.

Braine, M., & Rumain, B. (1981). Children's comprehension of 'or': Evidence for a sequence of competences. *Journal of Experimental Child Psychology, 31*, 46–70.

Breheny, R., Katsos, N., & Williams, J. (2006). Are generalised scalar implicatures generated by default? An on-line investigation into the role of context in generating pragmatic inferences. *Cognition, 100*, 434–463.

Bright-Paul, A., Jarrold, C., & Wright, D. B. (2005). Age-appropriate cues facilitate source-monitoring and reduce suggestibility in 3- to 7-year-olds. *Cognitive Development, 20*, 1–18.

Carston, R. (1998). Informativeness, relevance and scalar implicature. In R. Carston & S. Uchida (Eds.), *Relevance theory: Applications and implications* (pp. 179–236). Amsterdam: Benjamins.

Carston, R. (2002). *Thoughts and utterances: The pragmatics of explicit communication.* Oxford: Blackwell.

Clark, E. V. (1997). Conceptual perspective and lexical choice. *Cognition, 64,* 1–37.

Clark, H. H. (1996). *Using language.* New York: Cambridge University Press.

Courtin, C., & Melot, A-M. (2005). Metacognitive development of deaf children: Lessons from the appearance–reality and false belief tasks. *Developmental Science, 8,* 16–25.

Deák, G. O., & Narasimham, G. (2003). Is perseveration caused by inhibition failure? Evidence from preschool children's inferences about word meanings. *Journal of Experimental Child Psychology, 86,* 194–222.

Deák, G. O., Ray, S. D., & Brenneman, K. (2003). Children's perseverative appearance–reality errors are related to emerging language skills. *Child Development, 74,* 944–964.

Deák, G. O., Ray, S. D., & Pick, A. D. (2004). Effects of age, reminders, and task difficulty on young children's rule-switching flexibility. *Cognitive Development, 19,* 385–400.

Deák, G. O., Yen, L., & Pettit, J. (2001). By any other name: when will preschoolers produce several labels for a referent? *Journal of Child Language, 28,* 787–804.

Donaldson, M. (1978). *Children's minds.* Glasgow: Fontana.

Fay, A. L., & Klahr, D. (1996). Knowing about guessing and guessing about knowing: Preschoolers' understanding of indeterminacy. *Child Development, 67,* 689–716.

Flavell, J. H., Green, F. L., & Flavell, E. R. (1986). Development of the appearance–reality distinction. *Monographs of the Society for Research in Child Development, 51* (Serial No. 212).

Friedman, O., & Leslie, A. M. (2004). Mechanisms of belief–desire reasoning. *Psychological Science, 15,* 547–552.

Fritzley, V. H., & Lee, K. (2003). Do young children always say yes to yes–no questions? A metadevelopmental study of the affirmation bias. *Child Development, 74,* 1297–1313.

Gauvain, M., & Greene, J. K. (1994). What do children know about objects? *Cognitive Development, 9,* 311–329.

Gazdar, G. (1979). *Pragmatics.* New York: Academic Press.

Gelman, R., Meck, E., & Merkin, S. (1986). Young children's numerical competence. *Cognitive Development, 1,* 1–29.

Gelman, S. A. (2000). The role of essentialism in children's concepts. *Advances in Child Development and Behavior, 27,* 55–98.

Gelman, S. A. (2003). *The essential child.* New York: Oxford University Press.

Gelman, S. A., & Bloom, P. (2000). Young children are sensitive to how an object was created when deciding what to name it. *Cognition, 76,* 91–103.

Gelman, S. A., & Ebeling, K. S. (1998). Shape and representational status in children's early naming. *Cognition, 66,* B35–B47.

German, T., & Leslie, A. M. (2001). Children's inferences from *knowing* to *pretending* and *believing. British Journal of Developmental Psychology, 19,* 59–83.

Glucksberg, S. (2003). The psycholinguistics of metaphor. *Trends in Cognitive Sciences, 7,* 92–96.

Goetz, P. J. (2003). The effects of bilingualism on theory of mind development. *Bilingualism, 6,* 1–15.

Grice, H. P. (1975). Logic and conversation. In P. Cole & J. L. Morgan (Eds.), *Syntax and semantics: Vol. 3. Speech acts* (pp. 41–58). New York: Academic Press.

Grice, H. P. (1989). *Studies in the way of words.* Cambridge, MA: Harvard University Press.

Gualmini, A., Crain, S., & Meroni, L. (2001). At the semantic/pragmatic interface in child language. *Proceedings of Semantics and Linguistic Theory XI.* Ithaca, NY: CLC Publications.

Hamburger, H., & Crain, S. (1984). Acquisition of cognitive compiling. *Cognition, 17,* 85–136.

Hansen, M. B., & Markman, E. M. (2005). Appearance questions can be misleading: A discourse-based account of the appearance–reality problem. *Cognitive Psychology, 50,* 233–263.

Harris, P. L. (1996). Desires, beliefs, and language. In P. Carruthers & P. K. Smith (Eds.), *Theories of Theory of Mind* (pp. 200–220). New York: Cambridge University Press.

Harris, P. L., de Rosnay, M., & Pons, F. (2005). Language and children's understanding of mental states. *Current Directions in Psychological Science, 14,* 69–73.

Hayes, B. K., Goodhew, A., Heit, E., & Gillan, J. (2003). The role of diverse instruction in conceptual change. *Journal of Experimental Child Psychology, 86,* 253–276.

Horn, L. R. (1989). *A natural history of negation.* Chicago: University of Chicago Press.

Howie, P., Sheehan, M., Mojarrad, T., & Wrzesinska, M. (2004). 'Undesirable' and 'desirable' shifts in children's responses to repeated questions: Age differences in the effect of providing a rationale for repetition. *Applied Cognitive Psychology, 18,* 1161–1180.

Ingram, N., & Butterworth, G. E. (1989). The young child's representation of depth in drawing: process and product. *Journal of Experimental Child Psychology, 47,* 356–369.

Jolley, R., Knox, E., & Foster, S. (2000). The relationship between children's production and comprehension of realism in drawing. *British Journal of Developmental Psychology, 18,* 557–582.

Joseph, R. M. (1998). Intention and knowledge in preschoolers' conception of pretend. *Child Development, 69,* 966–980.

Keysar, B., & Henly, A. S. (2002). Speakers' overestimation of their effectiveness. *Psychological Science, 13,* 207–212.

Leslie, A. M. (1987). Pretense and representation: The origins of 'theory of mind'. *Psychological Review, 94,* 412–426.

Leslie, A. M., Friedman, O., & German, T. P. (2004). Core mechanisms in 'theory of mind.' *Trends in Cognitive Sciences, 8,* 528–533.

Leslie, A. M., German, T. P., & Polizzi, P. (2005). Belief–desire reasoning as a process of selection. *Cognitive Psychology, 50,* 45–85.

Levinson, S. (2000). *Presumptive meanings.* Cambridge, MA: MIT Press.

Matthei, E. M. (1981). The acquisition of prenominal modifier sequences. *Cognition, 11,* 301–332.

Medin, D. L. (1989). Concepts and conceptual structure. *American Psychologist, 44,* 1469–1481.

Martin, I., & McDonald, S. (2003). Weak coherence, no theory of mind, or executive dysfunction? Solving the puzzle of pragmatic language disorders. *Brain and Language, 85,* 451–466.

Meroni, L., & Crain, S. (2003). On not being led down the kindergarten path. *Proceedings of the 25th Annual Boston University Conference on Language Development.* Somerville, MA: Cascadilla Press.

Merriman, W. E., Jarvis, L. H., & Marazita, J. M. (1995). How shall a deceptive thing be called? *Journal of Child Language, 22,* 129–149.

Mill, J. S. (1867). *An Examination of Sir William Hamilton's Philosophy* (3rd ed.). London: Longman.

Miyake, A., Friedman, N. P., Emerson, M. J., Witzki, A. H., & Howerter, A. (2000). The unity and diversity of executive functions and their contributions to complex "frontal lobe" tasks: A latent variable analysis. *Cognitive Psychology, 41,* 49–100.

Morris, B. J., & Sloutsky, V. (2002). Children's solutions of logical versus empirical problems: What's missing and what develops? *Cognitive Development, 16,* 907–928.

Nadig, A. S., & Sedivy, J. C. (2002). Evidence of perspective-taking constraints in children's on-line reference resolution. *Psychological Science, 13,* 329–336.

Nelson, K., Skwerer, D. P., Goldman, S., Henseler, S., Presler, N., & Walkenfeld, F. F. (2003). Entering a community of minds: An experiential approach to 'theory of mind.' *Human Development, 46*, 24–46.

Ninio, A., & Snow, C. E. (1996). *Pragmatic development.* Boulder, CO: Westview Press.

Nobes, G., Martin, A., & Panagiotaki, G. (2005). The development of scientific knowledge of the earth. *British Journal of Developmental Psychology, 23*, 47–64.

Noveck, I. (2001). When children are more logical than adults: Experimental investigation of scalar implicatures. *Cognition, 78*, 165–188.

Noveck, I. A., & Posada, A. (2003). Characterizing the time course of an implicature: An evoked potentials study. *Brain and Language, 85*, 203–210.

Osherson, D., & Markman, E. (1975). Language and the ability to evaluate contradictions and tautologies. *Cognition, 86*, 213–226.

Panagiotaki, G., Nobes, G., & Banerjee, R. (2006). Children's representations of the earth: A methodological comparison. *British Journal of Developmental Psychology, 24*, 353–372.

Papafragou, A., & Musolino, J. (2003). Scalar implicatures: experiments at the semantics–pragmatics interface. *Cognition, 86*, 253–282.

Papafragou, A., & Tantalou, N. (2004). Children's computation of implicatures. *Language Acquisition, 12*, 71–82.

Pipe, M. E., Lamb, M. E., Orbach, Y., & Esplin, P. W. (2004). Recent research on children's testimony about experienced and witnessed events. *Developmental Review, 24*, 440–468.

Pouscoulous, N., & Noveck, I. A. (2004). Implicature et développement. *Psychologie Francaise, 49*, 193–207.

Rice, C., Koinis, D., Sullivan, K., Tager-Flusberg, H., & Winner, E. (1997). When 3-year-olds pass the appearance–reality test. *Developmental Psychology, 33*, 54–61.

Robinson, E. J., Goelman, H., & Olson, D. (1983). Children's understanding of the relation between expressions (what was said) and intentions (what was meant). *British Journal of Developmental Psychology, 1*, 75–86.

Sapp, F., Lee, K., & Muir, D. (2000). Three-year-olds' difficulty with the appearance–reality distinction: Is it real or is it apparent? *Developmental Psychology, 36*, 547–560.

Scholnick, E. K., & Wing, C. S. (1991). Speaking deductively: Preschoolers use of *If* in conversation and in conditional inference. *Developmental Psychology, 27*, 249–258.

Schoultz, J., Saljo, R., & Wyndhamn, J. (2001). Heavenly talk: Discourse, artifacts, and children's understanding of elementary astronomy. *Human Development, 44*, 103–118.

Sekerina, I. A., Stromswold, K., & Hestvik, A. (2004). How do adults and children process referentially ambiguous pronouns? *Journal of Child Language, 31*, 123–152.

Sharpe, D., Eakin, L., Saragovi, C., & Macnamara, J. (1996). Adults' and preschoolers' ability to cope with non-classical negation. *Journal of Child Language, 23*, 675–691.

Shatz, M. (1978). On the development of communicative understandings: An early strategy for interpreting and responding to messages. *Cognitive Psychology, 10*, 271–301.

Shatz, M. (1994). *A toddler's life.* New York: Oxford University Press.

Shatz, M., & McCloskey, L. (1984). Answering appropriately: A developmental perspective on conversational knowledge. In S. A. Kuczaj II (Ed.), *Discourse development* (pp. 19–36). New York: Springer-Verlag.

Siegal, M. (1997). *Knowing children: Experiments in conversation and cognition* (2nd ed.). Philadelphia: Psychology Press.

Siegal, M. (1999). Language and thought: The fundamental significance of conversational awareness for cognitive development. *Developmental Science, 2*, 1–34.

Siegal, M., & Beattie, K. (1991). Where to look first for children's knowledge of false beliefs. *Cognition, 38*, 1–12.

Siegal, M., Butterworth, G., & Newcombe, P. A. (2004). Culture and children's cosmology. *Developmental Science, 7*, 308–324.

Siegal, M., & Surian, L. (in press). Modularity in language and theory of mind: What is the evidence? In P. Carruthers, S. Laurence, & S. Stich (Eds.), *The innate mind: Culture and cognition.* New York: Oxford University Press.

Siegal, M., & Varley, R. (2002). Neural systems involved in 'theory of mind'. *Nature Reviews Neuroscience, 3*, 463–471.

Smith, C. (1980). Quantifiers and question-answering in young children. *Journal of Experimental Child Psychology, 30*, 191–205.

Smith, C. L., Solomon, G. E. A., & Carey, S. (2005). Never getting to zero: Elementary school students' understanding of the infinite divisibility of number and matter. *Cognitive Psychology, 51*, 101–140.

Sperber, D., & Wilson, D. (1995). *Relevance: Communication and cognition* (2nd ed.). Oxford: Blackwell.

Sperber, D., & Wilson, D. (2002). Pragmatics, modularity and mindreading. *Mind and Language, 17*, 3–23.

Surian, L. (1995). Children's ambiguous utterances – a reexamination of processing limitations on production. *Journal of Child Language, 22*, 151–169.

Surian, L., & Job, R. (1987). Children's use of conversational rules in a referential communication task. *Journal of Psycholinguistic Research, 16*, 369–382.

Surian, L., & Leslie, A. M. (1999). Competence and performance in false belief understanding: A comparison of autistic and normal 3-year-old children. *British Journal of Developmental Psychology, 17*, 141–155.

Trueswell, J. C., Sekerina, I., Hill, N. M., & Logrip, M. L. (1999). The kindergarten-path effect: studying on-line sentence processing in young children. *Cognition, 73*, 89–134.

Vosniadou, S., & Brewer, W. F. (1992). Mental models of the earth: A study of conceptual change in childhood. *Cognitive Psychology, 24*, 535–585.

Vosniadou, S., Skopeliti, I., & Ikospentaki, K. (2004). Modes of knowing and ways of reasoning in elementary astronomy. *Cognitive Development, 19*, 203–222.

Waterman, A. H., Blades, M., & Spencer, C. (2001). Interviewing children and adults: The effect of question format on the tendency to speculate. *Applied Cognitive Psychology, 15*, 1–11.

Waterman, A. H., Blades, M., & Spencer, C. (2004). Indicating when you do not know the answer: The effect of question format and interviewer knowledge on children's 'don't know' responses. *British Journal of Developmental Psychology, 22*, 335–348.

Whalen, J., Talbot, P., Eskritt, M., & Lee, K. (2002). *Recognition of the Gricean Maxims by 3- to 5- year-olds.* Paper presented at the Biennial Meeting of the International Society for the Study of Behavioral Development, Ottawa.

Wilson, D., & Sperber, D. (2004). Relevance theory. In G. Ward & L. Horn (Eds.), *Handbook of pragmatics* (pp. 607–632). Oxford: Blackwell.

Winner, E. (1988). *The point of words: Children's understanding of metaphor and irony.* Cambridge, MA: Harvard University Press.

Woolfe, T., Want, S. C., & Siegal, M. (2002). Signposts to development: Theory of mind in deaf children. *Child Development, 73*, 768–778.

Yazdi, A. A., German, T. P., Defeyer, M., & Siegal, M. (2006). Competence and performance in belief–desire reasoning across two cultures: The truth, the whole truth, and nothing but the truth about false belief? *Cognition, 100*, 343–368.

16

Bilingual First Language Acquisition

Fred Genesee and Elena Nicoladis

This chapter focuses on the simultaneous acquisition of two languages from birth, or what is generally referred to as bilingual first language acquisition (BFLA). A major question in studies of BFLA, and a focus of our review, is whether the developmental path and timecourse of language development in BFL learners is the same as that of children learning only one language. Underlying this question is the theoretical issue of whether children's ability to learn language is challenged in any way by the acquisition of two languages at the same time. Evidence that the rate of language development is slowed down in BFL learners compared with monolingual learners would argue that the ability that all children have to learn language is compromised by the challenge of learning more than one language at the same time. An additional issue is whether exposure to two languages simultaneously influences the pattern of development so that it differs from that observed in monolingual learners. Evidence that the patterns are different could give us insights as to how the processes that underlie language acquisition cope with dual language input.

The study of BFLA has had a remarkably long history. In 1913, Ronjat published a detailed description of his son Louis' simultaneous acquisition of French and German. Louis showed remarkable progress in both his languages and little sign of confusion. Ronjat attributed Louis' lack of confusion to both parents' use of only one language with him. This conclusion was brought into doubt in 1949 when Leopold published the last volume of a detailed diary of his daughter's (Hildegard) simultaneous acquisition of English and German. Leopold claimed that the parents were insistent on a one parent–one language rule. Yet Hildegard passed through a stage when she used words from both languages, a fact that Leopold interpreted as a sign that she had confused her two languages and was functioning as a monolingual. These diarists set the tone for the study of BFLA to this day. That BFL learners might go through an initial monolingual stage, as initially proposed by Leopold, is but one instance of the more general concern that BFLA strains the child's language learning capacity, leading to delayed and even impaired forms of language development (e.g., see Smith, 1935, for an early expression of this view). This concern has been expressed in a number of ways: BFLA might result in impaired cognitive, as well as linguistic, development (Bialystok, 2001); bilingual education puts children at risk for academic failure or delay (e.g., Macnamara, 1966); or BFL learners will be socio-cultural misfits, identifying strongly with neither language group (Diebold, 1968).

Different criteria have been proposed to distinguish simultaneous from successive dual language learners. De Houwer (1995) has proposed the stringent cut-off of exposure to two languages within one month of birth, while McLaughlin (1978), in an early review of bilingual acquisition research, proposed the much more lenient cut-off of exposure to two languages before 3 years of age. Whether acquisition of an additional language within one, two, or three years of birth entails different processes and outcomes is an empirical question with important theoretical implications. We limit our discussion to simultaneous acquisition from birth to about 4 years of age. Even with these limits, there is considerable heterogeneity among BFL learners because BFLA is impacted by all those factors that can affect monolingual acquisition as well as bilingual-specific factors, such as different language combinations and differences in the amount, consistency, and contexts of language exposure.

Our review of the research on BFLA is organized around three topics: (1) the development of morphosyntax, the lexicon, and phonology, (2) code-mixing, and (3) communicative competence.

The Development of Two Languages Simultaneously

Much of the research on the development of two languages simultaneously has been motivated by the unitary language system hypothesis according to which children exposed to two languages go through an initial stage when the languages are not differentiated (Leopold, 1949; Volterra & Taeschner, 1978; see Genesee, 1989, for a review). The most explicit formulation of this hypothesis was presented by Volterra and Taeschner (1978, p. 312):

> In the first stage the child has one lexical system which includes words from both languages . . . in this stage the language development of the bilingual child seems to be like the language development of the monolingual child . . .
>
> In the second stage, the child distinguishes two different lexicons, but applies the same syntactic rules to both languages.
>
> In the third stage the child speaks two languages differentiated both in lexicon and syntax . . .

Volterra and Taeschner's hypothesis, in effect, proposed that the initial state of the developing bilingual child is essentially monolingual. A corollary issue is whether the two languages of bilingual children develop autonomously or interdependently (Paradis & Genesee, 1996). Interdependent development would result from systemic influence of one language on the development of the other, resulting in patterns or rates of development that differ from what would be expected in monolingual children.

These theoretical and practical concerns have resulted in research that compares the development of bilingual children with that of monolingual children acquiring the same languages. On the one hand, this may be an inappropriate frame of reference because it stigmatizes bilingual patterns of development and risks attributing differences that bilingual children exhibit to deficits in children's capacity to acquire two languages at the same time (Cook, 2002). Alternatively, the linguistic competencies of bilingual children, like those of bilingual adults, should be examined and evaluated on their own merit (Grosjean, 1997). On the other hand, such comparisons are widespread in clinical and lay-communities and, thus, can have important real-world implications. Scientific comparisons between bilingual and monolingual children can reveal the extent to which BFLA actually differs from monolingual acquisition and, most importantly, what such differences mean.

Morphosyntax

Most of the research on BFLA of morphosyntax has examined production rather than perception (see Gerken, this volume, for research on related aspects of early monolingual language development). Contrary to the claims of the unitary language system hypothesis, there is widespread agreement that BFL learners acquire language-specific properties of the target languages early in development and these correspond, for the most part, to those exhibited by same-age monolingual children (see De Houwer, 1990, 2005; Deuchar & Quay, 2000; Genesee, 2001; Meisel, 2001, for reviews). Paradis and Genesee (1996), for example, found that 2- to 3-year-old French–English bilingual children: (1) used finite verb forms earlier in French than in English[1]; (2) used subject pronouns in French exclusively with finite verbs but subject pronouns in English with both finite and non-finite verbs, in accordance with the status of subject pronouns in French as clitics (or agreement markers); and (3) placed verbal negatives after lexical verbs in French (e.g., *n'aime pas*) but before lexical verbs in English (*do not like*). These patterns characterize the performance of monolingual children acquiring these languages. Findings from research on BFLA also generally indicate that bilingual children exhibit the same rate of morphosyntactic development as monolingual children, at least in their dominant language (see reviews in De Houwer, 2005; Nicoladis & Genesee, 1997; Paradis & Genesee, 1996; but see Oller & Jarmulowicz, this volume, for different results). This is evident even in bilingual children who are identified as having a specific language impairment. More specifically, Paradis, Crago, Genesee, and Rice (2003) found that French–English bilingual children in Quebec with specific language impairment exhibited the same pattern and degree of impairment in each language as similarly impaired monolingual English and French children of the same age.

At the same time, there is evidence of cross-linguistic transfer of specific morphosyntactic features from one language into the other (Döpke, 2000; Hulk & van der Linden, 1996; Müller, 1999; Nicoladis, 2002, 2003; Paradis & Navarro, 2003; Yip & Matthews, 2000). Döpke (2000), for example, found that Australian children learning English and

German simultaneously used -VO word order much more in all verbal clauses in their German than native, monolingual speakers of German. German uses both -VO and -OV word order: -VO in main clauses and both -VO and -OV word order in subordinate clauses; English, in contrast, uses -VO order in main and subordinate clauses. Working within the competition model of Bates and MacWhinney (1987), Döpke argued that her young subjects were prone to overgeneralize -VO word order in their German because the -VO order was reinforced on the surface of both the German and the English input they heard whereas -OV order appeared in only a limited number of subordinate German clauses. Working within a Universal Grammar framework, Hulk and Müller (2000, p. 229) have similarly argued that "there has to be a certain overlap[2] of the two systems at the surface level" for cross-linguistic syntactic transfer to occur. These explanations have been questioned, given that children sometimes show signs of cross-linguistic transfer for non-overlapping morphosyntactic structures (Nicoladis, 2002).

A mitigating factor in cross-linguistic transfer could be language dominance. Children might be more likely to incorporate structures from their dominant into their weaker language than vice versa (Döpke, 1998; Petersen, 1988; Yip & Matthews, 2000). For example, Yip and Matthews found evidence of transfer from Cantonese to English in a Cantonese–English learning child during a period when he was dominant in Cantonese. Matthews and Yip (2003) have suggested another mitigating factor, namely that asynchronous development of two languages with respect to specific features (e.g., relative clause constructions in Chinese and English) might also result in transfer of a structure that is normally acquired earlier in one language (e.g., Chinese) to the language in which the corresponding structure is normally acquired later (e.g., English) (see also Gawlitzek-Maiwald & Tracy, 1996; Paradis & Genesee, 1996). Dominance alone cannot explain all manifestations of cross-linguistic transfer observed thus far (Müller, 1999; Nicoladis, 2002). Instances of cross-linguistic transfer that have been reported are restricted. They pertain to specific aspects of the child's developing grammars and they appear to occur only under certain circumstances, as noted previously.

Lexicon

Studies that have examined age of first word production report that bilingual children produce their first words at about the same age as monolingual children – 12 to 13 months (Genesee, 2003a; Patterson & Pearson, 2004). Other milestones of lexical acquisition in bilingual and monolingual children are also similar – bilingual children's rates of vocabulary acquisition generally fall within the range reported for same-age monolinguals, as long as both languages are considered for bilinguals (Pearson, Fernández, & Oller, 1993), and the distribution of lexical categories (e.g., noun, verb, etc.) in the early lexicons of bilingual children is similar to that observed in monolingual children (Nicoladis, 2001). The relative amount of time spent in each language can affect the relative vocabulary size in each language of a bilingual (Pearson, Fernández, Lewedag, & Oller, 1997).

It is well established that monolingual children's acquisition of new words is guided by the principle of mutual exclusivity, or the assumption that new words tend to refer to new referents (Markman, Wasow, & Hansen, 2003). Bilingual children's acquisition of translation equivalents (words in each language that have the same referential meaning) is of interest because, prima facie, this would violate the principle of mutual exclusivity. However, evidence that bilingual children acquire translation equivalents could be used to argue that they are not acquiring one language, but two (Patterson & Pearson, 2004). A number of researchers have reported that bilingual children produce translation equivalents from the time they first begin to speak (Pearson, Fernández, & Oller, 1995) or at least by 8 months on (Deuchar & Quay, 2000; Genesee, Paradis, & Wolf, 1995; Nicoladis, 1998; Nicoladis & Genesee, 1996; Quay, 1995). Lanvers (1999) and Nicoladis and Secco (2000) found further that bilingual children used relatively few translation equivalents before the age of 1;5, but the percentage of translation equivalents in their two languages jumped subsequently to around 20–25% of their total vocabulary words thereafter. The high rate of translation equivalents, a clear violation of mutual exclusivity, suggests that at least from this age on children have two distinct lexical systems. It is possible that the ability to violate mutual exclusivity may be learned through experience of interpreting people's intentions about what words mean (Deuchar & Quay, 2000).

Phonology

Researchers have been interested in whether children with simultaneous dual language exposure exhibit the same patterns of phonological development and progress at the same rate as children with monolingual exposure, in terms of both perception and production (see also Polka, Rvachew, and Mattock; Gerken, this volume, for further discussion of related issues). A corollary issue in the production studies has been when children with dual language exposure give evidence of having two phonological systems. Most of the research on phonological development has been carried out in the last 10 years and must be interpreted with caution because it is diverse in linguistic focus and in the ages of the children who have been studied. Nevertheless, the picture that is emerging indicates that bilingual children show a tendency for different patterns of development in both prosodic (at the level of the syllable, such as rhythm) and segmental (at the level of the phoneme, such as phonemic discrimination) phonology compared with monolingual children (Vihman, 1996).

Research on speech perception during the preverbal stage of development has shown that monolingual infants can differentiate between their native (input) language and a "foreign language" (Mehler, Dupoux, Nazzi, & Dehaene-Lambertz, 1996) if the languages belong to different rhythmic groups (e.g., French and Russian), and they can differentiate between languages within the same rhythmic group (e.g., Spanish and Catalan) by 4.5 months of age (Bosch & Sebastián-Gallés, 1997; see Polka et al., this volume). Bosch and Sebastián-Gallés (1997) have found that 4-month-old infants exposed to both Spanish and Catalan have similar language differentiation abilities, indicating that reduced exposure to each language does not delay the emergence of this ability in bilinguals (see Sebastián-Gallés & Bosch, 2005, for a detailed review of these studies). The ability to distinguish between two languages early in development provides an important part of the foundation for building separate linguistic systems.

Research that has examined the early perception of segmental features of speech has found that children with dual language exposure from birth exhibit the same abilities as monolingual children but at a somewhat later age (see Polka et al.; Gerken, this volume). Monolingual infants are initially able to discriminate phonetic contrasts that are not necessarily phonemic in their native language (see Vihman, 1996, for a review). However, their discrimination abilities become language-specific during the second half of the first year of life so that they continue to discriminate contrasts that are phonemic in their native language, but cannot discriminate contrasts that are not phonemic. Vowel contrasts are perceived phonemically earlier (by 6–8 months of age; Bosch & Sebastián-Gallés, 2003; Kuhl, Williams, Lacerda, Stevens, & Lindblom, 1992) than consonant contrasts (by 8–10 months of age; Werker & Tees, 1984). Bilingual first language children go through a similar reorganization in speech perception but exhibit language-specific effects somewhat later than has been reported for monolinguals – by 12 months of age for vowel contrasts (Bosch & Sebastián-Gallés, 2003) and by 14 to 21 months of age for consonant contrasts (Burns, Werker, & McVie, 2002).

Children with dual language exposure have similarly shown a delay in the ability to use phonetic contrasts in word learning. More specifically, Fennel, Polka, and Werker (2002) found that while monolingual children were able to associate new words that differed by a minimal consonant contrast (i.e., /bih–dih/) with novel shapes at 17 months of age, bilingual children were able to do so only by 20 months of age. By contrast, research on word segmentation by Polka and Sundara (2003) found that French–English bilingual children were able to segment words from continuous speech in both their native languages by 7 months of age, like monolingual children. At the same time, early recognition of word forms in bilingual (and even monolingual) children may be sensitive to amount of exposure. Vihman and her colleagues report that 11-month-old bilingual Welsh–English children in Wales failed to show differential preference for familiar over unfamiliar words in a headturn preference study, while monolingual English children of the same age did (Vihman, Lum, Thierry, Nakai, & Keren-Portnoy, 2005). Vihman also reports that 11-month-old monolingual Welsh-speaking children failed to demonstrate a preference and suggests that the bilingual and monolingual children's performance with respect to Welsh might be due to the relatively low status and associated lower level of usage of Welsh compared with English.

Turning to production, Oller, Eilers, Urbano, and Cobo-Lewis (1997) found that the age of onset of canonical babbling was the same (i.e., around 27 weeks of age) for a group of bilingual English–Spanish children and English monolinguals, and Maneva and Genesee (2002) report evidence of differentiated babbling by a 10- to 15-month-old French–English bilingual child that corresponded to patterns attested in monolingual French and English babbling. These researchers analyzed prosodic features of babbling, such as utterance length and syllable structure (e.g., open/closed syllables). By contrast, Poulin-Dubois and Goodz (2001) failed to find language-specific differences in the babbling of French–English bilinguals of the same age when they examined segmental features (i.e., differences in place and manner of articulation). When BFL children start producing words, they sometimes show signs of prosodic differentiation from quite early in development. For example, Paradis (2001) found that 2-year-old French–English bilinguals were more likely to omit syllables from novel four-syllable words in each language based on the typical stress patterns of that language.

Whether and/or when BFL children have two language-specific segmental phonological repertoires is not clear. In some studies, bilingual children's segmental phonology has been reported to be similar to same-age monolingual children throughout the preschool years with respect to phonetic substitutions (e.g., substituting [l] for [r] in the Spanish word "cruz"; from Barlow, 2002; Bell, Müller, & Munro, 2001; Holm & Dodd, 1999), voice onset times (Johnson & Wilson, 2002; Kehoe, Lleó, & Rakow, 2004), and consonant harmony and syllable reduplication (Brulard & Carr, 2003; Johnson & Lancaster, 1998; Schnitzer & Krasinski, 1996). Other studies have pointed to delays or differences relative to monolingual children on some of the very same measures (Deuchar & Clark, 1996; Johnson & Wilson, 2002; Schnitzer & Krasinski, 1994).

The variability observed in the phonological development of BFL learners could be linked to multiple influences, some that are the same as those that influence monolingual phonological development and some that are particular to BFLA. Those that are the same include general developmental factors that are maturationally based (e.g., maturation of articulators that are linked to the onset of canonical babbling) and individual differences (compare Schnitzer & Krasinski, 1994, and Schnitzer & Krasinski, 1996; see also Kehoe et al., 2004). Those that are particular to BFLA include unequal or limited exposure to or practice with each language (e.g., Arnberg, 1981; Bell et al., 2001; Paradis, 2001), asynchronous development that reflects normal language-specific differences in the pattern of emergence of phonological abilities (Matthews & Yip, 2003, have proposed this for morphosyntax), cross-linguistic transfer (Holm & Dodd, 1999; Paradis, 2001), and idiosyncrasies in the distributional and/or qualitative properties of bilingual speech input (Sebastián-Gallés & Bosch, 2005; Polka et al., this volume).

Child Bilingual Code-Mixing

Code-mixing is ubiquitous among bilinguals – adults and children alike. It is the use of elements (phonological, lexical, morphosyntactic) from two languages in the same utterance or stretch of conversation. It can occur within an utterance (intra-utterance mixing – e.g., "see cheval" [horse]) or between utterances (inter-utterance mixing). Rates of code-mixing in children vary depending on the form of mixing (intra- vs. inter-utterance), the nature of the mixed element (function vs. content words), the language of the conversation (the child's less vs. the child's more proficient language), and the context (with interlocutors who are bilingual vs. those who are monolingual, for example). Individual differences in both rates and style of mixing are widely reported, even within the same family (see Vihman, 1998). Adult bilinguals also code-mix (Myers-Scotton, 1993; Poplack, 1980), and research has shown that adult bilinguals code-switch for a variety of meta-communicative purposes – for example, to mark ethnic identities or affiliations, to negotiate social roles and status, and to establish interpersonal intimacy or distance (Myers-Scotton, 1993; Poplack, 1987); and their mixing is grammatically constrained. In brief, code-mixing is a useful, sophisticated, and rule-governed feature of language use among adult bilinguals. By contrast, child bilingual code-mixing has often been interpreted as a sign of incompetence and even confusion (e.g., Volterra & Taeschner, 1978). Research on child bilingual code-mixing has been pursued with two primary goals in mind – to identify (1) its grammatical and (2) its functional properties in order to determine if it is rule-governed or a sign of confusion.

Grammatical properties

When two languages are used in the same utterance, grammatical incompatibilities between the languages could arise (e.g., different word orders); these in turn could result in patterns of language use that are awkward or illicit. Indeed, the commonly held perception of code-mixing is that it is an ungrammatical form of language use. Although this is not an appropriate characterization of adult code-mixing, questions remain about child bilingual code-mixing. In particular, are there grammatical constraints on child bilingual code-mixing? What form do they take? When in development are they evident? In order to code-mix in ways that respect the grammars of the participating languages the child has to acquire language-specific grammars and must also be able to coordinate them during production. Thus, evidence of grammatical constraints on the code-mixing of young bilingual children would provide important insights into their capacity to learn and use two languages at the same time. If constraints are operative from the outset of two- and multi-word productions and if they are essentially the same as those attested in adult code-mixing, this would suggest that code-mixing grammatically emerges with bilingual grammatical development.

Researchers have examined grammatical constraints on intra-utterance code-mixing by bilingual children learning a number of different language pairs: French and German (Köppe, in press; Meisel, 1994), French and English (Paradis, Nicoladis, & Genesee, 2000; Sauve & Genesee, 2000); English and Norwegian (Lanza, 1997a); English and Estonian (Vihman, 1998), and Inuktitut and English (Allen, Genesee, Fish, & Crago, 2002). These researchers all conclude that child bilingual code-mixing is grammatically constrained because children usually mix the two languages at points in an utterance where the grammar of both languages is concordant; they seldom mix at points where the grammar is not concordant.[3] Most researchers also report that the constraints that operate on child bilingual code-mixing are essentially the same as those that have been reported in adults (except see Meisel, 1994; and Köppe, in press). Meisel and Köppe argue that the constraints that operate on code-mixing in child bilinguals reflect their level of grammatical development and, thus, might differ from those that operate in adult bilinguals (see Lanza, 1997a, for an alternative view). More specifically, they argue that the operation of constraints based on abstract notions of grammar is most evident in bilingual children once they exhibit such knowledge in their actual language use (as marked by agreement, for example), usually around 2;6 years of age and older for children learning English, while the operation of constraints that reflect surface features of grammar (such as word order) is evident even earlier in development. There does not appear to be a stage in development when grammatical constraints do not operate, albeit the nature of the constraints may change as their grammars change. These findings reinforce results reviewed earlier indicating that, for the most part, bilingual children acquire language-specific morphosyntactic properties in each language early in development and, moreover, they can access these constraints simultaneously during production.

Functional properties

If code-mixing is not due to lack of differentiation of the two languages, the question remains: Why do bilingual children code-mix? Research on the functional properties of child bilingual code-mixing indicates that there are multiple explanations that are often related to performance factors.

Gap-filling.   A common explanation of child bilingual code-mixing is that it serves to fill gaps in the developing child's lexicons and grammars. On this view, code-mixing reflects the developing bilingual child's use of all linguistic resources to express him- or herself when mastery of each language is incomplete. According to the lexical-gap hypothesis, bilingual children mix words from language X when using language Y because they do not know the appropriate word in language Y. In support of this possibility, it has been found that young bilingual children mix more when they use their less proficient than their more proficient language (Genesee, Nicoladis, & Paradis, 1995; Lanvers, 2001). In a direct test of the lexical-gap hypothesis, Genesee et al. (1995) found that two young BFL learners (mean length of utterance ranged from 1.09 to 1.55) were more likely to code-mix words for which they did not know translation equivalents – this was true for Wayne 100% of the time and for Felix 65% of the time (see also Nicoladis & Secco, 2000). While mixing to fill lexical gaps because of incomplete mastery of their languages is one explanation of child code-mixing, it can also be true for otherwise fully proficient, older bilinguals because lexical knowledge in both languages of the bilingual is seldom equivalent, as noted previously.

Evidence for grammatical gap-filling comes from Petersen (1988) and Lanza (1997b) who report that bilingual children often mix function words and inflectional morphemes from their more proficient language with content words from their less proficient language, but seldom the reverse, and from Gawlitzek-Maiwald and Tracy (1996) who argue that young bilingual children use syntactic patterns from their stronger language to bootstrap into the grammar of their less proficient language. Both lexical and morphosyntactic mixing attest to the young bilingual child's ability to access and use creatively the lexical and morphosyntactic resources of both languages on-line during language production.

Context-sensitivity.   There is considerable evidence that bilingual children's code-mixing is sensitive to contextual variables, including those related to interlocutor (Deuchar & Quay, 2000; Genesee, Boivin, & Nicoladis, 1996; Genesee et al., 1995; Lanza, 1997b; Meisel, 1990; Vihman, 1998, among others), topic (Lanvers, 2001), and the purpose of the interaction (Vihman, 1998). Evidence that child bilingual code-mixing is sensitive to interlocutor variables is well documented. Most researchers report that bilingual children tend to use their languages appropriately with different interlocutors so that, for example, children who are raised in bilingual homes where parents tend to use only their native/dominant language with the child generally use more of each parent's language with that parent than with the other parent (e.g., De Houwer, 1990; Deuchar & Quay, 2000; Genesee et al., 1995; Lanza, 1997b; Vihman, 1998). Additional evidence of context-sensitive use of code-mixing is presented in the next section.

There is also evidence, from somewhat older bilingual children, that their use of code-mixing is sensitive to situational factors. Sprott and Kemper (1987) found that 3- and 6-year-old Spanish–English bilingual children were significantly less likely to code-mix with an adult during an interview to screen the children for participation in the study, based on their language ability, and more likely to mix when playing with other children, drawing pictures of their homes and families. Vihman (1998) notes that her two bilingual children's (2;8 to 9;10) code-mixing was sensitive to the presence of parents or the tape recorder and suggests that they used English and Estonian to mark the purpose of an activity as either "fantasy play" or "business matters," respectively.

Pragmatic and symbolic functions.   Code-mixing has also been associated with a variety of pragmatic functions, even in quite young bilingual children. Lanvers (2001) reports that her two German–English children (1;6 to 2;11) used language for emphasis (see also Goodz, 1989) and appeal, to quote a parent, and for topic shift (see also Vihman, 1998). It has also been noted that bilingual children make choices between their languages for what might be considered symbolic–identity reasons. Thus, Vihman (1998) notes that the unmarked language choice for her bilingual children when playing together was a mixture of English and Estonian, arguably a reflection of their dual identity with the Estonian and English speakers in their lives. By contrast, Estonian tended to prevail when with their parents, the primary sources of input in that language. In a related vein, in a study of 10 Mandarin–English bilingual children (4;0 to 6;0) in the United States, Pan (1995) found that, when interacting with their parents, the children tended to switch more frequently from Mandarin to English than did their parents and, moreover, they were more likely to maintain the switch to English than were their parents. Pan conjectures that differences in the children's and parents' switching patterns could be linked to their differential identity with and efforts to maintain Mandarin in contrast to English, the language of wider communication in the community. Pragmatic and symbolic functions that have been noted in these cases are often characteristic of somewhat older children (Zentella, 1999). Developmental studies with larger sample sizes are needed to document and clarify these developmental trends.

Communicative Competence

Bilingual children face the same communication challenges as monolingual children, namely, production of target-like language forms that are comprehensible to others; getting one's meaning across when language acquisition is incomplete; and use of language in socially appropriate ways. At the same time, the ability to communicate appropriately and effectively in two languages entails an understanding of interpersonal communication that exceeds that required for monolingual communication, including, among others, that breakdowns in communication may be due to language choice. Examining the development of communicative competence in bilingual children provides a window into their cognitive capacities as well as their linguistic competencies insofar as these bilingual-specific abilities implicate cognitive-developmental issues that go beyond strictly linguistic ones. In question is how bilingual children accommodate the specific demands of bilingual communication and when in development they do so.

Fundamental to bilingual communicative competence is the ability to make appropriate language choices with different interlocutors. Bilingual first language learners have been shown to possess such competence in a variety of ways. As noted previously, bilingual children in the one- and early two-word stages of development are able to use their languages differentially and appropriately with parents who habitually speak different languages with them (Nicoladis & Genesee, 1996); they demonstrate similar sensitivity when interacting with strangers with whom they have had no prior experience (Genesee et al., 1996); and they can adjust their rates of code-mixing to match those of unfamiliar interlocutors who change rates of mixing from one occasion to another (Comeau, Genesee, & Lapaquette, 2003; see Petitto et al., 2001, for similar evidence from children learning oral and sign languages simultaneously). Responsiveness to the linguistic preferences or proficiency of unfamiliar interlocutors indicates that bilingual children's ability to use their developing languages appropriately reflects true communicative competence; that is, the ability to make on-line adjustments to accommodate interlocutors' language preferences and/or abilities without the benefit of previous experience or learning.

The question arises of how do young bilingual children know which language is appropriate; and what does this tell us about their cognitive capacity to manage the additional demands of bilingual communication. Lanza (1997a, 2001) argues that bilingual children's understanding of appropriate language choices in the home arises from the same fundamental processes of language socialization that have been shown to influence the development of communication skills in monolingual children (Döpke, 1992). In particular, parents who adopt what Lanza dubs "bilingual discourse strategies," such as "move-on" or "expressed guess" strategies that imply that the parent has understood what the children are saying when they code-mix, tolerate and encourage further code-mixing. By contrast, parents who adopt monolingual strategies, such as requesting clarification of an utterance in the non-target language in response to their child's mixing, are likely to discourage their children from code-mixing. Indeed, in a longitudinal study of an English–Norwegian bilingual 2-year-old, Lanza notes that the child mixed her two languages more with her Norwegian-speaking father, who used bilingual strategies when she mixed, than with her English-speaking mother, who often pretended not to understand when the child spoke Norwegian (see Kasuya, 1998, for similar findings with English–Japanese bilingual children; but Nicoladis & Genesee, 1998, failed to find such a relationship). Similarly, in a study of English–German families in Australia, Döpke (1992) noted that families who were successful at getting their children to use German despite their tendency to favor English used explicit discourse strategies that obliged the children to use German. Parental discourse strategies may, therefore, be one way in which children learn to make appropriate language choices, at least with familiar interlocutors, and as well offers an explanation of some of the variation that characterizes children in different families. Language socialization is also a likely explanation of variation in code-mixing patterns in bilinguals who are raised in communities with different norms for code-mixing (see Poplack, 1987, and Myers-Scotton, 1993, for examples based on adult language patterns). Studies of language socialization of children in communities with different code-mixing norms are lacking at present.

However, language socialization cannot explain children's performance with unfamiliar interlocutors where prior experience and knowledge are lacking; as noted previously, bilingual children can exhibit appropriate language choices with strangers and they can match their rates of mixing with those of strangers. Comeau et al. (2003) report that bilingual children may use a language-contingent strategy to match language choices with unfamiliar interlocutors. Evidence for this comes from a turn-by-turn analysis of bilingual children's language choices with an unfamiliar interlocutor who changed her rates of mixing from 15% to 40% and back to 15% over three successive sessions. The children tended to switch languages in the turn after the interlocutor had switched languages and, thus, were able to achieve a rate of mixing that closely matched that of their conversational partner. The results of this study are of additional interest in that they indicate that BFL children can track language choices by their interlocutors and can alter their language choices accordingly.

Bilingual children are also responsive to feedback from interlocutors about the appropriateness of their language choices. Comeau and Genesee (2001) report that English–French BFL learners (average mean ages of 2;7 and 3;1) changed the language of their message following a request for clarification from an unfamiliar adult interlocutor whenever they used an inappropriate language with her. Most of the children's changes in language were made following implicit requests for clarification that did not specify the source of the breakdown (e.g., "what?"). Moreover, the children, even the youngest ones, virtually never changed languages when repairing a breakdown that was due to reasons other than language choice (e.g., inaudible utterance or incomprehensible word choice). It is noteworthy that the base (or "appropriate") language of the interaction was the less proficient language of the children so that using the appropriate language meant using their less proficient language. These findings suggest that 2- to 3-year-old bilingual children can infer the meaning of non-specific feedback regarding the appropriateness of their language choice, and they can use such feedback as cues to the appropriateness of their language choices.

Conclusions

In the previous sections, we have reviewed findings that indicate that bilingual first language acquisition is the same in some significant respects as monolingual acquisition and different in others. In this section, we explore explanations of the similarities and the differences. Starting with the similarities: in spite of less exposure to each language, bilingual children reach a number of important milestones within the same age span as their monolingual peers, such as the onset of canonical babbling (Oller et al., 1997), first words (see Nicoladis & Genesee, 1997), and overall rate of vocabulary growth (Pearson et al., 1997). As well, their morphosyntactic development resembles that of monolinguals for the most part and appears to occur within the same timeframe, at least in their dominant language (Paradis & Genesee, 1996). These aspects of language development may be relatively robust in the face of considerable variation in input because biological or cognitive maturation plays an important role in these developmental milestones (Oller et al., 1997; Wexler, 1998).

Nevertheless, some differences between bilingual and monolingual children have been observed. Differences in vocabulary size in each language are most likely attributable to differences in frequency of exposure and, in some cases, differences in context of exposure (Pearson et al., 1997). Children who receive primary input in each language from different interlocutors (e.g., mother, father, siblings) may acquire different lexical repertoires in each language because different people talk about different things (De Houwer, 1990). In a related vein, Sebastián-Gallés and Bosch (2005) have suggested that delays in bilingual children's discrimination of some segmental features may be attributable to the distributional properties of the input that arise when children are exposed to two closely related languages. Bilingual first language learners may not be exposed to clearly discernible phonemic contrasts in the input because the features in question (e.g., /e–ɛ/) form a unimodal distribution in the input (see Polka et al., this volume). Bilingual first language children hear less of either language than monolinguals, which could lead to delays relative to monolingual children in any aspect of acquisition that is frequency-dependent (e.g., Marchman, Martínez-Sussmann, & Dale, 2004).

It is also noteworthy that BFL learners acquire the additional skills that are required to manage and use two languages for communicative purposes. From a very early age, they know when to use each language and when to code-mix and how much, even with unfamiliar interlocutors. They are also able to identify breakdowns in communication that are due to inappropriate language choice; they can do so even if feedback is implicit and unspecified; and they have strategies for repairing such breakdowns. As Lanza (1997b) has pointed out, bilingual children's use of their two languages is subject to the same socialization processes as for monolingual children.

Other differences appear to be linked to transfer. Transfer itself can be linked to structural differences, surface level or abstract, of the target languages that are ambiguous from a learnability point of view. The probability that such structural differences result in transfer may be heightened if the child is dominant or more proficient in one language (Gawlitzek-Maiwald & Tracy, 1996; Matthews & Yip, 2003; Paradis & Genesee, 1996; cf. Müller, 1999; Nicoladis, 2002). Dominance is also implicated when BFL learners use lexical items (Nicoladis & Secco, 2000) from one language when speaking the other in order to fill gaps in vocabulary knowledge. To date, transfer has often been applied post hoc as an explanation of atypical morphosyntactic patterns in individual BFL learner's development. Predictive studies in which children are learning languages that are conducive to transfer are called for if we are to get beyond post hoc explanations.

Whether one focuses on the similarities or differences between BFL learners and monolinguals, the picture that emerges depicts BFLA as an active, creative process that draws on the linguistic, communicative, and cognitive resources of the developing child (Genesee, 2003a). Bilingual first language learners' resourcefulness is evident in their code-mixing to fill lexical gaps in their developing competence; in their transfer of morphosyntactic structures from one language to another in grammatically constrained ways; and in their competence in managing their two languages for communicative purposes.

There is much more to be learned, of course. We still need to learn much more about the first two years of development and, in particular, early speech perception and production; we need studies with larger sample sizes with detailed descriptions of language input that will permit us to examine the role of input more carefully; we need studies with more language combinations that will permit us to explore the limits and nature of transfer; we need studies of children who are at-risk for language delay or impairment for specific linguistic reasons or cognitive reasons (Genesee, 2003b); and we need more research that maps out BFL learners' development from the preschool to school years.

Notes

1   Finite verb forms are marked for tense (e.g., *he goes*) and non-finite verb forms are not (*he go*). English- and French-learning children usually use non-finite forms before they use finite forms.
2   Number (singular, plural) and counting in English and Japanese are examples of forms that do not overlap. Number in English is marked by a [-s] suffix on nouns, and if you count the noun, you put the numeral word in the noun phrase; for example, "[three pencils] are on the desk." In Japanese, the noun does not take any plural marking, and you cannot put a numeral word in the noun phrase. In Japanese, you need to add a new phrase to the sentence, with a classifier word appropriate for the noun for pencils. In Japanese, you would say something like, "[pencil], [three long pointy things] on the desk are."
3   A concordant grammatical structure is one that is the same in both languages (e.g., in both English and French articles appear before nouns); a non-concordant structure is one that differs in the two languages (e.g., in English object pronouns occur after the verb (*He likes them*) while in French they come before the verb (e.g., *Il les aime* [He them likes])).

References

Allen, S. E. M., Genesee, F. H., Fish, S. A., & Crago, M. B. (2002). Patterns of code mixing in English–Inuktitut bilinguals. In M. Andronis, C. Ball, H. Elston, & S. Neuvel (Eds.), *Proceedings of the 37th Annual Meeting of the Chicago Linguistic Society: Vol. 2* (pp. 171–188). Chicago, IL: Chicago Linguistic Society.

Arnberg, L. (1981). *A longitudinal study of language development in four young children exposed to English and Swedish in the home*. Linköping, Sweden: Linköping University, Department of Education.

Barlow, J. A. (2002). Error patterns and transfer in Spanish–English bilingual phonological development. In B. Skarbela et al. (Eds.), *Boston University Conference on Language Development 26 Proceedings* (pp. 60–71). Somerville, MA: Cascadilla Press.

Bates, E., & MacWhinney, B. (1987). Competition, variation, and language learning. In B. MacWhinney (Ed.), *Mechanisms of language acquisition* (pp. 157–194). Hillsdale, NJ: Lawrence Erlbaum.

Bell, M. J., Müller, N., & Munro, S. (2001). The acquisition of rhotic consonants by Welsh–English bilingual children. *International Journal of Bilingualism, 5*, 71–86.

Bialystok, E. (2001). *Bilingualism in development: Language, literacy, and cognition.* New York: Cambridge University Press.

Bosch, L., & Sebastián-Gallés, N. (1997). Native language recognition abilities in four-month-old infants from monolingual and bilingual environments. *Cognition, 65*, 33–69.

Bosch, L., & Sebastián-Gallés, N. (2003). Simultaneous bilingualism and the perception of a language-specific vowel contrast in the first year of life. *Language and Speech, 46*, 217–243.

Brulard, I., & Carr, P. (2003). French–English bilingual acquisition of phonology: One production system or two? *International Journal of Bilingualism, 7*, 177–202.

Burns, T. C., Werker, J. F., & McVie, K. (2002, November). *Development of phonetic categories in infants raised in bilingual and monolingual homes.* Paper presented at the 27th Annual Boston University Conference on Language Development, Boston, MA.

Comeau, L., & Genesee, F. (2001). Bilingual children's repair strategies during dyadic communication. In J. Cenoz & F. Genesee (Eds.), *Trends in bilingual acquisition* (pp. 231–256). Amsterdam: John Benjamins.

Comeau, L., Genesee, F., & Lapaquette, L. (2003). The modeling hypothesis and child bilingual code-mixing. *International Journal of Bilingualism, 7*, 113–126.

Cook, V. (2002). Background to the L2 user. In V. Cook (Ed.), *Portraits of the L2 user* (pp. 1–28). Clevedon, UK: Multilingual Matters.

De Houwer, A. (1990). *The acquisition of two languages from birth: A case study.* Cambridge: Cambridge University Press.

De Houwer, A. (1995). Bilingual language acquisition. In P. Fletcher & B. MacWhinney (Eds.), *The handbook of child language* (pp. 219–250). Oxford: Blackwell.

De Houwer, A. (2005). Early bilingual acquisition: Focus on morphosyntax and the separate development hypothesis. In J. Kroll & A. De Groot (Eds.), *The handbook of bilingualism* (pp. 30–48). Oxford: Oxford University Press.

Deuchar, M., & Clark, A. (1996). Early bilingual acquisition of the voicing contrast in English and Spanish. *Journal of Phonetics, 24*, 351–365.

Deuchar, M., & Quay, S. (2000). *Bilingual acquisition: Theoretical implications of a case study.* Oxford: Oxford University Press.

Diebold, A. R. (1968). The consequences of early bilingualism on cognitive development and personality formation. In E. Norbeck, D. Price-Williams, & W. M. McCord (Eds.), *The study of personality: An inter-disciplinary appraisal* (pp. 218–245). New York: Holt, Rinehart, & Winston.

Döpke, S. (1992). *One parent one language: An interactional approach.* Amsterdam: John Benjamins.

Döpke, S. (1998). Competing language structures: The acquisition of verb placement by bilingual German–English children. *Journal of Child Language, 25*, 555–584.

Döpke, S. (2000). Generation of and retraction from cross-linguistically motivated structures in bilingual first language acquisition. *Bilingualism: Language and Cognition, 3*, 209–226.

Fennel, C. T., Polka, L., & Werker, J. (2002, May). *Bilingual early word learner's ability to access phonetic detail in word forms.* Paper presented at the Fourth International Symposium on Bilingualism, Tempe, AZ.

Gawlitzek-Maiwald, I., & Tracy, R. (1996). Bilingual bootstrapping. *Linguistics, 34*, 901–926.

Genesee, F. (1989). Early bilingual development: One language or two? *Journal of Child Language, 16,* 161–179.

Genesee, F. (2001). Bilingual first language acquisition: Exploring the limits of the language faculty. In M. McGroarty (Ed.), *21st Annual Review of Applied Linguistics* (pp. 153–168). Cambridge: Cambridge University Press.

Genesee, F. (2003a). Rethinking bilingual acquisition. In J. M. deWaele (Ed.), *Bilingualism: Challenges and directions for future research* (pp. 158–182). Clevedon, UK: Multilingual Matters.

Genesee, F. (2003b). Bilingualism and language impairment. In R. D. Kent (Ed.), *MIT encyclopedia of communication disorders* (pp. 275–278). Cambridge, MA: MIT Press.

Genesee, F., Boivin, I., & Nicoladis, E. (1996). Talking with strangers: A study of bilingual children's communicative competence. *Applied Psycholinguistics, 17,* 427–442.

Genesee, F., Nicoladis, E., & Paradis, J. (1995). Language differentiation in early bilingual development. *Journal of Child Language, 22,* 611–631.

Genesee, F., Paradis, J., & Wolf, L. (1995). *The nature of the bilingual child's lexicon.* Unpublished research report, Psychology Department, McGill University, Montreal, Quebec, Canada.

Goodz, N. S. (1989). Parental language mixing in bilingual families. *Journal of Infant Mental Health, 10,* 25–44.

Grosjean, F. (1997). The bilingual individual. *Interpreting, 2,* 163–187.

Holm, A., & Dodd, B. (1999). A longitudinal study of the phonological development of two Cantonese–English bilingual children. *Applied Psycholinguistics, 20,* 349–376.

Hulk, A., & Müller, N. (2000). Bilingual first language acquisition at the interface between syntax and pragmatics. *Bilingualism: Language and Cognition, 3,* 227–244.

Hulk, A. C. J., & van der Linden, E. (1996). Language mixing in a French–Dutch bilingual child. In E. Kellerman et al. (Eds.), *Eurosla 6: A selection of papers* (pp. 89–103). Amsterdam: John Benjamins.

Johnson, C., & Lancaster, P. (1998). The development of more than one phonology: A case study of a Norwegian–English bilingual child. *International Journal of Bilingualism, 2,* 265–300.

Johnson, C. E., & Wilson, I. L. (2002). Phonetic evidence for early language differentiation: Research issues and some preliminary data. *International Journal of Bilingualism, 6,* 271–289.

Kasuya, H. (1998). Determinants of language choice in bilingual children: The role of input. *International Journal of Bilingualism, 2,* 327–346.

Kehoe, M. M., Lleó, C., & Rakow, M. (2004). Voice onset time in bilingual German–Spanish children. *Bilingualism: Language and Cognition, 7,* 71–88.

Köppe, R. (in press). Is codeswitching acquired? In J. MacSwan (Ed.), *Grammatical theory and bilingual codeswitching.* Cambridge, MA: MIT Press.

Kuhl, P., Williams, K. A., Lacerda, F., Stevens, K. N., & Lindblom, B. (1992). Linguistic experience alters phonetic perception in infants by 6 months of age. *Science, 255,* 606–608.

Lanvers, U. (1999). Lexical growth patterns in a bilingual infant: The occurrence and significance of equivalents in the bilingual lexicon. *International Journal of Bilingual Education and Bilingualism, 2,* 30–52.

Lanvers, U. (2001). Language alternation in infant bilinguals: A developmental approach to codeswitching. *International Journal of Bilingualism, 5,* 437–464.

Lanza, E. (1997a). Language contact in bilingual two-year-olds and code-switching: Language encounters of a different kind? *International Journal of Bilingualism, 1,* 135–162.

Lanza, E. (1997b). *Language mixing in infant bilingualism: A sociolinguistic perspective.* Oxford: Clarendon Press.

Lanza, E. (2001). Bilingual first language acquisition: A discourse perspective on language contact in parent–child interaction. In J. Cenoz & F. Genesee (Eds.), *Trends in bilingual acquisition* (pp. 201–230). Amsterdam: John Benjamins.

Leopold, W. (1949). *Speech development of a bilingual child: Vol. 4.* Evanston, IL: Northwestern University Press.

Macnamara, J. (1966). *Bilingualism and primary education.* Edinburgh: Edinburgh University Press.

Maneva, B., & Genesee, F. (2002). Bilingual babbling: Evidence for language differentiation in dual language acquisition. In B. Skarbela et al. (Eds.), *Boston University Conference on Language Development 26 Proceedings* (pp. 383–392). Somerville, MA: Cascadilla Press.

Marchman, V. A., Martínez-Sussmann, C., & Dale, P. (2004). The language-specific nature of grammatical development: Evidence from bilingual language learners. *Developmental Science, 7,* 212–224.

Markman, E. M., Wasow, J. L., & Hansen, M. B. (2003). Use of the mutual exclusivity assumption by young word learners. *Cognitive Psychology, 47,* 241–275.

Matthews, S., & Yip, V. (2003). Relative clauses in early bilingual development: Transfer and universals. In A. G. Ramat (Ed.), *Typology and second language acquisition* (pp. 39–81). Berlin: Mouton de Gruyter.

McLaughlin, B. (1978). *Second language acquisition in childhood.* Hillsdale, NJ: Lawrence Erlbaum.

Mehler, J., Dupoux, E., Nazzi, T., & Dehaene-Lambertz, G. (1996). Coping with linguistic diversity: The infant's viewpoint. In J. L. Morgan & K. Demuth (Eds.), *Signal to syntax* (pp. 101–116). Mahwah, NJ: Lawrence Erlbaum.

Meisel, J. M. (1990). *Two first languages: Early grammatical development in bilingual children.* Dordrecht: Foris.

Meisel, J. M. (1994). Code-switching in young bilingual children: The acquisition of grammatical constraints. *Studies in Second Language Acquisition, 16,* 413–441.

Meisel, J. M. (2001). The simultaneous acquisition of two first languages: Early differentiation and subsequent development of grammars. In J. Cenoz & F. Genesee (Eds.), *Trends in bilingual acquisition* (pp. 11–42). Amsterdam: John Benjamins.

Müller, N. (1999). Transfer in bilingual first language acquisition. *Bilingualism: Language and Cognition, 1,* 151–171.

Myers-Scotton, C. (1993). *Social motivation for codeswitching: Evidence from Africa.* Oxford: Oxford University Press.

Nicoladis, E. (1998). First clues to the existence of two input languages: Pragmatic and lexical differentiation in a bilingual child. *Bilingualism: Language and Cognition, 1,* 105–116.

Nicoladis, E. (2001). Finding first words in the input. In J. Cenoz & F. Genesee (Eds.), *Trends in bilingual acquisition* (pp. 131–147). Amsterdam: John Benjamins.

Nicoladis, E. (2002). What's the difference between "toilet paper" and "paper toilet"? French–English bilingual children's crosslinguistic transfer in compound nouns. *Journal of Child Language, 29,* 843–863.

Nicoladis, E. (2003). Cross-linguistic transfer in deverbal compounds of preschool bilingual children. *Bilingualism: Language and Cognition, 6,* 17–31.

Nicoladis, E., & Genesee, F. (1996). A longitudinal study of pragmatic differentiation in young bilingual children. *Language Learning, 46,* 439–464.

Nicoladis, E., & Genesee, F. (1997). Language development in preschool bilingual children. *Journal of Speech-Language Pathology and Audiology, 21,* 258–270.

Nicoladis, E., & Genesee, F. (1998). Parental discourse and code-mixing in bilingual children. *International Journal of Bilingualism, 2,* 85–100.

Nicoladis, E., & Secco, G. (2000). The role of a child's productive vocabulary in the language choice of a bilingual family. *First Language*, *58*, 3–28.

Oller, D. K., Eilers, R. E., Urbano, R., & Cobo-Lewis, A. B. (1997). Development of precursors to speech in infants exposed to two languages. *Journal of Child Language*, *24*, 407–425.

Pan, B. A. (1995). Code negotiation in bilingual families: "My body starts speaking English". *Journal of Multilingual and Multicultural Development*, *16*, 315–327.

Paradis, J. (2001). Do bilingual two-year olds have separate phonological systems? *International Journal of Bilingualism*, *5*, 19–38.

Paradis, J., Crago, M., Genesee, F., & Rice, M. (2003). Bilingual children with specific language impairment: How do they compare with their monolingual peers? *Journal of Speech, Language and Hearing Research*, *46*, 113–127.

Paradis, J., & Genesee, F. (1996). Syntactic acquisition in bilingual children: Autonomous or interdependent? *Studies in Second Language Acquisition*, *18*, 1–25.

Paradis, J., & Navarro, S. (2003). Subject realization and crosslinguistic interference in the bilingual acquisition of Spanish and English: What is the role of the input? *Journal of Child Language*, *30*, 371–393.

Paradis, J., Nicoladis, E., & Genesee, F. (2000). Early emergence of structural constraints on code-mixing: Evidence from French–English bilingual children. *Bilingualism: Language and Cognition*, *3*, 245–261.

Patterson, J. L., & Pearson, B. Z. (2004). Bilingual lexical development: Influences, contexts, and processes. In B. A. Goldstein (Ed.), *Bilingual language development and disorders in Spanish–English speakers* (pp. 77–104). Baltimore, MD: Paul H. Brookes.

Pearson, B. Z., Fernández, S. C., Lewedag, V., & Oller, D. K. (1997). The relation of input factors to lexical learning by bilingual infants (ages 10 to 30 months). *Applied Psycholinguistics*, *18*, 41–58.

Pearson, B. Z., Fernández, S. C., & Oller, D. K. (1993). Lexical development in bilingual infants and toddlers: Comparison to monolingual norms. *Language Learning*, *43*, 93–120.

Pearson, B. Z., Fernández, S. C., & Oller, D. K. (1995). Cross-language synonyms in the lexicons of bilingual infants: One language or two? *Journal of Child Language*, *22*, 345–368.

Petersen, J. (1988). Word-internal code-switching constraints in a bilingual child's grammar. *Linguistics*, *26*, 479–493.

Petitto, L. A., Katerelos, M., Levy, B. G., Gauna, K., Tetreault, K., & Ferraro, V. (2001). Bilingual signed and spoken language acquisition from birth: Implications for the mechanism underlying early bilingual language acquisition. *Journal of Child Language*, *28*, 453–496.

Polka, L., & Sundara, M. (2003). Word segmentation in monolingual and bilingual infant learners of English and French. In M. J. Solé, D. Recasens, & J. Romero (Eds.), *Proceedings of the International Congress of Phonetic Sciences*, *15*, 1021–1024.

Poplack, S. (1980). "Sometimes I start a sentence in English y termino en Espanol": Toward a typology of code-switching. *Linguistics*, *18*, 581–618.

Poplack, S. (1987). Contrasting patterns of code-switching in two communities. In E. Wande, J. Anward, B. Nordberg, L. Steensland, & M. Thelander (Eds.), *Aspects of multilingualism* (pp. 51–77). Uppsala: Borgströms, Motala.

Poulin-Dubois, D., & Goodz, N. (2001). Language differentiation in bilingual infants: Evidence from babbling. In J. Cenoz & F. Genesee (Eds.), *Trends in bilingual acquisition* (pp. 95–106). Amsterdam: John Benjamins.

Quay, S. (1995). The bilingual lexicon: Implications for studies of language choice. *Journal of Child Language*, *22*, 369–387.

Ronjat, J. (1913). *Le développement du langage observé chez un enfant bilingue*. Paris: Champion.

Sauve, D., & Genesee, F. (2000, March). *Grammatical constraints on child bilingual code-mixing.* Paper presented at the Annual Conference of the American Association for Applied Linguistics, Vancouver, Canada.

Schnitzer, M. L., & Krasinski, E. (1994). The development of segmental phonological production in a bilingual child. *Journal of Child Language, 21,* 585–622.

Schnitzer, M. L., & Krasinski, E. (1996). The development of segmental phonological production in a bilingual child: A contrasting second case. *Journal of Child Language, 23,* 547–571.

Sebastián-Gallés, N., & Bosch, L. (2005). Phonology and bilingualism. In J. F. Kroll & A. M. B. D. Groot (Eds.), *Handbook of bilingualism: Psycholinguistic approaches* (pp. 68–87). Oxford: Oxford University Press.

Smith, M. E. (1935). A study of the speech of eight bilingual children of the same family. *Child Development, 6,* 19–25.

Sprott, R. A., & Kemper, S. (1987). The development of children's code-switching: A study of six bilingual children across two situations. *Working Papers on Language Development, 2,* 116–134.

Vihman, M. M. (1996). *Phonological development.* Cambridge, MA: Blackwell Publishers.

Vihman, M. (1998). A developmental perspective on codeswitching: Conversations between a pair of bilingual siblings. *International Journal of Bilingualism, 2,* 45–84.

Vihman, M. M., Lum, J. A. G., Thierry, G., Nakai, S., & Keren-Portnoy, T. (2005). *Cross-linguistic experiments in infant word form recognition.* Unpublished manuscript, School of Psychology, University of Wales, Bangor.

Volterra, V., & Taeschner, T. (1978). The acquisition and development of language by bilingual children. *Journal of Child Language, 5,* 311–326.

Werker, J. F., & Tees, R. C. (1984). Cross-language speech perception: Evidence for perceptual reorganization during the first year of life. *Infant Behavior and Development, 7,* 49–63.

Wexler, K. (1998). Very early parameter setting and the unique checking constraint: A new explanation of the optional infinitive stage. *Lingua, 106,* 23–79.

Yip, V., & Matthews, S. (2000). Syntactic transfer in a Cantonese–English bilingual child. *Bilingualism: Language and Cognition, 3,* 193–208.

Zentella, A. C. (1999). *Growing up bilingual.* Malden, MA: Blackwell.

PART IV

Language Development after Early Childhood

Introduction

The chapters in this Part move beyond the period of early childhood to discuss language development in children who have, essentially, already acquired language as the field typically conceived it. Berman describes the developmental changes in language knowledge and language use that occur from middle childhood to adolescence. Descriptions of vocabulary, morphosyntax, and stylistic features of language use at the beginning of this age range (9–10 years) make the point that a great deal changes after the basics of language have been acquired. Not only does speech make use of a larger vocabulary and more complex syntax, but there are also changes in the type of vocabulary used (e.g., nominalized forms such as *desire* and *unwillingness*) and in the relations among syntactic structures (e.g., subordinate clauses may depend on other subordinate clauses, not just on the main clause of the sentence). Other major topics in the study of later language development are the use and comprehension of figurative language, the acquisition of literacy, and the development of a literate style of spoken language. Echoing the conclusions of earlier chapters, Berman argues that these depend both on internal cognitive and social developments and on external, experiential factors.

Oller and Jarmulowicz take on the topic of language and literacy development in children who are bilingual, thus picking up the story line begun by Genesee and Nicoladis in Chapter 16. Unlike the simultaneous bilinguals in Genesee and Nicoladis, however, the children in focus in Oller and Jarmulowicz's chapter have primary competence in one language but receive schooling in another language that they know less well. Two competing viewpoints dominate academic and political discussion of bilingualism in such children, who typically are born to immigrant parents and hear their parents' language at home more than they hear the language in which they will be schooled. One view is that this bilingual situation places the children at an academic disadvantage because they have less experience in the language of schooling. The other viewpoint emphasizes evidence that there is ultimately an advantage to being bilingual with respect to some cognitive and linguistic tasks. Oller and Jarmulowicz take on both views. They argue that the evidence that bilingual children trail monolingual children on some language measures has been "drastically misinterpreted" (p. 370) and offer instead an approach to considering the competence of bilingual children that takes into account their knowledge in both languages. They argue that the benefits of bilingualism are not just in ultimate metalinguistic and metacognitive effects but, more concretely, that knowledge of one language supports competency in another language to the degree that the two languages share structures. Thus, they argue for and illustrate a more concrete approach that asks not about general effects of bilingualism but instead about how knowing language A affects the acquisition of oral competence and literacy in language B.

Paradis focuses on children who are first exposed to a second language after they have some established proficiency in a first language and on the course of oral language development in that second language. Although it is widely believed that children have a special language acquisition capacity that adults do not have, that children soak up languages like little sponges, that children effortlessly and rapidly acquire native-like competence in a newly encountered language, the research Paradis reports suggests a more complex picture: obtaining oral language proficiency in a second language that is on a par with native speakers can take several years. Reviewing the evidence from this new field of study, Paradis finds that some aspects of language take as long to acquire in a second language as in a first. For example, first language learners of English master the plural form approximately 20 months after they begin speaking, and children who are second language learners of English master that form approximately 20 months after their first exposure. Other aspects of language are mastered more quickly by second language learners, suggesting there are some advantages for second language learning of being cognitively more mature and/or having already mastered something in another language. A hallmark of second language acquisition in childhood is variability. The range in the time it takes to learn a language and the ultimate degree of success is more variable in second language acquisition than in first. Paradis reviews the evidence regarding sources of these individual differences, finding some commonalities with first language acquisition (input matters) and differences as well (there are transfer effects). Paradis also discusses a frequent, and politically charged, consequence of second language acquisition: loss of competence in the first language.

Together the chapters in this Part move beyond the study of first language acquisition in monolingual children during the first 4 years of life. They describe an outcome that is richer and also more variably expressed in the population, thereby presenting new explanatory challenges for the theory of the human language faculty.

17

Developing Linguistic Knowledge and Language Use Across Adolescence

Ruth A. Berman

Developmental psycholinguistics since the 1960s has focused on preschool acquisition, rarely going beyond age 5. This is largely motivated by the Chomsky-inspired view of language acquisition as a rapid and efficient transition from the initial to the final state, and the recognition that "By 3 to 3.5 years of age, most normal children have mastered the basic morphological and syntactic structures of their language" (Bates & Goodman, 1999, p. 39). Preschoolers remain to this day the center of "natural," or untutored, language acquisition research, including from a usage-based perspective.

This chapter considers how language continues to develop across the school years, in the domain of *later language development* (Nippold, 1988). My point of departure is a key finding of cross-linguistic research on narrative development (Berman & Slobin, 1994). Asked to tell a story based on a picture book describing the adventures of a boy and his dog in search of a runaway frog, even children aged 3 to 4 years produced texts that were syntactically constructed according to the grammar of their language – confirming the Chomskyan view that language acquisition is a short-lived process. Yet the narratives of 9- to 10-year-old schoolchildren differed markedly from those of adults, in grammar and vocabulary as well as in narrative structure and content. We concluded that while becoming a *native* speaker is largely accomplished before school age, becoming a *proficient* speaker is a far more protracted process. This chapter elaborates on the finding that linguistic forms have "a long developmental history" (Berman & Slobin, 1994, pp. 593–594) and it reviews research which shows that becoming a proficient *user* of one's language across different communicative contexts continues into adolescence and beyond.

The scope of later language development has been specified as "language development after age 5" (Karmiloff-Smith, 1986a) or beyond "preliterate knowledge of language" (Berman, 1997), extending to "ages 9 to 19" (Nippold, 1988) or "the school-age and adolescent years" (Nippold, 1998). The focus of this chapter is developments from middle childhood to adolescence (Berman, 2004a). At the one end, age 9 to 10 years has been a helpful point for comparing preschool with school-age acquisition in both derivational morphology (e.g., Clark & Berman, 1984, 1987) and narrative development (Peterson & McCabe, 1983). By age 10 years, children have internalized a narrative schema, they have mastered reference to time, place, and participants in discourse (Hickmann, 2003), and by fourth grade, writing "as a notational system" is well established (Ravid & Tolchinsky, 2002; Tolchinsky, 2003).

At the other end, adolescence is a major developmental cut-off point for language as for other cognitive domains. High school speaker–writers of different languages differ markedly from younger schoolchildren in lexical expression, syntax, and style (Berman & Nir-Sagiv, 2004; Jisa & Viguié, 2005; Tolchinsky & Rosado, 2005). Besides, in terms of Piagetian cognitive maturation, adolescents have attained abstract thinking and have well-established metacognitive skills, developments that both enable and are fostered by advances in linguistic knowledge. This does not mean that later language development culminates in a clear *end-state*. Rather, the process continues across the lifespan, since the language used by adult speaker–writers of a standard dialect differs in significant ways from that of high school seniors (Ravid, 2004b; Reilly, Zamora, & McGivern, 2005).

This chapter focuses on psycholinguistic and developmental issues, while acknowledging the importance of research with clinical (e.g., Scott, 2004; Scott & Windsor, 2000) or pedagogical motivations (Cazden & Beck, 2003; Yearwood, 1979), or combinations of the two (Butler & Silliman, 2002). To illustrate, *spelling* was traditionally treated as a stumbling-block for poor students in gaining command of writing. By contrast, today, psycholinguists treat spelling as a source of insight into questions of implicit versus explicit knowledge, the mental representation of writing systems (e.g., Nunes, Bryant, & Bindman, 1997; Pacton & Fayol, 2004), and language-specific versus universal strategies in acquiring different orthographies (e.g., Gillis & Ravid, 2001). Against this background, the present chapter considers language development across the school years in vocabulary and syntax; non-literal language use and metalinguistic awareness; and extended discourse.

Language Knowledge – What Evolves?

This section considers the *what* rather than the *how* of later language development. An alternative route is to trace the developmental history of *particular constructions* across school age, to characterize what it means for a language learner to have "acquired" a linguistic form. Relatively few studies provide detailed developmental accounts along these lines (e.g., Berman, 2004b; Jisa, 2004). In place of detailed tracking of specific linguistic constructions from early emergence to late mastery, this section reviews general developments in vocabulary and syntax across the school years.

Vocabulary development

Vocabulary growth is the most salient and easily measurable facet of school-age language development. In *quantity*, the vocabulary of English-speaking children grows by several words per day, yielding an increase of thousands of words each year (Anglin, 1993). Numerous studies support the claim that "rate of acquisition [of meaning recognition vocabulary] during late elementary and high school years has been estimated at between 3,000 and 5,400 words per year (10–15 per day)" (Landauer & Dumais, 1997). This increase occurs largely without direct instruction in vocabulary, through indirect or incidental learning by exposure to a variety of knowledge-based and written language materials (Carlisle, Fleming, & Gudbrandsen, 2000; Dockrell & Messer, 2004).

School-age vocabulary also reflects a considerable change in *quality*. Advanced vocabulary involves items that are more *marked*, that is, greater in length, less frequent, semantically more specialized, and on a more formal level of usage than the everyday oral vocabulary of younger children (Anglin, 1993; Carlisle, 2000). In structure, derivational morphology – word-formation by means of affixing and compounding – plays an increasing role in more sophisticated vocabulary, with greater surface length and word-internal complexity of items like *lead-er-ship*, *desir-abil-ity*, *deriv-ation-al* (Ravid, 2004a). In content, advanced vocabulary learning involves changes in the representational status and semantics of lexical items. Knowledge of words extends beyond basic word meanings to varied senses of a single term, including synonymy – for example, the terms *doctor* and *physician* may both be used to refer to the same person – and polysemy – for example, *lesson* as both a school-based activity and a moral to infer (Booth & Hall, 1995; Keil, 1979).

Between grade and high school age, vocabulary use shows increasing sensitivity to level of usage or linguistic *register*, alternating between everyday colloquial language and slang usages in casual conversation and higher-register, more formal usages in academic, expository discourse (Biber, 1995; Ravid & Berman, submitted). In English, this involves relying more on words of Latinate origin rather than the everyday Germanic word-stock, most significantly from high school on, in writing compared with speech, and in expository compared with narrative discourse (Bar-Ilan & Berman, in press). For example, while preschoolers are familiar with denominal adjectives of Germanic origin (e.g., *dirty*, *rainy*, *sandy*), only school-age children use adjectives derived from Latinate nouns like *considerable*, *industrial*, *military* (Berman, 2004b; Clark, 1995).

These different aspects of school-age vocabulary development are reflected in text-embedded measures analyzing lexical *diversity* – the proportion of different words in a given text (Malvern, Richards, Chipere, & Durán, 2004); lexical *density* – the proportion of content words out of total words in a given text (Strömqvist et al., 2002); and lexical *complexity* – relative polysyllabicity of the words appearing in a text (Berman, Nir-Sagiv, & Bar-Ilan, in press). These converging trends are illustrated by expository texts produced by English-speaking students from three age groups (Grade IV, VII, and XI) asked to discuss the topic of "problems between people."[1] Content words (nouns, verbs, and adjectives) in (1) to (3) below are in italics.

(1) **Text written by fourth-grade English-speaking girl**
   I do not *think fighting* is *good*. You do not *make friends* that *way*.
   If you do not *fight*, you can have many many *friends*, but when you *fight*, you can *hurt* the *person's feelings* you are *fighting* with. You should always be *nice* and *respectful* to other *people*, and if you are not *nice*, you will *end* up not having any *friends*.

In lexical density, only one quarter of the 70 words in (1) are content words, and around half occur more than once. The text contains only one word of more than two syllables (*respectful*), and only five words of Latinate origin. This contrasts with the text in (2), written by a seventh grader at the same school.

(2)   **Essay of seventh-grade English-speaking girl**
      The *world* was not the *same* in the *earlier days*. *People trusted people better*. They *knew* everyone they are around. *People start thinking* about some *things* that they have *seen adults* do, and *automatically assume* it is okay. Many *conflicts* some *people* have *revolve* around *drugs*. For *example*, *cigarettes*, *alcohol*, and *weed* are the most *common*. Also, when you *reach* my *age*, there are *conflicts involving boyfriends* or *girlfriends*. *Friends* who have been *friends* for a *long time* begin to *fight* because they *change* at a *faster* or *slower rate*.

The text in (2) differs markedly from the fourth-grade text in (1). Nearly half of its 90 words are open class, and only seven of these are used more than once, far beyond (1) in both lexical density and diversity. Six words are more than two syllables long, there are five different adjectives, and the content vocabulary divides almost equally between the Latinate and Germanic strata of English. These developments are even more marked in (3), the first half of the *oral* text of a high school adolescent.

(3)   **Talk given by 11th-grade English-speaking boy**
      Okay, well, I *guess conflicts* are something that nobody *enjoys*, that nobody really *thinks* of as being *necessary*, but they're kind of a *necessary evil*, they help *identify people* through *difference* – *differences* of *opinion* as well as *different moral standards* and *things* of that *kind*. They're not always *completely bad*. I couldn't *think* of any *specific examples*, but *conflicts* of *opinion* usually *result* in the *bettering* of one *party involved*. I *guess* one *example*, not *necessarily* a *good* one, would be in the pol – the *American political system* between the *different political parties* that *run* for *office*. *Conflicts* of *opinion* often *arise* in *politics* and the *way* the *system* is *supposed* to *work* is the *party* who can *evolve* their *opinions* and *thoughts* to *match* those of the *people* most *correctly* is *elected* to *office*, and that's one *way* that *conflict* can be *useful*.

This text has two features typical of spoken compared with written usage, even though it is a discussion of an abstract topic: It contains numerous lexical repetitions, false starts, and informal discourse marker expressions like *okay, well, kind of, really*, and so it is lower in lexical diversity than the seventh-grader's written text in (2). But the vocabulary in (3) is more sophisticated than that of the younger children: The text has high lexical density – nearly half its 148 words are italicized content words – around one third of these are three or more syllables long, the bulk are Latinate in origin, and they include several adjectives and numerous abstract nouns.

   Such changes in lexical density and diversity across the school years are statistically supported by current research (Berman et al., in press; Malvern et al., 2004). Other advances include the fact that older children use far more abstract, non-imageable nouns like *evil, standards* and nouns used in a non-basic sense like *parties, office* (3 above); their verbs include conceptually more complex terms like *identify, arise, evolve* in the same text (Olson & Astington, 1986); lexical usage becomes semantically more specific, for example, not only *fall* but verbs like *topple, tumble, plummet*; and it includes metaphorical extension of more basic senses (e.g., not only *the boy's fall from the cliff* but also *the fall of Rome, his fall from grace*, or *fall in love, fall on hard times*). An expanding repertoire of set expressions (e.g., *conflicts of opinion arise, people are elected to office, a system is supposed to work*) reflects facility with idiomatic language and sensitivity to collocational appropriateness.

Several interrelated developments underlie these school-age advances in vocabulary. Increased familiarity with different types of written materials underlies achievement of a *literate lexicon*. This experiential basis combines with cognitive developments that enable older students to expand their repertoire along conceptually sophisticated lines. For example, use of *metacognitive* terms like *analogy, assume, interpret* in reading poetry indicates the emergence of critical thinking (Peskin & Olson, 2004). Moreover, lexical development interacts importantly with advances in other linguistic domains, particularly morphosyntax.

Syntactic development

The number of words per sentence is a reliable, rough and ready measure of developing syntax across the school years. Different analyses – for example, in terms of a T-unit (*terminable unit*) by Hunt (1965), as analyzed in Malvern et al. (2004, pp. 162–164); or a C-unit (*communication unit*), as in Nippold (1998, pp. 156–175) – reveal mean length of utterances and of sentences as increasing steadily across the school years. Defining an "utterance" or a "sentence" is problematic, especially in comparing spoken and written language. Below we use as our basic unit of analysis the *clause*, defined as "a single unified predication" (Berman & Slobin, 1994, pp. 660–663), as it is an easily identifiable and reliable unit for syntactic, semantic, and discursive analyses in different discourse genres and both speech and writing across languages.

Thus, the 14 clauses in the fourth-grade narrative in (1) and the 16 clauses in the seventh-grade essay in (2) both average five words per clause, compared with seven words per clause in the excerpt from the high school narrative in (3) (and over eight per clause in his written essay). High school students consistently produce longer, more densely packaged clauses than younger children, while expository texts average longer clauses than narratives, and written longer than spoken texts (Malvern et al., 2004; Ravid, 2004b). Research thus shows that *mean clause length* is a reliable if superficial criterion of *syntactic density*, comparable to mean length of utterance for grammatical complexity in early child language.

Qualitative analyses reveal that later developing grammatical constructions are more marked, they interact closely with the lexicon, and there is a big gap between initial emergence and eventual command of their use. In studying oral narrative development, we defined as "later developing linguistic forms" constructions that were absent from the texts produced by preschool children, rare in those of the 9-year-olds, and quite common with adults (Berman & Slobin, 1994). Examples in the (American) English sample were use of *past perfect* forms and *syntactic passives* with the auxiliary *be* rather than *get*. These results are supported by findings from the oral and written texts across adolescence. For example, in English-language narratives, use of the past progressive decreased and use of past perfect rose from fourth grade to high school, and high school and adult speaker–writers of different languages use passives far more than fourth and seventh graders (Jisa, Reilly, Verhoeven, Baruch, & Rosado, 2002; Reilly et al., 2005). Past perfect and syntactic passives, then, are marked constructions. The surface forms may emerge even at preschool age, but command of their use in discourse-embedded contexts continues into high school and beyond.

Another more advanced syntactic construction is non-finite subordination for textual connectivity – for example, the little boy climbed the rock <u>to search for his frog</u>, or <u>searching for his frog</u>, *the boy fell from the tree* in oral storybook narratives (Berman, 1998), or the infinitival <u>to match those of the people</u> in the text in (3). Use of infinitives, participles, and gerunds as main verbs increases significantly with age and schooling in English (Berman & Nir-Sagiv, in press), French (Gayraud, Jisa, & Viguié, 1999), and Spanish (Kupersmitt, 2006). The high school narrative in (4) – where clause boundaries are marked by], embedded clauses are in angled brackets, and clauses linked together into "packages" are indicated by a period – includes <u>underlined</u> non-finite subordination in one third of its clauses, and also wide use of past perfect forms (in italics).

(4) **Story written by 11th-grade English-speaking boy**
     A conflict arose the night of my best friend's 18th birthday party.] One of the guests *had been* in a bad mood all day] and thus by the end of the night *had sunk* into a state of depression.] Two of the other guests, ⟨<u>both having been good friends for some time</u>⟩, began to argue over the depressed guest's emotions.] One said] the guest should leave] or at least cheer up], as the party was supposed to be fun]. The other defended the guest], <u>saying</u>] we should feel sympathetic towards him.] The lack of rational communication ⟨that *had been* present between the two⟩, ⟨<u>coupled with some pent-up aggression</u>⟩, began to escalate the verbal conflict]. <u>Being an observer</u>] <u>to my friends' acting like this</u>], I began to worry.] I believed] that the situation would not escalate to physical conflict], but the situation looked grim]. Suddenly one friend pushed the other], <u>knocking him down</u>. I jumped out of the car] I *had been* in] and grabbed my fallen friend], <u>restraining him</u>] <u>from retaliating physically</u>]. Eventually we all calmed down], and I played the role of the rational thinker], <u>helping my friends</u>] sort out their emotions in a constructive and healthy way.]

The marked reliance on non-finite forms and high-level vocabulary (*escalate*, *retaliate*, *rational*) in (4) suggests a self-conscious attempt by high school students to attain a formal style of writing, differing from both the "plain English" of more competent writers and from their own casual spoken usage. Developmentally, however, younger children, including junior high schoolers, simply do not use these marked constructions, even in writing, relying instead on more basic constructions like active voice, simple past tense, and finite subordination. A key feature of advanced syntax, then, is the use of a broader, more marked repertoire of *expressive options* to meet the discourse functions of tighter connectivity, richer temporal texture, and a more formally distanced discourse stance (Berman, 2005a; Hickmann, 2003).

Sophisticated lexical devices are also deployed for advanced syntax. An example is use of *nominalized forms* of verbs and adjectives to create heavy noun phrases in place of finite clauses (cf. the following underlined forms from the expository text of the 11th-grade boy whose story is given in (4): *An <u>unwillingness</u> to listen can often escalate to both verbal and even physical <u>aggression</u>. An open mind and a <u>desire</u> to think the situation through rationally might possibly have prevented the <u>confrontation</u> from occurring in the first place*). Nominalizations are a mark of high-level, formal prose style and a very late morphosyntactic development in different languages (Comrie & Thompson, 1985; Ravid & Cahana-Amitay, 2005). Moreover, with age, constructions like passive voice and grammatical modals are used increasingly with less concrete nouns as their subject arguments – for example, *the issue was resolved* versus *my dress got torn*; *the situation may improve* versus *the train may be late* (e.g., Reilly, Baruch, Jisa, & Berman, 2002). The internal structure and content of noun phrases provide a qualitative means of evaluating syntactic density, for example "heavy noun phrases" such as *another <u>source</u> of conflict, close <u>contact</u> with someone unknown, the <u>relationships</u> in which they are involved* (from the essay of the boy whose story is excerpted in (4) above). Multidimensional analyses – including abstractness of head nouns, length in words, and amount, types, and depth of modifiers – reveal that the proportion of complex noun phrases increases markedly as a function of age, particularly from high school up (Berman, 2005b; Ravid et al., 2002).

The two-way interaction between an advanced lexicon and later developing syntax is also revealed through *clause-linkage* (Haiman & Thompson, 1988), also termed *syntactic packaging* or *connectivity* (Berman, 1998). Preschoolers can use complement, adverbial, and even relative clauses (De Villiers & De Villiers, 1985), but advances in use of these constructions require an expanded lexicon. For example, complement clauses occur with more sophisticated speech act verbs along with basic *say, tell, ask* – verbs like *announce, inform, demand*, which require more complex morphosyntactic constructions as complements. Adverbial clauses are extended from simple temporal subordinating conjunctions like *when, after* to *while, in the course of,* and clauses expressing causality are supplemented by concessives and conditionals with *although* and *unless*, while relative clauses use more marked relative pronouns like *which, whom, whose*. At the same time, textual connectivity is achieved by sophisticated sentence connectors like *however, on the other hand, instead* and by complex correlative constructions such as *if . . . then, only when . . . do they*, as in (4). Such constructions are the hallmark of a literate, academic style and they occur only from high school on.

Advanced syntax shows an increase in the number of clauses per package as well as in *depth of connectivity*, with coordinate and subordinate clauses dependent not on the main clause but on each other. This complex linking of different types of clauses nested inside each other is illustrated in the story written by a high school boy in (4) above.

Complex syntactic packaging is also found in the expository text in (5), translated freely from the original Hebrew.[2]

(5) **Expository essay written by 11th-grade Hebrew-speaking girl**
In the contemporary world (there) exist many social problems that we encounter daily and sometimes even ignore. They begin with words, insults, yelling and badmouthing in class, at home, all over, and end up with acts of physical violence. The problem is

that these things turn into something routine and normal in our society and that nobody attaches much importance to them, with the result that eventually the problems are not solved but persist.

The complex packaging of such high school texts derives not so much from the *number* of clauses linked together (typically only three or four clauses per package) as from the type of devices used for clause-linkage: non-finite clauses (*being an observer* . . .), center-embedded clauses, combinations of subordinate and coordinate clauses such as *One said that*] *the guests should leave*] *or at least cheer up*] and also *I believed that* . . . *but* in (4), and coordinated complement clauses in (5) in the sentence *The problem is that* . . . *and that*. In sum, sophisticated clause-linkage in discourse involves not only more clauses per sentence, or subordination as well as coordination. Rather, it means combining a variety of constructions instead of linking one clause to the next in a uniformly linear fashion.

This reflects a key feature of later developing linguistic knowledge and of advanced syntax in particular: Much of what children learn in the school years is not acquiring new forms as such, but how to deploy familiar forms for novel functions and to recruit new forms for available functions (Slobin, 1985). Thus, coordinate and subordinate constructions that children know from preschool age are later combined to form new types of complex sentences. Concurrently, new word-forms and expressions serve to elaborate familiar constructions, while new constructions trigger novel uses of earlier acquired lexical items.

As an example of this flourishing of morphosyntactic form–function interrelations from childhood to adolescence, take the use of the suffix *-ing*, among the earliest inflections acquired by English-speaking children (Brown, 1973). Later developments reveal a superficially U-shaped curve (Berman & Slobin, 1994, pp. 137–142): Juvenile use of these forms in isolation is supplemented by the auxiliary *be* – initially in present only much later in past progressive; these later recur in non-finite form – as complements of perception verbs (*see someone running*), later as nominalized forms (e.g., *fighting is not good*), and even later for non-finite subordination in adverbial clauses (*Running to meet her, he fell and twisted his ankle*) or relative clauses (*an issue requiring a solution*) – as in the high school text in (4). These findings for the multifunctional *-ing* forms illustrate the long route from initial emergence to eventual discourse-embedded command of grammatical forms and syntactic constructions. And they demonstrate the value of tracking the path of a particular linguistic construction from its initial preschool emergence to use by maturely proficient speaker–writers.

Linking Language Knowledge and Use

This section considers figurative language and consolidation of metalinguistic awareness as a bridge between linguistic and pragmatic development in the school years. A key facet of late-developing language use is the ability to comprehend and make appropriate use of non-literal language – jokes and riddles, similes and metaphors, idioms and proverbs – with "mastery of figurative language [is] a landmark in later language development" (Tolchinsky, 2004). It involves understanding different types of linguistic *ambiguity* – both lexical, as in "The first horse motel was opened to provide animals with a stable environment," and structural, as in "Did you hear about the cannibal who wanted to stop where they serve truck drivers?" (Ashkenazi & Ravid, 1998), and also *getting the point* of a joke or riddle and recognizing what is meant by "a sharp tongue" or "the pot calling the kettle black." Non-literal usages like these require that children understand the difference between *saying* and *meaning*, between the literal and the intended sense of an utterance (Lee, Torrance, & Olson, 2001; Levorato & Cacciari, 2002). This ability emerges as early as age 4 to 5, along with the ability to take into account the state of both one's own knowledge and that of the interlocutor or what psychologists term Theory of Mind (Astington, Harris, & Olson, 1988; Kuhn, 2000).

Nonetheless, even schoolchildren tend to process language in a largely literal sense. Thus, "While by second or third grade, children can clearly differentiate what is said from what is meant, they still have difficulty when this involves more complex tasks such as identifying inferences made in text understanding . . . And they are still in the early stages of developing the ability to say what they mean in their own writing and editing" (Peskin & Olson, 2004, p. 226). It takes until well after the early school years – in some domains such as irony, even beyond adolescence – for children to assign appropriate interpretations to different facets of non-literal language, including idioms (Cacciari & Levorato, 1989; Nippold & Taylor, 2002), metaphors (Gentner, 1988; Vosniadou, 1987), and different types of linguistic humor ranging from obvious to subtle (Mahoney & Mann, 1992). And the ability to comprehend and interpret poetry, the highest level of non-literal language, continues beyond adolescence and may even require special training (Peskin, 1998).

Metalinguistic awareness – being able to think about language as an object from without (Gombert, 1992; Olson, 1996a) – is another requirement for comprehension and production of figurative language and making inferences (Beal, 1990). Sophisticated metacognitive strategies are needed in order to go beyond the literal in interpreting speaker–writer intentions (Karmiloff-Smith, 1986b). As noted in Levorato and Cacciari's study of figurative language produced by schoolchildren, adolescents, and adults, "the metalinguistic awareness necessary to use figurative language in a creative way is acquired late, and is subsequent to the ability to comprehend and produce figurative expressions" (Levorato & Cacciari, 2002, p. 127). Between ages 7 and 17, considerable advances take place in processes of what Karmiloff-Smith (1992) terms "representational redescription" – contrasting with mere surface behavioral changes – in the shift from implicit knowledge to reflection on and explicit formulation of knowledge. Across the school years, such analytical metalinguistic awareness consolidates in phonology, lexicon, morphosyntax, and pragmatics (Carlisle, 2000; Demont & Gombert, 1996; Gillis & Ravid, 2003), ultimately being integrated across these domains.

Underlying these developments are general socio-cognitive abilities that emerge in middle childhood and consolidate across adolescence (Flavell, Miller, & Miller, 1993). These include the ability to shift from what Kuhn (2001) terms an "absolutist" to a "multiplist" level of thinking in order to interpret and encode states of affairs and

linguistic data from alternative perspectives (Ginsburg & Opper, 1988; Light & Littleton, 1999), and to literal thinking so as to contemplate abstractions (Inhelder & Piaget,
1958). Research in different languages points to the development of a more distant,
abstract, and impersonal discourse stance in different kinds of texts (Berman, 2005a)
and to a shift from judgmentally prescriptive, socially motivated to cognitively driven
epistemic attitudes – expressed linguistically by imperatives and prohibitions, on the one
hand, versus possibility and likelihood, on the other (Reilly et al., 2002). In sum, the
ability to relate to language beyond the basic, literal level of expression, and to regard it
as an object of reflection as well as a medium of use, are milestones of later language
that depend crucially on internal cognitive developments. Yet, as argued below, the fact
that linguistic knowledge becomes more analytic and explicit across the school years also
depends on experience with different contexts of language use and development of
literacy.

Development of Language Use

School-age language use involves both "linguistic literacy" – command of school language and academic-style discourse – and "discursive literacy" – pragmatic development
and communicative competence.

Developing linguistic literacy

Linguistic literacy involves "gaining increased control over a larger and more flexible
linguistic repertoire and simultaneously becoming more aware of one's own spoken and
written language systems" (Ravid & Tolchinsky, 2002, p. 420). It involves both linguistic variation – access to a range of different types of language use from everyday conversation to academic writing (Biber, 1988; Swales, 1990) – and metalinguistic awareness,
in order to learn from one's own linguistic output and input.

Linguistic literacy entails the impact of writing on knowledge of language and development of writing as a special style of discourse. Vygotsky (1962) early on recognized
that the act of writing imparts reflective awareness. Knowledge of writing promotes
awareness of the structural features of language, and the linguistic knowledge of literate
speaker–writers differs critically from that of less educated members of the speech community (Olson, 1996b, 2003). Some even claim that writing changes people's ways of
thinking in general (Donald, 1991; Goody, 1977).

Going beyond acquisition of writing as a notational system to mastering written language as a special discourse style is another important facet of later language development. It involves the ability to read *and* write in different genres, from sources of
interactive communication and information accessing like e-mail and Internet to the
academic-style language needed for school studies. Linguistic literacy is essential for
command of "book language" (Blank, 2002), and to be an educated member of a given
speech community.

Current research reveals an interesting interaction between speech and writing across the school years. In the early years of grade school, children tend to be preoccupied with the technicalities of writing (Wengelin & Strömqvist, 2004), and their written language is anchored in speech – although even fourth graders make some distinction between the two (for example, they avoid colloquial, interactive discourse markers such as *okay, and all that stuff, that's that,* when they write; Ravid & Berman, 2006). By high school, written and spoken usage diverges increasingly, with complex, higher-level vocabulary and syntax preferred for writing. Eventually, the way educated adults write will affect how they speak in more formal settings such as debating or giving a talk on an abstract topic (e.g., Strömqvist, Nordqvist, & Wengelin, 2004).

Developing discourse abilities

Discursive literacy also has a long developmental path. Defined as the ability "to interpret and construct extended discourse in genre-appropriate forms" (Blum-Kulka, 2004, p. 192), it proceeds from heavily scaffolded caretaker–child interchanges via peer-based communicative interaction to extended texts. Preschool pragmatic development is anchored in interactive conversation, while "autonomous," monologic discourse develops later (Ninio & Snow, 1996; Pellegrini & Galda, 1998). Research on school-age conversational interaction has focused largely on issues of gender, adolescent identity, or socialization rather than language development as such (e.g., Bailey, 2000; Cooper & Anderson-Inman, 1988; Zarbatany, McDougall, & Hymel, 2000). Blum-Kulka (2004, p. 194) and Donahue (2002, p. 240) note the relative paucity of developmentally oriented studies in this area, although several touch on language-related topics like conversations among friends, in the family, or teenage gossip (e.g., Blum-Kulka, 1997; Eckert, 1990; Gottman & Parker, 1986). Research on analyses of *classroom discourse* (e.g., Cazden & Beck, 2003; Mehan, 1985; Wells, 1993) indicates that school-based input from the teacher – as both "ruler of classroom conversation" and "facilitator of student participation" (Paoletti & Fele, 2004, p. 80) – might usefully be reconsidered as analogous to the role of scaffolding by caretaker input in early child talk.

Development of monologic text construction has been studied mainly with respect to narrative discourse.[3] This is conceptually well motivated by Bruner's (1986) distinction between the narrative and logico-scientific modes of thought and it is empirically supported by the early emergence of *inter-genre distinctiveness.* Even young school-age children can distinguish, for example, between personal-experience narratives and scripts (Hudson & Shapiro, 1991), storytelling and pretend play (Benson, 1993), fictional narrative and description (Tolchinsky & Sandbank, 1994), and prose narratives and nursery rhymes (Lee et al., 2001). And 9- to 10-year-old fourth-grade speakers of English, Hebrew, and Spanish express themselves differently in personal-experience narratives compared with expository discussions (e.g., Berman & Nir-Sagiv, 2004; Kupersmitt, 2006; Reilly et al., 2005), while English-speaking 10- and 12-year-olds distinguish similarly in producing fictional narratives compared with descriptive texts (Scott & Windsor, 2000). Thus, genre recognition is psychologically real and cognitively accessible from at least early school age.

There is extensive psycholinguistic research on the *narrative* genre before and across the school years. Even 3-year-olds are familiar with the narrative mode of discourse, at an age when storytelling is construed as typically interactive in both input and output (Blum-Kulka, 1997; Miller & Sperry, 1988). Between preschool age and middle childhood, narrative construction proceeds from immature linking of isolated events to fully-blown narratives with initial setting, episodic events, and resolution (Berman, 1995; Mandler, 1987). Research on oral narratives in different languages shows that by age 9 to 10 years, a *narrative schema* has consolidated (e.g., in personal-experience accounts – Peterson & McCabe, 1983; describing picture-series – Berman & Katzenberger, 1998; Hickmann & Hendriks, 1999; and a pictured storybook – Berman & Slobin, 1994; Reilly, 1992). And this is also generally manifested in stories that are *written* by fourth graders.

Yet command of fully proficient narrative production in different narrative subgenres continues into adolescence, in content as well as expression. Story openings provide more relevant information on background circumstances and motivations (Berman, 2001; Berman & Katzenberger, 2004; Tolchinsky, Johansson, & Zamora, 2002); appropriate reference is made to participants in the events (Bamberg, 1987; Hickmann, 2003); and, with age, the event-based storytelling of younger children is elaborated by a web of interpretive evaluations of the events recounted (Eaton, Collis, & Lewis, 1999; Ravid & Berman, 2006; Reilly, 1992). Only in adolescence will narratives reflect sophisticated storytelling skills going beyond structural well-formedness – in rhetorical expressiveness, metacognitive interpretations of events and participant behavior, and metatextual perspectives on discourse as an object of reflection.

Other developments in "discursive literacy" pertain to Bruner's (1986) non-narrative "logico-scientific mode of thinking." In considering non-narrative "reasoned discourse," Nippold (1998) analyzes *persuasion* and *negotiation* as two types of interactive oral discourse that involve both socially motivated communicative skills and cognitive abilities for logical argumentation, demonstrating that the shift from "adjusting to listener characteristics" or "taking the social perspective of another" to being able to control a discourse assertively or showing willingness to compromise follows a long developmental route from late preschool to adolescence. Relatedly, Goetz and Shatz's (1999) study of *justifications* used by 8- to 12-year-old children in peer interaction concludes that "the process of making justifications involves the complex interactions of linguistic, social, and cognitive abilities" (p. 747).

Monologic expository discourse is particularly relevant to school-based, academic language use. Psycholinguistic research in this domain has focused on cognitive processes of inferencing and causal reasoning in text comprehension (e.g., Graesser & Bertus, 1998; Noordman, Vonk, & Kempff, 1992; Singer & O'Connell, 2003). Convergent findings for how schoolchildren and adolescents *construct* non-narrative texts (Berman & Verhoeven, 2002; Scott & Windsor, 2000) show that being able to write an essay or give a talk discussing an abstract general problem such as "violence in schools" (Gayraud et al., 1999) or "conflicts between people" (Tolchinsky et al., 2002) is a more demanding task than constructing a story about these topics. On the one hand, as noted, young children use distinct forms of expression in narratives compared with expository discussion, and older schoolchildren rely increasingly on higher-register, more complex vocabulary and syntax when writing expository essays compared with telling a story (Ravid, 2004b). On the other hand, while 9- to 10-year-olds produce well-structured narratives, only high school adolescents can organize the content of their expository texts appropriately, by integrating top-down generalizations with bottom-up reference to subcategories and specific instances (Berman & Nir-Sagiv, in press; Katzenberger, 2004). The ability to construct an expository essay discussing an abstract topic is a hallmark of later-learned academic, school-type language. It requires socio-cognitive maturation of the type noted earlier for metalinguistic command of non-literal language. And it both depends on and feeds into the development of linguistic literacy.

In sum, discourse development across the school years departs from early concretely anchored conversational interactions, via personal experience and fictive narration, culminating in the ability to discuss abstract topics in formal communicative contexts such as giving talks and writing essays. Across high school and into adulthood, educated native language use becomes increasingly differentiated from that of early to middle childhood. It involves going beyond the home language and the language of the neighborhood to command of the approved *standard language* and culturally accepted norms of the speech community. This involves flexible alternations in level and type of language usage to suit varying communicative contexts and discourse purposes – including classroom language and other more formal styles of oral intercourse, on the one hand, and using different genres of written language and non-interactive discourse to both gain access and give expression to different knowledge domains, on the other.

Concluding Remarks

Knowledge and use of language thus develop into adolescence and beyond in vocabulary size and quality, clause-level and inter-clausal syntax, non-literal language, metalinguistic awareness, written language, and extended discourse. Different explanations have been proposed to account for these developments (summarized, for example, in Gillis & Ravid, 2003, Section 6.1; Tolchinsky, 2004, pp. 234–235). Clearly, no single factor can explain the complex and protracted route from preschool interactive language use to command of formal book language. Growth in *command of linguistic forms* and structures is an obvious prerequisite, but its pattern is not simply cumulative. Rather, forms previously used in restricted contexts and for limited functions are extended to new metaphorical and communicative contexts, while initially restricted discursive functions are expressed by means of an expanding repertoire of linguistic forms. Together, these developments underlie discursive literacy and the flourishing of rhetorical expressiveness in different communicative settings, from everyday conversation to expository essay writing.

These abilities depend crucially on *internal cognitive and social developments* in such domains as consideration of shared knowledge; re-representation of knowledge to enable metalinguistic reflection on earlier acquired linguistic structures; increased information processing capacities for comprehension and construction of complex discourse; the mental flexibility needed to alternate perspectives on different types of language use appropriate to different discourse goals; and the social maturity required for sensitivity to interlocutor needs and communicative goals.

These developments are also critically affected by *external, experiential factors* in the form of growing exposure to different types of discourse both inside and beyond the classroom. With age, new social experiences, extensive participation in peer culture, and a more independent lifestyle in schoolyard, neighborhood, and beyond provide contexts for different types of interactive language use. Concurrently, formal schooling provides students with opportunities for observing different varieties of language use – from informational prose to poetry – as both an object of reflection and a tool for acquiring new world knowledge. Classroom activities also promote use of more formal styles of language, more abstract vocabulary, and more complex syntax – including when dealing with problems in a "non-linguistic" area like mathematics (Lord, 2002). In these settings, linguistic literacy is inculcated, expanded, and exploited.

In all these respects – a growing repertoire of linguistic devices, social and cognitive developments, and increased schooling – *adolescence* constitutes a watershed in later developing knowledge and use of language. Research converges to reveal a significant cut-off point between grade school and junior high school children, on the one hand, and high school students, on the other, in: use of more advanced and higher-level lexicon and syntax; access to more communicatively appropriate levels of usage; expository compared with narrative discourse; and writing compared with speech. While these abilities emerge in early school age, command of appropriately varied language use – both socially effective peer interaction and carefully monitored, literate expository discourse – continues into adolescence. Maturely proficient knowledge and use of language require years of cognitive and linguistic maturation and experience with literacy-related school-based activities before attaining mastery.

Notes

1 Sample texts are from an international project on developing text production abilities funded by a Spencer Foundation Major Grant (Berman & Katzenberger, 2004; Berman & Verhoeven, 2002), with English data collection supervised by Judy S. Reilly, San Diego State University. Each participant produced an oral and written narrative and an oral and written expository text. Of the four text types, *written expository texts* consistently show the most complex, high-level, and self-consciously formal use of language.

2 Target language typology and rhetorical preferences affect the clause-combining strategies that are preferred. Hebrew reflects the classical Biblical style of parataxis, stringing parallel constructions by coordination, whereas Spanish favors non-finite subordination and embedded adverbial and relative clauses. Sandbank (2004) found such differences from the youngest age group in her study (first graders) and across the grade school years.

3 The term *monologic* is preferred here to *autonomous* or *decontextualized*, since most studies of narrative development use semi-structured elicitations. Besides, narrative production emerges in the context of interactive conversation, the most natural setting for storytelling across the lifespan.

References

Anglin, J. M. (1993). Vocabulary development: A morphological analysis. *Monographs of the Society for Research in Child Development, 58*, 10.

Ashkenazi, O., & Ravid, D. (1998). Children's understanding of linguistic humor: An aspect of metalinguistic awareness. *Current Psychology of Cognition* [Special Issue on Language Play in Children], *17*, 367–387.

Astington, J. W., Harris, P. L., & Olson, D. R. (Eds.). (1988). *Developing theories of mind.* New York: Cambridge University Press.

Bailey, B. (2000). Language and negotiation of ethnic/racial identity among Dominican Americans. *Language in Society, 29*, 555–582.

Bamberg, M. (1987). *The acquisition of narratives: Learning to use language.* Berlin: Mouton de Gruyter.

Bar-Ilan, L., & Berman, R. A. (in press). Developing register differentiation: The Latinate–Germanic divide in English. *Linguistics.*

Bates, E., & Goodman, J. (1999). The emergence of grammar from the lexicon. In B. MacWhinney (Ed.), *The emergence of language* (pp. 27–80). Mahwah, NJ: Lawrence Erlbaum.

Beal, C. R. (1990). Development of knowledge about the role of inference in text comprehension. *Child Development, 61*, 1011–1023.

Benson, M. S. (1993). 4- and 5-year-olds' narratives in pretend play and storytelling. *First Language, 13*, 203–224.

Berman, R. A. (1995). Narrative competence and storytelling performance: How children tell stories in different contexts. *Journal of Narrative and Life History, 5*, 285–313.

Berman, R. A. (1997). Preliterate knowledge of language. In C. Portecovo (Ed.), *Writing development: An interdisciplinary view* (pp. 61–76). Amsterdam: John Benjamins.

Berman, R. A. (1998). Typological perspectives on connectivity. In N. Dittmar & Z. Penner (Eds.), *Issues in the theory of language acquisition* (pp. 203–224). Bern: Peter Lang.

Berman, R. A. (2001). Setting the narrative scene: How children begin to tell a story. In A. Aksu-Koç, C. Johnson, & K. Nelson (Eds.), *Children's language: Vol. 10* (pp. 1–31). Mahwah, NJ: Lawrence Erlbaum.

Berman, R. A. (Ed.). (2004a). *Language development across childhood and adolescence. Trends in language acquisition research: Vol. 3.* Amsterdam: John Benjamins.

Berman, R. A. (2004b). Between emergence and mastery: The long developmental route of language acquisition. In R. A. Berman (Ed.), *Language development across childhood and adolescence* (pp. 9–34). Amsterdam: John Benjamins.

Berman, R. A. (2005a). Introduction: Developing discourse stance in different text types and languages. *Journal of Pragmatics, 37*, 2 [Special Issue on Developing Discourse Stance across Adolescence], 105–124.

Berman, R. A. (2005b, July). *Symposium on noun phrase structure and content in later language development: Text-based crosslinguistic analyses* [with H. Jisa, A. Mazur, D. Ravid, L. Tolchinsky, & N. Salas]. International Association for the Study of Child Language, Berlin.

Berman, R. A., & Katzenberger, I. (1998). Cognitive and linguistic factors in development of picture-series narration. In A. G. Ramat & M. Chini (Eds.), *Organization of learners' texts, 27*, 21–47.

Berman, R. A., & Katzenberger, I. (2004). Form and function in introducing narrative and expository texts: A developmental perspective. *Discourse Processes, 38*, 57–94.

Berman, R. A., & Nir-Sagiv, B. (2004). Linguistic indicators of inter-genre differentiation in later language development. *Journal of Child Language, 31*, 339–380.

Berman, R. A., & Nir-Sagiv, B. (in press). Comparing expository and narrative text construction across adolescence: Developmental paradoxes. *Discourse Processes.*

Berman, R. A., Nir-Sagiv, B., & Bar-Ilan, L. (in press). Vocabulary development across adolescence: Text-based analyses. In I. Kupferberg & A. Stavans (Eds.), *Language education in Israel: Papers in honor of Elite Olshtain.* Jerusalem: Magnes Press.

Berman, R. A., & Slobin, D. I. (1994). *Relating events in narrative: A crosslinguistic developmental study.* Hillsdale, NJ: Lawrence Erlbaum.

Berman, R. A., & Verhoeven, L. (2002). Developing text-production abilities across languages, genre, and modality. *Written Languages and Literacy, 5,* 1–22.

Biber, D. (1988). *Variation across spoken and written English.* Cambridge: Cambridge University Press.

Biber, D. (1995). *Dimensions of register variation: A crosslinguistic comparison.* Cambridge: Cambridge University Press.

Blank, M. (2002). Classroom discourse: A key to literacy. In K. D. Butler & E. R. Silliman (Eds.), *Speaking, reading, and writing in children with language learning disabilities* (pp. 151–174). Mahwah, NJ: Lawrence Erlbaum.

Blum-Kulka, S. (1997). *Dinner talk: Cultural patterns of sociability and socialization in family discourse.* Mahwah, NJ: Lawrence Erlbaum.

Blum-Kulka, S. (2004). The role of peer interaction in later pragmatic development: In R. A. Berman (Ed.), *Language development across childhood and adolescence* (pp. 191–210). Amsterdam: John Benjamins.

Booth, J. R., & Hall, W. S. (1995). Development of the understanding of the polysemous meanings of the mental-state verb *know. Cognitive Development, 10,* 529–549.

Brown, R. (1973). *A first language: The early stages.* Cambridge, MA: Harvard University Press.

Bruner, J. (1986). *Actual minds, possible worlds.* Cambridge, MA: Harvard University Press.

Butler, K. D., & Silliman, E. R. (Eds.). (2002). *Speaking, reading, and writing in children with language learning disabilities.* Mahwah, NJ: Lawrence Erlbaum.

Cacciari, C., & Levorato, M. C. (1989). How children understand idioms in discourse. *Journal of Child Language, 16,* 387–405.

Carlisle, J. F. (2000). Awareness of the structure and meaning of morphologically complex words: Impact on reading. *Reading and Writing, 12,* 169–190.

Carlisle, J. F., Fleming, J. E., & Gudbrandsen, B. (2000). Incidental word learning in science classes. *Contemporary Educational Psychology, 25,* 184–211.

Cazden, C. B., & Beck, S. W. (2003). Classroom discourse. In A. C. Graesser, M. A. Gernsbacher, & S. R. Goldman (Eds.), *Handbook of discourse processes* (pp. 165–198). Mahwah, NJ: Lawrence Erlbaum.

Clark, E. V. (1995). Later lexical development and word formation. In P. Fletcher & B. MacWhinney (Eds.), *The handbook of child language* (pp. 393–412). Cambridge: Cambridge University Press.

Clark, E. V., & Berman, R. A. (1984). Structure and use in the acquisition of word-formation. *Language, 60,* 542–590.

Clark, E. V., & Berman, R. A. (1987). Types of linguistic knowledge: Interpreting and producing compound nouns. *Journal of Child Language, 14,* 547–568.

Comrie, B., & Thompson, S. A. (1985). Lexical nominalization. In T. Shopen (Ed.), *Language typology and syntactic description: Vol. III* (pp. 349–398). Cambridge: Cambridge University Press.

Cooper, D. C., & Anderson-Inman, L. (1988). Language and socialization. In M. Nippold (Ed.), *Later language development: Ages nine through nineteen* (pp. 225–246). Austin, TX: Pro-Ed.

De Villiers, J. G., & De Villiers, P. A. (1985). The acquisition of English. In D. I. Slobin (Ed.), *The cross-linguistic study of language acquisition: Vol. I* (pp. 27–140). Hillsdale, NJ: Lawrence Erlbaum.

Demont, E., & Gombert, J.-E. (1996). Phonological awareness as a predictor of recoding skills and syntactic awareness as a predictor of comprehension skills. *British Journal of Educational Psychology, 66*, 315–332.

Dockrell, J., & Messer, D. (2004). Lexical acquisition in the early school years. In R. A. Berman (Ed.), *Language development across childhood and adolescence* (pp. 35–52). Amsterdam: John Benjamins.

Donahue, M. (2002). "Hanging with friends": Making sense of research on peer discourse in children with language and learning disabilities. In K. G. Butler & E. R. Silliman (Eds.), *Speaking, reading, and writing in children with language learning disabilities* (pp. 239–258). Mahwah, NJ: Lawrence Erlbaum.

Donald, M. (1991). *Origins of the modern mind: Three stages in the evolution of culture and cognition.* Cambridge, MA: Harvard University Press.

Eaton, J. H., Collis, G. M., & Lewis, V. A. (1999). Evaluative explanations in children's narratives of a video sequence without dialogue. *Journal of Child Language, 26*, 699–720.

Eckert, P. (1990). Cooperative competition in adolescent "girl talk". *Discourse Processes, 13*, 91–122.

Flavell, J. H., Miller, P. H., & Miller, S. A. (1993). *Cognitive development* (3rd ed.). Englewood Cliffs, NJ: Prentice Hall.

Gayraud, F., Jisa, H., & Viguié, A. (1999). The development of syntactic packaging in French children's written and spoken texts. In R. Aisenman (Ed.), *Developing literacy across genres, modalities, and languages. Working papers: Vol. I* (pp. 169–181). Tel Aviv University: International Literacy Project.

Gentner, D. (1988). Metaphor as structure mapping: The relational shift. *Child Development, 59*, 47–59.

Gillis, S., & Ravid, D. (2001). Language-specific effects on the development of written morphology. In S. Bendjaballah, W. U. Dressler, O. Pfeiffer, & M. Voeikova (Eds.), *Morphology 2000* (pp. 129–136). Amsterdam: John Benjamins.

Gillis, S., & Ravid, D. (2003). Language acquisition. In J. Verschueren, J.-O. Östman, J. Blommaert, & C. E. Bulcaen (Eds.), *Handbook of pragmatics* (pp. 1995–2013). Amsterdam: John Benjamins.

Ginsburg, H. P., & Opper, S. (1988). *Piaget's theory of intellectual development* (3rd ed.). Englewood Cliffs, NJ: Prentice Hall.

Goetz, P. J., & Shatz, M. (1999). When and how peers give reasons: justifications in the talk of middle school children. *Journal of Child Language, 26*, 721–748.

Gombert, J. E. (1992). *Metalinguistic development.* New York: Harvester Wheatsheaf.

Goody, J. (1977). *The domestication of the savage mind.* Cambridge: Cambridge University Press.

Gottman, J. M., & Parker, J. G. (1986). *Conversations of friends: Speculations on affective development.* Cambridge: Cambridge University Press.

Graesser, A. C., & Bertus, E. L. (1998). The construction of causal inferences while reading expository texts on science and technology. *Scientific Studies of Reading, 2*, 247–269.

Haiman, J., & Thompson, S. A. (Eds.). (1988). *Clause combining in grammar and discourse.* Amsterdam: John Benjamins.

Hickmann, M. (2003). *Children's discourse: Person, place, and time across languages.* Cambridge: Cambridge University Press.

Hickmann, M., & Hendriks, H. (1999). Cohesion and anaphora in children's narratives: A comparison of English, French, German, and Chinese. *Journal of Child Language, 26,* 419–452.

Hudson, J. A., & Shapiro, L. R. (1991). From knowing to telling: The development of children's scripts, stories, and personal narratives. In A. McCabe & C. Peterson (Eds.), *Developing narrative structure* (pp. 89–135). Hillsdale, NJ: Lawrence Erlbaum.

Hunt, K. W. (1965). *Grammatical structures written at three grade levels. Research Report #3.* Champaign, IL: National Council on the Teaching of English.

Inhelder, B., & Piaget, J. (1958). *The growth of logical thinking from childhood to adolescence.* New York: Basic Books.

Jisa, H. (2004). Growing into academic French. In R. A. Berman (Ed.), *Language development across childhood and adolescence* (pp. 135–162). Amsterdam: John Benjamins.

Jisa, H., Reilly, J., Verhoeven, L., Baruch, E., & Rosado, E. (2002). Cross-linguistic perspectives on the use of passive constructions in written texts. *Written Language and Literacy, 5,* 163–181.

Jisa, H., & Viguié, A. (2005). Developmental perspectives on the role of French *on* in written and spoken expository texts. *Journal of Pragmatics, 37, 2* [Special Issue on Developing Discourse Stance across Adolescence], 125–142.

Karmiloff-Smith, A. (1986a). Some fundamental aspects of language development after age 5. In P. Fletcher & M. Garman (Eds.), *Language acquisition* (2nd ed., pp. 455–474). Cambridge: Cambridge University Press.

Karmiloff-Smith, A. (1986b). From meta-processes to conscious access: Evidence from children's metalinguistic and repair data. *Cognition, 23,* 95–147.

Karmiloff-Smith, A. (1992). *Beyond modularity: A developmental perspective on cognitive science.* Cambridge, MA: MIT Press.

Katzenberger, I. (2004). The development of clause packaging in spoken and written expository texts. *Journal of Pragmatics, 36,* 1921–1948.

Keil, F. C. (1979). *Semantic and conceptual development: An ontological perspective.* Cambridge, MA: Harvard University Press.

Kuhn, D. (2000). Theory of mind, metacognition, and reasoning: A lifelong perspective. In P. Mitchell & K. J. Riggs (Eds.), *Children's reasoning and the mind* (pp. 301–326). Hove, UK: Psychology Press.

Kuhn, D. (2001). How do people know? *Psychological Science, 12,* 1–8.

Kupersmitt, J. (2006). *Developing text-embedded linguistic temporality in three languages.* Bar-Ilan University doctoral dissertation.

Landauer, T. K., & Dumais, S. T. (1997). A solution to Plato's problem: The Latent Semantic Analysis theory of acquisition, induction and representation of knowledge. *Psychological Review, 104,* 211–240.

Lee, E., Torrance, N., & Olson, D. (2001). Young children and the *say/mean* distinction: Verbatim and paraphrasing recognition in narrative and nursery rhyme contexts. *Journal of Child Language, 28,* 531–543.

Levorato, M., & Cacciari, C. (2002). The creation of new figurative expressions: Psycholinguistics evidence in Italian children, adolescents and adults. *Journal of Child Language, 20,* 127–150.

Light, P., & Littleton, K. (1999). *Social processes in children's learning.* Cambridge: Cambridge University Press.

Lord, C. (2002). Are subordinate clauses more difficult? In J. Bybee & M. Noonan (Eds.), *Complex sentences in grammar and discourse* (pp. 224–233). Amsterdam: John Benjamins.

Mahoney, D. L., & Mann, V. A. (1992). Using children's humour to clarify the relationship between linguistic awareness and early reading ability. *Cognition, 45,* 163–186.

Malvern, D. D., Richards, B. J., Chipere, N., & Durán, P. (2004). *Lexical diversity and language development: Quantification and assessment.* Basingstoke, Hampshire: Palgrave Macmillan.

Mandler, J. (1987). On the psychological reality of story structure. *Discourse Processes, 10,* 1–30.

Mehan, H. (1985). The structure of classroom discourse. In T. A. van Dijk (Ed.), *Handbook of discourse analysis: Vol. III* (pp. 119–131). London: Academic Press.

Miller, P. J., & Sperry, L. L. (1988). Early talk about the past: Origins of conversational stories of personal experience. *Journal of Child Language, 15,* 293–315.

Ninio, A., & Snow, C. (1996). *Pragmatic development.* Boulder, CO: Westview Press.

Nippold, M. A. (Ed.). (1988). *Later language development: Ages nine through nineteen.* Austin, TX: Pro-Ed.

Nippold, M. A. (1998). *Later language development: The school age and adolescent years* (2nd ed.). Austin, TX: Pro-Ed.

Nippold, M. A., & Taylor, C. L. (2002). Judgments of idiom familiarity and transparency: A comparison of children and adolescents. *Journal of Speech, Language, and Hearing Research, 45,* 384–391.

Noordman, L., Vonk, W., & Kempff, H. (1992). Causal inferences during the reading of expository texts. *Journal of Memory and Language, 31,* 573–590.

Nunes, T., Bryant, P., & Bindman, M. (1997). Morphological spelling strategies: Developmental stages and processes. *Developmental Psychology, 33,* 637–649.

Olson, D. R. (1996a). Literate mentalities: Literacy consciousness of language, and modes of thought. In D. R. Olson (Ed.), *Modes of thought* (pp. 141–151). Cambridge: Cambridge University Press.

Olson, D. R. (1996b). *The world on paper: The conceptual and cognitive implications of writing and reading.* Cambridge: Cambridge University Press.

Olson, D. R. (2003). The cognitive consequences of literacy. In T. Nunes & P. Bryant (Eds.), *Handbook of children's literacy* (pp. 539–555). Dordrecht: Kluwer Academic.

Olson, D., & Astington, J. (1986). Children's acquisition of metalinguistic and metacognitive verbs. In W. Demopoulos & A. Marras (Eds.), *Language learning and concept acquisition: Fundamental issues* (pp. 184–199). Norwood, NJ: Ablex.

Pacton, S., & Fayol, M. (2004). Learning to spell in a deep orthography: The case of French. In R. A. Berman (Ed.), *Language development across childhood and adolescence* (pp. 163–176). Amsterdam: John Benjamins.

Paoletti, I., & Fele, G. (2004). Order and disorder in the classroom. *Pragmatics, 14,* 69–86.

Pellegrini, A. D., & Galda, L. (1998). *The development of school-based literacy.* London: Routledge.

Peskin, J. (1998). Constructing meaning when reading poetry: An expert–novice study. *Cognition and Instruction, 16,* 235–263.

Peskin, J., & Olson, D. R. (2004). On reading poetry: Expert and novice knowledge. In R. A. Berman (Ed.), *Language development across childhood and adolescence* (pp. 211–232). Amsterdam: John Benjamins.

Peterson, C., & McCabe, A. (1983). *Developmental psycholinguistics: Three ways of looking at children's narratives.* New York: Plenum.

Ravid, D. (2004a). Derivational morphology revisited: Later lexical development in Hebrew. In R. A. Berman (Ed.), *Language development across childhood and adolescence* (pp. 53–82). Amsterdam: John Benjamins.

Ravid, D. (2004b). Emergence of linguistic complexity in later language development: Evidence from expository text construction. In D. Ravid & H. Bat-Zeev Shyldkrot (Eds.), *Perspectives on language and language development* (pp. 337–356). Dordrecht: Kluwer.

Ravid, D., & Berman, R. A. (2006). Information density in the development of spoken and written narratives in English and Hebrew. *Discourse Processes* [Special Issue on Surface Cues of Content and Tenor in Texts, eds. L. Lagerwerf, W. Spooren, & L. Degand], *41*, 117–149.

Ravid, D., & Berman, R. A. (submitted). Developing linguistic register across text types: The case of Modern Hebrew.

Ravid, D., & Cahana-Amitay, D. (2005). Verbal and nominal expressions in narrating conflict situations in Hebrew. *Journal of Pragmatics*, *37, 2* [Special Issue on Developing Discourse Stance across Adolescence], 157–184.

Ravid, D., & Tolchinsky, L. (2002). Developing linguistic literacy: A comprehensive model. *Journal of Child Language*, *29*, 419–448.

Ravid, D., van Hell, J., Rosado, E., & Zamora, A. (2002). Subject NP patterning in the development of text production in speech and writing. *Written Language and Literacy*, *5*, 69–94.

Reilly, J. S. (1992). How to tell a good story: The intersect of language and affect in children's narratives. *Journal of Narrative and Life History*, *2*, 355–377.

Reilly, J. S., Baruch, E., Jisa, H., & Berman, R. A. (2002). Propositional attitudes in written and spoken language. *Written Language and Literacy*, *5*, 183–218.

Reilly, J. S., Zamora, A., & McGivern, R. F. (2005). Acquiring perspective in English: The development of stance. *Journal of Pragmatics*, *37, 2* [Special Issue on Developing Discourse Stance across Adolescence], 185–208.

Sandbank, A. (2004). *Writing narrative text: A developmental and crosslinguistic study*. Unpublished doctoral dissertation, Tel Aviv University.

Scott, C. M. (2004). Syntactic ability in children and adolescents with language and learning disabilities. In R. A. Berman (Ed.), *Language development across childhood and adolescence* (pp. 111–134). Amsterdam: John Benjamins.

Scott, C. M., & Windsor, J. (2000). General language performance measures in spoken and written narrative and expository discourse in school-age children with language learning disabilities. *Journal of Speech, Language, and Hearing Research*, *43*, 324–339.

Singer, M., & O'Connell, G. (2003). Robust inference processes in expository text comprehension. *European Journal of Cognitive Psychology*, *15*, 607–631.

Slobin, D. I. (1985). Crosslinguistic evidence for the language-making capacity. In *The crosslinguistic study of language acquisition: Vol. II* (pp. 1159–1256). Hillsdale, NJ: Lawrence Erlbaum.

Strömqvist, S., Johansson, V., Kriz, S., Ragnarsdóttir, H., Aisenman, R., & Ravid, D. (2002). Toward a cross-linguistic comparison of lexical quanta in speech and writing. *Written Language and Literacy*, *5*, 45–69.

Strömqvist, S., Nordqvist, Å., & Wengelin, Å. (2004). Writing the frog story: Developmental and cross-modal perspectives. In S. Strömqvist & L. Verhoeven (Eds.), *Relating events in narrative: Typological and contextual perspectives* (pp. 359–394). Mahwah, NJ: Lawrence Erlbaum.

Swales, J. M. (1990). *Genre analysis: English in academic and research settings*. Cambridge: Cambridge University Press.

Tolchinsky, L. (2003). *The cradle of culture: What children know about writing and numbers before being taught*. Mahwah, NJ: Lawrence Erlbaum.

Tolchinsky, L. (2004). The scope of later language development. In R. A. Berman (Ed.), *Language development across childhood and adolescence* (pp. 233–248). Amsterdam: John Benjamins.

Tolchinsky, L., Johansson, V., & Zamora, A. (2002). Text openings and closings: Textual autonomy and differentiation. *Written Language and Literacy*, *5*, 219–254.

Tolchinsky, L., & Rosado, E. (2005). The effect of literacy, text type, and modality on the use of grammatical means for agency alternation in Spanish. *Journal of Pragmatics, 37, 2* [Special Issue on Developing Discourse Stance across Adolescence], 209–238.

Tolchinsky, L., & Sandbank, A. (1994). Text production and text differentiation: Developmental changes and educational influences. In S. Strauss (Ed.), *Learning environments and psychological development*. Norwood, NJ: Ablex.

Vosniadou, S. (1987). Children and metaphor. *Child Development, 58*, 870–885.

Vygotsky, L. S. (1962). *Thought and language*. Cambridge, MA: MIT Press. [Translated from 1934 Russian edition.]

Wells, G. (1993). Reevaluating the IRF sequence: A proposal for the articulation of theories of activity and discourse for the analysis of teaching and learning in the classroom. *Linguistics and Education, 5*, 1–37.

Wengelin, Å., & Strömqvist, S. (2004). Text-writing development viewed through on-line pausing in Swedish. In R. A. Berman (Ed.), *Language development across childhood and adolescence* (pp. 177–190). Amsterdam: John Benjamins.

Yearwood, B. (1979). *Sentence-combining in grade eight. Curriculum units by Fellows of the Yale-New Haven Teachers Institute: Vol. IV.* Yale, NH: New Haven Teachers Institute.

Zarbatany, L., McDougall, P., & Hymel, S. (2000). Gender-differentiated experience in the peer culture: Links to intimacy in preadolescence. *Social Development, 9*, 62–79.

18

Language and Literacy in Bilingual Children in the Early School Years

D. Kimbrough Oller and Linda Jarmulowicz

Background and Goals

Importance of research on literacy in bilingual children

Research on reading development in bilingual children is motivated by important questions about the nature of early reading and the skills on which it depends (see, e.g., Bialystok & Herman, 1999). Bilingual reading acquisition provides the opportunity to evaluate the components of language and reading skill required for different linguistic and writing systems, and research may help tease these components apart. Research on bilingual reading is also motivated by political concerns. For Hispanic immigrants to the United States, by far the largest group of second language learners, drop-out rates have long represented a social problem; lack of success in literacy (Frase, Kaufman, & Klein, 1999; Smith, 1995) is often assumed to be an important cause. Much effort has been devoted to investigating early phases of language and literacy acquisition in a second language for Hispanic children (see, e.g., August et al., 2003; Miccio, Tabors, Paez, Hammer, & Wagstaff, 2003).

Early intervention to prevent school drop-out may do well to focus on reading, because reading is crucial for further education and because there is evidence that Hispanic immigrants trail non-Hispanics in reading from early elementary school. School failure among immigrant children is not unique to the United States, and finding an explanation may be critical to provide a basis for early identification of problems in language and literacy and for early intervention (see, e.g., Verhoeven, 1994).

Goal of the chapter

This chapter is about interactions between differing linguistic and writing systems in the context of bilingual literacy in elementary school, and about how these interactions make bilingual literacy acquisition both similar to and different from monolingual learning. Most of the studies to be addressed concern children schooled in and learning to read in the second language only, but in some cases, to be specified as we go, both second language (L2) and first language (L1) education and reading are involved. The review emphasizes differences in early bilingual skill in various domains of learning with respect to monolinguals. Bilingual children in a variety of circumstances of schooling perform much better with respect to monolinguals on certain language and literacy tasks than on others (Oller & Eilers, 2002; Verhoeven, 1994). These "profile effects" in bilingual children's performance must be taken into account in any theory of bilingual learning. The goal of the review is to illustrate profiles of learning and to provide an interpretation of how these profiles are influenced by the particular relations between the two languages.

The principle that plays the largest role in relative bilingual and monolingual performance in each task type is based on the extent to which the two languages share concrete structures (phonological elements, letters of an alphabet, words, etc.). If the two languages have much in common (as when languages share many phonological elements), bilingual children do well compared with monolinguals, profiting from transfer across languages. If the two languages share little in a particular domain, there is little basis for sharing, and especially if the task of learning is large (as with vocabulary learning), bilingual children may trail monolinguals in both languages.

The present view contrasts with two widely publicized viewpoints. The first viewpoint emphasizes costs of bilingual learning, while the second emphasizes global benefits that have been widely reported to occur in successful bilingual learners. The first viewpoint emphasizes "time on task"; it notes that immigrant bilingual children often do not learn as much about L2 as monolinguals, because bilinguals may spend time learning L1, both at home and at school (Rossell & Baker, 1996). This first viewpoint also emphasizes evidence that immigrant children often trail monolinguals in academic tasks, and supporters argue for education of immigrant children in L2 only (Baker & de Kanter, 1981).

The second viewpoint emphasizes evidence that suggests bilingual children *ultimately* gain advantages by maintenance of L1, even if they initially trail monolinguals (Lambert, 1977; Swain, 1979). Late elementary school academic outcomes have been reported to be excellent in bilinguals, and consequently, supporters of the second view argue for education of immigrant children in both L1 and L2. Explanations about why long-term academic outcomes might be favorable for bilingual children have focused on *global* advantages of the bilingual experience, including metalinguistic advantages where children are thought to gain special insight in language (Bialystok, 1988). According to the reasoning, a "common underlying proficiency" emerges in bilinguals based on global perspectives attributable to the combination of linguistic and cognitive products of the two languages (Fitzgerald, 1995). Since monolinguals have only one language, their underlying proficiency is more limited. Successful bilinguals, in the second viewpoint, are predicted ultimately to *outperform* monolinguals in many linguistic and cognitive tasks.

Clearly bilingualism has practical advantages. But our concern in this chapter is not to create a case for bilingual education, a case effectively presented elsewhere (e.g., Krashen & Biber, 1988; Ramírez, Pasta, Yuen, Billings, & Ramey, 1991; Swain, 1979). Rather, we seek to clarify outcomes of bilingual learning of language and literacy. Here we differ from both the first and second viewpoints. The first is too narrow to offer a useful scientific assessment of bilingualism. Although elementary school bilingual children trail monolinguals in certain domains (especially vocabulary), this pattern has been drastically misinterpreted by advocates of the first viewpoint as underachievement. In fact a bilingual child's vocabulary capability cannot be determined by merely assessing performance in either language and comparing with monolinguals. The appropriate approach must consider *both* languages, a point illustrated below in discussion on the "distributed characteristic" of bilingual knowledge (Oller, 2005).

On the second viewpoint, we provide a contrasting interpretation de-emphasizing metalinguistic effects, and emphasizing concrete sharing of linguistic structures. The extent to which sharing occurs is determined by the extent to which structures are similar across the languages. This extent of sharing accounts for the primary profile effects seen in bilingual children in elementary school. The overwhelming patterns of differentiation between monolinguals and bilinguals can be understood only by explicitly accounting for concrete sharing of information across languages along with transfer effects that such sharing engenders.

Skills and Factors in Reading

Factors related to reading success

Learning to read, either as a monolingual or as a bilingual, involves a variety of language-based subskills. Reading is highly predicted by phonological awareness, the metaphonological ability to access and manipulate sounds in words. This includes phonological units of different sizes (i.e., syllables, onset-rimes, and phonemes), and may be measured by tasks such as clapping (where the child indicates how many syllables or phonemes are in a word), oddity (where the child names the word that differs from the others in onset, rime, or vowel as in "ball, boy, kite"), elision (where the child says a word such as "dog" without the first sound), or sound-matching (where the child might be asked to name the word that starts with the same sound as "dog": "pan, boy or dip"). Children who perform well in such tasks tend to perform well in reading (Bradley & Bryant, 1983; Fox & Routh, 1975; Juel, Griffith, & Gough, 1986; Liberman, Shankweiler, & Liberman, 1989; Tunmer, Herriman, & Nesdale, 1988; Vellutino & Scanlon, 1987; Wagner & Torgeson, 1987).

Reading is also predicted by at least three other factors: phonological memory (short-term memory for sounds), rapid automatized naming capability (speed of retrieval and production of words), and oral vocabulary knowledge (ability to recognize words and their meanings or produce words appropriately in naming tasks). While these abilities are all correlated with each other, each contributes unique variance to reading (Hansen & Bowey, 1994; Manis, Doi, & Bhadha, 2000; Wagner, Torgeson, & Rashotte, 1999).

In addition, tacit knowledge of a phonological system (i.e., command of perception and production of phonemic units and allophonic variants in a language) is believed to provide the foundation for much of the skill required in tasks such as phonological awareness, phonological memory, rapid naming, or oral vocabulary (see Goswami, 2000, for overview). Furthermore, lexical and phonological systems interact, such that vocabulary appears to affect phonological organization and specification (Goswami, 2000; Metsala & Walley, 1998). All these factors must be taken into account to explain reading acquisition in bilinguals or monolinguals. Higher-level functions of language, such as derivational morphology, syntax, and self-regulation, also play roles in reading acquisition, but these tend to show stronger effects relatively late in elementary school, when reading skills become more complex (Carlisle, 2000; Catts & Kamhi, 2005; Scott, 2005; Tyler & Nagy, 1990; Waltzman & Cairns, 2000; Westby, 2005).

Language interactions in bilingualism

To understand reading acquisition in bilinguals, we look to the unique character of bilingual knowledge. Research in bilingualism focuses heavily on interactions between languages (Cummins, 1979; Lambert, 1977). Bilingual individuals do not possess two independent monolingual capabilities, but rather an interactive system; when speech is perceived or produced in either language, the two language capabilities influence each other (see, e.g., Jared & Kroll, 2001). For example, hearing or seeing a word in one language makes remembering a related word in the other language more likely (Van Wijnendaele & Brysbaert, 2002). Multiple activation is also supported by latency-to-response effects; recognizing a word may be different in bilinguals and monolinguals, presumably because lexical storage in both languages must be referenced whenever a word in either language is retrieved by a bilingual (see, e.g., Carlo, 1995; Jared & Szucs, 2002).

The interaction between languages can have both positive and negative effects. Positive transfer effects occur when second language learners utilize knowledge of similar elements from L1 in learning L2. For example, if L1 has an [s], L2 learners may not need to acquire anything new to command a similar [s] in L2. This benefit is important, because [s] is typically late to appear in first language acquisition (see, e.g., Ingram, Christensen, & Veach, 1980). Many theorists (e.g., MacWhinney, 1999) assume that whenever elements of L2 are similar to those of L1, the L1 elements are imported. Empirical evidence supports the supposition of positive transfer. MacWhinney calls L2 learning "parasitic" on L1, transferring all similar elements.

At a later stage the learner must build a "firewall" between the languages, to allow differences between the two to be instantiated. For example, an element may exist in L2 that is absent in L1; English has a rare "r" which is produced as a semivowel [ɹ] with tongue retroflexion. Learners are often confounded by the English "r" and adapt the sound to their L1 by producing taps (from Spanish or Arabic, for example), trills (from Spanish or Italian, for example), labial glides (from Hebrew, for example), velar/uvular fricatives (from French or German, for example), or even glottal fricatives (from Brazilian Portuguese or Puerto Rican Spanish, for example). Languages can also differ in that two elements may exist in the one, where only one exists in the other. For instance, English has two vowels [i] and [I] (as in "beet" and "bit") that are often both adapted in Spanish-speaking learners to the Spanish [i] because no [I] exists in Spanish. Even [i] is not identical in the two languages, but represents a compromise that Spanish-speaking learners often adopt to substitute for both English vowels. In this way, contrastive information about words can be lost; "beet" and "bit" are pronounced indistinguishably to the English listener. This is negative transfer or interference.

If L2 learners are to become native or near-native speakers of L2, they must overcome effects of interference. Tracing acquisition of L2, accounting for L1 interference and its waning effects as learners progress, is a major task of research. Because reading depends upon knowledge of the language (including the phonology) in which reading is conducted, understanding bilingual reading skills requires understanding bilingual capability in the languages in question in terms of both auditory perception and speech production. The specifics of how L2 knowledge is structured at various points in learning must be understood to clarify how literacy is established in L2, and how it can go awry.

Theories and Evidence in Early Bilingual Language and Literacy

On interdependence and literacy development in bilingual children

Considerable research on transfer effects in bilingualism has been pursued in the context of the idea of "interdependence" (Cummins, 1979, 1981, 1991), implying that L1 and L2 knowledge can be mutually *supportive*. Interdependence implies that, in the right circumstances, bilingual performance can exceed monolingual performance on academic tasks. The reasoning suggests that interference between languages stimulates the bilingual learner to think in new and subtle ways, to recognize shades of meaning, and to make comparisons among linguistic structures (Stern, 1919).

Evidence of bilingual advantages has been compiled for generations. Sandra Ben Zeev, for example, produced and reviewed findings suggesting that bilingual children, although trailing monolinguals in vocabulary size, outperformed them in many tasks involving verbal reasoning (Ben Zeev, 1977b). Among the tasks where bilinguals performed particularly well were ones involving cognitive/verbal flexibility. Individuals quickly named as many uses as they could for a common object. Children answered questions requiring reasoning about the relation between words and their meanings. Children substituted words into sentence positions that produced ungrammatical sequences. Successful bilinguals outperformed monolinguals in these tasks. Importantly, bilinguals have been reported to perform as well as, or better than, monolinguals in reading for L2 after they have had 5 to 7 years to learn L2 in school, as long as L1 is substantially supported by instruction throughout the years of schooling (Collier, 1987, 1989; Fitzgerald, 1995).

Bilingual advantages in both oral and written modalities are often attributed to transfer occurring at a "metalinguistic" level (Bialystok, 1991, 2001). Research showing positive effects of interdependence has also been interpreted to imply development of a "common underlying proficiency" making mental capabilities of the two languages applicable to a variety of academic tasks (Fitzgerald, 1995).

Still, enthusiasm for bilingualism should not obscure the fact that it costs time and energy to learn a second language. These costs must be overcome if bilingual advantages are to occur. The idea of metalinguistic advantage in bilingualism implies that costs entailed by learning two languages may be *counterbalanced* by higher-order gains at a general level of verbal cognition. In this review, we sift evidence related to bilingual advantages and disadvantages in language and literacy.

Profile effects in bilingualism and interdependence

The idea of interdependence is taken to imply that verbal cognition advantages should accrue in bilingualism, at least in optimal circumstances of schooling, where both L1 and L2 are taught. But the generality of possible verbal cognition effects is challenged both empirically and conceptually. The empirical challenges concern "profile effects" (Oller, 2005) where bilingual learners perform much better on some tasks than others when compared with monolinguals. The large discrepancies in scores on different tests are not consistent with the idea of general verbal cognition advantages in bilingualism. An explanatory framework for profile effects in bilinguals requires focus on shared information in the structures of the two languages and on concrete circumstances of learning that differ for the languages. Below we review recent evidence related to tasks and circumstances that yield both high and low performance in bilinguals.

The conceptual challenges to the interdependence framework as traditionally presented are also substantial. Vehoeven has highlighted the criticism that Cummins' view "has been so broadly defined that it can hardly be tested empirically" (Verhoeven, 1994, p. 388). Consider, for example, Cummins' suggestions that interdependence effects should be strongest for academic tasks since these tend to involve *context-reduction* and *high cognitive demands*.

In fact, context-reduced communication is extremely common in *non-academic* settings. For example, a great deal of conversation is gossip (Dunbar, 1993, 1996, 2004), requiring context-reduction because its focus is persons not involved in the conversational context. Further, speakers report on current events, share information about new gadgets, make plans for meetings, criticize the government, and evangelize.

Although context-reduced discourse may be uncommon in preschoolers, context-reduced discourse develops steadily in elementary school (Nippold, 1998; Scott, 1994). Narratives become more context-reduced and develop in conjunction with improving presuppositional skills, lexical and syntactic maturity, and mastery of narrative genres (Scott, 1994). Both conversational and narrative discourse develop in conjunction with children's ability to read and function in context-reduced circumstances in school.

Emphasis on context-reduction of communication in school settings may be overplayed in the interdependence hypothesis given that the opposite, *context-embedding*, is a primary method used in school to help launch children's abilities to understand complex language and to read. Children are systematically presented with pictorial representations, demonstrations, or play-acting to support learning of new words and concepts and to support literacy acquisition. Further, imitation and repetitive practice are encouraged in circumstances designed to augment contextual support. Moreover, language directed toward children in elementary school often includes terminology and syntax appropriate to transmit immediate procedural information about how to act. When the kindergarten teacher says, "Everybody please be seated," a child who only partially understands the words and syntax may grasp the meaning by observation of what other children do. When the second-grade teacher says, "Please be quiet while I write the instructions on the board," understanding may be supported by observation of what the teacher does. This sort of information is richly context-embedded. Furthermore, effort is often made in school settings to provide children with instructional feedback when they fail to understand, thus providing contextual support within the academic setting. Children are often encouraged to personalize new information thereby making it more contextualized.

The same concern applies to the suggestion in the traditional reasoning about interdependence that bilingual advantages apply especially in circumstances of *high active cognitive involvement*, posited to be specific to the academic setting. In fact, high cognitive involvement is present in a wide variety of settings. Mature speakers talk about complicated matters involving political life, how to manipulate software, who is related to whom and so on. Whenever speakers introduce new information or attempt to interpret, analyze, correct misconception, convince or persuade, they invoke high cognitive demands.

As in the case of adult communication, cognitive demands for children in tasks outside of school may also be as high as demands in the academic setting. The fact that curricula are designed often to systematically use contextual support suggests that school-based communications might (from the child's perspective) be *less* rather than more cognitively demanding than communications outside of school.

This reasoning does not contradict the idea that the bulk of children's communications outside of school may be context-embedded in cultural expectations and experiences, or schemas formed as a result of culturally embedded experiences. Much of what is not explicit in a communicative exchange can be filled in by conversation partners with similar experiences. In contrast to monolingual peers, bilingual children may arrive at school with different cultural expectations and interpretations of communication. Nevertheless, both monolingual and bilingual children are required to navigate cultural and academic expectations. The challenge for the interdependence hypothesis, with its emphasis on complex school tasks and their role in reported bilingual advantages, is that active cognitive and complex cultural interpretation apply to *both* monolingual and bilingual children in *both* school and non-school settings.

On the domain specificity of transfer between languages

Transfer of linguistic skills seems to occur most effectively when there are concrete similarities between languages that can be exploited in transfer. More abstract interdependence effects on verbal cognition implied by the terms "metalinguistic" or "common underlying proficiency" appear also to exist, but their effect sizes tend to be relatively small, and their consistency across studies is often shaky. On the other hand, many profile effects that suggest domain specificity in patterns of bilingual learning show consistent outcomes and large effect sizes in elementary school.

The strongest language and literacy transfer tendencies appear to be compatible with interpretations that emphasize transfer of concrete structural elements that are shared between languages (as when two languages have certain very similar phonological elements); we see weaker (or lack of) effects of language and literacy transfer when sharing is limited to more abstract characteristics of language and literacy (as for example when languages share a writing system that is alphabetical, although composed of different letters). Thus, the strongest effects of bilingual performance in elementary school may be based on sharing of elements and may require no appeal to metalinguistic effects of interdependence.

The problem of tracing bilingual literacy development and its relation to both L1 and L2 development of language *per se* is, then, complicated by the fact that transfer does not occur to the same degree in all domains of language and literacy, and this is true whether children learn to read in one or both languages. In fact, recent evidence suggests stark differences across domains of function in the degree to which transfer between languages occurs. For example, the large-scale correlational research of Verhoeven (1994) determined that for Turkish–Dutch bilingual children, whether schooled in Dutch only or in Dutch and Turkish in early elementary school, transfer occurred for phonological skills, for certain discourse capabilities, and for literacy. However, lexical and syntactic learning were largely independent across languages. Subsequent work (Verhoeven, 2000), also based on a large sample, indicated that bilingual minority students (Turkish, Moroccan, and Caribbean) trailed monolingual Dutch children substantially in lexical knowledge, but that their decoding skills were comparable with those of monolinguals. Effect sizes in the Verhoeven work differed sharply across domains of testing: "The vocabulary scores for the minority children were more than two standard deviations below those for their native Dutch peers" (Verhoeven, 2000, p. 326). Decoding skills were essentially the same in monolinguals and bilinguals, but a variety of additional tasks (e.g., spelling and reading comprehension) showed discrepancy between bilinguals and monolinguals (though not as much as in vocabulary), with bilinguals trailing by half a standard deviation or more.

In a large study in Miami, early elementary bilinguals in Spanish and English, some studying in both languages, some in English only, also showed high correlations across languages for early literacy skills (e.g., reading comprehension, phonics, writing), but low correlations for oral language skills (e.g., oral picture naming, oral vocabulary reasoning). Further, bilinguals showed profile effects indicating low oral vocabulary compared with monolinguals, even though their levels of decoding in simple reading tasks were comparable with those of monolinguals in both languages (see Cobo-Lewis, Pearson, Eilers, & Umbel, 2002a, 2002b; Oller & Eilers, 2002).

As in the case of the Verhoeven studies, effect sizes in the Miami work suggested large differences favoring monolinguals for vocabulary knowledge (both receptive and productive) in both languages, much smaller differences favoring monolinguals for oral language reasoning, writing skill, and reading comprehension, but no discernible differences between monolinguals and bilinguals in word decoding. Importantly, the pattern of profiles with high bilingual scores in word decoding, low scores in vocabulary, and intermediate scores in oral reasoning and reading was consistent across eight subgroups of bilingual subjects (groups: high vs. low socio-economic status, two-way vs. English immersion instruction, and English-only at home vs. Spanish and English at home) (Oller, Cobo-Lewis, & Pearson, 2004). Furthermore, the profile differences applied to tests in both English and Spanish.

Possible bases of the profile effects

If subtractive bilingualism or failure to provide training in L1 were the sources of low scores on some tests in the Miami study, then (in accord with interdependence reasoning) we should expect low scores in the English immersion groups only. But in fact the low scores of bilinguals with respect to monolinguals in both languages in the Miami study applied strongly to both two-way and English immersion education. The pattern thus cannot be attributed simply to subtractive bilingualism or to a schooling method that failed to support L1. Children in both schooling groups showed profiles with large effect sizes at both second and fifth grade and in both English and Spanish.

It is well known that socio-economic status (SES) plays an important role in school success. Again, associated with the interdependence claim, it has been suggested that immigrant children from low socio-economic background may fail in school and in attaining high levels of bilingualism for reasons related to low social support for learning at home, social status at school, and access to educational resources associated with high SES. Yet, although bilingual children from high SES subgroups in Miami substantially outperformed low SES subgroups overall, both groups showed profile effects where word decoding performance was comparable to performance of monolinguals but vocabulary performance was much lower than that in monolinguals. In all comparisons, both high and low SES bilinguals' reading comprehension proved to be intermediate in comparison with monolinguals. These robust outcomes are not, then, the result of low SES in the bilingual sample.

The profile outcomes of these large-scale investigations suggest powerful effects that are not explained by the traditional interdependence view. The results are instead consistent with the idea that certain kinds of learning are transferable across languages *because of the nature of the material to be transferred*. In recent interpretations, Oller and colleagues (Oller, 2005; Oller et al., 2004) have argued that decoding skills transfer well for English–Spanish bilinguals because the languages largely *share an alphabet* and because there is a finite size to learning phonology and graphemic–phonemic mappings in both languages.

On the other hand, vocabulary learning requires open-ended acquisition of items that are unshared across languages. Partly because vocabularies are open-ended and partly because of differences in circumstances of learning for the two languages (for example, somewhat different words are learned at home and at school), lexical knowledge of a bilingual tends to be distributed across the two languages (Oller & Pearson, 2002) such that only some words are known in both languages as "doublet" vocabulary. Other words are known in one language or the other as "singlet" vocabulary, because the words tend to be used in settings where one of the languages is preferentially spoken. This "distributed characteristic" of bilingual lexical knowledge results in lower scores in vocabulary for both languages compared with monolingual peers (Ben Zeev, 1977a; Fernández, Pearson, Umbel, Oller, & Molinet-Molina, 1992; Rosenblum & Pinker, 1983; Umbel, Pearson, Fernández, & Oller, 1992). At the same time, bilinguals actually may have as many or more concepts lexicalized across the two languages as monolinguals do in their single language (Pearson, 1998; Pearson, Fernández, & Oller, 1995; Pearson, Umbel, Andrews de Flores, & Cobo-Lewis, 1999). The results suggest *not* that bilinguals are poor vocabulary learners, but that learning two languages results in a distributed pattern that thwarts the attempt to compare general learning abilities of bilingual and monolingual children based on comparisons of performance in vocabulary to monolingual norms.

In most cases, vocabulary knowledge is not amenable to transfer because word-forms are different across languages. Only in the case of cognate words can transfer be expected, and even there, special semantic learning is often necessary. The fact that vocabularies of natural languages are huge imposes on the bilingual learner a requirement to learn enormous numbers of lexicalizations twice.

Phonological systems include a tiny fraction of the number of elements that occur in lexicons, and notably phonological systems all over the world draw from a common base of universal phonological elements. So there is always a set of syllables and phonemes that are shared across languages. Further, among the language-specific phonological elements that each language possesses, there may be additional sharing of elements, especially among related languages.

As for graphemic elements, languages vary tremendously, and there are no universal graphemes. Still, many languages use essentially the same alphabets for writing. For example, the great bulk of the European languages use a Latin-based graphemic system, with only a few alterations. So there is a vast contrast in degree of amenability for transfer across languages in vocabulary versus decoding. The former depends on individual item learning in each language for huge numbers of words that cannot be shared, while the latter depends on learning of a much smaller set of elements that *can be* predominantly shared across languages.

The reasoning of Oller and colleagues suggests that the difference in outcomes for transfer across languages is most extreme for decoding (where transfer is high and scores for bilinguals are high) and vocabulary (where transfer is low and scores for bilinguals are low). Other skills, such as reading comprehension, show intermediate scores in bilinguals according to the reasoning because they recruit a combination of skills including vocabulary knowledge (which is low in bilinguals) and decoding (which is high). Oral vocabulary reasoning (determining synonyms or antonyms, or assessing oral analogies) produces intermediate scores also because it recruits a combination of skills, including raw vocabulary knowledge (which is low in bilinguals) and reasoning abilities about known vocabulary (which are presumably unimpaired in bilinguals).

Transfer of phonological awareness and decoding skills across languages

Much research has addressed whether positive transfer occurs between languages in phonological awareness, which is known to be related to word decoding skills in languages with alphabetical writing systems. On the whole, evidence favors the idea that bilinguals whose languages have related alphabetical writing systems may indeed experience benefits from transfer across the languages. For example, Bruck and Genesee (1995) found that French–English bilingual kindergarteners and first graders had generally good phonological awareness skills but showed mixed outcomes on individual subtests. Bilinguals scored better than monolinguals in syllable segmentation, but monolinguals outperformed bilinguals in phoneme awareness. The two groups performed similarly on onset-rime awareness. The authors interpreted the outcome as reflecting a role for L2 input in phonological awareness, but the results cannot be interpreted to indicate an overall enhancement in phonological awareness in bilinguals since the outcomes were mixed. Rather, the results are most appropriately interpreted to indicate that bilinguals are roughly on par with monolinguals in phonological awareness in the French–English case.

On the other hand, Bialystok, Majumder, and Martin (2003) found that Spanish–English bilinguals between kindergarten and second grade outperformed English monolinguals on a phoneme segmentation task, suggesting that the experience of learning to read in both languages fostered positive transfer. However, Chinese–English bilinguals did not show the same effect, but were outperformed by monolinguals on phoneme segmentation.

French and English share the Latin alphabet, whereas Chinese uses a character-based ideographic system that is largely morphosyllabic and non-alphabetic. The combination of results from Bruck and Genesee and Bialystok et al. may be interpreted to mean that transfer of phonological awareness skills is more likely to occur *when the two languages share an alphabetical system* around which the transfer can be built. Note that this outcome is compatible with the notion that transfer is a product of specific element sharing across languages rather than being a product of abstract knowledge of reading, or common underlying language proficiency.

Additional studies support the idea that when two languages largely share an alphabetical system, transfer of phonological awareness skills can occur (Bruck & Genesee, 1995, for English–French bilinguals; Campbell & Sais, 1995, and D'Angiulli, Siegel, & Serra, 2001, for English–Italian; Baum Bursztyn, 1999, Durgunoglu, Nagy, & Hancin-Bhatt, 1993, Lindsey, Manis, & Bailey, 2003, and Quiroga, Lemos-Britton, Mostafapour, Abbott, & Berninger, 2002, for Spanish–English).

Transfer of reading skills across languages with alphabetical writing systems

Of special interest is the possibility that there might be transfer of phonological awareness or decoding skills across languages that do not share a specific alphabet, but that both possess alphabets of some kind. This is the circumstance with English and Urdu. Urdu writing is an adaptation of Persian. Both English and Urdu possess alphabets, but letters in English and Urdu are different in every instance. Also, the mapping from graphemes to phonemes in Urdu is regular, although each grapheme has potential variations by position of occurrence (initial, medial, final). English on the other hand has many irregularities: phonemes have multiple graphemic representations and vice versa.

Mumtaz and Humphreys (2002) studied immigrant children in England, reporting that strongly bilingual Urdu–English children were better readers of nonsense words and real words than immigrant children who were more like monolingual English speakers (having low Urdu vocabulary), as long as the words followed regular patterns of graphemic–phonemic relation, as occurs in Urdu. The same advantage did not apply if words were irregular in graphemic–phonemic relation, as commonly occurs in English. On irregular words, children with low Urdu vocabulary performed better in reading. One interpretation of the study is that the children abstracted principles of graphemic–phonemic relation, as long as the language being learned presented regular graphemic–phonemic relations, and that learning these principles in one language encouraged acquisition of regular graphemic–phonemic relations in the other language. The results suggest that principles thus learned do not apply to learning the more complex mappings found in an irregular orthographic system (English). On the contrary, if irregular mappings occur, learning them may result in better performance in English, but at the expense of poorer ability to read words with regular patterns. Reading in a language like English appears to require two strategies, one for regular mappings (an alphabetical strategy) and another for irregular ones (a strategy based on memorization of written word-shapes); the results of the Urdu work suggest that bilinguals may acquire different degrees of balance with regard to which strategy is emphasized depending on the degree of experience they have with the two languages.

Mumtaz and Humphreys' study does not suggest a simple interdependence advantage. Rather it suggests *transfer effects that depend on the specific experiences*. Since the two languages in this case do not share an alphabet, but merely an alphabetical principle, transfer can occur at the level of the principle rather than at the level of particular units (because there are no shared letters to transfer in this case). But even at the level of the alphabetical principle, the differences between the systems of writing result in different strategies (one emphasizing regular relations and one emphasizing irregular ones), and use of these strategies depends on the degree that bilingual children are exposed to each of the languages.

Further evidence regarding effects of bilingualism in languages with different alphabetically based writing systems is found in Arab-Moghaddam and Sénéchal (2001), who evaluated Persian–English bilinguals learning to read in the two languages with their different alphabets. The results of the large-scale study showed very high within-language correlations between reading measures (for example, reading real words vs. nonsense words, .67 and .87 for Persian and English, respectively, correcting for grade level), usually accounting for more than half the variance, but much lower between-language correlations on the same measures (.24 and .25), accounting for less than 7% of variance. The authors evaluated numerous high correlations for within-language and low correlations for between-language measures, and concluded that "concurrent acquisition of literacy skills in two languages that bear no visual resemblance to each other might occur fairly independently for the two languages" (p. 145).

Mumtaz and Humphreys' study agreed with that of Arab-Moghaddam and Sénéchal in showing high correlations for reading measures within language (ranging from .66 to .93), but across-language correlations depended upon whether words could be read according to regular grapheme–phoneme mappings. There were high correlations for reading regular English words and words in Urdu (where all words are regular) (values from .62 to .68). At the same time, correlations between reading irregular English words and reading Urdu words were very low indeed, averaging .10. The correlations suggest selective transfer effects for reading skills, where the determining factor is not general metalinguistic ability, but the degree of sharing of specific strategies required to read in each language.

The Mumtaz and Humphreys results suggest that the lower between-language correlations for reading in the Arab-Moghaddam and Sénéchal study may have been the result of combined effects of two correlational subcomponents pertaining to grapheme–phoneme correspondences: one high value, corresponding to correlations of regular mappings across the two languages, and one low value, corresponding to correlations for irregular mappings in English with regular mappings in Persian.

These results also should be considered in the context of correlational outcomes for languages that share an alphabet, letters and all. For example, the Miami project, with Spanish–English bilinguals, showed high correlations between languages on reading measures (Cobo-Lewis, Eilers, Pearson, & Umbel, 2002), but much lower correlations for oral vocabulary or oral language reasoning. The outcome appears to mean that when children learn two systems with shared alphabets, a great deal of information can transfer. Other studies on Spanish–English bilingual children provide supporting evidence (Carlisle, Beeman, Davis, & Spharim, 1999; Lindsey et al., 2003; Riccio et al., 2001; Varona-Vicente, 2001).

To summarize, there is much evidence that cross-language transfer in phonological awareness and decoding is facilitated when two languages share an alphabet. On the other hand, if one has an alphabet and the other an ideographic system, there may be little or no transfer, even though evidence suggests that is a predictor of reading ability in both languages (McBride-Chang & Kail, 2002). If languages share the alphabetic principle, but have different alphabets, the outcome seems to depend upon the degree of regularity of mappings within the alphabetical systems, and the degree to which individual children learn the two languages. The general pattern of transfer for phonological awareness and decoding skills indicates that the more two languages share in concrete elements and principles of writing, the more basis there is for transfer. The simple sharing principle in transfer suggests it may not be necessary to invoke either general interdependence or a metalinguistic principle to account for it.

The Balance of Evidence on Advantages of Bilingualism

Of course, the evidence reviewed here does not rule out the possibility that a more general interdependence or metalinguistic principle may operate in many cases. The profile effects may obscure subtle effects of metalinguistic advantage. In fact, such advantages may not always be subtle. Many articles report bilingual children performing well compared with monolinguals in tasks involving metalinguistic skills (e.g., Edwards & Christophersen, 1988; Francis, 1999; Lindsey et al., 2003). Minimal exposure to a second language may improve performance on metalinguistic tasks in the short term, although these benefits do not appear to be sustained (Yelland, Pollard, & Mercuri, 1993). Bialystok provides substantial and well-reasoned reviews of research suggesting general cognitive advantages in successful bilingualism (Bialystok, 1999, 2001).

The proviso that it is "successful" or relatively "balanced" bilingualism that correlates with bilingual advantages in cognition suggests an interpretation that is not often emphasized. Perhaps successful bilinguals are more talented in some fundamental way than those who fail to become balanced bilinguals. Paradis (this volume) outlines characteristics of successful bilinguals. The importance of individual differences in successful L2 acquisition is emphasized by Cummins (1991) as well. Balanced bilingualism is rare. Children learning a second language in the United States usually experience subtractive rather than additive bilingualism, and thus do not usually become balanced bilinguals. Consequently, better performance on general cognitive tasks by successful bilinguals could be the result of these individuals' greater innate talents for language learning and other academic skills, rather than being the result of bilingualism *per se* (Hakuta, 1987).

Our overall conclusion is that the primary patterns reported in large-scale and well-controlled studies of transfer across two languages may be largely based on sharing in the bilingual mind of linguistic structures held in common by the two languages. If structures are not held in common, there is little basis for transfer. The primary patterns of transfer are not easily explained by general interdependence based on metalinguistic advantages. While the present view contrasts with the traditional interpretation of interdependence, it does *not* argue against bilingualism or bilingual education as a social goal. There are many advantages to being bilingual. So even if there are some costs to bilingual learning in elementary school, it is crucial that we continue to evaluate the nature of learning to speak and read in multiple languages and to support bilingualism as a way of life.

Note

This article was supported by NICHD (R01 HD046947 to D. Kimbrough Oller, PI) and by the Plough Foundation.

References

Arab-Moghaddam, N., & Sénéchal, M. (2001). Orthographic and phonological processing skills in reading and spelling in Persian/English bilinguals. *International Journal of Behavioral Development, 25,* 140–147.

August, D., Tabors, P. O., Calderon, M., Howard, E. R., Kenyon, D., Genesee, F., et al. (2003). *Colloquium: Linguistic and developmental influences on the English literacy acquisition of native Spanish speakers.* Tempe, AZ: 4th International Symposium on Bilingualism.

Baker, K., & de Kanter, A. (1981). *Effectiveness of bilingual education: A review of the literature. Final draft report.* Washington, DC: Office of Technical and Analytic Systems, U.S. Department of Education.

Baum Bursztyn, S. E. (1999). Phonological awareness and reading ability in bilingual native Spanish and monolingual English-speaking children. *Dissertation Abstracts International: Series B: The Sciences and Engineering, 59*(8-B), 4496.

Ben Zeev, S. (1977a). The influence of bilingualism on cognitive strategy and cognitive development. *Child Development, 48,* 1009–1018.

Ben Zeev, S. (1977b). Mechanisms by which childhood bilingualism affects understanding of language and cognitive structures. In P. A. Hornby (Ed.), *Bilingualism* (pp. 29–55). New York: Academic Press, Inc.

Bialystok, E. (1988). Levels of bilingualism and levels of linguistic awareness. *Developmental Psychology, 24,* 560–567.

Bialystok, E. (1991). Metalinguistic dimensions of bilingual language proficiency. In E. Bialystok (Ed.), *Language processing in bilingual children* (pp. 113–140). Cambridge: Cambridge University Press.

Bialystok, E. (1999). Cognitive complexity and attentional control in the bilingual mind. *Child Development, 70,* 636–644.

Bialystok, E. (2001). *Bilingualism in development: Language, literacy and cognition.* Cambridge: Cambridge University Press.

Bialystok, E., & Herman, J. (1999). Does bilingualism matter for early literacy? *Bilingualism, 2,* 35–44.

Bialystok, E., Majumder, S., & Martin, M.-M. (2003). Developing phonological awareness: Is there a bilingual advantage? *Applied Psycholinguistics, 24,* 27–44.

Bradley, L., & Bryant, P. E. (1983). Categorising sounds and learning to read: A causal connexion. *Nature, 301,* 419–421.

Bruck, M., & Genesee, F. (1995). Phonological awareness in young second language learners. *Journal of Child Language, 22,* 307–324.

Campbell, R., & Sais, E. (1995). Accelerated metalinguistic (phonological) awareness in bilingual children. *British Journal of Developmental Psychology, 13,* 61–68.

Carlisle, J. F. (2000). Awareness of the structure and meaning of morphologically complex words: Impact on reading. *Reading and Writing: An Interdisciplinary Journal, 12,* 169–190.

Carlisle, J. F., Beeman, M., Davis, L. H., & Spharim, G. (1999). Relationship of metalinguistic capabilities and reading achievement for children who are becoming bilingual. *Applied Psycholinguistics, 20,* 459–478.

Carlo, M. S. (1995). The effects of cross-language orthographic structure similarity on native language word recognition processes of English–Spanish bilinguals. *Dissertation Abstracts International: Series B: The Sciences and Engineering, 55*(11-B), 5102.

Catts, H. W., & Kamhi, A. G. (Eds.). (2005). *Language and reading disabilities* (2nd ed.). Needham, MA: Allyn and Bacon.

Cobo-Lewis, A., Eilers, R. E., Pearson, B. Z., & Umbel, V. C. (2002). Interdependence of Spanish and English knowledge in language and literacy among bilingual children. In D. K. Oller & R. E. Eilers (Eds.), *Language and literacy in bilingual children.* Clevedon, UK: Multilingual Matters.

Cobo-Lewis, A., Pearson, B. Z., Eilers, R. E., & Umbel, V. C. (2002a). Effects of bilingualism and bilingual education on oral and written English skills: A multifactor study of standardized test outcomes. In D. K. Oller & R. E. Eilers (Eds.), *Language and literacy in bilingual children.* Clevedon, UK: Multilingual Matters.

Cobo-Lewis, A., Pearson, B. Z., Eilers, R. E., & Umbel, V. C. (2002b). Effects of bilingualism and bilingual education on oral and written Spanish skills: A multifactor study of standardized test outcomes. In D. K. Oller & R. E. Eilers (Eds.), *Language and literacy in bilingual children*. Clevedon, UK: Multilingual Matters.

Collier, V. (1987). Age and rate of acquisition of second language for academic purposes. *TESOL Quarterly, 21*, 617–641.

Collier, V. P. (1989). How long? A synthesis of research on academic achievement in a second language. *TESOL Quarterly, 23*, 509–531.

Cummins, J. (1979). Linguistic interdependence and the educational development of bilingual children. *Review of Educational Research, 49*, 222–251.

Cummins, J. (1981). Age on arrival and immigrant second language learning in Canada: A reassessment. *Applied Linguistics, 2*, 131–149.

Cummins, J. (1991). Interdependence of first- and second-language proficiency in bilingual children. In E. Bialystok (Ed.), *Language processing in bilingual children*. Cambridge: Cambridge University Press.

D'Angiulli, A., Siegel, L. S., & Serra, E. (2001). The development of reading in English and Italian in bilingual children. *Applied Psycholinguistics, 22*, 479–507.

Dunbar, R. (1993). Coevolution of neocortical size, group size, and language in humans. *Behavioral and Brain Sciences, 16*, 681–735.

Dunbar, R. (1996). *Gossiping, grooming and the evolution of language*. Cambridge, MA: Harvard University Press.

Dunbar, R. I. M. (2004). Language, music and laughter in evolutionary perspective. In D. K. Oller & U. Griebel (Eds.), *The evolution of communication systems: A comparative approach* (pp. 257–274). Cambridge, MA: MIT Press.

Durgunoglu, A. Y., Nagy, W. E., & Hancin-Bhatt, B. J. (1993). Cross-language transfer of phonological awareness. *Journal of Educational Psychology, 85*, 453–465.

Edwards, D., & Christophersen, H. (1988). Bilingualism, literacy and meta-linguistic awareness in preschool children. *British Journal of Developmental Psychology, 6*, 235–244.

Fernández, M. C., Pearson, B. Z., Umbel, V. M., Oller, D. K., & Molinet-Molina, M. (1992). Bilingual receptive vocabulary in Hispanic preschool children. *Hispanic Journal of Behavioral Sciences, 14*, 268–276.

Fitzgerald, J. (1995). English-as-a-second-language learners' cognitive reading processes: A review of research in the United States. *Review of Educational Research, 65*, 145–190.

Fox, B., & Routh, D. K. (1975). Analysing spoken language into words, syllables and phonemes: A developmental study. *Journal of Psycholinguistic Research, 4*, 331–342.

Francis, N. (1999). Bilingualism, writing, and metalinguistic awareness: Oral-literate interactions between first and second languages. *Applied Psycholinguistics, 20*, 533–561.

Frase, M., Kaufman, P., & Klein, S. (1999). *Drop-out rates in the United States, 1997*. Washington, DC: National Center for Education Statistics, Doc. # 1999-082. URL: http://nces.ed.gov/pubsearch/pubsinfo.asp?pubid=1999082

Goswami, U. (2000). Phonological and lexical processes. In M. L. Kamil, P. B. Mosenthal, P. D. Pearson, & R. Barr (Eds.), *Handbook of reading research: Vol. III*. Mahwah, NJ: Erlbaum.

Hakuta, K. (1987). Degree of bilingualism and cognitive ability in mainland Puerto Rican children. *Child Development, 58*, 1372–1388.

Hansen, J., & Bowey, J. A. (1994). Phonological analysis skills, verbal working memory and reading ability in second grade children. *Child Development, 65*, 938–950.

Ingram, D., Christensen, L., & Veach, S. (1980). The acquisition of word-initial fricatives and affricates in English by children between two and six. In G. Yeni-Komshian, J. Kavanagh, & C. Ferguson (Eds.), *Child phonology: Vol. 1. Production*. New York: Academic Press.

Jared, D., & Kroll, J. F. (2001). Do bilinguals activate phonological representations in one or both of their languages when naming words? *Journal of Memory and Language, 44,* 2–31.

Jared, D., & Szucs, C. (2002). Phonological activation in bilinguals: Evidence from interlingual homograph naming. *Bilingualism: Language and Cognition, 5,* 225–239.

Juel, C., Griffith, P. L., & Gough, P. B. (1986). Acquisition of literacy: A longitudinal study of children in first and second grade. *Journal of Educational Psychology, 78,* 243–255.

Krashen, S. D., & Biber, D. (1988). *On course: Bilingual education's success in California*. Sacramento, CA: California Association for Bilingual Education.

Lambert, W. E. (1977). Effects of bilingualism on the individual: Cognitive and sociocultural consequences. In P. A. Hornby (Ed.), *Bilingualism: Psychological, social, and educational implications* (pp. 15–28). New York: Academic Press.

Liberman, I. Y., Shankweiler, D., & Liberman, A. M. (1989). The alphabetic principle and learning to read. In D. Shankweiler & I. Y. Liberman (Eds.), *Phonology and reading disability* (pp. 1–33). Ann Arbor, MI: University of Michigan Press.

Lindsey, K. A., Manis, F. R., & Bailey, C. E. (2003). Prediction of first-grade reading in Spanish-speaking English-language learners. *Journal of Educational Psychology, 95,* 482–494.

MacWhinney, B. (1999). Second language acquisition and the competition model. In A. M. d. Groot & J. F. Kroll (Eds.), *Tutorials in bilingualism: Psycholinguistic perspectives* (pp. 113–142). Hillsdale, NJ: Lawrence Erlbaum Associates, Inc.

Manis, F. R., Doi, L. M., & Bhadha, B. (2000). Naming speed, phonological awareness, and orthographic knowledge in second graders. *Journal of Learning Disabilities, 33,* 325–333.

McBride-Chang, C., & Kail, R. V. (2002). Cross-cultural similarities in the predictors of reading acquisition. *Child Development, 73,* 1392–1408.

Metsala, J. L., & Walley, A. C. (1998). Spoken vocabulary growth and the segmental restructuring of lexical representations: Precursors to phonemic awareness and early reading ability. In J. L. Metsala & L. C. Erhi (Eds.), *Word recognition in beginning literacy*. Mahwah, NJ: Erlbaum.

Miccio, A., Tabors, P. O., Paez, M., Hammer, C. S., & Wagstaff, D. (2003). *Vocabulary development in Spanish-speaking Head Start children of Puerto Rican descent*. Tempe, AZ: 4th International Symposium on Bilingualism.

Mumtaz, S., & Humphreys, G. W. (2002). The effect of Urdu vocabulary size on the acquisition of single word reading in English. *Educational Psychology, 22,* 165–190.

Nippold, M. A. (1998). *Later language development: The school-age and adolescent years* (2nd ed.). Austin, TX: Pro-Ed.

Oller, D. K. (2005). The distributed characteristic in bilingual learning. In J. Cohen, K. T. McAlister, K. Rolstad, & J. MacSwan (Eds.), *Proceedings of the 4th International Symposium on Bilingualism, Tempe, AZ* (pp. 1744–1749). Somerville, MA: Cascadilla Press.

Oller, D. K., Cobo-Lewis, A. B., & Pearson, B. Z. (2004). *Profiles in early bilingual learning: Vocabulary acquisition and the distributed characteristic*. Lafayette, LA: International Clinical Phonetics and Linguistics Association.

Oller, D. K., & Eilers, R. E. (2002). *Language and literacy in bilingual children*. Clevedon, UK: Multilingual Matters.

Oller, D. K., & Pearson, B. Z. (2002). Assessing the effects of bilingualism: A background. In D. K. Oller & R. E. Eilers (Eds.), *Language and literacy in bilingual children* (pp. 3–21). Clevedon, UK: Multilingual Matters.

Pearson, B. Z. (1998). Assessing lexical development in bilingual babies and toddlers. *International Journal of Bilingualism, 2*, 347–372.

Pearson, B. Z., Fernández, S., & Oller, D. K. (1995). Cross-language synonyms in the lexicons of bilingual infants: One language or two? *Journal of Child Language, 22*, 345–368.

Pearson, B. Z., Umbel, V. C., Andrews de Flores, P., & Cobo-Lewis, A. (1999). *Measuring cross-language vocabulary in childhood bilinguals at different stages of development.* Austin, TX: Texas Research Symposium on Language Diversity.

Quiroga, T., Lemos-Britton, Z., Mostafapour, E., Abbott, R. D., & Berninger, V. W. (2002). Phonological awareness and beginning reading in Spanish-speaking ESL first graders: Research into practice. *Journal of School Psychology, 40*, 85–111.

Ramírez, J. D., Pasta, D. K., Yuen, S. D., Billings, D. K., & Ramey, D. R. (1991). *Final report on the Longitudinal study of structured English immersion strategy, early-exit and late-exit transitional bilingual education programs for language-minority children (Contract No. 300-87-0156): Vol. II.* San Mateo, CA: Aguirre International.

Riccio, C. A., Amado, A., Jimenez, S., Hasbrouck, J. E., Imhoff, B., & Denton, C. (2001). Cross-linguistic transfer of phonological processing: Development of a measure of phonological processing in Spanish. *Bilingual Research Journal, 25*, 583–603.

Rosenblum, T., & Pinker, S. A. (1983). Word magic revisited: Monolingual and bilingual children's understanding of the word–object relationship. *Child Development, 53*, 773–780.

Rossell, C. H., & Baker, K. (1996). The effectiveness of bilingual education. *Research in the Teaching of English, 30*, 7–74.

Scott, C. (1994). A discourse continuum for school-age students: Impact of modality and genre. In G. P. Wallach & K. G. Butler (Eds.), *Language learning disabilities in school-age children and adolescents.* New York: Merrill/Macmillan.

Scott, C. (2005). Syntactic contributions to literacy learning. In C. A. Stone, E. R. Silliman, B. J. Ehren, & K. Apel (Eds.), *Handbook of language and literacy: Development and disorders.* New York: Guilford Press.

Smith, T. (1995). *Findings from The Condition of Education, 1995, Number 4: The Educational Progress of Hispanic Students.* Washington, DC: National Center for Education Statistics, Doc. # 95-767. URL: http://nces.ed.gov/pubsearch/pubsinfo.asp?pubid=95767

Stern, W. (1919). Die Erlenung und Beherrschung fremder Sprachen. *Zeitschrift für Paedagogische Psychologie, 20*, 104–108.

Swain, M. (1979). Bilingual education: Research and its implications. In C. A. Yorio, K. Perkins, & J. Schacter (Eds.), *On Tesol '79: The learner in focus.* Washington, DC: Teachers of English to Speakers of Other Languages.

Tunmer, W. E., Herriman, M. L., & Nesdale, A. R. (1988). Metalinguistic abilities and beginning reading. *Reading Research Quarterly, 23*, 134–158.

Tyler, A., & Nagy, W. (1990). Use of derivational morphology during reading. *Cognition, 36*, 17–34.

Umbel, V. M., Pearson, B. Z., Fernández, M. C., & Oller, D. K. (1992). Measuring bilingual children's receptive vocabularies. *Child Development, 63*, 1012–1020.

Van Wijnendaele, I., & Brysbaert, M. (2002). Visual word recognition in bilinguals: Phonological priming from the second to the first language. *Journal of Experimental Psychology: Human Perception and Performance, 28*, 616–627.

Varona-Vicente, E. (2001). Similarities and differences in phonological awareness, word reading and spelling acquisition between Spanish-speaking and English-speaking first graders. *Dissertation Abstracts International: Series A: Humanities and Social Sciences, 61*(11-A), 4289.

Vellutino, F., & Scanlon, D. (1987). Phonological coding, phonological awareness, and reading ability: Evidence from a longitudinal and experimental study. *Merrill-Palmer Quarterly, 33,* 321–363.

Verhoeven, L. (1994). Transfer in bilingual development: The linguistic interdependence hypothesis revisited. *Language Learning, 44,* 381–415.

Verhoeven, L. (2000). Components in early second language reading and spelling. *Scientific Studies of Reading, 4,* 313–330.

Wagner, R. K., & Torgeson, J. K. (1987). The nature of phonological processing and its causal role in the acquisition of reading skills. *Psychological Bulletin, 101,* 192–212.

Wagner, R. K., Torgeson, J. K., & Rashotte, C. A. (1999). *CTOPP: Comprehensive Test of Phonological Processing.* Austin, TX: Pro-Ed.

Waltzman, D. E., & Cairns, H. S. (2000). Grammatical knowledge of third grade good and poor readers. *Applied Psycholinguistics, 21,* 263–284.

Westby, C. (2005). A language perspective on executive functioning, metacognition, and self-regulation in reading. In C. A. Stone, E. R. Silliman, B. J. Ehren, & K. Apel (Eds.), *Handbook of language and literacy: Development and disorders.* New York: Guilford Press.

Yelland, G. W., Pollard, J., & Mercuri, A. (1993). The metalinguistic benefits of limited contact with a second language. *Applied Psycholinguistics, 14,* 423–444.

19

Second Language Acquisition in Childhood

Johanne Paradis

Second language (L2) acquisition in children has been seldom studied as a subfield with its own issues and questions separate from adult L2 acquisition on the one hand, or bilingualism and educational outcomes on the other. Consequently, we know little about second language acquisition (SLA) issues, such as individual differences, as they pertain to child as opposed to adult learners, and we know less about the developing oral language proficiency of L2 children than we know about their literacy development. Research on child L2 learners received a great deal of attention in the 1970s because SLA was emerging as a field of inquiry, and because educational programs such as French immersion in Canada and bilingual programs for Spanish-speaking children in the United States were being developed. There has been a recent resurgence of interest in this population of children in large measure due to clinical and special education researchers who seek to understand how to distinguish between language difference and language disorder in multilingual populations. This renewed interest in child L2 learners has come with a focus on oral language proficiency, because this is essential for assessment and intervention, as well as concern for issues that are more important to L2 learning by children rather than adults, such as the impact of languages spoken in the home on both first language (L1) and L2 development. This review discusses research on L2 children in terms of questions that are particularly relevant to child rather than adult SLA, and to oral language rather than literacy development: (1) Are child L2 acquisition patterns and rates similar to those for L1 acquisition? (2) How do child L2 learners compare with native speakers of the target language their own age? (3) What happens to the L1 development of minority children learning a L2 that is the majority language of the community?

The term "child bilingual" is often used synonymously with "child L2 learner," but they do not necessarily denote the same population. Simultaneous bilingual children learn both their languages in the preschool years (see Genesee & Nicoladis, this volume), while L2 children have established one language before they begin learning the other, and typically speak the L1 at home and the L2 at school. English L1 children who acquire French or Spanish as a L2 through immersion schooling are L1 majority L2 learners. By contrast, children who speak a minority language at home, such as Spanish, Chinese, or Arabic, and attend school in the majority language alongside English native speakers are L1 minority L2 learners. This chapter is concerned mainly with development of the L2 and L1 of minority children, but some research on L1 majority L2 children is discussed.

Initial Exposure to the Second Language

Tabors (1997) noted the following early stages in L2 development, based on observing minority children in an English preschool in the United States: (1) home-language use, (2) non-verbal period, (3) formulaic and telegraphic use, and (4) productive language use. Children initially use their native language in the L2 environment, but this stage is very brief because within a few days they realize that using their native language will not facilitate communication in the new context. By contrast, the subsequent non-verbal period can last a few weeks or extend to several months, and younger children seem to stay longer in this stage than older ones (Tabors, 1997; Winitz, Gillespie, & Starcev, 1995). During this stage, children produce few or no utterances in the L2, often make use of gestural communication, and may be silent for longer in a group rather than a one-on-one context.

L2 children's first utterances in English tend to be either formulaic or telegraphic, meaning that children rely heavily on memorized or unanalyzed phrases and use few grammatical morphemes. Tabors (1997) noted that the first utterances produced by the children in English were mainly single-words like object and color names, or counting sequences. Wong Fillmore (1979) lists several common formulas used repeatedly by the L2 children she observed in the early stages, for example *lookit, wait a minute, lemme see,* or *whaddya wanna do?* L2 children's transition from Tabors' stage (3) to the period of productive language is marked by their increasing use of novel concatenations of content and grammatical morphemes. Tabor's stage (4) resembles what L2 researchers traditionally call *interlanguage* (e.g., Selinker, Swain, & Dumas, 1975). Interlanguage describes L2 learner language that is reasonably fluent and is the product of an underlying productive linguistic system, but differs from the target language; it is a dynamic system balancing L1 transfer processes with target language developmental processes that gradually moves closer to the target language system.

Phonological Acquisition in the Second Language

Influence of the L1 is highly apparent in L2 phonology. According to Flege's Speech Learning Model, the starting point for L2 speech development is the L1 phonetic categories (Flege, 1999). For example, Spanish L1–English L2 children aged 4 to 7 years were found to be more accurate in their production of phonemes that are shared between the two languages than of phonemes that are present only in the English L2 (Goldstein, 2004). This initial L1 influence can be life-long, even for child L2 learners. Retrospective developmental studies show that adults who began to acquire their L2 as early as 6 to 8 years of age can have a perceptible foreign accent (Flege, 1999; Flege & Fletcher, 1992). With respect to acoustic properties like voice onset time (VOT), Spanish L1–English L2 children can eventually develop two systems for marking the phonemic voicing distinction in their production of stop consonants, short-lag versus long-lag (English) and pre-voiced versus short-lag (Spanish); however, their perception of VOT-signaled contrasts may not display the language-specific and separate boundaries found in monolinguals for each language, and thus bilingual VOT perceptual systems may be intertwined (Watson, 1991).

In addition to examining the role of the L1, researchers have also asked whether child L2 learners are faster to acquire L2 phonology than adult learners. Snow and Hoefnagel-Höhle (1977) studied the pronunciation of Dutch words by 47 English speakers aged 3 to 60 years learning Dutch as a L2 in the Netherlands. During the first 11 months of exposure to the L2, the children did not receive higher accuracy scores on pronunciation of individual target phonemes than the adults. Subsequent studies have shown that after 12 to 18 months of exposure to the target language, children's rate of phonological acquisition begins to outstrip adult learners because their foreign accent diminishes much more rapidly after that time (Flege, 2004; Winitz et al., 1995).

Adult Italian–English bilinguals were found to have lower pronunciation accuracy with vowels that are present in English but not in Italian, compared with vowels present in both languages, even though they had begun learning English as young children (Flege, 1999). Furthermore, Flege and Fletcher (1992) found that Chinese L1 adults had more perceptible foreign accents than Spanish L1 adults, even though both groups had been immersed in a majority English environment from 5 to 8 years of age.

Lexical Acquisition in the Second Language

Building a lexicon is an important task for L1 minority children not only for achieving adequate oral proficiency in their L2, but also for performance in a majority L2 school since vocabulary knowledge is an important component in literacy development. Umbel, Pearson, Fernández, and Oller (1992) studied the vocabulary knowledge of 151 dual language children in first grade in Miami, some of whom had been introduced to English at school (L2), and some of whom had been exposed to both English and Spanish at home before school entry (bilingual). Umbel et al. (1992) found that the English L2 learners scored lower than the bilinguals on the English standardized tests, both groups scored the same on the Spanish standardized tests, and both groups scored higher in Spanish than in English. Neither the L2 learners nor the bilinguals scored at the mean for monolinguals in the English norming sample; whereas both groups scored close to the mean for the monolingual Spanish norming sample. This study indicates that vocabulary accumulation in the majority language for both L2 and bilingual learners is a gradual process, but at the same time, exposure to English did not adversely affect the children's ability to maintain age appropriate vocabulary knowledge in their minority L1 into first grade. It is important to point out that using monolingual norms of vocabulary size to measure dual language children's development in both L1 and L2 might not sufficiently take into account context-dependent compositional differences between the monolingual and bilingual lexicons for a target language, and alternative methods of scoring tests and understanding lexical development for dual language children have been proposed (Patterson & Pearson, 2004; Peña & Kester, 2004).

As L2 children are accumulating vocabulary, the communicative demands on them in school and from native-speaker peers are often in advance of what they can produce. Harley (1992) presented English L1 children in French immersion, and French monolingual children, with cartoon story sequences to describe. The L2 children used a smaller number of different words overall than native speakers, and Harley noted three phenomena indicating that the L2 children were stretching their lexical resources in French. First, the L2 children often used non-specific verbs to describe specific actions; for example, in describing a picture of a man diving, an L2 child said *il va dans l'eau* "he goes into the water," while native-speaker age peers used the precise verb, *plonger* "to dive." Second, the L2 children were more likely to use sound symbolism, so another child described the diving picture as *il* [pløß] *dans l'eau* "he [sound effect] in the water." Finally, some children would codeswitch to English to be more precise, for example one child said *il va, um, sauter, euh* <u>dive</u> "he goes, um, jump, uh, <u>dive</u>." The L2 children also used more non-specific nominals than native speakers, such as *une chose* "a thing" or the deictic pronoun *ça* "that." Interestingly, there are similarities between these early L2 lexical strategies and those employed in the context of L1 attrition discussed below.

L2 lexical learning differs from L1 in that the child is more cognitively mature when the process starts, and also has an existing lexicon in their L1 to draw upon for insight into conceptual–lexical mappings; therefore, it is possible that child L2 learners accumulate vocabulary faster than younger L1 learners for the same target language. Winitz et al. (1995) found that the Polish L1 child they studied advanced four developmental years in vocabulary knowledge within one chronological year of exposure to English, as shown by age-equivalency scores on the Peabody Picture Vocabulary Test (PPVT). Following the same logic, PPVT age-equivalent scores and chronological ages were compared from 24 children participating in an ongoing longitudinal study of English L2 development in Edmonton, Canada (see Paradis, 2005, for details), to ascertain whether rate of vocabulary development is generally faster for L2 than L1 acquisition. At 9 (SD = 4.2) months of exposure to English (MOE), the mean chronological age of the children was 66.21 months (SD = 11.14), and the mean PPVT age-equivalency score was 44.33 months (SD = 20.16), nearly 22 months below chronological age. At 21 MOE (SD = 4), the mean chronological age was 75.9 months (SD = 9.97), with mean age equivalency on PPVT at 66.2 (SD = 18.76), nearly 10 months below chronological age. Thus, the children gained 12 months developmentally in vocabulary knowledge within 12 chronological months of exposure. Even though the overall rate of vocabulary accumulation for the group was similar to the rate for L1 acquisition, there were individual cases of remarkably rapid vocabulary acquisition. For example, two children's age-equivalency scores increased 40 months in the 12-month chronological interval. Also, the children's ages were positively and significantly correlated with the PPVT raw scores at 9 MOE ($r = .498$, $p = .0287$) and 21 MOE ($r = .553$, $p = .0128$). In sum, precocious vocabulary development appears to be an individual rather than a group trait for child L2 learners, but older child L2 learners may be faster than younger L2 learners.

Lexical processing, which consists of the ability to recognize, access, and produce words in the target language in a time dependent way, is a skill that continues to develop gradually in monolingual children until adolescence, and so it could be expected to also develop gradually in a child's L2, in tandem with vocabulary growth (Kohnert, 2004). Kohnert and colleagues studied picture-naming and picture-word verification in 100 Spanish L1 children and adolescents aged 5 to 16 in California (Kohnert & Bates, 2002; Kohnert, Bates, & Hernandez, 1999). The participants' accuracy with picture-naming and picture verification in their English L2 was superior in comprehension than production, and both continued to increase until the 14 to 16 age range, when accuracy reached 90% or greater. Response times in both tasks continually decreased until ages 14 to 16. Similar protracted development for lexical processing was also found for German L1–Swedish L2 children (Mägiste, 1992). Therefore, children's L2 lexical processing develops very gradually throughout elementary school and is consistent with known patterns for monolinguals (Kohnert, 2004).

Morphosyntactic Acquisition in the Second Language

Foundational studies on L2 morphosyntactic development examined children's errors with grammatical morphemes and syntactic structures, mainly for the purpose of determining whether interlanguage errors were developmental or transfer-based in this domain of acquisition, and whether the developmental sequence for grammatical morphemes mirrored L1 acquisition (Dulay & Burt, 1973, 1974). Dulay and Burt (1973) found that 85% of the errors in spoken English by 145 Spanish L1–English L2 children were developmental in origin, in other words, not traceable to Spanish, and were mainly errors with grammatical morphemes. Transfer from Spanish was expected for a variety of structures, for example, use of *have* in *he has hunger* instead of *he is hungry*, or use of noun–adjective word order, *the man skinny* instead of *the skinny man*. In their follow-up study with both Spanish and Chinese L1 children, they found again that the major source of difficulty for both L1 groups was developmental errors with grammatical morphology, demonstrating that the learner's L1 was not the principal source of the errors in their interlanguage (Dulay & Burt, 1974). In addition, Dulay and Burt (1973, 1974) and Dulay, Burt, and Krashen (1982) show that order sequence of morpheme acquisition is similar to that found in L1 English: for example, early-acquired morphemes in English L2 are progressive [-ing] and plural [-s]; late-acquired morphemes are past tense [-ed] and third person singular [-s]. More recent research confirms the special difficulty of grammatical morphemes in child English L2 acquisition, and the dominance of developmental, mainly omission, errors in children's interlanguage (Ionin & Wexler, 2002; Jia, 2003; Paradis, 2005; Paradis, Rice, Crago, & Richman, 2004). Here are some examples of omission and commission errors in child L2 English: *we playing hide and seek*; *he want some ice cream*; *how you say that?*; *I didn't sawed*, and *there's are not maths in my school* (Genesee, Paradis, & Crago, 2004, pp. 124–125).

Building on the notion of early-versus late-acquired morphemes, recent research shows that omission of tense/agreement (finiteness) markers in particular is a significant characteristic of child L2 interlanguage, whether the L2 is French, German, or English, regardless of the L1 background, and for both L1 majority and minority children (Grondin & White, 1996; Haznedar, 2001; Ionin & Wexler, 2002; Lakshmanan, 1994; Paradis, 2005; Paradis & Crago, 2000, 2004; Paradis, Le Corre, & Genesee, 1998; Prévost & White, 2000). More specifically, finite verb morphology in English and French is acquired later by child L2 learners than non-finiteness-related morphology, and this directly parallels L1 acquisition patterns for early- versus late-acquired morphemes (Paradis, 2005; Paradis & Crago, 2000, 2004). One exception is that the verb *BE* emerges relatively early for a finiteness-marking morpheme (Haznedar, 2001; Ionin & Wexler, 2002; Paradis et al., 2004).

Concerning other L1–L2 acquisition comparisons, researchers have found parallels in how grammatical aspect is acquired by child L1 and L2 learners of English and French (Gavruseva, 2002; Harley, 1992), and how object pronouns are acquired in child L1 and L2 French (Paradis, 2004). Child L2 learners have also been found to make similar errors in morphosyntax as monolingual children the same age with language impairment, with either English or French as the target language (Paradis, 2004, 2005; Paradis & Crago, 2000, 2004). Such an overlap between a clinical and typically developing population has practical consequences for differential diagnosis in multilingual contexts, as well as posing challenges for theories of language impairment aimed at identifying linguistic characteristics that circumscribe the clinical population among same-aged children.

Differences between L1 and child L2 acquisition have also been found. L2 children display a larger proportion of commission errors than younger L1 learners, and the phenomenon of *BE*-overgeneration appears to be unique to child L2 (Ionin & Wexler, 2002; Paradis et al., 2004). *BE*-overgeneration consists of using this morpheme in contexts not permitted in adult English, possibly as a general-all-purpose finiteness marker, for example *I'm sit down on my spot* or *you're win*, and has been documented in children with various L1 backgrounds. Another difference between L1 and L2 concerns the appearance of subjects. Null subjects appear widely in the speech of young children cross-linguistically, even when the target language does not permit null subjects, like English. However, in the L2 acquisition of English, null subjects are infrequent or non-existent, even when the children's L1 permits null subjects (Haznedar, 2001; Ionin & Wexler, 2002; Lakshmanan, 1994). Perhaps the cognitive immaturity of very young learners is the source of the null subjects stage in L1 acquisition.

As with lexical acquisition, researchers have asked whether morphosyntactic acquisition is faster for the more cognitively mature L2 children than for younger L1 learners. Jia (2003) found that it took an average of 20 months of exposure (range 7–33) for nine Mandarin L1 children to master the use of plural [-s] in their English L2 (mastery = 80% use or greater). Assuming 12 months to be the onset of language production, Jia (2003) reckoned the L1 average for mastery of plural [-s] is 17 to 21 months after production begins, making it similar to the L2 average, although the range might be broader for L2 children. The Edmonton ESL study supports Jia's (2003) findings with a larger sample, and with children from various L1 backgrounds. At 21 MOE (SD = 4), the children used plural [-s] 79.85% (SD = 15.05) correct in obligatory context, similar to L1 acquisition. Regarding a more global measure of morphosyntactic development, the Edmonton ESL children had an average mean length of utterance (MLU) of 4.66 (SD = .89) at 21 MOE. Assuming production to begin at 12 months, the majority of English L1 children reach this milestone after 29 months of production (Miller & Chapman, 1981), while these L2 children reached it 8 months earlier. In fact, 5/24 ESL children had an MLU of 4.5 or higher at 9 MOE. Perhaps already having a language established and being more cognitively mature accelerates development of utterance length in L2 acquisition.

While Dulay et al. (1982) argued that L1 transfer does not play a dominant role in L2 acquisition of morphosyntax, L1 influence can determine some interlanguage patterns. Paradis (2004) found that error patterns with object pronouns in child L2 French reflected possible transfer from English. Harley (1989) compared the use of verbs and prepositions in sixth grade by monolingual French native speakers and English L1 children in French immersion. The French L2 learners differed systematically from the monolingual French children in ways that reflected properties of English. For example, to describe the rescue of a cat from a tree, native speakers would often choose a verb with directionality encoded into it, *elle descendit le chat* "she brought the cat down," where the L2 learners often chose to use a prepositional phrase in their expression of this event, *il le pris dans ses bras* "he took him in his arms" (Harley, 1989, p. 14; see also Harley, 1992).

Child Second Language Learners Compared with Monolingual Age Peers

A substantial body of research indicates that it takes 5 to 7 years in English school for L2 children to have academic verbal skills on par with native speakers (Cummins, 2000), but there has been less research focused on the time it takes to master oral language. Hakuta, Goto Butler, and Witt (2000) examined standardized measures of English oral proficiency for 1,872 L1 minority children in San Francisco, and concluded that it took approximately 5 years of schooling in English for children to score in the native-speaker range. Looking at vocabulary in particular, Cobo-Lewis, Pearson, Eilers, and Umbel (2002) and Eilers, Pearson, and Cobo-Lewis (2006) report that Spanish-at-home/English-at-school children in Miami scored below monolingual English children on standardized tests for productive and receptive vocabulary throughout elementary school, although the gap narrowed by fifth grade. Scoring within the monolingual range occurred more often for receptive than productive vocabulary.

How long it takes for L2 children to perform within the normal range for native speakers may differ depending on the aspect of language being examined on the standardized measure. In the Edmonton ESL study, after 21 MOE (SD = 4), 40% of the children performed within the normal range of monolinguals for grammatical morpheme production, 65% for receptive vocabulary, and 90% for story grammar in a narrative. One reason why these L2 children achieved monolingual norms so rapidly for story grammar could be because the conceptual underpinnings of storytelling abilities could easily transfer from their native language.

Unlike comparisons based on standardized tests, direct comparisons between L2 learners and native speakers can provide more specific information about qualitative differences in linguistic competence between these groups. Flege (2004) compared foreign accent ratings for Korean and Japanese L1–English L2 children and age-matched English native speakers and found differences between the groups even after 5 years' exposure to the English L2. These findings suggest that L2 phonological development takes a long time to reach native-speaker levels, and as mentioned above, some differences between the speech of monolinguals and early-onset bilinguals may be life-long. Gathercole (2002a, 2002b) elicited grammaticality judgments for English morphosyntactic structures that differ with Spanish in Spanish-at-home/English-at-school children and monolingual English children in Miami. At second grade, the L2 children made fewer correct judgments of acceptable/non-acceptable structures in English than the monolinguals; however, differences between the groups narrowed considerably by fifth grade. Gathercole raises the important issue of whether bilingual children ever develop identical competencies to monolinguals (difference), or whether they are simply slower to develop these competencies because of the reduced amount of input in each language (delay). Kohnert and Windsor (2004) also present research addressing the "difference or delay?" question. They examined word recognition and picture-naming in Spanish L1–English L2 learners and English native speakers aged 8 to 13. The L2 learners performed similarly to the native speakers in both accuracy and response time for word recognition; in contrast, the English native speakers outperformed the English L2 group for picture-naming accuracy and response time. It is possible that the L2 children will catch up with the monolinguals in production abilities, but on the other hand, longer latencies might be typical of lexical production in all bilinguals. In sum, all these studies point to the possibility that bilinguals are not just two-monolinguals-in-one; the dual language experience of L2 children may cause their pronunciation, grammatical competence, and processing abilities to possess some different characteristics (but see Gathercole, 2002b).

Sources of Individual Differences in Child Second Language Acquisition

There are striking individual differences in rates of child L2 acquisition, even for children with similar amounts of classroom exposure to the L2 and similar instructional programs (Paradis, 2005; Wong Fillmore, 1983). Individual differences have a more prominent focus in L2 than L1 acquisition research, possibly because young L2 learners have more potential sources of individual differences in acquisition than L1 learners. For example, child L2 learners have more variation in their target language input than L1 learners because the input amount is divided between two languages (and often between two contexts), they come in contact with the target language at various ages instead of uniformly at birth, and they already have another developing language when L2 learning begins. Research aimed at determining the sources of individual differences in L2 acquisition rates and ultimate attainment has looked at various factors ranging from internal psychological and cognitive characteristics to external variables like social context of target language input.

Motivation

Motivation is a set of attitudes, affective variables, and beliefs toward the target cultural group and learning the target language that consistently predict differences in achievement across numerous studies of L2 learners (Dörnyei & Skehan, 2003; Gardner, 1980; Skehan, 1991). It is easy to understand why internal attitudes and beliefs would exert an effect on the outcomes of adult learners who have chosen to acquire a L2. However, it is possible that attitudinal variables are less likely to predict outcomes in younger children because they may not have a developed view of intergroup and cultural differences (Genesee & Hamayan, 1980). Furthermore, motivation is even less of a concern for L1 minority children who, generally speaking, demonstrate a strong desire to assimilate to the new language and culture. On the other hand, Wong Fillmore (1979) argues that motivation to integrate with the host society may explain some individual differences in L2 development among L1 minority children who are in communities where the L1 is spoken outside their homes.

Aptitude

Language aptitude consists of several analytic and working memory abilities pertinent to acquiring language structures and individual words, as measured by tests like the Modern Languages Aptitude Test (Carroll & Sapon, 1959), and is related to, but not the same as, verbal and non-verbal intelligence (Dörnyei & Skehan, 2003; Sawyer & Ranta, 2001). Language aptitude is considered to be a relatively stable and inherent characteristic, predictive of both L1 and L2 development (Skehan, 1991). Language aptitude is one of the most reliable factors explaining individual differences in L2 success among adolescent and adult learners, along with motivation (Dörnyei & Skehan, 2003; Gardner, 1980; Skehan, 1991). Ranta (2002) examined language analytic aptitude and L2 attainment in French-speaking sixth grade children from the French-majority province of Québec in Canada who were enrolled in an intensive English immersion program. Results showed that high and low language aptitude was associated with high and low L2 attainment in the 5-month program. Harley and Hart (1997) studied language aptitude and L2 proficiency in two groups of adolescent English L1 French immersion students in Canada: those who began learning the L2 in seventh grade (late immersion) and those who began learning the L2 in first grade (early immersion). They found that memory-based aptitude skills better predicted L2 proficiency in the early-immersion group whereas language analytic aptitude skills better predicted L2 proficiency in the late-immersion group. Harley and Hart (1997) suggest that the memory component of language aptitude may be more relevant to L2 acquisition in young children. By contrast, Genesee and Hamayan (1980) found that a general analytical skill, non-verbal reasoning, predicted success in verbal academic skills, vocabulary, and listening comprehension in French by English L1 children in first grade immersion.

Personality characteristics

Personality characteristics such as outgoingness or assertiveness are predicted to lead to success in L2 learning because an individual who possesses such characteristics is expected to experience more frequent and high quality interactions with native speakers of the target language. Research investigating the relationship between personality variables and L2 outcomes has shown mixed results (Dörnyei & Skehan, 2003; Sawyer & Ranta, 2001; Strong, 1983); however, Strong (1983) argues that studies that measured natural communicative language are those that consistently found a relationship between personality variables and L2 outcomes. Two studies looking at L1 minority children in particular suggest social–personality variables play some role in determining individual differences (Strong, 1983; Wong Fillmore, 1983). Wong Fillmore (1983) reported that the most successful L2 learners in her study of 48 children had one of two personality types. One type of successful learner was highly social and outgoing and sought out opportunities to speak English through peer interaction. The other type of successful learner was shy and not sociable, but seemed to otherwise compensate by demonstrating strong cognitive abilities and attentiveness to the teacher in the classroom. Strong (1983) found that personality variables associated with amount of social contact with native speakers, namely talkativeness, responsiveness, and gregariousness, were significantly correlated with higher achievement on English grammar, vocabulary, and pronunciation measures gathered through natural child–child interactions in kindergarten.

First language typology

Typological similarities and differences between the L1 and L2 could affect rate of development and ultimate attainment in the L2. As mentioned earlier, adult Italian–English bilinguals were found to have lower pronunciation accuracy with vowels that are present in English but not in Italian, compared with vowels present in both languages, even though they had begun learning English as young children (Flege, 1999). Furthermore, Flege and Fletcher (1992) found that Chinese L1 adults had more perceptible foreign accents than Spanish L1 adults, even though both groups had been immersed in a majority English environment from 5 to 8 years of age. In the lexical domain, overlap between L1 and L2 in vocabulary may have a facilitating effect because school-age children can make effective use of cognates in their acquisition of L2 vocabulary (Patterson & Pearson, 2004). Whether typological distance between L1 and L2 causes variation in morphosyntactic acquisition is more controversial. Dulay and Burt (1974) found that Chinese L1 learners of English had somewhat lower accuracy scores with grammatical morphemes than the Spanish L1 learners of English. By contrast, Paradis (2005) found

that at 9 MOE (SD = 4.2), Chinese L1 children, whose native language has few inflections and no grammatical tense, produced tense morphemes in English with the same
accuracy as children with more richly inflected native languages. Turning to ultimate
attainment, Bialystok and Miller (1999) found that when exposure to English began
before 8 years of age, adult Chinese L1 and Spanish L1 speakers of English performed
virtually the same on their grammaticality judgment task as English native speakers.
However, McDonald (2000) compared the grammaticality judgment performance of
Spanish L1 and Vietnamese L1 adults whose exposure to English began around 5 years
of age. The Spanish L1 bilinguals performed like English native speakers in terms of
accuracy and response times, but the Vietnamese L1 bilinguals had lower accuracy and
slower response times.

Age of acquisition

The existence of age effects in L2 acquisition is not controversial. It is exceptional for a
late onset L2 learner to appear indistinguishable from native speakers even in informal
conversation, let alone in a more sensitive experimental context. The question being
continually debated is what the source of these effects is; more specifically, whether it is
a biological critical period that ends around puberty. Age of acquisition may not seem
relevant in the context of child L2 acquisition; however, much research indicates that in
contrast to the assumption of a critical period at puberty, individual differences in ultimate attainment emerge depending on what age in the pre-puberty years L2 learning
begins. Jia (2003) reported differences in the acquisition of plural [-s] in English by
Mandarin L1 children based on their age of first exposure to English. Several studies
employing a retrospective developmental design have also found gradient age effects
within the pre-puberty period on English language attainment in both phonology and
morphosyntax (Bialystok & Miller, 1999; Flege, 1999; McDonald, 2000; Weber-Fox &
Neville, 1999, 2001). Gradient age effects within the pre-puberty period are not apparent
for all aspects of language, however. Weber-Fox and Neville (1999, 2001) found no differences in event-related potential (ERP) measurements for open class word processing
or in performance on grammaticality judgments of semantic (lexical choice) violations
for Chinese L1 adult speakers of English whose first exposure to English ranged between
1 and 16 years of age. By contrast, these researchers found differences both in ERP
measurements of closed class word processing and in grammaticality judgments of syntactic violations between adult Chinese L1 speakers who were first exposed to English
before age 7, and those first exposed to English between 7 and 10 years of age. Bialystok
and Miller (1999) and Jia (2003) argue that the existence of gradient age effects within
the pre-puberty period on L2 attainment is evidence against the notion of a biological
critical period.

Socio-economic status

The socio-economic status (SES) of a child's family, as measured by parental level
of education or family income, has been widely studied as a predictor of individual

differences in L1 acquisition. Family SES is rarely considered as a source of individual variation in adult SLA, but it has been considered in some child SLA research, and it seems to make a difference. The Miami studies reported above on vocabulary and grammatical acquisition found that low SES children performed worse than high SES children on the oral language measures from second grade to fifth grade (Cobo-Lewis et al., 2002; Eilers et al., 2006; Gathercole, 2002a, 2002b). Hakuta et al. (2000) examined the impact of SES in their data on oral English proficiency in San Francisco area minority children. They examined the level of school poverty as measured by percentage enrollment in school free lunch programs and found that children at schools with 70% enrollment lagged behind children in the other schools at achieving native-speaker levels of proficiency.

Quality and context of second language input

Researchers have looked beyond broad measures of amount of input, such as age of arrival in the English majority society or years spent in an English classroom, and explored other facets of the L2 input to see if they impact on children's rate of L2 acquisition. Jia (2003) and Jia and Aaronson (2003) measured richness of the English L2 environment outside the classroom for Chinese L1 children using a composite score based on information about hours of English TV watched weekly, number of English books read, number of English native-speaker friends, and the percentage of time they spoke English at home. Jia (2003) found that faster acquisition of the plural [-s] in English was associated with increasing richness of the L2 environment over time. However, the richness of the L2 environment may have non-straightforward effects on children's L2 acquisition when it occurs at the expense of rich input in the L1 at home. In the Edmonton ESL study, information on amount of English spoken in the home was calculated as a percent mean across the percent each household member reported using English versus the native language. This is a different home language measure from the one used by Jia (2003) and Jia and Aaronson (2003), which focused on the child's use and preference only. When MOE in the classroom was held constant at two academic years (20 months), English home language use varied considerably among the children's families, 23% to 80% (mean = 47%), and was significantly and negatively correlated with children's raw scores on the PPVT ($rho = -.501$, $z = -2.242$, $p = .0250$), and significantly and negatively correlated with years of parental education ($rho = -.568$, $z = -2.538$, $p = .0111$). This finding is not surprising when one considers the quality of the L2 input children might be getting from their non-native-speaker parents. Children need exposure to rich and diverse vocabulary in order to build their English lexicons, and their parents may not be able to provide this when speaking their L2. In addition, this finding suggests that the rich vocabulary parents provide when they use their native language could have a positive impact on L2 lexical growth through a positive impact on L1 lexical growth (see Cummins' (2000) discussion of the interdependence hypothesis).

The L2 classroom is a primary source of input, and children may make differential use of this input depending on how they interact in the classroom context. Wong Fillmore (1983) argued that teacher-centered versus group-oriented classrooms yield different sources of input that suit different learner needs. Outgoing learners can gain a great deal from group-oriented classrooms because more peer interaction means more L2 input. By contrast, teacher-centered classrooms may provide a consistent source of input for shy, less sociable learners. Genesee and Hamayan (1980) found that one of the strongest predictors of success in French language learning by first grade immersion students was how actively individuals participated in class, practiced French in class, and used French in the halls and at recess, as measured by teacher questionnaires.

Language Shift and First Language Loss

While acquiring their L2, minority children's dominant, or most proficient/preferred, language typically shifts from the L1 to the L2. Language shift can result in maintenance of the L1, albeit as the less dominant language, but it can also result in gradual L1 loss, a process often described as L1 attrition. A shift in dominance or loss of L1 proficiency does not occur for L1 majority children acquiring a minority L2 at school, which underscores the importance of sociolinguistic context on dual language learning outcomes in children (Genesee et al., 2004).

Research on dominant language shift indicates that this can occur gradually and need not be accompanied by precipitous loss of the L1, particularly if children reside in communities where their L1 is spoken outside the home. Kohnert and colleagues found that Spanish L1–English L2 children's lexical processing skills were superior in Spanish until they had approximately 7 to 10 years' experience with English in school in California, at which point abilities in both languages were fairly balanced, followed by the emerging superiority of the English skills (Kohnert & Bates, 2002; Kohnert et al., 1999). In addition, Pease-Alvarez, Hakuta, and Bayley (1996) found that lexical knowledge and grammatical abilities in Spanish L1 children aged 8 to 10 attending English schools in California still met age expectations for Spanish monolinguals. However, the dominant language shift may occur faster in younger L2 children. In Mägiste's (1992) study of lexical processing in German L1–Swedish L2 children, it was found that the switch to the L2 as the superior language in lexical processing occurred after 4 years' residence for the young children but after 6 years for the adolescents. Jia and Aaronson (2003) also found that the switch in preference from the L1 to the L2, as measured through questionnaires, occurred more rapidly for the Mandarin L1 children who were younger than 9 years old when they arrived.

Even when the L1 is maintained, the variety used by minority children may become distinct from that of monolinguals. Anderson (2004) reviews several studies reporting on lexical/semantic and morphosyntactic characteristics of Spanish L1 children acquiring English in the United States. The lexical characteristics are mainly compensatory strategies used when the child does not know the precise word in Spanish, for example general-all-purpose demonstrative pronouns like *esto* "this one." Some grammatical changes appear to be the result of transfer from the English L2, such as rigid Subject–Verb–Object word order, while others appear to consist of simplification of paradigms, such as the use of the third person singular as a default verb form. Anderson also notes lexical borrowing and code-mixing into English as a vocabulary gap-filling strategy (see Genesee & Nicoladis, this volume). While these characteristics are typically accepted as examples of L1 attrition, it is not always possible to tease apart something that was learned in the L1 and then lost (attrition) versus something that was never completely learned in the first place (incomplete acquisition) due to a change in quality or quantity of L1 input (Anderson, 2004; Montrul, 2002).

Why do some minority children lose their L1, and others undergo a more gradual shift to become L2-dominant bilinguals? Wong Fillmore (1991) pointed to early onset of English acquisition as a major factor contributing to L1 attrition. Results of this large-scale survey showed that 73% of the children who attended English-only or bilingual preschool used some English in the home, while this was true for only 48% of the children in Spanish-only preschool programs. Parents of the children in the English-only preschool programs were six to eight times more likely to describe their children's abilities in the native language as deficient or non-existent. By contrast, Winsler, Díaz, Espinosa, and Rodríguez (1999) found that early onset of English L2 acquisition did not adversely affect native language maintenance in Spanish L1 children because the English preschool group in this study did not perform worse in Spanish in kindergarten than the at-home group. One reason for these discrepant findings could be that Wong Fillmore's (1991) sample of children included some who had little community support for their L1, while Winsler et al. (1999), as well as the studies by Kohnert and Hakuta and colleagues discussed above, examined children from communities where Spanish was widely spoken (see also Anderson, 2004). Furthermore, Jia and Aaronson (2003) discuss the dynamic interrelationship between age of L2 onset and other factors, such as positive attitudes toward the L2 and host culture, the social network in the L2, and L1 proficiency, as predictive of L1 maintenance. In a nutshell, the earlier the age of arrival, the more likely a child is to have positive attitudes toward the host culture and language, which in turn increases the likelihood of a larger social network of L2 speakers. This increased experience with and attraction toward the L2 underlies the shift in preference from L1 to L2, and, potentially, loss or stagnation of L1 proficiency. Diminished proficiency in the L1 then becomes another factor pushing the minority child toward the host culture and language. Finally, Hakuta and colleagues found that immigration depth of family (i.e., generations born in the United States) and personal commitment to Spanish were inter-related and predictive of the amount of Spanish spoken in the home, which was in turn predictive of L1 maintenance in the children (Hakuta & D'Andrea, 1992; Hakuta & Pease-Alvarez, 1994; Pease-Alvarez et al., 1996). Eilers et al. (2006) found that immigration depth interacted with SES in predicting Spanish language maintenance in Miami, where low SES families with parents born in the United States were less likely to maintain Spanish as the home language.

Summary

Let us return to the three questions posed at the outset and consider some possible answers. (1) Are child L2 acquisition patterns and rates similar to those for L1 acquisition? Patterns and rates are highly similar overall between L1 and L2; for example, difficult and late-acquired morphosyntax is the same for L1 and L2, and rates of vocabulary accumulation in L1 and L2 appear to be the same for children as a group. Some notable exceptions include patterns potentially caused by L1 transfer, which is prominent in phonological development, and the absence of L1 patterns like subject omission and short MLUs, possibly due to the greater cognitive maturity of L2 learners. In addition, individual variation in patterns and rates is possibly more pronounced for child L2 acquisition because there are more sources of variation than in L1 acquisition. (2) How do child L2 learners compare with native speakers of the target language their own age? It is commonly believed that child L2 learners, unlike adults, acquire a L2 quickly and with uniform native-speaker ultimate attainment; however, research does not substantiate these beliefs. In particular, the cognitive maturity of these learners does not seem to confer advantages as a group in rate of development, with the exception of MLU, and obtaining oral language proficiency in the L2 on par with native speakers can take most of the elementary school years. It is also important to consider that some discrepancies in performance between native speakers and L2 children might be due to the different, that is, bilingual, nature of their language competence, rather than being a mark of inferiority with respect to monolinguals. (3) What happens to the L1 development of minority children learning a L2 that is the majority language of the community? L1 minority children experience a shift in dominant language from L1 to L2, whose rapidity and effect on long-term proficiency in L1 is determined by a combination of social and psychological factors, chief among which is community support for the L1.

Understanding child SLA is crucial to developing a complete understanding of children's language development in the school years because dual language children are the majority globally (Tucker, 1998), and thus their experiences and outcomes are neither marginal nor abnormal. It is hoped that in the future child SLA will be examined with less emphasis on deviation from the monolingual situation, and with greater acceptance of bilingualism as a healthy and advantageous developmental path.

References

Anderson, R. (2004). First language loss in Spanish-speaking children: Patterns of loss and implications for clinical practice. In B. Goldstein (Ed.), *Bilingual language development and disorders in Spanish–English speakers* (pp. 187–212). Baltimore, MD: Brookes.

Bialystok, E., & Miller, B. (1999). The problem of age in second language acquisition: Influences from language, structure and task. *Bilingualism: Language and Cognition, 2*, 127–145.

Carroll, J., & Sapon, S. (1959). *The Modern Languages Aptitude Test*. San Antonio, TX: Psychological Corporation.

Cobo-Lewis, A., Pearson, B., Eilers, R., & Umbel, V. (2002). Effects of bilingualism and bilingual education on oral and written English skills: A multifactor study of standardized test outcomes. In D. K. Oller & R. Eilers (Eds.), *Language and literacy in bilingual children* (pp. 64–97). Clevedon, UK: Multilingual Matters.

Cummins, J. (2000). *Language, power and pedagogy: Bilingual children in the crossfire*. Clevedon, UK: Multilingual Matters.

Dörnyei, Z., & Skehan, P. (2003). Individual differences in second language learning. In C. Doughty & M. Long (Eds.), *The handbook of second language acquisition* (pp. 589–630). Oxford: Blackwell.

Dulay, H., & Burt, M. (1973). Should we teach children syntax? *Language Learning, 24,* 245–258.

Dulay, H., & Burt, M. (1974). Natural sequences in child second language acquisition. *Language Learning, 24,* 37–53.

Dulay, H., Burt, M., & Krashen, S. (1982). *Language two.* Oxford: Oxford University Press.

Eilers, R., Pearson, B., & Cobo-Lewis, A. (2006). The social circumstances of bilingualism: The Miami experience. In P. McCardle & E. Hoff (Eds.), *Child bilingualism* (pp. 68–90). Clevedon, UK: Multilingual Matters.

Flege, J. (1999). Age of learning and second language speech. In D. Birdsong (Ed.), *Second language acquisition and the critical period hypothesis* (pp. 101–132). Mahwah, NJ: Lawrence Erlbaum.

Flege, J. (2004). *Second language speech learning.* Paper presented at Laboratory Approaches to Spanish Phonology and Phonetics, Indiana University.

Flege, J., & Fletcher, K. (1992). Talker and listener effects on degree of perceived foreign accent. *Journal of the Acoustical Society of America, 91,* 370–389.

Gardner, R. (1980). On the validity of affective variables in L2 acquisition: conceptual, contextual, and statistical considerations. *Language Learning, 30,* 255–270.

Gathercole, V. (2002a). Command of the mass/count distinction in bilingual and monolingual children: an English morphosyntactic distinction. In D. K. Oller & R. Eilers (Eds.), *Language and literacy in bilingual children* (pp. 175–206). Clevedon, UK: Multilingual Matters.

Gathercole, V. (2002b). Monolingual and bilingual acquisition: Learning different treatments of that-trace phenomena in English and Spanish. In D. K. Oller & R. Eilers (Eds.), *Language and literacy in bilingual children* (pp. 220–254). Clevedon, UK: Multilingual Matters.

Gavruseva, E. (2002). Is there primacy of aspect in child L2 English? *Bilingualism: Language and Cognition, 5,* 109–130.

Genesee, F., & Hamayan, E. (1980). Individual differences in second language learning. *Applied Psycholinguistics, 1,* 95–110.

Genesee, F., Paradis, J., & Crago, M. (2004). *Dual language learning and disorder: A handbook on bilingualism and second language learning.* Baltimore, MD: Brookes.

Goldstein, B. (2004). Phonological development and disorders. In B. Goldstein (Ed.), *Bilingual language development and disorders in Spanish–English speakers* (pp. 259–286). Baltimore, MD: Brookes.

Grondin, N., & White, L. (1996). Functional categories in child L2 acquisition of French. *Language Acquisition, 5,* 1–34.

Hakuta, K., & D'Andrea, D. (1992). Some properties of bilingual maintenance and loss in Mexican background high-school students. *Applied Linguistics, 13,* 72–99.

Hakuta, K., Goto Butler, Y., & Witt, D. (2000). *How long does it take English learners to attain proficiency?* Policy Report, the University of California Linguistic Minority Research Institute. Retrieved March 31, 2004, from http://www.stanford.edu/~hakuta/.

Hakuta, K., & Pease-Alvarez, L. (1994). Proficiency, choice and attitudes in bilingual Mexican-American children. In G. Extra & L. Verhoeven (Eds.), *The cross-linguistic study of bilingual development* (pp. 145–164). Amsterdam: Royal Netherlands Academy of Arts and Sciences.

Harley, B. (1989). Transfer in the written compositions of French immersion students. In H. Dechert & M. Raupach (Eds.), *Transfer in language production* (pp. 3–19). Norwood, NJ: Ablex Publishing Corporation.

Harley, B. (1992). Patterns of second language development in French immersion. *French Language Studies, 2,* 159–183.

Harley, B., & Hart, D. (1997). Language aptitude and second language proficiency in classroom learners of different starting ages. *Studies in Second Language Acquisition, 19,* 379–400.

Haznedar, B. (2001). The acquisition of the IP system in child L2 English. *Studies in Second Language Acquisition, 23,* 1–39.

Ionin, T., & Wexler, K. (2002). Why is "Is" easier than "-s"? – Acquisition of tense/agreement morphology by child L2-English learners. *Second Language Research, 18,* 95–136.

Jia, G. (2003). The acquisition of the English plural morpheme by native Mandarin Chinese-speaking children. *Journal of Speech, Language, and Hearing Research, 46,* 1297–1311.

Jia, G., & Aaronson, D. (2003). A longitudinal study of Chinese children and adolescents learning English in the United States. *Applied Psycholinguistics, 24,* 131–161.

Kohnert, K. (2004). Processing skills in early sequential bilinguals. In B. Goldstein (Ed.), *Bilingual language development and disorders in Spanish–English speakers* (pp. 53–76). Baltimore, MD: Brookes.

Kohnert, K., & Bates, E. (2002). Balancing bilinguals II: Lexical comprehension and cognitive processing in children learning Spanish and English. *Journal of Speech, Language, and Hearing Research, 45,* 347–359.

Kohnert, K., Bates, E., & Hernandez, A. (1999). Balancing bilinguals: Lexical-semantic production and cognitive processing in children learning Spanish and English. *Journal of Speech, Language, and Hearing Research, 42,* 1400–1413.

Kohnert, K., & Windsor, J. (2004). The search for common ground: Part I. Lexical performance by linguistically diverse learners. *Journal of Speech, Language, and Hearing Research, 47,* 877–890.

Lakshmanan, U. (1994). *Universal grammar in child second language acquisition.* Amsterdam: John Benjamins.

Mägiste, E. (1992). Second language learning in elementary and high school students. *European Journal of Cognitive Psychology, 4,* 355–365.

McDonald, J. L. (2000). Grammaticality judgments in a second language: Influences of age of acquisition and native language. *Applied Psycholinguistics, 21,* 395–423.

Miller, J., & Chapman, R. (1981). The relation between age and mean length of utterance. *Journal of Speech, Language, and Hearing Research, 24,* 154–161.

Montrul, S. (2002). Incomplete acquisition and attrition of Spanish tense/aspect distinctions in adult bilinguals. *Bilingualism: Language and Cognition, 5,* 39–68.

Paradis, J. (2004). On the relevance of specific language impairment to understanding the role of transfer in second language acquisition. *Applied Psycholinguistics, 25,* 67–82.

Paradis, J. (2005). Grammatical morphology in children learning English as a second language: Implications of similarities with specific language impairment. *Language, Speech, and Hearing Services in Schools, 36,* 172–187.

Paradis, J., & Crago, M. (2000). Tense and temporality: Similarities and differences between language-impaired and second-language children. *Journal of Speech, Language, and Hearing Research, 43,* 834–848.

Paradis, J., & Crago, M. (2004). Comparing L2 and SLI grammars in French: Focus on DP. In J. Paradis & P. Prévost (Eds.), *The acquisition of French in different contexts: Focus on functional categories* (pp. 89–108). Amsterdam: John Benjamins.

Paradis, J., Le Corre, M., & Genesee, F. (1998). The emergence of tense and agreement in child L2 French. *Second Language Research, 14,* 227–257.

Patterson, J., & Pearson, B. (2004). Bilingual lexical development: Influences, contexts, and processes. In B. Goldstein (Ed.), *Bilingual language development and disorders in Spanish–English speakers* (pp. 77–104). Baltimore, MD: Brookes.

Paradis, J., Rice, M., Crago, M., & Richman, A. (2004). *Missing inflection or (extended) optional infinitives? Comparing child L2 English with English SLI.* Paper presented at the 29th Annual Boston University Conference on Language Development, Boston University.

Pease-Alvarez, L., Hakuta, K., & Bayley, R. (1996). Spanish proficiency and language use in a California Mexicano community. *Southwest Journal of Linguistics, 15*, 137–151.

Peña, E., & Kester, E. (2004). Semantic development in Spanish–English bilinguals. In B. Goldstein (Ed.), *Bilingual language development and disorders in Spanish–English speakers* (pp. 105–128). Baltimore, MD: Brookes.

Prévost, P., & White, L. (2000). Accounting for morphological variation in second language acquisition: truncation or missing inflection? In M.-A. Friedemann & L. Rizzi (Eds.), *The acquisition of syntax* (pp. 202–235). Harlow, UK: Longman.

Ranta, L. (2002). The role of learners' language analytic ability in the communicative classroom. In P. Robinson (Ed.), *Individual differences and instructed language learning* (pp. 159–181). Amsterdam: John Benjamins.

Sawyer, M., & Ranta, L. (2001). Aptitude, individual differences, and instructional design. In P. Robinson (Ed.), *Cognition and second language instruction* (pp. 319–353). Cambridge: Cambridge University Press.

Selinker, L., Swain, M., & Dumas, G. (1975). The interlanguage hypothesis extended to children. *Language Learning, 25*, 139–152.

Skehan, P. (1991). Individual differences in second language learning. *Studies in Second Language Acquisition, 13*, 275–298.

Snow, C., & Hoefnagel-Höhle, M. (1977). Age differences in the pronunciation of foreign sounds. *Language and Speech, 20*, 357–365.

Strong, M. (1983). Social styles and the second language acquisition of Spanish-speaking kindergartners. *TESOL Quarterly, 17*, 241–258.

Tabors, P. (1997). *One child, two languages: A guide for preschool educators of children learning English as a second language.* Baltimore, MD: Brookes.

Tucker, G. R. (1998). A global perspective on multilingualism and multilingual education. In J. Cenoz & F. Genesee (Eds.), *Beyond bilingualism: Multilingualism and multilingual education* (pp. 3–15). Clevedon, UK: Multilingual Matters.

Umbel, V., Pearson, B., Fernández, M., & Oller, D. K. (1992). Measuring bilingual children's receptive vocabularies. *Child Development, 63*, 1012–1020.

Watson, I. (1991). Phonological processing in two languages. In E. Bialystok (Ed.), *Language processing in bilingual children* (pp. 25–48). Cambridge: Cambridge University Press.

Weber-Fox, C., & Neville, H. (1999). Functional neural subsystems are differentially affected by delays in second language immersion: ERP and behavioral evidence in bilinguals. In D. Birdsong (Ed.), *Second language acquisition and the critical period hypothesis* (pp. 23–38). Mahwah, NJ: Lawrence Erlbaum.

Weber-Fox, C., & Neville, H. (2001). Sensitive periods differentiate processing of open- and closed-class words: An ERP study of bilinguals. *Journal of Speech, Language, and Hearing Research, 44*, 1338–1353.

Winitz, H., Gillespie, B., & Starcev, J. (1995). The development of English speechpatterns of a 7-year-old Polish-speaking child. *Journal of Psycholinguistic Research, 24*, 117–143.

Winsler, A., Díaz, R., Espinosa, L., & Rodríguez, J. (1999). When learning a second language does not mean losing the first: Bilingual language development in low-income, Spanish-speaking children attending bilingual preschool. *Child Development, 70*, 349–362.

Wong Fillmore, L. (1979). Individual differences in second language acquisition. In C. Fillmore et al. (Eds.), *Individual differences in language ability and language behavior* (pp. 203–227). New York: Academic Press.

Wong Fillmore, L. (1983). The language learner as an individual: Implications of research on individual differences for the ESL teacher. In M. Clarke & J. Handscombe (Eds.), *On TESOL '82: Pacific Perspectives on Language Learning and Teaching*. Washington, DC: TESOL.

Wong Fillmore, L. (1991). When learning a second language means losing the first. *Early Childhood Research Quarterly*, 6, 323–346.

PART V

Atypical Language Development

Introduction

The axiom that guides much of the research in language development is that language is robust. But sometimes, language development is not so robust. The chapters in this Part consider the cases in which language and the language-related accomplishment of literacy do not develop as they typically do. Rice considers those children who seem unimpaired in all other domains and whose difficulties seem specific to language. Tager-Flusberg considers cases in which atypical language development accompanies another developmental disorder: autism, Williams syndrome, or Down syndrome. Lyytinen and colleagues discuss the development of reading and reading disorders (dyslexia).

Besides completing the Handbook's coverage of the field by considering the exceptions to the rule of robustness, these chapters address basic questions of how language is acquired and how language development is related to competencies in other domains. The research reviewed in these chapters applies the logic that study of a process that has gone awry provides clues to how that process operates when it is successful. Each of these chapters also provides ties to the chapters in Part I, on basic foundations, as they describe research that seeks causes of disordered development in neurodevelopmental and genetic bases and in social and cognitive prerequisites to language development. These chapters all forcefully make the point that, effects of input notwithstanding, biology constrains what is possible with respect to language development.

The neurodevelopmental and genetic bases of language are revealed in evidence of the heritability of specific language impairment (SLI) (Rice) and dyslexia (Lyytinen et al.) and of specific genotype–phenotype linkages in some cases of SLI and in Williams and Down syndrome (Tager-Flusberg). Underlying neuropathology is also implicated in many of these cases of atypical language development. Another tie to the foundational work presented in Part I is in the connections Rice makes between a description of the phenotype of SLI in the terminology of generative grammar and proposed biological and genetic bases of language.

These chapters present findings with provocative implications for understanding the processes of both atypical and typical language development. The evidence with respect to SLI suggests that genes play a greater role in determining language impairment than they do in accounting for variation within the normal range of variability, consistent, perhaps, with the notion that given species-characteristic learning capacities, differences in language development are a function, to a significant degree, of differences in input, but where the genetic endowment is less than the normal learning capacity, variations in input may make less of a difference. The disordered pragmatics that is characteristic of children with autism provides compelling evidence that social understandings are prerequisite to normal language development. On the other hand, the language development that children with autism do accomplish suggests language is not the product of a purely social process. Some children with autism who have near normal intelligence do acquire a vocabulary and a grammar. These acquisitions must reflect an underlying process that does not fully depend on a social base. The research on reading disorders reported by Lyytinen et al. makes the point that language development not only rests on previously existing foundations, it is also itself a foundation for later developments.

These chapters also say something about what we do not know. We do not know why the population of children with SLI is so heterogeneous. Although we know that language impairments, both specific and as part of other syndromes, have a genetic basis, we do not fully understand how the particular genetic differences become manifest as particular language differences. Although we know, from studies of children with Williams syndrome and Down syndrome, that IQ is not a reliable predictor of language learning capacity, we do not know exactly what underlying inabilities explain the language problems displayed by children with Williams or Down syndrome. Together, the chapters in this Part both add to the database from which to build an account of how children acquire language and point out the need, to echo Rice's conclusion, for a theory of language acquisition that is sufficiently robust to account for its disruptions and delays as well as its typical successes.

20

Children with Specific Language Impairment: Bridging the Genetic and Developmental Perspectives

Mabel L. Rice

It is widely understood that children's language acquisition is a remarkably robust phenomenon. A valuable scientific generalization is that youngsters share a nearly universal aptitude for the acquisition of their native language during the first few years of life. As documented in this volume, there is now a large literature that provides descriptive benchmarks, pegged to chronological age, that describe children's language development across different linguistic dimensions and social contexts of use; the ways in which children may or may not draw upon one dimension, such as semantic development, to build another, such as syntax; and the ways in which children's social contexts contribute to their development.

Some years ago, Steven Pinker succinctly captured a predominant view of the robustness of children's language acquisition abilities: "In general, language acquisition is a stubbornly robust process; from what we can tell there is virtually no way to prevent it from happening short of raising a child in a barrel" (Pinker, 1984, p. 29). Opposition to his perspective came from scholars who argued for more influence attributable to variations in environmental exposure that are less extreme than total deprivation (cf. Snow, 1996). From either perspective, a corollary was implied: If a child did not develop language readily, there must have been something significantly deficit about the child's environment (barring no obvious concomitant conditions such as severe mental retardation or hearing loss that would impair a youngster's abilities to acquire language).

Children with specific language impairment (SLI) are significant exceptions to this assumption. Children with SLI do not keep up with their age peers in their language development, although there is no obvious reason for them to fall behind. To understand these youngsters, the perspective shifts from central tendencies across all children to individual differences characteristic of a subgroup of children; from an assumption of tightly intertwined dimensions of language to consideration of possible disruptions in synchrony; and from an emphasis on shared or nonshared social environments to possible inherited limitations in language acquisition mechanisms.

These variations from the normative developmental assumptions are evident in the clinical, developmental, and genetic perspectives of SLI, each of which is summarized in this chapter. It is suggested that a bridge between the genetic and developmental perspectives is needed and the notion of maturational mechanisms could serve such a bridging function. There is a long-standing interest in the possible causes of SLI. The momentum of modern genetics inquiry is profoundly shaping the fundamental work of description of the symptoms of language impairment in SLI and interpretive frameworks. In many ways the new genetics investigations sharpen the need for solid empirical work across the wide range of language phenomena. This includes a need for developmental studies that capture the growth trajectories of language with careful attention to central tendencies within age levels and individual variations, and interpretive frameworks that aim to integrate growth mechanisms with etiological factors.

The chapter begins with conventional operational definitions of SLI, followed by a brief overview of the history of investigations of this condition. Then the clinical, genetic, and developmental perspectives are briefly explained, and why they are in need of bridging. This is followed by a review of the research that aims to describe the phenotype (behavioral symptoms thought to be related to genetic influences), with an emphasis on growth trajectories. The next section reviews the recent genetics advances. The following section lays out some basic parameters of a maturational perspective of inherited timing mechanisms and developmental change. The chapter concludes with a section on the implications of the SLI research for general models of language development.

Definition of Specific Language Impairment

The commonly accepted research definition of SLI invokes inclusionary and exclusionary criteria. Inclusionary criteria are intended to establish that the affected youngsters have language impairments relative to age expectations. Typically, this is determined by performance on a standardized omnibus language assessment instrument, with "impairment" defined as performance of −1 standard deviation or more below the age mean, or, roughly, at the 15th percentile or below of the child's age group. Depending upon the purpose of a given investigation, the definition is sometimes further specified according to receptive versus expressive language abilities, and according to whether or not the children have accompanying speech impairments. For example, in studies of morphological impairments it is important to control for phonological/speech impairments, in order to avoid confounding estimates of morphological impairments with phonological or speech impairments. This is typically done by means of a pretest designed to elicit word final consonants in single words (cf. Rice & Wexler, 2001). Another example is the need to control for speech impairments in imitation tasks; without such control, it is not possible to tell if poor performance is attributable to poor speech skill or poor memory of speech/phonological units.

The exclusionary criteria are intended to select affected children whose developmental impairment is specific to language (see Rice & Warren, 2004, and Rice, Warren, & Betz, 2005, for information about language disorders across different clinical groups). Children with hearing loss are excluded. Children diagnosed with syndromic conditions, such as Williams syndrome, Down syndrome, and fragile X syndrome, are excluded. Conventionally, children diagnosed as autistic have been excluded, although in the recent shift to the broader clinical category of autism spectrum disorders (ASD) the diagnostic boundary between SLI and autism is somewhat blurred and is currently a matter of active investigation (see Tager-Flusberg, 2004, 2005, for overviews). The issue is the extent to which children with language impairments show overlap, either in genetic risk indicators (i.e., family aggregation) or in behavioral symptoms. Mental retardation is usually ruled out via exclusion of children whose nonverbal IQ performance levels are 85 or below. The range between 70 and 85 nonverbal IQ is sometimes invoked as acceptable for the label of SLI, although it is preferable to label this range as "nonspecific language impairment" (NLI) (Tomblin & Zhang, 1999) and treat children in this range as a separate clinical group, in order to avoid error attributable to too much heterogeneity (and unknown sources of error variance) in the grouping criteria (e.g., Miller, Kail, Leonard, & Tomblin, 2001; Rice, Tomblin, Hoffman, Richman, & Marquis, 2004). Finally, children with known neurological conditions, such as epilepsy, are routinely excluded from the SLI research groups. In actual clinical practice the generic label of "language impairment" is sometimes used to collapse across the exclusionary criteria to create an inclusive clinical group that is more diffuse than the controlled research groupings.

There is long-standing recognition of the need to avoid confusing dialectal differences in linguistic systems with linguistic differences indicative of language impairment. Conventional standardized language assessments have been widely criticized as inappropriate for dialect speakers. With support from the National Institute of Deafness and Communication Disorders, investigators have developed new assessment systems designed to differentiate dialectal differences from language disorders in young children (Seymour, Roeper, & de Villiers, 2003), or have adapted existing measures and methods to use as culturally valid language screenings (Oetting & McDonald, 2002; Washington & Craig, 2004). Research standards are moving toward explicit control of dialectal differences in studies of children with SLI, that is, to treat dialect as an exclusionary variable for studies of the linguistic dimensions affected by the dialect or to use dialect as a grouping variable.

A recent epidemiological investigation generated an estimate of 7% of children (8% for boys and 6% for girls) aged 5 to 6 years as meeting the definition of SLI (Tomblin et al., 1997). This investigation also established that in the general population clinically significant speech impairments are orthogonal to language impairments (Shriberg, Tomblin, & McSweeny, 1999). This outcome was surprising, because children with speech impairments are more likely to be identified for clinical services. Thus, children with speech and language problems are over-represented in clinical caseloads, creating the impression of considerable overlap. It is worth noting that because children with SLI who participate in research studies are often recruited out of clinical caseloads, children who participate in scientific studies may be likely to have speech as well as language impairments, although it is often difficult to establish this because speech status is not always described. These sampling issues are important to keep in mind because the clinical samples may not be representative of the general population of children with language impairments; speech and language impairments are not intrinsically linked in the condition of language impairment; and the co-occurrence of speech and language impairments can introduce confounds in some tasks.

Another important outcome of the epidemiological study was that affected children were unlikely to be identified and enrolled in clinical services. Tomblin et al. (1997) report that the parents of 29% of the affected children reported that they had previously been informed that their child had a speech or language problem. Thus, our best current information suggests that about 70% of affected children are not identified and enrolled in appropriate intervention during their kindergarten year of school.

Collectively, these observations point toward a clinical condition of unexpected variation in children's language acquisition aptitude that is: (1) more prevalent in the general population than widely assumed; (2) likely to be confused with speech impairments and/or possible concomitant developmental deficits such as low cognitive ability, social deficits, or reading impairment; and (3) often undiagnosed. These facts certainly contribute to the challenges involved in careful investigation of this clinical condition, and perhaps to the inconsistencies in the scientific literature insofar as the difficulties conspire to increase the likelihood of heterogeneity in the affected groups and an imprecise calibration across studies of children labeled as SLI. This becomes especially relevant to etiological investigations, as discussed below. At the same time, there are areas of convergent and replicated findings that contribute to a strong sense of momentum.

History of Studies of SLI

The study of SLI has roots at least as far back as the beginnings of modern descriptive medicine and psychology, to the early years of the 1800s. A case description by Gall in 1822 is widely cited as the earliest description in the modern literature (Gall, 1835, English translation). Subsequent entries in the literature generated a variety of labels for the condition, ranging from "congenital word deafness" to the widespread extensions of the term "aphasia" in the 1900s. "Developmental aphasia" (Eisenson, 1968) and "developmental dysphasia" (Clahsen, 1989) are immediate antecedents of the current term. By the 1980s, researchers began to adopt "specific language impairment" as an etiologically neutral term, without assumption of neurological impairments of the same sort as associated with aphasia or cortical lesions (e.g., Leonard, 1981). In the current literature, "specific language impairment" is in widespread use by investigators, although a variety of diagnostic labels appear in clinical manuals and across different clinical settings (cf. Leonard, 1998, pp. 5–8).

In the context of this chapter, two points are of note. One is that the unexpected variation in children's language acquisition has been documented for a significant length of time. The other is that, historically, the labels vary as a consequence of the scholarly context of the observer. The condition of SLI falls at the margin of the focal points of studies of child development, child health/disease, and children with disabilities. The disciplines of psychology, medicine, education, and, more recently, speech/language pathology, linguistics, and genetics have contributed to the literature that bears on SLI. It remains to be seen if the label stays constant or if new labels appear for new distinctions. What is essential is the need to explicate the core phenomenon, that is, how it is that children who seem to have all the prerequisite abilities and environmental resources in place nevertheless do not develop language in the expected robust fashion.

Clinical, Genetic, and Developmental Perspectives: A Need for Bridging

From the outset there has been a great interest in the factors that cause SLI. This is apparent in early studies of the genetics of language, dating from the beginning of the 1900s (e.g., Orton, 1930). Much of the early period of investigation established that individuals with speech and language impairments tended to cluster in families. Lenneberg (1967) foresaw the current program of investigation in his description of "congenital language disability" involving "delayed onset of speech, protracted articulatory difficulties in childhood, congenital expressive disorders" (p. 349).

With the advent of the modern explosion in behavioral and molecular genetics, the search for a genetic contribution to individual variation in language aptitude has taken on new momentum. Studies of the genetic contributions to SLI are moving on multiple fronts, with the most striking advances in DNA analyses of affected cases and family members (for an overview of current methods and research directions, see Rice & Smolik, in press, Smith, 2004, and Smith & Morris, 2005). Twin studies are also contributing valuable new information. There is growing consensus that genetic factors contribute to SLI, although it is thought that the genetics underlying SLI are complex, involving several genes that are likely to interact with each other and with a child's linguistic environment (cf. SLI Consortium, 2004). Although it is early in this line of investigation, there is reason to suspect that the genetic contributions are probably not uniform across linguistic dimensions or related cognitive variables.

A vital element of the emerging genetics studies is the characterization of the behavioral phenotype that is thought to be a core deficit of SLI (cf. Smith, 2004; Smith & Morris, 2005). Measures to identify affected individuals must be sensitive to the disorder (i.e., able to identify a high percentage of affected individuals), and they must be specific (i.e., able to identify a high percentage of unaffected individuals). Further, a good phenotype has validity for interpretation of the nature of the disorder. Operationally, this amounts to a search for clinical markers that yield little overlap of affected and unaffected groups of children.

The prevailing methods have relied on samples of affected children identified on the basis of comparison with age-level peers. Such methods are essential for establishing appropriate levels of sensitivity and selectivity. At the same time, they do not capture well the ways in which the linguistic system of affected children is similar to or different from that of unaffected children over a developmental trajectory, nor the ways in which an affected child's linguistic system does or does not fully approximate the expected end-state grammar. Recent studies of the acquisition of finite verb morphology show how a developmental perspective of SLI can bring together the accounts of unaffected, typically developing children with accounts of the nature of language impairment. A further advantage of the developmental perspective is that it could provide a developmentally calibrated phenotype, such that a person's affectedness could be described quantitatively as a slope of the acquisition trajectory and/or age of asymptote (cf. Francis, Shaywitz, Stuebing, Shaywitz, & Fletcher, 1996, for a study of reading disability with a similar developmental perspective). This possible refinement of phenotype definition has yet to be formally evaluated, but it is clearly on the horizon for future work.

Tracking the Developmental Course of SLI Relative to Normative Development: Delay versus Disruptions in Language Acquisition

An important distinction in the study of children with SLI is the notion of delayed language acquisition versus deviant or disrupted acquisition. It is possible that affected children are like younger typically developing children, that is, that there is a general immaturity in the language acquisition system. This model is a conservative model, in that it assumes that the mechanisms of language acquisition, once activated, are very similar in affected and unaffected children. Experimentally, a delay model is evaluated by means of a control group of younger children at equivalent levels of general language acquisition, most often benchmarked during the preschool years as equivalent levels of mean length of utterance (MLU). This sets up a three-group design in studies of SLI that has proven to be very informative, comprised of an affected group, an age comparison group, and a language equivalent group. If the SLI group is at lower levels than the age comparison group but equivalent to the younger language equivalent group, this is generally viewed as a pattern attributable to the generally lower language competencies of the affected group, more like that of younger children.

By contrast, there are two versions of a nondelay model. One proposes that the language of affected children is "deviant," in the sense that it is qualitatively different from that of unaffected children (cf. Karmiloff & Karmiloff-Smith, 2001). The deviant model, while very interesting, will not be discussed further here, because of space limitations. The alternative nondelay model is one of "disruption" (referred to as a "delay within a delay" model in Rice, 2003, and updated to a "disruption" notion in Rice, 2004a). In this model, some elements of language are out of harmony, or disrupted, relative to others, leading to a lack of synchrony in the overall linguistic system. Evidence for this possibility is lower performance of the SLI group than either of the control groups on a given linguistic dimension, indicating that affected children's low performance extends beyond that expected for a general immaturity relative to age expectations. Such an asynchrony is a good candidate for a clinical marker, because the affected children's performance is not likely to overlap with unaffected age peers (cf. Rice, 2000). Areas of disrupted synchrony are of theoretical interest, because they show how the linguistic dimensions that are tightly intertwined in typically developing children are to some extent independent elements that can be selectively affected and fall behind in acquisition.

Delayed Onset: Late Talkers

Some otherwise healthy children are slow to begin talking, as is evident in smaller vocabularies than their peers at 24 months of age. These children are referred to as "late talkers." Late onset of language is a hallmark characteristic of children with language impairments. In the case of children with SLI, late talking can be the first diagnostic symptom. Tager-Flusberg and Cooper (1999) called for studies of early identification of SLI, "with particular emphasis on predicting which late talkers develop SLI" (p. 1277). Estimates of proportions of 2-year-olds who are late talkers have been hampered by limitations of ascertainment. Until recently, the available evidence was drawn from self-selected, predominantly middle class families. A new investigation by Zubrick, Taylor, Rice, and Slegers (under review) reports outcomes from an epidemiologically ascertained sample of 1,766 children of 24 months old for whom there were parent reports of vocabulary and first word combinations, as well as a six-item rating scale for general communication abilities, including early receptive language. In this large sample, 13% of the children met the definition of "late talker." Further, there was extensive information about maternal, family, and child characteristics. It is noteworthy that in this large sample, variables associated with home resources (cf. Entwhistle & Astone, 1994), including mother's education, family income, socio-economic status, parental mental health, parenting style, and family functioning, did not predict late talker status. The significant predictors were only a handful out of a large number of variables: gender (2.74 times the risk for boys than girls); the family history of speech and language delays (2.11 times the risk for families with a positive history); number of children in the family (double the risk for families with two or more children); perinatal status (1.8 times the risk for children with a low percentage of expected birth weight or gestation age less than 37 weeks); and the child's early neuromotor skills (more than double the risk for children somewhat late in developing motor skills, although it must be emphasized that the late talker children's motor development is within normative expectations). These outcomes suggest that a child's genetic make-up and certain constitutional attributes are associated with the timing of language onset.

The available evidence about the longitudinal outcomes for children who are late talkers is comprised of very small samples of children followed over time, drawn from a restricted range of mothers who agreed to participate: Rescorla (2002) followed 34 children; Paul (1996), 31; Whitehurst and Fischel (1994), 37; Thal, Tobias, and Morrison (1991), 10 children. The data are complicated further by some differences in the arbitrary means of identifying affected children. Keeping the limitations in mind, the best estimate for children with a history of late talker status who are classified as SLI at age 6 years seems to be in the range of 17–25% (cf. Paul, 1996; Rescorla, 2002).

The other approach to exploring the full growth trajectory of children with SLI is to ascertain children in the 5- to 6-year age range, follow them over time, and project the obtained growth curves to an earlier period of development. In the following section, we see that this method also points toward delayed onset as part of the overall picture of SLI, and in addition it reveals important areas of disrupted language growth, out of sync with the rest of the language system.

Delays in the Language Growth Trajectories of SLI

Evidence of a consistent pattern of language delay is evident in the growth of MLU and receptive vocabulary in children with SLI. Rice, Redmond, and Hoffman (in press) followed a group of 21 five-year-old children with expressive/receptive SLI (screened for speech impairment) and 20 MLU equivalent children who were two years younger. The children were assessed at 6-month intervals for MLU, for a total of nine data points over 5 years. The two groups showed remarkable parallels in MLU growth. They were at equivalent levels of MLU at each time of measurement, ranging from ~3.7 to ~5.2 from the first to last time of measurement. Growth curve modeling showed that there were no group differences in the growth trajectories; each group showed linear and quadratic growth, with negatively accelerating growth such that at the later times of measurement there was less of an increase in the MLU between times of measurement. It is as if the mechanisms that guide increased utterance length are working in the same way in the two groups over the observed time, even though the affected children are two years older than the controls, were enrolled in language intervention at the outset, and were at higher levels of formal education. Projecting the growth trajectories downward, and assuming the continued parallel growth patterns early on, there is strong implication of a delayed onset of the system of combining words into phrases and clauses for affected children.

Growth in receptive vocabulary was tracked in the two groups, as well. Receptive vocabulary was measured annually by the raw score on the Peabody Picture Vocabulary Test-Revised (Dunn & Dunn, 1981). The groups were not initially selected for equivalency on receptive vocabulary. At the outset, the affected group had a small but statistically significant numerical advantage ($M = 32$ raw score vs. 25 for the MLU equivalent group). At the end, the affected group had a small but statistically significant numerical disadvantage ($M = 80$ for the SLI group vs. 89 for the MLU equivalent group). The groups did not differ in the intervening times of measurement. In the growth model, there were significant linear and quadratic growth parameters, with group differences at the intercept (outset) and in linear rates, such that the MLU equivalent group overcame the initial lower level of performance with a greater degree of linear change subsequently. It is as if the affected children benefited from the two years' age difference at the outset, in the experience needed to acquire new words, but this advantage was overcome by a slightly better rate of learning new words in the younger group.

So the picture of synchrony/asynchrony is mixed during this observation period – receptive vocabulary and MLU growth are not exactly aligned in the same ways across the two groups in the observed period of acquisition, and yet for the middle two years the groups remain equivalent for vocabulary as well as MLU. It seems overly strong to characterize the general vocabulary development of affected children during this time as "disrupted" from the general growth in language competency as indicated by MLU, given this mid period of alignment. At the same time, there are some indications that younger, MLU equivalent children may be better than affected children in quick incidental learning of new vocabulary items, a learning advantage that could accumulate over time to generate the higher receptive vocabulary levels at the last time of measurement. MLU equivalent children, as a group, are somewhat better than affected children in using syntactic cues in their acquisition of new words (cf. Rice, Cleave, & Oetting, 2000), although they are similar in their need for frequent exposures to novel words in order to store them in memory (cf. Rice, Oetting, Marquis, Bode, & Pae, 1994). Oetting (1999) found that 6-year-old affected children used cues to interpret verb meaning as well as younger MLU equivalent controls, but the affected children were less able to retain new verbs than the younger group. Other studies report mixed outcomes for the SLI/MLU group comparison (cf. Hoff-Ginsberg, Kelly, & Buhr, 1996; O'Hara & Johnston, 1997; Van der Lely, 1994), which Oetting (1999) suggests may be attributable to task differences and memory demands. Overall, the cross-sectional outcomes are consistent with the longitudinal outcomes in suggesting that if there are differences between affected and younger children in the synthesis of general language growth, as indexed by MLU and lexical acquisition, then the differences are relatively subtle, and not yet well replicated.

Disruptions in the Language Growth of Children with SLI: Finiteness Marking

In contrast to the lexical picture, there is robust documentation of notable disruption in the linguistic system of affected children for the grammatical function of finiteness marking. For some time there had been accumulating evidence that morphology associated with verbs was especially problematic for children with SLI, although morphology was widely viewed as a problem of lexical stem + affix, and surface characteristics of morphology, such as perceptual salience, were accorded a strong role in accounting for affected children's limitations (cf. Leonard, 1998). Recent advances in linguistic theory allowed for a more precise characterization of the nature of the impairments. Finiteness involves tense and agreement features on verbs in main clauses, features that interact with syntactic requirements of clause structures, hence the term "morphosyntax" to capture the close connection of morphology and syntax.

A thumbnail sketch of the adult grammar from this theoretical perspective can lay out some features of interest in children's grammars. For a more complete description, see Haegemann (1994); for the theory as applied to child grammar, see Guasti (2002); for a short but technically sound synopsis, see Schütze (2004). It is hypothesized that features such as *tense*, *agreement*, and *case marking* are tightly interrelated in the syntax of clause structure. Essentially, the term "finiteness" involves "tense" and "agreement." Note that the term "tense" is used in two ways: it can refer to the semantics of reference to temporal dimensions (as in "present" vs. "past" tense), and it also has a second sense of a required grammatical property which is not so tightly linked to temporal dimensions (e.g., the need to insert auxiliary *DO* in questions). Further, agreement involves person and number marking on nouns, markings which are "copied over" onto verbs, where they do not add additional meanings to the verbs. Such features are distinguished from other properties of the underlying syntax.

This framework captures some of the following facts about English grammar. Finiteness is marked by the following morphemes: Third person singular present tense *-s* as in "Patsy runs home every day"; past tense *-ed* or irregular past tense, as in "Patsy walked/ran home yesterday"; copula or auxiliary *BE* as in "Patsy is happy" or "Patsy is running"; and auxiliary *DO*, as in "Does Patsy like to run?" In a simple clause there is only one site for finiteness marking and no more than one finiteness marker can appear, as shown in the following examples where an asterisk is inserted to indicate ungrammatical clauses: *Runs Patsy home every day; *Does Patsy likes to run?; *Patsy is runs home every day; *Does Patsy is happy? Note that the set of morphemes is not limited to verbal affixes but instead includes irregular stem-internal morphophonological variants and free-standing morphemes as well.

Subject–verb agreement requires agreement of the person/number features on the noun and verb. These sentences violate that requirement: *Patsy are happy; *I runs home every day. English requires an overt subject for a well-formed clause, as shown by this ungrammatical utterance: *runs home every day. Pronoun case assignment differentiates nominative and accusative case, which is determined by syntactic position, as in "She likes him," and not "*Her likes he." It is thought that the tense feature of English is linked to the requirement of overt subjects (in contrast to languages that do not require overt subjects, such as Italian), and the agreement feature is linked to the requirement of nominative case, although the precise technical details of these interpretations are under investigation (cf. Schütze, 2004).

This perspective allows for some fine-grained distinctions to be applied to child grammars, and to interpretations of the locus of disruptions in the grammars of children with SLI. As expressed very succinctly by Schütze (2004, p. 355), ". . . it is possible for children with normal syntactic structures to sound very unlike adults, because in their lexicon certain morphemes either are missing or have incorrect features associated with them." Finiteness came to the attention of scholars with the observation that in many languages children show an acquisition period in which they produce infinitival forms of verbs where finite forms are required in the adult grammar. At the same early period of word combinations, English-speaking children produce uninflected verbal forms, such as "*Patsy go home" and "*Patsy happy." Wexler and others recognized that the uninflected verbal forms of English were the English variants of infinitives in other early child grammars, thereby unifying the observations across languages and relating the child grammars to the end-state adult grammar.

Wexler initially labeled this an *optional infinitive stage* (Wexler, 1991, 1994, 1996) which was later amended to an *agreement tense omission model* (ATOM) (Schütze & Wexler, 1996; Wexler, Schütze, & Rice, 1998) and then to a *unique checking constraint model* (Wexler, 1998) as the theory evolved to account for a wider range of phenomena across languages. The basic claims about finiteness in English-speaking children, however, remained the same as the theory evolved. The fundamental notion is that, in some languages, young children go through a period in which they seem to treat finiteness marking as optional, although it is obligatory in the adult grammar; at the same time they know many other properties of clausal construction. In the normative literature, this phenomenon is widely accepted as a general description of young children's grammars. There are ongoing discussions and debates about the nature of the underlying linguistic representations, reasons this period is evident in some but not all languages, and the way in which finiteness is linked to null subjects and case marking.

The theory was extended to children with SLI in the prediction that their long delay in the acquisition of verbal morphology is an extension of a phase that is part of younger children's grammatical development (Rice, Wexler, & Cleave, 1995). Early on, it was pointed out that this is, in effect, an enriched *extended development model* (cf. Rice & Wexler, 1996a), which recognizes the many ways in which the language of children with SLI is similar to younger unaffected children, but with a greatly protracted period of incomplete acquisition of grammatical tense marking.

The theory offers some explicit predictions of particular relevance here. One is that the domain of finiteness marking could be uncoupled from other semantic and syntactic properties, in that under this theoretical perspective the computational requirements of tense and agreement checking are distinct from the lexical/semantic elements of the grammar and also are distinct from other syntactic dimensions (cf. Chomsky, 1995; Schütze, 2004). In the context of the discussion here of delay versus disruption of linguistic synchronies, this model allows for a disruption as well as delays. Another prediction is that a set of surface morphemes will cluster together in their performance levels in children, based on their shared underlying function in the adult grammar. This set includes bound as well as free morphemes. Further, at an empirical level, the association among morphemes allows for the calculation of composite variables that enhance psychometric robustness. A third prediction is that although weakness in the finiteness domain can be evident, at the same time other syntactic mechanisms can be unaffected. This translates to the expectation that affected children should be unlikely to make errors indicative of basic syntactic limitations.

Let us consider the first two predictions. These are testable within the three-group design for studies of SLI. Further, longitudinal observations pose an empirically rigorous test of the extent to which the expected associations within the morpheme set are observed, and the extent to which the disruption persists. The children who participated in the longitudinal study of MLU and receptive vocabulary described above also received tasks to measure finiteness marking. The results revealed multiple ways in which the affected group did not perform as well as the MLU equivalent group. Each of the target morphemes showed such a deficit at almost each and every measurement point. Further, the set of morphemes showed strong associations among the items. Finally, the difference was evident across tasks: spontaneous language samples, elicited production tasks, and grammatical judgment tasks yielded the same pattern of outcome. The effect sizes for the group differences are relatively robust, that is, eta square values in the range of 28–54% relative to the younger group, and 31–85% for the age comparison group (Rice, Wexler, & Hershberger, 1998). Models of growth were the same for the two groups, indicating linear and quadratic components for both groups. The predictor relationships were also the same across groups: growth was not predicted by a child's nonverbal intelligence, mother's education, or PPVT-R vocabulary scores at the outset, although a child's initial MLU did predict rate of acquisition. The findings replicated for irregular past tense, when irregular accuracy was calculated as finiteness marking by regarding over-regularizations as finiteness markers (albeit ones in which the phonological requirements of morphology were not fully worked out) (Rice, Wexler, Marquis, & Hershberger, 2000). Further, the replicated findings with judgment tasks establish that the effects are not restricted to production demands but also are evident in children's likelihood to accept utterances as well formed with the same kinds of omissions that they produce (Rice, Wexler, & Redmond, 1999).

There are also cross-sectional replications from other labs of the basic finding that children with SLI, as a group, are likely to perform less accurately than younger controls on morphemes associated with the finiteness marker (cf. Bedore & Leonard, 1998; Conti-Ramsden, Botting, & Faragher, 2001; Eadie, Fey, Douglas, & Parsons, 2002; Grela & Leonard, 2000; Joseph, Serratrice, & Conti-Ramsden, 2002; Leonard, Eyer, Bedore, & Grela, 1997; Marchman, Wulfeck, & Ellis Weismer, 1999; Oetting & Horohov, 1997). Thus the empirical phenomenon is well established, although there is a lively and flourishing dialog about the interpretation.

To return to the predictions, the first two are well supported by available empirical evidence, to the effect that the grammars of children with SLI show a protracted period of delayed acquisition of finiteness marking relative to their age peers and, more remarkable, relative to younger children. There is strong reason to consider this a disruption rather than a general immaturity, in that performance in this area lags behind general indices of language acquisition such as MLU and receptive vocabulary (at least in some portions of the period between 3 and 7 years of typical development). This part of the grammar is not in full synchrony with other dimensions of language growth in affected children.

Let us return to the third prediction. As noted by Schütze (2004), the theory carries further requirements of clause-by-clause inspection to determine if there are errors of morpheme use that would indicate underlying syntactic deficiencies. Such analyses are laborious and often not done, but in the studies of English-speaking children that carefully code for such possibilities, the general finding is that there are very few errors of usage. More particularly, errors of subject–verb agreement are at best only a very small proportion out of all possible occurrences; errors of word order placement are rare or nonexistent as are violations of the requirement that there can be only a single instance of finiteness marking within a main clause. In short, in the studies carried out in the Rice lab, errors are overwhelmingly likely to be constrained to omissions in obligatory contexts. Leonard, Camarata, Brown, and Camarata (2004) report a similar outcome for the observed error patterns in an intensive training study.

Further, the prediction that there should be an association of pronoun case marking with finiteness marking is also evident in children with SLI, such that "she runs home" is much more likely than "*her runs home" (cf. Wexler et al., 1998; also see Charest & Leonard, 2004, for a detailed analysis of tense vs. agreement as the source of case assignment in affected children). Collectively, such observations indicate that large portions of the underlying syntactic system must be operating in an unimpaired way in children with SLI. This does not necessarily imply that all syntactic dimensions are robust (cf. the arguments of van der Lely and others that a condition described as "grammatical

SLI," thought to be a subset of the generic SLI clinical group, can include syntactic limitations).

There are many complexities yet to be addressed. One is the extent to which similar linguistic symptoms and developmental benchmarks appear in different languages. Although the bulk of the available SLI literature involves English-speaking children, studies of other languages are entering the literature, including French, German, Italian, Spanish, Hebrew, Swedish, Greek, and Cantonese. It is beyond the scope of this chapter to address the outcomes in detail. In general, as expected, there are differences across languages in which elements of the linguistic system are vulnerable, although there is also a growing understanding of how the underlying finiteness system is affected even if the surface manifestations are not the same. A most interesting example is the work on bilingual French/English children with SLI who have been studied in Canada (Paradis, Crago, Genesee, & Rice, 2003). An elegant design feature is the use of balanced bilingual children as participants. This means that the language comparisons are not confounded with extraneous variables that are difficult to control when comparing groups across languages. These French/English bilingual children showed grammatical impairments in both languages, and a problem with finiteness marking in both languages, although the precise symptoms varied according to the rules for English and French. Furthermore, the age benchmarks for affected children were similar across the two languages; 8-year-old French-speaking children continue to show deficits in their levels of finiteness marking as do English-speaking children. This is interesting because unaffected French-speaking children master finiteness marking at an earlier age than English-speaking unaffected children. So the delay of finiteness is actually greater in the French-speaking children with SLI, relative to normative expectations. Another important outcome was that bilingual French/English children with SLI do not show a deficit attributable to the bilingualism; their performance was comparable to monolingual French- or English-speaking children with SLI.

As these examples attest, there is much to be gained from cross-linguistic studies and investigations of bi- or multilingual children with SLI. Early findings are yielding some surprising indications of unexpected robustness as well as important documentation of how the symptoms will interact with the structure of the child's native language.

Genetics of SLI: Focus on the Phenotype

The recent reports of DNA analyses of affected cases and family members are harbingers of an oncoming wave of genetic information. At this early stage of investigation, the findings are mixed but promising. As a higher order cognitive trait, language acquisition is complex, and there are multiple possible ways of defining affectedness. Part of the inconsistency in the current findings is likely to be related to the diversity in definitions. A descriptive review of the evidence is beyond the scope of this paper (see Rice & Smolik, in press, for further details).

A brief summary is as follows. New findings link sites on chromosome 16q and 19q to SLI (SLI Consortium, 2004). The findings are complicated by a lack of replication across subsamples of the participants, inconsistencies between nonword repetition and an omnibus expressive language measure, and possible age effects, such that the genetic influences are more detectable in children older than 8 years than in younger children. These sites are different from the well-reported FOXP2 gene discovery on chromosome 7, first documented in a large extended family in English, referred to as the KE family (see Fisher, 2005, and Vargha-Khadem, Gadian, Copp, & Mishkin, 2005, for clear overviews). Although the ways in which speech and language are affected in the KE family are still debated, the one way in which the affected members of the family are different from unaffected members is a developmental dyspraxia of the orofacial system, such that all affected members have difficulty in controlling the complex mouth movements that generate speech. Thus, dyspraxia is established as a core deficit, although candidates for additional, independent core deficits include "rule-based learning, lexical acquisition and retrieval, and non-verbal cognition" (Vargha-Khadem et al., 2005). It is worth noting that dyspraxia is ruled out in the definition of SLI, although the other candidate core deficits are implicated in the condition of SLI.

A recent twin study (Bishop, Adams, & Norbury, 2005) evaluated the heritability of tense marking and nonword repetition ability (as an index of phonological short-term memory) in a sample of 173 six-year-old twin pairs. Disrupted development in the finiteness-marking element of grammar is predicted to be related to underlying genetic factors (Rice, 1996, 2000, 2003, 2004a, 2004b; Rice & Wexler, 1996b; Wexler, 1996, 1998, 2003). Nonword repetition is an index of phonological short-term memory that is of interest because it is associated with language impairments and is a candidate clinical marker for SLI (Bishop, North, & Conlan, 1996; Gathercole, Willis, Baddeley, & Emslie, 1994; Tager-Flusberg & Cooper, 1999). Bishop et al. (2005) found that impairments in both areas were significantly heritable, although there was minimal phenotypic and etiological overlap between the two deficits. They conclude: "Our findings are also in agreement with predictions made by Rice and colleagues, in confirming that deficits in use of verb inflections commonly persist beyond the age of 4 years in children with language impairments and are heritable. Most crucially, this study reveals that impairments in use of verb inflections have distinctive genetic origins and cannot be explained away as secondary consequences of limitations of phonological short term memory." Thus, although it is early on in the investigation of the inherited elements of SLI, these new discoveries point toward the viability of this line of study, and the promise of such investigations.

Putting it Together: A Maturational Perspective of Inherited Timing Mechanisms and Developmental Change

As matters now stand, the genetics studies employ a wide range of language phenotypes, most of which define affectedness by reference to age peers. Although this approach has psychometric value and is beginning to uncover potential genetic linkages, it does not capture well the ways in which the linguistic systems of children with SLI share fundamental growth properties with the linguistic systems of unaffected children, nor the ways in which the linguistic system can be less synchronized in affected youngsters, nor the ways in which inherited mechanisms can be influencing the growth. An alternative framework is a maturational perspective, suggested by the delays and disruptions within the grammatical system of children with SLI.

A maturational account posits that there are powerful timing mechanisms that activate the onset of language that can be delayed in onset for affected children (cf. Rice, 2003, 2004a, 2004b; Wexler, 2003). Once language onset is activated, there is an expected synchrony in the emerging system that unfolds in typically developing children, in a close interaction with environmental input, including the child's native language and the ways in which adults and familiar people in a child's home environment interact with him or her. Twin studies indicate that the relative contribution of genetics and environment loads more heavily toward genetics than environment for children at the lower levels of language performance during the 2- to 4-year age period, implicating genetic contributions to onset mechanisms that are especially significant for children who start late (Dale et al., 1998; Viding et al., 2004). Under a maturational model, it is predicted that environmental factors would show weaker relationships to onset timing in affected children insofar as the delayed onset is more driven by constitutional weaknesses than insufficiencies in the environment (assuming no gross violation of environmental resources).

For children with SLI, the finiteness-marking component seems to be under different timing mechanisms such that the clock for this linguistic element is running out of sync with the other elements. Bishop et al. (2005) are the first to document a positive genetic contribution to this particular phenotype, in a cross-sectional study of 6-year-old twins. A recent training study provides evidence that if children have not yet started to use the finiteness markers, the effects of intensive training are modest at best. After 48 individual intervention sessions for 31 children with SLI ages 3;0 to 4;4, as a group, the treated children did not move beyond optional use of third person singular present tense *-s* or auxiliary *BE* (Leonard et al., 2004). The maturational model would predict that the mechanisms guiding components of the linguistic system are not necessarily in sync, such that some elements can lag behind, although the general pattern of change mirrors that of unaffected children. The environmental manipulations involved in language intervention would not be likely to reset the acquisition curves if intervention antedates the expected deflection points in the acquisition curve that mark a transition in aptitude for change. As noted by Leonard et al. (2004), language training is not likely to be effective if the children are not ready for the targeted grammatical forms.

Although maturational models have been out of favor as a developmental account, the condition of SLI is calling for a reconsideration of the feasibility of such models and how they can be carefully evaluated. Much of modern genetics is moving toward explicit investigations of the timing mechanisms, that is, the internal clock that is intrinsic to cellular growth and the timing of genetic effects (cf. Purnell, 2003; Rice, 2004a, 2004b). Although studies of language acquisition have been highly sensitive to the need for age-referenced benchmarks in language acquisition, there has been surprisingly little serious attention given to the ways these benchmarks are tied into children's biological guidance mechanisms in interaction with the environmental influences.

Among the benefits of a developmental perspective on language impairment of this sort is that it can be applied more broadly to language impairments in other clinical conditions. Rice (2004a, 2004b) argues that consideration of the delay-with-disruption model focuses attention on the onset, growth trajectories, and possible plateaus of language acquisition. These three elements in turn can be explored across conditions. It may well be the case that a common feature of language impairment is a delayed onset, which in turn may be vulnerable to multiple sources of genetic dysfunction. Delayed development may be more characteristic of some conditions whereas disruption may be more operative in others. Comparison with a language-equivalent, as well as an age-equivalent, control group could help clarify language impairments in disorders beyond SLI.

Implications for Models of Language Development

Perhaps one of the biggest paradoxes of the study of children with SLI is that the research focus on the ways in which these youngsters are different from unaffected children has also led to an increased appreciation of the many ways in which these youngsters are also attuned to the developmental mechanisms that guide language acquisition in unaffected children. This suggests that the scientific problem is not so much about how to develop different theories for different groups of children, but how to develop theories robust enough to capture loci of possible delay and disruption within the linguistic system, as well as the exquisitely finely integrated system of language acquisition in general. Contemporary lines of investigation promise to generate progress toward this goal.

Note

Preparation of this paper was supported by the Merrill Advanced Studies Center at the University of Kansas and grants from the National Institutes of Health to the University of Kansas through the Mental Retardation and Developmental Disabilities Research Center (P30HD002528), the Center for Biobehavioral Neurosciences in Communication Disorders (P30DC005803), R01DC001803, and R01DC005226.

References

Bedore, L. M., & Leonard, L. B. (1998). Specific language impairment and grammatical morphology: A discriminant function analysis. *Journal of Speech, Language, and Hearing Research*, *41*, 1185–1192.

Bishop, D. V. M., Adams, C. V., & Norbury, C. F. (2005). Distinct genetic influences on grammar and phonological short-term memory deficits: evidence from 6-year-old twins [Electronic version]. Genes, Brain and Behavior. (Preprint of an accepted article, doi:10.1111/

j.1601-183X.2005.00148.x. Retrieved in August 2005 from http://www.blackwell-synergy.com/toc/gbb/0/0.)

Bishop, D. V. M., North, T., & Conlan, C. (1996). Nonword repetition as a behavioral marker for inherited language impairment: Evidence from a twin study. *Journal of Child Psychology and Psychiatry, 37,* 391–403.

Charest, M. J., & Leonard, L. B. (2004). Predicting tense: finite verb morphology and subject pronouns in the speech of typically-developing children and children with specific language impairment. *Journal of Child Language, 31,* 231–246.

Chomsky, N. (1995). *The minimalist program.* Cambridge, MA: MIT Press.

Clahsen, H. (1989). The grammatical characterization of developmental dysphasia. *Linguistics, 27,* 897–920.

Conti-Ramsden, G., Botting, N., & Faragher, B. (2001). Psycholinguistic markers for specific language impairment. *Journal of Child Psychology and Psychiatry, 42,* 741–748.

Dale, P. S., Simonoff, E., Bishop, D. V. M., Eley, T. C., Oliver, B., Price, T. S., et al. (1998). Genetic influence on language delay in two-year-old children. *Nature Neuroscience, 1,* 324–328.

Dunn, L. M., & Dunn, L. M. (1981). *Peabody Picture Vocabulary Test-Revised.* Circle Pines, MN: American Guidance Service.

Eadie, P. A., Fey, M. E., Douglas, J. M., & Parsons, C. L. (2002). Profiles of grammatical morphology and sentence imitation in children with specific language impairment and Down syndrome. *Journal of Speech, Language, and Hearing Research, 45,* 720–732.

Eisenson, J. (1968). Developmental aphasia: A speculative view with therapeutic implications. *Journal of Speech and Hearing Disorders, 33,* 3–13.

Entwhistle, D. R., & Astone, N. M. (1994). Some practical guidelines for measuring youths' race/ethnicity and socioeconomic status. *Child Development, 65,* 1521–1540.

Fisher, S. E. (2005). Dissection of molecular mechanisms underlying speech and language disorders. *Applied Psycholinguistics, 26,* 111–128.

Francis, D. J., Shaywitz, K. K., Stuebing, B. A., Shaywitz, B. A., & Fletcher, J. M. (1996). Developmental lag versus deficit models of reading disability: A longitudinal, individual growth curves analysis. *Journal of Educational Psychology, 88,* 3–17.

Gall, F. (1835). *The function of the brain and each of its parts: 5. Organology.* Boston: Marsh, Capen, & Lyon.

Gathercole, S. E., Willis, C., Baddeley, A. D., & Emslie, H. (1994). The children's test of nonword repetition: A test of phonological working memory. *Memory, 2,* 103–127.

Grela, B., & Leonard, L. B. (2000). The influence of argument structure complexity on the use of auxiliary verbs by children with SLI. *Journal of Speech, Language, and Hearing Research, 43,* 1115–1125.

Guasti, M. T. (2002). *Language acquisition: The growth of grammar.* Cambridge, MA: MIT Press.

Haegemann, L. (1994). *Introduction to government and binding theory* (2nd ed.). Cambridge, MA: Blackwell.

Hoff-Ginsberg, E., Kelly, D., & Buhr, J. (1996). Syntactic bootstrapping by children with SLI: Implications for a theory of specific language impairment. In *Proceedings of the 20th Annual Boston University Conference on Language Development* (pp. 329–339). Somerville, MA: Cascadilla Press.

Joseph, K. L., Serratrice, L., & Conti-Ramsden, G. (2002). Development of copula and auxiliary BE in children with specific language impairment and younger unaffected controls. *First Language, 22,* 137–172.

Karmiloff, K., & Karmiloff-Smith, A. (2001). *Pathways to language*. Cambridge, MA: Harvard University Press.

Lenneberg, E. (1967). *Biological foundations of language*. New York: Wiley.

Leonard, L. B. (1981). Facilitating linguistic skills in children with specific language impairment. *Applied Psycholinguistics, 2*, 89–118.

Leonard, L. B. (1998). *Children with specific language impairment*. Cambridge, MA: MIT Press.

Leonard, L. B., Camarata, S. M., Brown, B., & Camarata, M. N. (2004). Tense and agreement in the speech of children with specific language impairment: Patterns of generalization through intervention. *Journal of Speech, Language, and Hearing Research, 47*, 1363–1379.

Leonard, L. B., Eyer, J., Bedore, L., & Grela, B. (1997). Three accounts of the grammatical morpheme difficulties of English-speaking children with specific language impairment. *Journal of Speech, Language, and Hearing Research, 40*, 741–753.

Marchman, V. A., Wulfeck, B., & Ellis Weismer, S. (1999). Morphological productivity in children with normal language and SLI: A study of the English past tense. *Journal of Speech, Language, and Hearing Research, 42*, 206–219.

Miller, C. A., Kail, R., Leonard, L. G., & Tomblin, J. B. (2001). Speed of processing in children with specific language impairment. *Journal of Speech, Language, and Hearing Research, 44*, 416–433.

Oetting, J. B. (1999). Children with SLI use argument structure cues to learn verbs. *Journal of Speech, Language, and Hearing Research, 42*, 1261–1274.

Oetting, J. B., & Horohov, J. E. (1997). Past-tense marking by children with and without specific language impairment. *Journal of Speech, Language, and Hearing Research, 40*, 62–74.

Oetting, J. B., & McDonald, J. L. (2002). Nonmainstream dialect use and specific language impairment. *Journal of Speech, Language, and Hearing Research, 45*, 505–518.

O'Hara, M., & Johnston, J. (1997). Syntactic bootstrapping in children with SLI. *European Journal of Disorders of Communication, 32*, 189–205.

Orton, S. T. (1930). Familial occurrence of disorders in acquisition of language. *Eugenics, 3*(4), 140–147.

Paradis, J., Crago, M., Genesee, F., & Rice, M. L. (2003). French–English bilingual children with SLI: How do they compare with their monolingual peers? *Journal of Speech, Language, and Hearing Research, 46*, 113–127.

Paul, R. (1996). Clinical implication of the natural history of slow expressive language development. *American Journal of Speech-Language Pathology, 5*, 5–21.

Pinker, S. (1984). *Language learnability and language development*. Cambridge, MA: Harvard University Press.

Purnell, B. (2003). To every thing there is a season. *Science, 301*, 325.

Rescorla, L. (2002). Language and reading outcomes to age 9 in late-talking toddlers. *Journal of Speech, Language, and Hearing Research, 45*, 360–371.

Rice, M. L. (1996). Of language, phenotypes, and genetics: Building a cross-disciplinary platform for inquiry. In M. L. Rice (Ed.), *Toward a genetics of language* (Preface, pp. xi–xxv). Mahwah, NJ: Lawrence Erlbaum.

Rice, M. L. (2000). Grammatical symptoms of specific language impairment. In D. V. M. Bishop & L. B. Leonard (Eds.), *Speech and language impairments in children: Causes, characteristics, intervention and outcome* (pp. 17–34). East Sussex, UK: Psychology Press Ltd.

Rice, M. L. (2003). A unified model of specific and general language delay: Grammatical tense as a clinical marker of unexpected variation. In Y. Levy & J. Schaeffer (Eds.), *Language competence across populations: Toward a definition of specific language impairment* (pp. 63–95). Mahwah, NJ: Lawrence Erlbaum.

Rice, M. L. (2004a). Growth models of developmental language disorders. In M. L. Rice & S. F. Warren (Eds.), *Developmental language disorders: From phenotypes to etiologies* (pp. 207–240). Mahwah, NJ: Lawrence Erlbaum.

Rice, M. L. (2004b). Language growth of children with SLI and unaffected children: Timing mechanisms and linguistic distinctions. In A. Brugos, L. Micciulla, & C. Smith (Eds.), *Proceedings of the 28th Annual Boston University Conference on Language Development*. Somerville, MA: Cascadilla Press.

Rice, M. L., Cleave, P. L., & Oetting, J. B. (2000). The use of syntactic cues in lexical acquisition by children with SLI. *Journal of Speech, Language, and Hearing Research, 43*, 582–594.

Rice, M. L., Oetting, J. B., Marquis, J., Bode, J., & Pae, S. (1994). Frequency of input effects on word comprehension of children with specific language impairment. *Journal of Speech and Hearing Research, 37*, 106–122.

Rice, M. L., Redmond, S. M., & Hoffman, L. (in press). MLU in children with SLI and younger control children shows concurrent validity, stable and parallel growth trajectories. *Journal of Speech, Language, and Hearing Research*.

Rice, M. L., & Smolik, F. (in press). Genetics of language disorders: Clinical conditions, phenotypes, and genes. In G. Gaskell (Ed.), *Oxford handbook of psycholinguistics*. Oxford: Oxford University Press.

Rice, M. L., Tomblin, J. B., Hoffman, L. M., Richman, W. A., & Marquis, J. (2004). Grammatical tense deficits in children with SLI and nonspecific language impairment: Relationships with nonverbal IQ over time. *Journal of Speech, Language, and Hearing Research, 47*, 816–834.

Rice, M. L., & Warren, S. F. (2004). *Developmental language disorders: From phenotypes to etiologies*. Mahwah, NJ: Lawrence Erlbaum.

Rice, M. L., Warren, S. F., & Betz, S. K. (2005). Language symptoms of developmental language disorders: An overview of autism, Down syndrome, fragile X, specific language impairment, and Williams syndrome. *Applied Psycholinguistics, 26*, 7–28.

Rice, M. L., & Wexler, K. (1996a). Toward tense as a clinical marker of specific language impairment in English-speaking children. *Journal of Speech and Hearing Research, 39*, 1239–1257.

Rice, M. L., & Wexler, K. (1996b). A phenotype of specific language impairment: Extended optional infinitives. In M. L. Rice (Ed.), *Toward a genetics of language* (pp. 215–237). Mahwah, NJ: Lawrence Erlbaum.

Rice, M. L., & Wexler, K. (2001). *Rice/Wexler Test of Early Grammatical Impairment*. San Antonio, TX: The Psychological Corporation.

Rice, M. L., Wexler, K., & Cleave, P. L. (1995). Specific language impairment as a period of extended optional infinitive. *Journal of Speech and Hearing Research, 38*, 850–863.

Rice, M. L., Wexler, K., & Hershberger, S. (1998). Tense over time: The longitudinal course of tense acquisition in children with specific language impairment. *Journal of Speech, Language, and Hearing Research, 41*, 1412–1431.

Rice, M. L., Wexler, K., Marquis, J., & Hershberger, S. (2000). Acquisition of irregular past tense by children with SLI. *Journal of Speech, Language, and Hearing Research, 43*, 1126–1145.

Rice, M. L., Wexler, K., & Redmond, S. M. (1999). Grammaticality judgments of an extended optional infinitive grammar: Evidence from English-speaking children with specific language impairment. *Journal of Speech, Language, and Hearing Research, 42*, 943–961.

Schütze, C. T. (2004). Morphosyntax and syntax. In R. D. Kent (Ed.), *The MIT encyclopedia of communication disorders* (pp. 354–358). Cambridge, MA: MIT Press.

Schütze, C. T., & Wexler, K. (1996). Subject case licensing and English root infinitives. In A. Stringfellow, D. Cahana-Amitay, E. Hughes, & A. Zukowski (Eds.), *BUCLD 20 Proceedings*. Somerville, MA: Cascadilla Press.

Seymour, H. N., Roeper, T. W., & de Villiers, J. (2003). *Diagnostic Evaluation of Language Variation* (DELV). San Antonio, TX: The Psychological Corporation.

Shriberg, L. D., Tomblin, J. B., & McSweeny, J. L. (1999). Prevalence of speech delay in 6-year-old children and comorbidity with language impairment. *Journal of Speech, Language, and Hearing Research, 42*, 1461–1481.

SLI Consortium. (2004). Highly significant linkage to the SLI1 locus in an expanded sample of individuals affected by specific language impairment. *American Journal of Human Genetics, 74*, 1225–1238.

Smith, S. D. (2004). Localization and identification of genes affecting language and learning. In M. L. Rice & S. F. Warren (Eds.), *Developmental language disorders: From phenotypes to etiologies* (pp. 329–354). Mahwah, NJ: Lawrence Erlbaum.

Smith, S. D., & Morris, C. A. (2005). Planning studies of etiology. *Applied Psycholinguistics, 26*, 97–110.

Snow, C. E. (1996). Toward a rational empiricism: Why interactionism is not behaviorism any more than biology is genetics. In M. L. Rice (Ed.), *Toward a genetics of language* (pp. 377–396). Mahwah, NJ: Lawrence Erlbaum.

Tager-Flusberg, H. (2004). Do autism and specific language impairment represent overlapping language disorders? In M. L. Rice & S. F. Warren (Eds.), *Developmental language disorders: From phenotypes to etiologies* (pp. 31–52). Mahwah, NJ: Lawrence Erlbaum.

Tager-Flusberg, H. (2005). Designing studies to investigate the relationships between genes, environments, and developmental language disorders. *Applied Psycholinguistics, 26*, 29–40.

Tager-Flusberg, H., & Cooper, J. (1999). Present and future possibilities for defining a phenotype for specific language impairment. *Journal of Speech, Language, and Hearing Research, 42*, 1275–1278.

Thal, D. S., Tobias, S., & Morrison, D. (1991). Language and gesture in late talkers: A one year follow-up. *Journal of Speech and Hearing Research, 34*, 604–612.

Tomblin, J. B., & Zhang, X. (1999). Language patterns and etiology in children with specific language impairment. In H. Tager-Flusberg (Ed.), *Neurodevelopmental disorders* (pp. 361–382). Cambridge, MA: MIT Press.

Tomblin, J. B., Records, N. L., Buckwalter, P., Zhang, X., Smith, E., & O'Brien, M. (1997). The prevalence of specific language impairment in kindergarten children. *Journal of Speech, Language, and Hearing Research, 40*, 1245–1260.

Van der Lely, H. (1994). Canonical linking rules: Forward versus reverse linking in normally developing and specifically language-impaired children. *Cognition, 51*, 29–72.

Vargha-Khadem, F., Gadian, D. G., Copp, A., & Mishkin, M. (2005). *FOXP2* and the neuroanatomy of speech and language. *Nature Reviews/Neuroscience, 6*, 131–138.

Viding, E., Spinath, F. M., Price, T. S., Bishop, D. V. M., Dale, P. S., & Plomin, R. (2004). Genetic and environmental influence on language impairment in 4-year-old same-sex and opposite-sex twins. *Journal of Child Psychology and Psychiatry, 45*, 315–325.

Washington, J. A., & Craig, H. K. (2004). A language screening protocol for use with young African American children in urban settings. *American Journal of Speech-Language Pathology, 13*, 329–340.

Wexler, K. (1991). On the argument from the poverty of the stimulus. In A. Kasher (Ed.), *The Chomskyan turn*. Cambridge, MA: Blackwell.

Wexler, K. (1994). Optional infinitives, head movement and the economy of derivations. In D. Lightfoot & N. Hornstein (Eds.), *Verb movement* (pp. 305–350). Cambridge: Cambridge University Press.

Wexler, K. (1996). The development of inflection in a biologically based theory of language acquisition. In M. L. Rice (Ed.), *Toward a genetics of language* (pp. 113–144). Mahwah, NJ: Lawrence Erlbaum.

Wexler, K. (1998). Very early parameter setting and the unique checking constraint: a new explanation of the optional infinitive stage. *Lingua, 106,* 23–79.

Wexler, K. (2003). Lenneberg's dream: Learning, normal language development and specific language impairment. In Y. Levy & J. Schaeffer (Eds.), *Language competence across populations: Toward a definition of specific language impairment* (pp. 11–61). Mahwah, NJ: Lawrence Erlbaum.

Wexler, K., Schütze, C. T., & Rice, M. L. (1998). Subject case in children with SLI and unaffected controls: Evidence for the Agr/Tns omission model. *Language Acquisition, 7,* 317–344.

Whitehurst, G. J., & Fischel, J. E. (1994). Early developmental language delay: What, if anything, should the clinician do about it? *Journal of Child Psychology and Psychiatry, 35,* 613–648.

Zubrick, S., Taylor, K., Rice, M. L., & Slegers, D. (under review). An epidemiological study of late-talking 24-month-old children: Prevalence and predictors.

21

Atypical Language Development: Autism and Other Neurodevelopmental Disorders

Helen Tager-Flusberg

The field of language acquisition has long been enriched by the study of language in atypical children. From the Wild Boy of Aveyron (Lane, 1976) to Genie (Curtiss, 1977), our fascination with atypical individuals can offer significant insights for theories about the mechanisms that underlie how all children acquire language. Children with neurodevelopmental disorders provide clues about the organizational structure and representation of language, as well as the relation between language and other cognitive systems. For example, children with autism show striking asynchronies in the development of pragmatics and syntax (Tager-Flusberg, 1994), and research across different syndromes provides evidence that lexical semantic development is more closely tied to general cognitive capacities than other components of language. Research on atypical children contributes to our understanding of the universal and non-universal aspects of language and the process of acquisition. For the majority of children with different neurodevelopmental disorders the onset of language milestones is delayed, the period of acquisition is protracted, and in many cases language never reaches the mature state. This slowed rate of development provides us with the opportunity to view stages of development within and across different aspects of language in greater detail and to investigate variability among children in acquiring language.

In this chapter I review the literature on language acquisition in three different neurodevelopmental disorders: autism, Williams syndrome, and Down syndrome. These syndromes all have a strong genetic component and involve neurodevelopmental pathology that probably begins early in the prenatal period. In all three syndromes language is only one of several cognitive systems that is affected, in contrast to specific language impairment (SLI). The majority of, but not all, individuals with autism, Williams syndrome, or Down syndrome have varying degrees of mental retardation. Thus, research on these populations illuminates the role of general intellectual ability in the acquisition of language. For each syndrome, research on the acquisition of the major domains of language will be reviewed with a special focus on profiles of synchrony and asynchrony in developmental patterns across these domains.

Autism

Autism is a complex neurodevelopmental disorder, with core impairments in reciprocal social interaction, language, and communication, and a restricted repertoire of activities and interests (American Psychiatric Association, 1994). Family studies have shown that autism has a strong genetic component (Santangelo & Folstein, 1999), although no specific genes have yet been identified. One of the hallmark features of autism is the significant heterogeneity found across the spectrum of children and adults with a diagnosis of autism or related disorders (including Asperger syndrome and pervasive developmental disorder-not otherwise specified). The majority of children with autism have mental retardation, although there are high-functioning individuals whose IQ scores are in the normal or above normal range. There are also widely varying language abilities found in autism (Tager-Flusberg, Paul, & Lord, 2005). Although most studies of language and communicative impairment in autism focus on verbal autistic children, it is important to note that about half the population never acquires functional language (Bailey, Phillips, & Rutter, 1996). Studies of autism have investigated specific cognitive impairments that may underlie the core symptoms in this disorder, highlighting the role of theory of mind and executive dysfunction in understanding the social, communicative, and behavioral deficits in autism (Joseph, McGrath, & Tager-Flusberg, 2005). Studies of language and communication have focused in particular on the relationships between language and theory of mind in autism (e.g., Happé, 1993; Tager-Flusberg, 1997).

Vocal and phonological development in autism

Because autism is never diagnosed during infancy, there are no studies of very early vocal development in this population. One study investigated the early vocal behavior of young preverbal children with autism (Sheinkopf, Mundy, Oller, & Steffens, 2000). They found that the children with autism exhibited normal canonical babbling but exhibited highly atypical vocal quality.

Several studies have investigated phonological development in verbal children with autism. Controlled studies have found that their phonological skills are relatively unimpaired (e.g., Kjelgaard & Tager-Flusberg, 2001). Error patterns are similar to those reported in the literature on normal development (Bartolucci & Pierce, 1977). By middle childhood, as in normally developing children, children with autism who develop some functional language generally have mature phonological systems, but their voice quality and intonation patterns remain atypical, for example, abnormal volume control, nasal voice quality, or monotonic speech prosody. These problems appear to persist through adulthood (Shriberg et al., 2001).

Communicative and pragmatic development in autism

The development of prelinguistic social-communicative development in infants with autism is significantly impaired. While some infants, who are later diagnosed autistic, apparently enjoy a normal first year of life, others show obvious deficits, almost from birth. These infants with autism are described as showing little or no interest in people and some parents report, retrospectively, that it was difficult to maintain eye contact or engage in interaction with their babies (Ornitz, Guthrie, & Farley, 1977). Unlike typically developing children, prelinguistic children with autism show no preference to listen to their own mothers' speech (Klin, 1991) and may have idiosyncratic means of conveying different needs, which their mothers find difficult to interpret (Ricks & Wing, 1976).

These deficits culminate in their well-documented problems in joint attention (Loveland & Landry, 1986; Mundy, Sigman, & Kasari, 1990). These problems are perhaps the earliest manifestation of specific deficits in their acquisition of a theory of mind (Baron-Cohen, 1993). Studies of non-verbal intentional communication in autistic children consistently show that while they do produce and understand requests, proto-declarative comments are virtually absent (Mundy, Sigman, & Kasari, 1994). Longitudinal studies of young children with autism suggest that these early deficits in joint attention and protodeclarative communication are correlated with later language development (Mundy et al., 1990; Sigman & Ruskin, 1999).

Given the known deficits in theory of mind that characterize autism, it is not surprising that researchers have identified pragmatics as the aspect of language that is most seriously impaired in autism (Baltaxe, 1977; Tager-Flusberg et al., 2005). Wetherby and Prutting (1984) examined the range of speech acts expressed by children with autism in both gestural and spoken language at early stages of development. They found that the children with autism were unimpaired in their use of language for requests for objects or actions, protests, and self-regulation (e.g., *Don't do that*). However, comments, showing off, acknowledging the listener, and requesting information were virtually absent in these children (see also Loveland, Landry, Hughes, Hall, & McEvoy, 1988). The speech acts missing from the conversations of children with autism all have in common an emphasis on *social* rather than environmental uses of language (Wetherby, 1986). More specifically, they entail a more sophisticated mentalistic understanding of other people, not simply a view of people as a means for meeting a behavioral goal (Tager-Flusberg, 1993). Thus, children with autism who in the prelinguistic stage exhibit serious deficits in joint attention continue to show language deficits at the level of speech act usage. These deficits reflect their fundamental impairment in the ability to process information about others' mental states.

A few studies have investigated conversational skills in children with autism. Tager-Flusberg and Anderson (1991) reported significant differences between young children with autism and with Down syndrome, in whom social adaptive skills are a relative strength, in their ability to maintain conversational topic while they were interacting with their mothers. The children with autism often did not respond in a topic-related way to their mothers' utterances; instead they would introduce irrelevant or repetitive comments. Even when the children with autism did respond on topic, they did not develop the capacity to expand or elaborate on the information provided by their mothers. Capps, Kehres, and Sigman (1998) replicated these findings in older children, who were engaged in conversation with an experimenter. In a larger sample of children with autism, Hale and Tager-Flusberg (2005) found that these conversational deficits were significantly correlated with performance on theory of mind tasks, independent of IQ and overall levels of language ability.

Several studies have also investigated more advanced discourse skills, including narrative skills, in higher-functioning autistic children. Loveland and her colleagues investigated narrative ability by asking groups of individuals with autism and Down syndrome, matched on age, IQ, and language skills, to retell the story they were shown in the form of a puppet show or video sketch (Loveland, McEvoy, Tunali, & Kelley, 1990). Compared with the controls, the children with autism were more likely to exhibit pragmatic violations including bizarre or inappropriate utterances and were less able to take into consideration the listener's needs. Some of the children with autism in this study even failed to understand the story as a representation of meaningful events, suggesting that they lacked a cultural perspective underlying narrative (Loveland & Tunali, 1993). Loveland et al. (1990) concluded that narrative discourse problems in autism reflect deficits in theory of mind. In a later study Tager-Flusberg and Sullivan (1995) provided support for the relationship between narrative impairments and theory of mind in children with autism.

Lexical development in autism

In most children with autism spectrum disorders the onset of first words is delayed. However, once children begin to acquire words, the pattern of development is similar to normally developing children (Tager-Flusberg et al., 1990). Studies have shown that verbal children with autism use semantic groupings (e.g., *bird, boat, food*) in very similar ways to categorize and to retrieve words (Boucher, 1988; Tager-Flusberg, 1985). The majority of high-functioning children and adolescents with autism score quite well on standardized vocabulary tests, indicating an unusually rich knowledge of words (Jarrold, Boucher, & Russell, 1997; Kjelgaard & Tager-Flusberg, 2001). Lexical knowledge can be an area of relative strength for some individuals with autism.

At the same time, it appears that certain classes of words may be under-represented in the vocabularies of children with autism. For example, Tager-Flusberg (1992) found that the children participating in a longitudinal language study used hardly any mental state terms, particularly terms for cognitive states (e.g., *know, think, remember, pretend*). These findings were replicated in research including older children with autism. Other studies suggest that children with autism have particular difficulties understanding social–emotional terms as measured on standardized vocabulary tests (Eskes, Bryson, & McCormick, 1990; Hobson & Lee, 1989; van Lancker, Cornelius, & Needleman, 1991). Thus, while overall lexical knowledge may be a relative strength in autism, the acquisition of words that map onto mental state concepts may be specifically impaired in this disorder.

There is also wide variation in lexical use among individuals with autism, even those who acquire functional language. For example, individuals with autism often misuse words and phrases, producing idiosyncratic terms and neologisms (Volden & Lord, 1991) or *metaphorical language*, as Kanner (1946) described it. Rutter (1987) suggests that these abnormal uses of words may be functionally similar to the kinds of early word meaning errors made by young normally developing children. It is their persistence in autistic children that defines them as abnormal, and they may reflect the fact that autistic children are not sensitive to the corrective feedback provided by their parents because of their social impairments.

Morphological and syntactic development in autism

There are still relatively few studies investigating grammatical development in autism. One longitudinal study found that young children with autism followed the same developmental path as Down syndrome comparison children who were part of the study, and as normally developing children drawn from the extant literature (Tager-Flusberg et al., 1990). Not surprisingly, however, for most of the children the *rate* of growth was slower than in normally developing children. The autistic and Down syndrome children acquired grammatical structures in the same order as normally developing children. These findings confirm other early studies that found grammatical development in children with autism did not involve deficits that were unique to this disorder, because the children with autism were not different in their performance to the control groups matched on language and general cognitive ability (e.g., Bartolucci, Pierce, & Streiner, 1980; Pierce & Bartolucci, 1977).

Kjelgaard and Tager-Flusberg (2001) investigated language profiles in a large group of verbal children with autism using standardized language tests. This study highlighted the heterogeneity of language skills among verbal children with autism. About one-quarter of the children in this study had no grammatical impairments; the remaining three-quarters of the children were significantly impaired. These impaired children had distinctive profiles of performance across the language measures, including spared articulation but impaired performance on tests of vocabulary, nonsense word repetition, and higher-order syntax and semantics, suggesting that they formed a subtype of children with autism *and* language impairment. Tager-Flusberg and Joseph (2003) proposed that this group of children was similar in their language profile to children with SLI, who have the same pattern of impairments on language tests, especially difficulties with aspects of grammatical morphology and nonsense word repetition (Tager-Flusberg & Cooper, 1999; Tomblin & Zhang, 1999). Follow-up studies have found that this subtype of children with autism and language impairment show the same difficulties on experimental tasks tapping tense morphology as do children with SLI (Roberts, Rice, & Tager-Flusberg, 2004).

Summary of language acquisition in autism

Delays and deficits in acquiring language are among the core features of autism. There is enormous variation in this domain, ranging from no functional language and very limited communicative ability to performance in the high normal range on standardized language measures. Across the spectrum of autism, there are selective deficits in those aspects of communication and language use that entail a theory of mind. There is more variability in the acquisition of vocabulary and grammar, with evidence for distinct subtypes among children with autism: some have normal linguistic skills, while others have language impairments which parallel those found in SLI.

Williams Syndrome

Williams syndrome is a rare genetic disorder, occurring in only 1 in 7,500 births. It is characterized by a set of unusual facial characteristics (called "elfin facies"), physical problems, and a unique cognitive profile (Williams, Barratt-Boyes, & Lowe, 1961). This set of characteristics is now known to be causally related to a small deletion on chromosome 7, which involves about 20 genes (Ewart et al., 1993). This syndrome has captured the interest of developmental psycholinguists because part of the cognitive phenotype appears to involve relatively spared language abilities (e.g., Bellugi, Wang, & Jernigan, 1994). Along with good language skills, individuals with Williams syndrome are unusually interested in people, highly sociable or even overly friendly, and have relatively spared face recognition and auditory memory skills (Bellugi et al., 1994; Mervis, Morris, Bertrand, & Robinson, 1999). By contrast, they have extremely deficient visual–spatial constructive abilities and are usually retarded in the mild/moderate range (Mervis et al., 1999). Studies of children and adults with Williams syndrome have focused on whether their language skills are significantly better than would be predicted from their mental age, suggesting a genuine dissociation of language from other cognitive abilities, and whether, because of their unusual cognitive profile, they acquire language in unique ways.

Vocal and phonological development in Williams syndrome

Until recently, Williams syndrome was usually not diagnosed at birth so there has been limited opportunity to study early vocal development in this population. Mervis and Bertrand (1997) report on the early development of two infants who reached the stage of canonical babbling slightly later than normally developing infants: one at 7 months and one at 8 months of age, at the same time as they began rhythmic hand banging.

Although there have not been any detailed studies of phonological development in children with Williams syndrome, they do not appear to have particular problems with articulation. One study of a relatively large sample of children with Williams syndrome found that their articulation was significantly better than a mental-age matched group of children with non-specific retardation, suggesting that this is an area of strength for this population relative to other groups with neurodevelopmental disorders (Gosch, Städing, & Pankau, 1994).

Communicative and pragmatic development in Williams syndrome

Young children with Williams syndrome are extremely interested in people, and spend extended periods of time looking intently at other people's faces (Bellugi, Bihrle, Neville, Jernigan, & Doherty, 1992). One girl with Williams syndrome was followed for a year beginning when she was 20 months old (Mervis & Bertrand, 1997). During this period, she showed intense interest in both familiar and unfamiliar faces, in ways that seemed quite inappropriate in both quality and quantity. It is not clear how this unusual pattern of social attention influences early communicative development in Williams syndrome.

One study of early communicative development in children with Williams syndrome, which used a parent report measure, found that compared with children with Down syndrome at the same mental age level, the children with Williams syndrome appeared to be impoverished in their use of gestures (Singer, Bellugi, Bates, Jones, & Rossen, 1994). Another study, which followed a group of children longitudinally, found that they did not produce a referential pointing gesture until well after the onset of language (Mervis & Bertrand, 1997). Not only did these children not produce pointing gestures, it appeared that they did not understand and were unable to respond appropriately to pointing gestures produced by their mothers, at the same time as they were beginning to speak referentially. The absence of pointing in Williams syndrome remains poorly understood.

Studies on pragmatic functioning in children with Williams syndrome provide a mixed picture. Kelley and Tager-Flusberg (1995) explored the discourse characteristics in spontaneous speech of children with Williams syndrome. The children were relatively good at providing responses to requests for clarification, and were able to maintain a topic over several turns, adding more information to the ongoing discourse. Reilly and her colleagues (Reilly, Klima, & Bellugi, 1990) found that older children with Williams syndrome were relatively good at narrating coherent stories, and showed an unusual ability to express affective engagement in their narratives.

On the other hand, Volterra and her colleagues report that their larger sample of children with Williams syndrome showed certain deficits in their narratives, and they often were not able to directly respond to questions, suggesting other discourse-level difficulties (Volterra, Sabbadini, Capirci, Pezzini, & Ossella, 1995). Some researchers have described the language of children with Williams syndrome as "cocktail party" speech, which is filled with stereotypic social phrases, little content, and is not well tuned to their conversational partner (Udwin & Yule, 1991), and Laws and Bishop (2004) found significant pragmatic deficits in children and young adults with Williams syndrome, according to parent or teacher report.

Lexical development in Williams syndrome

In the previous section it was noted that children with Williams syndrome begin acquiring words before they are able to use or understand a referential point or other gestures.

Mervis and Bertrand (1997) suggest that although episodes of joint attention are critical for acquiring lexical knowledge, especially object labels, children with Williams syndrome depend on means other than referential pointing for achieving joint attention. In an experimental study, Rowe, Peregrine, and Mervis (2004) found that young children with Williams syndrome are less reliant than comparison children on using speaker gaze as a clue to object labeling. During the early stages of lexical development in Williams syndrome children appear to be highly dependent on their parents' facilitating the acquisition of new words by labeling objects their children are attending to or manipulating. Parents seem to compensate for their children's poor use of gaze cues to interpret a speaker's intentions.

Mervis and her colleagues have also explored whether children with Williams syndrome use operating principles to constrain the meanings of newly acquired words. Using both parental report data and direct observations of the children in their longitudinal study, Mervis and Bertrand (1997) found that like normally developing children, children with Williams syndrome almost always acquire the basic level names for objects before either the subordinate or superordinate label, they learn words for whole objects long before they learn any attribute or object part names, and they are able to fast map the meaning of new words. However, in contrast to normally developing children, in all but one of the children with Williams syndrome in Mervis and Bertrand's longitudinal study the vocabulary spurt began at least 6 months *before* they could sort objects exhaustively into categories. Mervis and Bertrand (1997) suggest that for children with Williams syndrome, an increase in auditory memory for words or greater attention to verbal input may be more important for the onset of the vocabulary spurt than other factors, suggesting alternative developmental routes to lexical growth.

As children with Williams syndrome get older, they continue to acquire a rich vocabulary. Indeed, lexical knowledge appears to be a genuine strength in this population (Mervis et al., 1999), with almost half the population scoring within the normal range on standardized tests. These findings confirm other reports in the literature on older individuals with Williams syndrome (Bellugi et al., 1994). In general, experimental studies have demonstrated that semantic organization is not deviant in Williams syndrome (Laing et al., 2005; Mervis et al., 1999).

In sum, studies of lexical development in children with Williams syndrome suggest that this domain is an area of genuine strength for this population. Although they are delayed relative to age matched normally developing children, they begin acquiring words during the toddler years. In certain respects, they show similar patterns of development as other groups of young children, but in other ways they seem to follow a more unique path, for example beginning to speak before they use pointing gestures, and reaching the vocabulary spurt before they sort objects exhaustively.

Morphological and syntactic development in Williams syndrome

Early reports of children and adolescents with Williams syndrome identified grammar as an area of strength in their language profile, and indeed the descriptions of these individuals using fluent complex syntactic constructions despite moderate levels of retardation were taken as evidence for the dissociation between grammar and general cognitive abilities (Bellugi et al., 1992). More recent studies have questioned these conclusions, but the finding of relatively good syntactic ability has generally been supported.

A cross-sectional study of a large group of children with Williams syndrome ranging widely in age found that the children with Williams syndrome were delayed on measures of mean length of utterance, relative to normally developing children; however, there was a close relation between utterance length and grammatical knowledge (Mervis et al., 1999). Using a standardized measure of grammatical comprehension, the Test for Reception of Grammar, or TROG (Bishop, 1989), Mervis and her colleagues (1999) found that there was continued growth in syntactic knowledge through adolescence, with about half the sample scoring within the normal range. However, many older adolescents with Williams syndrome were still unable to correctly understand the most complex embedded sentences. Overall, grammatical ability among the participants in this study was at the same level as general cognitive abilities, supporting other studies by Gosch et al. (1994) and Udwin and Yule (1991). Robinson, Mervis, and Robinson (2003) found that receptive grammatical skills using the TROG were more highly correlated with both working memory (measured by digit span) and phonological short-term memory for children with Williams syndrome compared with normal controls, suggesting that people with Williams syndrome may be especially reliant on working memory to acquire grammatical knowledge.

Studies of English-speaking children with Williams syndrome generally find that they have no difficulties acquiring grammatical morphology (Clahsen & Almazan, 1998; Rice, 2003). Research by Zukowski (2004) found that English-speaking adolescents with Williams syndrome have subtle difficulties interpreting complex relative clauses, but their pattern of performance on experimental tasks of relative clause comprehension and production of complex questions was similar to that of normally developing younger children. By contrast, for children acquiring other languages, including French (Karmiloff-Smith et al., 1997), Italian (Volterra et al., 1995), and Hebrew (Levy & Hermon, 2003), languages that have much richer grammatical morphology than English, the evidence is that children with Williams syndrome show more significant delays. One longitudinal study of two Hebrew-speaking children found atypical linguistic profiles of development, marked by significant strength in marking gender and agreement, but weaknesses in pragmatics and word usage. The error patterns for these children were similar to those reported during early developmental stages for normally developing children acquiring Hebrew (Levy, 2004), leading Levy to conclude that Williams syndrome is characterized by asynchronies that are related to differences in developmental timing for formal linguistic versus semantic–pragmatic aspects of language, rather than deviant acquisition patterns (Levy & Hermon, 2003).

Summary of language acquisition in Williams syndrome

Studies of children and adolescents with Williams syndrome have demonstrated that, in general, language is an area of relative strength for this population, especially in contrast to their impaired visual–spatial constructive abilities (Bellugi et al., 1994; Mervis et al.,

1999). The onset of first words and word combinations is delayed, though appears to be commensurate with mental age levels. This continues to hold through childhood and adolescence, with grammatical comprehension and production closely tied to mental age level. By contrast, children and adults with Williams syndrome show genuine strength, greater than predicted for their mental age levels, in lexical knowledge. Studies by Mervis and her colleagues (Mervis & Bertrand, 1997; Mervis et al., 1999) suggest that children with Williams syndrome may follow an unusual pathway in acquiring lexical knowledge, and that their strong language abilities may be closely tied to their relatively intact working memory (Robinson et al., 2003).

Down Syndrome

Down syndrome is the most common neurodevelopmental disorder, occurring in about 1 in 800 live births. Down syndrome is associated with the presence of a third chromosome 21. As in all syndromes, despite the relative uniformity of the underlying etiology, the phenotype varies quite broadly, with IQ scores ranging from near-normal levels to the severely retarded range, with the majority of children with Down syndrome having moderate levels of retardation. There are controversies surrounding the ability to identify a unique behavioral phenotype for Down syndrome (Flint, 1996), but studies suggest that language is relatively more impaired than other cognitive functions, though the sources and nature of this deficit have still not been clearly resolved (Chapman & Hesketh, 2000).

Vocal and phonological development in Down syndrome

Research on babbling in infants with Down syndrome has shown that there are delays in the onset of canonical babbling in Down syndrome infants. Steffens and colleagues (Steffens, Oller, Lynch, & Urbano, 1992) compared infants with Down syndrome with a group of normally developing infants: the age of onset for the infants with Down syndrome was about 2 months behind the normally developing infants. Once canonical babbling began in the Down syndrome infants, it was significantly less stable than for the normally developing infants. Studies have also shown that the onset of canonical babbling in infants with Down syndrome emerges at the same time as rhythmic hand banging, as has been found for normally developing infants (and Williams syndrome), suggesting that both milestones reflect underlying rhythmic behavior (Cobo-Lewis, Oller, Lynch, & Levine, 1995). Lynch, Oller, Eilers, and Basinger (1990) suggest that the delays in canonical babbling in Down syndrome might be related to the motor delays and hypotonicity that are characteristic of this population (Wishart, 1988).

Problems in expressive language continue in children with Down syndrome, as they typically have difficulties with the phonological aspects of language, once they begin producing words. Dodd (1976) compared the phonological errors produced by severely retarded children with Down syndrome, children with non-specific retardation, and normally developing children, matched on overall cognitive mental age. The children with Down syndrome produced more errors overall, and more different error types, and their phonological development lagged significantly behind their cognitive level. Similar findings were obtained by Stoel-Gammon (1980). Articulation difficulties often persist in older children and adolescents with Down syndrome (Chapman & Hesketh, 2000). They contribute to the reduced intelligibility of individuals with Down syndrome (Abbeduto & Murphy, 2004), and are not simply attributable to anatomical features such as enlarged tongue (Margar-Bacal, Witzel, & Munro, 1987).

Communicative and pragmatic development in Down syndrome

Young infants with Down syndrome show delays in the onset of mutual eye contact (Berger & Cunningham, 1981), they vocalize much less than other infants (Berger & Cunningham, 1983), and their dyadic interactions with their mothers are less well coordinated (Jasnow et al., 1988). However, by the second half of the first year, infants with Down syndrome catch up, and they then show significantly higher levels of mutual eye contact with their caregivers than age matched normally developing infants.

These early differences in the social patterns of Down syndrome and typically developing infants continue to be reflected in play and intentional communication in the second year of life. Mundy and his colleagues conducted a comprehensive study comparing a large group of toddlers with Down syndrome with mental-age matched subjects with non-specific retardation and normally developing children on the Early Social Communication Scales (Mundy, Sigman, Kasari, & Yirmiya, 1988). Compared with the other groups, the children with Down syndrome showed higher frequencies of social interaction behaviors, but lower frequencies of object request behaviors. Other studies have found that communicative intents tended to be expressed in the Down syndrome children only through gesture, rather than the more typical pattern of gestures combined with vocalization or word (Greenwald & Leonard, 1979; Singer et al., 1994), which is consistent with their vocal and phonological difficulties.

Pragmatic skills appear to be an area of relative strength for children with Down syndrome. Coggins, Carpenter, and Owings (1983) found that at the early stages of language development children with Down syndrome expressed the same range of communicative intents as the normally developing children. However, they used relatively fewer requesting behaviors than the normally developing children, perhaps reflecting lower arousal or greater passivity, whereas the frequencies of comments, answers, and protests were similar. This asymmetric pattern was also reported in a larger study of children with Down syndrome (Beeghly, Weiss-Perry, & Cicchetti, 1990). Young children with Down syndrome are relatively more focused on the use of communication to interact and engage socially with other people than on regulating their environment.

As typically developing children become more advanced in their conversation skills they are more contingent in their responding (Bloom, Rocissano, & Hood, 1976) and maintain a topic over an increasing number of turns (Brown, 1980). Beeghly et al. (1990) found that their children with Down syndrome spent significantly more turns on the same topic than language matched controls. Similarly, Tager-Flusberg and Anderson

(1991) found that children with Down syndrome had higher levels of contingent responding than the typically developing children studied by Bloom and her colleagues, suggesting that this aspect of language is a genuine strength for this population. Children with Down syndrome are also surprisingly good at conversational repairs. Coggins and Stoel-Gammon (1982) found that even at early stages, young children with Down syndrome revise, rather than simply repeat, their messages in response to requests for clarification from an adult conversational partner (see also Scherer & Owings, 1984). However, lack of intelligibility and limited syntactic knowledge can interfere with the expression of pragmatic intent: older children who used primarily single-word sentences were fairly limited in the success of their repair strategies, depending more on sign than on speech to accomplish their goals (Bray & Woolnough, 1988).

Older children and adolescents with Down syndrome provide socially appropriate responses in discourse contexts (Loveland & Tunali, 1991) and in more structured referential communication tasks (e.g., Jordan & Murdoch, 1987). Adults with Down syndrome also show extended discourse coherence in conversations with their caregivers (Bennett, 1976). However, not surprisingly, on discourse tasks that depend on expressive language ability, such as storytelling, adolescents with Down syndrome perform less well than mental-age matched controls. They also have difficulty meeting the informational needs of their social partner in a structured interaction (Abbeduto & Murphy, 2004). Thus across the lifespan, we see that pragmatic aspects of language are relatively spared in Down syndrome, although very young children may distribute their communicative acts in unique ways, and subtle problems are found among adolescents.

Lexical development in Down syndrome

Children with Down syndrome are significantly delayed in the onset of first words (Berglund, 2001), but most studies have found that vocabulary development is a relative strength compared with grammatical development. Moreover, children with Down syndrome rely on the same principles for acquiring new words as do typically developing children. In a longitudinal study of six young children with Down syndrome, Mervis and her colleagues (Cardoso-Martins, Mervis, & Mervis, 1985; Mervis, 1990) found that all the children's early object labels were at the basic level, as has been found for normally developing children. Even in older children with Down syndrome who had quite large vocabularies, comprehension of words at the basic level was significantly better than at either the subordinate or superordinate levels (Tager-Flusberg, 1985), and objects were almost always named at the basic level (Tager-Flusberg, 1986).

Lexical operating principles known to be important early in normal development have also been found to constrain the word meanings acquired by children with Down syndrome. Longitudinal observational and cross-sectional experimental studies by Mervis and her colleagues have confirmed that children with Down syndrome extend the meanings of words to other objects in the same basic level category, based on their similarity to the prototype for that category (Cardoso-Martins et al., 1985; Mervis, 1990; Mervis & Bertrand, 1995). In relation to vocabulary growth, some young children with Down syndrome develop vocabularies at a rate that is comparable to their mental age level, while others appear to be significantly delayed, perhaps because of their additional articulation deficits (Miller, Sedley, Miolo, Murray-Branch, & Rosin, 1992).

Morphological and syntactic development in Down syndrome

We have already noted the significant delays and specific impairments in the expressive language of children with Down syndrome (Chapman, 1995). Studies also suggest that there are comprehension impairments in Down syndrome, particularly for complex sentences (Abbeduto et al., 2003; Chapman, Schwartz, & Kay-Raining Bird, 1991). These deficits have been directly linked to specific deficits in acquiring grammatical aspects of language.

Studies of young children with Down syndrome have found widely varying rates of change in mean length of utterance (MLU) within this population, which are only partially explained by individual differences in chronological age and IQ (Beeghly et al., 1990; Fowler, Gelman, & Gleitman, 1994). Fowler et al. (1994) report on one young girl with Down syndrome who did not begin combining words productively into two-word utterances until about the age of 48 months. Yet her rate of development after this point was rapid, and not that different from normal, at least until her MLU reached 3.5 when she was 5.5 years. Similar relatively rapid rates of development during these early stages of syntactic growth were found by Tager-Flusberg and her colleagues for two out of six young children with Down syndrome, who were followed longitudinally (Tager-Flusberg et al., 1990). Most other children with Down syndrome, particularly those whose IQ scores are below 50 (Fowler, 1988), may not begin combining words until the age of 5 or 6. Their rate of development is very slow, and children with Down syndrome may never develop beyond the early stages of grammatical development (Miller, 1988). However, in general, the complexity of their sentences is commensurate to MLU, indicating that utterance length reflects the same level of linguistic knowledge in Down syndrome as in typically developing children (Thordardottir, Chapman, & Wagner, 2002).

These findings confirm other studies reporting significant delays in syntactic development in Down syndrome. They often omit sentence arguments, especially subjects (Grela, 2003). Most children with Down syndrome fail to acquire knowledge of more complex grammatical constructions, and Fowler (1990) argues that they generally do not progress much beyond an MLU level of about 3.0. Moreover, children with Down syndrome frequently omit grammatical morphemes, especially those that mark tense (Eadie, Fey, Douglas, & Parsons, 2002; Laws & Bishop, 2003). There does not, however, appear to be an absolute ceiling on the levels of language that are achieved by older children with Down syndrome, and development continues through the adolescent years. For example, Chapman and her colleagues found that MLU continues to increase through the adolescent years, and more complex sentences appear in the narratives of older adolescents (Chapman, 1995).

What might account for the specific deficits that have been identified in the grammatical development of children with Down syndrome? One hypothesis is that specific weaknesses in auditory or phonological working memory might explain the language deficits, and there is strong evidence to support the view that phonological memory is closely associated with deficits in expressive grammar in this population (Jarrold, Baddeley, & Hewes, 2000; Laws, 2004). This hypothesis is consistent with the vocal and phonological impairments discussed earlier, and provides some support for the widely used intervention approach of teaching sign language skills to children with Down syndrome.

Summary of language acquisition in Down syndrome

The phenotype of Down syndrome typically involves specific delays and deficits in the acquisition of language, relative to other cognitive domains. While lexical and pragmatic development appear to be closely tied to overall cognitive levels, most children show more profound delays in phonological and grammatical aspects of language acquisition. Receptive skills are highly correlated with non-verbal IQ (Abbeduto et al., 2003), whereas expressive grammar is more closely associated with phonological memory.

Conclusions

The general picture of language acquisition across different populations of atypical children provides evidence for both important differences as well as similarities among children with various neurodevelopmental disorders. The most striking findings are the contrasting profiles that are found between populations across domains of language. These asynchronies among phonological, lexical, and morphosyntactic development are the hallmark of language acquisition in atypical children (Tager-Flusberg, 1988).

The comparisons between, for example, Williams syndrome and Down syndrome suggest a dissociation between developments in grammar and pragmatics. Studies of grammatical development have revealed different developmental profiles in Down syndrome and Williams syndrome, relative to other aspects of language development. These differences parallel the findings on phonological development in these populations in that impairments in phonology tend to co-occur with impairments in morphosyntactic aspects of language. Together, these findings suggest that the formal linguistic aspects of language are impaired in Down syndrome but relatively spared in Williams syndrome. In autism there are distinct subgroups: some children have impairments in grammatical development similar to those found in SLI, while others have no deficits in morphosyntax. Impairments to the computational aspects of language are associated with impairments in auditory working memory, while populations who show relative strengths in acquiring phonology and grammar also have relatively intact phonological working memory. This relation between a non-linguistic cognitive skill and a specific component of language suggests that there may be important integral neurobiological connections between the substrates that serve these cognitive functions.

Studies of pragmatic abilities have shown that this is a domain of relative strength in Down syndrome. By contrast, from the beginning, pragmatic abilities are significantly impaired in autism. These patterns highlight the central role of social functioning, particularly theory of mind, in the acquisition of the communicative aspects of language.

Finally, it is interesting to note that across the syndromes considered in this chapter one consistent finding was the relative strength in lexical development. Because lexical knowledge is closely tied to general cognitive level, one would expect a fairly close relationship between the lexicon and mental age measures, and indeed, this was a consistent finding across studies with different populations.

The asynchronies across different populations that have been documented in this chapter underscore the need for a complex model of language acquisition. This model involves the interaction of several partially independent mechanisms that process different types of linguistic information. This chapter has illustrated some of these asynchronies, which suggest that in different syndromes different mechanisms may be impaired. Thus, in autism, impairments are primarily to theory of mind mechanisms that play a role in language and communication, whereas in Down syndrome there are impairments in the computational mechanisms that underlie the processing of grammatical information, which may be linked to working memory.

To what extent does language development in children with neurodevelopmental disorders provide support for the modularity hypothesis of language? Early research on Williams syndrome was viewed as showing that language was significantly more advanced than general cognitive abilities, and taken as strong support for the view that language may be independent of other aspects of cognition (e.g., Bellugi et al., 1992). However, later research found that language was highly correlated with non-linguistic abilities in Williams syndrome and that verbal working memory was a strong predictor of performance on standardized language measures (Mervis et al., 1999), demonstrating that in Williams syndrome language is tied to certain aspects of cognition. Nevertheless, the kinds of developmental asynchronies found *within* the language system, for example between formal linguistic and semantic or pragmatic components, suggest a modified view of modularity, although this perspective has been criticized by Thomas and Karmiloff-Smith (2005), who argue that children with neurodevelopmental disorders exhibit atypical patterns of development that reflect fundamentally different ways in which their brains are organized for processing language.

Research on atypical children has highlighted some of the universal constraints that operate on the acquisition of certain aspects of phonology, semantics, and grammar. Within each of these domains there are uniform sequences of development, and key principles that constrain the process of development. There are not multiple alternative ways of acquiring language (but cf. Thomas & Karmiloff-Smith, 2005), though as these components develop over time they may become integrated in different ways, which leads to syndrome-specific profiles. As knowledge of the genetic and neurobiological bases of neurodevelopmental disorders advances, future research on autism, Williams syndrome, and Down syndrome will begin to illuminate the specific genes and neuropathologies that underlie the complex language phenotypes associated with these syndromes.

Note

This chapter was written with grant support from the NIDCD (U19 DC 03610), and NICHD (RO1 HD 33470).

References

Abbeduto, L., & Murphy, M. (2004). Language, social cognition, maladaptive behavior, and communication in down syndrome and fragile X syndrome. In M. L. Rice & S. Warren (Eds.), *Developmental language disorders: From phenotypes to etiologies*. Mahwah, NJ: Erlbaum.

Abbeduto, L., Murphy, M., Cawthon, S., Richmond, E., Weissman, M., Karadottir, S., & O'Brien, A. (2003). Receptive language skills of adolescents and young adults with down or fragile X syndrome. *American Journal of Mental Retardation, 108*, 149–160.

American Psychiatric Association. (1994). *Diagnostic and Statistical Manual of Mental Disorders (DSM-IV)* (4th ed.). Washington, DC: APA.

Bailey, A., Phillips, W., & Rutter, M. (1996). Autism: towards an integration of clinical, genetic, neuropsychological, and neurobiological perspectives. *Journal of Child Psychology and Psychiatry, 37*, 89–126.

Baltaxe, C. A. M. (1977). Pragmatic deficits in the language of autistic adolescents. *Journal of Pediatric Psychology, 2*, 176–180.

Baron-Cohen, S. (1993). From attention-goal psychology to belief-desire psychology: The development of a theory of mind and its dysfunction. In S. Baron-Cohen, H. Tager-Flusberg, & D. J. Cohen (Eds.), *Understanding other minds: perspectives from autism* (pp. 59–82). Oxford: Oxford University Press.

Bartolucci, G., & Pierce, S. (1977). A preliminary comparison of phonological development in autistic, normal, and mentally retarded subjects. *British Journal of Disorders of Communication, 12*, 134–147.

Bartolucci, G., Pierce, S., & Streiner, D. (1980). Cross-sectional studies of grammatical morphemes in autistic and mentally retarded children. *Journal of Autism and Developmental Disorders, 10*, 39–50.

Beeghly, M., Weiss-Perry, B., & Cicchetti, D. (1990). Beyond sensorimotor functioning: Early communicative and play development of children with down syndrome. In D. Cicchetti & M. Beeghly (Eds.), *Children with Down syndrome: A developmental perspective* (pp. 329–368). New York: Cambridge University Press.

Bellugi, U., Bihrle, A., Neville, H., Jernigan, T., & Doherty, S. (1992). Language, cognition and brain organization in a neurodevelopmental disorder. In M. Gunnar & C. Nelson (Eds.), *Developmental behavioral neuroscience* (pp. 201–232). Hillsdale, NJ: Erlbaum.

Bellugi, U., Wang, P., & Jernigan, T. (1994). Williams syndrome: An unusual neuropsychological profile. In S. Broman & J. Grafman (Eds.), *Atypical cognitive deficits in developmental disorders: Implications for brain function* (pp. 23–56). Hillsdale, NJ: Erlbaum.

Bennett, T. (1976). Code-switching in down's syndrome. *Proceedings of the Second Annual Meeting of the Berkeley Linguistics Society*. Berkeley, CA.

Berger, J., & Cunningham, C. (1981). The development of eye contact between mothers and normal versus Down's syndrome infants. *Developmental Psychology, 17*, 678–689.

Berger, J., & Cunningham, C. (1983). The development of early vocal behaviors and interactions in Down syndrome and non-handicapped infant–mother pairs. *Developmental Psychology, 19*, 322–331.

Berglund, E. (2001). Parental reports of spoken language skills in children with Down syndrome. *Journal of Speech, Language, and Hearing Research, 44*, 179–191.

Bishop, D. (1989). *Test for the reception of grammar*. Manchester: Chapel Press.

Bloom, L., Rocissano, L., & Hood, L. (1976). Adult–child discourse: Developmental interaction between information processing and linguistic knowledge. *Cognitive Psychology, 8*, 521–552.

Boucher, J. (1988). Word fluency in high functioning autistic children. *Journal of Autism and Developmental Disorders, 18*, 637–645.

Bray, M., & Woolnough, L. (1988). The language skills of children with Down's syndrome aged 12 to 16 years. *Child Language Teaching and Therapy, 4*, 311–324.

Brown, R. (1980). The maintenance of conversation. In D. R. Olson (Ed.), *The social foundations of language and thought* (pp. 187–210). New York: Norton.

Capps, L., Kehres, J., & Sigman, M. (1998). Conversational abilities among children with autism and children with developmental delays. *Autism, 2*, 325–344.

Cardoso-Martins, C., Mervis, C., & Mervis, C. (1985). Early vocabulary acquisition by children with Down syndrome. *American Journal of Mental Deficiency, 90*, 177–184.

Chapman, R. (1995). Language development in children and adolescents with Down syndrome. In P. Fletcher & B. MacWhinney (Eds.), *The handbook of child language* (pp. 641–663). Oxford: Blackwell.

Chapman, R., & Hesketh, S. (2000). Behavioral phenotype of individuals with Down syndrome. *Mental Retardation and Developmental Disabilities Research Reviews, 6*, 84–95.

Chapman, R., Schwartz, S., & Kay-Raining Bird, E. (1991). Language skills of children and adolescents with Down syndrome: I. Comprehension. *Journal of Speech and Hearing Research, 34*, 1106–1120.

Clahsen, H., & Almazan, M. (1998). Syntax and morphology in Williams syndrome. *Cognition, 68*, 167–198.

Cobo-Lewis, A. B., Oller, K., Lynch, M., & Levine, S. L. (1995). *Relationships among motor and vocal milestones in normally developing infants and infants with Down syndrome.* Gatlinburg Conference on Research and Theory in Mental Retardation and Developmental Disabilities, Gatlinburg, TN.

Coggins, T., Carpenter, R., & Owings, N. (1983). Examining early intentional communication in Down's syndrome and nonretarded children. *British Journal of Disorders of Communication, 18*, 99–107.

Coggins, T., & Stoel-Gammon, C. (1982). Clarification strategies used by four Down's syndrome children for maintaining normal conversational interaction. *Education and Training of the Mentally Retarded, 16*, 65–67.

Curtiss, S. (1977). *Genie: A psycholinguistic study of a modern day "wild child".* New York: Academic Press.

Dodd, B. J. (1976). A comparison of the phonological systems of mental-age-matched severely subnormal, and Down's syndrome children. *British Journal of Disorders of Communication, 11*, 27–42.

Eadie, P., Fey, M., Douglas, J., & Parsons, C. (2002). Profiles of grammatical morphology and sentence imitation in children with specific language impairment and Down syndrome. *Journal of Speech, Language, and Hearing Research, 45*, 720–732.

Eskes, G. A., Bryson, S. E., & McCormick, T. A. (1990). Comprehension of concrete and abstract words in autistic children. *Journal of Autism and Developmental Disorders, 20*, 61–73.

Ewart, A., Morris, C. A., Atkinson, D., Jin, W., Sternes, K., Spallone, P., et al. (1993). Hemizygosity at the elastin locus in a developmental disorder, Williams syndrome. *Nature Genetics, 5*, 11–16.

Flint, J. (1996). Annotation: Behavioral phenotypes: a window onto the biology of behavior. *Journal of Child Psychology and Psychiatry, 37*, 355–367.

Fowler, A. (1988). Determinants of rate of language growth in children with Down syndrome. In L. Nadel (Ed.), *The psychobiology of Down syndrome* (pp. 217–245). Cambridge, MA: MIT Press.

Fowler, A. (1990). Language abilities in children with Down syndrome: Evidence for a specific syntactic delay. In D. Cicchetti & M. Beeghly (Eds.), *Children with Down syndrome: A developmental perspective* (pp. 302–328). New York: Cambridge University Press.

Fowler, A., Gelman, R., & Gleitman, L. (1994). The course of language learning in children with Down syndrome: Longitudinal and language level comparisons with young normally developing children. In H. Tager-Flusberg (Ed.), *Constraints on language acquisition: Studies of atypical children* (pp. 91–140). Hillsdale, NJ: Erlbaum.

Gosch, A., Städing, G., & Pankau, R. (1994). Linguistic abilities in children with Williams-Beuren syndrome. *American Journal of Medical Genetics, 52,* 291–296.

Greenwald, C. A., & Leonard, L. (1979). Communicative and sensorimotor development of Down's syndrome children. *American Journal of Mental Deficiency, 84,* 296–303.

Grela, B. (2003). Do children with Down syndrome have difficulty with argument structure? *Journal of Communication Disorders, 36,* 263–279.

Hale, C. M., & Tager-Flusberg, H. (2005). Social communication in children with autism: The relationship between theory of mind in discourse development. *Autism, 9,* 157–178.

Happé, F. (1993). Communicative competence and theory of mind in autism: A test of relevance theory. *Cognition, 48,* 101–119.

Hobson, R. P., & Lee, A. (1989). Emotion-related and abstract concepts in autistic people: Evidence from the British Picture Vocabulary Scale. *Journal of Autism and Developmental Disorders, 19,* 601–623.

Jarrold, C., Baddeley, A., & Hewes, A. (2000). Verbal short term memory deficits in Down syndrome: A consequence of problems in rehearsal? *Journal of Child Psychology and Psychiatry, 40,* 233–244.

Jarrold, C., Boucher, J., & Russell, J. (1997). Language profiles in children with autism: Theoretical and methodological implications. *Autism, 1,* 57–76.

Jasnow, M., Crown, C. L., Feldstein, S., Taylor, L., Beebe, B., & Jaffe, J. (1988). Coordinated interpersonal timing of Down-syndrome and nondelayed infants with their mothers: Evidence for a buffered mechanism of social interaction. *Biological Bulletin, 175,* 355–360.

Jordan, F. M., & Murdoch, B. E. (1987). Referential communication skills of children with Down syndrome. *Australian Journal of Human Communication Disorders, 15,* 47–59.

Joseph, R. M., McGrath, L., & Tager-Flusberg, H. (2005). Executive dysfunction and its relation to language ability in verbal school-age children with autism. *Developmental Neuropsychology, 27,* 361–378.

Kanner, L. (1946). Irrelevant and metaphorical language. *American Journal of Psychiatry, 103,* 242–246.

Karmiloff-Smith, A., Grant, J., Berthoud, I., Davies, M., Howling, P., & Udwin, O. (1997). Language and Williams syndrome: How intact is "intact"? *Child Development, 68,* 246–262.

Kelley, K., & Tager-Flusberg, H. (1995). Discourse characteristics of children with Williams syndrome: Evidence of spared theory of mind abilities. *Genetics Counseling, 6,* 169–170.

Kjelgaard, M., & Tager-Flusberg, H. (2001). An investigation of language impairment in autism: Implications for genetic subgroups. *Language and Cognitive Processes, 16,* 287–308.

Klin, A. (1991). Young autistic children's listening preferences in regard to speech: A possible characterization of the symptom of social withdrawal. *Journal of Autism and Developmental Disorders, 21,* 29–42.

Laing, E., Grant, J., Thomas, M., Parmigiani, C., Ewing, S., & Karmiloff-Smith, A. (2005). Love is . . . an abstract word: The influence of lexical semantics on verbal short-term memory in Williams syndrome. *Cortex, 41,* 169–179.

Lane, H. (1976). *The wild boy of Aveyron*. Cambridge, MA: Harvard University Press.

Laws, G. (2004). Contributions of phonological memory, language comprehension and hearing to the expressive language of adolescents and young adults with Down syndrome. *Journal of Child Psychology and Psychiatry, 45*, 1085–1095.

Laws, G., & Bishop, D. (2003). A comparison of language in adolescents with Down syndrome and children with specific language impairment. *Journal of Speech, Language, and Hearing Research, 46*, 1324–1339.

Laws, G., & Bishop, D. (2004). Pragmatic language impairment and social deficits in Williams syndrome: A comparison with Down's syndrome and specific language impairment. *International Journal of Language and Communication Disorders, 39*, 45–64.

Levy, Y. (2004). A longitudinal study of language development in two children with Williams syndrome. *Journal of Child Language, 31*, 287–310.

Levy, Y., & Hermon, S. (2003). Morphological abilities of Hebrew-speaking adolescents with Williams syndrome. *Developmental Neuropsychology, 23*, 59–83.

Loveland, K., & Landry, S. (1986). Joint attention and language in autism and developmental language delay. *Journal of Autism and Developmental Disorders, 16*, 335–349.

Loveland, K., Landry, S., Hughes, S., Hall, S., & McEvoy, R. (1988). Speech acts and the pragmatic deficits of autism. *Journal of Speech and Hearing Research, 31*, 593–604.

Loveland, K. A., McEvoy, R. E., Tunali, B., & Kelley, M. L. (1990). Narrative story telling in autism and Down's syndrome. *British Journal of Developmental Psychology, 8*, 9–23.

Loveland, K., & Tunali, B. (1991). Social scripts for conversational interactions in autism and Down syndrome. *Journal of Autism and Developmental Disorders, 21*, 177–186.

Loveland, K., & Tunali, B. (1993). Narrative language in autism and the theory of mind hypothesis: a wider perspective. In S. Baron-Cohen, H. Tager-Flusberg, & D. J. Cohen (Eds.), *Understanding other minds: perspectives from autism*. Oxford: Oxford University Press.

Lynch, M., Oller, K., Eilers, R., & Basinger, D. (1990). *Vocal development of infants with Down's syndrome*. Symposium for Research on Child Language Disorders, Madison, WI.

Margar-Bacal, F., Witzel, M., & Munro, I. (1987). Speech intelligibility after partial glossectomy in children with Down's syndrome. *Plastic and Reconstructive Surgery, 79*, 44–49.

Mervis, C. (1990). Early conceptual development of children with Down syndrome. In D. Cicchetti & M. Beeghly (Eds.), *Children with Down syndrome: a developmental perspective* (pp. 252–301). New York: Cambridge University Press.

Mervis, C., & Bertrand, J. (1995). Acquisition of the novel name-nameless category (N3C) principle by young children who have Down syndrome. *American Journal of Mental Retardation, 100*, 231–243.

Mervis, C., & Bertrand, J. (1997). Relations between cognition and language: A developmental perspective. In L. B. Adamson & M. A. Romski (Eds.), *Research on communication and language disorders: Contributions to theories of language development*. Baltimore, MD: Paul Brookes Publishing.

Mervis, C., Morris, C., Bertrand, J., & Robinson, B. (1999). Williams syndrome: Findings from an integrated program of research. In H. Tager-Flusberg (Ed.), *Neurodevelopmental disorders: contributions to a new framework from the cognitive neurosciences*. Cambridge, MA: MIT Press.

Miller, J. (1988). The developmental asynchrony of language development in children with Down syndrome. In L. Nadel (Ed.), *The psychobiology of Down syndrome* (pp. 167–198). Cambridge, MA: MIT Press.

Miller, J., Sedley, A., Miolo, G., Murray-Branch, J., & Rosin, M. (1992). *Longitudinal investigation of vocabulary acquisition in children with Down syndrome*. Symposium on Research in Child Language Disorders, Madison, WI.

Mundy, P., Sigman, M., & Kasari, C. (1990). A longitudinal study of joint attention and language development in autistic children. *Journal of Autism and Developmental Disorders, 20,* 115–123.

Mundy, P., Sigman, M., & Kasari, C. (1994). Joint attention, developmental level and symptom presentation in autism. *Development and Psychopathology, 6,* 389–401.

Mundy, P., Sigman, M., Kasari, C., & Yirmiya, N. (1988). Nonverbal communication skills in Down syndrome children. *Child Development, 59,* 235–249.

Ornitz, E., Guthrie, D., & Farley, A. J. (1977). Early development of autistic children. *Journal of Autism and Childhood Schizophrenia, 7,* 207–229.

Pierce, S., & Bartolucci, G. (1977). A syntactic investigation of verbal autistic, mentally retarded, and normal children. *Journal of Autism and Childhood Schizophrenia, 7,* 121–134.

Reilly, J., Klima, E. S., & Bellugi, U. (1990). Once more with feeling: affect and language in atypical populations. *Development and Psychopathology, 2,* 367–391.

Rice, M. (2003). A unified model of specific and general language delay: Grammatical tense as a clinical marker of unexpected variation. In Y. Levy & J. Schaeffer (Eds.), *Language competence across populations: Toward a definition of specific language impairment* (pp. 63–95). Mahwah, NJ: Erlbaum.

Ricks, D., & Wing, L. (1976). Language, communication and the use of symbols. In L. Wing (Ed.), *Early childhood autism: Clinical, educational, and social aspects* (2nd ed., pp. 93–134). New York: Pergamon Press.

Roberts, J., Rice, M., & Tager-Flusberg, H. (2004). Tense marking in children with autism. *Applied Psycholinguistics, 25,* 429–448.

Robinson, B., Mervis, C., & Robinson, B. (2003). The roles of verbal short-term memory and working memory in the acquisition of grammar by children with Williams syndrome. *Developmental Neuropsychology, 23,* 13–31.

Rowe, M., Peregrine, E., & Mervis, C. B. (2004). *Role of intention reading in word learning by children with Williams syndrome.* Tenth International Professional Conference on Williams Syndrome, Grand Rapids, MI.

Rutter, M. (1987). The "what" and "how" of language development: a note on some outstanding issues and questions. In W. Yule & M. Rutter (Eds.), *Language development and disorders* (pp. 159–170). London: MacKeith Press.

Santangelo, S., & Folstein, S. (1999). Autism: A genetic perspective. In H. Tager-Flusberg (Ed.), *Neurodevelopmental disorders* (pp. 431–447). Cambridge, MA: MIT Press.

Scherer, N., & Owings, N. (1984). Learning to be contingent: Retarded children's responses to their mothers' requests. *Language and Speech, 27,* 255–267.

Sheinkopf, S., Mundy, P., Oller, K., & Steffens, M. (2000). Vocal atypicalities of preverbal autistic children. *Journal of Autism and Developmental Disorders, 30,* 345–354.

Shriberg, L., Paul, R., McSweeney, J., Klin, A., Cohen, D., & Volkmar, F. (2001). Speech and prosody characteristics of adolescents and adults with high-functioning autism and AS. *Journal of Speech, Language, and Hearing Research, 44,* 1097–1115.

Sigman, M., & Ruskin, E. (1999). Continuity and change in the social competence of children with autism, Down syndrome and developmental delays. *Monographs of the Society for Research in Child Development, 64* (Serial No. 256).

Singer, N. G., Bellugi, U., Bates, E., Jones, W., & Rossen, M. (1994). *Contrasting profiles of language development in children with Williams and Down syndromes.* Technical Report #9403, Project in Cognitive and Neural Development, University of California, San Diego, CA.

Steffens, M. L., Oller, K., Lynch, M., & Urbano, R. (1992). Vocal development in infants with Down syndrome and infants who are developing normally. *American Journal of Mental Retardation, 97,* 235–246.

Stoel-Gammon, C. (1980). Phonological analysis of four Down's syndrome children. *Applied Psycholinguistics, 1*, 31–48.

Tager-Flusberg, H. (1985). The conceptual basis for referential word meaning in children with autism. *Child Development, 56*, 1167–1178.

Tager-Flusberg, H. (1986). Constraints on the representation of word meaning: Evidence from autistic and mentally retarded children. In S. A. Kuczaj & M. Barrett (Eds.), *The development of word meaning* (pp. 139–166). New York: Springer-Verlag.

Tager-Flusberg, H. (1988). On the nature of a language acquisition disorder: The example of autism. In F. Kessel (Ed.), *The development of language and language researchers* (pp. 249–267). Hillsdale, NJ: Erlbaum.

Tager-Flusberg, H. (1992). Autistic children's talk about psychological states: Deficits in the early acquisition of a theory of mind. *Child Development, 63*, 161–172.

Tager-Flusberg, H. (1993). What language reveals about the understanding of minds in children with autism. In S. Baron-Cohen, H. Tager-Flusberg, & D. J. Cohen (Eds.), *Understanding other minds: perspectives from autism* (pp. 138–157). Oxford: Oxford University Press.

Tager-Flusberg, H. (1994). Dissociations in form and function in the acquisition of language by autistic children. In H. Tager-Flusberg (Ed.), *Constraints on language acquisition: Studies of atypical children* (pp. 175–194). Hillsdale, NJ: Erlbaum.

Tager-Flusberg, H. (1997). Language acquisition and theory of mind: Contributions from the study of autism. In L. B. Adamson & M. A. Romski (Eds.), *Research on communication and language disorders: Contributions to theories of language development.* Baltimore, MD: Paul Brookes Publishing.

Tager-Flusberg, H., & Anderson, M. (1991). The development of contingent discourse ability in autistic children. *Journal of Child Psychology and Psychiatry, 32*, 1123–1134.

Tager-Flusberg, H., Calkins, S., Nolin, T., Baumberger, T., Anderson, M., & Chadwick-Dias, A. (1990). A longitudinal study of language acquisition in autistic and Downs syndrome children. *Journal of Autism and Developmental Disorders, 20*, 1–21.

Tager-Flusberg, H., & Cooper, J. (1999). Present and future possibilities for defining a phenotype for specific language impairment. *Journal of Speech, Language, and Hearing Research, 42*, 1275–1278.

Tager-Flusberg, H., & Joseph, R. M. (2003). Identifying neurocognitive phenotypes in autism. *Philosophical Transactions of the Royal Society, Series B, 358*, 303–314.

Tager-Flusberg, H., Paul, R., & Lord, C. E. (2005). Language and communication in autism. In F. Volkmar, R. Paul, A. Klin, & D. J. Cohen (Eds.), *Handbook of autism and pervasive developmental disorder: Vol. 1* (3rd ed., pp. 335–364). New York: Wiley.

Tager-Flusberg, H., & Sullivan, K. (1995). Attributing mental states to story characters: A comparison of narratives produced by autistic and mentally retarded individuals. *Applied Psycholinguistics, 16*, 241–256.

Thomas, M., & Karmiloff-Smith, A. (2005). Can developmental disorders reveal the component parts of the human language faculty? *Language Learning and Development, 1*, 65–92.

Thordardottir, E., Chapman, R., & Wagner, L. (2002). Complex sentence production by adolescents with Down syndrome. *Applied Psycholinguistics, 23*, 163–183.

Tomblin, J. B., & Zhang, X. (1999). Language patterns and etiology in children with specific language impairment. In H. Tager-Flusberg (Ed.), *Neurodevelopmental disorders* (pp. 361–382). Cambridge, MA: MIT Press.

Udwin, O., & Yule, W. (1991). A cognitive and behavioral phenotype in Williams syndrome. *Journal of Clinical and Experimental Neuropsychology, 13*, 232–244.

Van Lancker, D., Cornelius, C., & Needleman, R. (1991). Comprehension of verbal terms for emotions in normal, autistic, and schizophrenic children. *Developmental Neuropsychology, 7,* 1–18.

Volden, J., & Lord, C. (1991). Neologism and idiosyncratic language in autistic speakers. *Journal of Autism and Developmental Disorders, 21,* 109–130.

Volterra, V., Sabbadini, L., Capirci, O., Pezzini, G., & Ossella, T. (1995). Language development in Italian children with Williams syndrome. *Genetics Counseling, 6,* 137–138.

Wetherby, A. (1986). Ontogeny of communication functions in autism. *Journal of Autism and Developmental Disorders, 16,* 295–316.

Wetherby, A. M., & Prutting, C. A. (1984). Profiles of communicative and cognitive-social abilities in autistic children. *Journal of Speech and Hearing Research, 27,* 364–377.

Williams, J., Barratt-Boyes, B. G., & Lowe, J. B. (1961). Supravalvular aortic stenosis. *Circulation, 24,* 1311–1318.

Wishart, J. G. (1988). Early learning in infants and young children with Down syndrome. In L. Nadel (Ed.), *The psychobiology of Down syndrome* (pp. 7–50). Cambridge, MA: MIT Press.

Zukowski, A. (2004). Investigating knowledge of complex syntax: Insights from experimental studies of Williams syndrome. In M. L. Rice & S. Warren (Eds.), *Developmental language disorders: From phenotypes to etiologies.* Mahwah, NJ: Erlbaum.

22

Reading and Reading Disorders

Heikki Lyytinen, Jane Erskine, Mikko Aro, and Ulla Richardson

This chapter explores four major research issues relative to typical and atypical language development in the school years. In tracking the development from newborn to reading age, the first topic examines the developmental prerequisites of reading, through speech perception and language development, toward the development of phonological awareness as the primary precursor to reading acquisition. The second issue examines whether reading develops similarly in all languages. The third issue explores why some children, despite adequate instruction and opportunity, fail to learn to read and are consequently deemed to be dyslexic. The fourth issue details what can be done to support such children who fail to learn to read. In the closing section and within the context of the Jyväskylä Longitudinal Study of Dyslexia, some answers and solutions to these important issues are offered.

Secondary language skills (reading and writing) are founded on primary language skills (speaking and listening) (Mattingly, 1972). Primary skills develop remarkably implicitly, while secondary skills require more explicit learning and the diversion of attention toward the sound structure – phonology. Reading requires "awareness" and the ability to manipulate the phonological information contained in spoken language. In general, this awareness of phonemes is acquired by all those who are exposed to reading instruction within the context of an alphabetic orthography. Morais, Cary, Alegria, and Bertelson (1979) clearly demonstrated the reciprocal and dependent relationship between phonological awareness and reading by showing that illiterate adults could not perform tasks requiring the manipulation of phonemes.

The majority of previous research has been conducted within the remit of the alphabetic languages, especially the English language. Alphabetic writing systems are based on symbols (letters) which represent the smallest and most important segments (phonemes) of a spoken language. The relationship between the letter(s), or graphemes, which represent these phonemes, is either direct (as in consistent languages) or indirect (as in inconsistent languages). English is an inconsistent orthography and boasts many complexities in the mapping between its graphemes and phonemes. For example, in the reading direction, one grapheme may represent numerous phonemes and in the spelling direction, a single phoneme may represent numerous graphemes. However, the relationship between these graphemes and phonemes may be entirely different as a function of the direction of translation. English therefore qualifies as a bidirectionally inconsistent orthography. It is our intention to accommodate differences between alphabetic orthographies, but we focus especially on reading acquisition in the consistent Finnish orthography where the relationship between letter and sound is straightforward in that one grapheme corresponds to one phoneme and that same phoneme corresponds to the same grapheme (e.g., Finnish qualifies as a bidirectionally consistent orthography). This will help the reader to appreciate that reading acquisition and reading problems are not independent of the system of the connections between the spoken and the written system of the language. Furthermore, comprehension may be detrimentally affected if reading is insufficiently fluent. For the most part, research has focused on reading accuracy in the context of English. However, in more consistent orthographies, the focus is moving toward the accommodation of reading fluency as a more primary feature of both skilled and disabled reading.

Western society is strongly dependent on the use of literacy as a cultural, educational, and social medium. Olson (2002) observes that the vast majority of the world's population does not read because they live in an environment where no script exists, or reading has no role in their society. The second largest population with compromised reading skill concerns those who fail to receive adequate reading instruction because they lack access to necessary factors such as school, instruction, or societal or familial support. If afforded adequate opportunity, then the majority of children in the developed world learn to read. However, in global terms, a miniscule population has poor reading ability of initial genetic and/or brain-related etiology which predisposes them toward reading failure. Our concern here is this small portion.

Reading skill shows a continuous distribution and thus the criteria of reading difficulty (dyslexia) today are still arbitrary and predominantly based on social diagnosis – social, in the sense that it is the degree of deviance from others rather than either a quantified detriment resulting from poor skill or an observed biological difference. The most typical ways in which to define the problem in both research and clinical terms is to use a critical deviation criterion of 1 to 2 standard deviations below the mean of the same age population. The definition may include one or more criterion variables. Research on English typically emphasizes accuracy of reading and/or spelling, but it is increasingly common, particularly in research on more consistent orthographies, to employ fluency of reading or a combination of reading fluency and accuracy scores as criteria.

In addressing these contemporary issues in the field of reading development and reading disability, the Jyväskylä Longitudinal Study of Dyslexia has followed children at familial risk for dyslexia and their controls from birth to school age (for a recent review of results, see Lyytinen et al., 2004). The results partially replicate many of the findings of the only completed similar study by Scarborough (1990) in showing that different early language-related weaknesses anticipate reading disorder. In such a context, we offer a new perspective with regard to the characteristics, early identification, and prevention of compromised reading.

How Does Reading Develop?

Phonological skills are the most influential pre-reading skills and the strongest predictors of English reading and spelling skills in both children and adults (e.g., Bradley & Bryant, 1983; Lundberg, Olofsson, & Wall, 1980; for a review, see Vellutino, Fletcher, Snowling, & Scanlon, 2004). Phonological awareness is held to comprise a range of subskills which reflect awareness of different sound units, including small units (phonemes) (Snowling, 1980) and larger units, such as onsets or rimes (Goswami & Bryant, 1990a) – both arguably helpful foci in terms of reading instruction in inconsistent orthographies such as English. Another factor of reading skill, letter knowledge, has until recently received less attention in terms of its relationship to skilled reading. However, it is increasingly apparent that skills associated with phonological development can be identified before children are exposed to or interested in the symbols used in writing.

One of the first indications of phonological development is that infants are drawn to the speech rhythm of their native language as opposed to non-native language (Ramus & Mehler, 1999). Perception of native (but not non-native) language contrasts is also predictive of the ease of reading acquisition at later pre-reading ages (Burnham, 2003). Infants are also born with the ability to discriminate small differences between speech sounds (spectral and durational; spectral referring to the quality of speech sounds and durational to the temporal aspect of sounds) (Eimas, Sigueland, Jusczyck, & Vigorito, 1971; Leppänen, Pihko, Eklund, & Lyytinen, 1999). Speech perception is language specific from a very early age. In studies of categorization skills, not only are infants able to utilize general speech rhythm, but they have also been shown to use successfully the suprasegmental features of speech to categorize words according to phonological quantity (e.g., sound duration) at 6 months of age (Leppänen et al., 2002; Richardson, Leppänen, Leiwo, & Lyytinen, 2003). In Finnish, phonological quantity is indicated orthographically by the doubling of letters (e.g., *mato* [worm] – *matto* [carpet]). It is realized in speech as longer duration of the sound, and this contrast is phonemic, affecting a large number of Finnish words.

By 9 months, infants pay increasing attention to the meaningful differences at the segmental level and ignore those that are unimportant to their native language (Werker & Tees, 1987). Such phonological sensitivity is important for the development of the foundation skills for reading, as children must learn to consciously segment words into smaller chunks in order to reach the level where they are able to assemble pronunciation from small grapheme-size chunks.

The first substantial growth in vocabulary (lexicon) size, which typically occurs around the age of 1.5 to 2 years, induces children to process phonological sub-lexical units. For example, Metsala and Walley's (1998) "Lexical Restructuring Model" advocates that the lexicon is constantly restructured as a combined result of increasing vocabulary size and growing awareness of the phonological similarities between words (initially through larger lexical units, e.g., word, syllable, onset and rime, toward more "fine-grained" segmentation of phoneme unit sizes), gained through familiarity and experience with spoken language (Walley, 1993; Stoel-Gammon & Sosa, this volume). In order to learn new words that are phonologically similar to those in the existing lexicon, children must master the differentiation of sub-lexical units. Children acquiring the highly inflected languages where a number of variants of the same words often differ only by one phoneme are usually able to produce and comprehend the segment size differences at a very early age. Thus, in Finnish, 2-year-olds can comprehend and produce the inflected variants of, for example, the word *talo* (house) *talossa* (in the house) and *talosta* (from the house; Lyytinen & Lyytinen, 2004).

The above-mentioned skills are acquired implicitly in the context of language learning. Children become explicitly "aware" of phonemes (i.e., able to manipulate the phonemic size units outside the meaning of the word by attending to the sound only) mostly through the process of learning to read (Morais, 1991; Vellutino, Scanlon, & Chen, 1995; Wagner, Torgesen, & Rashotte, 1994). However, bringing such units to the fore with appropriate "phonological training" may facilitate earlier acquisition of reading, even if this training is conducted orally and without the involvement of letters (Lundberg et al., 1980).

Does Reading Develop the Same Way in All Languages?

Not only is reading acquisition determined by the competency of the beginning reader, it is also determined by the qualities and features of the language and orthography to be mastered (for a review of such qualities see, e.g., deFrancis, 1989). The majority of research has targeted the beginning reader and predominantly the reader of English (see Marsh, Friedman, Welch, and Desberg's (1981) cognitive developmental theory; Frith's (1985) three-stage strategy, six-step model; Goswami and Bryant's (1990b) causal model). Less attention has been paid to the language context or the interaction between language and orthography. Furthermore, the degree of differences among different alphabetic writing systems has rarely been considered in the literature.

While all alphabetic orthographies share similar basic principles in terms of marking the phonemes into script, the numerous differences between orthographies may also impact on the process of reading acquisition. Such differences extend to the language-specific phonological and morphological properties that may be differentially responsible for posing obstacles to the reader. Nonetheless, perhaps the most relevant difference between orthographies, from the point of view of the beginning reader, concerns the transparency of the grapheme–phoneme correspondence system, which varies greatly among alphabetic orthographies.

Although comprehensive indices for the assessment of this transparency are scarce (but see Borgwaldt, Hellwig, & de Groot, 2004; Seymour, Aro, & Erskine, 2003; Ziegler, Jacobs, & Stone, 1996; Ziegler, Stone, & Jacobs, 1997), there is consensus regarding the orthographies that fall at the extremes of this continuum (Frost, Katz, & Bentin, 1987). English is generally thought to be the most opaque alphabetic orthography, with complex and context-sensitive grapheme–phoneme pairings, multi-letter graphemes, and inconsistencies. At the opposite end of the continuum are orthographies such as Finnish, Italian, and Spanish, where the correspondences are more consistent, allowing simple rule-based learning of these associations.

Developmentally, the typical rate at which children's phonological skills develop follows a path which is not necessarily universal and which produces considerable variation between individuals. In general, however, the order in which the different elements of phonology are acquired is relatively stable, even across languages: phonetic development is similar, as are the phonological processes (e.g., cluster reduction, vowel harmony, assimilation, substitution, voicing, etc.), albeit they follow the characteristics of a given language. Generally speaking, therefore, by the age of 5 years typically developing children have acquired the basic principles of the phonology of their language and their use of speech sounds is more or less organized in a similar way to adult speakers of the same language. If not, then the development could be considered to be delayed or deficient and will most likely affect the literacy skills of these children.

Phonological sensitivity to different sizes of speech units in segmental and suprasegmental levels at different stages of reading acquisition is a good predictor of reading acquisition across languages (Goswami, 2003; Goswami, Gombert, & Barrera, 1998; Goswami, Ziegler, Dalton, & Schneider, 2001; Richardson, Thomson, Scott, & Goswami, 2004), at least in inconsistent orthographies such as English. In consistent orthographies such as Finnish, their predictive role may last a shorter time as it is not the accuracy which requires further honing after 1 to 2 years of instruction, but fluency. Automatization seems to be affected, not only by phonological skills, but also by speed factors related to retrieval from memory. This is why naming fluency, independent of whether it is based on visual language, seems also to be predictively associated with reading fluency. Naming fluency is typically measured with a task where the subject has to name a series of familiar items (such as digits, numbers, colors, or objects) as fast as possible. The time used for the naming task is supposed to be an index of the ease and automaticity with which the phonological representations can be retrieved from memory. Whether phonological skills and naming fluency are both based on some third factor connected to the phonological domain is currently unclear, but for practical purposes naming fluency makes a clear contribution to the prediction of reading failure associated with automatization. This differentiation is important because fluency of reading skill naturally affects reading comprehension, the ultimate goal of reading. Wolf and Katzir-Cohen (2001) define fluent reading as a level of reading in which accuracy and rate are such that decoding is relatively effortless and attention can be allocated to comprehension.

Cross-linguistic findings have consistently shown that, in terms of reading accuracy, English-speaking children lag behind their peers who are learning to read in more consistent orthographies (as shown in Figure 22.1). In collaboration with a European network of reading and dyslexia researchers, we recently carried out a comprehensive cross-linguistic assessment of early reading acquisition (Seymour et al., 2003). The theoretical context of the study was provided by Seymour's (1999) foundation literacy framework which proposes that letter-sound knowledge serves as the basis for two processes involved in early reading development: alphabetic and logographic processes. In the collaborative study, letter knowledge, word recognition and decoding skills were compared at the end of the first grade in 13 different European orthographies. Results revealed no differences in letter knowledge, children in all orthographies having achieved letter knowledge of 90% or better. However, there were large differences in word recognition and decoding skills. The accuracy, especially of English-speaking children, but also

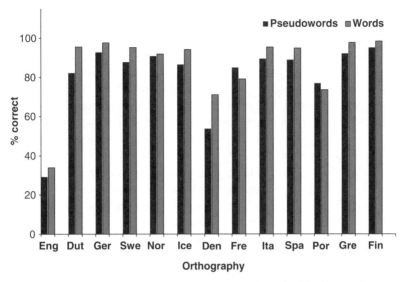

Figure 22.1 Accuracy of word and pseudoword reading at the end of the first grade in 13 orthographies, according to Seymour et al. (2003).

Danish, French, and Portuguese children, was reduced in comparison to the accuracy of children reading in more consistent orthographies (see Figure 22.1). As shown by the figure, the time required to establish basic reading skills varies according to orthographic depth. It could be estimated that English-speaking children require 2.5 years of reading instruction to reach the level of accuracy attained by children in consistent orthographies at some point during the first grade.

Seymour et al. (2003) interpreted the results to reflect a qualitative difference in the reading acquisition processes depending on the consistency of the orthography: in consistent orthographies, where the relationship between letter and sound is straightforward, alphabetic processing skills are sufficient for reading acquisition. By contrast, in more inconsistent orthographies, dual routes to reading are required in terms of supplementing the alphabetic skills with logographic skills (relying on memory for recognition of larger units such as whole words), especially when these words do not conform to regular letter–sound correspondences (e.g., as in the spelling "yacht"). The differences in the time taken to acquire the foundation reading skills reflect these differences. This has been observed in a number of studies comparing two (Cossu, Shankweiler, Liberman, Katz, & Tola, 1988; Thorstad, 1991; Wimmer & Goswami, 1994) or more orthographies (Aro & Wimmer, 2003; Seymour et al., 2003). Although differences among the orthographies are apparent in terms of typical reading development, such differences are also apparent in the profiles of atypical or dyslexic readers. A difference between orthographies has also been observed in the performance of English and German dyslexic readers, with German children being more accurate readers despite the implementation of comparable diagnostic procedures for the two groups (Landerl, Wimmer, & Frith, 1997).

Why Do Some Children Fail to Read?

It is estimated that, despite adequate schooling, between 5% and 20% of the Western population have difficulty in acquiring basic literacy skills. Current definitions of dyslexia are still embroiled in issues of *exclusion* (Critchley & Critchley, 1978), *discrepancy* between expected and actual ability (Reynolds, 1984), or, more recently, accommodation of the *distal* and *proximal* factors associated with literacy difficulty (Coltheart & Jackson, 1998). Exclusionary definitions make reference to symptoms and a cognitive-genetic basis but the diagnosis is attained only by merit of persistence when all other possible causal factors have been excluded. Discrepancy definitions are a product of the exclusionary philosophy and rely on the regression approach in positing that dyslexia is marked by a discrepancy between obtained and expected ability (Stanovich & Siegel, 1994). A discrepancy is usually claimed if individual performance on one factor (such as reading ability) is significantly discrepant (more than 2 standard deviations below the mean) (Snowling, 1998) from performance predicted by a second correlating factor (such as IQ; Nelson & McKenna, 1975). Coltheart and Jackson (1998) assert the need to accommodate the *proximal* and *distal* causes of dyslexia. The distal causes are functions which are distinct from reading and spelling but which nonetheless disrupt the development of those processes. The proximal causes are the functions which are directly involved in the orthographic processes underlying competence in reading and spelling.

In terms of isolating a biological basis, the heterogeneous nature of dyslexia currently defies neurology and genetics in their search to link distal mechanisms with proximal outcomes. Nonetheless, advances in neuroimaging techniques are beginning to propose specific neural structures as distal candidates for the different proximal features (visual and auditory, orthographic and phonological) that constitute the mosaic that is dyslexia.

Previous and current causal theories of dyslexia are too numerous and diverse to elaborate here in detail. Briefly, early pathological studies of dyslexic brains showed structural and functional differences (Galaburda, Sherman, Rosen, Aboitiz, & Geschwind, 1985; Livingstone, Rosen, Drislane, & Galaburda, 1991) such as ectopias, anatomical neuronal abnormalities believed to result from atypical cell migration. There is evidence to support a strong familial basis (Gilger, Pennington, & De Fries, 1991; Hallgren, 1950; Scarborough, 1989) and a genetic basis (e.g., Cardon, Smith, Fulker, et al., 1994; Grigorenko et al., 1997; Smith, Kimberling, Pennington, & Lubs, 1983), or even a role of a single candidate gene (the first one identified by Taipale et al., 2003). Visual (Breitmeyer, 1993; Lovegrove, Martin, & Slaghuis, 1986; Stein & Fowler, 1981) and auditory (Studdert-Kennedy, 2002; Tallal, 1980), as well as multi-faceted explanations (Ramus et al., 2003, but see Ramus, 2003, for the evidence supporting the most extensively validated views) of dyslexia have also been the focus of more contemporary research.

Over the last few decades, the "core phonological deficit" (Stanovich, 1986) has been promoted as underlying developmental dyslexia (Bradley & Bryant, 1983; Vellutino, 1979). Snowling (1998, p. 5) suggests that this core deficit is a result of "poorly specified phonological representations [which] underlie reading and spelling, [and] compromise literacy development by placing limitations on [the] ability to establish the mappings between letter strings and phonology that are critical for learning to read."

By a process known as double dissociation whereby patterns of disruption or residual function are confirmed or refuted by the nature of their antithetical comparison, characteristic error patterns make it possible to identify specific types of dyslexic impairment; specifically, the surface (Coltheart, Masterson, Byng, Prior, & Riddoch, 1983; Marshall & Newcombe, 1973) and phonological (Beauvois & Derouesné, 1979; Castles & Coltheart, 1993) subtypes. This dichotomy is held to represent the two routes (lexical, non-lexical) (Ellis & Young, 1988) to reading that are available, at least to the reader of English, and the subtypes are claimed on the basis of selective impairment to either the lexical–visual (surface) or non-lexical–auditory (phonological) route to reading. In English, surface-type errors reflect difficulty with the application of visual memory-based strategies, especially in the context of reading unfamiliar irregularly spelled words. Phonological-type errors reflect difficulty with the application of decoding rules in the context of reading unfamiliar or non-words. The heterogeneous nature and often-time absence of "pure" subtypes has led researchers to question their existence. Nonetheless, recent technological improvements in neuroimaging have resurrected questions relative to the "visual" versus "auditory" routes to reading (Ramus et al., 2003; Stein, 2001).

The phonological–surface error-based distinction is therefore of possible relevance to inconsistent orthographies that require, in addition to decoding skill, the ability to recognize irregularly spelled words with reliance on visual lexical memory. In consistent orthographies, the phenotype of these subtypes is likely to differ. It could be hypothesized that, whereas phonological-type errors would be similar, irrespective of the orthography, in consistent orthographies the additional subtype problems manifest as slow decoding speed.

There is also ongoing debate as to whether the surface subtype is simply a form of "developmental delay" (Snowling, Goulandris, & Defty, 1998; Stanovich, Siegel, & Gottardo, 1997), which is more susceptible to the influence of environmental factors (Castles, Datta, Gayan, & Olson, 1999). Nonetheless, recent suggestions of a wider spread deficit incorporating both the visual and auditory systems and extending to the cerebellum, described by Stein (e.g., 2001) as the "brain's main timing device," better accommodate the heterogeneous nature of proximal difficulties in dyslexia, including difficulties with the establishment of reading fluency (i.e., automatization, Nicolson & Fawcett, 1990; Wolf & Bowers, 1999), motor/coordination problems (Nicolson, Fawcett, & Dean, 2001), and orthographic skill and rapid naming (Eckert et al., 2003). The prevalence of these visual or auditory-based difficulties is still being debated (see Ramus et al., 2003).

What Can Be Done to Support Children Who Fail to Read?

The implications that definitions of reading disorder have for practice, comprise, for example, the apparently different ways in which poor accuracy or fluency can be remediated. If accuracy is overemphasized, the reader who has a severe "bottleneck" in his/her acquisition of reading skill may never become fully interested in reading. Failure to attain sufficient reading speed may inhibit enjoyment from reading comprehension (Leinonen et al., 2001). Share's (1995) "self-teaching mechanism" advocates that children acquire knowledge of words (orthographic representations) by a process of self-teaching through their experience of recoding phonological information when attempting unfamiliar words. Ultimately, with experience and practice, we know that it is this "self-teaching mechanism" or, more concretely, reading practice whose application, in the end, is a prerequisite to the acquisition of automatized fluent reading.

Research shows that dyslexic readers can improve their reading accuracy, but continue to lack fluency in their reading (Lefly & Pennington, 1991). Furthermore, the inefficiency of phonological-based treatments in terms of improving rate-related reading problems has redirected attention toward reading fluency. This increased attention is also reflected in the definition of dyslexia; in their update of a working definition of dyslexia, Lyon, Shaywitz, and Shaywitz (2003) recognize reading fluency problems as characteristic of dyslexic individuals, especially adolescents and adults.

While this emphasis toward rate-related aspects of reading performance is not new (see, e.g., subtype models by Boder, 1973, and Lovett, 1987), Wolf and Katzir-Cohen (2001) describe the interest in fluency research as spasmodic. The role of reading speed as a characteristic of dyslexia has been more acknowledged in languages with more consistent orthographies than in English (e.g., Wimmer, 1993). This difference has also been reflected in diagnostic methods. In English, reading speed has often been overlooked in diagnostic procedures that emphasize accuracy, whereas in consistent orthographies most reading tests explicitly include a rate component. However, the speed deficit in reading has also been shown to be a dominant factor in defining compromised reading in English, as shown by, for example, Ziegler, Perry, Ma-Wyatt, Ladner, and Schulte-Körne (2003) and Erskine and Seymour (2005). These differences should be taken into account when developing remedial practices in different orthographies.

The fundamental aim of the most widely supported phonics instruction (and by proxy phoneme awareness instruction) is to make children aware of correspondences between graphemes and phonemes and to relate these to reading and spelling. Previous research (Share, Jorm, Maclean, & Matthews, 1984; see deJong & Olson, 2004, for a review) focusing on English and current research conducted in the authors' laboratory reflecting the results from a highly consistent orthography has shown that letter knowledge (Lyytinen, Ronimus, Alanko, Taanila, & Poikkeus, submitted), phonological awareness (Puolakanaho, Poikkeus, Ahonen, Tolvanen, & Lyytinen, 2004), and naming fluency (Lyytinen et al., 2004) are the best predictors of children's reading acquisition and, where relevant, their failure to do so. Ehri et al. (2001) undertook an extensive review of the literature concerning the efficacy of different phonological and phonics approaches (including synthetic, analytic, and no-phonics approaches). Systematic phonics instruction is a "put-together" approach that encourages the word to be recognized through the building of its constituent sounds. By contrast, analytic phonics is a "break-down" approach with analysis of the constituent sounds after the word has been recognized. No-phonics approaches commonly involve "whole-language" methods of reading, including reading words by sight.

These findings showed that systematic phonics instruction was more effective in teaching children to read than non-systematic or non-phonics instruction, especially in the early years. Moreover, this meta-analysis of the studies showed that children, both with a risk for reading problems and developing typically, were shown to benefit from systematic phonics instruction. Recent results reporting training effects of reading English emphasize explanation of the phonological units and their connection to writing (Hatcher, Hulme, & Snowling, 2004).

Grapheme–phoneme learning is straightforward in highly consistent orthographies. In less consistent orthographies, often the sound can only be connected consistently to larger units containing several letters. Children learning English can be effectively trained by using a synthetic phonics instruction system supported by oral phonological training (as opposed to simple training in phonological awareness) or analytical phonics instruction methods (see, e.g., Hatcher et al., 2004). Such a system is typically based on a method similar to that used in more consistent orthographies and involves the teaching of small groups or clusters of letters. Interestingly, Hutzler, Ziegler, Perry, Wimmer, and Zorzi (2004) have recently suggested that the advantages shown for reading in a more consistent orthography, at least between German and English, should be described as an interaction between the consistency of the mapping between grapheme and phoneme and teaching methods (phonics vs. whole word).

The Jyväskylä Longitudinal Study of Dyslexia

The results of the Jyväskylä Longitudinal Study of Dyslexia (JLD) show that, despite a writing and teaching system which is highly effective in terms of helping most children to attain full reading accuracy within the first 3 to 4 months of schooling, the acquisition of skilled reading may still fail to proceed normally for some children. Such a short period of instruction is usually sufficient because the relation between the 24 independent letters and phonemes is bidirectionally consistent. Children have mastered most of the letter–sound correspondences already before school entry. After learning letter-sounds the only other requirement for reading is to invent how to assemble these learned letter-sounds. In a fully consistent orthography, this process simply entails the sequencing of these letters/phonemes in the same order that they are written/heard in order to be able to produce/identify the word that they represent (Lyytinen, Aro, et al., 2005).

Why, then, should it be the case that prevalence rates for reading failure are similar across different languages, irrespective of the consistency of the orthography? We attempt to answer this question below. Almost half of the children who are at familial risk face problems in reading Finnish and close to 10% of the controls clearly differ from the typical majority in terms of acquiring accuracy within the expected time and especially in terms of the development of fluency.

Very early predictors of reading acquisition

In the JLD, very early speech processing or discrimination of speech sounds reflected in brain indices (event-related brain potentials, Guttorm, Leppänen, Richardson, &

Lyytinen, 2001; Leppänen et al., 2002) and behaviorally assessed speech perception (using a head turn paradigm, Richardson et al., 2003) gave the first indications of the differential language development of the children who were at risk for dyslexia because of their family history. However, surprisingly, even a very good start in early language development cannot always shield against early reading failure (Lyytinen, Erskine, et al., 2006). Our behavioral and psychophysiological studies have shown that infants as young as 6 months can categorize speech sounds according to sound duration (Leppänen et al., 2002; Richardson et al., 2003). Significantly, our recent analyses of the JLD data indicate that infants' ability to process features of speech predicts their acquisition of early reading skills. Consequently, readiness to process speech signals in infancy is an important factor in relation to the foundations of reading acquisition (for the earliest JLD publication to support this argument, see Guttorm et al., 2005; see also Molfese, 2000).

Early language predictors and early reading predictors (individual variation)

In addition to receptive language, expressive indices (such as maximum sentence length at 2 years of age) of language (Lyytinen & Lyytinen, 2004), inflectional (Lyytinen & Lyytinen, 2004), phonological (Puolakanaho et al., 2004), and naming skills (Lyytinen et al., 2004) from 3 years of age showed increasingly atypical development among at risk children and also predicted reading acquisition. The early delay in expressive language (late talking) seems to predict continuing delay in language development and difficulties in reading acquisition, especially if it is associated with early delay in receptive language (Lyytinen, Eklund, & Lyytinen, 2005). The single most accurate predictor to emerge, however, was the development of letter knowledge during the years before the start of formal reading instruction. All but one of the children who encountered reading acquisition difficulties that persisted for more than one year after beginning school had experienced difficulties in learning letter names, irrespective of whether they also showed similar delays in phonological measures and/or rapid naming tasks. In fact, 10% of these children showed a delay in letter knowledge only. However, letter knowledge was also poor among those children who additionally achieved low scores in phonological awareness measures from age 3.5 years and in rapid naming from age 5 years. Naturally, these three characteristics – low letter knowledge, mostly together with low phonological awareness and/or rapid naming skill – characterized children most severely delayed in their reading acquisition. These predictive indices match those observed commonly in English (e.g., Wagner et al., 1994). Of these three characteristics, the learning of the connections between written and spoken items has not received the attention it deserves. The Finnish data show that, potentially, the primary problem is rooted in the ease of learning the letter-sounds, because problems emerge even in the case when the connections are very few in number (24) and very consistent. In short, impaired acquisition of letter knowledge is a good predictor and, ultimately, failure to overcome any initial difficulty in the acquisition of letter-sounds, even with intensive training of the connections between written and spoken language, can only result in compromised reading skill.

The central role in terms of building the connection between written and spoken items is also seen in English, not only via their higher count (at least hundreds) but also at the primary grapheme–phoneme level, whereby findings show that controlling for letter knowledge tends to partial out the effects of phonological awareness from the prediction of early reading skill (e.g., Blaiklock, 2004). It has been shown convincingly that knowledge for letters precedes explicit phonological awareness (Johnston, Anderson, & Holligan, 1996; Stahl & Murray, 1994), and is a more powerful predictor of reading (Gallagher, Frith, & Snowling, 2000; Pennington & Lefly, 2001) and a central mediator of the phonological manipulation skill that forms the basis of reading (Johnston et al., 1996; see Hammill, 2004, for a recent review).

Notably, in the highly consistent Finnish orthography, mere informal home and kindergarten practices related to written language are sufficient for more than one third of children without any formal school instruction to acquire accurate decoding skill. Happily, most of those (about 10%) children for whom reading acquisition is initially difficult during the first grades can be helped to compensate for their difficulties and attain if not adequate, then at least almost adequate reading skill. This conclusion is also valid with regard to reading acquisition in English (Vellutino et al., 2004).

Computer intervention

Failure to attain fluent reading skills is detrimental to the further development of reading with comprehension and to children's spontaneous engagement in reading. Current theories describing the acquisition of fully specified orthographic representations stress the role of accurate identification of words on a number of different occasions during text reading, via a self-teaching mechanism (e.g., Share, 1995). Torgesen, Rashotte, and Alexander (2001) have summarized evidence showing vast differences in the amount of reading practice between good and poor readers. These differences make it difficult for slow readers to close the gap in reading skills with typically achieving children.

The core knowledge required for reading comprises grapheme–phoneme connections. As letter naming seems to be difficult for those who fail to acquire reading at the expected age, this means that learning the letter-sounds is also more challenging. In fact, we have increasingly observed this initial learning among children with low initial letter knowledge and found that these children require much more intensive exposure to these connections in order to successfully start their reading career. Letter-sounds are abstract and are not naturally of interest to children. Consequently, introducing the learning of these sounds in a computer game context can make this learning enjoyable and greatly assist those who are unable to master the connections without extensive repetition. In just such a computer game context, developed within the remit of the JLD, each child receives training on items which he or she is just learning to master. The game adapts to the individual level of ability and this ensures that players are supported by maximum positive feedback and the child's interest in further playing (and consequently, learning) is sustained. Such an early boost seems to assist children at familial risk for dyslexia and those who also show a developmental delay in phonological skills. The provision of vast numbers of well-targeted repetitions within a sufficiently enjoyable game environment may also aid learning of the connections between larger units of written and spoken language (necessary for learning the connections characteristic of inconsistent orthographies) and also automatize the retrieval of those items to which a child requires speedy access in order to acquire fluent reading.

Concluding Remarks

In detailing language development in the school years, this chapter has addressed current issues in terms of how reading develops, its development in different languages, why some children fail to learn to read and what can be done to support such children. Over the past decade, the Jyväskylä Longitudinal Study of Dyslexia has, in following the development of children at familial risk for dyslexia, examined these main themes in an attempt to identify the precursors and developmental pathways to reading and to provide remedial solutions for those children who deviate from the typical path in their journey from birth to reading.

Apparently, the initial cause of dyslexic difficulty is in the genes. The knowledge is fast accumulating in brain research concerning the correlates of reading, but as yet provides little in terms of understanding the gene–brain connection. However, it may elaborate upon the identification of subtypes of developmental dyslexia whose phenotypes have been studied using behavioral indices for a long time. During the last two decades, the neurobiological foundations of reading and especially dyslexia have been the focus of substantial genetic (see Fisher & DeFries, 2002, for a review) and brain research (see Lyytinen, Guttorm, et al., 2005, for a review). It is clear that a number of candidate genes will be identified in the near future and these may help target research toward promising aspects of brain functioning. The hopes are that this will lead to a richer understanding of the inter-individual variation in the types of reading failure. Today, the best guess seems to be that at least one of the following components of the known functional reading system is affected: the left inferior frontal area, the left parietal/temporal reading pathway, and the left inferior temporal/occipital area (Demonet, Taylor, & Chaix, 2004; Pugh, Sandak, Frost, Moore, & Mencl, 2005). It may not be a single locus of anatomical malfunction that makes the neural transmission non-optimal, but rather the functional connection between areas associated with reading-related processing, including those supporting fluency (McCrory, Mechelli, Frith, & Price, 2005). The same functional architecture likely explains reading failures characteristic of readers of both consistent and inconsistent orthographies (Paulesu et al., 2001).

Our current understanding concerning the bottlenecks hindering acquisition of fluent and accurate reading skill is based on behavioral data. The cognitive and reading skill based profiles have been identified without redress to diagnostic categories that entail more than decoding- and comprehension-based reading failures (dyslexia and hyperlexia). However, we know from research that certain language based developmental delays, such as that of receptive language, comprise these bottlenecks and make reading acquisition much more difficult. We have long believed that phonological skills form a central basis of reading, but recent research seems to cast some doubt on the variant of this theory emphasizing that oral phonological training also suffices in terms of surmounting reading disorder.

The early research by Lundberg et al. (1980) was first to show that oral phonological training can prepare for reading acquisition. However, current knowledge emanating from similar experimental research with children at high risk for dyslexia fails to show that these gains endure for more than 1 to 2 years (e.g., Torgesen et al., 2001; Wise, Ring, & Olson, 1999; see also reviews and meta-analyses by Bus & van IJzendoorn, 1999, and Ehri et al., 2001) if the training is not also focused toward grapheme–phoneme associations and orthographic issues. Such a combination results in more long range effects (Blachman, 1994; Borstrom & Elbro, 1997; Bradley & Bryant, 1983; Schneider, Roth, & Ennemoser, 2000) although even these effects have not been very satisfactory. Thus, on top of phonological and orthographic training *per se*, we may need more, a third factor (Scarborough, 2001).

Nevertheless, it seems that the core deficit is in learning. This comes as no surprise after dyslexia has been referred to as a learning disorder for such a long time. Byrne, Fielding-Barnsley, and Ashley (2000) showed that early responsiveness to phonics-type instruction is a good predictor of the gains that a child can obtain from training and a general learning-rate factor associated with learning of both phonological and orthographic skills necessary for fluent reading. Thus, the simple conclusion is that vulnerable children, may their difficulties result from poor speech perception, as suggested by the JLD (Lyytinen et al., 2004; see also Serniclaes, van Heghe, Mousty, Carre, & Sprenger-Charolles, 2004), or some other cause, simply require more practice to reach a sufficient level of reading skill. If traditional methods are used, the typical 30 to 60 hours' training should possibly be increased to 80 to 100 hours – the number of hours which has resulted in optimistic conclusions concerning the treatability of dyslexia (Vellutino et al., 2004).

In consistent orthographies, where the acquisition of accurate reading skill is much faster than in English (Seymour et al., 2003), a shorter period of intervention may suffice if initiated sufficiently early to interest the child in reading. This allows the self-teaching mechanism to support fluency training, which is the most challenging aspect of reading in relatively consistent (Wimmer, 1993, for German) and highly consistent (Holopainen, Ahonen, & Lyytinen, 2001, for Finnish) writing systems.

The remaining question then concerns training which could lead to compensation for the dysfunctions associated with reading which are likely of innate origin. We can be optimistic because, independent of the writing system (for English see Lefly & Pennington, 1991, and for Finnish see Lyytinen et al., 1995), approximately 20% of adults with early reading difficulties have acquired fluent reading skills by adulthood, irrespective of severe familial risk. Practice is the key factor. Preventive training will be a realistic possibility in treating reading disorder when we soon learn to identify children at risk before school age. If the foundation skills of grapheme–phoneme retrieval can be automatized with early practice, the motivation to continue reading can be more easily guaranteed and this subsequent interest in reading then helps most, if not all, to practice their reading to the extent that they become fluent readers.

Note

This article was supported by grants from the Academy of Finland to Heikki Lyytinen and the European Commission's FP6, Marie Curie Excellence Grants (MCEXT-CE-2004-014203) to Ulla Richardson.

References

Aro, M., & Wimmer, H. (2003). Learning to read: English in comparison to six more regular orthographies. *Applied Psycholinguistics, 24*, 621–635.

Beauvois, M. F., & Derouesné, J. (1979). Phonological alexia: Three dissociations. *Journal of Neurology, Neurosurgery, and Psychiatry, 42*, 1115–1124.

Blachman, B. A. (1994). What we have learned from longitudinal studies of phonological processing and reading, and some unanswered questions: A response to Torgesen, Wagner, and Roshotte. *Journal of Learning Disabilities, 27*, 287–289.

Blaiklock, K. (2004). The importance of the letter knowledge in the relationship between phonological awareness and reading. *Journal of Research in Reading, 27*, 36–57.

Boder, E. (1973). Developmental dyslexia: A diagnostic approach based on three atypical reading–spelling patterns. *Developmental Medicine and Child Neurology, 15*, 663–687.

Borgwaldt, S. R., Hellwig, F. M., & de Groot, A. (2004). Word initial entropy in five languages: Letter to sound, and sound to letter. *Written Language and Literacy, 7*, 165–184.

Borstrom, I., & Elbro, C. (1997). Prevention of dyslexia in kindergarten: Effects of phoneme awareness training with children of dyslexic parents. In C. Hulme & M. Snowling (Eds.), *Dyslexia: Biology, cognition and intervention* (pp. 235–253). London: Whurr Publishers.

Bradley, L., & Bryant, P. E. (1983). Categorising sounds and learning to read: A connection. *Nature, 301*, 419–421.

Breitmeyer, B. G. (1993). Sustained (P) and transient (M) channels in vision. In D. M. Willows, R. S. Kruk, & E. Corcos (Eds.), *Visual processes in reading and reading disabilities.* Hillsdale, NJ: Lawrence Erlbaum Associates.

Burnham, D. (2003). Language specific speech perception and the onset of reading. *Reading and Writing, 16*, 573–609.

Bus, A. G., & van IJzendoorn, M. H. (1999). Phonological awareness and early reading: A meta-analysis of experimental training studies. *Journal of Educational Psychology, 91*, 403–414.

Byrne, B., Fielding-Barnsley, R., & Ashley, L. (2000). Effects of preschool phoneme identity training after six years: Outcome level distinguished from rate of response. *Journal of Educational Psychology, 92*, 659–667.

Castles, A., & Coltheart, M. (1993). Varieties of developmental dyslexia. *Cognition, 47*, 149–180.

Cardon, L. R., Smith, S. D., Fulker, F. W., et al. (1994). Quantitative trait locus for reading disability on chromosome 6. *Science, 266*, 276–279.

Castles, A., Datta, H., Gayan, J., & Olson, R. K. (1999). Varieties of developmental reading disorder: genetic and environmental influences. *Journal of Experimental Child Psychology, 72*, 73–94.

Coltheart, M., & Jackson, N. E. (1998). Defining dyslexia. *Child Psychology and Psychiatry Review, 3*, 12–16.

Coltheart, M., Masterson, J., Byng, S., Prior, M., & Riddoch, J. (1983). Surface dyslexia. *Quarterly Journal of Experimental Psychology, 35A*, 469–495.

Cossu, G., Shankweiler, D., Liberman, I. Y., Katz, L., & Tola, G. (1988). Awareness of phonological segments and reading ability in Italian children. *Applied Psycholinguistics, 9,* 1–16.

Critchley, M., & Critchley, E. (1978). *Dyslexia defined.* London: Heinemann Medical Books.

DeFrancis, J. (1989). *Visible language: The diverse oneness of writing systems.* Honolulu: The University of Hawaii Press.

DeJong, P. F., & Olson, R. K. (2004). Early predictors of letter knowledge. *Journal of Experimental Child Psychology, 88,* 254–273.

Demonet, J.-F., Taylor, M., & Chaix, Y. (2004). Developmental dyslexia. *The Lancet, 363,* 1451–1460.

Eckert, M. A., Leonard, C. M., Richards, T. L., Aylward, E. H., Thomson, J., & Berninger, V. W. (2003). Anatomical correlates of dyslexia: frontal and cerebellar findings. *Brain, 126,* 482–494.

Ehri, L. C., Nunes, S. R., Willows, D. M., Schuster, B. V., Yaghoub-Zadeh, Z., & Shanahan, T. (2001). Phonemic awareness instruction helps children learn to read: Evidence from the National Reading Panel's meta-analysis. *Reading Research Quarterly, 36,* 250–287.

Eimas, P. D., Sigueland, E. R., Jusczyck, P., & Vigorito, J. (1971). Speech perception in infants. *Science, 171,* 303–306.

Ellis, A. W., & Young, A. W. (1988). *Human cognitive neuropsychology* (p. 222). London: Lawrence Erlbaum Associates.

Erskine, J. M., & Seymour, P. H. K. (2005). Proximal analysis of developmental dyslexia in adulthood: the cognitive mosaic model. *Journal of Educational Psychology, 97,* 406–424.

Fisher, S. E., & DeFries, J. C. (2002). Developmental dyslexia: genetic dissection of a complex cognitive trait. *Nature Reviews, Neuroscience, 3,* 767–780.

Frith, U. (1985). Beneath the surface of developmental dyslexia. In K. Patterson, J. C. Marshall, & M. Coltheart (Eds.), *Surface dyslexia* (pp. 301–330). London: Routledge & Kegan Paul.

Frost, R., Katz, L., & Bentin, S. (1987). Strategies for visual word recognition and orthographical depth: A multilingual comparison. *Journal of Experimental Psychology: Human Perception and Performance, 13,* 104–115.

Galaburda, A. M., Sherman, G. F., Rosen, G. D., Aboitiz, F., & Geschwind, N. (1985). Developmental dyslexia: Four consecutive patients with cortical anomalies. *Annals of Neurology, 18,* 222–233.

Gallagher, A., Frith, U., & Snowling, M. (2000). Precursors of literacy delay among children at genetic risk of dyslexia. *Journal of Child Psychology and Psychiatry, 41,* 203–213.

Gilger, J. W., Pennington, B. F., & De Fries, J. (1991). Risk for reading disability as a function of parental history in three family studies. *Reading and Writing: An Interdisciplinary Journal, 3,* 205–217.

Goswami, U. (2003). Phonology, learning to read and dyslexia: a cross-linguistic analysis. In V. Csepe (Ed.), *Dyslexia: Different brain, different behavior* (pp. 1–40). Neuropsychology and Cognition Series. Dordrecht: Kluwer.

Goswami, U., & Bryant, P. B. (Eds.). (1990a). *Phonological skills and learning to read.* London: Lawrence Erlbaum Associates.

Goswami, U., & Bryant, P. B. (1990b). Theories about learning to read. In U. Goswami & P. B. Bryant (Eds.), *Phonological skills and learning to read.* London: Lawrence Erlbaum Associates.

Goswami, U., Gombert, J., & Barrera, F. (1998). Children's orthographic representations and linguistic transparency: Nonsense word reading in English, French and Spanish. *Applied Psycholinguistics, 19,* 19–52.

Goswami, U., Ziegler, J., Dalton, L., & Schneider, W. (2001). Pseudohomophone effects and phonological recoding procedures in reading development in English and German. *Journal of Memory and Language, 45*, 648–664.

Grigorenko, E. L., Wood, F. B., Meyer, M. S., Hart, L. A., Speed, W. C., Shuster, A., & Pauls, D. L. (1997). Susceptibility loci for distinct components of developmental dyslexia on chromosomes 6 and 15. *American Journal of Human Genetics, 60*, 27–39.

Guttorm, T. K., Leppänen, P. H. T., Poikkeus, A-M., Eklund, K. M., Lyytinen, P., & Lyytinen, H. (2005). Brain event-related potentials (ERPs) measured at birth predict later language development in children with and without familial risk for dyslexia. *Cortex, 41*, 291–303.

Guttorm, T. K., Leppänen, P. H. T., Richardson, U., & Lyytinen, H. (2001). Event-related potentials and consonant differentiation in newborns with familial risk for dyslexia. *Journal of Learning Disabilities, 34*, 534–544.

Hallgren, B. (1950). Specific dyslexia: a clinical and genetic study. *Acta Psychiatrica et Neurologica Scandinavia, 65 (Suppl.)*, 1–287.

Hammill, D. (2004). What we know about correlates of reading. *Exceptional Children, 70*, 453–468.

Hatcher, P. J., Hulme, C., & Snowling, M. J. (2004). Explicit phoneme training combined with phonic reading instruction helps young children at risk of reading failure. *Journal of Child Psychology and Psychiatry, 45*, 338–358.

Holopainen, L., Ahonen, T., & Lyytinen, H. (2001). Predicting delay in reading achievement in a highly transparent language. *Journal of Learning Disabilities, 34*, 401–413.

Hutzler, F., Ziegler, J. C., Perry, C., Wimmer, H., & Zorzi, M. (2004). Do current connectionist learning models account for reading development in different languages? *Cognition, 91*, 273–296.

Johnston, R., Anderson, M., & Holligan, C. (1996). Knowledge of the alphabet and explicit awareness of phonemes in pre-readers: The nature of the relationship. *Reading and Writing: An Interdisciplinary Journal, 8*, 217–234.

Landerl, K., Wimmer, H., & Frith, U. (1997). The impact of orthographic consistency on dyslexia: A German–English comparison. *Cognition, 63*, 315–334.

Lefly, D. L., & Pennington, B. F. (1991). Spelling errors and reading fluency in compensated adult dyslexics. *Annals of Dyslexia, 41*, 143–162.

Leinonen, S., Müller, K., Leppänen, P. H. T., Aro, M., Ahonen, T., & Lyytinen, H. (2001). Heterogeneity in adult dyslexic readers: Relating processing skills to the speed and accuracy of oral text reading. *Reading and Writing: An Interdisciplinary Journal, 14*, 265–296.

Leppänen, P. H. T., Pihko, E., Eklund, K. M., & Lyytinen, H. (1999). Cortical responses of infants with and without a genetic risk for dyslexia: II. Group effects. *NeuroReport, 10*, 901–905.

Leppänen, P. H. T., Richardson, U., Pihko, E., Eklund, K. M., Guttorm, T., Aro, M., & Lyytinen, H. (2002). Brain responses reveal temporal processing differences in infants at risk for dyslexia. *Developmental Neuropsychology, 22*, 407–422.

Livingstone, M. S., Rosen, G. D., Drislane, F. W., & Galaburda, A. M. (1991). Physiological and anatomical evidence for a magnocellular defect in developmental dyslexia. *Proceedings of the National Academy of Sciences of the USA, 88*, 7943–7947.

Lovegrove, W., Martin, F., & Slaghuis, W. (1986). A theoretical and experimental case for a visual deficit in specific reading disability. *Cognitive Neuropsychology, 3*, 225–267.

Lovett, M. W. (1987). A developmental approach to reading disability: Accuracy and speed criteria of normal and deficient reading skill. *Child Development, 58*, 234–260.

Lundberg, I., Olofsson, Å., & Wall, S. (1980). Reading and spelling skills in the first school years predicted from phonemic awareness in kindergarten. *Scandinavian Journal of Psychology, 21,* 159–173.

Lyon, G. R., Shaywitz, S. E., & Shaywitz, B. A. (2003). A definition of dyslexia. *Annals of Dyslexia, 53,* 1–14.

Lyytinen, H., Aro, M., Eklund, K., Erskine, J., Guttorm, T. K., Laakso, M.-L., et al. (2004). The development of children at familial risk for dyslexia: birth to school age. *Annals of Dyslexia, 54,* 185–220.

Lyytinen, H., Aro, M., Holopainen, L., Leiwo, M., Lyytinen, P., & Tolvanen, A. (2005). Children's language development and reading acquisition in a highly transparent orthography. In R. M. Joshi & P. G. Aaron (Eds.), *Handbook of orthography and literacy* (pp. 47–62). Mahwah, NJ: Lawrence Erlbaum Associates.

Lyytinen, H., Erskine, J., Tolvanen, A., Torppa, M., Poikkeus, A-M., & Lyytinen, P. (2006). Trajectories of reading development: A follow-up from birth to school age of children with and without risk for dyslexia. *Merrill-Palmer Quarterly, 52,* 514–546.

Lyytinen, H., Guttorm, T. K., Huttunen, T., Hämäläinen, J., Leppänen, P. H. T., & Vesterinen, M. (2005). Psychophysiology of developmental dyslexia: A review of findings including studies of children at risk for dyslexia. *Journal of Neurolinguistics, 18,* 167–195.

Lyytinen, H., Leinonen, S., Nikula, M., Aro, M., & Leiwo, M. (1995). In search of the core features of dyslexia: Observations concerning dyslexia in the highly orthographically regular Finnish language. In V. W. Berninger (Ed.), *The varieties of orthographic knowledge II: Relationships to phonology, reading, and writing* (pp. 177–204). Dordrecht: Kluwer.

Lyytinen, H., Ronimus, M., Alanko, A., Taanila, M., & Poikkeus, A-M. (submitted). Early identification and prevention of dyslexia.

Lyytinen, P., Eklund, K., & Lyytinen, H. (2005). Language development and literacy skills in late-talking toddlers with and without familial risk for dyslexia. *Annals of Dyslexia, 55,* 166–192.

Lyytinen, P., & Lyytinen, H. (2004). Growth and predictive relations of vocabulary and inflectional morphology in children with and without familial risk for dyslexia. *Applied Psycholinguistics, 25,* 397–411.

Marsh, G., Friedman, M. P., Welch, V., & Desberg, P. (1981). A cognitive-developmental approach to reading acquisition. In T. Waller & G. E. MacKinnon (Eds.), *Reading research: Advances in theory and practice: Vol. 2.* New York: Academic Press.

Marshall, J. C., & Newcombe, F. (1973). Patterns of paralexia: a psycholinguistic approach. *Journal of Psycholinguistic Research, 2,* 175–199.

Mattingly, I. G. (1972). Reading, the linguistic process, and linguistic awareness. In J. F. Kavanagh & I. G. Mattingly (Eds.), *Language by ear and by eye: The relationships between speech and reading.* Cambridge, MA: MIT Press.

McCrory, D., Mechelli, A., Frith, U., & Price, C. (2005). Words: a common neural basis for reading and naming deficits in developmental dyslexia. *Brain, 128,* 261–267.

Metsala, J. L., & Walley, A. C. (1998). Spoken vocabulary growth and the segmental restructuring of lexical representations: Precursors to phonemic awareness and early reading ability. In J. L. Metsala & L. C. Ehri (Eds.), *Word recognition in beginning literacy* (pp. 89–120). Hillsdale, NJ: Lawrence Erlbaum Associates.

Molfese, D. (2000). Predicting dyslexia at 8 years of age using neonatal brain responses. *Brain and Language, 72,* 238–245.

Morais, J. (1991). Phonological awareness: A bridge between language and literacy. In D. Sawyer & B. Fox (Eds.), *Phonological awareness in reading: The evolution of current perspectives* (pp. 31–71). New York: Springer-Verlag.

Morais, J., Cary, L., Alegria, J., & Bertelson, P. (1979). Does awareness of speech as a sequence of phones arise spontaneously? *Cognition, 7,* 323–331.

Nelson, H. E., & McKenna, P. (1975). The use of current reading ability in the assessment of dementia. *British Journal of Social and Clinical Psychology, 14,* 259–267.

Nicolson, R. I., & Fawcett, A. J. (1990). Automaticity: a new framework for dyslexia research? *Cognition, 35,* 159–182.

Nicolson, R. I., Fawcett, A. J., & Dean, P. (2001). Developmental dyslexia: the cerebellar deficit hypothesis. *Trends in Neurosciences, 24,* 515–516.

Olson, D. R. (2002). Literacy in the past millennium. In E. Hjelmqvuist & C. von Euler (Eds.), *Dyslexia and literacy* (pp. 23–38). London: Whurr Publishers.

Paulesu, E., Démonet, J., Fazio, F., McCrory, E., Chanoine, V., Brunswick, N., et al. (2001). Dyslexia: Cultural diversity and biological unity. *Science, 291,* 2165–2167.

Pennington, B., & Lefly, D. L. (2001). Early reading development in children at family risk for dyslexia. *Child Development, 72,* 816–833.

Pugh, K. R., Sandak, R., Frost, S. J., Moore, D., & Mencl, W. E. (2005). Examining reading development and reading disability in English language learners: Potential contributions from functional neuroimaging. *Learning Disabilities Research and Practice, 20,* 24–30.

Puolakanaho, A., Poikkeus, A.-M., Ahonen, T., Tolvanen, A., & Lyytinen, H. (2004). Emerging phonological awareness as a precursor of risk in children with and without familial risk for dyslexia. *Annals of Dyslexia, 54,* 221–243.

Ramus, F. (2003). Developmental dyslexia: specific phonological deficit or general sensorimotor dysfunction? *Current Opinion in Neurobiology, 13,* 1–7.

Ramus, F., & Mehler, J. (1999). Language identification with suprasegmental cues: A study based on speech re-synthesis. *Journal of the Acoustical Society of America, 105,* 512–521.

Ramus, F., Rosen, S., Dakin, S. C., Day, B. L., Castellote, J. M., White, S., & Frith, U. (2003). Theories of developmental dyslexia: Insights from a multiple case study of dyslexic adults. *Brain, 126,* 841–865.

Reynolds, C. (1984). Critical measurement issues in learning disabilities. *Journal of Special Education, 18,* 451–476.

Richardson, U., Leppänen, P. H. T., Leiwo, M., & Lyytinen, H. (2003). Speech perception of infants with high familial risk for dyslexia differ at the age of six months. *Developmental Neuropsychology, 23,* 385–397.

Richardson, U., Thomson, J., Scott, S. K., & Goswami, U. (2004). Auditory processing skills and phonological representation in dyslexic children. *Dyslexia, 10,* 215–233.

Scarborough, H. S. (1989). Prediction of reading disability from familial and individual differences. *Journal of Educational Psychology, 81,* 101–108.

Scarborough, H. S. (1990). Very early language deficits in dyslexic children. *Child Development, 61,* 1728–1743.

Scarborough, H. S. (2001). Connecting early language and literacy to later reading (dis)abilities: Evidence, theory, and practice. In S. Neuman & D. Dickinson (Eds.), *Handbook for research in early literacy* (pp. 97–110). New York: Guilford Press.

Schneider, W., Roth, E., & Ennemoser, M. (2000). Training phonological skills and letter knowledge in children at risk for dyslexia: A comparison of three kindergarten intervention programs. *Journal of Educational Psychology, 92,* 284–295.

Serniclaes, W., van Heghe, S., Mousty, P., Carre, R., & Sprenger-Charolles, L. (2004). Allophonic mode of speech perception in dyslexia. *Journal of Experimental Child Psychology, 87,* 336–361.

Seymour, P. H. K. (1999). Cognitive architecture of early reading. In I. Lundberg, F. E. Tønnessen, & I. Austad (Eds.), *Dyslexia: Advances in theory and practice* (pp. 59–73). Dordrecht: Kluwer.

Seymour, P. H. K., Aro, M., & Erskine, J. M. (2003). Foundation literacy acquisition in European orthographies. *British Journal of Psychology, 94*, 143–174.

Share, D. (1995). Phonological recoding and self-teaching: Sine qua non of reading acquisition. *Cognition, 55*, 151–218.

Share, D., Jorm, A., Maclean, R., & Matthews, R. (1984). Sources of individual differences in reading achievement. *Journal of Educational Psychology, 76*, 1309–1324.

Smith, S. D., Kimberling, W. J., Pennington, B. F., & Lubs, H. A. (1983). Specific reading disability: identification of an inherited form through linkage analysis. *Science, 219*, 1345–1347.

Snowling, M. J. (1980). The development of grapheme–phoneme correspondences in normal and dyslexic readers. *Journal of Experimental Child Psychology, 29*, 294–305.

Snowling, M. J. (1998). Dyslexia as a phonological deficit: Evidence and implications. *Child Psychology and Psychiatry Review, 3*, 4–11.

Snowling, M. J., Goulandris, N., & Defty, N. (1998). Development and variation in developmental dyslexia. In C. Hulme & R. M. Joshi (Eds.), *Reading and spelling: Development and disorders*. Hillsdale, NJ: Lawrence Erlbaum Associates.

Stahl, S. A., & Murray, B. A. (1994). Defining phonological awareness and its relationship to early reading. *Journal of Educational Psychology, 86*, 221–234.

Stanovich, K. E. (1986). Cognitive processes and the reading problems of learning disabled children: Evaluating the assumption of specificity. In J. K. Torgesen & B. Y. L. Wong (Eds.), *Psychological and educational perspectives on learning disabilities* (pp. 87–131). San Diego, CA: Academic Press.

Stanovich, K. E., & Siegel, L. S. (1994). Phenotypic performance profile of children with reading disabilities: A regression-based test of the phonological-core variable-difference model. *Journal of Educational Psychology, 86*, 24–53.

Stanovich, K. E., Siegel, L. S., & Gottardo, A. (1997). Progress in the search for dyslexia subtypes. In C. Hulme & M. Snowling (Eds.), *Dyslexia: Biology, cognition and intervention* (pp. 108–130). London: Whurr Publishers.

Stein, J. (2001). The sensory basis of reading problems. *Developmental Neuropsychology, 20*, 509–534.

Stein, J., & Fowler, M. S. (1981). Visual dyslexia. *Trends in Neurological Sciences, 4*, 77–80.

Studdert-Kennedy, M. (2002). Deficits in phoneme awareness do not arise from failures in rapid auditory processing. *Reading and Writing, 15*, 5–14.

Taipale, M., Kaminen, N., Nopola-Hemmi, J., Haltia, T., Myllyluoma, B., Lyytinen, H., et al. (2003). A candidate gene for developmental dyslexia encodes a nuclear tetratricopeptide repeat domain protein dynamically regulated in brain. *Proceedings of the National Academy of Sciences of the USA, 100*, 11553–11558.

Tallal, P. (1980). Auditory temporal perception, phonics, and reading disabilities in children. *Brain and Language, 9*, 182–198.

Thorstad, G. (1991). The effect of orthography on the acquisition of literacy skills. *British Journal of Psychology, 82*, 527–537.

Torgesen, J. K., Rashotte, C. A., & Alexander, A. (2001). Principles of fluency instruction in reading: Relationships with established empirical outcomes. In M. Wolf (Ed.), *Dyslexia, fluency, and the brain*. Parkton, MD: York Press.

Vellutino, F. R. (1979). *Dyslexia: Theory and research*. Cambridge, MA: MIT Press.

Vellutino, F. R., Fletcher, J. M., Snowling, M. J., & Scanlon, D. M. (2004). Specific reading disability (dyslexia): what have we learned in the past four decades? *Journal of Child Psychology and Psychiatry, 45*, 2–40.

Vellutino, F. R., Scanlon, D. M., & Chen, R. S. (1995). The increasing inextricable relationship between orthographic and phonological coding in learning to read: Some reservations about current methods of operationalizing orthographic coding. In V. W. Berninger (Ed.), *The varieties of orthographic knowledge II: Relationships to phonology, reading, and writing* (pp. 47–111). Dordrecht: Kluwer.

Wagner, R., Torgesen, J., & Rashotte, C. (1994). Development of reading-related phonological processing abilities: New evidence of bidirectional causality from a latent variable longitudinal study. *Developmental Psychology, 30*, 73–87.

Walley, A. C. (1993). The role of vocabulary development in children's spoken word recognition and segmentation ability. *Developmental Review, 13*, 284–350.

Werker, J. F., & Tees, R. C. (1987). Speech perception in severely disabled and average reading children. *Canadian Journal of Psychology, 41*, 48–61.

Wimmer, H. (1993). Characteristics of developmental dyslexia in a regular writing system. *Applied Psycholinguistics, 14*, 1–33.

Wimmer, H., & Goswami, U. (1994). The influence of orthographic consistency on reading development: Word recognition in English and German children. *Cognition, 51*, 91–103.

Wise, B. W., Ring, J., & Olson, R. K. (1999). Training phonological awareness with and without explicit attention to articulation. *Journal of Experimental Child Psychology, 72*, 271–304.

Wolf, M., & Bowers, P. G. (1999). The double-deficit hypothesis for the developmental dyslexias. *Journal of Educational Psychology, 91*, 415–438.

Wolf, M., & Katzir-Cohen, T. (2001). Reading fluency and its intervention. *Scientific Studies of Reading, 5*, 211–239.

Ziegler, J. C., Jacobs, A. M., & Stone, G. O. (1996). Statistical analysis of the bidirectional inconsistency of spelling and sound in French. *Behavior Research Methods, Instruments, and Computers, 28*, 504–515.

Ziegler, J. C., Perry, C., Ma-Wyatt, A., Ladner, D., & Schulte-Körne, G. (2003). Developmental dyslexia in different languages: Language-specific or universal? *Journal of Experimental Child Psychology, 86*, 169–193.

Ziegler, J. C., Stone, G. O., & Jacobs, A. M. (1997). What is the pronunciation for -ough and the spelling for /u/? A database for computing feed forward and feedback consistency in English. *Behavior Research Methods, Instruments, and Computers, 29*, 600–618.

Author Index

Subject Index